HORNGREN'S
ACCOUNTING

HORNGREN'S ACCOUNTING

TRACIE L. MILLER-NOBLES
Austin Community College

BRENDA MATTISON
Tri-County Technical College

ELLA MAE MATSUMURA
University of Wisconsin—Madison

CAROL A. MEISSNER
Georgian College

JO-ANN L. JOHNSTON
British Columbia Institute of Technology

PETER R. NORWOOD
Langara College

VOLUME TWO

11TH CANADIAN EDITION

Pearson Canada Inc., 26 Prince Andrew Place, North York, Ontario M3C 2H4.

ISBN 9780134790107

Library and Archives Canada Cataloguing in Publication

Miller-Nobles, Tracie L., author
    Horngren's accounting / Tracie Miller-Nobles,
Texas State University-San
Marcos [and five others]. — 11th Canadian edition.

Includes indexes.
ISBN 978-0-13-479010-7 (v. 2 : softcover)

    1. Accounting--Textbooks. 2. Textbooks.
I. Title. II. Title: Accounting.

HF5636.M54 2019   657   C2018-906037-9

In memory of *Charles T. Horngren* 1926–2011

Whose vast contributions to the teaching and learning of accounting impacted and will continue to impact generations of accounting students and professionals.

I would like to thank my students for keeping me on my toes. Hearing their new ideas and how they think about accounting makes teaching such a wonderful job.

Carol A. Meissner

I would like to thank my husband, Bill, and my family for their encouragement and support.

Jo-Ann L. Johnston

I would like to thank my wife, Helen, and my family very much for their support and encouragement.

Peter R. Norwood

Brief Contents

VOLUME 1

Part 1 The Basic Structure of Accounting

1 Accounting and the Business Environment *2*
2 Recording Business Transactions *56*
3 Measuring Business Income: The Adjusting Process *112*
4 Completing the Accounting Cycle *172*
5 Merchandising Operations *242*
6 Accounting for Merchandise Inventory *322*
7 Accounting Information Systems *370*

Part 2 Accounting for Assets and Liabilities

8 Internal Control and Cash *430*
9 Receivables *492*
10 Property, Plant, and Equipment; and Goodwill and Intangible Assets *550*
11 Current Liabilities and Payroll *602*

Appendix A: **Indigo Books and Music Inc. 2017 Annual Report** A-1

Appendix B: **Typical Chart of Accounts for Service Proprietorships** B-1

VOLUME 2

Part 3 Accounting for Partnerships and Corporate Transactions

12 Partnerships *658*
13 Corporations: Share Capital and the Balance Sheet *712*
14 Corporations: Retained Earnings and the Income Statement *762*
15 Long-Term Liabilities *818*
16 Investments and International Operations *886*

Part 4 Analysis of Accounting Information

17 The Cash Flow Statement *946*
18 Financial Statement Analysis *1030*

Appendix A: **Indigo Books and Music Inc. 2017 Annual Report** A-1

Appendix B: **Typical Chart of Accounts for Corporations** B-1

Contents

Part 3 Accounting for Partnerships and Corporate Transactions

12 Partnerships 658

Characteristics of a Partnership 661
Advantages and Disadvantages of Partnerships 663
Types of Partnerships 664
Partnership Financial Statements 665
Forming a Partnership 666
Sharing Partnership Profits and Losses 667
Partner Withdrawals (Drawings) 673
Admission of a Partner 674
Withdrawal of a Partner from the Business 678
Liquidation of a Partnership 682

  Summary Problem for Your Review 686

  Summary 688

  Assignment Material 691

  Extending Your Knowledge 708

13 Corporations: Share Capital and the Balance Sheet 712

Corporations 714
Shareholders' Equity 717
Issuing Shares 720
Organization Costs 726
Accounting for Cash Dividends 727
Different Values of Shares 730
Accounting for Business Transactions 730
Evaluating Operations 732

  Summary Problem for Your Review 735

  Summary 737

  Assignment Material 741

  Extending Your Knowledge 760

14 Corporations: Retained Earnings and the Income Statement 762

Retained Earnings 764
Stock Dividends 765
Stock Splits 767
Repurchase of Its Shares by a Corporation 769
The Corporate Income Statement 774
Statement of Retained Earnings 780
Statement of Shareholders' Equity 780
Restrictions on Retained Earnings 782
Changing Financial Statements 783

  Summary Problem for Your Review 788

  Summary 790

  Assignment Material 793

  Extending Your Knowledge 814

15 Long-Term Liabilities 818

Bonds: An Introduction 820
Bonds 822
Issuing Bonds to Borrow Money 824
Amortization of a Bond Discount and a Bond Premium 829
Adjusting Entries for Interest Expense 836
Retirement of Bonds 839
Convertible Bonds and Notes 840
Advantages and Disadvantages of Issuing Bonds
  Versus Shares 841
Mortgages and Other Long-Term Liabilities 842
Lease Liabilities 844

  Summary Problem for Your Review 849

  Summary 851

  Assignment Material 855

  Extending Your Knowledge 872

    Chapter 15 Appendix: Time Value of Money:
    Future Value and Present Value 873

16 Investments and International Operations 886

Share Investments 888
Accounting for Short-Term Investments 890
Long-Term Equity Investments Without Significant
  Influence 894
Long-Term Share Investments with Significant Influence 896
Long-Term Share Investments Accounted for by the
  Consolidation Method 898
Consolidated Financial Statements 899
Investments in Bonds 906
Foreign-Currency Transactions 910

Summary Problem for Your Review 916

Summary 918

Assignment Material 922

Extending Your Knowledge 941

Part 4 Analysis of Accounting Information

17 The Cash Flow Statement 946

The Cash Flow Statement: Basic Concepts 949
Purpose of the Cash Flow Statement 950
Format of the Cash Flow Statement 952
Operating, Investing, and Financing Activities 952
Measuring Cash Adequacy: Free Cash Flow 955
The Cash Flow Statement: The Indirect Method 956
Computing Individual Amounts for the Cash Flow
  Statement 961

Summary Problem for Your Review 965

Summary 968

Chapter 17 Appendix: The Cash Flow Statement:
The Direct Method 969

Summary Problem For Your Review 983

Assignment Material 987

Extending Your Knowledge 1026

18 Financial Statement Analysis 1030

Objectives of Financial Statement Analysis 1032
Methods of Analysis 1033
Horizontal Analysis 1033
Vertical Analysis 1037
Common-Size Statements 1040
Using Ratios to Make Decisions 1044
Limitations of Financial Analysis 1055
Investor Decisions 1055

Summary Problem for Your Review 1059

Summary 1061

Assignment Material 1065

Extending Your Knowledge 1097

Appendix A: Indigo Books and Music Inc. 2017 Annual
            Report A-1

Appendix B: Typical Chart of Accounts for
            Corporations B-1

Glossary G1
Index I1

About the Authors

TRACIE L. MILLER-NOBLES, CPA, received her bachelor's and master's degrees in accounting from Texas A&M University and is currently pursuing her Ph.D. in adult education also at Texas A&M University. She is an associate professor at Austin Community College, Austin, Texas. Previously she served as a senior lecturer at Texas State University, San Marcos, Texas, and she has taught as an adjunct at University of Texas-Austin. Tracie has public accounting experience with Deloitte Tax LLP and Sample & Bailey, CPAs.

Tracie is a recipient of the following awards: American Accounting Association J. Michael and Mary Anne Cook prize, Texas Society of CPAs Rising Star TSCPA Austin Chapter CPA of the Year, TSCPA Outstanding Accounting Educator, NISOD Teaching Excellence and Aims Community College Excellence in Teaching. She is a member of the Teachers of Accounting at Two Year Colleges, the American Accounting Association, the American Institute of Certified Public Accountants, and the Texas State Society of Certified Public Accountants. She is currently serving on the board of directors as secretary/webmaster of Teachers of Accounting at Two Year Colleges and as a member of the American Institute of Certified Public Accountants financial literacy committee. In addition, Tracie served on the Commission on Accounting Higher Education: Pathways to a Profession.

Tracie has spoken on such topics as using technology in the classroom, motivating non-business majors to learn accounting, and incorporating active learning in the classroom at numerous conferences. In her spare time she enjoys camping and hiking and spending time with friends and family.

BRENDA L. MATTISON, CMA, has a bachelor's degree in education and a master's degree in accounting, both from Clemson University. She is currently an accounting instructor at Tri-County Technical College in Pendleton, South Carolina. Brenda previously served as accounting program coordinator at TCTC and has prior experience teaching accounting at Robeson Community College, Lumberton, North Carolina; University of South Carolina Upstate, Spartanburg, South Carolina; and Rasmussen Business College, Eagan, Minnesota. She also has accounting work experience in retail and manufacturing businesses and is a Certified Management Accountant.

Brenda is a member of the American Accounting Association, Institute of Management Accountants, South Carolina Technical Education Association, and Teachers of Accounting at Two Year Colleges. She is currently serving on the board of directors as vice-president of Conference Administration of Teachers of Accounting at Two Year Colleges.

Brenda previously served as Faculty Fellow at Tri-County Technical College. She has presented at state, regional, and national conferences on topics including active learning, course development, and student engagement.

In her spare time, Brenda enjoys reading and spending time with her family. She is also an active volunteer in the community, serving her church and other organizations.

ELLA MAE MATSUMURA, PH.D., is a professor in the Department of Accounting and Information Systems in the School of Business at the University of Wisconsin–Madison, and is affiliated with the university's Center for Quick Response Manufacturing. She received an A.B. in mathematics from the University of California, Berkeley, and M.Sc. and Ph.D. degrees from the University of British Columbia. Ella Mae has won two teaching excellence awards at the University of Wisconsin–Madison and was elected as a lifetime fellow of the university's Teaching Academy, formed to promote effective teaching. She is a member of the university team awarded an IBM Total Quality Management Partnership grant to develop curriculum for total quality management education.

Ella Mae was a co-winner of the 2010 Notable Contributions to Management Accounting Literature Award. She has served in numerous leadership positions in the American Accounting Association (AAA). She was coeditor of *Accounting Horizons* and has chaired and served on numerous AAA committees. She has been secretary-treasurer and president of the AAA's Management Accounting Section. Her past and current research articles focus on decision making, performance evaluation, compensation, supply chain relationships, and sustainability. She coauthored a monograph on customer profitability analysis in credit unions.

About the Canadian Authors

CAROL A. MEISSNER is a professor in both Business and Management Studies and the Automotive Business School of Canada at Georgian College in Barrie, Ontario. She teaches in the Accounting Diploma, Automotive Business Diploma, and business degree programs.

Carol has always been a teacher. She started as a part-time college instructor when she completed her first degree and has taught full time since 2005. In 2014, Carol was awarded the Georgian College Board of Governors' Award of Excellence Academic for outstanding contributions to the college and an ongoing commitment to excellence.

Her "real world" experience includes car dealership controllership and self-employment as a part-time controller and consultant for a wide variety of businesses.

Carol has broad experience in curriculum development. She has been a curriculum chair, program coordinator, member of several curriculum committees, and has been involved in writing and renewing degree, diploma, and graduate certificate programs.

A self-professed "learning junkie," Carol holds a Bachelor of Commerce degree, a Master of Business Administration degree, a Master of Arts degree in Education (Community College concentration), and a CPA designation. She has also earned Georgian College's Professional Development Teaching Practice Credential and is a graduate of Georgian's Aspiring Leaders program. She is a regular attendee and occasional presenter at conferences related to teaching, accounting, and the automotive industry. Outside of work she is an esports mom who spends many hours watching tournaments online.

JO-ANN JOHNSTON is an instructor in the Accounting, Finance and Insurance Department at the British Columbia Institute of Technology (BCIT). She obtained her Diploma of Technology in Financial Management from BCIT, her Bachelor in Administrative Studies degree from British Columbia Open University, and her Master of Business Administration degree from Simon Fraser University. She is also a certified general accountant, has CPA designation, and completed the Canadian securities course.

Prior to entering the field of education, Jo-Ann worked in public practice and industry for over 10 years. She is a past member of the board of governors of the Certified General Accountants Association of British Columbia and has served on various committees for the association. She was also a member of the board of directors for the BCIT Faculty and Staff Association and served as treasurer during that tenure.

In addition to teaching duties and committee work for BCIT, Jo-Ann is the financial officer for a family-owned business.

PETER R. NORWOOD is an instructor in accounting and coordinator of the Accounting program at Langara College in Vancouver. A graduate of the University of Alberta, he received his Master of Business Administration from the University of Western Ontario. He is a CPA, a fellow of the Institute of Chartered Accountants of British Columbia, a certified management accountant, and a fellow of the Society of Management Accountants of Canada.

Before entering the academic community, Peter worked in public practice and industry for over 15 years. He is a past president of the Institute of Chartered Accountants of British Columbia and chair of the Chartered Accountants School of Business (CASB). He is also the chair of the Chartered Accountants Education Foundation for the British Columbia Institute of Chartered Accountants and has been active on many provincial and national committees, including the Board of Evaluators of the Canadian Institute of Chartered Accountants. Peter is also a sessional lecturer in the Sauder School of Business at the University of British Columbia.

Changes to This Edition

General

Revised end-of-chapter starters, exercises, practice sets, challenge exercises, ethical issues, problems, challenge problems, decision problems, and financial statement cases.

Moved IFRS Mini-Cases and Comprehensive Problems for each Part to MyLab Accounting.

Learning Objectives in all chapters have been reviewed against current CPA competencies and correlation provided at the beginning of each chapter. Many of the problems in the text (Beyond the Numbers, Ethical issues, Decision Problems, Financial Statements Cases) give opportunities to develop CPA competencies, in particular Enabling Competencies, such as Communication, Problem Solving, and Professional and Ethical Behaviour.

- **NEW! Using Excel.** This end-of-chapter exercise in select chapters introduces students to Excel to solve common accounting problems as they would in the business environment.
- **NEW! Serial Exercises.** Serial exercises in all chapters expose students to recording entries for a service company, which grows to become a merchandiser later in the text.
- **NEW! Ethics box.** This feature provides common questions and potential solutions business owners face. Students are asked to determine the course of action they would take based on concepts covered in the chapter and are then given potential solutions. Available in most chapters.
- **NEW!** List of acronyms has been expanded and added to inside back cover for easier student reference.

Chapter 12
- Additional starters and exercises.

Chapter 13
NEW! chapter-opening vignette.

- Made examples more continuous so they are easier to follow (fewer companies in examples).

Chapter 14
- Updated corporate information in opening vignette.
- Split errors and changes into separate learning objectives so easier for faculty to teach one or both.
- Additional starters and exercises.

Chapter 15
NEW! chapter-opening vignette.

- Streamlined bonds introduction.
- Schedules now in Excel.
- Improved presentation and consistency in mortgage schedules.

Chapter 16
NEW! chapter-opening vignette.

- Additional starters and exercises.
- Removed Joint Ventures – the new S2056 for Joint Arrangements is too complex for an introductory course.
- Moved summaries of types of investments to beginning of the equity sections.
- Separated equity and consolidation information into different learning objectives so schools that don't cover consolidations can omit them easier.

Chapter 17
NEW! chapter-opening vignette.

- Focused chapter on the indirect method for the cash flow statement and moved the direct method to an appendix. Easier for schools only covering one, though all content is still there for those who cover both methods.
- Additional starters, exercises and problems.

Chapter 18
NEW! chapter-opening vignette.

- Expanded explanations for days sales in inventory and debt/equity ratio.
- Additional starters and exercises.

Horngren's Accounting ...
Expanding on Proven Success

Accounting Cycle Tutorial

This interactive tutorial in MyLab Accounting helps students master the Accounting Cycle for early and continued success in introduction to accounting courses. The tutorial, accessed by computer, smartphone, or tablet, provides students with brief explanations of each concept of the Accounting Cycle through engaging, interactive activities. Students are immediately assessed on their understanding, and their performance is recorded in the MyLab gradebook. Whether the Accounting Cycle Tutorial is used as a remediation self-study tool or course assignment, students have yet another resource within MyLab to help them be successful with the accounting cycle.

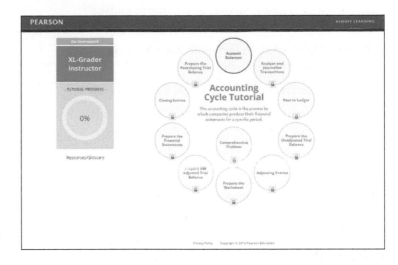

NEW! ACT Comprehensive Problem

The Accounting Cycle Tutorial now includes a comprehensive problem that allows students to work with the same set of transactions throughout the accounting cycle. The comprehensive problem, which can be assigned at the beginning or the end of the full cycle, reinforces the lessons learned in the Accounting Cycle Tutorial activities by emphasizing the connections between the accounting cycle concepts.

Study Plan

The Study Plan acts as a tutor, providing personalized recommendations for each of your students based on his or her ability to master the learning objectives in your course. This allows students to focus their study time by pinpointing the precise areas they need to review and allowing them to use customized practice and learning aids–such as videos, eText, tutorials, and more–to get them back on track. Using the report available in the gradebook, you can then tailor course lectures to prioritize the content where students need the most support–offering you better insight into classroom and individual performance.

Dynamic Study Modules

New! Chapter-specific Dynamic Study Modules help students study effectively on their own by continuously assessing their activity and performance in real time. Here's how it works: students complete a set of questions with a unique answer format that also asks them to indicate their confidence level. Questions repeat until the student can answer them all correctly and confidently. Dynamic Study Modules explain the concept using materials from the text. These are available as graded assignments and are accessible on smartphones, tablets, and computers.

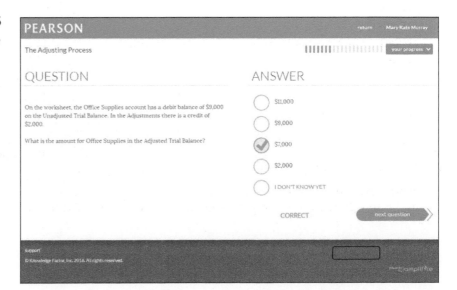

Learning Catalytics

Text-specific Learning Catalytics helps you generate class discussion, customize your lecture, and promote peer-to-peer learning with real-time analytics. As a student response tool, Learning Catalytics uses students' smartphones, tablets, or laptops to engage them in more interactive tasks and thinking.

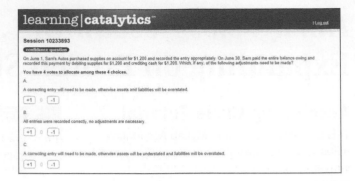

- **NEW!** Upload a full PowerPoint® deck for easy creation of slide questions.

- Help your students develop critical thinking skills.

- Monitor responses to find out where your students are struggling.

- Rely on real-time data to adjust your teaching strategy.

- Automatically group students for discussion, teamwork, and peer-to-peer learning.

Pearson Etext

Pearson eText gives students access to their textbook anytime, anywhere. In addition to note-taking, highlighting, and bookmarking, the Pearson eText offers interactive and sharing features. Instructors can share their comments or highlights, and students can add their own, creating a tight community of learners within the class.

Textbook Features

Making Connections

CONNECTING CHAPTER boxes appear at the beginning of each chapter. This feature combines the chapter outline with the learning objectives, key questions, and page references.

18 Financial Statement Analysis

CONNECTING CHAPTER 18

LEARNING OBJECTIVES

① Perform a horizontal analysis of financial statements

How do we compare several years of financial information?

Objectives of Financial Statement Analysis, page 1032
Methods of Analysis, page 1033
Horizontal Analysis, page 1033
   Trend Percentages

② Perform a vertical analysis of financial statements

What is vertical analysis, and how do we perform one?

Vertical Analysis, page 1037

③ Prepare and use common-size financial statements

What are common-size financial statements, and how do we use them?

Common-Size Statements, page 1040
   Benchmarking

④ Compute the standard financial ratios

How do we compute standard financial ratios, and what do they mean?

Using Ratios to Make Decisions, page 1044
   Measuring the Ability to Pay Current Liabilities
     (Liquidity)
   Measuring the Ability to Sell Inventory and Collect
     Receivables (Efficiency)
   Measuring the Ability to Pay Long-Term Debt
     (Solvency)
   Measuring Profitability
   Analyzing Shares as an Investment (Value)
Limitations of Financial Analysis, page 1055
Investor Decisions, page 1055
   Annual Reports
   Red Flags in Analyzing Financial Statements

⑤ Describe the impact of IFRS on financial statement analysis

What is the impact of IFRS on financial statement analysis?

The Impact of IFRS on Financial Statement Analysis, page 1058

The **Summary** for Chapter 18 appears on page 1061.
Key Terms with definitions for this chapter's material appears on page 1063.

LEARNING OBJECTIVES provide a roadmap showing what will be covered and what is especially important in each chapter.

PAGE REFERENCES give students the ability to quickly connect to the topic they are seeking within the chapter.

KEY QUESTIONS are questions about the important concepts in the chapter, expressed in everyday language.

CPA competencies

This text covers material outlined in **Section 1: Financial Reporting of the CPA Competency Map**. The Learning Objectives for each chapter have been aligned with the CPA Competency Map to ensure the best coverage possible.

1.1.2 Evaluates the appropriateness of the basis of financial reporting

1.4.4 Interprets financial reporting results for stakeholders (internal or external)

CPA COMPETENCY MAP Each chapter's Learning Objectives have been aligned with the latest CPA competencies, which are provided here.

CHAPTER OPENERS · · · · · · · · · · · · · · · · · · ·

Chapter openers set up the concepts to be covered in the chapter using stories students can relate to. The implications of those concepts on a company's reporting and decision-making processes are then discussed.

When Danielle Rodriguez started her business in January 2015, she wasn't thinking about accounting. As an IT professional, she was looking to combine her business skills with her love of dogs. Her "fur babies," Zoey and Maggie Mae, are an important part of her #Barknfun Team.

Her business, The Bark'N Fun Company, is a monthly subscription box service that offers premium toys, treats, and accessories for dogs and puppies. The business is online, but her office is located in the small town of Courtice, Ontario.

The majority of small businesses fail within the first three years. So how has The Bark'N Fun Company stayed in business in a competitive online market for luxury items? Danielle, The Bark'N Fun Company's owner, uses accounting information to make her business decisions. Is she an accountant? No! She is a smart businessperson who knows that she needs to understand the business's monthly revenues and expenses so that her business can survive in the short-term and thrive in the long-term. The Bark'N Fun Company needs to know if the prices of their toys and treats are high enough to cover operating expenses, or if they can afford to offer free shipping. Is it working? Yes. The Bark'N Fun Company has not only been able to stay in business but also supports charities that are important to dogs, such as canine rescue organizations and humane society shelters.

This chapter shows how The Bark'N Fun Company and other businesses record their transactions and update their financial records. The procedures outlined in this chapter are followed by businesses ranging in size from giant multinational corporations like PetSmart Inc. to micro-enterprises like The Bark'N Fun Company and Hunter Environmental Consulting, who we will continue to follow through this chapter.

57

SPREADSHEET FORMATS USED IN EXHIBITS ·

NEW! Excel-based financial documents are used so students will familiarize themselves with the accounting information used in the business world.

EXHIBIT 10–6 | Units-of-Production Amortization for a Truck

	A	B	C	D	E	F	G	H	I
1			**Amortization for the Year**						
2 3	**Date**	**Asset Cost**	**Amortization Per Kilometre**		**Number of Kilometres**		**Amortization Expense**	**Accumulated Amortization**	**Asset Book Value**
4	Jan. 1, 2020	$65,000	❶		❷				$65,000
5	Dec. 31, 2020		$0.15	×	90,000	=	$13,500	$13,500	51,500
6	Dec. 31, 2021		0.15	×	120,000	=	18,000	31,500	33,500
7	Dec. 31, 2022		0.15	×	100,000	=	15,000	46,500	18,500
8	Dec. 31, 2023		0.15	×	60,000	=	9,000	55,500	9,500
9	Dec. 31, 2024		0.15	×	30,000	=	4,500	60,000	5,000

Residual value

EXHIBIT 2–8 | The Journal

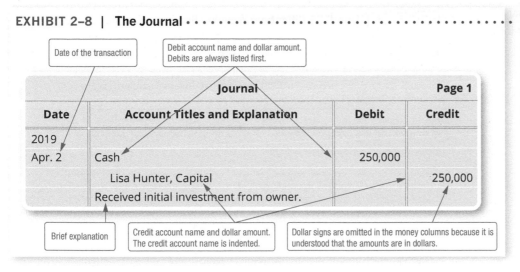

Date of the transaction

Debit account name and dollar amount. Debits are always listed first.

Journal			Page 1
Date	Account Titles and Explanation	Debit	Credit
2019			
Apr. 2	Cash	250,000	
	Lisa Hunter, Capital		250,000
	Received initial investment from owner.		

Brief explanation

Credit account name and dollar amount. The credit account name is indented.

Dollar signs are omitted in the money columns because it is understood that the amounts are in dollars.

ANNOTATED EXHIBITS More annotated exhibits have been developed for this edition to improve clarity and reduce related explanations in the text.

INSTRUCTOR TIPS & TRICKS Found throughout the text, these handwritten notes mimic the experience of having an experienced teacher walk a student through concepts on the "board." Many include mnemonic devices or examples to help students remember the rules of accounting.

One way to memorize this is to use an acronym, such as AWE ROL. In this case, the (A)sset, (W)ithdrawal, and (E)xpense accounts all have debit balances, while the (R)evenue, (O)wner's Equity, and (L)iability accounts all have credit balances. Or memorize which side has the "+" (increase), and then all the "−" (decreases) are the opposite. This way you only have to memorize half of them! Try DR. AWE—the debits (dr) belong with the (A)sset, (W)ithdrawal, and (E)xpense accounts.

EXHIBIT 2–6 | Expanded Accounting Equation

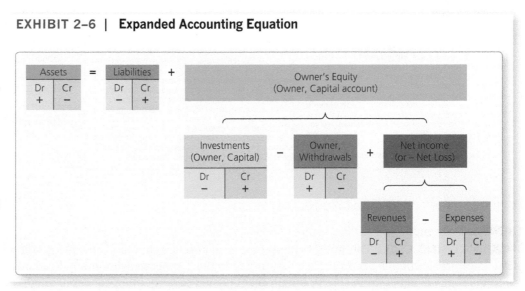

TRY IT! BOXES Found after each learning objective, Try It! boxes give students opportunities to apply the concept they've just learned by completing an accounting problem. Links to these exercises appear throughout the eText, allowing students to practise in MyLab Accounting without interruption.

8. Using the following accounts and their balances, prepare the unadjusted trial balance for Cooper Furniture Repair as of December 31, 2018. All accounts have normal balances.

Cash	$ 7,000	Advertising Expense	$ 1,200
Unearned Revenue	4,500	Utilities Expense	800
Equipment	10,000	Rent Expense	5,000
Service Revenue	8,000	Accounts Payable	2,300
M. Cooper, Capital	12,200	M. Cooper, Withdrawals	3,000

Solutions appear at the end of this chapter and on **MyLab Accounting**

IFRS/ASPE COMPARISON . . . . . .
Provides guidance on how IFRS
differs from ASPE.

EXHIBIT 1–16 | How IFRS Differ from What We See in the Chapter

ASPE	IFRS
In Canada, both International Financial Reporting Standards (IFRS) and Accounting Standards for Private Enterprises (ASPE) are prepared under the authority of the **Accounting Standards Board** and are published as part of the CPA *Canada Handbook*.	
Sole proprietorships follow ASPE, which are simpler and less costly to implement. Private corporations can choose to follow ASPE or IFRS.	Publicly accountable enterprises or those planning to become one must follow IFRS.
Financial reports contain less information under ASPE because readers have more access to the details themselves.	Financial reports under IFRS contain more detailed information than under ASPE because users do not have easy access to the information.
Companies reporting under either method must also provide notes to the financial statements, which include significant accounting policies and explanatory information.	

ETHICS | Are receipts really important? ·

Elijah Morris, assistant manager for Red's Big Burger Restaurant, is responsible for purchasing equipment and supplies for the restaurant. Elijah recently purchased a $4,000 commercial-grade refrigerator for the restaurant, but he can't find the receipt. Elijah purchased the refrigerator with personal funds and is asking to be reimbursed by the restaurant. Hannah, the restaurant's accountant, has said that she is unsure if the business can reimburse Elijah without a receipt. Elijah suggests: "Hannah, it won't really matter if I have a receipt or not. You've seen the refrigerator in the restaurant, so you know I purchased it. What difference is a little receipt going to make?"

What should Hannah do? What would you do?

Solution

Hannah should not reimburse Elijah until she receives the receipt—the source document. Elijah could have purchased the refrigerator for less than the amount he is asking in reimbursement. Source documents provide the evidence of the amount of the transaction. If either an auditor or the owner of the restaurant investigated the $4,000 purchase, he or she would need to see the source document to verify the transaction. If Elijah truly cannot find the receipt, Hannah should ask for an alternative source document such as a credit card or bank statement that shows evidence of the purchase. In addition, Elijah should be warned about using personal funds to purchase equipment for the business.

· · · ETHICS BOXES This feature provides common questions and potential solutions business owners face. Students are asked to determine the course of action they would take based on concepts covered in the chapter and are then given potential solutions.

NEW! **USING EXCEL** This end-of-chapter exercise in select chapters introduces students to Excel to solve common accounting problems as they would in the business environment. Students will work from a template that will aid them in solving the problem related to accounting concepts taught in the chapter.

NEW! **SERIAL EXERCISE** starts in Chapter 1 and run through Volume 1, exposing students to recording entries for a service company and then moving into recording transactions for a merchandiser later in the text.

NEW! **PRACTICE SET** The Practice Set for Chapters 2–9 provide another opportunity for students to practise the entire accounting cycle. The practice set uses the same company in each chapter, but is often not as extensive as the serial exercise.

Acknowledgments for *Horngren's Accounting*, Eleventh Canadian Edition

Acknowledgements for *Horngren's Accounting*, Eleventh Canadian Edition

Horngren's Accounting, Eleventh Canadian Edition, is the product of a rigorous research process that included multiple reviews in the various stages of development to ensure the revision meets the needs of Canadian students and instructors. The extensive feedback from the following reviewers helped shape this edition into a clearer, more readable and streamlined textbook in both the chapter content and assignment material:

- Gregory Springate, Red Deer College
- Deirdre Fitzpatrick, George Brown College
- Joan Baines, Red River College
- Robert Cinapri, Humber College
- Arsineh Garabedian, Douglas College
- Darlene Lowe, MacEwan University
- Jerry Aubin, Algonquin College
- Meredith Delaney, Seneca College
- Heather Cornish, Northern Alberta Institute of Technology
- Cheryl Wilson, Durham College

We would also like to thank the late Charles Horngren and Tom Harrison for their support in writing the original material.

We would like to give special thanks to Chris Deresh, CPA, Manager, Curriculum Content, at Chartered Professional Accountants of Canada for his guidance and technical support. His willingness to review and discuss portions of the manuscript was generous and insightful, and it is gratefully acknowledged.

The Chartered Professional Accountants, as the official administrator of generally accepted accounting principles in Canada, and the *CPA Canada Handbook*, are vital to the conduct of business and accounting in Canada. We have made every effort to incorporate the most current *Handbook* recommendations in this new edition of *Accounting*. We would also like to thank Sarah Magdalinski, Northern Alberta Institute of Technology, for her work in assessing and adapting this edition's Serial Exercises.

Thanks are extended to Indigo Books & Music Inc. and TELUS Corporation for permission to use portions of their annual reports in Volumes I and II of this text and on MyLabAccounting. We acknowledge the support provided by the websites of various news organizations and by the annual reports of a large number of public companies.

We would like to acknowledge the people of Pearson Canada, in particular senior portfolio manager Keara Emmett and marketing manager Darcey Pepper. Special thanks to Suzanne Simpson Millar, Queen Bee at Simpson Editorial Services, who was an awesome content developer on this edition. Thanks also to Sarah Gallagher, project manager; Nicole Mellow and Sogut Gulec, content managers, for their diligence in keeping everything on track.

Our task is to provide educational material in the area of accounting to instructors and students to aid in the understanding of this subject area. We welcome your suggestions and comments on how to serve you better.

12 Partnerships

CONNECTING CHAPTER 12

LEARNING OBJECTIVES

(1) Identify the characteristics of a partnership

What are the characteristics of a partnership?

Characteristics of a Partnership, page 661
    The Written Partnership Agreement
    Limited Life
    Mutual Agency
    Unlimited Liability
    Co-ownership of Property
    No Partnership Income Tax

Advantages and Disadvantages of Partnerships, page 663

Type of Partnerships, page 664
    General Partnerships
    Limited Partnerships

Partnership Financial Statements, page 665

(2) Account for partners' initial investments in a partnership

How do we account for partners' investments in a partnership?

Forming a Partnership, page 666

(3) Allocate profits and losses to the partners by different methods

How can we allocate profits and losses to the partners?

Sharing Partnership Profits and Losses, page 667
    Sharing Based on a Stated Fraction
    Sharing Based on Capital Investments

    Sharing Based on Capital Investments and on Service
    Sharing Based on Service and Interest
    Allocation of a Net Loss

Partner Withdrawals (Drawings), page 673

(4) Account for the admission of a new partner

How do we account for a new partner?

Admission of a Partner, page 674
    Admission by Purchasing a Partner's Interest
    Admission by Investing in the Partnership

(5) Account for the withdrawal of a partner

How do we account for the withdrawal of a partner?

Withdrawal of a Partner from the Business, page 678
    Withdrawal at Book Value
    Withdrawal at Less than Book Value
    Withdrawal at More than Book Value
    Death of a Partner

(6) Account for the liquidation of a partnership

How do we account for the ending of a partnership?

Liquidation of a Partnership, page 682
    Sale of Assets at a Gain
    Sale of Assets at a Loss
    Capital Deficiencies

The **Summary** for Chapter 12 appears on page 688.

Key Terms with definitions for this chapter's material appears on page 689.

CPA competencies

This text covers material outlined in **Section 1: Financial Reporting of the CPA Competency Map**. The Learning Objectives for each chapter have been aligned with the CPA Competency Map to ensure the best coverage possible.

1.3.1 Prepares financial statements

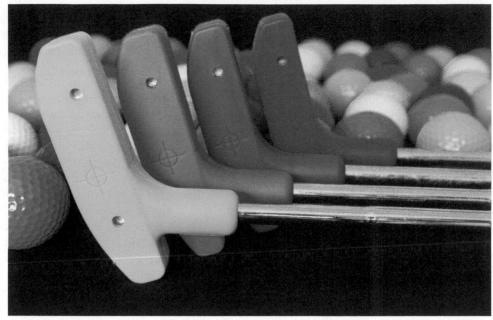

Mylitleye/Fotolia

Jenny Lo and Sam Lachlan are considering opening a miniature golf course in Wasaga Beach, Ontario. The golf course will have 18 holes with dinosaurs, wind-mills, water features, and more. Jenny has been carefully evaluating the tourism industry in the town and believes that the golf course will be busy enough during the summer tourist season to close during the winter months, allowing Jenny and Sam plenty of time to ski and snowboard in the off season.

Jenny and Sam are considering organizing the business as a partnership. Jenny is willing to contribute a piece of property in the prime downtown area that she just inherited. She is also interested in managing the day-to-day operations of the business. Sam, with his degree in accounting, has agreed to handle the accounting and business aspects of the golf course.

Now all Jenny and Sam need to decide is how the partnership will be organized. Some questions they are considering include, What are the specific responsibilities of each partner? How should profits and losses be shared between the partners? What if one of the partners wants out of the partnership in the future? How would the partnership add a new partner?

A **partnership** is an association of two or more persons who co-own a business for profit. This definition is common to the various provincial partnership acts, which tend to prescribe similar rules with respect to the organization and operation of partnerships in their jurisdictions.

Forming a partnership is easy. It requires no permission from government authorities and involves no legal procedures, with the exception that most provinces require partnerships to register information such as the names of the partners and the name under which the business will be conducted.[1] When two people decide to go into business together, a partnership is automatically formed.

A partnership combines the assets, talents, and experience of the partners. Business opportunities closed to an individual may open up to a partnership. As the chapter-opening story illustrates, this is an important characteristic of a partnership. The miniature golf course will likely be successful because it is able to combine the skills of its two owners. It is unlikely that Jenny or Sam would be able to operate the business as well if either tried to do it on his or her own.

Partnerships come in all sizes. Many partnerships have fewer than 10 partners. Some medical practices may have 10 or more partners, while some of the largest law firms in Canada have more than 500 partners. The largest accounting firm in Canada has more than 800 partners. Exhibit 12–1 lists the 10 largest public accounting firms in Canada. The majority of them are partnerships.

EXHIBIT 12–1 | The 10 Largest Accounting Firms in Canada (by Number of Partners in 2015)

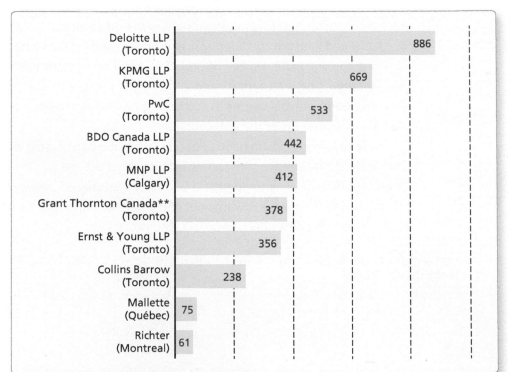

Firm	Partners
Deloitte LLP (Toronto)	886
KPMG LLP (Toronto)	669
PwC (Toronto)	533
BDO Canada LLP (Toronto)	442
MNP LLP (Calgary)	412
Grant Thornton Canada** (Toronto)	378
Ernst & Young LLP (Toronto)	356
Collins Barrow (Toronto)	238
Mallette (Québec)	75
Richter (Montreal)	61

Source: Data from Statista, Top 20 accounting firms in the United States in 2018, by U.S. revenue (in billion U.S. dollars), Retrieved from https://www.statista.com/statistics/478912/number-of-partners-at-leading-accounting-firms-canada/

---

[1] Smyth, J.E., D.A. Soberman, A.J. Easson, and S.S. McGill, *The Law and Business Administration in Canada,* 13th ed. (Toronto: Pearson Canada Inc., 2013), 598–602.

Beginning with this chapter, you will learn more about the different types of organization structures that were first introduced in Chapter 1. So far, we have only really looked at accounting for proprietorships.

The good news is that the principles and concepts in the accounting framework you have learned apply equally to all types of organizations.

Characteristics of a Partnership

Starting a partnership is voluntary. A person cannot be forced to join a partnership, and partners cannot be forced to accept another person as a partner (unless existing partners vote and the majority accept the new partner). The following characteristics distinguish partnerships from proprietorships and from corporations.

LO (1)
What are the characteristics of a partnership?

The Written Partnership Agreement

A business partnership is somewhat like a marriage. To be successful, the partners must cooperate. However, business partners do not vow to remain together for life. To make certain that each partner fully understands how the partnership operates, partners should draw up a **partnership agreement**. Although the partnership agreement may be oral, a written agreement between the partners reduces the chance of a misunderstanding. This agreement is a contract between the partners, so transactions under the agreement are governed by contract law. The provincial legislatures in Canada have passed their respective versions of a partnership act, the terms of which apply in the absence of a partnership agreement or in the absence of particular matters in the partnership agreement.[2]

The partnership agreement should specify the following points:

A partnership is not required to have a formal written agreement. But a written agreement prevents confusion as to the sharing of profits and losses, partners' responsibilities, admission of new partners, how the partnership will be liquidated, and so on. However, there can still be disagreements even when there is a written agreement.

- Name, location, and nature of the business
- Name, capital investment, and duties of each partner
- Procedures for admitting a new partner
- Method of sharing profits and losses among the partners
- Withdrawals of assets allowed to the partners
- Procedures for settling disputes among the partners
- Procedures for settling with a partner who withdraws from the firm
- Procedures for removing a partner who will not withdraw or retire from the partnership voluntarily
- Procedures for liquidating the partnership—selling the assets, paying the liabilities, and giving any remaining cash to the partners

Limited Life

A partnership has a limited life. If one partner withdraws from the business or dies, the partnership dissolves and its books are closed. If the remaining partners want to continue as partners in the same business, they form a new partnership with a new set of financial records and a new partnership agreement. **Dissolution** is the ending of a partnership and does not require liquidation; that is, the assets need

---

[2] Ibid., 598–618.

not be sold to outside parties for a new partnership to be created. Often the new partnership continues the former partnership's business, and the new partnership may choose to continue to use the dissolved partnership's name. Some types of large partnerships, such as Deloitte LLP, retain the firm name even after partners resign from the firm.

Mutual Agency

Mutual agency means that every partner is a mutual agent of the firm. Any partner can bind the business to a contract within the scope of the partnership's regular business operations. If a partner enters into a contract with a person or another business to provide a service, then the firm—not just the partner who signed the contract—is bound to provide that service. If the partner signs a contract to buy her own car, however, the partnership is not liable because the car is a personal matter; it is not within the scope of the regular business operations of the partnership.

The following example shows the impact mutual agency can have on a partnership. Richard Harding and Simon Davis formed a partnership to deal in lumber and other building materials. The partners agreed that their company should not handle brick or any stone materials and that neither partner had the right to purchase these commodities. While Harding was away during the summer, Davis purchased a quantity of these materials for the company because he could buy them at a cheap price. Two months later, when Harding returned, business was very slow, and brick and stone were selling at a price lower than Davis had paid for them. Harding, therefore, refused to accept any more deliveries under the contract. Harding argued that Davis had no authority to buy these goods since the partnership was not organized to deal in brick and stone. The supplier of the brick and stone said that he did not know the partnership was not in the brick and stone business. In fact, he believed that it did handle these goods since all of the other lumber companies in the area bought or sold brick and stone. Because the supplier acted in good faith, he claimed that Harding and Davis should accept the remaining deliveries of brick and stone according to the agreement that was made. Who is correct? Under normal circumstances, the brick and stone supplier is correct because the mutual agency characteristic of a partnership allows partners to bind each other in business contracts. The agreements made within the partnership would not be known by an outside party like the supplier, so the supplier would have a solid case and could sue the partnership to abide by the contract.[3]

Unlimited Liability

Chapter 1 introduced these concepts for a sole proprietorship. You may want to go back and review them now.

Each partner has **unlimited personal liability** for the debts of the business. When a partnership cannot pay its debts with business assets, the partners must pay with their personal assets. (There are exceptions, which are described in the section, Types of Partnerships.) If either partner is unable to pay his or her part of the debt, the other partner (or partners) must make payment.

Unlimited liability and mutual agency are closely related. A dishonest partner or a partner with poor judgment may commit the partnership to a contract under which the business loses money. In turn, creditors may force *all* the partners to pay the debt from their personal assets. Hence, a business partner should be chosen with great care.

---

[3] This case is based on the scenario described at ChestofBooks.com, "B. Apparent Scope of Authority," http://chestofbooks.com/business/law/Case-Method/B-Apparent-Scope-Of-Authority.html#ixzz1qimHxY2o, accessed July 1, 2018.

Co-ownership of Property

Any asset—cash, inventory, machinery, computers, and so on—that a partner invests into the partnership becomes the joint property of all the partners. The partner who invested the asset is no longer its sole owner.

There is a way for a partner to allow the partnership to use a personal asset, such as a car or money, without losing his or her claim to that asset: The partner could lease the car to the partnership. If the partnership ended, the car would have to be returned to its owner. The partner could also lend money to the partnership instead of investing it. The partnership would have to repay the loan to the lending partner before any distribution of capital to the partners.

No Partnership Income Tax

The partnership *reports* its income to the government tax authority (the Canada Revenue Agency), but the partnership pays *no* income tax. The net income of the partnership is divided and flows through the business to the partners, who pay personal income tax on their share.

For example, suppose that the Willis & Jones partnership earned net income of $150,000, shared equally by the two partners. The partnership would pay no income tax *as a business entity*. However, each partner would pay income tax *as an individual* on his or her $75,000 share of partnership income.

ETHICS | Should Erik buy the new equipment?

Erik Morales was very angry with his brother. He had just come from a partnership meeting concerning the purchase of new equipment for their recording studio. His brother, Juan, disagreed about purchasing the new equipment, stating that the business didn't have enough cash to purchase the equipment without incurring additional debt. After thinking about their conversation, Erik decided that he would secure a loan to purchase the equipment. Erik knew that if his brother could just see how well the new equipment worked, Juan would change his mind. Should Erik buy the new equipment? What would you do?

Solution

Mutual agency allows Erik to act as an agent of the partnership and secure debt for the purchase of new equipment. However, the fact that his partner, Juan, does not agree with incurring additional debt should discourage Erik from taking out the loan. Erik should consider that the partnership's debt becomes a personal liability not only to Erik, but also to Juan. If the partnership can't repay the debt, then Erik and Juan must use personal assets to meet the debt. Erik could not only endanger the liquidity of the partnership by taking out a loan, but also risk his relationship with his brother. Erik should not go behind his brother's back to purchase the equipment, even though he thinks it will be a good decision in the long run.

Advantages and Disadvantages of Partnerships

Exhibit 12–2 lists the advantages and disadvantages of partnerships (compared with proprietorships and corporations). Most features of a proprietorship also apply to a partnership, most importantly:

- Limited life
- Unlimited liability
- No business income tax

EXHIBIT 12–2 | Advantages and Disadvantages of Partnerships

Partnership Advantages	Partnership Disadvantages
Versus Proprietorships: • A partnership can raise more capital since capital comes from more than one person. • A partnership brings together the abilities of more than one person. • Partners working well together can achieve more than by working alone: $1 + 1 > 2$ in a good partnership. *Versus Corporations:* • A partnership is less expensive to organize than a corporation, which requires articles of incorporation from a province or the federal government. • A partnership is subject to fewer governmental regulations and restrictions than a corporation.	• A partnership agreement may be difficult to formulate. Each time a new partner is admitted or a partner leaves the partnership, the business needs a new partnership agreement. • Relationships among partners may be fragile. It is hard to find the right partner. • Mutual agency and unlimited liability create personal obligations for each partner. • Lack of continuity of the business is faced by a partnership but not a corporation.

Types of Partnerships

There are two basic types of partnerships: general and limited.

General Partnerships

A **general partnership** is the basic form of partnership organization. Each partner is a co-owner of the business with all the privileges and risks of ownership. The general partners share the profits, losses, and the risks of the business.

Limited Partnerships

Since all partners are personally liable for any debt of the business, it is extremely important to choose a partner carefully. This is one reason some investors/partners prefer the limited partnership form of business organization.

Partners can avoid unlimited personal liability for partnership obligations by forming a *limited partnership*. A **limited partnership** has at least two classes of partners:

• There must be at least one *general partner*, who takes primary responsibility for the management of the business. The general partner also takes most of the risk of failure if the partnership goes bankrupt (liabilities exceed assets). In some limited partnerships, such as real estate limited partnerships, the general partner often invests little cash in the business. Instead, the general partner's contribution is her or his skill in managing the organization. Usually, the general partner is the last owner to receive a share of partnership profits and losses. But the general partner may earn all excess profits after the limited partners get their share of the income.

• The *limited partners* are so named because their personal obligation for the partnership's liabilities is limited to the amount they have invested in the business. Limited partners have limited liability similar to the limited liability that shareholders in a corporation have. Usually, the limited partners have invested the bulk of the partnership's assets and capital. They therefore usually have the first claim to partnership profits and losses, but only up to a specified limit. In exchange for their limited liability, their potential for profits usually has a limit as well.

Limited Liability Partnerships Many professionals, such as doctors, lawyers, and most public accounting firms in Canada—including most of those in Exhibit 12–1—are now organized as **limited liability partnerships (LLPs)**. An LLP can only be used by eligible professions (such as accounting) and is designed to protect innocent partners from negligence damages that result from another partner's actions. This means that each partner's personal liability for other partners' negligence is limited to a certain dollar amount, although liability for a partner's own negligence is still unlimited. The LLP must carry an adequate amount of malpractice insurance or liability insurance to protect the public.

Partnership Financial Statements

Partnership financial statements are much like those of a proprietorship. Exhibit 12–3 compares partnership statements (in Panel A) against the same reports for a sole proprietorship (in Panel B).

The key differences between a proprietorship's and a partnership's financial statements are as follows:

- A partnership income statement includes a section showing the division of net income to the partners.

- A partnership balance sheet reports a separate Capital account for each partner in the section now called Partners' Equity. Large partnerships may show one balance, the total for all partners, and provide the details in a separate report, also shown in Exhibit 12–3, called a statement of partners' equity.

EXHIBIT 12–3 | **Financial Statements of a Partnership and a Proprietorship (all amounts in thousands of dollars)**

Panel A—PARTNERSHIP

KIM & GALARZA
Income Statement
For the Year Ended December 31, 2020

Revenues		$460
Expenses		270
Net income		$190
Allocation of net income:		
To Su-min Kim	$114	
To Luis Galarza	76	$190

KIM & GALARZA
Statement of Partners' Equity
For the Year Ended December 31, 2020

	Kim	Galarza	Total
Capital, January 1, 2020	$ 50	$ 40	$ 90
Additional investments	10	—	10
Net income	114	76	190
Subtotal	174	116	290
Less: Withdrawals	72	48	120
Capital, December 31, 2020	$102	$ 68	$170

KIM & GALARZA
Balance Sheet
December 31, 2020

Assets		
Cash and other assets	$170	
Total assets		$170
Partners' Equity		
Su-min Kim, capital	$102	
Luis Galarza, capital	68	
Total partners' equity		$170
Total liabilities and equity		$170

Panel B—PROPRIETORSHIP

GALARZA CONSULTING
Income Statement
For the Year Ended December 31, 2020

Revenues	$460
Expenses	270
Net income	$190

GALARZA CONSULTING
Statement of Owner's Equity
For the Year Ended December 31, 2020

Capital, January 1, 2020	$ 90
Additional investments	10
Net income	190
Subtotal	290
Less: Withdrawals	120
Capital, December 31, 2020	$170

GALARZA CONSULTING
Balance Sheet
December 31, 2020

Assets	
Cash and other assets	$170
Total assets	$170
Owner's Equity	
Luis Galarza, capital	$170
Total liabilities and equity	$170

Try It!

Forming a Partnership

LO ②

How do we account for partners' investments in a partnership?

Let's examine the startup of a partnership. Partners in a new partnership may invest assets and their related liabilities in the business. These contributions are journalized in the same way as for proprietorships, by debiting the assets and crediting the liabilities at their agreed-upon values. Each person's net contribution—assets minus liabilities—is credited to the equity account for that person. Often the partners hire an independent firm to *appraise* their assets and liabilities at current market value at the time a partnership is formed. This outside evaluation assures an objective valuation for what each partner brings into the business.

Suppose Katie Wilson and Dan Chao form a partnership on June 1, 2020, to develop and sell computer software. The partners agree on the following values based on an independent appraisal:

Wilson's contributions

- Cash, $10,000; inventory, $40,000; and accounts payable, $80,000
- Computer equipment: cost, $800,000; accumulated amortization, $200,000; current market value, $450,000

Chao's contributions

- Cash, $5,000
- Computer software: cost, $50,000; current market value, $100,000

The partnership entries are as follows:

The partnership records receipts of the partners' initial investments at the current market values of the assets and liabilities because, in effect, the partnership is buying the assets and assuming the liabilities at their current market values.

	Wilson's investment		
Jun. 1	Cash	10,000	
	Inventory	40,000*	
	Computer Equipment	450,000*	
	Accounts Payable		80,000*
	Katie Wilson, Capital		420,000
	To record Wilson's investment in the partnership ($500,000 − $80,000).		
	Chao's investment		
Jun. 1	Cash	5,000	
	Computer Software	100,000*	
	Dan Chao, Capital		105,000
	To record Chao's investment in the partnership.		

*Current market values are used.

The initial partnership balance sheet appears in Exhibit 12–4.

EXHIBIT 12–4 | Partnership Balance Sheet

WILSON AND CHAO Balance Sheet June 1, 2020			
Assets		**Liabilities**	
Cash	$ 15,000	Accounts payable	$ 80,000
Inventory	40,000	**Partners' Equity**	
Computer equipment	450,000	Katie Wilson, capital	420,000
Computer software	100,000	Dan Chao, capital	105,000
		Total partners' equity	525,000
Total assets	$605,000	Total liabilities and equity	$605,000

Try It!

3. Marty Kaur invests land in a partnership with Lee Manors. Kaur purchased the land in 2014 for $20,000. Three independent real estate appraisers now value the land at $50,000. Kaur wants $50,000 capital in the new partnership, but Manors objects. Manors believes that Kaur's capital investment should be measured by the book value of his land. Manors and Kaur seek your advice.
   a. Which value of the land is appropriate for measuring Kaur's capital: book value or current market value?
   b. Give the partnership's journal entry to record Kaur's investment in the business on September 1, 2020.

Solutions appear at the end of this chapter and on **MyLab Accounting**

Sharing Partnership Profits and Losses

Allocating profits and losses among partners can be challenging and can be a major source of disputes. Any division of profits and losses is allowed as long as the partners agree and it is in the partnership agreement. Typical arrangements include the following:

LO ③

How can we allocate profits and losses to the partners?

- Sharing profits and losses based on a stated fraction for each partner, such as 50/50, or 2/3 and 1/3, or 4:3:3 (which means 40 percent to Partner A, 30 percent to Partner B, and 30 percent to Partner C)
- Sharing based on each partner's capital investment
- Sharing based on each partner's service
- Sharing based on a combination of stated fractions, investments, service, and other items

If the partners have not drawn up an agreement, or if the agreement does not state how the partners will divide profits and losses, then, by law, the partners must share profits and losses equally. If the agreement specifies a method for sharing profits but not losses, then losses are shared in the same proportion as profits. For example, a partner receiving 75 percent of the profits would likewise absorb 75 percent of any losses.

In some cases an equal division is not fair. One partner may perform more work for the business than the other partner, or one partner may make a larger capital contribution. In the preceding example, Dan Chao might agree to work longer hours for the partnership than Katie Wilson in order to earn a greater share of profits. Wilson could argue that she should receive more of the profits because she contributed more net assets ($420,000) than Chao did ($105,000). Chao might contend that his computer software program is the partnership's most important asset, and that his share of the profits should be greater than Wilson's share. Arriving at fair sharing of profits and losses in a partnership may be difficult.

We now demonstrate how to account for some options available in determining partners' shares of profits and losses using several different partnerships.

Sharing Based on a Stated Fraction

The partnership agreement may state each partner's fraction of the total profits and losses. Suppose the partnership agreement of Shannon Kerry and Raoul Calder allocates two-thirds of the business profits and losses to Kerry and one-third to Calder. This sharing rule can also be expressed as 2:1.

Net Income If net income for the year is $60,000, and all revenue and expense accounts have been closed, the Income Summary account has a credit balance of $60,000 prior to its closing.

Income Summary

	Bal. 60,000

The ratio of 2:1 is equal to fractions of 2/3 and 1/3, where the denominator of the fraction is the sum of the numbers in the ratio. The ratio of 2:1 is also a 66.7%: 33.3% percent sharing ratio.

The entry to close this account and allocate the net income to the partners' Capital accounts is as follows:

Dec. 31	Income Summary	60,000	
	Shannon Kerry, Capital		40,000
	Raoul Calder, Capital		20,000
	To allocate net income to partners. (Kerry: $60,000 × ⅔; Calder: $60,000 × ⅓)		

The income summary account was introduced in Chapter 4. It holds profits/losses until distributed to owners.

Suppose Kerry's beginning Capital balance was $50,000 and Calder's was $10,000. After posting, the accounts appear as follows:

Income Summary		**Shannon Kerry, Capital**		**Raoul Calder, Capital**	
Clo. 60,000	Bal. 60,000		Bal. 50,000		Bal. 10,000
			Clo. 40,000		Clo. 20,000
			Bal. 90,000		Bal. 30,000

Net Loss If the partnership had a net loss of $15,000, the Income Summary account would have a debit balance of $15,000. In that case, the closing entry to allocate the loss to the partners' Capital accounts would be:

Dec. 31	Shannon Kerry, Capital	10,000	
	Raoul Calder, Capital	5,000	
	Income Summary		15,000
	To allocate net loss to partners.		
	(Kerry: $15,000 × ⅔; Calder: $15,000 × ⅓)		

> A profit or loss will increase or decrease each partner's Capital account, but cash will not change hands. The **Withdrawals** account records the cash each partner takes from the partnership.

Sharing Based on Capital Investments

Profits and losses are often allocated in proportion to the partners' capital investments in the business. Suppose John Abbot, Erica Baxter, and Tony Craven are partners in ABC Company. Their Capital accounts at the end of the first year of business have the following balances, before closing entries. These amounts are equal to the original capital investments for each of the partners since there were no additional investments during the year and no earnings or withdrawals have yet been posted to these accounts.

John Abbot, Capital	$120,000
Erica Baxter, Capital	180,000
Tony Craven, Capital	150,000
Total Capital balances	$450,000

Assume that the partnership earned a profit of $300,000 for the year. To allocate this amount based on capital investments, each partner's percentage share of the partnership's total capital investment amount must be computed.

We divide each partner's investment by the total capital investment amount:

Abbot:	($120,000 ÷ $450,000)	= 26.6667%
Baxter:	($180,000 ÷ $450,000)	= 40%
Craven:	($150,000 ÷ $450,000)	= 33.3333%

Do not round the interim percentages. For this chapter, round only the final dollar amount to the nearest whole dollar.

These figures, multiplied by the $300,000 profit amount, yield each partner's share of the year's profits:

Abbot:	$300,000 × 26.6667%	= $80,000.10, round to $80,000
Baxter:	$300,000 × 40%	= $120,000
Craven:	$300,000 × 33.3333%	= $99,999.90, round to $100,000

Or it can be calculated in one step as follows:

Abbot:	($120,000 ÷ $450,000) × $300,000	= $ 80,000
Baxter:	($180,000 ÷ $450,000) × $300,000	= $120,000
Craven:	($150,000 ÷ $450,000) × $300,000	= $100,000
	Net income allocated to partners	= $300,000

The closing entry to allocate the profit to the partners' Capital accounts is:

Dec. 31	Income Summary	300,000	
	John Abbot, Capital		80,000
	Erica Baxter, Capital		120,000
	Tony Craven, Capital		100,000
	To allocate net income to partners.		

After this closing entry, the partners' Capital balances are:

John Abbot, Capital	$200,000	$120,000 + $80,000
Erica Baxter, Capital	300,000	$180,000 + $120,000
Tony Craven, Capital	250,000	$150,000 + $100,000
Total Capital balances after allocation of net income	$750,000	

Sharing Based on Capital Investments and on Service

One partner, regardless of his or her capital investment, may put more work into the business than the other partners. Even among partners who log equal service time, one person's superior experience and knowledge may be worth more to the firm. To reward the harder-working or more valuable person, the profit-and-loss-sharing method may be based on a combination of partner capital investments *and* **service** to the business. In this case, the partners are allocated predetermined sums to be withdrawn. These are *not* employee salaries, but they are sometimes referred to as a **salary allowance**.

Assume Michelle Wallas and Carolyn Borugian formed a partnership in which Wallas invested $50,000 and Borugian invested $50,000, a total of $100,000. Borugian devotes more time to the partnership and earns the larger income allocation from the partnership. Accordingly, the two partners have agreed to share profit as follows:

❶ The first $40,000 of partnership profit is to be allocated based on the partners' capital investments in the business.

❷ The next $60,000 of profit is to be allocated based on service (Wallas works 40 percent of the time and Borugian works 60 percent of the time), with Wallas receiving $24,000 and Borugian receiving $36,000.

❸ Any remaining profit is allocated equally.

If net income for the first year is $125,000, the partners' shares of this profit are computed as follows:

	A	B Wallas	C Borugian	D Total
1		**Wallas**	**Borugian**	**Total**
2	Total net income			$125,000
3	❶ Sharing the first $40,000 of net income,			
4	based on capital investments:			
5	Wallas ($50,000 ÷ $100,000 × $40,000)	$20,000		
6	Borugian ($50,000 ÷ $100,000 × $40,000)		$20,000	
7	Total			40,000
8	Net income remaining for allocation			85,000
9	❷ Sharing of next $60,000, based on service:			
10	Wallas	24,000		
11	Borugian		36,000	
12	Total			60,000
13	Net income remaining for allocation			25,000
14	❸ Remainder shared equally:			
15	Wallas ($25,000 × ½)	12,500		
16	Borugian ($25,000 × ½)		12,500	
17	Total			25,000
18	Net income remaining for allocation			$ 0
19	Net income allocated to the partners	$56,500	$68,500	$125,000

The net income (loss) allocated to each partner should always equal the total net income (loss). $56,500 + $68,500 = $125,000

On the basis of this allocation, the closing entry is as follows:

Dec. 31	Income Summary	125,000	
	Michelle Wallas, Capital		56,500
	Carolyn Borugian, Capital		68,500
	To allocate net income to partners.		

Sharing Based on Service and Interest

Partners may be rewarded for their service and their capital investments to the business in other ways. In the sharing plan we just saw, the capital investment was recognized with a lump-sum payment. Another option is to allocate an **interest allowance** calculated as a percentage of their Capital balances. It is important to remember that the service (salaries) and interest amounts discussed above are not the business expenses for salaries and interest in the usual sense. Service and interest in partnership agreements are ways of expressing the allocation of profits and losses to the partners. The service component rewards work done for the partnership. The interest component rewards a partner's investment of cash or other assets in the business. But the partners' service and interest amounts are *not* salary expense and interest expense in the partnership's accounting or tax records.

Allocation of Profit   Assume Edward Meyers and Pierre Zrilladich form an oil-exploration partnership. Their partnership agreement outlines the following income allocation:

❶ The partnership agreement allocates an annual "salary" of $107,000 to Meyers and $88,000 to Zrilladich.

❷ After these amounts are allocated, each partner earns 8 percent interest on his beginning Capital balance. At the beginning of the year, their Capital balances are $200,000 and $250,000, respectively.

❸ Any remaining net income is divided equally.

Partnership profit of $240,000 for the current year will be allocated as follows:

	A	B	C	D
		Meyers	**Zrilladich**	**Total**
1				
2	Total net income			$240,000
3	❶ Allocation for service:			
4	Meyers	$107,000		
5	Zrilladich		$ 88,000	
6	Total			195,000
7	Net income remaining for allocation			45,000
8	❷ Interest on beginning capital balances:			
9	Meyers ($200,000 × 0.08)	16,000		
10	Zrilladich ($250,000 × 0.08)		20,000	
11	Total			36,000
12	Net income remaining for allocation			9,000
13	❸ Remainder shared equally:			
14	Meyers ($9,000 × ½)	4,500		
15	Zrilladich ($9,000 × ½)		4,500	
16	Total			9,000
17	Net income remaining for allocation			$ 0
18	Net income allocated to the partners	$127,500	$112,500	$240,000

Allocation of a Negative Remainder   In the preceding illustration, net income exceeded the sum of service and interest. If the partnership profit is less than the allocated sum of service and interest, a negative remainder will occur at some stage in the allocation process. Even so, the partners use the same method for allocation purposes. For example, assume that Meyers and Zrilladich Partnership earned only $205,000 in the current year.

	A	B	C	D
1		**Meyers**	**Zrilladich**	**Total**
2	Total net income			$205,000
3	❶ Allocation for service:			
4	Meyers	$107,000		
5	Zrilladich		$88,000	
6	Total			195,000
7	Net income remaining for allocation			10,000
8	❷ Interest on beginning capital balances:			
9	Meyers ($200,000 × 0.08)	16,000		
10	Zrilladich ($250,000 × 0.08)		20,000	
11	Total			36,000
12	Net income (loss) remaining for allocation			(26,000)
13	❸ Remainder shared equally:			
14	Meyers [($26,000) × ½]	(13,000)		
15	Zrilladich [($26,000) × ½]		(13,000)	
16	Total			(26,000)
17	Net income remaining for allocation			$ 0
18	Net income allocated to the partners	$110,000	$95,000	$205,000

Allocation of a Net Loss

A net loss would be allocated to Meyers and Zrilladich in the same manner outlined for net income. The sharing procedure would begin with the net loss and then allocate service interest and any other specified amounts to the partners.

For example, assume that Meyers and Zrilladich Partnership had a loss of $30,000 in the current year.

	A	B	C	D
1		**Meyers**	**Zrilladich**	**Total**
2	Total net income (loss)			($ 30,000)
3	❶ Allocation for service:			
4	Meyers	$107,000		
5	Zrilladich		$ 88,000	
6	Total			195,000
7	Net income (loss) remaining for allocation			(225,000)
8	❷ Interest on beginning Capital balances:			
9	Meyers ($200,000 × 0.08)	16,000		
10	Zrilladich ($250,000 × 0.08)		20,000	
11	Total			36,000
12	Net income (loss) remaining for allocation			(261,000)
13	❸ Remainder shared equally:			
14	Meyers [($261,000) × ½]	(130,500)		
15	Zrilladich [($261,000) × ½]		(130,500)	
16	Total			(261,000)
17	Net income remaining for allocation			$ 0
18	Net income (loss) allocated to the partners	($ 7,500)	($ 22,500)	($ 30,000)

In this case, Zrilladich might be surprised to be allocated such a large share of the loss. It is important for partners to understand the partnership agreement and what it might mean in case of a loss.

Partner Withdrawals (Drawings)

Partners need cash for personal living expenses like anyone else. Partnership agreements usually allow partners to withdraw cash or other assets from the business. These withdrawals are sometimes called *drawings* and are recorded in a separate Withdrawals or Drawings account for each partner. (Drawings from a partnership are recorded exactly as they are for a proprietorship.) Assume that both Edward Meyers and Pierre Zrilladich are allowed a monthly withdrawal of $12,500. The partnership records the March withdrawal with this entry:

According to the Income Tax Act, partners are taxed on their share of partnership income, not on the amount of their withdrawals.

Mar. 31	Edward Meyers, Withdrawals	12,500	
	Cash		12,500
	Monthly partner withdrawal of cash—cheque #789.		
Mar. 31	Pierre Zrilladich, Withdrawals	12,500	
	Cash		12,500
	Monthly partner withdrawal of cash—cheque #790.		

During the year, each partner's Withdrawals account accumulates 12 such amounts, a total of $150,000 ($12,500 × 12). At the end of the year, the general ledger shows the following account balances immediately after net income has been closed to the partners' Capital accounts.

Assume the January 1 balances for Meyers and Zrilladich are shown below and that at the end of the year $205,000 of profit has been allocated on the basis of the illustration on page 671.

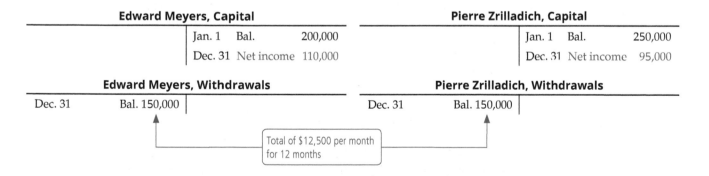

The Withdrawals accounts must be closed at the end of the period:

Dec. 31	Edward Meyers, Capital	150,000	
	Edward Meyers, Withdrawals		150,000
	To close the Withdrawals account to Capital.		
Dec. 31	Pierre Zrilladich, Capital	150,000	
	Pierre Zrilladich, Withdrawals		150,000
	To close the Withdrawals account to Capital.		

Withdrawals are closed to the Capital account as part of the closing process. See Chapter 4.

After posting the final closing entry, the balances in the capital accounts for each partner are as follows:

Edward Meyers, Capital			
	Jan. 1 Bal.	200,000
	Dec. 31 Net income	110,000
Dec. 31 Withdraw. 150,000		
	Bal.	160,000

Pierre Zrilladich, Capital			
	Jan. 1 Bal.	250,000
	Dec. 31 Net income	95,000
Dec. 31 Withdraw. 150,000		
	Bal.	195,000

The amount of the withdrawal does not depend on the partnership's income or loss for the year. In fact, it is possible for a partner to withdraw more than the balance in the Capital account if, for example, profits were expected to be higher than they proved to be and withdrawals were made in anticipation of these high profits. This situation can only occur if the partnership has the cash required for the withdrawal and the other partners agree with the withdrawal and the ending Capital balance.

Try It!

4. Calculate the net income or net loss to be allocated to each partner under the following partnership agreements:
   a. Burns and White share profits and losses 60/40. Net partnership income was $50,000.
   b. Betty, Luella, and Pius share profits and losses 3:4:3. Net partnership loss was $200,000.
   c. Locke and Barnel share profits 1/3 and 2/3. The partnership agreement does not address the sharing of losses. Net partnership loss was $60,000.
   d. Hampton and Kirk do not have a partnership agreement. Hampton does one-third of the work and Kirk does two-thirds of the work. Partnership net income was $90,000.

Solutions appear at the end of this chapter and on **MyLab Accounting**

Admission of a Partner

LO ④

How do we account for a new partner?

A partnership lasts only as long as its current set of partners remain in the business. Admitting a new partner dissolves the old partnership and begins a new one.

Often the new partnership continues the former partnership's business. In fact, the new partnership may choose to retain the dissolved partnership's name, as is the case with accounting firms. Ernst & Young LLP, for example, is an accounting firm that retires and admits many partners during the year. The former partnership dissolves and a new partnership begins many times. The business, however, retains the name and continues operations. Other partnerships may dissolve and then re-form under a new name. Let's look at the ways that a new owner can be added to a partnership.

Admission by Purchasing a Partner's Interest

A person can become a member of a partnership by purchasing an existing partner's interest in the business. First, however, the new person must gain the approval of the other partners.

Let's assume that Stephanie Spelacy and Carlo Lowes have a partnership with the following account balances:

Cash	$ 40,000	Total liabilities	$120,000
Other assets	360,000	Stephanie Spelacy, capital	170,000
		Carlo Lowes, capital	110,000
Total assets	$400,000	Total liabilities and equity	$400,000

Purchase of interest for more than capital balance Business is so successful that Spelacy receives an offer from Linda Drake, an outside party, to buy her $170,000 interest in the business for $200,000. Lowes approves Drake as a new partner, and Spelacy agrees to accept $200,000. The firm records the transfer of capital with this entry:

Apr. 16	Stephanie Spelacy, Capital	170,000	
	Linda Drake, Capital		170,000
	To transfer Spelacy's equity to Drake.		

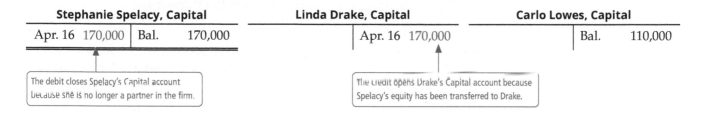

Stephanie Spelacy, Capital			Linda Drake, Capital		Carlo Lowes, Capital	
Apr. 16 170,000	Bal. 170,000		Apr. 16 170,000		Bal. 110,000	

The debit closes Spelacy's Capital account because she is no longer a partner in the firm.

The credit opens Drake's Capital account because Spelacy's equity has been transferred to Drake.

The entry amount is Spelacy's Capital balance ($170,000) and not the $200,000 price that Drake paid Spelacy to buy into the business. The full $200,000 goes to Spelacy because the partnership does not receive cash. The transaction was between Drake and Spelacy, not between Drake and the partnership.

Purchase of interest for less than capital balance Suppose Drake pays Spelacy less than Spelacy's Capital balance. The entry on the partnership books is not affected. Spelacy's equity is transferred to Drake at book value ($170,000).

The profit or loss on the sale of a partnership interest belongs personally to the partner selling the interest and will not appear on the partnership's books.

Admission by Investing in the Partnership

A person may be admitted as a partner by investing directly in the partnership rather than by purchasing an existing partner's interest. The new partner invests assets—for example, cash, inventory, equipment, or a patent—in the business. Let's consider several possible independent investment scenarios for a new partner.

Admission by Investing in the Partnership at Book Value—No Bonus Assume that the partnership of Robin Hardy and Michael May has the following assets, liabilities, and capital:

Cash	$ 20,000	Total liabilities	$ 60,000
Other assets	200,000	Robin Hardy, capital	70,000
		Michael May, capital	90,000
Total assets	$220,000	Total liabilities and equity	$220,000

Devan Mann wants to join the Hardy and May partnership. Mann can invest equipment with a market value of $80,000. Hardy and May agree to dissolve their partnership and to start up a new one, giving Mann one-third interest in exchange for the contributed asset, as follows:

Partnership capital before Mann is admitted ($70,000 + $90,000)	$160,000
Mann's investment in the partnership	80,000
Partnership capital after Mann is admitted	$240,000
One-third interest is ($240,000 × ⅓). Share to Mann.	$ 80,000

Always add the new partner's investment to the existing partners' capital total first before calculating the new partner's ownership interest amount in the partnership.

Notice that Mann is buying into the partnership at book value because her one-third investment ($80,000) equals one-third of the new partnership's total capital ($240,000).

The partnership's entry to record Mann's investment is:

Jul. 18	Equipment	80,000	
	Devan Mann, Capital		80,000
	To admit D. Mann as a partner with a one-third interest in the business.		

After this entry, the partnership books show the following:

Cash	$ 20,000	Total liabilities	$ 60,000
Equipment	80,000	Robin Hardy, capital	70,000
Other assets	200,000	Michael May, capital	90,000
		Devan Mann, capital	80,000
Total assets	$300,000	Total liabilities and equity	$300,000

Mann's one-third interest in the partnership does not necessarily entitle her to one-third of the profits. The sharing of profits and losses is a separate element in the partnership agreement.

Admission by Investing in the Partnership—Bonus to the Old Partners If the partnership is successful, a new partner may be required to make a higher payment to enter the business. The old partners may demand a bonus, which will increase their Capital accounts. The bonus is allocated to partners based on their profit-and-loss-sharing ratio.

Suppose that Hiro Nagasawa and Lisa Wendt's partnership has earned above-average profits for 10 years. The two partners share profits and losses equally. The balance sheet carries these figures:

Cash	$ 40,000	Total liabilities	$100,000
Other assets	210,000	Hiro Nagasawa, capital	70,000
		Lisa Wendt, capital	80,000
Total assets	$250,000	Total liabilities and equity	$250,000

Nagasawa and Wendt agree to admit Alana Moor to a one-fourth interest in return for Moor's cash investment of $90,000. Moor's Capital balance on the new partnership books is only $60,000, computed as follows:

Partnership capital before Moor is admitted ($70,000 + $80,000)	$ 150,000
Moor's investment in the partnership	90,000
Partnership capital after Moor is admitted	$ 240,000
One-quarter interest ($240,000 × ¼). Share to Moor.	$ 60,000
Bonus to the old partners ($90,000 − $60,000)	$ 30,000

In effect, Moor had to buy into the partnership at a price ($90,000) which is above the book value of her one-fourth interest ($60,000). Moor's greater-than-book-value investment of $30,000 creates a bonus for Nagasawa and Wendt.

The entry on the partnership books to record Moor's investment is:

Mar. 1	Cash	90,000	
	Alana Moor, Capital		60,000
	Hiro Nagasawa, Capital		15,000
	Lisa Wendt, Capital		15,000
	To admit A. Moor as a partner with a one-fourth interest in the business. Nagasawa and Wendt each receive a bonus of $15,000 ($30,000 × 1/2) because bonus is split based on the profit-and-loss-sharing ratio.		

Notice that Nagasawa's and Wendt's Capital accounts increased because of Moor's investment but that Nagasawa and Wendt have not received cash. All the cash went into the partnership.

Moor's Capital account is credited for her one-fourth interest in the partnership. The bonus is allocated to the original partners (Nagasawa and Wendt) based on their profit-and-loss-sharing ratio.

The new partnership's balance sheet reports these amounts:

$40,000 + $90,000

Cash	$130,000	Total liabilities	$100,000
Other assets	210,000	Hiro Nagasawa, capital	85,000
		Lisa Wendt, capital	95,000
		Alana Moor, capital	60,000
Total assets	$340,000	Total liabilities and equity	$340,000

$70,000 + $15,000

$80,000 + $15,000

Admission by Investing in the Partnership—Bonus to the New Partner   A potential new partner may be so important that the old partners offer a partnership share that includes a bonus to the new partner. A law firm may desire a former premier, cabinet minister, or other official as a partner because of the person's reputation. A restaurant owner may want to go into partnership with a famous sports personality like Sidney Crosby or a musician like Deadmau5.

Suppose Jan Page and Miko Goh have a restaurant. Their partnership balance sheet appears as follows:

Cash	$140,000	Total liabilities	$120,000
Other assets	360,000	Jan Page, capital	230,000
		Miko Goh, capital	150,000
Total assets	$500,000	Total liabilities and equity	$500,000

$380,000

The partners admit Martin Santiago, a famous hockey player, as a partner with a one-third interest in exchange for Santiago's cash investment of $100,000. At the time of Santiago's admission, the firm's capital is $380,000. Page and Goh share profits and losses in the ratio of two-thirds to Page and one-third to Goh. The computation of Santiago's equity in the new partnership is as follows:

Partnership capital before Santiago is admitted ($230,000 + $150,000)	$380,000
Santiago's investment in the partnership	100,000
Partnership capital after Santiago is admitted	$480,000
One-third interest ($480,000 × 1/3). Share to Santiago.	$160,000
Bonus to new partner ($160,000 − $100,000)	$ 60,000

In this case, Santiago entered the partnership at a price ($100,000) below the book value of his equity ($160,000). The Capital accounts of Page and Goh are debited for the $60,000 difference between the new partner's equity ($160,000) and his investment ($100,000). The old partners share this decrease in capital, which is accounted for as though it were a loss, based on their profit-and-loss-sharing ratio. The entry to record Santiago's investment is:

Aug. 24	Cash	100,000	
	Jan Page, Capital	40,000	
	Miko Goh, Capital	20,000	
	Martin Santiago, Capital		160,000
	To admit M. Santiago as a partner with a one-third interest in the business. Split loss according to profit-and-loss-sharing ratio: Page: $60,000 × ⅔ and Goh: $60,000 × ⅓		

The new partnership's balance sheet reports these amounts:

$140,000 + $100,000

Cash	$240,000	Total liabilities	$120,000	
Other assets	360,000	Jan Page, capital	190,000	$230,000 − $40,000
		Miko Goh, capital	130,000	$150,000 − $20,000
		Martin Santiago, capital	160,000	
Total assets	$600,000	Total liabilities and equity	$600,000	

Try It!

5. Tina and Jean are partners with Capital balances of $25,000 and $75,000, respectively. They share profits and losses in a 30:70 ratio. Tina and Jean admit Phyllis to a 10 percent interest in a new partnership when Phyllis invests $20,000 in the business.
   a. Compute the bonus to Tina and Jean.
   b. Journalize the partnership's receipt of Phyllis's investment on June 12.
   c. What is each partner's Capital in the new partnership?
6. Refer to the data in the previous question. If Phyllis had invested only $10,000 into the partnership for a 10 percent interest, journalize the partnership's receipt of Phyllis's investment.

Solutions appear at the end of this chapter and on **MyLab Accounting**

Withdrawal of a Partner from the Business

LO (5)

How do we account for the withdrawal of a partner?

A partner may leave the business for many reasons, including retirement or a dispute with the other partners. The withdrawal of a partner dissolves the old partnership. The partnership agreement should specify how to split the partnership assets and liabilities with a withdrawing partner.

In the simplest case, a partner may withdraw by selling his or her interest to another party in a personal transaction. This is the same as admitting a new person who purchases an old partner's interest, as we saw earlier. The journal entry simply debits the withdrawing partner's Capital account and credits the new partner's Capital account. The dollar amount of the entry is the old partner's Capital balance, regardless of the price paid by the purchaser, as illustrated for Spelacy and Drake on page 675.

Another option would be for a current partner to buy a second partner's interest. This is recorded the same way as when an outside party buys a current partner's interest.

The two main steps that must be completed prior to identifying how much is owed to the withdrawing partner are as follows:

1. Close the books. If the partner withdraws in the middle of the accounting period, the partnership books should be updated to determine the withdrawing partner's Capital balance. The business must measure net income or net loss for the fraction of the year up to the withdrawal date and allocate profit or loss according to the existing ratio.

2. If it is in the partnership agreement, the settlement procedure may specify an independent appraisal of the assets to determine their current market value of the assets. In that case, the partnership must update the value of the assets in the accounting records. This is known as an **asset revaluation**. The partners share any market value changes according to their profit-and-loss-sharing ratio.

Terminology alert! Notice that here the term *withdrawal* refers to a partner who is leaving and not the "drawings" that were discussed earlier.

Withdrawal at Book Value

Suppose Ben Wolfe is retiring in the middle of the year from the partnership of Sheldon, Greis, and Wolfe. After the books have been adjusted for partial-period income but before the asset appraisal, revaluation, and closing entries are recorded, the balance sheet reports the following:

When a partner leaves a partnership, she or he ceases to be an agent and no longer has the authority to bind the business to contracts. Third parties with whom the partnership has dealt should be notified that the exiting partner can no longer bind the partnership. All others can be informed with a newspaper advertisement.

Cash		$ 70,000	Total liabilities		$ 80,000
Inventory		40,000			
Land		50,000			
Building	$90,000		Joan Sheldon, capital		50,000
Less: Accumulated			George Greis, capital		40,000
amortization	60,000	30,000	Ben Wolfe, capital		20,000
Total assets		$190,000	Total liabilities and equity		$190,000

An independent appraiser revalues the inventory at $34,000 (down from $40,000) and the land at $100,000 (up from $50,000). The partners share the differences between market value and book value based on their profit-and-loss sharing ratio of 1:2:1.

We identify what share each partner has for the revaluation:

The ratios of 1:2:1 is the same as a ¼, ½, ¼ fraction. It is also the same as a 25 percent, 50 percent, 25 percent sharing ratio.

These figures, multiplied by the gain or loss in value from the revaluation, yield each partner's share.

Ratio of 1:2:1 means of the 4 "shares", the first person gets 1 of 4, the second gets 2 of 4 and the third gets 1 of 4.

Inventory − $6,000 decrease ($40,000 − $34,000):

Sheldon:	$6,000 × ¼ = $1,500
Greis:	$6,000 × ½ = $3,000
Wolfe:	$6,000 × ¼ = $1,500

Land − $50,000 increase ($100,000 − $50,000):

Sheldon:	$50,000 × ¼ = $12,500
Greis:	$50,000 × ½ = $25,000
Wolfe:	$50,000 × ¼ = $12,500

The entries to record the revaluation of the inventory and land are as follows:

Jun. 30	Joan Sheldon, Capital	1,500	
	George Greis, Capital	3,000	
	Ben Wolfe, Capital	1,500	
	Inventory		6,000
	To revalue the inventory and allocate the loss in value to the partners.		

Jun. 30	Land	50,000	
	Joan Sheldon, Capital		12,500
	George Greis, Capital		25,000
	Ben Wolfe, Capital		12,500
	To revalue the land and allocate the gain in value to the partners.		

After the revaluations, the partnership balance sheet reports the following:

Cash		$70,000	Total liabilities	$80,000	
Inventory		34,000			
Land		100,000			
Building	$90,000		Joan Sheldon, capital	61,000	$50,000 − $1,500 + $12,500
Less: Accumulated			George Greis, capital	62,000	$40,000 − $3,000 + $25,000
amortization	60,000	30,000	Ben Wolfe, capital	31,000	$20,000 − $1,500 + $12,500
Total assets		$234,000	Total liabilities and equity	$234,000	

As the balance sheet shows, Wolfe has a claim to $31,000 in partnership assets. Now we can account for Wolfe's withdrawal from the business.

If Ben Wolfe withdraws by taking cash equal to the book value of his owner's equity, the entry would be:

Jun. 30	Ben Wolfe, Capital	31,000	
	Cash		31,000
	To record the withdrawal of B. Wolfe from the partnership.		

This entry records the payment of partnership cash to Wolfe and the closing of his Capital account upon his withdrawal from the business.

Ben Wolfe, Capital

		Begin.	20,000
Inventory adj.	1,500	Land adj.	12,500
Withdraw.	31,000	Bal.	31,000

The double underline is a shortcut used in earlier chapters to indicate a zero balance.

Withdrawal at Less than Book Value

The withdrawing partner may be so eager to depart that she or he is willing to take less than her or his equity. Assume Ben Wolfe withdraws from the business and agrees to receive cash of $10,000 and a $15,000 note payable from the new partnership. This $25,000 settlement is $6,000 less than Wolfe's $31,000 equity in the business. The remaining partners share this $6,000 difference—which is a bonus to them—according to their profit-and-loss-sharing ratio.

Because Wolfe has withdrawn from the partnership, Wolfe's capital account is closed, and Greis and Sheldon may or may not continue the partnership. Assuming they agree to form a new partnership, a new agreement—and a new profit-and-loss-sharing ratio—is needed. In forming a new partnership, Greis and Sheldon may decide on any ratio they wish. Assume Greis and Sheldon agree on a profit-and-loss-sharing ratio of ⅔ for Greis and ⅓ for Sheldon.

The entry to record Wolfe's withdrawal at less than book value is as follows:

Jun. 30	Ben Wolfe, Capital	31,000	
	Cash		10,000
	Note Payable to Ben Wolfe		15,000
	Joan Sheldon, Capital		2,000
	George Greis, Capital		4,000
	To record withdrawal of B. Wolfe from the partnership. Sheldon's bonus is $2,000 ($6,000 × ⅓) and Greis's bonus is $4,000 ($6,000 × ⅔).		

> Even though Ben agrees to a $25,000 settlement, the balance in his Capital account must be cleared.

Withdrawal at More than Book Value

A withdrawing partner may receive assets worth more than the book value of their equity. This situation creates:

- A bonus to the withdrawing partner
- A decrease in the remaining partners' Capital accounts, shared in their profit-and-loss ratio

The accounting for this situation follows the pattern illustrated previously for withdrawal at less than book value—with one exception. In this situation, the remaining partners' Capital accounts are debited because they are paying a bonus to the withdrawing partner.

Refer back to our previous example. Suppose Wolfe withdraws from the partnership and agrees to receive only $40,000 cash. Greis and Sheldon agree that Greis will get two-thirds of the new partnership's profits and losses and Sheldon one-third. The entry to record Wolfe's withdrawal at more than book value is:

Jun. 30	Ben Wolfe, Capital	31,000	
	Joan Sheldon, Capital	3,000	
	George Greis, Capital	6,000	
	Cash		40,000
	To record withdrawal of B. Wolfe from the partnership. Sheldon's Capital is reduced by $3,000 ($9,000 × ⅓) and Greis's Capital is reduced by $6,000 ($9,000 × ⅔).		

Death of a Partner

As with any other form of partnership withdrawal, the death of a partner dissolves a partnership. The partnership accounts are adjusted to measure net income or loss for the fraction of the year up to the date of death. The accounts are then closed to determine all partners' Capital balances on that date. Settlement with the deceased partner's estate is based on the partnership agreement. There may or may not be an asset revaluation. The estate commonly receives partnership assets equal to the partner's Capital balance.

Alternatively, a remaining partner may purchase the deceased partner's equity. The deceased partner's Capital account is debited and the purchaser's Capital account is credited. The amount of this entry is the ending Capital balance of the deceased partner.

> Partners commonly carry life insurance on themselves, with the partners as beneficiaries. In the event of a death, the partners receive the cash flow necessary to settle with the deceased partner's estate, without putting the partnership into financial jeopardy.

Try It!

7. Suppose Ruth is withdrawing from the partnership of Ruth, Nick, and Adriana. The partners share profits and losses in a 1:2:3 ratio for Ruth, Nick, and Adriana, respectively. After the revaluation of assets, Ruth's Capital balance is $40,000, and the other partners agree to pay her $50,000. Nick and Adriana agree to a new profit-and-loss-sharing ratio of 2:3 for Nick and Adriana, respectively. Journalize the payment to Ruth for her withdrawal from the partnership on August 31.

Solutions appear at the end of this chapter and on **MyLab Accounting**

Liquidation of a Partnership

LO 6

How do we account for the ending of a partnership?

As we have seen, the admission or withdrawal of a partner dissolves the partnership. However, the business may continue operating with no apparent change to outsiders such as customers and creditors. In contrast, business **liquidation** is the process of going out of business by selling the entity's assets and paying its liabilities. The business shuts down. Before the business is liquidated, the books must be adjusted and closed.

Liquidation of a partnership includes three basic steps:

1. Sell the assets. Allocate the gain or loss to the partners' Capital accounts based on the profit-and-loss-sharing ratio.
2. Pay all the partnership's liabilities.
3. Pay the remaining cash to the partners in proportion to their Capital balances.

The liquidation of a business can stretch over weeks or months, even years for a large company. Selling every asset and paying every liability of the entity takes time.

To avoid excessive detail in our illustrations, we include only two asset categories—Cash and Noncash Assets—and a single liability category—Liabilities. Our examples also assume that the business sells the assets in a single transaction and then pays the liabilities at once. (In actual practice, each asset and its related amortization would be accounted for separately when it is sold, and each liability would be accounted for separately when it is paid.)

Assume that Ryan Lauren, Alexis Andrews, and Scott Benroudi have shared profits and losses in the ratio of 3:1:1. The partners decide to liquidate their partnership. After the books are adjusted and closed, these accounts remain:

Cash	$ 10,000	Liabilities	$ 30,000
Noncash assets	90,000	Ryan Lauren, capital	40,000
		Alexis Andrews, capital	20,000
		Scott Benroudi, capital	10,000
Total assets	$100,000	Total liabilities and equity	$100,000

Sale of Assets at a Gain

❶ Sell the Assets and Allocate Gain to Partners Assume the Lauren, Andrews, and Benroudi partnership sells its noncash assets for $150,000 (book value, $90,000). The partnership realizes a gain of $60,000, which is allocated to the partners based on their profit-and-loss-sharing ratio.

This could be broken down into two steps: recording the gain or loss on liquidation and recording the allocation of the gain or loss to the partners. The journal entries would be:

Oct. 31	Cash	150,000	
	Noncash Assets		90,000
	Gain on Liquidation		60,000
	To sell noncash assets in liquidation.		
31	Gain on Liquidation	60,000	
	Ryan Lauren, Capital		36,000
	Alexis Andrews, Capital		12,000
	Scott Benroudi, Capital		12,000
	To allocate gain to partners. Lauren's share of the gain is $36,000 ($60,000 × 0.60), Andrew's and Benroudi's are $12,000 each ($60,000 × 0.20).		

The ratio of 3:1:1 is equal to 3/5, 1/5, 1/5, or a 60 percent, 20 percent, 20 percent sharing ratio.

Now the partners' Capital accounts have the following balances:

Ryan Lauren, Capital		
	Begin.	40,000
	Oct. 31	36,000
	Bal.	76,000

Alexis Andrews, Capital		
	Begin.	20,000
	Oct. 31	12,000
	Bal.	32,000

Scott Benroudi, Capital		
	Begin.	10,000
	Oct. 31	12,000
	Bal.	22,000

❷ Pay All the Partnership Liabilities

Oct. 31	Liabilities	30,000	
	Cash		30,000
	To pay liabilities in liquidation.		

❸ Pay the Remaining Cash to the Partners in Proportion to Their Capital Balances
The amount of cash left in the partnership is $130,000, as follows:

Cash			
Begin.	10,000		
Sale of assets	❶ 150,000	Payment of liabilities	❷ 30,000
Bal.	❸ 130,000		

Upon liquidation, gains and losses on the sale of assets are shared based on profit-and-loss sharing ratio. The cash balance is used to pay out the partners' Capital account balances.

The partners divide the remaining cash according to their Capital balances:

Oct. 31	Ryan Lauren, Capital	76,000	
	Alexis Andrews, Capital	32,000	
	Scott Benroudi, Capital	22,000	
	Cash		130,000
	To disburse cash to partners in liquidation.		

A convenient way to summarize the transactions in a partnership liquidation is given in Exhibit 12–5.

EXHIBIT 12–5 | Partnership Liquidation—Sale of Assets at a Gain

	A	B	C	D	E	F	G	H	I	J	K	L
										Capital		
1												
2								**Lauren**		**Andrews**		**Benroudi**
3		**Cash**	**+**	**Noncash Assets**	**=**	**Liabilities**	**+**	**(60%)**	**+**	**(20%)**	**+**	**(20%)**
4	Balances before sale of assets	$ 10,000		$90,000		$30,000		$40,000		$20,000		$10,000
5	❶ Sale of assets and sharing of gain	150,000		(90,000)				36,000		12,000		12,000
6	Balances	160,000		0		30,000		76,000		32,000		22,000
7	❷ Payment of liabilities	(30,000)				(30,000)						
8	Balances	130,000		0		0		76,000		32,000		22,000
9	❸ Disbursement of cash to partners	(130,000)						(76,000)		(32,000)		(22,000)
10	Balances	$ 0		$ 0		$ 0		$ 0		$ 0		$ 0

After the disbursement of cash to the partners, the business has no assets, liabilities, or equity. All final balances are zero.

Sale of Assets at a Loss

Liquidation of a business often includes the sale of assets at a loss. When a loss occurs, the partners' Capital accounts are debited based on the profit-and-loss sharing ratio. Otherwise, the accounting follows the pattern illustrated for the sale of assets at a gain.

Suppose the Lauren, Andrews, and Benroudi partnership sold its noncash assets for $30,000 and all other details in Exhibit 12–5 remained the same. This creates a loss of $60,000 on the sale of the noncash assets. Exhibit 12–6 summarizes the transactions in a partnership liquidation when the assets are sold at a loss.

EXHIBIT 12–6 | Partnership Liquidation—Sale of Assets at a Loss

	A	B	C	D	E	F	G	H	I	J	K	L
										Capital		
1												
2								**Lauren**		**Andrews**		**Benroudi**
3		**Cash**	**+**	**Noncash Assets**	**=**	**Liabilities**	**+**	**(60%)**	**+**	**(20%)**	**+**	**(20%)**
4	Balances before sale of assets	$10,000		$90,000		$30,000		$40,000		$20,000		$10,000
5	❶ Sale of assets and sharing of loss	30,000		(90,000)				(36,000)		(12,000)		(12,000)
6	Balances	40,000		0		30,000		4,000		8,000		(2,000)
7	❷ Payment of liabilities	(30,000)				(30,000)						
8	Balances	10,000		0		0		4,000		8,000		(2,000)
9	❸ Disbursement of cash to partners	(10,000)						(4,000)		(8,000)		2,000
10	Balances	$ 0		$ 0		$ 0		$ 0		$ 0		$ 0

This is called a capital deficiency.

Capital Deficiencies

When a business liquidates, there may not be enough cash from the sale of the assets to pay the liabilities. The partners (who are personally liable for the partnership debts) must contribute cash on the basis of their profit-and-loss-sharing ratio to cover unpaid debts. Notice that Benroudi's Capital account has a negative balance. This is known as a **capital deficiency**. The capital deficiency must be dealt with *before* the ending cash is distributed. One way of dealing with the $2,000 capital deficiency in Benroudi's Capital account is for Benroudi to contribute $2,000 of assets to the partnership to erase his capital deficiency. If Benroudi contributes cash, the journal entry to record this is:

Oct. 31	Cash	2,000	
	Scott Benroudi, Capital		2,000
	Contributed cash to cover capital deficiency on liquidation.		

Another option for dealing with Benroudi's $2,000 capital deficiency is for Benroudi's partners, Lauren and Andrews, to agree to absorb Benroudi's capital deficiency by decreasing their own Capital balances in proportion to their remaining profit-and-loss-sharing percentages: Lauren, 60/80; Andrews, 20/80. The journal entry to record this is:

Oct. 31	Ryan Lauren, Capital	1,500	
	Alexis Andrews, Capital	500	
	Scott Benroudi, Capital		2,000
	To absorb the Benroudi capital deficiency by decreasing remaining partners' Capital balances. Lauren $1,500 ($2,000 × 60/80) and Andrews $500 ($2,000 × 20/80)		

How do partners deal with a situation where two of the three partners have capital deficiencies? Both partners could contribute assets in the amount of their deficiencies to the third partner. However, if the deficient partners cannot contribute personal assets, then the deficits must be absorbed by the remaining partner. If the remaining partner then still has a balance in his or her Capital account, any remaining cash balance would be paid to that partner.

Try It!

8. Refer to the Lauren, Andrews, and Benroudi partnership on page 682. Suppose the partnership sold its noncash assets for $20,000 and all other details in Exhibit 12–5 remained the same.
   a. What is the profit or loss created on the sale of the noncash assets?
   b. Allocate the profit or loss calculated in part (a) to the partners.
   c. How can the partnership deal with any capital deficiencies in this situation?

Solutions appear at the end of this chapter and on **MyLab Accounting**

Summary Problem for Your Review

The partnership of Anderssen and Wang admits Sony Pappachan as a partner on January 2, 2020. The partnership has these balances on that date:

ANDERSSEN & WANG Balance Sheet January 2, 2020			
Cash	$ 9,000	Total liabilities	$ 50,000
Other assets	110,000	Magnus Anderssen, capital	45,000
		Songyao Wang, capital	24,000
Total assets	$119,000	Total liabilities and equity	$119,000

Their partnership agreement states that Magnus Anderssen's share of profits and losses is 60 percent and Songyao Wang's share is 40 percent. They are looking to increase the total assets of the partnership so they are considering two different scenarios for admitting a partner.

Required

1. Suppose Pappachan pays Wang $30,000 to acquire Wang's interest in the business after Anderssen approves Pappachan as a partner.
   a. Record the transfer of owner's equity on the partnership books.
   b. Prepare the partnership balance sheet immediately after Pappachan is admitted as a partner.

2. Suppose instead that Pappachan becomes a partner by investing $31,000 cash to acquire a one-fourth interest in the business.
   a. Compute Pappachan's Capital balance and determine whether there is any bonus. If so, who gets the bonus?
   b. Record Pappachan's investment in the business.
   c. Prepare the partnership balance sheet immediately after Pappachan is admitted as a partner.

3. Which way of admitting Pappachan to the partnership increases its total assets? Give your reason.

SOLUTION

Requirement 1

a.

When a new partner acquires an old partner's interest, the new partner purchases the old partner's equity balance on the books and *replaces* the old partner. Any amount paid in excess goes to the old partner personally.

Jan. 2	Songyao Wang, Capital	24,000	
	Sony Pappachan, Capital		24,000
	To transfer Wang equity in the partnership to Pappachan.		

b.

ANDERSSEN & PAPPACHAN Balance Sheet January 2, 2020			
Cash	$ 9,000	Total liabilities	$ 50,000
Other assets	110,000	Magnus Anderssen, capital	45,000
		Sony Pappachan, capital	24,000
Total assets	$119,000	Total liabilities and equity	$119,000

The balance sheet for the partnership of Anderssen and Pappachan is identical to the balance sheet given for Anderssen and Wang in the problem, except Sony Pappachan's name replaces Songyao Wang's name in the title and in the listing of Capital accounts.

Requirement 2

a. Computation of Pappachan's Capital balance and bonus to old partners:

Partnership capital before Pappachan is admitted ($45,000 + $24,000)	$ 69,000
Pappachan's investment in the partnership	31,000
Partnership capital after Pappachan is admitted	$100,000
Pappachan's capital in the partnership ($100,000 × ¼)	$ 25,000
Bonus to the old partners ($31,000 − $25,000)	$ 6,000

When a new partner acquires an interest in a partnership, the new partner *joins the existing partners* by adding cash to the pool of capital, then dividing the pool among the old and new partners. Any amount paid in excess increases the old partners' Capital balances.

b.

Jan. 2	Cash	31,000	
	Sony Pappachan, Capital		25,000
	Magnus Anderssen, Capital		3,600
	Songyao Wang, Capital		2,400
	To admit Pappachan as a partner with a one-fourth interest in the business. Anderssen's bonus is $3,600 ($6,000 × 0.60) and Wang's bonus is $2,400 ($6,000 × 0.40).		

The $6,000 bonus is split based on the profit-and-loss-sharing ratio in place before the new partner joined.

c.

ANDERSSEN, WANG, AND PAPPACHAN Balance Sheet January 2, 2020			
Cash	$ 40,000	Total liabilities	$ 50,000
Other assets	110,000	Magnus Anderssen, capital	48,600
		Songyao Wang, capital	26,400
		Sony Pappachan, capital	25,000
Total assets	$150,000	Total liabilities and equity	$150,000

$9,000 + $31,000 = $40,000

$45,000 + $3,600 = $48,600

$24,000 + $2,400 = $26,400

The Cash and Capital accounts will change when a new partner joins existing partners. Add the bonus to each of the old partners' Capital balances and add the new partner's Capital balance, all from the January 2, 2020, journal entry.

Requirement 3

Pappachan's investment in the partnership increases its total assets by the amount of his contribution. Total assets of the business are $150,000 after his investment, compared with $119,000 before. By contrast, Pappachan's purchase of Wang's interest in the business is a personal transaction between the two individuals. It does not affect the assets of the partnership, regardless of the amount Pappachan pays Wang.

A partnership's total assets are increased only when a new partner joins existing partners, not when a new partner replaces an old partner by purchasing the old partner's Capital.

Summary

Learning Objective

① Identify the characteristics of a partnership Pg. 661

What are the characteristics of a partnership?
- A *partnership* is a business co-owned by two or more persons for profit.
- The characteristics of partnerships are:

  - Ease of formation
  - Limited life
  - Mutual agency

  - Unlimited liability
  - Co-ownership of property
  - No partnership income taxes

- In a *limited partnership,* the limited partners have limited personal liability for the obligations of the business.
- A written *partnership agreement* establishes procedures for admission of a new partner, withdrawal of a partner, and the sharing of profits and losses among the partners.
- When a new partner is admitted to the firm or an existing partner withdraws, the old partnership is *dissolved*, or ceases to exist. A new partnership may or may not emerge to continue the business.

② Account for partners' initial investments in a partnership Pg. 666

How do we account for partners' investments in a partnership?
- Accounting for a partnership is similar to accounting for a proprietorship. However, a partnership has more than one owner.
- Each partner has an individual Capital account and a Withdrawal account; the Capital accounts for each partner are shown on the balance sheet.
- The partnership income statement includes a section showing the division of net income to the partners.

③ Allocate profits and losses to the partners by different methods Pg. 667

How can we allocate profits and losses to the partners?
- Partners share net income or loss in any manner they choose.
- Common sharing agreements base the *profit-and-loss sharing ratio* on:
  - A stated fraction
  - Partners' capital investments
  - Other methods, including a combination of service and interest, which, despite their name, are not expenses of the business.

④ Account for the admission of a new partner Pg. 674

How do we account for a new partner?
- An outside person may become a partner by:
  - Purchasing a current partner's interest (the transaction is between the partners and does not increase the total partnership equity)
  - Investing in the partnership (the transaction increases the total partnership equity by the amount of the investment)
- In some cases, the new partner must pay the current partners a bonus to join. In other situations, the new partner may receive a bonus to join.

⑤ Account for the withdrawal of a partner Pg. 678

How do we account for the withdrawal of a partner?
- The two steps prior to accounting for the withdrawal of a partner are:
  1. Adjust and close the books up to the date of the partner's withdrawal from the business.
  2. Appraise the assets and the liabilities to determine their current market value. Allocate the gain or loss in value to the partners' Capital accounts based on their profit-and-loss-sharing ratio.
- Then account for the partner's withdrawal
  - a At book value (no change in remaining partners' Capital balances)
  - b At less than book value (increase the remaining partners' Capital balances)
  - c At greater than book value (decrease the remaining partners' Capital balances)

⑥ Account for the liquidation of a partnership Pg. 682

How do we account for the ending of a partnership?
- In *liquidation*, a partnership goes out of business by:
  - ❶ Selling the assets
  - ❷ Paying the liabilities
  - ❸ Paying any remaining cash to the partners based on their capital balances

Key Terms for the chapter are shown next and are in the **Glossary** at the back of the book. **Similar Terms** are shown after **Key Terms**.

KEY TERMS

Asset revaluation Adjusting asset values to reflect current market values, usually based on an independent appraisal of the assets *(p. 679)*.

Capital deficiency A partnership's claim against a partner occurs when a partner's Capital account has a debit balance *(p. 685)*.

Dissolution Ending a partnership *(p. 661)*.

General partnership A form of partnership in which each partner is an owner of the business, with all the privileges and risks of ownership *(p. 664)*.

Interest allowance An interest component that rewards a partner with an allocation because of his or her investment in the business. This is not the same as interest expense paid on a loan *(p. 671)*.

Limited liability partnership (LLP) A partnership in which each partner's personal liability for other partners' negligence is limited to a certain dollar amount, although liability for a partner's own negligence is still unlimited. *(p. 664)*.

Limited partnership A partnership with at least two classes of partners: a general partner and limited partners *(p. 664)*.

Liquidation The process of going out of business by selling the entity's assets and paying its liabilities. The final step in liquidation of a business is the distribution of any remaining cash to the partners *(p. 682)*.

Mutual agency Every partner can bind the business to a contract within the scope of the partnership's regular business operations *(p. 662)*.

Partnership An unincorporated business with two or more owners *(p. 660)*.

Partnership agreement An agreement that is the contract between partners specifying such items as the name, location, and nature of the business; the name, capital investment, and duties of each partner; and the method of sharing profits and losses by the partners *(p. 661)*.

Salary allowance Another term for *service (p. 670)*.

Service An allocation to a partner based on his or her service to the partnership. This is not the same as salary expense for an employee *(p. 670)*.

Unlimited personal liability When a partnership (or a proprietorship) cannot pay its debts with business assets, the partners (or the proprietor) must use personal assets to meet the debt *(p. 662)*.

SIMILAR TERMS

Limited liability partnership	LLP
Liquidation	Shutting down the business; going out of business
Partners' equity	Partners' capital; Capital
Service	Salary allowance
Withdrawals	Drawings

SELF-STUDY QUESTIONS

Test your understanding of the chapter by marking the correct answer for each of the following questions:

1. Which of these characteristics identifies a partnership? *(p. 661)*
   a. Unlimited life
   b. No income tax paid by the business entity
   c. Limited personal liability
   d. All of the above

2. A partnership records a partner's investment of assets in the business at *(p. 666)*
   a. The partner's book value of the assets invested
   b. The market value of the assets invested
   c. A special value set by the partners
   d. Any of the above, depending upon the partnership agreement

3. The partnership of Malik, Dingle, and West divides profits in the ratio of 4:5:3. There is no provision for losses. During 2020, the business earned $40,000. West's share of this income is (p. 667)
   a. $10,000
   b. $13,333
   c. $16,000
   d. $16,667

4. The partners of Martin, Short, and Chase share profits and losses 1/5, 1/6, and 19/30. During 2020, the first year of their partnership, the business earned $120,000, and each partner withdrew $50,000 for personal use. What is the balance in Chase's Capital account after all closing entries? (p. 668)
   a. Not determinable because Chase's beginning Capital balance is not given
   b. Minus $10,000
   c. Minus $50,000
   d. $26,000

5. Partner withdrawals (p. 673)
   a. Decrease partnership capital
   b. Increase partnership liabilities
   c. Decrease partnership net income
   d. Increase partnership capital

6. Elaine Robinson buys into the partnership of Quantz and Goodwin by purchasing a one-third interest for $55,000. Prior to Robinson's entry, Edward Quantz's Capital balance was $46,000 and Louisa Goodwin's balance was $52,000; profits and losses were shared equally. The entry to record Robinson's buying into the business is (p. 674)

a.	Cash	55,000	
	Elaine Robinson, Capital		55,000

b.	Edward Quantz, Capital	27,500	
	Louisa Goodwin, Capital	27,500	
	Elaine Robinson, Capital		55,000

c.	Cash	55,000	
	Elaine Robinson, Capital		51,000
	Edward Quantz, Capital		2,000
	Louisa Goodwin, Capital		2,000

d.	Cash	51,000	
	Edward Quantz, Capital	2,000	
	Louisa Goodwin, Capital	2,000	
	Elaine Robinson, Capital		55,000

7. The partners of Tsui, Valik, and Wollenberg share profits and losses equally. Their Capital balances are $40,000, $50,000, and $60,000, respectively, when Wollenberg sells her interest in the partnership to Valik for $90,000. Tsui and Valik continue the business. Immediately after Wollenberg's retirement, the total assets of the partnership are (p. 678)
   a. Increased by $30,000
   b. Increased by $90,000
   c. Decreased by $60,000
   d. The same as before Wollenberg sold her interest to Valik

8. Prior to Felix Lengyel's withdrawal from the partnership of Lengyel, Iorio, and Dahlstrom, the partners' Capital balances were $140,000, $110,000 and $250,000, respectively. The partners share profits and losses 1/3, 1/4, and 5/12 respectively. The appraisal indicates that assets should be written down by $36,000. Arthur Iorio's share of the writedown is (p. 678)
   a. $7,920
   b. $9,000
   c. $12,000
   d. $18,000

9. The process of closing the business, selling the assets, paying the liabilities, and disbursing remaining cash to the owners is called (p. 682)
   a. Dissolution
   b. Forming a new partnership
   c. Withdrawal
   d. Liquidation

10. Mike Marr and Pamela Coombs have shared profits and losses equally. Immediately prior to the final cash disbursement in a liquidation of their partnership, the books show:
    Cash $100,000 = Liabilities $0 + Mike Marr, Capital $60,000 + Pamela Coombs, Capital $40,000
    How much cash should Marr receive? (p. 682)
    a. $40,000
    b. $50,000
    c. $60,000
    d. None of the above

Answers to Self-Study Questions
1. b   2. b   3. a ($40,000 × 3/12 = $10,000)   4. a   5. a.
6. c [($46,000 + $52,000 + $55,000) × 1/3 = $51,000; $55,000 − $51,000 = $4,000; $4,000 + 2 = $2,000 each to Quantz and Goodwin]
7. d   8. b ($36,000 × 1/4 = $9,000)   9. d   10. c

Assignment Material

QUESTIONS

1. List at least five items that the partnership agreement should specify.

2. Ron Montgomery, who is a partner in M&N Associates, commits the firm to a contract for a job within the scope of its regular business operations. What term describes Montgomery's ability to obligate the partnership?

3. If a partnership cannot pay a debt, who must make payment? What term describes this obligation of the partners?

4. How is income of a partnership taxed?

5. Identify the advantages and disadvantages of the partnership form of business organization.

6. Most professionals in Canada, such as doctors, lawyers, and public accounting firms, are organized as limited liability partnerships (LLPs). Explain the fundamental concept that governs an LLP.

7. Compare and contrast the financial statements of a proprietorship and a partnership.

8. Chris Loranger and Mei Ling want to form a partnership to open a restaurant. They are considering bringing in a third partner who does not want any day-to-day responsibility for managing the operations; he or she may simply want to receive a return on his or her investment. Describe the type of partner this person would be.

9. Chris Higgins and Taylor Pyett's partnership agreement states that Higgins gets 60 percent of profits and Pyett gets 40 percent. If the agreement does not discuss the treatment of losses, how are losses shared? How do the partners share profits and losses if the agreement specifies no profit-and-loss-sharing ratio?

10. What determines the amount of the credit to a partner's Capital account when the partner contributes assets other than cash to the business?

11. Do partner withdrawals of cash for personal use affect the sharing of profits and losses by the partner? If so, explain how. If not, explain why not.

12. Briefly describe how to account for the purchase of an existing partner's interest in the business.

13. Jeff Malcolm purchases Sheila Wilson's interest in the Wilson & Conners partnership. What right does Malcolm obtain from the purchase? What is required for Malcolm to become Paula Conners's partner?

14. Sal Assissi and Hamza Zahari each have capital of $150,000 in their business. They share profits in the ratio of 55:45. Sheetal Kaur acquires a one-fifth share in the partnership by investing cash of $100,000. What are the Capital balances of the three partners immediately after Kaur is admitted?

15. Name two events that can cause the dissolution of a partnership.

16. Distinguish between dissolution and liquidation of a partnership.

17. Name the three steps in liquidating a partnership.

18. The partnership of Ralls and Sauls is in the process of liquidation. How do the partners share (a) gains and losses on the sale of noncash assets and (b) the final cash disbursement?

19. Summarize the situations in which partnership allocations are based on (a) the profit-and-loss-sharing ratio and (b) the partners' Capital balances.

20. When does a capital deficiency occur?

STARTERS

S12–1 For both of the independent situations below, indicate if you would recommend the partnership form of business organization. State the reasons for your recommendation.

The partnership form of business

1. Philip Harcourt just joined the law practice of Osler and Hoskins. He thinks he will be making a huge salary and is worried about the tax effects of this income. He thinks the partners should incorporate the partnership and avoid the tax bill.

2. Fred Klaus and Felix Cadeau would like to form a construction company. Fred has the contacts, cash, and estimating skills, while Felix has equipment and field experience. There will be minimal profits until the business has a few projects.

①

Statement of equity

Won, $80,100

S12–2 Tarlier and Won are partners. Using the following information, prepare a statement of partner's equity on December 31, 2020, for the T&W Partnership:

	Capital Jan. 1, 2020	Capital Contributions	Net Income Allocated	Partner Drawings
Tarlier	$45,000	$10,000	$33,900	$12,000
Won	$60,000	$10,000	$22,100	$12,000

②

Partnership formation

1. S. Knoll, Capital, $470,000

S12–3 Susan Knoll and Emerson Wyndon are forming a partnership to develop a craft beer brewing company. Knoll contributes cash of $300,000 and land appraised at $80,000 with a building that has a current market value of $200,000. When Knoll purchased the land and building in 2014, its cost was $250,000. The partnership will assume Knoll's mortgage on the property in the amount of $110,000. Wyndon contributes cash of $500,000 and equipment with a current market value of $90,000.

1. Journalize the partnership's receipt of assets and liabilities on October 15. Record this as a compound journal entry for both partners.

2. Compute the partnership's total assets, total liabilities, and total partners' equity immediately after organizing.

②

Partnership balance sheet

Total partners' equity, $400,000

S12–4 On June 30, 2019, Rick Reeves, Jason Bateman, and Oliver Morali started a partnership called RJO Enterprises. Prepare an opening balance sheet showing their investments:

R. Reeves --------- Land appraised at $150,000

J. Bateman --------- Cash, $175,000

O. Morali --------- Inventory, $105,000; accounts payable $30,000

③

Partners' profits, losses, and Capital balances

2. Baker Capital, $58,000

S12–5 Abel and Baker decided to form a partnership. Abel contributed equipment (book value $65,000), inventory (paid $20,000), and $10,000 cash. The equipment and inventory have a current market value of $40,000 and $15,000, respectively. Abel also had a debt of $20,000 for the equipment. Baker contributed office equipment (book value $20,000) and cash of $50,000. The current market value of the office equipment is $10,000. The two partners fail to agree on a profit-and-loss-sharing ratio. For the first month (June), the partnership lost $4,000.

1. How much of this loss goes to Abel? How much goes to Baker?

2. The partners withdrew no assets during June. What is each partner's Capital balance at June 30? Prepare a T-account for each partner's Capital.

③

Dividing partnership profits based on capital contributions and service

Friesen, $43,000

S12–6 Friesen, Walters, and Onley have Capital balances of $12,000, $6,000, and $6,000, respectively. The partners share profits and losses as follows:

a. The first $40,000 is divided based on the partners' capital investments.

b. The next $30,000 is based on service, shared equally by Friesen and Onley.

c. The remainder is divided equally.

Compute each partner's share of the $94,000 net income for the year.

① ② ③

Partnership income statement

Net income for Je-hong, $36,000

S12–7 The partnership of Je-hong and Barton had these balances at September 30, 2020:

Cash	$ 20,000	Service Revenue	$145,000
Liabilities	40,000	Je-hong, Capital	30,000
Barton, Capital	10,000	Total expenses	85,000
Other assets	120,000		

Je-hong gets 60 percent of profits and losses, and Barton gets 40 percent. Prepare the partnership's income statement and ending Capital balances for the year ended September 30, 2020.

④

Admitting a partner who purchases an existing partner's interest

S12–8 Todd has a Capital balance of $60,000; Carlson's balance is $55,000. Reynaldo pays $175,000 to Carlson to purchase Carlson's interest in the Todd & Carlson partnership.

Journalize the partnership's transaction to admit Reynaldo to the partnership on August 1.

S12-9 The partnership of Evans and Falconi has these Capital balances:

- Judy Evans $60,000
- Julie Falconi $80,000

Joan Gray invests cash of $70,000 to acquire a one-third interest in the partnership.

1. Does Gray's investment in the firm provide a bonus to the partners? Show your work.
2. Journalize the partnership's receipt of the $70,000 from Gray on February 1.

④
Admitting a partner who invests in the business
1. No bonus

S12-10 Bo and Go have partner Capital balances of $115,000 and $75,000, respectively. Bo gets 60 percent of profits and losses, and Go gets 40 percent. Assume Mo invests $70,000 to acquire a 20 percent interest in the new partnership of Bogomo. Is there a bonus? If so, who gets it? Journalize the partnership's receipt of cash from Mo on May 21.

④
Admitting a new partner; bonus to the old partners
Bonus for Go, $7,200

S12-11 Adams, Everett, and Chapman each have a $75,000 Capital balance. They share profits and losses as follows: 25 percent to Adams, 50 percent to Everett, and 25 percent to Chapman. Suppose Chapman is withdrawing from the business, and the partners agree that no appraisal of assets is needed. How much in assets can Chapman take from the partnership? Give the reason for your answer. What role does the profit-and-loss-sharing ratio play in this situation?

⑤
Withdrawal of a partner

S12-12 Suppose Sean is withdrawing from the partnership of Sean, Mohid, and Beth. The partners share profits and losses in a 1:2:3 ratio for Sean, Mohid, and Beth, respectively. After the revaluation of assets, Sean's Capital balance is $40,000, and the other partners agree to pay him $30,000. Mohid and Beth agree to a new profit-and-loss-sharing ratio of 2:3 for Mohid and Beth, respectively. Journalize the payment to Sean for his withdrawal from the partnership on August 31.

⑤
Journalize withdrawal of a partner

S12-13 Simpson, Locke, and Job each have a $27,000 Capital balance. Simpson is retiring from the business. The partners agree to revalue the assets at current market value. A real estate appraiser values the land at $70,000 (book value is $50,000). The profit-and-loss-sharing ratio is 1:2:1. Journalize (a) the revaluation of the land on July 31, and (b) a payment of $32,000 to Simpson upon his retirement the same day.

⑤
Withdrawal of a partner; asset revaluation
(a) Debit Land, $20,000

S12-14 Suppose the partnership of Ryan Lauren, Alexis Andrews, and Scott Benroudi introduced in Exhibit 12–5 liquidates by selling all noncash assets for $80,000. Complete the liquidation schedule as shown in Exhibit 12–5 with this new information.

⑥
Liquidation of a partnership at a loss
Lauren, $34,000

S12-15 After completing the liquidation schedule in S12–14, journalize the partnership's (a) sale of noncash assets for $80,000 (use a single account for Noncash Assets), (b) payment of liabilities, and (c) payment of cash to the partners on October 31. Include an explanation with each entry.

⑥
Liquidation of a partnership

S12-16 What if instead of the result you calculated in S12–14, you notice that Benroudi has a final balance of negative $8,000. What are the options for dealing with this capital deficit?

⑥
Capital deficit upon liquidation of a partnership

EXERCISES

E12-1 Mark Giltrow and Denise Chan are forming a business to imprint T-shirts. Giltrow suggests that they organize as a partnership to avoid the unlimited liability of a proprietorship. According to Giltrow, partnerships are not very risky.

Giltrow explains to Chan that if the business does not succeed, each partner can withdraw from the business, taking the same assets that she or he invested at its beginning. Giltrow states that the main disadvantage of the partnership form of organization is double taxation: First, the partnership pays a business income tax; second, each partner also pays personal income tax on her or his share of the business's profits.

Correct the errors in Giltrow's explanation.

①
Partnership characteristics

①
Organizing a business as a partnership

E12–2 Joanna Volescu, a friend from college, approaches you about forming a partnership to export software. Since graduation, Joanna has worked for the World Bank, developing important contacts among government officials and business leaders in Poland and Hungary. Joanna believes she is in a unique position to capitalize on expanding markets. With your expertise in finance, you would have responsibility for accounting and finance in the partnership.

Required   Discuss the advantages and disadvantages of organizing the export business as a partnership rather than a proprietorship. Comment on the way partnership income is taxed.

②

Investments by partners

2. Total assets, $56 mil.

E12–3 Jackson Cooke and Julia Bamber are forming a partnership to develop an amusement park near Ottawa. Cooke contributes cash of $3 million and land valued at $30 million. When Cooke purchased the land, its cost was $16 million. The partnership will assume Cooke's $6 million note payable on the land. Bamber invests cash of $15 million and construction equipment that she purchased for $14 million (accumulated amortization to date is $6 million). The equipment's market value is equal to its book value.

Required

1. Journalize the partnership's receipt of assets and liabilities from Cooke and Bamber on November 10. Record each asset at its current market value with no entry to accumulated amortization.
2. Compute the partnership's total assets, total liabilities, and total equity immediately after organizing.

②

Combining proprietorships into a partnership

1. Demetrius, Capital $92,000

E12–4 On December 31, 2019, Demetrius and Garnett agree to combine their sole proprietorships into a partnership. Their balance sheets on December 31 are shown as follows:

	Demetrius's Business		Garnett's Business	
	Book Value	Current Market Value	Book Value	Current Market Value
Assets				
Cash	$ 9,000	$ 9,000	$ 3,000	$ 3,000
Accounts Receivable	23,000	21,000	16,000	14,000
Inventory	49,000	43,000	40,000	40,000
Vehicles, Net	126,000	108,000	54,000	58,000
Total Assets	$ 207,000	$ 181,000	$ 113,000	$ 115,000
Liabilities and Owner's Equity				
Accounts Payable	$ 23,000	$ 23,000	$ 12,000	$ 12,000
Other Accrued Payables	13,000	13,000		
Notes Payable	53,000	53,000		
Demetrius, Capital	118,000	?		
Garnett, Capital			101,000	?
Total Liabilities and Owner's Equity	$ 207,000	$ 181,000	$ 113,000	$ 115,000

Required

1. Journalize the contributions of Demetrius and Garnett to the partnership.
2. Prepare the partnership balance sheet at December 31, 2019.

E12–5 On January 1, 2019, Chris Hunts and Carol Lo formed the Chris and Carol Partnership by investing the following assets and liabilities in the business:

② Recording a partner's investment

Carol Lo, capital, $193,000

	Chris's Book Value	Carol's Book Value
Cash	$12,000	$18,500
Equipment	38,000	53,500
Accumulated amort.—equipment	8,200	9,900
Buildings	84,000	95,000
Accumulated amort.—buildings	25,000	35,000
Land	60,000	66,000
Accounts payable	35,000	35,000
Note payable	17,000	28,000

An independent appraiser was hired to provide the current market values of all assets. The values are: Chris's equipment $29,000, Carol's equipment $47,500, Chris's building $90,000, Carol's building $110,000, Chris's land $78,000, and Carol's land $80,000.

Chris and Carol agree to share profits and losses in a 60:40 ratio. During the first year of operations, the business net income is $74,000. Each partner withdrew $30,000 cash.

Required

1. Prepare the journal entries to record the initial investments in the business by Chris and Carol.

2. Prepare a balance sheet dated January 1, 2019, after the completion of the initial journal entries.

E12–6 Ken Danolo and Jim Goldman form a partnership, investing $96,000 and $168,000, respectively. Determine their shares of net income or net loss for each of the following situations:

③ Computing partners' shares of net income and net loss

c. Danolo, $104,000

a. Net loss is $124,800 and the partners have no written partnership agreement.

b. Net income is $105,600 and the partnership agreement states that the partners share profits and losses based on their capital investments.

c. Net income is $264,000. The first $132,000 is shared based on the partner's capital investments. The next $100,000 is shared based on partner service, with Danolo receiving 40 percent and Goldman receiving 60 percent. The remainder is shared equally.

E12–7 Harper, Cheves, and Calderon have capital investments of $20,000, $30,000, and $50,000, respectively. The partners share profits and losses as follows:

③ Share of income or loss for 3 partners

Cheves, $36,000

a. The first $40,000 is divided based on the partner's capital investments.

b. The next $40,000 is based on service, shared equally by Harper and Cheves.

c. The remainder is divided equally.

Compute each partner's share of the $92,000 net income for the year.

E12–8 Oscar and Elmo have formed a partnership and invested $50,000 and $70,000, respectively. They have agreed to share profits as follows:

③ Computing partners' share of a loss

Oscar, ($5,000)

a. Oscar is to receive an allocation of $25,000 for his service and Elmo is to receive an allocation of $15,000 for his service.

b. $12,000 is to be allocated according to their original capital contributions to the partnership.

c. The remainder is to be allocated 5:4 respectively.

Assuming that the business had a loss of $11,000, allocate the loss to Oscar and Elmo.

E12–9 The partnership of Danolo and Goldman reports the following information:

③ Computing partners' Capital balances

Overall effect, $4,000 decrease

• Ken Danolo withdrew cash of $148,000 for personal use.

• Jim Goldman withdrew cash of $120,000 during the year.

- Net income is $264,000. The first $132,000 is shared based on the partner's capital investments (Danolo $96,000; Goldman $168,000). The next $100,000 is shared based on partner service, with Danolo receiving 40 percent and Goldman receiving 60 percent. The remainder is shared equally. (If you completed E12–6 you can use the amounts calculated there.)

  Journalize the entries on December 31 to close to each Capital account with the net income to the partners, and to close the partners' Withdrawal accounts. Explanations are not required. Indicate the amount of increase or decrease in each partner's Capital balance. What was the overall effect on partnership capital?

④
Admitting a new partner
Neilson's equity, $14,100

E12–10 Goertz Accounting Services has a capital balance of $30,000 after adjusting assets to the fair market value. Leonard Goertz wants to form a partnership with Morley Neilson, who will receive a 30 percent interest in the new partnership. Neilson contributes $17,000 for his 30 percent interest. Determine Neilson's equity after admission and any bonus if applicable.

④
Admitting a new partner
1c. Wang, $47,500

E12–11 Joanna Wang is admitted to a partnership. Prior to the admission of Wang, the partnership books show Tanya Wird's Capital balance at $79,000 and Alan Bales's Capital balance at $39,500. Wird and Bales share profits and losses equally.

Required

1. Compute the amount of each partner's equity on the books of the new partnership under each of the following plans:

   a. Wang purchases Bales's interest in the business, paying $47,250 directly to Bales.

   b. Wang invests $39,500 to acquire a one-fourth interest in the partnership.

   c. Wang invests $71,500 to acquire a one-fourth interest in the partnership.

2. Make the partnership journal entry on March 4 to record the admission of Wang under plans (a), (b), and (c) in Requirement 1. Explanations are not required.

① ③ ④
Using a partnership financial statement, admitting a new partner
1. Harry Simra 40%;
Sunny Simra 60%

E12–12 The Simra Brothers Partnership had the following statement of partners' equity for the years ended December 31, 2019, and 2020. (This is similar to the statement of partners' equity shown in Exhibit 12–3 on page 665.)

SIMRA BROTHERS PARTNERSHIP
Statement of Partners' Equity
For the Years Ended December 31, 2019, and 2020

	Harry Simra, Capital	Sunny Simra, Capital	Amin Simra, Capital	Total Partnership Capital
Balance, Jan. 1, 2019	$ 75,000	$ 50,000		$125,000
Net income for 2019	20,000	30,000		50,000
Balance, Dec. 31, 2019	95,000	80,000		175,000
Amin's contribution	2,000	3,000	$45,000	50,000
Net income for 2020	8,000	56,000	16,000	80,000
Subtotal	105,000	139,000	61,000	305,000
Less: partner withdrawals	12,000	16,000	10,000	38,000
Balance, Dec. 31, 2020	$ 93,000	$123,000	$51,000	$267,000

Required

1. What was the profit-and-loss-sharing ratio in 2019?

2. Refer to Amin's contribution, which was made in cash. How much cash did Amin contribute to the partnership?

3. What percentage of interest did Amin obtain?

4. Why do Harry and Sunny have additions to their balances as a result of Amin's contribution?

5. What was the profit-and-loss-sharing ratio in 2020?

E12–13 After closing the books, Stihl & Laksa's partnership balance sheet reports owner's equity of $40,500 for Stihl and $54,000 for Laksa. Stihl is leaving the firm. He and Laksa agree to write down partnership assets by $18,000. They have shared profits and losses in the ratio of one-third to Stihl and two-thirds to Laksa. The partnership agreement states that a partner withdrawing from the firm will receive assets equal to the book value of his owner's equity.

Withdrawal of a partner from a business

2. $42,000

Required

1. How much will Stihl receive?

2. Laksa will continue to operate the business as a proprietorship. What is Laksa's beginning Capital on the proprietorship books?

E12–14 Alana Bruno is retiring from the partnership of Bruno, Kraft, and Hamelin on May 31. The partner Capital balances are Alana Bruno, $108,000; Robert Kraft, $153,000; and Rollon Hamelin, $66,000. The partners agree to have the partnership assets revalued to current market values. The independent appraiser reports that the book value of the inventory should be decreased by $24,000 and the book value of the land should be increased by $96,000. The partners agree to these revaluations. The profit-and-loss-sharing ratio has been 2:4:4 for Bruno, Kraft, and Hamelin, respectively. In retiring from the firm, Bruno received $180,000 cash.

Withdrawal of a partner

b. Debit Kraft, Capital, $28,800

Required Journalize (a) the asset revaluations and (b) Bruno's withdrawal from the firm.

E12–15 Jonas, Teese, and Moyer are liquidating their partnership. Before selling the noncash assets and paying the liabilities, the Capital balances are Jonas, $57,500; Teese, $34,500; and Moyer, $23,000. The partnership agreement divides profits and losses equally.

Liquidation of a partnership

2. Jonas, $53,500

Required

1. After selling the noncash assets and paying the liabilities, suppose the partnership has cash of $115,000. How much cash will each partner receive in final liquidation?

2. After selling the noncash assets and paying the liabilities, suppose the partnership has cash of $103,000. How much cash will each partner receive in final liquidation?

E12–16 Prior to liquidation, the accounting records of Garcia, Woods, and Mickelson included the following balances and profit-and-loss-sharing percentages:

Liquidation of a partnership

	A	B	C	D	E	F	G	H	I	J	K	L
1									Capital			
2				Noncash				Garcia		Woods		Mickelson
3			Cash	+	Assets	=	Liabilities	+	(40%)	+	(30%)	+	(30%)
4	Balances before sale of assets	$10,000		$62,500		$26,500		$20,000		$15,000		$11,000

The partnership sold the noncash assets for $78,500, paid the liabilities, and disbursed the remaining cash to the partners. Complete the summary of transactions in the liquidation of the partnership. Use the format illustrated in Exhibit 12–5.

E12–17 The partnership of Linus, Lebrun, and Beale is liquidating. Business assets, liabilities, and partners' Capital balances prior to dissolution are shown below. The partners share profits and losses as follows: Shelly Linus, 20 percent; Peter Lebrun, 30 percent; and Cathy Beale, 50 percent.

Liquidation of a partnership

Shelly Linus, Capital, $29,600

Chapter 12 Partnerships **697**

Required Create a spreadsheet or solve manually—as directed by your instructor—to show the ending balances in all accounts after the noncash assets are sold for $280,000. Determine the unknown amounts, represented by (?).

	A	B	C	D	E	F	G
1			Noncash		Shelly Linus,	Peter Lebrun,	Cathy Beale,
2		Cash	Assets	Liabilities	Capital	Capital	Capital
3							
4	Balance before sale of assets	$ 12,000	$252,000	$154,000	$24,000	$74,000	$12,000
5	Sale of assets	280,000	(252,000)		?†	?	?
6	Balances	$292,000	$ 0	$154,000	$?	$?	$?
7							

† ($B5 – $C5) * .2

USING EXCEL

③

Using Excel for partnerships

E12–18 *Download an Excel template for this problem online in MyLab Accounting.*

Green, White, and Cedar are partners in GWC Services, a consulting practice. The partnership agreement states any income or loss is to be distributed in the following order:

1. Services contributed by the partners

2. Interest on the capital balance—6%

3. Remaining net income/loss is to be allocated 3:2:1 to Green, White, and Cedar

Salaries and capital balance information:

	Green	White	Cedar
Salaries	$ 60,000	$ 30,000	$ 45,000
Capital balance	120,000	150,000	200,000

Required

1. Assume that during the year ended December 31, 2018, the partnership earned net income of $320,000. Allocate the net income among the three partners in accordance with the partnership agreement. Dollar amounts should be in whole dollars. Use dollar signs and double underlines where appropriate.

2. Assume instead the net income was $100,000 for the year. Allocate the net income among the three partners in accordance with the partnership agreement. Dollar amounts should be in whole dollars. Use dollar signs and double underlines where appropriate.

SERIAL EXERCISE

② ③ ⑤

Account for partners' initial investment, allocate profit and losses, account for the withdrawal of a partner

Jean Turner, Capital, December 31, 2021 $10,600

E12–19 *The Serial Exercise involves a company that will be revisited throughout relevant chapters in Volume 1 and Volume 2. You can complete the Serial Exercises using MyLab Accounting.*

This exercise continues recordkeeping for the Canyon Canoe Company. Students do not have to complete prior exercises in order to answer this question.

Amber Wilson, Jean Turner, and Oscar White decide to form a T-shirt design partnership. Wilson figures this T-shirt design business will help her other company, Canyon Canoe Company, with any T-shirt design needs. Additionally, Turner and White have connections with many companies, and can expand and grow this new partnership. Each of the three partners contributes $12,000 cash to start up the WTW partnership. They agree to share profits in two steps. First, Turner will receive $11,000 and White will receive $16,000 because they will do most of the graphic design work. Any remaining profits or losses will be shared 1:2:3 for Wilson, Turner, and White. The business starts on January 1, 2021. On December 31, 2021, the business posted a loss of $12,000. Wilson decides to withdraw from the partnership on December 31, 2021. Turner and White agree to give Wilson $4,000 for her equity interest.

Required

1. Journalize the contribution of the partners in the partnership on January 1, 2021.
2. Journalize the allocation of the loss from the Income Summary account.
3. Journalize the withdrawal of Wilson as a partner on December 31, 2021.
4. Calculate the ending balances in Turner's and White's capital accounts.

CHALLENGE EXERCISES

C12–20 On December 31, 2020, Jim Austin and Mike Mundy agree to combine their proprietorships as a partnership. Their balance sheets on December 31 are as follows:

②
Preparing a partnership balance sheet
Total assets, $1,425,000

	Austin's Business		Mundy's Business	
	Book Value	Current Market Value	Book Value	Current Market Value
Assets				
Cash	$ 30,000	$ 30,000	$ 25,000	$ 25,000
Accounts receivable (net)	110,000	100,000	40,000	35,000
Inventory	255,000	230,000	170,000	180,000
Equipment (net)	610,000	525,000	270,000	300,000
Total assets	$1,005,000	$885,000	$505,000	$540,000
Liabilities and Equity				
Accounts payable	$ 120,000	$120,000	$ 50,000	$ 50,000
Accrued expenses payable	10,000	10,000	10,000	10,000
Notes payable	275,000	275,000		
Jim Austin, capital	600,000	480,000		
Mike Mundy, capital			445,000	480,000
Total liabilities and equity	$1,005,000	$885,000	$505,000	$540,000

Required

1. Prepare the partnership balance sheet at December 31, 2020, in report format using two columns.
2. Assume John Allen wants to join the partnership by paying $212,000 for a 1/4 interest. The partnership equity before John joins is $960,000, and Jim Austin and Mike Mundy shared profits 60 percent for Austin and 40 percent for Mundy. Prepare the journal entry to record Allen's admission to the partnership on January 1, 2021.
3. What percentage of the profits will John Allen receive after becoming a partner?

BEYOND THE NUMBERS

① ⑤
Partnership issues

BN12–1

The following questions relate to issues faced by partnerships:

1. The text suggests that a written partnership agreement should be drawn up between the partners in a partnership. One benefit of an agreement is that it provides a mechanism for resolving disputes between the partners. What are five areas of dispute that might be resolved by a partnership agreement?

2. The statement has been made that "If you must take on a partner, make sure the partner is richer than you are." Why is this statement valid?

3. Frizzell, Clamath, & Legree is a partnership of lawyers. Clamath is planning to move to Australia. What are the options open to her to convert her share of the partnership assets to cash?

ETHICAL ISSUE

EI12–1

Feng Li and Tanya Ng operate The Party Centre, a party supply store in Mississauga, Ontario. The partners split profits and losses equally, and each takes an annual withdrawal of $90,000. To even out the workload, Ng does the buying and Li serves as the accountant. From time to time, they use small amounts of store merchandise for personal use. In preparing for a large private party, Li took engraved invitations, napkins, placemats, and other goods that cost $3,000. She recorded the transaction as follows:

Cost of Goods Sold	3,000	
Inventory		3,000

Required

1. How should Li have recorded this transaction?
2. Discuss the ethical dimension of Li's action.

PROBLEMS (GROUP A)

②
Investments by partners
2. Total assets, $252,000

P12–1A Vince Sharma and Klaus Warsteiner formed a partnership on January 1, 2020. The partners agreed to invest equal amounts of capital. Sharma invested his proprietorship's assets and liabilities (all accounts have normal balances):

	Sharma's Book Value	Current Market Value
Accounts receivable	$24,000	$20,000
Inventory	86,000	62,000
Prepaid expenses	13,000	12,000
Store equipment	72,000	52,000
Accounts payable	40,000	40,000

On January 1, Warsteiner invested cash in an amount equal to the current market value of Sharma's partnership capital. The partners decided that Sharma would earn 70 percent of partnership profits because he would manage the business. Warsteiner agreed to accept 30 percent of profits. During the period ended December 31, 2020, the partnership earned $432,000. Warsteiner's withdrawals were $128,000 and Sharma's withdrawals were $172,800.

Required

1. Journalize the partners' initial investments.
2. Prepare the partnership balance sheet immediately after its formation on January 1, 2020.
3. Calculate the partners' Capital balances on December 31, 2020.

P12–2A Sheila Sasso, Karen Schwimmer, and Jim Perry have formed a partnership. Sasso invested $60,000; Schwimmer, $120,000; and Perry, $180,000. Sasso will manage the store, Schwimmer will work in the store three-quarters of the time, and Perry will not work in the business.

Computing partners' shares of net income and net loss

1. b. Net income allocated to Sasso, $58,000

Required

1. Compute the partners' shares of profits and losses under each of the following plans:

   a. Net loss is $70,500, and the partnership agreement allocates 45 percent of profits to Sasso, 35 percent to Schwimmer, and 20 percent to Perry. The agreement does not discuss the sharing of losses.

   b. Net income for the year is $136,500. The first $45,000 is allocated on the basis of partners' Capital investments. The next $75,000 is based on service, with $45,000 going to Sasso and $30,000 going to Schwimmer. Any remainder is shared equally.

   c. Net loss for the year is $136,500. The first $45,000 is allocated on the basis of partners' Capital investments. The next $75,000 is based on service, with $45,000 going to Sasso and $30,000 going to Schwimmer. Any remainder is shared equally.

2. Revenues for the year were $858,000 and expenses were $721,500. Under plan (b), prepare the partnership income statement for the year. Assume a year end of September 30, 2020.

3. How will what you have learned in this problem help you manage a partnership?

P12–3A SAC Company is a partnership owned by K. Santiago, R. Astorga, and J. Camino, who share profits and losses in the ratio of 1:3:4. The adjusted trial balance of the partnership (in condensed form) at June 30, 2020, follows:

Capital amounts for the balance sheet of a partnership

2. K. Santiago, Capital, $41,500

SAC COMPANY Adjusted Trial Balance June 30, 2020		
Cash	$ 166,000	
Noncash assets	800,000	
Liabilities		$ 690,000
K. Santiago, capital		152,000
R. Astorga, capital		282,000
J. Camino, capital		428,000
K. Santiago, withdrawals	126,000	
R. Astorga, withdrawals	272,000	
J. Camino, withdrawals	312,000	
Revenues		748,000
Expenses	624,000	
Totals	$2,300,000	$2,300,000

Required

1. Prepare the June 30, 2020, entries to close the Revenues, Expenses, Income Summary, and Withdrawals accounts.

2. Using T-accounts, insert the opening balances in the partners' Capital accounts, post the closing entries to the Capital accounts, and determine each partner's ending Capital balance.

④
Admitting a new partner
c. B. Ratta, Capital, $20,000

P12–4A Toronto Skytop Resort is a partnership, and its owners are considering admitting Bharat Ratta as a new partner. On July 31, 2020, the Capital accounts of the three existing partners and their shares of profits and losses are as follows:

	Capital	Sharing Percentage
Eleanor Craven..............................	$20,000	20%
Navneet Shelmar..........................	30,000	30
Brian Harmon..............................	40,000	50

Required Journalize the admission of Ratta as a partner on July 31, 2020, for each of the following independent situations:

a. Ratta pays Harmon $55,000 cash to purchase Harmon's interest.

b. Ratta invests $30,000 in the partnership, acquiring a one-quarter interest in the business.

c. Ratta invests $30,000 in the partnership, acquiring a one-sixth interest in the business.

④ ⑤
Recording changes in partnership Capital
c. Debit Karen Tenne, Capital, $248,000

P12–5A Trail Equipment is a partnership owned by three individuals. The partners share profits and losses in the ratio of 30 percent to Karen Tenne, 40 percent to Frank Durn, and 30 percent to Erin Hana. At December 31, 2020, the firm has the following balance sheet amounts:

Cash		$ 354,000	Total liabilities		$ 520,000
Accounts receivable	$88,000				
Less: Allowance for doubtful accounts	4,000	84,000			
Inventory		432,000	Karen Tenne, capital		248,000
Equipment	460,000		Frank Durn, capital		160,000
Less: Accumulated amortization	132,000	328,000	Erin Hana, capital		270,000
Total assets		$1,198,000	Total liabilities and capital		$1,198,000

Karen Tenne withdraws from the partnership on December 31.

Required Record Tenne's withdrawal from the partnership under the following independent plans:

a. In a personal transaction, Tenne sells her equity in the partnership to Michael Adams, who pays Tenne $176,000 for her interest. Durn and Hana agree to accept Adams as a partner.

b. The partnership pays Tenne cash of $72,000 and gives her a note payable for the remainder of her book equity in settlement of her partnership interest.

c. The partnership pays Tenne $260,000 cash for her equity in the partnership.

d. The partners agree that the equipment is worth $548,000 (net). After the revaluation, the partnership settles with Tenne by giving her cash of $44,000 and inventory for the remainder of her book equity.

② ③ ④ ⑤
Accounting for partners' investments; allocating profits and losses; accounting for the admission of a new partner; accounting for the withdrawal of a partner; preparing a partnership balance sheet
2. A. Buckner, Capital, $387,209

P12–6A

2017

Jun. 10   Adam Buckner and Amber Kwan have agreed to pool their assets and form a partnership to be called B&K Consulting. They agree to share all profits equally and make the following initial investments:

	Buckner	Kwan
Cash...	$15,000	$30,000
Accounts receivable (net)......................	33,000	27,000
Office furniture.......................................	36,000	24,000

Dec. 31   The partnership's reported net income was $195,000 for the year
           ended December 31, 2014.

2018

Jan. 1   Buckner and Kwan agree to accept Heidi Nguen into the partnership
           with a $180,000 investment for 30 percent of the business. The partner-
           ship agreement is amended to provide for the following sharing of
           profits and losses:

	Buckner	Kwan	Nguen
Service..	$90,000	$120,000	$75,000
Interest on capital balance before allocation of income...........................	5%	5%	5%
Balance in ratio of...............................	3 :	2 :	5

Dec. 31   The partnership's reported net income was $480,000.

2019

Oct. 10   Buckner withdrew $84,000 cash from the partnership and Kwan with-
           drew $57,000 (Nguen did not make any withdrawals).
Dec. 31   The partnership's reported net income was $255,000.

2020

Jan. 2   After a disagreement as to the direction in which the partnership
           should be moving, Nguen decided to withdraw from the partnership.
           The three partners agreed that Nguen could take cash of $300,000 in
           exchange for her equity in the partnership.

Required

1. Journalize all of the transactions for the partnership.
2. Prepare the partners' equity section of the B&K Consulting balance sheet as of
   January 2, 2020.

P12–7A The partnership of Malkin, Neale, & Staal has experienced operating losses for three
consecutive years. The partners, who have shared profits and losses in the ratio of
Lisa Malkin, 20 percent, John Neale, 40 percent, and Brian Staal, 40 percent, are considering liquidating the business. They ask you to analyze the effects of liquidation
under various assumptions about the sale of the noncash assets. They present the
following partnership balance sheet amounts at December 31, 2020:

(6)
Liquidation of a partnership
1. a. Cash distributed to partners,
$310,000

Cash	$ 41,000	Liabilities	$151,000
Noncash assets	367,000	Lisa Malkin, capital	57,500
		John Neale, capital	158,500
		Brian Staal, capital	41,000
Total assets	$408,000	Total liabilities and equity	$408,000

Required

1. Prepare a summary of liquidation transactions (as illustrated in the chapter) for
   each of the following situations:
   a. The noncash assets are sold for $420,000.
   b. The noncash assets are sold for $338,000.
2. Make the journal entries to record the liquidation transactions in Requirement 1(b).

P12–8A The partnership of Telliher, Bachra, and Lang has experienced operating losses for
three consecutive years. The partners, who have shared profits and losses in the ratio
of Thea Telliher, 60 percent, Denis Bachra, 20 percent, and Alan Lang, 20 percent,
are considering liquidating of the business. They ask you to analyze the effects of
liquidation under various possibilities about the sale of the noncash assets. *Neither
Telliher nor Lang have personal assets if they go into a deficit financial position.* They present the following partnership balance sheet amounts at December 31, 2020:

(6)
Liquidation of a partnership
(deficits)
1. a. Loss allocated to Telliher,
$49,500

Cash	$ 6,750	Liabilities	$ 28,350
Noncash assets	118,800	Thea Telliher, capital	46,600
		Denis Bachra, capital	30,000
		Alan Lang, capital	20,600
Total assets	$125,550	Total liabilities and equity	$125,550

Required

1. Prepare a summary of liquidation transactions (as illustrated in Exhibit 12–6) for each of the following situations:

    a. The noncash assets are sold for $36,300.

    b. The noncash assets are sold for $27,600.

2. What legal recourse do the remaining partners have to be reimbursed for deficit balances?

PROBLEMS (GROUP B)

② Investments by partners

P12–1B On January 1, 2020, Svitlana Yaeger and Val Havlac formed a partnership. The partners agreed to invest equal amounts of capital. Havlac invested her proprietorship's assets and liabilities (all accounts have normal balances) as follows:

	Havlac's Book Value	Current Market Value
Accounts receivable	$20,200	$20,000
Inventory	44,000	48,000
Prepaid expenses	4,800	4,000
Office equipment	92,000	56,000
Accounts payable	48,000	48,000

On January 1, 2020, Yaeger invested cash in an amount equal to the current market value of Havlac's partnership capital. The partners decided that Havlac would earn two-thirds of partnership profits because she would manage the business. Yaeger agreed to accept one-third of profits. During the remainder of the year, the partnership earned $276,000. Havlac's withdrawals were $76,000, and Yaeger's withdrawals were $56,000.

Required

1. Journalize the partners' initial investments.

2. Prepare the partnership balance sheet immediately after its formation on January 1, 2020.

3. Calculate the partners' Capital balances at December 31, 2020.

② ③ Computing partners' shares of net income and net loss

P12–2B Sav Berlo, Silvio Felini, and Louis Valente have formed a partnership. Berlo invested $30,000, Felini $40,000, and Valente $50,000. Berlo will manage the store, Felini will work in the store half time, and Valente will not work in the business.

Required

1. Compute the partners' shares of profits and losses under each of the following plans:

    a. Net loss is $200,000, and the partnership agreement allocates 40 percent of profits to Berlo, 25 percent to Felini, and 35 percent to Valente. The agreement does not discuss the sharing of losses.

    b. Net income for the year is $354,000. The first $150,000 is allocated based on partner capital investments. The next $72,000 is based on service, with Berlo receiving $56,000 and Felini receiving $16,000. Any remainder is shared equally.

2. Revenues for the year were $1,014,000 and expenses were $660,000. Under plan (b), prepare the partnership income statement for the year. Assume a January 31, 2020, year end.

3. How will what you learned in this problem help you manage a partnership?

P12–3B SY&I is a partnership owned by T. Shitang, D. Yamamoto, and J. Ishikawa, who share profits and losses in the ratio of 2:3:5. The adjusted trial balance of the partnership (in condensed form) at September 30, 2020, follows:

(2) (3)
Capital amounts for the balance sheet of a partnership

SY&I Adjusted Trial Balance September 30, 2020		
Cash	$ 110,000	
Noncash assets	389,000	
Liabilities		$ 319,000
T. Shitang, capital		125,000
D. Yamamoto, capital		97,000
J. Ishikawa, capital		46,000
T. Shitang, withdrawals	99,000	
D. Yamamoto, withdrawals	81,000	
J. Ishikawa, withdrawals	40,000	
Revenues		928,000
Expenses	796,000	
Totals	$1,515,000	$1,515,000

Required

1. Prepare the September 30, 2020, entries to close the Revenues, Expenses, Income Summary, and Withdrawals accounts.

2. Using T-accounts, insert the opening Capital balances in the partner Capital accounts, post the closing entries to the Capital accounts and determine each partner's ending Capital balance.

P12–4B Pineridge Consulting Associates is a partnership, and its owners are considering admitting Helen Fluery as a new partner. On March 31, 2020, the Capital accounts of the three existing partners and their shares of profits and losses are as follows:

(4)
Admitting a new partner

	Capital	**Sharing Percentage**
Jim Zook	$ 50,000	40%
Richard Land	100,000	20
Jennifer Lowe	150,000	40

Required Journalize the admission of Fluery as a partner on March 31, 2020, for each of the following independent situations:

a. Fluery pays Lowe $200,000 cash to purchase Lowe's interest in the partnership.

b. Fluery invests $100,000 in the partnership, acquiring a one-fourth interest in the business.

c. Fluery invests $80,000 in the partnership, acquiring a one-fourth interest in the business.

P12–5B Vector Financial Planning is a partnership owned by three individuals. The partners share profits and losses in the ratio of 20 percent to Katherine Depatie, 40 percent to Sam Seamus, and 40 percent to Emily Hudson. At December 31, 2020, the firm has the following balance sheet amounts:

(4) (5)
Recording changes in partnership capital

Cash		$ 350,400	Total liabilities	$ 573,000
Accounts receivable	$ 92,400			
Less: Allowance for doubtful accounts	16,800	75,600		
Building	1,102,000		Katherine Depatie, capital	390,600
Less: Accumulated amortization	294,000	808,000	Sam Seamus, capital	210,000
Land		200,000	Emily Hudson, capital	260,400
Total assets		$1,434,000	Total liabilities and capital	$1,434,000

Seamus withdraws from the partnership on December 31, 2020, to establish his own consulting practice.

Required Record Seamus's withdrawal from the partnership under the following independent plans:

a. In a personal transaction, Seamus sells his equity in the partnership to Rea Pearlman. Depatie and Hudson agree to accept Pearlman as a partner.

b. The partnership pays Seamus cash of $163,000 and gives him a note payable for the remainder of his book equity in settlement of his partnership interest.

c. The partnership pays Seamus cash of $336,000.

d. The partners agree that the building is worth $682,000 (net). After the revaluation, the partnership settles with Seamus by giving him cash of $82,000 and a note payable for the remainder of his book equity.

② ③ ④ ⑤

Accounting for partners' investments; allocating profits and losses; accounting for the admission of a new partner; accounting for the withdrawal of a partner; preparing a partnership balance sheet

P12–6B

2017

Jun. 10 Steven Hodgson and Sarah Asham have agreed to pool their assets and form a partnership to be called H&A Distributors. They agree to share all profits equally and make the following initial investments:

	Hodgson	Asham
Cash	$21,000	$36,000
Accounts receivable (net)	42,000	21,000
Office furniture (net)	48,000	27,000

Dec. 31 The partnership's reported net income was $228,000 for the year.

2018

Jan. 1 Hodgson and Asham agree to accept Myra Sirroca into the partnership with a $210,000 investment for 40 percent of the business. The partnership agreement is amended to provide for the following sharing of profits and losses:

	Hodgson	Asham	Sirroca
Service	$120,000	$90,000	$80,000
Interest on end-of-period capital balance before allocation of income	10%	10%	10%
Balance in ratio of	2 :	3 :	5

Dec. 31 The partnership's reported net income is $570,000.

2019

Oct. 10 Hodgson withdrew $90,000 cash from the partnership and Asham withdrew $60,000 (Sirroca did not make any withdrawals).

Dec. 31 The partnership's reported net income is $225,000.

2020

Jan. 2   After a disagreement as to the direction in which the partnership should be moving, Sirroca decided to withdraw from the partnership. The three partners agreed that Sirroca could take cash of $510,000 in exchange for her equity in the partnership.

Required

1. Journalize all of the transactions for the partnership.
2. Prepare the partners' equity section of the balance sheet as of January 2, 2020.

P12–7B The partnership of Du, Chong, and Smith has experienced operating losses for three consecutive years. The partners, who have shared profits and losses in the ratio of Jia Du, 10 percent, Denis Chong, 30 percent, and Alan Smith, 60 percent, are considering liquidating the business. They ask you to analyze the effects of liquidation under various possibilities about the sale of the noncash assets. They present the following partnership balance sheet amounts at December 31, 2020:

⑥
Liquidation of a partnership

Cash	$ 70,000	Liabilities	$316,000
Noncash assets	526,000	Jia Du, capital	80,000
		Denis Chong, capital	102,000
		Alan Smith, capital	98,000
Total assets	$596,000	Total liabilities and equity	$596,000

Required

1. Prepare a summary of liquidation transactions (as illustrated in the chapter) for each of the following situations:
   a. The noncash assets are sold for $552,000.
   b. The noncash assets are sold for $448,000.
2. Make the journal entries to record the liquidation transactions in Requirement 1(b).

P12–8B The partnership of Pavelski, Ovechin, and Oh has experienced operating losses for three consecutive years. The partners, who have shared profits and losses in the ratio of Steven Pavelski, 60 percent, Eddie Ovechin, 20 percent, and Kwan Oh, 20 percent, are considering liquidating the business. They ask you to analyze the effects of liquidation under various possibilities about the sale of the noncash assets. *None of the partners has personal assets if they go into a deficit financial position.* They present the following partnership balance sheet amounts at December 31, 2020:

⑥
Liquidation of a partnership (deficit)

Cash	$ 27,000	Liabilities	$113,400
Noncash assets	475,200	Steven Pavelski, capital	186,400
		Eddie Ovechin, capital	120,000
		Kwan Oh, capital	82,400
Total assets	$502,200	Total liabilities and equity	$502,200

Required

1. Prepare a summary of liquidation transactions (as illustrated in Exhibit 12–6) for each of the following situations:
   a. The noncash assets are sold for $145,200.
   b. The noncash assets are sold for $110,400.
2. What legal recourse do the remaining partners have to be reimbursed for deficit balances?

CHALLENGE PROBLEMS

P12–1C Nancy Wesla and Jordon Dugger have been in a partnership for five years. The principal business of the partnership is systems design for financial institutions. Gross revenues have increased from $330,000 in 2016 to $3,800,000 in 2020, the year

① ②
Deciding on a capital structure

just ended. The number of employees has increased from two in the first year to nine in the most recent year. Wesla and Dugger realized that they had to build up the partnership's capital and have withdrawn only part of the annual profits. As a result, their Capital accounts have increased from $200,000 (Wesla, $140,000; Dugger, $60,000) in 2010 to $2,000,000 (Wesla, $1,080,000; Dugger, $920,000) in 2020.

The two partners realize that they must expand their capital base to expand their operations in order to meet the increasing demand for their systems designs. At the same time, they wish to take personal advantage of the partnership's earnings. They have been trying to determine whether they should continue the partnership and borrow the necessary funds, take on one or more partners (several of their employees have expressed interest and have capital to invest), or incorporate and sell a portion of the business to outsiders. With respect to incorporation, Faisal Jamal, a former classmate of Wesla's who works for a stockbroker, has indicated he knows of investors who would be interested in buying a share of the business.

Required   Wesla and Dugger have come to you to ask for advice. Provide an analysis of the situation and make a recommendation. In response to your questions, they indicate they will need additional capital of $1,600,000 to $2,000,000.

③

The effects of accounting decisions on profits

P12–2C Simone Perrier, Mary Salter, and Sean Patten have been partners in a systems design business for the past eight years. Perrier and Patten work full time in the business; Salter has a public accounting practice and works about 5 to 10 hours per week on the administrative side of the business. The business has been successful and the partners are considering expansion.

The partnership agreement states that profits will be distributed as follows:

1. Partners will get 6 percent interest on their average Capital balances.

2. Perrier will get a payment of $75,000 for her service; Salter will get a payment of $9,375 for her service; and Patten will get a payment of $75,000 for his service.

3. The balance remaining will be distributed on the basis of Perrier, 40 percent; Salter, 20 percent; and Patten, 40 percent.

The agreement also stipulates that the distributions outlined in parts 1 and 2 of the agreement will be made even if there are not sufficient profits and that any deficiency will be shared on the basis of part 3.

The capital structure was as follows at December 31, 2020, and reflects the average Capital balances for 2020:

Perrier	$ 228,750
Salter	1,091,250
Patten	491,250
Total	$1,811,250

There has been some stress in the partnership of late because Perrier believes that she is contributing a major part of the effort but is earning much less than Patten; Salter is upset because she believes that she is earning the least even though her capital is essentially funding the partnership.

Required   Perrier, Salter, and Patten have come to you to ask for advice as to how they might amicably settle the present dispute. Analyze the situation and make a recommendation. Assume net income in 2020 was $400,000.

Extending Your Knowledge

DECISION PROBLEM

DP12–1

③

Settling disagreements among partners

Lori Barclay invested $30,000 and Vanesa Resultan invested $15,000 in a public relations firm that has operated for 10 years. Neither partner has made an additional investment. They have shared profits and losses in the ratio of 2:1, which is the ratio of their investments in the business. Barclay manages the office, supervises the 16 employees, and does the accounting. Resultan, the moderator of a television talk show, is responsible for marketing. Her high profile generates important revenue for the business. During the year ended December 2020, the partnership earned net income of $75,000, shared in the 2:1 ratio. On December 31, 2020, Barclay's Capital balance was $152,500 and Resultan's Capital balance was $105,000.

Required

Respond to each of the following situations:
1. What explains the difference between the ratio of partner Capital balances at December 31, 2020, and the 2:1 ratio of partner investments and profit sharing?

2. Resultan believes the profit-and-loss-sharing ratio is unfair. She proposes a change, but Barclay insists on keeping the 2:1 ratio. What two factors may underlie Resultan's unhappiness?

3. During January 2020, Barclay learned that revenues of $24,000 were omitted from the reported 2019 income. She brings this to Resultan's attention, pointing out that her share of this added income is two-thirds, or $16,000, and Resultan's share is one-third, or $8,000. Resultan believes they should share this added income based on their Capital balances: 60 percent (or $14,400) to Barclay, and 40 percent (or $9,600) to Resultan. Which partner is correct? Why?

4. Assume that an account payable of $18,000 for an operating expense in 2019 was omitted from 2019 reported income. On what basis would the partners share this amount?

FINANCIAL STATEMENT CASE

FSC12–1

Lisogar, Philip, & Walters (LPW) is a regional accounting firm with four offices. Summary data from the partnership's annual report follow:

	Years Ended June 30 (dollars in thousands, except where indicated)				
	2020	**2019**	**2018**	**2017**	**2016**
Revenues					
Assurance services	$1,234	$1,122	$1,064	$1,093	$1,070
Consulting services	1,007	775	658	473	349
Tax services	743	628	567	515	557
Total Revenues	$2,984	$2,525	$2,289	$2,081	$1,976
Operating Summary					
Revenues	$2,984	$2,525	$2,289	$2,081	$1,976
Personnel costs	1,215	1,004	887	805	726
Other costs	712	630	517	458	415
Income to Partners	$1,057	$ 891	$ 885	$ 818	$ 835
Statistical Data					
Average number of partners	9	9	9	8	8

Required

1. What percentages of total revenues did LPW earn by performing assurance services (similar to auditing), consulting services, and tax services during 2016? What were the percentages in 2020? Which type of service grew the most from 2016 to 2020?

2. Compute the average revenue per partner in 2020. Assume each partner works 1,900 hours per year. On average, how much does each partner charge a client for one hour of time?

3. How much net income did each LPW partner earn, on average, in 2020?

Try It! Solutions for Chapter 12

1. The partnership agreement is a contract, so transactions under the agreement are governed by contract law. If or when disputes arise, both partners are legally protected. A partnership agreement should contain the following items:
   - Name, location, and nature of the business
   - Name, capital investment, and duties of each partner
   - Procedures for admitting a new partner
   - Method of sharing profits and losses among the partners
   - Withdrawals of assets allowed to the partners
   - Procedures for settling disputes among the partners
   - Procedures for settling with a partner who withdraws from the firm
   - Procedures for removing a partner who will not withdraw or retire from the partnership voluntarily
   - Procedures for liquidating the partnership

2. Advantages as compared to proprietorships are that partnerships can raise more capital, partnerships bring together the abilities of more than one person, and partners working well together can achieve more than by working alone. Compared to corporations, partnerships are less expensive to organize and are subject to fewer governmental regulations and restrictions.

   The main disadvantage of partnerships is that partnership agreements may be difficult to formulate. Each time a new partner is admitted or a partner leaves the partnership, the business needs a new partnership agreement. Other disadvantages are that relationships among partners may be fragile, and mutual agency and unlimited liability create personal obligations for each partner.

3. a. The appraised value or current market value is the appropriate value to use because that is what the land is worth now, and the current market value was verified by independent professionals.

   b.

Sep. 1	Land		50,000	
	Marty Kaur, Capital			50,000

4. a. Burns: $50,000 × 60% = $30,000 net income
      White: $50,000 × 40% = $20,000 net income
   b. Betty: $200,000 × 3/10 = $60,000 net loss
      Luella: $200,000 × 4/10 = $80,000 net loss
      Pius: $200,000 × 3/10 = $60,000 net loss
   c. Losses are shared the same way as profits.
      Locke: $60,000 × 1/3 = $20,000 net loss
      Barnel: $60,000 × 2/3 = $40,000 net loss
   d. When there is no agreement, profits and losses are shared equally.
      Hampton: $90,000 × 1/2 = $45,000 net income
      Kirk: $90,000 × 1/2 = $45,000 net income

5. a.

Partnership capital before Phyllis is admitted ($25,000 + $75,000)	$ 100,000
Phyllis's investment in the partnership	20,000
Partnership capital after Phyllis is admitted	$ 120,000
Phyllis's capital in the partnership ($120,000 × 1/10)	$ 12,000
Bonus to the old partners ($20,000 − $12,000)	$ 8,000

   b.

Jun. 12	Cash		20,000	
	Phyllis, Capital			12,000
	Tina, Capital			2,400
	Jean, Capital			5,600
	To admit Phyllis with a 10% interest in the business. Bonus to existing partners: Tina; $8,000 × 0.30 = $2,400 and Jean; $8,000 × 0.70 = $5,600			

   c.

Partners' capital balances on June 12:	
Tina, capital ($25,000 + $2,400)	$ 27,400
Jean, capital ($75,000 + $5,600)	80,600
Phyllis, capital	12,000
Total partnership capital	$ 120,000

6.

Partnership capital before Phyllis is admitted ($25,000 + $75,000)	$100,000
Phyllis's investment in the partnership	10,000
Partnership capital after Phyllis is admitted	$110,000
Phyllis's capital in the partnership ($110,000 × 1/10)	$ 11,000
Bonus to the new partner ($11,000 − $10,000)	$ 1,000

Jun. 12	Cash	10,000	
	Tina, Capital	300	
	Jean, Capital	700	
	Phyllis, Capital		11,000
	To admit Phyllis with a 10% interest in the business. Loss to existing partners: Tina; $1,000 × 0.30 = $300 and Jean; $1,000 × 0.70 = $700		

7.

Aug. 31	Ruth, Capital	40,000	
	Nick, Capital	4,000	
	Adriana, Capital	6,000	
	Cash		50,000
	To record withdrawal of Ruth from the business. Reduce Nick's Capital by $4,000 ($10,000 × 2/5) and Adriana's Capital by $6,000 ($10,000 × 3/5).		

8. a. The sale of the noncash assets for $20,000 creates a loss of $70,000 on the sale of noncash assets ($90,000 − $20,000 = $70,000).

   b.

	A	B	C	D	E	F	G	H	I	J	K	L
1										Capital		
2								Lauren		Andrews		Benroudi
3		Cash	+	Noncash Assets	=	Liabilities	+	(60%)	+	(20%)	+	(20%)
4	Balances before sale of assets	$ 10,000		$ 90,000		$ 30,000		$ 40,000		$20,000		$ 10,000
5	❶ Sale of assets and sharing of loss	20,000		(90,000)				(42,000)		(14,000)		(14,000)
6	Balances	30,000		0		30,000		(2,000)		6,000		(4,000)
7	❷ Payment of liabilities	(30,000)				(30,000)						
8	Balances	0		0		0		(2,000)		6,000		(4,000)
9	❸ Disbursement of cash to partners							2,000		(6,000)		4,000
10	Balances	$ 0		$ 0		$ 0		$ 0		$ 0		$ 0

   c. Lauren and Benroudi both have capital deficiencies. Both of these partners could contribute assets in the amount of their deficiencies to Andrews. However, if the deficient partners cannot contribute personal assets, then the deficits must be absorbed by Andrews. If Andrews absorbs the deficits, then she has a zero balance in her capital account. Since there is no remaining cash balance to distribute, she would be paid nothing more at liquidation.

13

Corporations: Share Capital and the Balance Sheet

CONNECTING CHAPTER 13

LEARNING OBJECTIVES

① Identify the characteristics of a corporation

What is a corporation, and why is it an important form of business?

Corporations, page 714
Characteristics of a Corporation
Organization of a Corporation
Share Capital

Shareholders' Equity, page 717
Contributed Capital
Retained Earnings
Dividends
Shareholders' Rights

② Record the issuance of shares and prepare the shareholders' equity section of a corporation's balance sheet

How do we record and present share information?

Issuing Shares, page 720
Common Shares
Preferred Shares
The Shareholders' Equity Section on a Balance Sheet
Debt versus Equity

Organization Costs, page 726

③ Account for cash dividends

What are cash dividends and how do we account for them?

Accounting for Cash Dividends, page 727
Dividend Dates
Declaring and Paying Dividends
Dividends on Cumulative and Noncumulative Preferred Shares

④ Use different share values in decision making

What is the difference between book value and market value of shares?

Different Values of Shares, page 730
Market Value
Book Value

⑤ Evaluate a company's ROA and ROE

What are the return on total assets (ROA) and the return on common shareholders' equity (ROE), and how do we calculate them?

Evaluating Operations, page 732
Return on Assets
Return on Common Shareholders' Equity

⑥ Identify the impact of IFRS on share capital

How does IFRS apply to share capital?

The Impact of IFRS on Share Capital, page 734

The **Summary** for Chapter 13 appears on pages 737–738.
Key Terms with definitions for this chapter's material appears on pages 738–739.

CPA competencies

This text covers material outlined in **Section 1: Financial Reporting of the CPA Competency Map**. The Learning Objectives for each chapter have been aligned with the CPA Competency Map to ensure the best coverage possible.

1.1.2 Evaluates the appropriateness of the basis of financial reporting

1.2.2 Evaluates treatment for routine transactions

1.4.4 Interprets financial reporting results for stakeholders (internal or external)

Aaron Vincent Elkaim/The Canadian Press

Canada Goose Holdings Inc. is famous for its incredibly warm down-filled coats. They are worn by both trekkers who need the functionality, and "Goose People" (brand ambassadors like José Bautista, Marc Jacobs, and Drake) who market its heritage and craftsmanship as a fashion statement. This global luxury brand is available in 36 countries.

Dani Reiss, president and CEO, still runs the company founded by his grandfather, Sam Tick, in 1957. At that time the business was called Metro Sportswear Ltd., and it made wool vests, raincoats, and snowsuits. The product line has expanded to include its signature product—their down coats—many of which retail for over $1,000 each. Their warmth comes from down that is purchased from Canadian Hutterite farmers' free-range birds.

To fund expansion, Bain Capital Investors, LLC purchased the majority of shares from Reiss in 2013. By 2016, the business had grown to $290.8 million in sales. The gross profit of $145.6 million means their gross margin was a strong 50.1%. Overall profits? A net income of $26.5 million for the year.

This success meant that the business would be able to raise even more funds to grow. This time, the company "went public" (started selling shares on a stock exchange) in March 2017. Since the *initial public offering* (IPO), its shares have been traded on the Toronto Stock Exchange and the New York Stock Exchange with the stock symbol GOOS.

So how can you use this information? You might want to invest in this business. Learning all about corporations in this chapter will help you make better decisions about personal investing as well as how the accounting is done.

Like Indigo Books & Music Inc. and TELUS Corporation, Canada Goose Holdings Inc. is a corporation. From this point forward, we will focus on corporations, so this chapter marks a turning point. Fortunately, most of the accounting you have learned thus far also applies to corporations.

Corporations

LO ①

What is a corporation, and why is it an important form of business?

Corporations dominate business activity in Canada. Although proprietorships and partnerships are more numerous, corporations transact more business and are larger in terms of total assets, sales revenue, and number of employees. Most well-known businesses, such as Canadian Tire Corporation, Limited and grocery store chain Loblaw Companies Limited are corporations. Their full names often include *Limited, Incorporated,* or *Corporation* (abbreviated *Ltd., Inc.,* or *Corp.*) to show they are corporations.

A corporation can be set up as a *public corporation,* such as the businesses just mentioned, or as a *private corporation.*

Public corporation A **public corporation** is a company organized as a corporation that is listed and sells its shares on a stock exchange. Canada Goose Holdings Inc. sells its shares on both the Toronto (TSX) and New York (NYSE) stock exchanges. Canadian generally accepted accounting principles (GAAP) require that these publicly accountable enterprises follow International Financial Reporting Standards (IFRS).

Just because a company is a private corporation does not mean it is small. According to their website, the Jim Pattison Group is the second largest private company in Canada, with sales over $10.1 billion and more than 45,000 employees in 2017.

Private corporation A **private corporation** is a company organized as a corporation that is not listed and does not sell its shares on a stock exchange. According to GAAP, private enterprises have the choice to follow either IFRS or Accounting Standards for Private Enterprises (ASPE). A company like Canada Goose was a private corporation from 1957 until 2017 when it *went public.*

The majority of this chapter will focus on ASPE and what is common between IFRS and ASPE. At the end of the chapter, a few differences between the standards will be highlighted.

Why It's Done This Way

As with partnerships, the principles and concepts in the accounting framework described in Chapter 1 apply equally to corporations.

Recall that the objective of financial reporting is to communicate useful information to users. With corporations, more information is presented because corporations can have more "owners" who may not have access to the financial details like a proprietor or a partner does.

The elements of financial statements (the accounts) do change a little. Accounting differences among types of organizations only relate to the equity section of the balance sheet, with corporations having contributed capital and retained earnings.

Characteristics of a Corporation

What makes the corporate form of organization so attractive? What are some of the reasons other forms of business organization are chosen?

Corporations can have one or more shareholders. For simplicity and ease of reading, this text will refer to "shareholders" rather than "shareholder(s)."

Separate Legal Entity A corporation is a separate legal entity formed under federal or provincial law. The government approves the **articles of incorporation**, which is a document giving the owners permission to form a corporation. Neither a proprietorship nor a partnership requires federal or provincial approval to do business, because in the eyes of the law the business and the owner or owners are not separate entities. From a legal perspective, a corporation is a distinct entity— an artificial person that exists apart from its owners, who are called **shareholders**.

A corporation has many of the rights that a person has. For example, a corporation can buy, own, and sell property. Assets and liabilities in the business belong to the corporation rather than to the corporation's owners. The corporation can also enter into contracts, sue, and be sued, just like an individual.

Continuous Life and Transferability of Ownership The owners' equity of a corporation is divided into **shares** of **stock**. The articles of incorporation specify how many shares the corporation can issue (sell) and lists the other details of its relationship with the federal or provincial government under whose laws it is incorporated. Most corporations have *continuous lives* regardless of changes in the ownership of their shares. In contrast, proprietorships and partnerships end when their ownership changes.

The US term for common shares is *common stock*.

The shareholders of Sleep Country Canada Inc, Canada Goose Holdings Inc. or any other corporation may sell or trade the shares to another person, give them away, bequeath them in a will, or dispose of them in any other way they desire. The transfer of the shares does not affect the continuity of the corporation.

No Mutual Agency **Mutual agency** means that all the owners act as agents of the business. A contract signed by one owner is binding for the whole company. Mutual agency operates in partnerships and proprietorships, but *not* in corporations. A shareholder of Imperial Oil Limited cannot commit the corporation to a contract (unless the shareholder is also an officer of the corporation).

Limited Liability of Shareholders Shareholders have **limited liability** for corporation debts. That means they have no personal obligation for corporation liabilities. The most that a shareholder can lose on an investment in a corporation's shares is the cost of the investment. In contrast, proprietors and partners are personally liable for all the debts of their businesses, unless the partnership is a limited partnership.

The combination of limited liability and no mutual agency means that investors can invest in a corporation without fear of losing all their personal wealth if the business fails. This feature enables a corporation to raise more money than proprietorships and partnerships can. Because of limited shareholder liability, many banks will lend money to a small corporation only if a third party (usually a corporate officer) guarantees payment of the loan personally in the event of default by the corporation.

Separation of Ownership and Management Shareholders own a corporation, but a *board of directors*—elected by the shareholders—appoints corporate officers to manage the business. Shareholders may invest any amount of money without having to manage the company.

Corporate Taxation Corporations are separate taxable entities. They pay a variety of taxes not required for proprietorships or partnerships, such as federal and provincial corporate income taxes. Corporate earnings are subject to some **double taxation**:

- First, corporations pay their own income taxes on corporate income.
- The shareholders then pay personal income tax on the dividends (distributions) that they receive from corporations, although the tax rate is usually lower than for regular income to minimize double taxation.

Proprietorships and partnerships pay no business income tax. Instead, owners are taxed on their share of the proprietorship or partnership income on their personal income tax return.

Government Regulation Because of shareholders' limited liability for corporation debts, outsiders doing business with the corporation can look no further than the corporation for payment of its debts. To protect people who lend money to a corporation or who invest in its shares, the federal and provincial governments monitor the affairs of corporations. This government regulation consists mainly of ensuring that corporations disclose adequate business information for investors and creditors. Public corporations are required to have an audit and to file certain reports with the applicable provincial securities commission. These requirements add to a corporation's expenses without increasing its income, but they are necessary.

Unique Costs for Corporations In Canada, legally, the directors of a corporation (defined below) have unlimited liability. However, insurance is available to cover any costs incurred by directors who may be sued by outsiders doing business with the corporation. If the corporation did not purchase this insurance for its directors, no one would agree to be a director of a corporation. In many small corporations there may only be one or a few shareholders, who would also be directors of the corporation. The cost for directors' insurance is unique to corporations—proprietorships or partnerships would not incur this cost.

Exhibit 13–1 summarizes the advantages and disadvantages of corporations.

EXHIBIT 13–1 | Advantages and Disadvantages of a Corporation

Corporation Advantages	Corporation Disadvantages
Can raise more money than a proprietorship or partnership.	Ownership and management are separated.
Has a continuous life.	Corporate earnings are subject to some double taxation.
Transferring ownership is easy.	Government regulation can be expensive.
No mutual agency exists among the shareholders.	Corporations may incur costs unique to corporations.
Shareholders have limited liability.	The board of directors often requires special insurance against lawsuits.

Organization of a Corporation

The process of creating a corporation begins when its organizers, called the *incorporators*, submit articles of incorporation to the federal or provincial government for approval. The articles of incorporation include the **authorization of shares** for the corporation to issue a certain number of shares of stock, which are shares of ownership in the corporation. The incorporators pay fees and file the required documents with the incorporating jurisdiction. Then the corporation comes into existence and becomes a legal entity. The incorporators agree to a set of **bylaws**, which act as the constitution for governing the corporation.

The ultimate control of the corporation rests with the shareholders, who usually receive one vote for each voting share they own. The shareholders elect the members of the **board of directors**, which has the following responsibilities:

- Sets policy for the corporation.
- Elects a **chairperson**, who is often the most powerful person in the corporation.
- Appoints (hires) the **president**, and other executive officers who are in charge of managing day-to-day operations.

Most corporations have a number of vice-presidents. Exhibit 13–2 shows a typical authority structure in a corporation.

EXHIBIT 13–2 | Typical Authority Structure in a Corporation

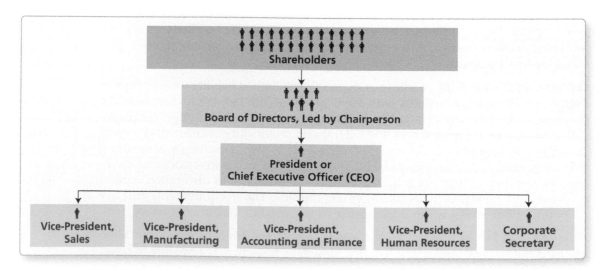

All corporations have an annual meeting at which the shareholders elect directors and make other shareholder decisions, such as appointing the external auditors. Shareholders unable to attend this annual meeting may vote on corporation matters by use of a **proxy**, which appoints another person to cast the vote on their behalf.

Share Capital

A corporation issues *share certificates* to its owners when they invest in the business. Shareholders rarely see or receive share certificates. Instead, their share purchase and sale transactions are listed on the monthly summary of activity in their brokerage or trading accounts. Because shares represent the corporation's capital, they are often called *share capital*. The basic unit of share capital is called a *share*. A corporation may issue a share certificate for any number of shares it wishes: 1 share, 100 shares, or any other number. Exhibit 13–3 depicts what a share certificate would look like and highlights key information found on it.

EXHIBIT 13-3 | Share Certificate

Used with permission from Smart Touch Learning.

Shareholders' Equity

A corporation reports assets and liabilities the same way as a proprietorship or a partnership. However, owners' equity of a corporation—called **shareholders' equity**—is reported differently. Business laws require corporations to report their sources of capital because some of the capital must be maintained by the company. The two most basic sources of capital are:

- **Contributed capital,** which represents investment amounts received from the shareholders of the corporation. Contributed surplus, which will be discussed in Chapter 14, is also a component of contributed capital.

- **Retained earnings,** which is capital earned from profitable operations.

While the Canada Business Corporations Act (CBCA) and several of the provincial incorporating acts use the term *stated capital* to describe share capital, this text

In a proprietorship, the owner's investment and earnings are both recorded in the Capital account. In a corporation, the owners' investment is called contributed capital *and the earnings not paid out to the owners (shareholders) are called* retained earnings.

will use the more common term *share capital*. Exhibit 13–4 is a summarized version of the shareholders' equity section of the balance sheet of Canada Goose Holdings Inc., which is used to show how to report these categories of shareholders' equity.

EXHIBIT 13–4 | Summarized Shareholders' Equity at March 31, 2018, of Canada Goose Holdings Inc. (adapted, amounts in thousands)

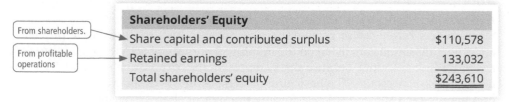

	Shareholders' Equity	
From shareholders. →	Share capital and contributed surplus	$110,578
From profitable operations →	Retained earnings	133,032
	Total shareholders' equity	$243,610

Contributed Capital

Common shares are regarded as the permanent capital of the business because the balance in the Common Shares account *cannot* be withdrawn by the shareholders. The entry to record the receipt of $200,000 cash and the issuance of 10,000 common shares to shareholders is as follows:

Oct. 20	Cash	200,000	
	Common Shares		200,000
	Issued 10,000 common shares.		

Issuing shares increases both the assets and the shareholders' equity of a corporation.

Retained Earnings

Retained Earnings is a part of shareholders' equity and therefore should have a normal credit balance A debit balance in Retained Earnings is called a deficit.

Profitable operations produce net income for the corporation, which increases shareholders' equity through a separate account called Retained Earnings.

Some people think of Retained Earnings as a fund of cash. It is not, because Retained Earnings is not an asset—it is an element of shareholders' equity. Retained earnings has no particular relationship to Cash or any other asset.

Corporations close their revenues and expenses into Income Summary, and then they close net income to Retained Earnings. To illustrate, let's consider a private corporation called Six Property Limited. Assume it had revenues for the year ended December 31, 2020, in the amount of $10,387,100 and expenses totalled $9,643,400. The closing entries would be:

Dec. 31	Revenues (detailed)	10,387,100	
	Income Summary		10,387,100
	To close revenue accounts.		
Dec. 31	Income Summary	9,643,400	
	Expenses (detailed)		9,643,400
	To close expenses.		

Now, Income Summary holds revenues, expenses, and net income:

Income Summary			
Expenses	9,643,400	Revenues	10,387,100
		Balance (net income)	743,700

Finally, the Income Summary's balance is closed to Retained Earnings:

Dec. 31	Income Summary	743,700	
	Retained Earnings		743,700
	To close net income to Retained Earnings.		

This closing entry completes the closing process. Income Summary is zeroed out, and Retained Earnings now holds net income.

If Six Property Limited had a net loss, Income Summary would have a debit balance. To close an assumed $100,000 loss, the closing entry credits Income Summary and debits Retained Earnings as follows:

Dec. 31	Retained Earnings	100,000	
	Income Summary		100,000
	To close Income Summary by transferring net loss to Retained Earnings.		

Negative Retained Earnings Is Called a Deficit   A loss or an accumulation of several years of losses may cause a debit balance in the Retained Earnings account. This condition—called a negative Retained Earnings or Accumulated **Deficit**—is reported as a negative amount in shareholders' equity. WeedMD Inc. reported the following (adapted) in its 2017 annual report:

	(in thousands of dollars)	
Shareholders' Equity	**December 31, 2017**	**December 31, 2016**
Common shares and contributed surplus	$41,525	$10,670
Deficit	(16,392)	(7,587)
Total shareholders' equity	$25,133	$ 3,083

Dividends

A profitable corporation may distribute retained earnings to its shareholders. Such distributions are called **dividends**. Dividends are similar to the withdrawals of cash made by the owner of a proprietorship or by a partner of a partnership. Dividends are discussed in detail later in this chapter.

Shareholders' Rights

The owner of a share has certain rights that are set out in the corporation's articles of incorporation; these vary from company to company, and even between classes of shares within a company. In addition, the shareholder may have other rights granted by the legislation under which the corporation wrote its articles. An example of a right under the CBCA is that the shareholders may require the directors of the corporation to call a meeting of the shareholders.

Some of the rights generally attached to common shares[1] are:

- The right to sell the shares.
- The right to vote at shareholders' meetings.
- The right to receive a **proportionate share** of any dividends declared by the directors for that class of shares.
- The right to receive a proportionate share of any assets on the winding-up of the company, after the creditors and any classes of shares that rank above that class have been paid. In reality, being last in line often means there is nothing left.

---

[1] For a more complete listing, the interested reader is referred to the Canada Business Corporations Act in *The Revised Statutes of Canada*.

- A **preemptive right**—the right to maintain one's proportionate ownership in the corporation. If a shareholder owns 5 percent of the outstanding common shares and the corporation decides to issue 100,000 new shares, the shareholder would be entitled to purchase 5,000 of the new shares ($0.05 \times 100,000$).

Try It!

1. Compare and contrast the characteristics of proprietorships and corporations.
2. Describe the authority structure of a corporation, starting with the group or position that has the greatest authority.

Solutions appear at the end of this chapter and on **MyLab Accounting**

Issuing Shares

LO ②
How do we record and present share information?

Large corporations such as Canada Goose Holdings Inc., Bombardier Inc., and Blackberry Inc. need huge quantities of money to operate. They cannot expect to finance all their operations through borrowing. They can raise these funds by issuing shares. The articles of incorporation include an *authorization of shares*—that is, a provision for the business to issue (sell) a certain number of shares.

Underwriters   Corporations may sell their shares directly to the shareholders; however, they typically use the services of an **underwriter** to sell their shares, such as the brokerage firm RBC Dominion Securities Inc. or CIBC World Markets Inc. The agreement between a corporation and its underwriter will vary, but typically the underwriter will commit to placing (selling) all of the share issue it can with its customers, and to buying any unsold shares for its own account. In another form of contract, the underwriter agrees to do its best to sell all of the share issue but makes no guarantees. The underwriter makes its money by selling the shares for a higher price than it pays to the corporation issuing the shares.

SEDAR   Companies often advertise the issuance of their shares to attract investors. A good source of such information is SEDAR (System for Electronic Document Analysis and Retrieval). SEDAR is a website developed under the authority of the Canadian Securities Administrators and administered by each of the provincial securities regulatory authorities.

IPO   Exhibit 13–5 on the next page, is a reproduction of a portion of the *prospectus* of Canada Goose Holdings Ltd.'s *initial public offering*. A **prospectus** is a required legal document that describes the investment offering to potential purchasers. It shows the *offering price* (the expected sales price), the number and type of shares being sold, and the names of the underwriters. An **initial public offering (IPO)** is the first time a corporation's shares are sold to investors or members of the public.

Number of Shares   The following diagram illustrates the relationship among the authorized, issued, and outstanding shares:

- *Authorized shares.* The maximum number of shares the corporation can issue according to the articles of incorporation are the **authorized shares**. Most corporations are authorized to issue many more shares than they intend to issue originally. Management may hold some shares back and issue them later if the need for additional capital arises. If the corporation wants to issue more than the authorized shares, the articles of incorporation must be changed. Amendment of the articles of incorporation requires shareholder approval and may require government approval as well.
- *Issued shares.* The shares that the corporation does issue to shareholders are called **issued shares**. Only by issuing shares—not by receiving authorization—does the corporation increase the asset and shareholders' equity amounts on its balance sheet.

EXHIBIT 13–5 | Announcement of IPO by Canada Goose Holdings Inc.

SUPPLEMENTED PREP PROSPECTUS

Initial Public Offering
and Secondary Offering

March 16, 2017

CANADA GOOSE HOLDINGS INC.
$340,000,000
20,000,000 Subordinate Voting Shares

This prospectus qualifies the distribution of an aggregate of 20,000,000 subordinate voting shares of Canada Goose Holdings Inc. offered at a price of $17.00 per subordinate voting share. This offering consists of an initial public offering of 6,308,154 subordinate voting shares by the company and a secondary offering of an aggregate of 13,691,846 subordinate voting shares by Brent (BC) Participation S.à r.l., an investment fund advised by Bain Capital L.P. and its affiliates, DTR LLC, an entity indirectly controlled by our President and Chief Executive Officer, the Combined Jewish Philanthropies of Greater Boston, Inc. and Fidelity Investments Charitable Gift Fund. See "Underwriting" and "Principal and Selling Shareholders."

We will not receive any proceeds from the subordinate voting shares sold by the selling shareholders. We will use the net proceeds from the offering as described in this prospectus. See "Use of Proceeds." The subordinate voting shares are being offered in Canada by CIBC World Markets Inc., Credit Suisse Securities (Canada), Inc., Goldman Sachs Canada Inc., RBC Dominion Securities Inc., Merrill Lynch Canada Inc., Morgan Stanley Canada Limited, Barclays Capital Canada Inc., BMO Nesbitt Burns Inc., TD Securities Inc., Wells Fargo Securities Canada, Ltd. and Canaccord Genuity Corp., referred to herein as the Canadian underwriters, and in the United States by certain U.S. broker-dealers.

Price: $17.00 per subordinate voting share

	Price to the Public[1]	Underwriters' Commissions	Net Proceeds to the Company[2]	Net Proceeds to Selling Shareholders[3]
Per subordinate voting share	$ 17.00	$ 1.1475	$ 15.8525	$ 15.8525
Total[3]	$340,000,000	$22,950,000	$100,000,011	$217,049,989

Canada Goose Holdings Inc, Subordinate Voting shares.https://www.sec.gov/Archives/edgar/data/1690511/000119312517084398/d289883d424b4.htm#toc

The price that the shareholder pays to acquire shares from the corporation is called the **issue price**. A combination of underwriter opinion and market factors—including the company's comparative earnings record, financial position, prospects for success, and general business conditions—determines issue price.

- *Outstanding shares.* Shares that have been sold to and are held by shareholders are considered **outstanding shares**. The total number of a corporation's shares outstanding at any time represents 100 percent of its ownership.

Canada Goose's IPO was for **subordinated shares**, which means they have fewer voting rights. GOOS's *multiple voting shares* have ten votes each, whereas these shares only have one vote each.

Common Shares

Every corporation issues *common shares*, the most basic form of share capital. The common shareholders are the owners of the business. Companies may issue different classes of common shares. For example, Rogers Communications Inc. has issued Class A common shares, which carry the right to vote, and Class B common shares, which are nonvoting. (Classes of common shares may also be designated Series A, Series B, and so on, with each series having unique features.) There is a separate general ledger account for each class of common shares.

Investors   Investors who buy common shares take a risk with a corporation. They are the owners of the business, but the corporation makes no promises to pay them. If the corporation succeeds, it may distribute dividends to its shareholders, but if Retained Earnings and Cash are too low, the shareholders may receive no dividends. The market value (selling price) of the shares of successful corporations increase, and investors enjoy the benefit of selling the shares at a gain. Thus, the holder of common shares can earn income both from dividends and from increases in the value of the shares.

But share prices can decrease, possibly leaving the investors with nothing of value. Because common shareholders take a risky investment position, they demand increases in share prices, high dividends, or both. If the corporation does not accomplish these goals and many shareholders sell their shares, the market price will fall. Short of bankruptcy, this is one of the worst things that can happen to a corporation because it means that the corporation cannot easily raise capital as needed. The period from the autumn of 2008 to the first part of 2009 highlighted this as most stock markets around the world saw share prices plummet. Exhibit 13–6 shows the performance of the Canadian stock market, represented by the performance of a group of corporate shares on the Toronto Stock Exchange. Notice the steep decline in values in 2008 and 2009. Imagine how difficult it must have been for shareholders and managers of corporations during that period.

EXHIBIT 13–6 | Canadian Stock Market Performance (TSX Composite Index)

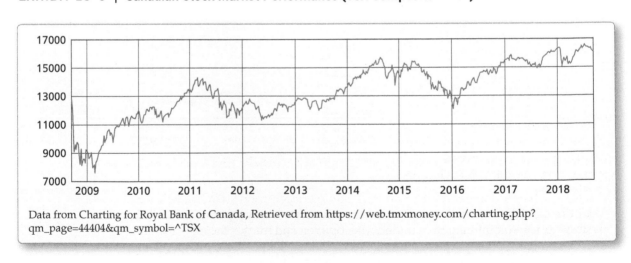

Data from Charting for Royal Bank of Canada, Retrieved from https://web.tmxmoney.com/charting.php?qm_page=44404&qm_symbol=^TSX

No-Par-Value Shares   **No-par-value shares** are shares that do not have a value assigned to them by the articles of incorporation. The CBCA requires all newly issued shares in Canada to be no-par-value. **Par value** is an arbitrary value assigned to each share, and it might be seen in Canadian corporations that were established before the CBCA came into effect or when certain complex tax-planning arrangements are made.

Stated Value of Shares   The board of directors may assign a value to the shares when they are issued; this value is known as the **stated value**. For Canada Goose Holding's IPO, the stated price shown in Exhibit 13–5 was $17. This is not the same as the market price. On the first day of sales, the market price was $23.

The full amount of the proceeds from the sale of shares by a company must be allocated to the capital account for those shares, as shown in the next section.

Issuing Common Shares at a Stated Value   Using the Canada Goose Holdings information found in Exhibit 13–5, the IPO share issuance entry (including fees and commissions) for only the first 6,308,154 shares in the IPO is:

Mar. 15	Cash	100,000,011	
	Discounts and Commissions Expense	7,238,607	
	Common Shares		107,238,618
	To issue 6,308,154 common shares at $17.00 per share, the stated value, less discounts and commissions expenses of $1.1475 per share.		

Issuance of new shares increases the corporation's assets and shareholders' equity. Sales of shares by shareholders after this date are not reflected in the corporation's balance sheet because they are sales between shareholders and the company is not involved.

The amount invested in the corporation, is called *share capital.* The credit to Common Shares records an increase in the share capital of the corporation.

Issuing Common Shares for Assets Other Than Cash   A corporation may issue shares in exchange for assets other than cash. It debits the assets received for their current market value and credits the Common Shares or Preferred Shares accounts accordingly. The assets' prior book value does not matter.

Suppose the company we discussed earlier, Six Property Limited, issued 25,000 common shares (of the 100,000 authorized) for equipment worth $25,000 plus a building worth $125,000 during 2020. The entry is:

Jun. 12	Equipment	25,000	
	Building	125,000	
	Common Shares		150,000
	To issue 25,000 common shares in exchange for equipment and a building.		

Common Shares increases by the amount of the assets' *current market value,* $150,000 in this case. The stated value, or value assigned to the shares, would be $6.00 ($150,000 ÷ 25,000) per share.

Preferred Shares

Preferred shares have special rights or preferences that give their owners certain advantages over common shareholders. Investors who buy preferred shares take less risk than common shareholders:

- Preferred shareholders receive dividends before the common shareholders. The preferred dividend may be a set amount or a fixed percentage of some number, such as the prime interest rate at the date of declaration of the dividend.
- Preferred shareholders receive assets before the common shareholders if the corporation liquidates.
- Corporations often pay a fixed dividend on preferred shares. Investors usually buy preferred shares to earn those fixed dividends.

Because of the preferred shareholders' priorities, common shares represent the *residual ownership* in the corporation's assets after the liabilities and the claims of preferred shareholders have been subtracted.

Classes   Often the right to vote is withheld from preferred shareholders. Companies may issue different classes of preferred shares (Class A and Class B or Series A and Series B, for example). Each class is recorded in a separate account. For

Another investment vehicle available to investors is called an income trust or investment trust. It is a portfolio of assets that is designed to provide safety of principal and a regular fixed income. An example of an income trust is Boston Pizza Royalties Income Fund. Unitholders receive monthly cash payments, but at the same time they maintain their equity position in the company. The monthly cash payments are roughly equivalent to dividends paid by corporations, but their tax treatment in the hands of unitholders is different.

example, Bombardier Inc.'s December 31, 2016, annual report showed the company had the following classes of common and preferred shares:

	Number of Shares Authorized	Number of Shares Issued and Outstanding	Dividends
Class A Shares (Multiple Voting)	3,592,000,000	313,900,550	—
Class B Shares (Subordinate Voting)	3,592,000,000	1,879,142,745	—
Series 2 Cumulative Redeemable Preferred	12,000,000	9,692,521	50–100% of the Canadian prime rate per annum payable monthly
Series 3 Cumulative Redeemable Preferred	12,000,000	2,307,479	3.134% or $0.7835 per share per annum payable quarterly until July '17
Series 4 Cumulative Redeemable Preferred	9,400,000	9,400,000	6.25% per annum or $1.5625 per share per annum payable quarterly

Investors Investors usually buy preferred shares to earn these fixed dividends. Preferred shares' market values do not fluctuate much, so investor income from owning preferred shares is mostly from dividends rather than share-price increases. Individuals might also prefer to hold preferred shares because the income tax rate they pay on dividends they receive is lower than the income tax rate they pay on interest they receive. It's for this reason that the dividend rate on a company's preferred shares is usually lower than the interest rate on bonds the company issues (the bonds pay interest; the preferred shares pay dividends).

Not all corporations issue preferred shares. However, all corporations must issue at least one common share.

Bonds are an alternative form of financing for corporations that will be discussed in detail in chapter 15.

Issuing Preferred Shares Accounting for preferred shares follows the pattern illustrated for common shares.

Assume Six Property Limited's articles of incorporation authorize issuance of 10,000 preferred shares with an annual dividend of $5.00 per share. On July 31, the company issues 1,000 shares at a stated price of $100.00 per share and receives a cash payment of $100,000. The issuance entry is:

Jul. 31	Cash	100,000	
	Preferred Shares		100,000
	To issue 1,000 preferred shares for $100.00 per share (1,000 × $100).		

Convertible Preferred Shares **Convertible preferred shares** are preferred shares that may be exchanged by the preferred shareholders, if they choose, for another specified class of shares in the corporation. For example, during the year, Six Properties Limited issued a new class of preferred shares that is convertible into the company's common shares. A note on Six Property's balance sheet describes the conversion terms as follows:

The ... preferred shares are convertible at the rate of 7.00 common shares for each preferred share outstanding.

If you owned 100 Six Property convertible preferred shares, you could convert them into 700 (100 × 7.00) common shares. Under what condition would you exercise the conversion privilege? You would do so if the market value of the common shares that you could receive from conversion was greater than the market value of the preferred shares that you presently hold. This way, you as an investor could increase your personal wealth.

If the convertible preferred shares were issued for $10,000, the conversion of the 100 preferred shares into 700 common shares would be recorded as follows:

No gain or loss is reported on a conversion of shares.

Dec. 7	Preferred Shares	10,000	
	Common Shares		10,000
	Conversion of preferred shares into common. (100 preferred shares converted into 700 common shares.)		

At this point, the new common shares cannot be converted back to preferred shares.

The balance sheet would be updated to show the change in the equity section by reflecting the new numbers of each type of share.

The Shareholders' Equity Section of a Balance Sheet

The shareholders' equity section of Six Property Limited's balance sheet at December 31, 2020, appears in Exhibit 13–7.

EXHIBIT 13–7 | Shareholders' Equity Section of a Balance Sheet

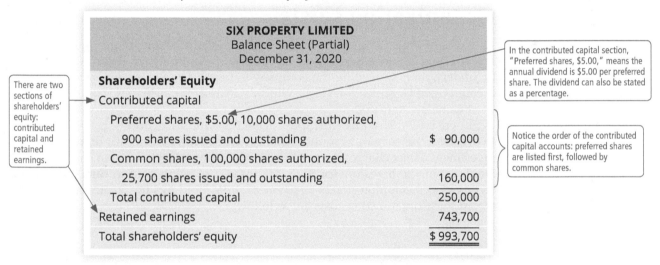

SIX PROPERTY LIMITED
Balance Sheet (Partial)
December 31, 2020

Shareholders' Equity

There are two sections of shareholders' equity: contributed capital and retained earnings.

Contributed capital

Preferred shares, $5.00, 10,000 shares authorized,

900 shares issued and outstanding — $ 90,000

Common shares, 100,000 shares authorized,

25,700 shares issued and outstanding — 160,000

Total contributed capital — 250,000

Retained earnings — 743,700

Total shareholders' equity — $ 993,700

In the contributed capital section, "Preferred shares, $5.00," means the annual dividend is $5.00 per preferred share. The dividend can also be stated as a percentage.

Notice the order of the contributed capital accounts: preferred shares are listed first, followed by common shares.

Debt versus Equity

Corporations are faced with a number of choices when raising capital. Some of the things a corporation should consider when choosing to sell shares or issue long-term debt include the following:

	Common Shares	Preferred Shares	Long-term Debt
Annual Cost/Liability	Flexible. There may be dividends but only if declared by the board of directors	Flexible. There may be dividends but only if declared by the board of directors	Required interest payment
Control	Vote	Usually no voting rights, so no change in control	Lenders have no voting rights, but may have influence through contracts
Repayment	No	No	Yes, fixed per terms of loan
Tax Implications for the Corporation	Dividends are not tax deductible because they are a distribution of earnings	Dividends are not tax deductible because they are a distribution of earnings	Interest is a deductible expense for tax purposes

ETHICS | What should the building be valued at when it is exchanged for shares?

Reed Hiller, the accountant for Snyder Corporation, is trying to decide how to record the company's most recent issuance of shares. Jack Chavez, a majority shareholder, has contributed a building in exchange for common shares. Jack believes that the building should be valued at $4 million, his evaluation of the building's market value. Jack argues that by recording the asset at such a large amount, the business will look more prosperous to investors. Reed is concerned that Jack is overvaluing the asset. What should Reed do?

Solution

Issuance of shares for cash poses no ethical challenge because the value of the asset received (cash) is clearly understood. Issuing shares for assets other than cash can pose a challenge, though. A company should record an asset received at its current market value or the market value of the shares issued, whichever is more clearly determinable. One person's evaluation of a building's market value can differ from another's. The ethical course of action is to record the current market value as determined by an independent appraiser. Alternatively, the company can use the market value of the shares issued to determine the value of the building. This would be appropriate if the shares are traded on an organized exchange.

Organization Costs

Corporations are rarely found guilty of understating their assets, but companies have been sued for overstating asset values.

The costs of organizing a corporation include legal fees for preparing documents and advising on procedures, fees paid to the incorporating jurisdiction, and charges by underwriters for selling the company's shares. These costs are grouped in an account titled Organization Costs, which is an asset because these costs contribute to a business's start-up.

Suppose BBV Holdings Inc. pays legal fees and incorporation fees of $5,000 to organize the corporation under the CBCA in Newfoundland. In addition, an investment dealer charges a fee of $15,000 for selling 30,000 common shares of BBV Holdings Inc. to investors for $225,000. Instead of being paid in cash, the broker receives 2,000 common shares as payment. BBV Holdings Inc.'s journal entries to record these organization costs are as follows:

Mar. 31	Organization Costs	5,000	
	Cash		5,000
	Legal fees and incorporation fees to organize the corporation.		
Apr. 3	Cash	225,000	
	Organization Costs	15,000	
	Common Shares		240,000
	To record receipt of funds from sale of 30,000 common shares and issue of 2,000 shares to investment dealer for selling shares in the corporation.		

Notice that there is no specific guidelines for how long to amortize the organization costs. As you learn more accounting, you will find there are fewer rules and more room for professional judgment when recording transactions.

Organization costs are an *intangible asset*, reported on the balance sheet along with patents, trademarks, goodwill, and any other intangibles. The Income Tax Act allows corporations to expense a portion of organization costs against taxable income. While the *CPA Canada Handbook* does not require them to be amortized, most companies amortize organization costs over a short time period because of their relatively small size. As is true with other intangibles, amortization expense for the year should be disclosed in the financial statements.

Try It!

Accounting for Cash Dividends

Corporations share their wealth with the shareholders through dividends. Corporations declare dividends from *retained earnings* and usually pay the dividends with *cash*. A corporation must have enough retained earnings to declare the dividend and also have enough cash to pay the dividend. In addition, section 42 of the CBCA goes further to require that a "corporation shall not declare or pay a dividend if there are reasonable grounds for believing that (a) the corporation is or would after payment be unable to pay its liabilities as they become due; or (b) the realizable value of the corporation's assets would thereby be less than the aggregate of its liabilities and stated capital."[2]

Companies also have the option to issue stock dividends, which are discussed in Chapter 14.

LO 3

What are cash dividends and how do we account for them?

Dividend Dates

A corporation must declare a dividend before paying it. The corporation has no obligation to pay a dividend until the board of directors declares one. However, once the dividend is declared, it becomes a legal liability. Three dates for dividends are relevant and are illustrated in Exhibit 13–8.

Dividend announcements are published in the financial press and online to ensure that shareholders or potential shareholders are kept fully aware of the corporation's dividend policy.

Dividends are *not an expense*, but a distribution of earnings to owners. Cash dividends, like withdrawals, reduce assets and shareholders' equity.

Some accountants debit an account called Dividends, a temporary account that is later closed to Retained Earnings, but most businesses debit Retained Earnings directly, as shown here.

Declaring and Paying Dividends

Let's continue with the Six Properties Limited example and see how their dividends would be recorded in late 2020 if they did not convert any shares. The dividend for 1,000 shares would be $5,000 ($5 × 1,000).

EXHIBIT 13–8 | Sample Dividend Notice

1 *Declaration date.* On the **declaration date**, the board of directors announces the intention to pay the dividend. The declaration creates a current liability called Dividends Payable for the corporation.

2 *Date of record.* Those shareholders holding the shares on the **date of record**—several weeks after declaration—will receive the dividend.

3 *Distribution date.* Payment of the dividend usually follows the record date by two to four weeks.

---

[2] Section 42 of Canada Business Corporations Act

① Declaration Date Declaration of a cash dividend is recorded by debiting Retained Earnings and crediting the current liability Dividends Payable as follows:

Oct. 3	Retained Earnings	5,000	
	Dividends Payable		5,000
	To declare a cash dividend for preferred shareholders on the October 31 date of record. Payment date is November 15.		

② Date of Record There is no journal entry on October 31, the date of record. Shareholders who own shares on this date will receive the dividend on November 15.

③ Distribution Date To pay the dividend on the payment date, the transaction is recorded as follows:

Nov. 15	Dividends Payable	5,000	
	Cash		5,000
	To pay a cash dividend.		

When a company has issued both preferred and common shares, the preferred shareholders receive their dividends first. The common shareholders receive dividends only if the total declared dividend is large enough to satisfy the preferred requirements.

Exhibit 13–9 shows the division of dividends between the preferred shares and common shares for two situations.

Dividends are paid based on the number of shares issued and outstanding.

EXHIBIT 13–9 | Dividing a Dividend between the Preferred Shares and Common Shares of Six Properties Limited

Case A:	Total dividend of $5,000	
	Preferred dividend (The full $5,000 goes to the preferred shares because the annual preferred dividend is $5,000 [$5.00 × 1,000].)	$ 5,000
	Common dividend (None, because the total dividend declared did not exceed the preferred dividend for the year.)	0
		$ 5,000
Case B:	**Total dividend of $30,000**	
	Preferred dividend ($5.00 × $1,000)	$ 5,000
	Common dividend ($30,000 − $5,000)	25,000
		$30,000

When a company has more than one class of preferred shares or common shares, the division of dividends among the various classes of shares depends on the order of priority created when each of the classes was established.

Dividends on Cumulative and Noncumulative Preferred Shares

Cumulative The allocation of dividends will involve additional calculations if the preferred shares are *cumulative*. If a corporation fails to declare the preferred dividend, the missed dividends are said to be in **arrears**. The owners of **cumulative preferred shares** must receive all dividends in arrears plus the current year's dividend before the corporation pays dividends to the common shareholders. *Cumulative* means that any dividends in arrears will accumulate, or carry over, to the future. The cumulative feature is not automatic to preferred shares but must be assigned to the preferred shares in the articles of incorporation. Common shares are never cumulative.

Let's assume the preferred shares of Six Properties Limited are cumulative and the company did not declare the 2020 preferred dividend of $5,000. If the business now declares a $40,000 dividend in 2021, how much of this dividend goes to the preferred shareholders if the preferred shares are cumulative?

$10,000 (the $5,000 in arrears + $5,000 for the current year)

How much goes to the common shareholders?

The remaining $30,000 ($40,000 − $10,000)

The entry to record the declaration of this dividend is:

May 31	Retained Earnings	40,000	
	Dividends Payable, Preferred Shares		10,000
	Dividends Payable, Common Shares		30,000
	To declare a cash dividend. Preferred dividends are $10,000 ($5,000 × 2); common dividends are $30,000 ($40,000 − $10,000)		

If the preferred shares are not designated as cumulative, the corporation is not obligated to pay any dividends in arrears.

Noncumulative   Suppose that the Six Properties Limited preferred shares were non-cumulative, and the company did not declare a dividend in 2020. The preferred share-holders would lose the 2020 dividend forever. Before paying any common dividends in 2021, the company would have to pay only the 2021 preferred dividend of $5,000.

Note Disclosure   Having dividends in arrears on cumulative preferred shares is *not* a liability to the corporation. (A liability for dividends arises only after the board of directors declares the dividend.) Nevertheless, a corporation must report cumulative preferred dividends in arrears in the notes to the financial statements. This information alerts common shareholders to how much in cumulative preferred dividends must be paid before the common shareholders will receive any dividends.

Note disclosure of cumulative preferred dividends might take the following form on the balance sheet at the end of 2021:

Preferred shares, $5.00, 10,000 shares authorized, 1,000 shares issued (Note 3)	$100,000
Common shares, 100,000 shares authorized, 25,000 shares issued	150,000
Retained earnings (Note 3)	962,400

Note 3: Cumulative preferred dividends in arrears. At December 31, 2021, dividends on the company's $5.00 preferred shares were in arrears for 2020 and 2021 in the amount of ($5.00 × 10,000 × 2 years).

Try It!

4. CRS Robotics Inc. was organized on January 1, 2019, with 500,000 shares authorized; 200,000 shares were issued on January 5, 2019. CRS Robotics Inc. earned $250,000 during 2019 and declared a dividend of $0.25 per share on December 16, 2019, payable to shareholders on January 6, 2020.
   a. Journalize the declaration and payment of the dividend.
   b. Compute the balance of Retained Earnings on December 31, 2019.
5. Trivision Corp. has outstanding 20,000 common shares and 10,000 $2.00 cumulative preferred shares. The company has declared no dividends for the past two years but plans to pay $90,000 this year.
   a. Compute the dividends for the preferred and common shares.
   b. By how much will the dividends reduce Retained Earnings?

Solutions appear at the end of this chapter and on **MyLab Accounting**

Different Values of Shares

LO (4)

What is the difference between book value and market value of shares?

The business community refers to several different *share values*. Both market value and book value are used for decision making.

Market Value

A share's **market value**, or *market price*, is the price for which a person can buy or sell a share. The issuing corporation's net income, financial position, future prospects, and the general economic conditions determine market value. Most companies' websites track their share prices, as do many business news sites and brokerage firms. *In almost all cases, shareholders are more concerned about the market value of a share than any other value.* At September 14, 2018, the common shares of Canada Goose Holdings Inc. were *listed at* (an alternative term is *quoted at*) $75.56, which meant they sold for, or could be bought for, $75.56 per share. The purchase of 100 common shares of Canada Goose Holdings would cost $7,556 ($75.56 × 100) plus a commission. If you were selling 100 common shares, you would receive cash of $7,556 less a commission. The commission is the fee an investor pays to a stockbroker for buying or selling the shares. If you buy shares in Canada Goose Holdings from another investor, Canada Goose Holdings gets no cash. The transaction is a sale between investors. Canada Goose Holdings records only the change in shareholder name.

Book Value

Book value per share uses the number of shares *outstanding*, not the number of shares authorized.

The **book value** of a share is the amount of shareholders' equity on the company's books for each share. If the company has only common shares outstanding, divide total shareholders' equity by the number of shares *outstanding*. If a company has both common shares and preferred shares, the preferred shareholders have the first claim to shareholders' equity. Therefore, the preferred shareholders' equity must be subtracted from total shareholders' equity to calculate the shareholders' equity available for the common shareholders. This is shown by the following formula:

$$\text{Book value per common share} = \frac{\text{Total shareholders' equity} - \text{Preferred equity}}{\text{Number of common shares outstanding}}$$

For example, a company with shareholders' equity of $180,000, no preferred shares, and 5,000 common shares outstanding has a book value of $36.00 per common share, calculated as follows:

$$\text{Book value per common share} = \frac{\text{Total shareholders' equity} - \text{Preferred equity}}{\text{Number of common shares outstanding}}$$

$$= \frac{\$180,000 - \$0}{5,000}$$

$$= \$36.00$$

If the company has both preferred and common shares outstanding, the preferred shareholders' equity must be calculated before the common shareholders' equity can be calculated. Ordinarily, preferred shares have a specified **liquidation value**, or redemption value, or call value. This is shown by the following formula:

$$\text{Book value per preferred share} = \frac{\text{Preferred equity}}{\text{Number of preferred shares outstanding}}$$

$$= \frac{\text{Liquidation value} + \text{Dividends in arrears}}{\text{Number of preferred shares outstanding}}$$

To illustrate, Garner Corp. reports the following amounts on their balance sheet:

Shareholders' Equity	
Contributed capital	
Preferred shares, $7.00, $90 liquidation value, 5,000 shares authorized, 1,000 shares issued and outstanding	$ 100,000
Common shares, 20,000 shares authorized, 5,000 shares issued and outstanding	150,000
Total contributed capital	250,000
Retained earnings	90,000
Total shareholders' equity	$ 340,000

Suppose that three years of cumulative preferred dividends are in arrears. The current year preferred dividend must also be paid.

The book value for the preferred shares must be calculated first:

$$\textbf{Book value per preferred share} = \frac{\textbf{Liquidation value} + \textbf{Dividends in arrears}}{\textbf{Number of preferred shares outstanding}}$$

$$= \frac{(\$90 \times 1{,}000) + (\$7.00 \times 1{,}000 \times 4^*)}{1{,}000}$$

$$= \frac{\$90{,}000 + \$28{,}000}{1{,}000}$$

$$= \frac{\$118{,}000}{1{,}000} \quad \longleftarrow \quad \boxed{\text{Preferred equity}}$$

$$= \$118.00$$

*4 years of dividends = 3 years in arrears + current year

The book value for the common shares can then be calculated, as follows:

$$\textbf{Book value per common share} = \frac{\textbf{Total shareholders' equity} - \textbf{Preferred equity}}{\textbf{Number of common shares outstanding}}$$

$$= \frac{\$340{,}000 - \$118{,}000}{5{,}000}$$

$$= \$44.40$$

Using Book Value in Decision Making   Book value may be a factor in determining the price to pay for a *closely held* corporation. A corporation is **closely held** when it is a private corporation that has only a few shareholders. A company may buy out a shareholder by agreeing to pay the book value of the shareholder's shares.

Some investors compare the book value of a share with its market value. The idea is that shares selling below book value are *underpriced* and thus are a *good buy*. But the relationship between book value and market value is far from clear. Other investors believe that if shares sell at a price below book value, the company must be experiencing difficulty. Exhibit 13–10 contrasts the book values and market prices for the common shares of three Canadian companies. In all cases, the share price, which is the market value, exceeds book value—a sign of success.

EXHIBIT 13–10 | Book Value and Market Value*

	Stock	Book Value per Share	Share Price
Canadian Tire Corporation Limited	CTC	$66.67	$155.87
Barrick Gold Corporation	ABX	$ 8.02	$ 13.19
Canada Goose Holdings Inc.	GOOS	$ 2.07	$ 75.56

* Retrieved September 14, 2018, from Yahoo! Finance.

Try It!

Evaluating Operations

LO ⑤

What are the return on total assets (ROA) and the return on total common shareholders' equity (ROE), and how do we calculate them?

Round final answers to 2 decimal places unless otherwise indicated.

Investors and creditors are constantly comparing companies' profits. However, the Canada Goose Holdings Ltd. net income may not be comparable to that of a company in the oil and gas industry, such as EnCana Corporation, or of a brewery, such as Sleeman Breweries Ltd. To compare companies, investors, creditors, and managers turn dollar amounts into ratios to look at the *relationship between* amounts rather than the exact dollar amounts. Two important ratios are the rate of return on total assets and the rate of return on common shareholders' equity. We will calculate both ratios using the figures from the TELUS Corporation Inc. 2016 annual report found on MyLab Accounting.

Return on Assets

The **rate of return on total assets**, or simply **return on assets (ROA)**, measures a company's success in using its assets to earn income. Two groups invest money to finance a corporation:

- Shareholders—they invest in shares and expect the company to earn net income.
- Creditors—they lend money to the corporation to earn interest.

The sum of net income and interest expense is the return to the two groups that have financed the corporation's assets, and this is the numerator of the return on assets ratio.

The rate of return on total assets is computed as follows (amounts in millions of dollars):

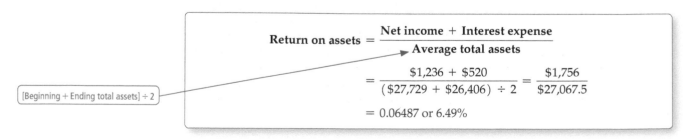

$$\text{Return on assets} = \frac{\text{Net income} + \text{Interest expense}}{\text{Average total assets}}$$

[Beginning + Ending total assets] ÷ 2

$$= \frac{\$1,236 + \$520}{(\$27,729 + \$26,406) \div 2} = \frac{\$1,756}{\$27,067.5}$$

$$= 0.06487 \text{ or } 6.49\%$$

Net income and interest expense are taken from the income statement (or in TELUS's case, from the consolidated statements of earnings and other comprehensive earnings). Average total assets are computed from the balance sheet (or the consolidated statements of financial position).

How is this profitability measure used in decision making? It is used to compare companies. By relating the sum of net income and interest expense to average total assets, we have a standard measure that describes the profitability of all types of companies.

What is a good rate of return on total assets? There is no single answer to this question because rates of return vary widely by industry. For example, consumer products companies earn much higher returns than utilities or grocery store chains. In most industries, a return on assets of 10 percent is considered very good.

Return on Common Shareholders' Equity

Rate of return on common shareholders' equity, often called **return on equity (ROE)**, shows the relationship between net income and average common shareholders' equity. The numerator is net income minus preferred dividends. This information is taken from the income statement and statement of retained earnings. Preferred dividends are subtracted because the preferred shareholders have the first claim to dividends from the company's net income. The denominator is average *common shareholders' equity*—total shareholders' equity minus preferred equity. TELUS's rate of return on common shareholders' equity is computed as follows (amounts in millions of dollars):

Preferred dividends in this formula are declared in the year or in arrears if they are cumulative.

$$\text{Return on common shareholders' equity} = \frac{\text{Net income} - \text{Preferred dividends}}{\text{Average common shareholders' equity}}$$

[Beginning + Ending average common shareholders' equity] ÷ 2

$$= \frac{\$1,236 - \$0}{(\$7,917 + \$7,672) \div 2} = \frac{\$1,236}{\$7,794.5}$$

$$= 0.15857 \text{ or } 15.86\%$$

Investors and creditors use return on common shareholders' equity in much the same way as they use return on total assets—to compare companies. The higher the rate of return, the more successful the company. A 12 percent return on common shareholders' equity is considered quite good in many industries. Investors also compare a company's return on shareholders' equity to interest rates available in the market. If interest rates are almost as high as return on equity, many investors will lend their money to earn interest or deposit it in a bank rather than invest in common shares. They choose to forgo the extra risk of investing in shares when the rate of return on equity is too low.

Leverage Observe that the return on equity (15.86 percent) is higher than the return on assets (6.49 percent). This difference results from the interest expense component of return on assets. Companies such as TELUS borrow at one rate, say 4.5 percent, and invest the funds to earn a higher rate, say 6.5 percent. Borrowing at a lower rate than the return on investments is called *using leverage*. During good times, **leverage** produces high returns for shareholders. However, too much borrowing can make it difficult to pay the interest on the debt. The company's creditors are guaranteed a fixed rate of return on their loans. The shareholders, conversely, have no guarantee that the corporation will earn net income, so their investments are riskier. Consequently, shareholders demand a higher rate of return than do creditors, and this explains why return on equity should exceed return on assets.

Try It!

8. The financial statements of Riley Resources Corp. reported the following:

	2020	2019
Net income	$ 80,000	$ 90,000
Interest expense	20,000	24,000
$6.00 preferred shares (1,000 shares)	100,000	100,000
Common shares	200,000	200,000
Retained earnings	180,000	160,000
Total assets	840,000	760,000

Dividends were paid to preferred shareholders in 2019 and 2020. Dividends of $54,000 were declared and paid to common shareholders in 2020. Compute the return on assets for 2020.

9. Refer to the Riley Resources Corp. financial information in the previous question. Compute the return on common shareholders' equity for 2020.

10. Refer to the previous two questions. Compare the return on assets (ROA) and return on equity (ROE). Is there a favourable or unfavourable relationship between the two ratios?

Solutions appear at the end of this chapter and on **MyLab Accounting**

LO 6

How does IFRS apply to share capital?

EXHIBIT 13–11 | The Impact of IFRS on Share Capital

ASPE	IFRS
The principles governing accounting for share capital are essentially the same under accounting standards for private enterprises (ASPE), as described in this chapter, and under IFRS.	
The requirements under ASPE are less rigorous—they only require that disclosure be made for classes of shares that have actually been issued.	Under IFRS, companies must make certain disclosures about *all* classes of shares authorized by the corporation, whether those classes of shares have been issued or not.
When shares are issued for non-cash items, use fair value of either the item received or the item given up. Choose the information that is most reliable to record the transaction.	First consider the fair value of the non-cash item received in exchange for shares. If its value cannot be reliably determined, then use the fair value of the shares when recording the transaction.
Organization costs are capitalized under ASPE—recorded as an intangible asset—and then amortized.	Under IFRS, organization costs are expensed.

Summary Problem for Your Review

Presented below are the accounts and related balances for ECOM Finance Ltd. at September 30, 2020:

Salary Payable..	$ 3,000
Cash..	15,000
Accounts Payable...	20,000
Retained Earnings...	80,000
Organization Costs, net..	1,000
Long-term Note Payable...	70,000
Common Shares, 60,000 shares authorized, 25,000 shares issued	95,000
Inventory..	85,000
Property, Plant, and Equipment, net...	204,000
Accounts Receivable, net	25,000
Income Tax Payable	12,000
Preferred Shares, $6.00, cumulative, 20,000 shares authorized, 3,000 shares issued	50,000

Required

1. Prepare the classified balance sheet at September 30, 2020. Use the account format for the balance sheet.

2. Are the preferred shares cumulative or noncumulative? How can you tell?

3. What is the total amount of the annual preferred dividend?

4. Assume the common shares were all issued at the same time. What was the selling price per share?

5. Compute the book value per share of the preferred shares and the common shares. No prior-year preferred dividends are in arrears, and ECOM Finance Ltd. has not declared the current-year dividend.

SOLUTION

1.

ECOM FINANCE LTD. Balance Sheet September 30, 2020			
Assets		**Liabilities**	
Current assets		Current liabilities	
Cash	$ 15,000	Accounts payable	$ 20,000
Accounts receivable, net	25,000	Salary payable	3,000
Inventory	85,000	Income tax payable	12,000
Total current assets	125,000	Total current liabilities	35,000
Property, plant, and equipment, net	204,000	Long-term note payable	70,000
Intangible assets		Total liabilities	105,000
Organization costs, net	1,000	**Shareholders' Equity**	
		Contributed capital	
		Preferred shares, $6.00, cumulative, 20,000 shares authorized, 3,000 shares issued	$ 50,000
		Common shares, 60,000 shares authorized, 25,000 shares issued	95,000
		Total contributed capital	145,000
		Retained earnings	80,000
		Total shareholders' equity	225,000
Total assets	$330,000	Total liabilities and shareholders' equity	$330,000

2. The preferred shares are cumulative, as is noted in their description.
3. Total annual preferred dividend: $18,000 (3,000 × $6.00)
4. Price per share: $3.80 ($95,000 ÷ 25,000 shares issued) ← Use the number of shares *issued*, not the number of shares authorized to calculate the share price.
5. Book values per share of preferred and common shares:

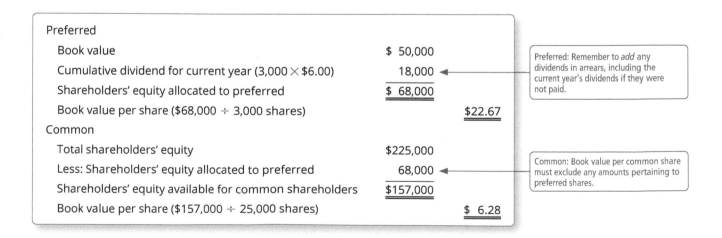

Preferred		
Book value	$ 50,000	
Cumulative dividend for current year (3,000 × $6.00)	18,000	← Preferred: Remember to *add* any dividends in arrears, including the current year's dividends if they were not paid.
Shareholders' equity allocated to preferred	$ 68,000	
Book value per share ($68,000 ÷ 3,000 shares)		$22.67
Common		
Total shareholders' equity	$225,000	
Less: Shareholders' equity allocated to preferred	68,000	← Common: Book value per common share must exclude any amounts pertaining to preferred shares.
Shareholders' equity available for common shareholders	$157,000	
Book value per share ($157,000 ÷ 25,000 shares)		$ 6.28

Summary

Learning Objectives

(1) Identify the characteristics of a corporation Pg. 714

What is a corporation, and why is it an important form of business?
- A corporation is a separate legal and business entity. Shareholders are the owners of a corporation.
- Advantages of a corporation:
  - Continuous life
  - Ease of raising large amounts of capital
  - Ease of transferring ownership
  - Limited liability
  - No mutual agency
- Disadvantages:
  - A degree of double taxation
  - Separation of ownership and management
  - Expensive government regulation
  - Additional costs (such as insurance)

(2) Record the issuance of shares and prepare the shareholders' equity section of a corporation's balance sheet Pg. 720

How do we record and present share information?
- Shares are classified as common or preferred, and there may be several classes or series. Preferred shares are further defined to include cumulative or noncumulative, and convertible.
- The balance sheet carries the capital raised through share issuance under the heading Contributed Capital in the shareholders' equity section. Preferred shares are shown first and then common shares. Retained earnings is listed last.

(3) Account for cash dividends Pg. 727

What are cash dividends and how do we account for them?
- There is a liability to pay dividends when the board of directors declares a dividend. Dividends are declared (announced) for shareholders who own shares on the date of record and are paid after the date of record.
- Preferred shares have priority over common shares when dividends are paid.
- Preferred dividends are usually stated as a dollar amount per share.
- Preferred shares have a claim to dividends in arrears if the preferred shares are cumulative.

(4) Use different share values in decision making Pg. 730

What is the difference between book value and market value of shares?
- A share's *market value* is the price for which a share may be bought or sold.
- *Book value* is the amount of shareholders' equity per share.

$$\text{Book value per common share} = \frac{\text{Total shareholder's equity} - \text{Preferred equity}}{\text{Number of common shares outstanding}}$$

$$\text{Preferred equity} = \text{Liquidation value} + \text{Dividends in arrears}$$

$$\text{Book value per preferred share} = \frac{\text{Liquidation value} + \text{Dividends in arrears}}{\text{Number of preferred shares outstanding}}$$

(5) Evaluate a company's ROA and ROE Pg. 732

What are the return on total assets (ROA) and the return on common shareholders' equity (ROE), and how do we calculate them?
- These are two standard measures of profitability. A healthy company's return on equity will exceed its return on assets.

$$\text{ROA} = \frac{\text{Net income} + \text{Interest expense}}{\text{Average total assets}}$$

$$\text{ROE} = \frac{\text{Net income} - \text{Preferred dividends}}{\text{Average common shareholders' equity}}$$

How does IFRS apply to share capital?
- The mechanics of accounting for shares under ASPE and IFRS is the same.
- IFRS requires fair market value of items received in exchange for shares to be considered first. If not reliable, then consider the fair market value of the shares as the transaction price.
- Organization costs are expensed under IFRS but capitalized as intangible assets and amortized under ASPE.

Key Terms for the chapter are shown next and are in the **Glossary** at the back of the book. **Similar Terms** are shown after **Key Terms**.

KEY TERMS

Arrears To be behind or overdue in a debt payment (p. 728).

Articles of incorporation The document issued by the federal or provincial government giving the incorporators permission to form a corporation (p. 714).

Authorization of shares A provision in a corporation's articles of incorporation that permits a corporation to sell a certain number of shares of stock (p. 716).

Authorized shares The number of shares a corporation is allowed to sell according to the articles of incorporation (p. 720).

Board of directors A group elected by the shareholders to set policy for a corporation and to appoint its officers (p. 716).

Book value The amount of shareholders' equity on the company's books for each of its shares (p. 730).

Bylaws The constitution for governing a corporation (p. 716).

Chairperson (of board) An elected person on a corporation's board of directors; usually the most powerful person in the corporation (p. 716).

Closely held Describes a corporation with only a few shareholders (p. 731).

Common shares The most basic form of share capital. In describing a corporation, the common shareholders are the owners of the business (p. 718).

Contributed capital A corporation's capital from investments by the shareholders. Also called *share capital* or *capital stock* (p. 717).

Convertible preferred shares Preferred shares that may be exchanged by the preferred shareholders, if they choose, for another class of shares in the corporation (p. 724).

Cumulative preferred shares Preferred shares whose owners must receive all dividends in arrears before the corporation pays dividends to the common shareholders (p. 728).

Date of record On this date, which is a few weeks after the declaration of the dividend, the list of shareholders who will receive the dividend is compiled (p. 727).

Declaration date The date on which the board of directors announces the dividend. There is a liability created on this date (p. 727).

Deficit A debit balance in the Retained Earnings account (p. 719).

Dividends Distributions of retained earnings by a corporation to its shareholders (p. 719).

Double taxation Corporations pay their own income taxes on corporate income. Then, the shareholders pay personal income tax on the cash dividends that they receive from corporations (p. 715).

Initial public offering (IPO) The first time a particular class of a corporation's shares are sold to investors (p. 720).

Issued shares Shares that are sold to investors (p. 720).

Issue price The price at which shareholders first purchase shares from the corporation (p. 721).

Leverage The use of financial instruments to increase the potential return on investment by earning more income on borrowed money than the related expense, thereby increasing the earnings for the owners of the business (p. 733).

Limited liability No personal obligation of a shareholder for corporation debts. The most that a shareholder can lose on an investment in a corporation's shares is the cost of the investment (p. 715).

Liquidation value (redemption value) The amount of capital that a preferred shareholder would receive per preferred share upon liquidation of the corporation (p. 730).

Market value The price for which a person could buy or sell a share (p. 730).

Mutual agency Every owner can bind the business to a contract within the scope of the business's regular operations. This does not exist in a corporation (p. 715).

No-par-value shares Shares that do not have a value assigned to them by the articles of incorporation (p. 722).

Organization costs The costs of organizing a corporation, including legal fees and charges by promoters for selling the shares. Organization costs are an intangible asset under ASPE but are written off as an expense under IFRS (p. 726).

Outstanding shares Shares in the hands of shareholders (p. 721).

Par value An arbitrary value assigned when certain shares are initially offered to the public; these types of shares are not common in Canada (p. 722).

Preemptive right Existing shareholders are given the right to purchase additional shares of the company before the shares are offered to others. This would give existing shareholders the opportunity to maintain the same percentage of ownership as they would have had before the new shares were issued (p. 720).

Preferred shares Shares of stock that give their owners certain advantages over common shareholders, such as the priority to receive dividends before the common shareholders and the priority to receive assets before the common shareholders if the corporation liquidates (p. 723).

President The person in charge of managing the day-to-day operations of a corporation (p. 716).

Private corporation A corporation whose shares are not traded on a stock exchange. (p. 714).

Proportionate share The same amount of shares in relation to others before and after an event such as a new issue of shares (p. 719).

Prospectus A mandatory legal document that describes an investment to potential purchasers (p. 720).

Proxy A formal appointment of one person to cast a vote for another person (p. 717).

Public corporation A corporation that issues shares that are traded on a stock exchange (p. 714).

Rate of return on common shareholders' equity Net income minus preferred dividends divided by average common shareholders' equity. A measure of profitability. Also called *return on equity (ROE)* or *return on common shareholders' equity* (p. 733).

Rate of return on total assets The sum of net income plus interest expense divided by average total assets. This ratio measures the success a company has in using its assets to earn income for the people who finance the business. Also called *return on assets (ROA)* (p. 732).

Retained earnings A corporation's capital that is earned through profitable operation of the business and is left in the business (p. 717).

Return on assets (ROA) Another name for *rate of return on total assets* (p. 732).

Return on equity (ROE) Another name for *rate of return on common shareholders' equity* (p. 733).

Shareholder A person or a company that owns shares in a corporation (p. 714).

Shareholders' equity Owners' equity of a corporation (p. 717).

Shares Units into which the owners' equity of a corporation is divided (p. 715).

Stated value An arbitrary amount assigned to a share of stock when it is issued (p. 722).

Stock Units of ownership into which the owners' equity of a corporation is divided (p. 715).

Subordinated shares Shares with fewer voting rights than other shares within the same corporation (p. 722).

Underwriter An independent firm that is hired to sell shares on a corporation's behalf (p. 720).

SIMILAR TERMS

CBCA	Canada Business Corporations Act
Corp.	Corporation
Inc.	Incorporated
Initial public offering	IPO
Issue	Sell
Liquidation value	Redemption value
Ltd.	Limited
Market value	Market price
NYSE	New York Stock Exchange
Rate of return on common shareholders' equity	Return on equity; ROE
Rate of return on total assets	Return on assets; ROA
Share capital	Capital stock; Stated capital
Shareholder	Stockholder (US terminology)
Stated capital	Share capital
TSX	Toronto Stock Exchange
Using leverage	Borrowing at a lower rate than the return on investments

SELF-STUDY QUESTIONS

Test your understanding of the chapter by marking the correct answer to each of the following questions:

1. Which characteristic of a corporation is most attractive to an owner (shareholder)? *(p. 714)*
   a. Limited liability
   b. Double taxation
   c. Mutual agency
   d. All of the above

2. The person with the most power in a corporation is often the *(p. 716)*
   a. Accountant
   b. Chairperson of the board
   c. President
   d. Vice-president

3. The dollar amount of the shareholder investments in a corporation is called *(p. 717)*
   a. Outstanding shares
   b. Total shareholders' equity
   c. Contributed capital
   d. Retained earnings

4. Retained earnings *(p. 717)*
   a. Is classified as an asset on the corporate balance sheet
   b. Is part of contributed capital
   c. Represents investments by the shareholders of the corporation
   d. Represents capital earned by profitable operations

5. Magnum Corporation receives a building for 10,000 common shares. The building's book value is $275,000 and its current market value is $640,000. This transaction increases Magnum's share capital by *(p. 723)*
   a. $0 because the corporation received no cash
   b. $365,000
   c. $275,000
   d. $640,000

6. Under ASPE, organization costs are classified as a(n) *(p. 726)*
   a. Operating expense
   b. Current asset
   c. Contra item in shareholders' equity
   d. None of the above

7. The 10,000 preferred shares of Glanville Inc. were issued at $55.00 per share. Each preferred share can be converted into 10 common shares. The entry to record the conversion of these preferred shares into common is *(p. 724)*

a.

Cash	550,000	
Preferred Shares		500,000
Common Shares		50,000

b.

Preferred Shares	500,000	
Cash		50,000
Common Shares		550,000

c.

Preferred Shares	550,000	
Common Shares		550,000

d.

Common Shares	550,000	
Preferred Shares		550,000

8. Glanville Inc. has 10,000 $3.50 cumulative preferred shares and 100,000 common shares issued and outstanding. Two years' preferred dividends are in arrears.

   Glanville Inc. declares a cash dividend large enough to pay the preferred dividends in arrears, the preferred dividend for the current period, and a $1.50 dividend per common share. What is the total amount of the dividend? *(p. 728)*
   a. $255,000
   b. $220,000
   c. $150,000
   d. $105,000

9. When an investor is buying shares as an investment, the value of most direct concern is *(p. 730)*
   a. Par value
   b. Market value
   c. Liquidation value
   d. Book value

10. Mist Corporation has the following data:

Net income	$ 24,000
Preferred dividends	$ 12,000
Average common shareholders' equity	$100,000

   Mist's return on common shareholders' equity is *(p. 733)*
   a. 24%
   b. 50%
   c. 12%
   d. 36%

Answers to Self-Study Questions

1. a   2. b   3. c   4. d   5. d   6. d Intangible asset   7. c
8. a [(10,000 × $3.50 × 3 = $105,000) + (100,000 × $1.50 = $150,000) = $255,000]   9. b   10. c.

Assignment Material

QUESTIONS

1. Identify the characteristics of a corporation.

2. Explain how corporate earnings are subject to a degree of double taxation.

3. Briefly outline the steps in the organization of a corporation.

4. Compare the characteristics of a partnership and a corporation.

5. Name the five rights of a common shareholder.

6. Are preferred shares automatically nonvoting?

7. Which event increases the assets of the corporation: authorization of shares or issuance of shares? Explain.

8. Suppose Recky Corp. issued 1,400 shares of its $4.50 preferred shares for $110.00 per share. By how much would this transaction increase the company's contributed capital? By how much would it increase retained earnings? By how much would it increase annual cash dividend payments?

9. United Inc. issued 150 common shares for $9.00 per share and 250 shares for $8.50 per share. What would be the journal entry to record the combined issue on July 6?

10. How does issuance of 1,500 common shares for land and a building, together worth $125,000, affect contributed capital?

11. List the following accounts in the order in which they would appear on the balance sheet: Common Shares, Preferred Shares, Retained Earnings, Dividends Payable. Also, give each account's balance sheet classification.

12. What type of account is Organization Costs? Briefly describe how to account for organization costs under ASPE.

13. Briefly discuss the three important dates for a dividend.

14. Tapin Inc. has 2,500 shares of its $1.75 preferred shares outstanding. Dividends for 2018 and 2019 are in arrears. Assume that Tapin Inc. declares total dividends of $35,000 at the end of 2020. Show how to allocate the dividends to preferred and common shareholders (a) if preferred shares are cumulative, and (b) if preferred shares are noncumulative.

15. As a preferred shareholder, would you rather own cumulative or noncumulative preferred shares? If all other factors are the same, would the corporation rather issue cumulative or noncumulative preferred shares? Give your reasons.

16. How are cumulative preferred dividends in arrears reported in the financial statements? When do dividends become a liability of the corporation?

17. Distinguish between the market value of shares and the book value of shares. Which is more important to investors?

18. How is book value per common share computed when the company has both preferred shares and common shares outstanding?

19. The _____ measures a company's success in using its assets to earn income for the stakeholders who are financing the business.

20. Why should a healthy company's rate of return on shareholders' equity exceed its rate of return on total assets?

STARTERS

S13–1 Answer these questions about corporations.:
    a. Who is the most powerful person in the corporation?
    b. What group holds the ultimate power in a corporation?
    c. Who is in charge of day-to-day operations?
    d. Who is in charge of accounting?

①
Authority structure in a corporation.

S13–2 How does a proprietorship's balance sheet differ from a corporation's balance sheet? How are the two balance sheets similar?

①
The balance sheets of a corporation and a proprietorship

S13–3 Grimreality Corp. has two classes of shares: common and preferred. Journalize the corporation's June 22 issuance of
    1. 3,000 common shares for $70.00 per share
    2. 1,500 preferred shares for a total of $32,000

②
Issuing shares

S13–4 At December 31, 2020, Thaler Corporation reported the following on its comparative

②

Issuing shares and analyzing
retained earnings

1. Increased $7,000

S13–4 At December 31, 2020, Thaler Corporation reported the following on its comparative
balance sheet, which included 2019 amounts for comparison:

	December 31,	
	2020	**2019**
Common shares		
Authorized: 10,000 shares		
Issued: 3,600 shares in 2020	$86,000	
3,190 shares in 2019		$79,000
Retained earnings	50,800	46,800

1. How much did Thaler Corporation's total contributed capital increase during
   2020? What caused total contributed capital to increase? How can you tell?

2. Assuming no dividends were declared during 2020, did Thaler Corporation have
   a profit or a loss for 2020? How can you tell?

②

Contributed capital for a
corporation

Total contributed capital, $515,000

S13–5 Assured Corp. has recently incorporated. The company issued common shares to a
lawyer who provided legal services worth $7,500 to help organize the corporation.
It issued common shares to another person in exchange for his patent with a market
value of $45,000. In addition, Assured Corp. received cash both for 2,500 of its $1.50
preferred shares at $10.00 per share and for 35,000 of its common shares at $12.50 per
share. Without making journal entries, determine the total contributed capital created
by these transactions.

②

Preparing the shareholders'
equity section of a balance
sheet

Total shareholder's equity, $47,500

S13–6 Shock Limited reported the following partial list of accounts:

Cost of Goods Sold	$29,400	Accounts Payable	$ 3,000
Common Shares,		Retained Earnings	18,000
40,000 shares issued		Unearned Revenue	2,600
and outstanding	29,500	Cash	12,000
Long-term Note Payable	3,800	Total assets	?

Identify the accounts which belong in the shareholders' equity section of the Shock
Limited balance sheet. Calculate the total shareholders' equity.

②

Raising capital

S13–7 Indicate whether each of the following supports the use of long-term debt to raise
capital or the issuance of common shares:
a. Annual payment is optional.
b. Money must be repaid.
c. Issuance means dilution of existing control.
d. Annual cost is tax deductible.

③

Accounting for cash dividends

Cash, Jan. 8, 2020, $45,000

S13–8 On December 10, HoHo Limited declared the annual cash dividend on its 5,000 $3.00
preferred shares and a $0.60 per share cash dividend on its 50,000 common shares.
HoHo Limited then paid the dividends on January 8, 2020. HoHo Limited earned
net income of $85,000 during the year ended December 31, 2019, and has sufficient
cash to pay the dividends.
1. Journalize the declaration of the cash dividends on December 10, 2019.
2. Journalize the payment of the cash dividends on January 8, 2020.

S13–9 Xiong Inc. has the following shareholders' equity:

Preferred shares, $0.025, cumulative, liquidation value $0.50, 50,000 shares authorized, 45,000 shares issued and outstanding	$ 20,000
Common shares, 1,000,000 shares authorized and issued and outstanding	200,000
Retained earnings	130,000
Total shareholders' equity	$350,000

③
Dividing cash dividends between preferred and common shares

3. Preferred, $3,375; Common, $13,625

Answer these questions about Xiong's dividends:
1. Are Xiong Inc.'s preferred shares cumulative or noncumulative? How can you tell? Assume there are no dividends in arrears.

2. Suppose Xiong Inc. declares cash dividends of $17,000 for 2020. How much of the dividends goes to preferred shares? How much goes to common shares? Assume that there are no dividends in arrears.

3. Suppose Xiong Inc. did not pay the preferred dividend in 2018 and 2019. In 2020, the company declares cash dividends of $17,000. How much of the dividends goes to preferred shares? How much goes to common shares?

S13–10 Refer to the shareholders' equity information of Xiong Inc. in S13–9. Xiong Inc. has not declared preferred dividends for five years (including the current year). Compute the book value per share of Xiong Inc.'s common shares. Round your answer to two decimal places.

④
Book value per common share

Book value per share, $0.32

S13–11 Midnight Distribution Corporation's balance sheet reported the following information at December 31, 2019:

④
Calculating book value

Common shares = $51.35

Preferred shares, $3, cumulative, 11,000 shares issued, liquidation value $55 per share	$ 605,000
Common shares, 75,000 shares issued	2,000,000
Total contributed capital	2,605,000
Retained earnings	1,950,000
Total shareholders' equity	$4,555,000

Assuming there are three years' dividends in arrears (including 2019), determine the book value per share of both preferred and common shares. Round your answers to the nearest cent.

S13–12 Tahini Inc.'s 2019 financial statements reported the following items—with 2018 figures given for comparison:

⑤
Computing return on assets

ROA, 13.86%

Balance sheet	2019	2018
Total assets	$49,000	$44,800
Total liabilities	$27,400	$25,800
Total shareholders' equity (all common)	21,600	19,000
Total liabilities and equity	$49,000	$44,800

Income statement	
Net sales	$39,130
Cost of goods sold	14,210
Gross margin	24,920
Selling and administrative expenses	14,000
Interest expense	400
All other expenses, net	4,420
Net income	$ 6,100

Compute Tahini Inc.'s return on assets for 2019. Round the answer to 2 decimal places.

S13–13 Myrna Inc.'s 2020 financial statements reported the following items—with 2019 figures given for comparison:

	2020	2019
Total assets	$41,000	$40,800
Total liabilities	$17,400	$18,000
Total shareholders' equity (all common)	23,600	22,800
Total liabilities and equity	$41,000	$40,800
Net income	$ 6,100	$ 7,200

Compute Myrna Inc.'s return on common shareholders' equity for 2020. Round the answer to 2 decimal places.

EXERCISES

E13–1 Suppose you are forming a business and you need some outside money from other investors. Assume you have decided to organize the business as a corporation that will issue shares to raise the needed funds. Briefly discuss your most important reason for organizing as a corporation rather than as a partnership. If you had decided to organize as a partnership, what would be your most important reason for not organizing as a corporation?

E13–2 David Johnston and Lisa Jacobs are opening a decorating business to be named Student Decor Ltd. They need outside capital, so they plan to organize the business as a corporation. Because your accounting course is next to their design class, they come to you for advice. Write a memorandum informing them of the steps in forming a corporation. Identify specific documents used in this process, and name the different parties involved in the ownership and management of a corporation.

E13–3 The co-op student working at Morneau Equipment Inc. prepared their adjusted trial balance in alphabetical order. All accounts have their normal balances.

Accounts Receivable	$ 56,000	Other Expenses	$ 35,400
Accumulated Amortization	14,000	Retained Earnings	78,400
Amortization Expense	1,800	Salaries Expense	199,000
Cash	122,000	Salaries Payable	3,400
Common Shares	50,000	Service Revenue	356,400
Computers & Equipment	74,800	Supplies	5,600
Interest Expense	18,800	Unearned Revenues	5,400
Interest Revenue	5,800		

Required

1. Prepare the appropriate closing entries for the January 31 year end.
2. What is the balance in the Retained Earnings account after the closing entries have been completed?

E13–4 Is each of the following statements true or false? For each false statement, explain why it is false.

a. A shareholder may bind (obligate) the corporation to a contract.

b. The policy-making body in a corporation is called the board of directors.

c. The owner of 100 preferred shares has greater voting rights than the owner of 100 common shares.

d. A company incorporated under the Canada Business Corporations Act must assign the proceeds of a share issue to the capital account for that type of share.

e. All common shares issued and outstanding have equal voting rights.

f. Issuance of 1,000 common shares at $12.00 per share increases shareholders' equity by $12,000.

g. The stated value of a share is the value assigned to the shares by the company issuing them at the date issued.

h. A corporation issues its preferred shares in exchange for land and a building with a combined market value of $200,000. This transaction increases the corporation's shareholders' equity by $200,000 regardless of the assets' prior book value.

E13–5 Shahidi Corporation engaged in the following share transactions in the first quarter of their fiscal year:

②
Issuing shares
2. Contributed capital, $143,500

Jan. 19   Issued 4,500 common shares for cash of $11.00 per share.

Feb. 3   Sold 1,000 $1.50 Class A preferred shares for $15,000 cash to new investors.

11   Received inventory valued at $20,000 and vehicles with market value of $17,000 for 5,800 common shares.

Mar. 15   Issued 3,000 $1.00 Class B preferred shares for $14.00 per share

Required

1. Journalize the transactions. Explanations are not required.

2. How much contributed capital did these transactions generate for Shahidi Corporation?

E13–6 Record the journal entries on April 18 for each of the following cases:

②
Issuing shares to finance the purchase of assets

Case A—Issue shares and buy the assets in separate transactions:
Kvissle Corp. issued 11,000 common shares for cash of $1,460,000. In a separate transaction, Kvissle then used the cash to purchase an office building for $900,000 and equipment for $560,000.

Case B—Issue shares to acquire the assets:
Kvissle Corp. issued 11,000 common shares to acquire an office building valued at $900,000 and equipment worth $560,000.

Compare the balances in all accounts in Case A and Case B. Are the account balances similar or different?

E13–7 Solve for the missing amounts in the partial balance sheet using the additional information provided below:

③
Calculating shareholders' equity data
D = $125,000

Shareholders' Equity	
Contributed capital	
Preferred shares, $2.50, (A) issued, outstanding	$175,000
Common shares, 150,000 issued and outstanding	(B)
Total contributed capital	(C)
Deficit	(D)
Total shareholders' equity	$500,000

All of the shares were issued at one time. Common shares were sold for $3.00 per share and preferred shares were sold for $5.00 each. No dividends were paid for the year.

Shareholders' equity section of a balance sheet

Total shareholders' equity, $284,500

E13–8 Skeet Corporation has the following selected account balances at June 30, 2020. Prepare the shareholders' equity section of the company's balance sheet.

Common Shares,			Inventory	$70,000
500,000 shares authorized,			Machinery and Equipment	82,500
100,000 shares issued	$100,000		Preferred Shares, $1.25,	
Accumulated Amortization—			100,000 shares authorized,	
Machinery and Equipment	32,500		10,000 shares issued	87,500
Retained Earnings	97,000		Organization Costs, net	2,500
Cost of Goods Sold	42,500			

Issuing shares and preparing the shareholders' equity section of the balance sheet

2. Total shareholders' equity, $435,000

E13–9 The articles of incorporation for Plum Corp. authorize the company to issue 100,000 $5 preferred shares and 500,000 common shares. During its first fiscal year of operations, Plum Corp. completed the following selected transactions:

2019

Dec.   4   Issued 5,000 common shares to the consultants who formed the corporation, receiving cash of $140,000.

       13   Issued 500 preferred shares for cash of $55,000.

       14   Issued 4,000 common shares in exchange for land valued at $120,000.

2020

Nov. 30   Earned a profit for the fiscal year and closed the $120,000 net income into Retained Earnings.

Required

1. Record the transactions in the general journal.

2. Prepare the shareholders' equity section of the Plum Corp. balance sheet at November 30, 2020.

Balance sheet presentation

Total assets, $4,634,000

E13–10 The following is an alphabetical list of accounts of Outlet Services Inc. as at January 31, 2019. The balances are *prior* to the closing journal entries. All accounts have normal balances.

Accrued Liabilities	$ 50,400
Accounts Payable	90,000
Accounts Receivable, net	318,000
Cash	494,000
Common Shares, 500,000 shares authorized; 200,000 shares issued	2,500,000
Interest Expense	29,000
Inventory	420,000
Long-term Note Payable	600,000
Organization Costs	18,000
Prepaid Expenses	3,600
Preferred Shares, $2.50, cumulative, 24,000 authorized and issued	240,000
Property, Plant, and Equipment, net	3,360,000
Retained Earnings	623,600
Trademark, net	20,400

Additional information:

Net income for 2019 was $530,000.

No new shares were issued in 2019.

Required Prepare a classified balance sheet as at January 31, 2019.

E13–11 Sydney Incorporated has 75,000 shares of $2 cumulative preferred shares outstanding as well as 110,000 common shares. There are no dividends in arrears on the preferred shares. The following transactions were reported during May 2020:

③
Accounting for cash dividends

Retained earnings, $101,800

May   1   Declared the required dividend on the preferred shares and a $0.23 per share dividend on the common shares.

14   The date of record for the dividend declared on May 1.

28   Paid the dividend declared on May 1.

31   Closed the Income Summary account. Net income for the year was $225,000.

Required

1. Prepare journal entries to record the above transactions. No explanations are required.
2. Assuming the balance of Retained Earnings on June 1, 2019, was $52,100, determine the balance of the account on May 31, 2020.

E13–12

③
Dividing cash dividends between preferred and common shares

4. Common, $35,000

FRESH START CORP. Balance Sheet (Partial) December 31, 2020	
Shareholders' Equity	
Contributed capital	
Preferred shares, $5.00, 10,000 shares authorized,	
1,000 shares issued and outstanding	$100,000
Common shares, 100,000 shares authorized,	
30,000 shares issued and outstanding	150,000
Total contributed capital	250,000
Retained earnings	661,000
Total shareholders' equity	$911,000

Answer these questions about Fresh Start Corp.'s dividends:

1. How much in dividends must Fresh Start declare each year before the common shareholders receive cash dividends for the year?
2. Suppose Fresh Start declares cash dividends of $20,000 for 2020. How much of the dividends go to preferred shareholders? How much goes to common shareholders?
3. Are Fresh Start's preferred shares cumulative or noncumulative? How can you tell?
4. Suppose Fresh Start did not pay the preferred dividend in 2018 and 2019. In 2020, Fresh Start declares cash dividends of $40,000. How much of the dividends go to preferred shareholders? How much goes to common shareholders?

E13–13 The following elements of shareholders' equity are adapted from the balance sheet of Brzynski Marketing Ltd.:

③
Computing dividends on preferred and common shares

Common gets $35,000

Shareholders' Equity	
Preferred shares, $0.10, cumulative, 100,000 shares authorized, 60,000 shares issued and outstanding	$ 60,000
Common shares, 2,000,000 shares authorized, 900,000 shares issued and outstanding	1,500,000

The company has paid all dividends through 2018.

Required Compute the dividends paid to preferred shareholders and to common shareholders for 2019 and 2020 if total dividends are $0 in 2019, and $47,000 in 2020. Round your answers to the nearest dollar.

④
Book value per share of preferred and common shares

Common, $12.10 per share

E13–14 The balance sheet of Pujari Sports Corp. reported the following:

Cumulative preferred shares, 300 shares issued and outstanding, liquidation value $15,000	$ 15,000
Common shares, 25,000 shares issued and outstanding	187,500

Assume that Pujari Sports had paid preferred dividends for the current year and all prior years (no dividends in arrears). Retained Earnings was $115,000.

Required Compute the book value per share of the preferred shares and the common shares.

③ ④
Book value per share of preferred and common shares; preferred dividends in arrears

Preferred, $78.00 per share; common, $11.76 per share

E13–15 Refer to E13–14. Compute the book value per share of the preferred shares and the common shares, assuming that four years of preferred dividends (including dividends for the current year) are in arrears. Assume the preferred shares are cumulative and their dividend rate is $7.00 per share.

⑤
Evaluating profitability

ROE, 6.73%

E13–16 Woldenga Consulting Ltd. reported the figures shown below for 2020 and 2019:

	2020	2019
Income statement		
Interest expense	$ 5,200	$ 3,700
Net income	3,250	5,200
Balance sheet		
Total assets	105,000	95,000
Preferred shares, $1.15,		
200 shares issued and outstanding	1,000	1,000
Common shareholders' equity	46,700	43,000
Total shareholders' equity	47,700	44,000

Required

1. Compute the return on total assets (ROA) and the return on common shareholders' equity (ROE) for 2020. Round your answers to two decimal places.
2. Do these rates of return suggest strength or weakness? Give your reasons.

E13–17 You have been asked to consider investing in ASAP Printing Services Inc.

⑤

Calculating ROA and ROE

ROA, 9.80%

ASAP Printing Services Inc.
Balance Sheet
December 31, 2019

Assets		Liabilities		
Current assets		Current liabilities		
Cash	$384,000	Accounts payable	$	90,000
Accounts receivable, net	318,000	Accrued liabilities		50,400
Inventory	420,000	Total current liabilities		$ 140,400
Prepaid expenses	3,600	Long-term note payable		600,000
Total current assets	$1,125,600	Total liabilities		$ 740,400
Property, plant, and equipment, net	3,360,000	**Shareholders' Equity**		
		Contributed capital		
Intangible assets		Preferred shares, $2.50, cumulative, 24,000, authorized and issued	$ 240,000	
Trademark, net	$ 20,400	Common shares, 300,000 shares authorized, 200,000 shares issued	2,500,000	
Organization costs	18,000	Total contributed capital	2,740,000	
Total intangible assets	38,400	Retained earnings	1,043,600	
		Total shareholders' equity		3,783,600
Total assets	$4,524,000	Total liabilities and shareholders' equity		$4,524,000

Additional information:

Total assets at January 1, 2019, were $4,050,000.

Net income for 2019 was $420,000.

No new shares were issued in 2019.

Required

1. Calculate the following for 2019, reporting the answers to two decimal places:
   a. Return on total assets
   b. Return on common shareholders' equity
2. If the minimum rate of return for each of the above ratios is 12 percent, will you invest in this business?

SERIAL EXERCISE

② ③
Record the issuance of shares and preparation of shareholders' equity, account for cash dividends

Total shareholders' equity
$672,000

E13–18 *The Serial Exercise involves a company that will be revisited throughout relevant chapters in Volume 1 and Volume 2. You can complete the Serial Exercises using MyLab Accounting.*

This exercise continues recordkeeping for the Canyon Canoe Company. Students do not have to complete prior exercises in order to complete this question.

Amber Wilson, owner of Canyon Canoe Company, decides to start a new company that will be operated as a corporation, Outdoor Equipment Incorporated (OEI). This company will sell outdoor clothing and equipment. The articles of incorporation for OEI authorize the company to issue 500,000 preferred shares that pay a dividend of $4.00 per year and 1,000,000 common shares.

OEI had the following select transactions in 2022:

Jan.   1   Issued 50,000 common shares for a total of $200,000.
      10   Issued 2,000 preferred shares in exchange for land with a market value of $70,000.
Dec. 15   Declared total cash dividends of $15,000.
      31   Paid the cash dividends.

Required

1. Journalize the transactions.
2. Calculate the balance in Retained Earnings on December 31, 2022. Assume net income for the year was $417,000.
3. Prepare the shareholders' equity section of the balance sheet as of December 31, 2022.

CHALLENGE EXERCISES

② ③
Accounting for shareholders' equity transactions

E13–19 Shredders Wintersports Inc. reported these comparative shareholders' equity data:

	December 31,	
	2020	**2019**
Common shares	$1,530,000	$ 300,000
Retained earnings	2,318,000	1,538,000

During 2020, Shredders Wintersports Inc. completed these transactions and events:

a. Net income, $1,430,000.
b. Cash dividends, $650,000.
c. Issuance of common shares for cash, 3,000 shares at $60.00 per share.
d. Issuance of common shares to purchase another company (Shredders debited the Investments account), 15,000 shares at $70.00 per share.

Required Without making journal entries, show how Shredders Wintersports Inc.'s 2020 transactions and events accounted for the changes in the shareholders' equity accounts. For each shareholders' equity account, start with the December 31, 2019, balance and work toward the balance at December 31, 2020.

BEYOND THE NUMBERS

BN13–1

② ④
Characteristics of corporations' shareholders' equity

Answer the following questions to enhance your understanding of the shareholders' equity of corporations:

1. Why do you think contributed capital and retained earnings are shown separately in the shareholders' equity section?
2. Ann Todt, owner of Dirt Girl Landscaping, proposes to sell some land she owns to her company for common shares. What problem does Dirt Girl Landscaping face in recording the transaction?

3. Preferred shares generally have preference over common shares for dividends and on liquidation. Why would investors buy common shares when preferred shares are available?

4. If you owned 100 shares of Canada Goose Holdings Inc. and someone offered to buy the shares for their book value, would you accept the offer? Why or why not?

5. What is a convertible preferred share? Why would an investor exercise the conversion privilege?

ETHICAL ISSUE

EI13-1

Note: This case is based on a real situation.

Jason Wertz paid $50,000 for a franchise that entitled him to market Success software programs in the countries of the European Union. Wertz intended to sell individual franchises for the major language groups of Western Europe—German, French, English, Spanish, and Italian. Naturally, investors considering buying a franchise from Wertz asked to see the financial statements of his business.

Believing the value of the franchise to be greater than $50,000, Wertz sought to capitalize his own franchise at $375,000. The law firm of St. Charles and LaDue helped Wertz form a corporation authorized to issue 500,000 common shares. Lawyers suggested the following chain of transactions:

1. A third party borrows $375,000 and purchases the franchise from Wertz.

2. Wertz pays the corporation $375,000 to acquire all its shares.

3. The corporation buys the franchise from the third party, who repays the loan.

In the final analysis, the third party is debt-free and out of the picture. Wertz owns all the corporation's shares, and the corporation owns the franchise. The corporation's balance sheet lists a franchise acquired at a cost of $375,000. This balance sheet is Wertz's most valuable marketing tool.

Required

1. What is unethical about this situation?

2. Who can be harmed? How can they be harmed? What role does accounting play?

PROBLEMS (GROUP A)

P13–1A Mark Mathews and Karen Willamas are opening a software company. They have developed a new and effective software to manage small business operations. Their most fundamental decision is how to organize the business. Mathews thinks the partnership form is best. Willamas favours the corporate form of organization. They seek your advice.

(1)
Organizing a corporation

Required Write a memo to Mathews and Willamas to make them aware of the advantages and the disadvantages of organizing the business as a corporation. Use the following format for your memo:

Date:	_____
To:	Mark Mathews and Karen Willamas
From:	[Student Name]
Subject:	Advantages and disadvantages of the corporate form of business organization

P13–2A The partnership of Nuan Zhang and Jen Phuah needed additional capital to expand into new markets, so the business incorporated as E-Z Services Inc. The articles of incorporation under the Canada Business Corporations Act authorize E-Z Services Inc. to issue 500,000 $2.50 preferred shares and 2,000,000 common shares. In its first year, E-Z Services Inc. completed the following share-related transactions:

2020

Aug.	2	Paid incorporation fees of $6,000 and paid legal fees of $16,000 to organize as a corporation.
	2	Issued 20,000 common shares to Zhang and 25,000 common shares to Phuah in return for cash. Zhang paid $150,000 cash, and Phuah paid $187,500 cash.
Dec.	10	Issued 1,000 preferred shares to acquire a computer system with a market value of $80,000.
	16	Issued 15,000 common shares for cash of $120,000.

Required

1. Record the transactions in the general journal.
2. Prepare the shareholders' equity section of the E-Z Services Inc. balance sheet at December 31, 2020. The ending balance in Retained Earnings is $145,000.

P13–3A Riverbend Inc. was organized in 2019. At December 31, 2019, Riverbend Inc.'s balance sheet reported the following shareholders' equity account information:

Preferred shares, $4.00, 200,000 shares authorized, none issued	$ 0
Common shares, 1,000,000 shares authorized, 150,000 shares issued and outstanding	225,000
Retained earnings (Deficit)	(50,000)

Required

Answer the following questions and make journal entries as needed:

1. What does the $4.00 mean for the preferred shares? If Riverbend Inc. issues 2,500 preferred shares, how much in cash dividends will it expect to pay?
2. At what average price per share did Riverbend Inc. issue the common shares during 2019?
3. Were first-year operations profitable? Give your reason.
4. Journalize the share transactions which took place during 2020. Explanations are not required.

Feb.	15	Issued for cash 1,500 preferred shares at $20.00 per share.
April	2	Issued for cash 5,000 common shares at a price of $1.75 per share.
June	1	Issued 100,000 common shares to acquire a building valued at $250,000.
Dec.	31	Net income for the year was $180,000, and the company declared no dividends. Make the closing entry for net income.

5. Prepare the shareholders' equity section of the Riverbend Inc. balance sheet at December 31, 2020.

P13–4A The following summaries for Ruby Distributors Ltd. and Gem Wholesalers Inc. provide the information needed to prepare the shareholders' equity section of each company's balance sheet. The two companies are independent.

Ruby Distributors Ltd. This company is authorized to issue 150,000 common shares. All the shares were issued at $3.00 per share. The company incurred a net loss of $75,000 in 2014 (its first year of operations) and a net loss of $30,000 in 2018. It earned net incomes of $35,000 in 2019 and $60,000 in 2020. The company declared no dividends during the four-year period.

Gem Wholesalers Inc. Gem Wholesalers Inc.'s articles of incorporation authorize the company to issue 200,000 cumulative preferred shares and 1,000,000 common shares. Gem Wholesalers Inc. issued 2,000 preferred shares at $12.50 per share. It issued 100,000 common shares for $300,000. The company's Retained Earnings balance at the beginning of 2020 was $75,000. Net income for 2020 was $50,000, and the company declared the specified preferred share dividend for 2020. Preferred share dividends for 2019 were in arrears. The preferred dividend was $1.10 per share per year.

Required For each company, prepare the shareholders' equity section of its balance sheet at December 31, 2020. Show the computation of all amounts. Journal entries are not required.

P13–5A Toluca Enterprises Inc. reported the following information in its October 31, 2019, annual report:

② ③
Analyzing the shareholders' equity of a corporation

2. $4.00 per share

Shareholders' Equity	
Preferred shares, $2.75, cumulative, 600,000 shares authorized, 100,000 shares issued and outstanding	$ 400,000
Common shares, unlimited number of shares authorized, 1,300,000 shares issued and outstanding	1,850,000
Retained earnings	5,850,000
Total shareholders' equity	$8,100,000

Required

1. Identify the different issues of shares that Toluca Enterprises Inc. has outstanding.

2. What is the average issue price per preferred share?

3. Make two summary journal entries to record issuance of all the Toluca shares for cash on March 1, 2020. Explanations are not required.

4. Assume no preferred dividends are in arrears. Journalize the declaration of a $400,000 dividend at March 31, 2020. Use separate Dividends Payable accounts for preferred and common shares. An explanation is not required.

P13–6A Rainy Day Corporation has 50,000 $0.50 preferred shares and 600,000 common shares issued and outstanding. During a three-year period, Rainy Day Corporation declared and paid cash dividends as follows: 2017, $0; 2018, $114,000; and 2019, $260,000.

③
Computing dividends on preferred and common shares

1. b. 2018: Preferred, $50,000

Required

1. Compute the total dividends to preferred shares and common shares for each of the three years if

   a. Preferred shares are noncumulative.

   b. Preferred shares are cumulative.

2. For requirement 1b, record the declaration of the 2019 dividends on December 22, 2019, and the payment of the dividends on January 12, 2020.

P13–7A The balance sheet of Tulameen Systems Inc. reported the following:

③ ④
Analyzing the shareholders' equity of a corporation

4. Book value per common share, $14.36

Shareholders' Equity	
Preferred shares, cumulative, convertible, authorized 25,000 shares	$200,000
Common shares, authorized 50,000 shares, issued 44,000 shares	528,000
Retained earnings	168,000
Total shareholders' equity	$896,000

Notes to the financial statements indicate that 10,000 $1.20 preferred shares were issued and outstanding. The preferred shares have a liquidation value of $24.00 per share. Preferred dividends are in arrears for two years, including the current year. On the balance sheet date, the market value of the Tulameen Systems Inc. common shares was $28.00 per share.

Required

1. Are the preferred shares cumulative or noncumulative? How can you tell?
2. What is the total contributed capital of the company?
3. What is the total market value of the common shares?
4. Compute the book value per share of the preferred shares and of the common shares.

(2) (3) (4)
Recording the issuance of shares; allocating cash dividends; calculating book value; preparing the liability and shareholders' equity sections of the balance sheet

4. Average price, $6.25/share

P13–8A At January 1, 2018, Cricket Corp.'s balance sheet reported the following shareholders' equity information:

Shareholders' Equity	
Contributed capital	
Preferred shares, $1.25, cumulative (2 years in arrears), liquidation price of $20, 100,000 shares authorized, 30,000 shares issued and outstanding	$ 200,000
Common shares	
Class A, 20,000 shares authorized and issued and outstanding	125,000
Class B, unlimited number of shares authorized, 150,000 shares issued and outstanding	1,500,000
Total contributed capital	1,825,000
Retained earnings	300,000
Total shareholders' equity	$2,125,000

The company had the following transactions on the dates indicated:

2018

Dec. 1 The company declared dividends of $180,000, payable on January 15, 2019, to the shareholders of record on December 31. Indicate the amount that would be payable to the preferred shareholders and to the common shareholders. The dividend rate for Class A and Class B shares is the same.

31 The company reported net income after taxes of $60,000 for the year and then closed the Income Summary account.

2019

Jan. 7 The company sold 10,000 preferred shares at $23.50 per share.

15 The company paid the dividend declared on December 1, 2018.

Feb. 14 The company sold 15,000 Class B common shares at $11.00 per share.

Dec. 2 The company declared dividends of $120,000, payable on January 15, 2020, to the shareholders of record on December 31, 2019. Indicate the amount that would be payable to the preferred shareholders and to the common shareholders.

31 The company reported net income after taxes of $145,000 and then closed the Income Summary account.

2020

Jan. 15 Paid the dividend declared on December 2, 2019.

Required

1. Record the transactions in the general journal.
2. Prepare the liability and shareholders' equity sections of the balance sheet as of the close of business on December 31, 2019.
3. Calculate the book value per share of the preferred shares and of the common shares (Class A and Class B combined) on December 31, 2019.
4. What was the average price at which the Class A common shares were issued?

P13–9A The following accounts and related balances of Etse Manufacturing Inc. at December 31, 2020 are arranged in no particular order:

② ⑤
Preparing a corporation's balance sheet; measuring profitability

Total assets, $759,000

Accrued Liabilities	$ 23,000	Accounts Payable	$ 36,000
Long-term Note Payable	100,500	Retained Earnings	?
Accounts Receivable, net	100,000	Interest Expense	10,850
Cash	35,000	Dividends Payable	4,500
Inventory	190,500	Total assets, Dec. 31, 2019	567,500
Property, Plant, and Equipment, net	381,000	Net income	140,750
Prepaid Expenses	15,500	Common Shareholders'	
Patent, net	37,000	Equity, Dec. 31, 2019	520,000
Common Shares, 100,000 shares authorized, 33,000 shares issued and outstanding		165,000	
Preferred Shares, $0.15, 25,000 shares authorized, 6,000 shares issued		30,000	

Required

1. Prepare the company's classified balance sheet in the report format at December 31, 2020.
2. Compute the return on total assets and the return on common shareholders' equity for the year ended December 31, 2020.
3. Do these rates of return suggest strength or weakness? Give your reason.

PROBLEMS (GROUP B)

P13–1B Jack Rudd and Pam Kines are opening an office supply store. The area where the store is located is growing, and no competitors are located in the immediate vicinity. Their most fundamental decision is how to organize the business. Rudd thinks the partnership form is best. Kines favours the corporate form of organization. They seek your advice.

①
Organizing a corporation

Required Write a memo to Rudd and Kines to make them aware of the advantages and disadvantages of organizing the business as a corporation. Use the following format for your memo:

Date:	_____
To:	Jack Rudd and Pam Kines
From:	[Student Name]
Subject:	Advantages and disadvantages of the corporate form of business organization

P13–2B Gingrich Solutions Ltd.'s articles of incorporation state that it is allowed to issue 90,000 $2.00 preferred shares and 150,000 common shares. In its first year, Gingrich Solutions Ltd. completed the following selected transactions:

②
Journalizing corporation transactions and preparing the shareholders' equity section of the balance sheet

2020

Jan.	2	Paid incorporation costs of $2,500 and legal fees of $6,000 to organize as a corporation.
	6	Issued 20,000 common shares for equipment with a market value of $175,000.
	12	Issued 100 preferred shares to acquire software with a market value of $19,500.
May	22	Issued 5,000 common shares for $7.00 cash per share.

Required

1. Record the transactions in the general journal.

2. Prepare the shareholders' equity section of the Gingrich Solutions Ltd. balance sheet at December 31, 2020. The ending Retained Earnings balance is $40,000.

P13–3B Sloboda Corporation was established in 2019. At December 31, 2019, Sloboda Corporation's balance sheet reported the following shareholders' equity account information:

Preferred shares, $0.20, 50,000 shares authorized, none issued	$ 0
Common shares, 100,000 shares authorized, 10,000 shares issued and outstanding	87,500
Retained earnings (Deficit)	(20,000)

Required

1. What does the $0.20 mean in the description of the preferred shares? If Sloboda Corporation issued 4,000 preferred shares, how much in cash dividends will Sloboda Corporation expect to pay per year?

2. At what average price per share did Sloboda Corporation issue the common shares?

3. Were first-year operations profitable? Give your reason.

4. Journalize the share transactions which took place during 2020. Explanations are not required.

Jan. 27	Issued for cash 10,000 preferred shares at $2.50 per share.
Apr. 4	Issued for cash 1,000 common shares at a price of $9.00 per share.
Sep. 15	Issued 25,000 common shares to acquire a building valued at $235,000.
Dec. 31	Net income for the year was $62,500, and the company declared no dividends. Make the closing entry for net income.

5. Prepare the shareholders' equity section of the Sloboda Corporation balance sheet at December 31, 2020.

P13–4B Shareholders' equity information is given for Kabaddi Corp. and Kerala Ltd. The two companies are independent.

Kabaddi Corp. Kabaddi Corp. is authorized to issue 100,000 common shares. All the shares were issued at $10.00 per share. The company incurred a net loss of $30,000 in 2018, its first year of business. It earned net income of $45,000 in 2019 and $50,000 in 2020. The company declared no dividends during the three-year period.

Kerala Ltd. Kerala Ltd.'s articles of incorporation authorize the company to issue 50,000 $1.25 cumulative preferred shares and 500,000 common shares. Kerala Ltd. issued 4,000 preferred shares at $10.00 per share. It issued 60,000 common shares for a total of $150,000. The company's Retained Earnings balance at the beginning of 2020 was $55,000, and net income for the year was $62,500. During 2020, the company declared the specified dividend on preferred shares and a $0.50 per share dividend on common shares. Preferred dividends for 2019 were in arrears.

Required For each company, prepare the shareholders' equity section of its balance sheet at December 31, 2020. Show the computation of all amounts. Journal entries are not required.

②

Issuing shares and preparing the shareholders' equity section of the balance sheet

② ③

Shareholders' equity section of the balance sheet

P13–5B Reckless Phones Ltd. included the following shareholders' equity on its year-end balance sheet at December 31, 2020:

② ③

Analyzing the shareholders' equity of a corporation

Shareholders' Equity	
Preferred shares, $0.25, cumulative, unlimited authorization, 10,000 shares issued and outstanding	$ 32,500
Common shares, unlimited authorization, 230,000 shares issued and outstanding	100,000
Retained earnings	1,000,000
Total shareholders' equity	$1,132,500

Required

1. Identify the different issues of shares that Reckless has outstanding.
2. Are the preferred shares cumulative or noncumulative? How can you tell?
3. Give two summary journal entries to record issuance of all the Reckless shares on August 31, 2020. All the shares were issued for cash. Explanations are not required.
4. Assume that preferred dividends are in arrears for 2019. Record the declaration of a $15,000 dividend on December 31, 2020. Use separate Dividends Payable accounts for preferred shares and common shares.

P13–6B Tijiu Broadcasting Inc. has 15,000 $2.50 preferred shares and 75,000 common shares outstanding. Tijiu Broadcasting Inc. declared and paid the following dividends during a three-year period: 2018, $45,000; 2019, $0; and 2020, $120,000.

③

Computing dividends on preferred and common shares

Required

1. Compute the total dividends on preferred shares and common shares for each of the three years if
   a. Preferred shares are noncumulative.
   b. Preferred shares are cumulative.
2. For Requirement 1(b), record the declaration of the 2020 dividends on December 28, 2020, and the payment of the dividends on January 17, 2021. Use separate Dividends Payable accounts for preferred shares and common shares.

P13–7B The balance sheet of OWL Corporation reported the following:

③ ④

Analyzing the shareholders' equity of a corporation

Shareholders' Equity	
Preferred shares, redeemable, nonvoting, cumulative, authorized 16,000 shares, liquidation value $350,000	$350,000
Common shares, authorized 200,000 shares, issued 90,000 shares	340,000
Retained earnings	120,000
Total shareholders' equity	$810,000

Notes to the financial statements indicate that 16,000 of the cumulative preferred shares were issued and outstanding. The shares paid a dividend of $1.40. Preferred dividends have not been paid for three years, including the current year. On the balance sheet date, the market value of OWL Corporation's common shares was $3.00 per share.

Required

1. Are the preferred shares cumulative or noncumulative? How can you tell?
2. Which class of shareholders controls the company? Give your reason.
3. What is the total contributed capital of the company?
4. What was the total market value of the common shares?
5. Compute the book value per share of the preferred shares and the common shares.

Recording the issuance
of shares; allocating cash
dividends; calculating
book value; preparing the
shareholders' equity section
of the balance sheet

P13–8B At January 1, 2018, Bohemia Nursery Ltd.'s balance sheet reported the following shareholders' equity:

Shareholders' Equity	
Contributed capital	
Preferred shares, $0.75, cumulative (3 years in arrears), liquidation price of $25, 100,000 shares authorized, 40,000 shares issued and outstanding	$ 800,000
Common shares: Class A, 15,000 shares authorized, issued, and outstanding	120,000
Class B, unlimited number of shares authorized, 75,000 shares issued and outstanding	375,000
Total contributed capital	1,295,000
Retained earnings	300,000
Total shareholders' equity	$1,595,000

The company had the following transactions on the dates indicated:

2018

Dec. 1   The company declared dividends of $170,000, payable on January 14, 2019, to the shareholders of record on December 31, 2018. Indicate the amount that would be payable to the preferred shareholders and to the common shareholders. Class A and Class B shares receive the same per-share dividend.

31   The company reported net income after taxes of $80,000 and closed the Income Summary account.

2019

Jan. 7   The company sold 10,000 preferred shares at $22.50 per share.

14   The company paid the dividend declared on December 1, 2018.

Feb. 14   The company sold 15,000 Class B common shares at $5.00 per share.

Dec. 2   The company declared dividends of $75,000, payable on January 13, 2020, to the shareholders of record on December 31, 2019. Indicate the amount that would be payable to the preferred shareholders and to the common shareholders.

31   The company reported net income after taxes of $63,000 and closed the Income Summary account.

2020

Jan. 13   Paid the dividend declared on December 2, 2019.

Required

1. Record the transactions in the general journal.
2. Prepare the shareholders' equity section of the balance sheet as of the close of business on December 31, 2019.
3. Calculate the book value per share of the preferred shares and of the common shares on December 31, 2019.
4. What was the average price at which the Class A common shares were issued?

P13–9B The accounts and related balances of EOC Corp. at June 30, 2020 are arranged in no particular order:

② ⑤
Preparing a corporation's balance sheet; measuring profitability

Common Shareholders' Equity, June 30, 2019	$200,000	Preferred Shares, $0.20, 10,000 shares authorized, issued and outstanding	29,500
Net income	25,000	Cash	15,000
Total assets, June 30, 2019	410,000	Accounts Receivable, net	52,500
Interest Expense	7,200	Accrued Liabilities	30,000
Property, Plant, and Equipment, net	300,000	Long-term Note Payable	48,500
Common Shares, 500,000 shares authorized; 272,000 shares issued and outstanding	300,000	Inventory	93,500
		Dividends Payable	10,500
Prepaid Expenses	12,000	Retained Earnings	?
Trademark, net	$19,000	Accounts Payable	36,000

Required

1. Prepare the company's classified balance sheet in report format at June 30, 2020.

2. Compute the return on total assets and the return on common shareholders' equity for the year ended June 30, 2020.

3. Do these rates of return suggest strength or weakness? Give your reason.

CHALLENGE PROBLEMS

P13–1C Your friend Bryan McNair has come to you for advice. He has a very successful antiques store that had sales of more than $800,000 in the year just ended. He would like to expand and will need to borrow $350,000 to finance an enlarged inventory. He has learned that he can buy the store adjoining his for $250,000 and estimates that $60,000 of renovations would be needed to make the store compatible with his present store. Expansion would mean adding three or four employees to the current two employees.

①
The pros and cons of incorporation

Bryan's accountant has suggested that he incorporate his business and that Bryan hold all the shares. He has cited several reasons to Bryan, including the benefits of limited liability. Bryan has talked to his banker about the possibility of incorporating; the banker has pointed out that if Bryan does incorporate, the bank will need personal guarantees for any loans Bryan arranges with the bank.

Required Consider Bryan's situation and discuss the pros and cons of incorporation for Bryan. What would you suggest?

P13–2C You have just received $4,000 from an uncle and you have decided to invest the money in shares of Electronic Recycling Inc. (ERI), a company that is listed on the Toronto Stock Exchange. ERI has common shares; cumulative preferred shares; noncumulative, convertible preferred shares; and noncumulative preferred shares.

④ ⑤
Deciding on an investment in shares; evaluating different types of shares

- Common shares are trading at $40.00 and currently are paying a dividend of $2.40 per share.
- Cumulative preferred shares are selling at $50.00 and have a stated dividend of $3.50.
- Convertible preferred shares are selling for $78.50 and are convertible at the rate of 2 common for 1 preferred; the dividend rate is $5.30.
- Noncumulative preferred shares are trading at $25.00 and have a dividend rate of $1.55.

Required Evaluate each of the four different shares as an investment opportunity. After performing your analysis, select which shares you will buy and explain your choice.

Extending Your Knowledge

DECISION PROBLEM

Evaluating alternative ways of raising capital

DP13-1

Kimberly Carlyle and Erron Friesen have written a spreadsheet program (Viacalc) to rival Excel. They need additional capital to market the product, and they plan to incorporate the business. They are considering the capital structure. Their primary goal is to raise as much capital as possible without giving up control of the business. Carlyle and Friesen plan to sell the Viacalc software to the corporation in exchange for 100,000 common shares. The partners have been offered $100,000 for the software.

The corporation's plans for the articles of incorporation include an authorization to issue 10,000 preferred shares and 1,000,000 common shares. Carlyle and Friesen are uncertain about the most desirable features for the preferred shares. Prior to incorporating, the partners have discussed their plans with two investment groups. The corporation can obtain capital from outside investors under either of the following plans:

Plan 1 Group 1 will invest $100,000 to acquire 1,000 shares of $7.50, cumulative preferred shares and $72,000 to acquire 60,000 common shares. Each preferred share will receive 50 votes if preferred dividends are more than two years in arrears.

Plan 2 Group 2 will invest $150,000 to acquire 1,200 shares of $8.50 nonvoting, noncumulative preferred shares.

Required Assume the corporation receives its articles of incorporation.

1. Journalize the issuance of common shares to Kimberly Carlyle and Erron Friesen on July 2.

2. Journalize the issuance of shares to the outsiders on July 3 under both plans.

3. Assume that net income for the first year is $184,000, and total dividends of $34,800 are properly subtracted from retained earnings. Prepare the shareholders' equity section of the corporation's balance sheet under both plans.

4. Recommend one of the plans to Carlyle and Friesen. Give your reasons.

FINANCIAL STATEMENT CASES

② ⑥

Shareholders' equity

2. Yes. Note 15.

FSC13-1

The Indigo Books & Music Inc. fiscal 2017 financial statements appear in Appendix A at the end of this book and on MyLab Accounting. Answer the following questions about the company's share capital:
1. Where can you find information about Indigo's share capital? What classes of shares does Indigo have issued and outstanding? How many shares are authorized and how many are issued and outstanding?

2. Were any shares issued during the year? How do you know?

② ⑥

Shareholders' equity

4. Basic EPS, $2.06

FSC13-2

The TELUS Communications Corp. 2016 financial statements appear on MyLab Accounting. Answer the following questions about the company's share capital:
1. What classes of shares has TELUS issued? How many shares are authorized and how many are issued and outstanding?

2. What change was made to the common shares?

3. What is the book value per share at December 31, 2016? The market price of the shares closed at $42.75 on that date. Why is the market price different from the book value per share?

4. What did TELUS earn per common share in 2016? Where did you find that information?

IFRS Mini-Cases are available in MyLab, Chapter Resources, for Chapters 13, 14, 15, 17, and 18, and highlight the similarities and differences between ASPE and IFRS.

IFRS MINI-CASE

The IFRS Mini-Case is now available online, at **MyLab Accounting** in Chapter Resources.

Try It! Solutions for Chapter 13

1. *Proprietorship*
   - Legally, the owner and the business are one entity.
   - Limited to the life of the proprietor.
   - Unlimited liability of the owner.
   - Management by owner.
   - Business income is included in calculating the owner's taxable income.

   Corporation
   - Separate legal entity.
   - Continuous life.
   - Limited liability of shareholders.
   - Often has separation of ownership and management.
   - Pays corporate income tax.
   - May incur additional costs compared to proprietorships
   - No mutual agency.
   - More government regulation.

2. The authority structure in a corporation typically begins with the *shareholders*, who have the ultimate control in a corporation. The shareholders elect a *board of directors*, who elect a *chairperson of the board*. The board and its chairperson elect a *president* or *chief executive officer (CEO)*, who manages day-to-day operations; then *vice-presidents* are hired.

3. a.

Jul. 31	Cash	200,000	
	Preferred Shares		100,000
	Common Shares		100,000
	To issue 1,000 preferred shares with a stated value of $100 per share, and 2,000 common shares at $50 per share.		

   b.

Contributed capital	
Preferred Shares	$100,000
Common Shares	100,000
Total contributed capital	200,000
Retained earnings	50,000
Total shareholders' equity	$250,000

   c. Converting preferred shares into common shares occurs at the original value of the preferred shares, not at their current market value.

Aug. 26	Preferred Shares	1,000	
	Common Shares		1,000
	To record conversion of 10 preferred shares into 20 common shares (10 preferred shares × $100 each)		

4. a.

2019			
Dec. 16	Retained Earnings	50,000	
	Dividends Payable		50,000
	To declare a dividend on common shares to be paid on January 6, 2020 (200,000 shares × $0.25 per share).		

2020			
Jan. 6	Dividends Payable	50,000	
	Cash		50,000
	To pay the dividend on common shares declared on December 16, 2019.		

   b. The balance in Retained Earnings is $200,000 ($250,000 − $50,000). The declaration on December 16, 2019—not the payment on January 6, 2020—reduces Retained Earnings.

5. a.

Preferred Shares	
Dividends in arrears ($2.00 × 10,000 × 2 years)	$40,000
Current dividend	20,000
Total to Preferred Shareholder	$60,000
Common Shares	
Remainder of dividend ($90,000 − $60,000)	30,000
Total dividend	$90,000

   b. Dividends will reduce Retained Earnings by $90,000.

6. Shareholders' equity allocated to preferred shareholders:

Preferred shares ($13 × 3,500)	$45,500
Dividends in arrears ($0.91 × 3,500 × 5 years)	15,925
Shareholders' equity for preferred shares	$61,425

7. Shareholders' equity allocated to common shareholders:

Total shareholders' equity	$380,000
Less: Shareholders' equity allocated to preferred shareholders	61,425
Shareholders' equity available for common shareholders	$318,575
Book value per common share = ($318,575 ÷ 140,000 shares)	$2.28

8. Return on assets is 12.5 percent:

   (Net income + Interest expense) ÷ Average total assets
   = ($80,000 + $20,000) ÷ [($840,000 + $760,000) ÷ 2]
   = $100,000 ÷ $800,000
   = 0.1250, or 12.50%

9. Return on equity is 20 percent:

   (Net income − Preferred dividends) ÷ Average common shareholders' equity
   = [$80,000 − ($6.00 × 1,000)] ÷ [($380,000 + $360,000) ÷ 2]
   = $74,000 ÷ $370,000
   = 0.2000, or 20.00%

10. The return on equity (ROE) is higher than the return on assets (ROA), which indicates that the company is using leverage favourably.

14 Corporations: Retained Earnings and the Income Statement

CONNECTING CHAPTER 14

LEARNING OBJECTIVES

① Account for stock dividends and stock splits

How do we account for stock dividends and stock splits?

Retained Earnings, page 764
Stock Dividends, page 765
  Reasons for Stock Dividends
  Recording Stock Dividends
Stock Splits, page 767
  Consolidation
  Similarities and Differences between Stock Dividends and Stock Splits

② Account for repurchased shares

Why are shares repurchased, and how do we account for them?

Repurchase of Its Shares by a Corporation, page 769
  Treasury Shares
  Share Repurchases
  Share Repurchase at Average Issue Price
  Share Repurchase below Average Issue Price
  Share Repurchase above Average Issue Price
  Recording the Sale of Repurchased Shares

③ Prepare a detailed corporate income statement

How do we prepare a corporate income statement?

The Corporate Income Statement, page 774
  Continuing Operations and Income Taxes
  Discontinued Operations
  Earnings per Share (EPS)

④ Prepare a statement of retained earnings and a statement of shareholders' equity

How do we prepare a statement of retained earnings and a statement of shareholders' equity?

Statement of Retained Earnings, page 780
Statement of Shareholders' Equity, page 780
  Variations in Reporting Shareholders' Equity
Restrictions on Retained Earnings, page 782
  Appropriations of Retained Earnings
  Limits on Dividends and Share Repurchases

⑤ Account for errors and changes in accounting policy and circumstances

How do we record or report errors or changes?

Changing Financial Statements, page 783
  Errors
  Change in Accounting Policy
  Change in Circumstances

⑥ Identify the impact of IFRS on the income statement and the statement of shareholders' equity

What is the impact of IFRS on the income statement and the statement of shareholders' equity?

The Impact of IFRS on the Income Statement and the Statement of Shareholders' Equity, page 786

The **Summary** for Chapter 14 appears on pages 790–791.
Key Terms with definitions for this chapter's material appear on pages 791–792.

CPA competencies

This text covers material outlined in **Section 1: Financial Reporting of the CPA Competency Map**. The Learning Objectives for each chapter have been aligned with the CPA Competency Map to ensure the best coverage possible.

1.1.2 Evaluates the appropriateness of the basis of financial reporting

1.2.2 Evaluates treatment for routine transactions

1.3.1 Prepares financial statements

Dollarama Inc., Canada's largest dollar store chain, is a retail success story in a market dominated by large American retailers. In 2018 it had over 1,000 locations across Canada. Dollarama carries seasonal and consumable products and general merchandise, all priced at $4 or less.

Dollarama Inc. (listed as DOL on the Toronto Stock Exchange) is a Canadian public corporation. The retail enterprise has its roots in a store started in 1910 by Salim Rossy. His chain of stores was expanded by his son George and again by George's son Larry, who founded Dollarama in its present form in 1992. In 2018 the family stopped managing the business when Larry Rossy was named chairman emeritus and is no longer chairman of the board.

The corporation went public in 2009. Since then, it has continued to be successful. In 2018, they reported a five year earnings per share growth rate of 25.36 percent. One way that companies share these profits is by issuing dividends. Dollarama's shareholders have received steady quarterly dividends each year. In 2018, the dividend was $0.12 per share ($0.48 per share annually), and Dollarama had its sixth consecutive year with a growth in the dividend payment.

Senior managers in a corporation have lots of choices available to help them keep investors interested in purchasing their shares. Dollarama has done this by paying dividends and by buying back shares. In 2017, Dollarama's management announced another "normal course issuer bid" to use the business' excess cash to repurchase 5% of the outstanding shares to cancel them. In 2018, management tried another tactic to keep shareholders happy — they did a stock split.

Chapter 13

introduced corporations and covered the basics of shareholders' equity. We saw that a corporation's balance sheet is the same as that for a proprietorship or a partnership except for the owner's equity section, which is called *shareholders' equity* for a corporation and has some different accounts. The topics covered in Chapter 13 apply to private corporations, whose shares tend to be held by a small number of shareholders and are not traded on a stock exchange, as well as public corporations, whose shares trade on stock exchanges.

All corporations' financial reporting is governed by Canadian generally accepted accounting principles (GAAP). Public corporations are governed by International Financial Reporting Standards (IFRS), which are discussed in Learning Objective 6 in this chapter. Private enterprises have a choice to follow either IFRS or Accounting Standards for Private Enterprises (ASPE). While ASPE forms the basis for this textbook, some examples in this chapter use public corporations to illustrate concepts more easily and to acknowledge that the accounting information students will see in the business press and in everyday dealings will be generated mainly by public corporations.

This chapter takes corporate equity a few steps further, as follows:

Chapter 13 covered	Chapter 14 covers
Contributed capital	Retained earnings
Issuing shares	Repurchasing shares
Cash dividends	Stock dividends and stock splits
Corporate balance sheet	Corporate income statement

Retained Earnings

We have seen that the contributed capital accounts and retained earnings make up the shareholders' equity section of a corporation's balance sheet. We studied contributed capital in Chapter 13. Now let's focus on retained earnings.

Retained Earnings carries the balance of the business's accumulated lifetime net income less all net losses from operations and less all dividends. *Retained* means "held onto" or "kept." The normal balance of Retained Earnings is a credit. A debit balance in Retained Earnings is called a *deficit*. Retained Earnings deficits are not common because they often indicate that the corporation may be facing corporate failure and bankruptcy.

When you read a balance sheet, remember these facts about retained earnings:

Retained Earnings

Net loss	Begin. bal.
Dividends	Net income
	End. bal.

- In a proprietorship, investments, net income, and withdrawals are all recorded in the Capital account. In a corporation, *shareholders' equity is split into contributed capital and retained earnings*. The contributed capital section holds capital invested, or contributed. Retained earnings is used to record net income, net loss, and dividends.

- *Credits to the Retained Earnings account arise only from net income.* Retained Earnings shows how much net income a corporation has earned and retained in the business. Its balance is the cumulative, lifetime earnings of the company less all net losses and all dividends.

- *The Retained Earnings account is not a reservoir of cash.* Retained Earnings represents no particular asset. In fact, the corporation may have a large balance in Retained Earnings but too little cash to pay a dividend.

Retained Earnings is not a cash account. A $500,000 balance in Retained Earnings means that $500,000 of capital has been created by profits left in or reinvested in the business over its lifetime.

  - To *declare* a dividend, the company must have a credit balance in Retained Earnings both before and after the declaration of dividends.

  - To *pay* the dividend, it must have the cash.

- *Retained Earnings' ending balance is computed as follows* (amounts assumed):

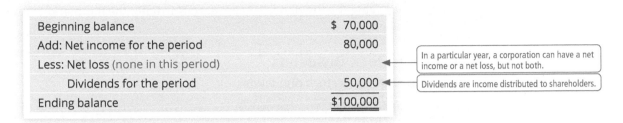

Beginning balance	$ 70,000
Add: Net income for the period	80,000
Less: Net loss (none in this period)	
Dividends for the period	50,000
Ending balance	$100,000

In a particular year, a corporation can have a net income or a net loss, but not both.

Dividends are income distributed to shareholders.

Stock Dividends

LO ①

How do we account for stock dividends and stock splits?

A **stock dividend**, also called a **share dividend**, is a distribution of a corporation's own shares to its shareholders. Stock dividends are fundamentally different from cash dividends because stock dividends do not give any cash to the shareholders. Stock dividends increase Common Shares and decrease Retained Earnings. Both of these accounts are elements of shareholders' equity, so total shareholders' equity is unchanged. There is merely a transfer from Retained Earnings to Common Shares.

To illustrate the effects of a stock dividend, assume Sugar Bay Parts Inc. offered a 10 percent stock dividend to its shareholders. Since 75,000 shares were issued and outstanding before the stock dividend, then 7,500 new shares would be issued as a result of the stock dividend (75,000 × 10% = 7,500). This gives a total of 82,500 shares issued and outstanding after the stock dividend (75,000 + 7,500 = 82,500). Assume the market price of the shares was $1.50 per share on the date of the stock dividend, so the total value of the new 7,500 shares is $11,250.

The shareholders' equity section of Sugar Bay Parts Inc. before and after the stock dividend appears in Exhibit 14–1. Notice the change in the Retained Earnings and Common Shares balances after the stock dividend—each balance has changed by the $11,250 value of the 7,500 shares from the stock dividend. Total shareholders' equity is unchanged.

EXHIBIT 14–1 | Effects of a 10% Stock Dividend

Before		After	
Shareholders' Equity		**Shareholders' Equity**	
Common shares (75,000)	100,000	Common shares (82,500)	$111,250
Retained earnings	$150,000	Retained earnings	$138,750
Total shareholders' equity	$250,000	Total shareholders' equity	$250,000

↑ by $11,250
↓ by $11,250

No change

Suppose you owned 20 percent of Sugar Bay Parts Inc.'s shares before the stock dividend, which is 15,000 shares (75,000 × 20% = 15,000). A 10 percent stock dividend gives you 1,500 new shares (15,000 × 10% = 1,500), for a total of 16,500 shares (15,000 + 1,500 = 16,500). After the stock dividend you still own 20 percent of the total shares (16,500 ÷ 82,500 = 20%). This proves that you are in the same relative ownership position (20 percent ownership) after the stock dividend as you were before the stock dividend.

When a shareholder receives a stock dividend, the shareholder's percentage ownership in the company does not change.

Amount of Retained Earnings Transferred in a Stock Dividend   Stock dividends are said to be **capitalized retained earnings** because they transfer an amount from retained earnings to contributed capital. The contributed capital accounts are more permanent than retained earnings because they cannot be paid out as dividends.

Many shareholders view stock dividends as distributions that are little different from cash dividends.

Stock dividends, like cash dividends, are taxable in the hands of the recipient. The value of the stock dividend is equal to the amount of the increase in the capital of the company paying the dividend. The increase is usually the fair market value of the shares issued.

Reasons for Stock Dividends

Why do companies issue stock dividends?

- *To continue dividends but conserve cash.* A company may wish to continue dividends in some form but may need to keep its cash in the business.

- *To reduce the market price per share of its shares.* For companies whose shares trade on a stock exchange, a stock dividend may cause the market price of a company's shares to fall because of the increased supply of the shares. Dollarama Inc.'s common shares traded at $104 in November 2014. When the company doubled the number of its shares outstanding by issuing a 100 percent stock dividend, the market price of the shares dropped by approximately half to $52.69 per share. The objective of such a large stock dividend would be to make the shares less expensive and thus more affordable and attractive to investors.

Recording Stock Dividends

As with a cash dividend, there are three key dates for a stock dividend:

① Declaration date. The board of directors announces stock dividends on the declaration date. The declaration of a stock dividend does *not* create a liability because the corporation is not obligated to pay out assets. (Recall that a liability is a claim on *assets*.) Instead, the corporation has declared its intention to distribute its shares.

② Date of record.

③ Distribution date.

One concern about stock dividends is how to determine the amount to transfer from Retained Earnings to the Common Shares account. The Canada Business Corporations Act suggests that the market value of the shares issued is the appropriate amount to transfer, while other incorporating acts allow the directors to set a value on the shares. If market value were to be used, it would be the market value on the date the dividend is declared. This is the valuation used in this text.

Assume Tweeter Corporation has the following shareholders' equity prior to a stock dividend:

A cash dividend involves the payment of a current asset (cash). A stock dividend is a distribution of a company's own shares, which are not an asset but rather a component of equity.

Shareholders' Equity	
Contributed capital	
Common shares, 100,000 shares authorized, 40,000 shares issued	$400,000
Retained earnings	100,000
Total shareholders' equity	$500,000

① **Declaration Date** Assume Tweeter Corporation declares a 10 percent common stock dividend on November 17. The company will distribute 4,000 (40,000 × 0.10) shares on December 12. On November 17, the market value of its common shares is $16.00 per share. Using the market value approach, Tweeter Corporation makes the following entry on the declaration date:

Nov. 17	Retained Earnings	64,000	
	Common Stock Dividend Distributable		64,000
	To declare a 10 percent common stock dividend. (40,000 × 0.10 × $16)		

If the company prepares financial statements after the declaration of the stock dividend but before issuing it, Common Stock Dividend Distributable is reported in the shareholders' equity section of the balance sheet immediately after Common Shares. However, this account holds the value of the dividend shares only from the declaration date to the date of distribution.

2 Date of Record No journal entry is made. A list of shareholders is created at this time and they are the ones who will receive the dividend.

3 Distribution Date On the distribution date, the company records issuance of the dividend shares as follows:

Dec. 12	Common Stock Dividend Distributable	64,000	
	Common Shares		64,000
	To issue common shares in a stock dividend.		

The following comparison shows the changes in shareholders' equity caused by the stock dividend:

Shareholders' Equity	Before the Dividend	After the Dividend	Change
Contributed capital			
Common shares, 100,000 shares authorized			
40,000 shares issued	$400,000		
44,000 shares issued		$464,000	Up by $64,000
Total contributed capital	400,000	464,000	**Up by $64,000**
Retained earnings	100,000	36,000	**Down by $64,000**
Total shareholders' equity	$500,000	$500,000	Unchanged

The stock dividend does not affect assets, liabilities, or total shareholders' equity. It merely rearranges the information within the shareholders' equity accounts.

Stock Splits

A **stock split** is fundamentally different from a stock dividend. A stock split increases the number of authorized and outstanding shares with a proportionate reduction in the book value per share. For example, if the company splits its stock 2 for 1, the number of outstanding shares is doubled and each share's book value is halved. Many large companies in Canada—such as Lululemon Athletica Inc., Scotiabank, Royal Bank of Canada, and Loblaw Companies Limited have split their stock.

Assume that the market price of one common share of Marcato Corp. is $100 and that the company wishes to decrease the market price to approximately $50. Marcato decides to split the common shares 2 for 1 in the expectation that the share's market price would fall from $100 to $50. A 2-for-1 stock split means that the company would have two times as many shares outstanding after the split as it had before and that each share's book value would be halved. Exhibit 14–2 shows how a 2-for-1 stock split affects Marcato Corp.'s shareholders' equity:

- It doubles the number of shares authorized and issued.
- It leaves all account balances and total shareholders' equity unchanged.

Stock splits are more common than stock dividends. In 2018, Dollarama chose to offer shareholders a 3-for-1 stock split.

EXHIBIT 14–2 | A 2-for-1 Stock Split

Shareholders' Equity before 2-for-1 Stock Split		Shareholders' Equity after 2-for-1 Stock Split	
Contributed capital		Contributed capital	
Common shares, unlimited number of shares authorized,		Common shares, unlimited number of shares authorized,	
400,000 shares issued and outstanding	$4,000,000	**800,000 shares issued and outstanding**	$4,000,000
Retained earnings	1,800,000	Retained earnings	1,800,000
Total shareholders' equity	$5,800,000	Total shareholders' equity	$5,800,000

Because the stock split affects no account balances, no formal journal entry is necessary. Instead, the split is often recorded in a **memorandum entry**—a note in the journal without debits or credits—such as the following:

Aug. 19	Distributed one new common share for each old share previously outstanding. This increased the number of common shares issued and outstanding from 400,000 to 800,000.

Consolidation

Canada Coal Inc., consolidated its shares in December 2017 when they were selling at 5 cents per share. The 1-for-2 consolidation raised the share price to 9.5 cents on the day of the transaction.

A company may engage in a **consolidation** (or **reverse split**) to decrease the number of shares outstanding and increase the market price per share. For example, Marcato Corp. could consolidate its stock 1 for 4, which would reduce the number of shares issued from 400,000 to 100,000 and increase the share price from, for example, $25 per share to $100 per share. Consolidations are rare but are sometimes done to allow companies to continue trading their shares on stock exchanges that require a minimum share price if the company's share price falls below the minimum.

Similarities and Differences between Stock Dividends and Stock Splits

A 2-for-1 stock split and a 100 percent stock dividend appear remarkably similar on the surface, but there are a number of differences between the two choices.

Similarities

- Both increase the number of shares owned per shareholder.
- Neither a stock dividend nor a stock split changes the investor's total cost of the shares owned. For example, assume you paid $32,000 to acquire 1,000 common shares of LOM Ltd. In both cases, your 1,000 shares increase to 2,000, but your total cost is still $32,000.
- Both a stock dividend and a stock split increase the corporation's number of shares issued and outstanding.
- Both double the outstanding shares and are likely to initially cut the market price per share in half.

Differences

- Stock splits increase the number of shared authorized. Stock dividends do not.
- Stock splits and stock dividends differ in the way they are treated for tax purposes.
  - A stock *split* does not create taxable income to the investor.
  - A stock *dividend* creates taxable income because stock dividends are taxed in the same way as cash dividends. The stock dividend is valued at the market value of the shares on the date the stock dividend is declared, and this amount is included as taxable income. This is one reason why stock dividends are less popular than stock splits; investors must pay income tax on a stock dividend even though no cash is received.
- A stock *dividend* shifts an amount from retained earnings to contributed capital, leaving the total book value unchanged. However, the book value *per share* will decrease because of the increased number of shares outstanding. A stock *split* affects no account balances whatsoever but instead changes the book value of each share.

Exhibit 14–3 provides a summary of the effects of all dividends and stock splits.

EXHIBIT 14–3 | Effects of Dividends and Stock Splits

Effect on:	Cash Dividend	Stock Dividend	Stock Split
Common Shares account	None	Increase	None
Number of common shares issued and outstanding	None	Increase	Increase
Number of shares authorized	None	None	Increase (except when an unlimited number of shares are authorized)
Retained earnings	Decrease	Decrease	None
Total shareholders' equity	Decrease	None	None
Taxes to be paid by a shareholder	Yes	Yes	No
Book value per share	No	Decrease	Decrease

Try It!

1. Beachcomber Pool Supply Inc. has 16,000 common shares outstanding for a total contributed capital value of $48,000. Beachcomber declares a 10 percent stock dividend on July 15 when the market value of its shares is $8 per share. The date of record is August 15 and the distribution date is August 31.

   a. Journalize the declaration of the stock dividend on July 15 and the distribution on August 31.
   b. What is the overall effect on Beachcomber's total assets? On total shareholders' equity? Explain using the accounting equation.
   c. If Beachcomber declared a 2-for-1 stock split instead of a stock dividend, what would be the journal entry on July 15? On August 31?
   d. What would be the effect of the stock split on shareholders' equity?

   Solutions appear at the end of this chapter and on **MyLab Accounting**

Repurchase of Its Shares by a Corporation

Corporations may **repurchase shares** from their shareholders for several reasons:

- The corporation may have issued all its authorized shares and need to recover shares for distributions to officers and employees under bonus plans or share purchase plans.
- The purchase may help support the shares' current market price by decreasing the supply of shares available to the public.
- Management may want a more tax-efficient means of sharing earnings. An increased share price will not trigger an income tax expense, but a cash dividend will.
- The corporation may need to meet share-ownership requirements or limits, which may be a percentage of the total for foreign ownership or some other legislated requirement.

The Canada Business Corporations Act requires a corporation that purchases its own shares to cancel them, or if the number of shares is limited, they maybe restored as authorized but unissued. Most incorporating acts do not permit a corporation to acquire its own shares if such reacquisition would result in the corporation

LO **2**

Why are shares repurchased, and how do we account for them?

It is not unusual for businesses to repurchase their own shares. A *normal course issuer bid* tells the public a repurchase will take place. This is what Dollarama did in 2017 when it bought and then cancelled its own shares.

putting itself into financial jeopardy and being unable to pay its liabilities as they become due.

Treasury Shares

Several of the provincial incorporating acts also require that the shares be cancelled, while other jurisdictions inside and outside of Canada permit the corporation to hold the shares as **treasury shares** (in effect, the corporation holds the shares in its treasury) and resell them. Because of the complex and varied treatment of treasury shares, they are covered more fully in intermediate and advanced accounting courses and will not be covered further in this text.

Share Repurchases

The first step in recording a share repurchase is to calculate the average cost per share. How a share repurchase is recorded depends on whether the shares are repurchased at a price equal to, less than, or greater than the average cost per share. We will examine each of these situations.

Share Repurchase at Average Issue Price

Assume the articles of incorporation for Dawson Resources Ltd., issued under the Canada Business Corporations Act, authorized it to issue 100,000 common shares. By February 29, 2020, Dawson Resources had issued 9,000 shares at an average issue price of $20.00 per share, and its shareholders' equity appeared as follows:

Shareholders' Equity	
Contributed capital	
Common shares, 100,000 shares authorized, 9,000 shares issued and outstanding	$180,000
Retained earnings	24,000
Total shareholders' equity	$204,000

On March 20, 2020, Dawson Resources Ltd. repurchases 1,000 shares at $20.00 per share, an amount equal to the average issue price. The company records the transaction as follows:

2020			
Mar. 20	Common Shares	20,000	
	Cash		20,000
	Purchased 1,000 shares at $20.00 per share.		

The repurchase of its own shares by a company decreases the company's assets (cash) and its shareholders' equity (common shares). The shareholders' equity section of Dawson Resources Ltd.'s balance sheet would appear as follows after the transaction:

Shareholders' Equity	
Contributed capital	
Common shares, 100,000 shares authorized, 8,000 shares issued and outstanding (Note 6)	$160,000
Retained earnings	24,000
Total shareholders' equity	$184,000

Note 6: During the year, the company acquired 1,000 common shares at a price of $20.00 per share; the shares had been issued at $20.00 per share.

Observe that the purchase of the shares decreased the number of shares issued and outstanding. Only *outstanding* shares have a vote, receive cash dividends, and share in assets if the corporation liquidates.

Share Repurchase below Average Issue Price

The *CPA Canada Handbook* requires a company that purchases its own shares at a price less than the *average issue price* to debit Common Shares (or Preferred Shares, as the case may be) for the average issue price. The excess of the average issue price over the purchase price should be credited to a new account: Contributed Surplus—Share Repurchase. (If the company has more than one class or series of shares, the Contributed Surplus—Share Repurchase account name would include the class or series.)

Let's continue the Dawson Resources Ltd. example. On April 30, 2020, Dawson repurchases 1,000 shares at $15.00 per share. The average issue price was $20.00 per share. The company records the transaction as follows:

2020			
Apr. 30	Common Shares	20,000	
	Contributed Surplus—Share Repurchase		5,000
	Cash		15,000
	Purchased 1,000 Shares at $15.00 per share, which is below the average issue price.		

Callouts: Issued at $20 × 1,000 — Excess of issue price over purchase price ($20,000 − $15,000)

The shareholders' equity section of Dawson Resources Ltd.'s balance sheet would appear as follows after the transaction:

Shareholders' Equity	
Contributed capital	
Common shares, 100,000 shares authorized, 7,000 shares issued and outstanding (Note 6)	$140,000
Contributed Surplus—Share Repurchase (Note 7)	5,000
Total contributed capital	145,000
Retained earnings	24,000
Total shareholders' equity	$169,000

Note 7: During the year, the company acquired 1,000 common shares at a price of $20.00 per share and 1,000 common shares at a price of $15.00 per share; the shares had been issued at $20.00 per share.

Dawson Resources Ltd. now has a balance in the Contributed Surplus—Share Repurchase account.

Share Repurchase above Average Issue Price

When a company purchases its own shares at a price greater than the average issue price, the excess should first be debited to Contributed Surplus—Share Repurchase to reduce the balance in this account to $0, and any remaining excess should then be debited to Retained Earnings.

Balance in the Contributed Surplus—Share Repurchase Account Let's continue the Dawson Resources Ltd. example. Suppose Dawson repurchased another 1,000 shares at $30.00 per share on May 10, 2020, and the Contributed Surplus—Share Repurchase account had the balance of $5,000 shown above. The company would reduce the balance in Contributed Surplus—Share Repurchase to nil before reducing the Retained Earnings account, as follows:

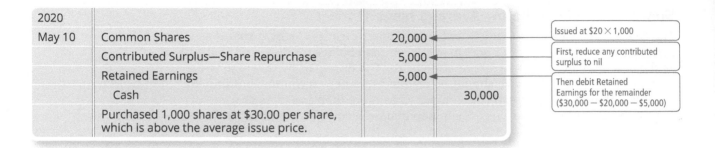

2020			
May 10	Common Shares	20,000	
	Contributed Surplus—Share Repurchase	5,000	
	Retained Earnings	5,000	
	Cash		30,000
	Purchased 1,000 shares at $30.00 per share, which is above the average issue price.		

- Issued at $20 × 1,000
- First, reduce any contributed surplus to nil
- Then debit Retained Earnings for the remainder ($30,000 − $20,000 − $5,000)

The shareholders' equity section of Dawson Resources Ltd.'s balance sheet would appear as follows after the transaction:

Shareholders' Equity	
Contributed capital	
Common shares, 100,000 shares authorized, 6,000 shares issued and outstanding (Note 6)	$120,000
Retained earnings	19,000
Total shareholders' equity	$139,000

Note 6: During the year, the company acquired 1,000 common shares at a price of $20.00 per share, 1,000 common shares at a price of $15.00 per share, and 1,000 common shares at a price of $30.00 per share; the shares had been issued at $20.00 per share.

No Balance in the Contributed Surplus—Share Repurchase Account Suppose Dawson Resources Ltd. had repurchased 1,000 of its shares at $30.00 per share on May 10, 2020, and did not have a balance in the Contributed Surplus—Share Repurchase account. Retained Earnings would be debited for the difference between the purchase price and the issue price, which in this case is $10,000 ($30,000 − $20,000). The journal entry would be as follows:

The repurchase and sale of its own shares do not affect a corporation's net income. A share repurchase affects balance sheet accounts, not income statement accounts.

2020			
May 10	Common Shares	20,000	
	Retained Earnings	10,000	
	Cash		30,000
	Purchased 1,000 shares at $30.00 per share, which is above the average issue price. There is no contributed surplus balance.		

Recording the Sale of Repurchased Shares

A company incorporated under the Canada Business Corporations Act may reissue the shares that it previously had repurchased. The sale would be treated like a normal sale of authorized but unissued shares. The Contributed Surplus—Share Repurchase account is *not* affected when a company sells its own repurchased shares.

Exhibit 14–4 summarizes the journal entries for share repurchases.

EXHIBIT 14–4 | Summary of Journal Entries for Share Repurchases

Repurchase at average issue price:

Date	Account Titles and Explanations	Debit	Credit
	Common Shares	Number repurchased × Average issue price per share	
	Cash		Number repurchased × Price paid per share

Repurchase below average issue price:

Date	Account Titles and Explanations	Debit	Credit
	Common Shares	Number repurchased × Average issue price per share	
	Contributed Surplus—Share Repurchase		Difference between Cash and Common Shares amounts
	Cash		Number repurchased × Price paid per share

Repurchase above average issue price:

Date	Account Titles and Explanations	Debit	Credit
	Common Shares	Number repurchased × Average issue price per share	
	Contributed Surplus—Share Repurchase	Use up the credit balance in this account first	
	Retained Earnings	The amount of any remaining difference (the "plug" amount)	
	Cash		Number repurchased × Price paid per share

In Canada, the maximum prison term for insider trading under the Criminal Code is 10 years.

ETHICS Playing Fair

What would happen if a company repurchased its own shares at $6.00 per share and one day later announced a technological breakthrough that would generate millions of dollars in new business and the share price doubled? The shareholder would claim that, with the knowledge of the technological advance, he or she would have held the shares until after the price increase and been able to sell the shares at a higher price.

Solution

Share repurchase transactions have a serious ethical and legal dimension. A company buying its own shares must be extremely careful that its disclosures of information are complete and accurate. Otherwise, a shareholder who sold shares back to the company may file a lawsuit to claim that he or she was deceived into selling the shares at too low a price.

To keep the stock markets fair for everyone, people who work for public corporations are not allowed to buy or sell shares of the company when the information they have is not available to the public. They may not share this information secretly with their friends. Insiders may buy and sell shares, but they must file reports with securities administrators or else be charged with **insider trading**.

Try It!

2. Whippet Industries Corporation has the following partial balance sheet information available at November 30, 2019:

Shareholders' Equity	
Contributed capital	
Common shares, 400,000 shares authorized, 150,000 shares issued and outstanding	$ 900,000
Retained earnings	700,000
Total shareholders' equity	$1,600,000

If Whippet Industries repurchased 20,000 common shares on March 1, 2020, at a price of $4.50 per share, prepare the journal entry for the transaction.

3. Refer to the previous question. Suppose Whippet Industries repurchased 20,000 shares on March 1, 2020, at a price of $8.25 per share instead of $4.50. Prepare the journal entry for this transaction.

4. Prepare the shareholders' equity section of the balance sheet in question 2 after the repurchase recorded in question 3.

Solutions appear at the end of this chapter and on **MyLab Accounting**

The Corporate Income Statement

LO (3)

How do we prepare a corporate income statement?

As we have seen, the shareholders' equity of a corporation is more complex than the capital of a proprietorship or a partnership. Also, a corporation's income statement includes some features that don't often apply to a proprietorship or a partnership. Most of the income statements you will see belong to corporations, so we turn now to the corporate income statement to explore these new features.

Net income is probably the most important piece of information about a company. Net income measures how successfully the company has operated. To shareholders, the larger the corporation's profit, the greater the likelihood of dividends or share-price increases. To creditors, the larger the corporation's profit, the better able it is to pay its debts. Net income builds up a company's assets and shareholders' equity. It also helps to attract capital from new investors who believe the company will be successful in the future.

A single-step income statement is illustrated in the Summary Problem at the end of this chapter. It does not show the gross margin calculation, nor does it break down other gains/ losses in the same amount of detail as shown here.

Suppose you are considering investing in the shares of Dollarama Inc., or a private corporation. You would examine these companies' income statements. Of particular interest is the amount of net income they can expect to earn year after year. To understand net income, let's examine Exhibit 14–5 (on the next page), which presents the multi-step income statement of KLR Technology Inc., a small manufacturer of electronic switching equipment that is owned by a few shareholders who run the company. Its shares do not trade on a stock exchange, so KLR Technology Inc. is a private corporation.

Continuing Operations and Income Taxes

Income from a business's continuing operations helps financial statement users make predictions about the business's future earnings. In the income statement of Exhibit 14–5, the top section reports income from continuing operations. This part of the business is expected to continue from period to period. We may use this information to try to predict that KLR Technology Inc. will earn income of approximately $117,000 next year.

The continuing operations of KLR Technology Inc. include three items deserving explanation:

❶ During 2020, the company had a $20,000 loss on restructuring operations. Restructuring costs include severance pay to laid-off workers, moving expenses for employees transferred to other locations, and environmental cleanup expenses. The restructuring loss is part of continuing operations because KLR Technology Inc. is remaining in the same line of business. But the restructuring loss is highlighted as an "other" item (unusual item) on the income statement because its cause—restructuring—falls outside KLR's main business endeavour, which is selling electronics equipment.

❷ KLR Technology Inc. had a gain on the sale of machinery ($42,000), which is also outside the company's core business activity. It is shown in the continuing operations section because it is related to the machinery, which is used in operations.

EXHIBIT 14–5 | Corporate Income Statement—Multi-Step Format

KLR TECHNOLOGY INC. Income Statement For the Year Ended December 31, 2020				Using two or three columns instead of one is based on preference and not on formatting rules.
Sales revenue			$1,000,000	
Cost of goods sold			480,000	
Gross margin			520,000	
Operating expenses (listed individually)			362,000	
Operating income			158,000	
Other gains (losses)				Continuing operations
❶ Loss on restructuring operations	($20,000)			
❷ Gain on sale of machinery	42,000		22,000	
Income from continuing operations before income tax			180,000	
❸ Income tax expense			63,000	
Income from continuing operations			117,000	
❹ Discontinued operations				
Operating income, $60,000, less income tax of $21,000	39,000			
Gain on disposal, $10,000, less income tax of $3,500	6,500		45,500	Discontinued operations
Net income			$ 162,500	
❺ Earnings per common share (60,000 shares outstanding)				
Income from continuing operations		$	1.95	
Income from discontinued operations			0.76	Earnings per share
Net income		$	2.71	

The gains or losses from any unusual or infrequent transactions that are outside a company's core business activity would be disclosed separately on the income statement as part of income from continuing operations. Other examples in addition to those shown in Exhibit 14–5 could include:

- Gains and losses due to lawsuits
- Losses due to employee labour strikes
- Losses due to floods, fire, or other forces of nature

These items are *not* shown net of tax effects.

❸ Income tax expense ($63,000) has been deducted in arriving at income from continuing operations. The tax corporations pay on their income is a significant expense. The combined federal and provincial income tax rates for corporations varies by the type and size of company, and from province to province. We will use an income tax rate of 35 percent in our illustrations. The $63,000 income tax expense in Exhibit 14–5 equals the pretax income from continuing operations multiplied by the tax rate ($180,000 \times 0.35 = $63,000$).

Businesses operate to generate profits; without profits, a business will not exist for long. The main source of income for an ongoing business must be from regular, continuing operations, not from sources such as selling off a business segment.

After continuing operations, an income statement may include a section for gains and losses from discontinued operations.

Discontinued Operations

Many corporations engage in several lines of business. For example, The Jim Pattison Group of Vancouver is the second largest private corporation in Canada and includes a diverse group of businesses. They include companies that sell illuminated signs, wholesale food, and retail automobiles, while others are involved in packaging, media, and periodical distribution, to name just a few. We call each significant part of a company a **segment of the business.**

A company may sell a segment of its business. Such a sale is not a regular source of income because a company cannot keep on selling its segments indefinitely. The sale of a business segment is viewed as a one-time transaction. Financial analysts and potential investors typically do not include income or loss on discontinued operations in their predictions about a company's future income. The discontinued segments will generate no income in the future.

④ The income statement presents information on the segment that has been disposed of under the heading Discontinued Operations. This section of the income statement is divided into two components:

- Operating income (or loss) from the segment that is disposed of
- Gain (or loss) on the disposal

It is necessary to separate discontinued operations into these two components because the company may operate the discontinued segment for part of the year. This is the operating income (or loss) component; it should include the results of operations of the segment from the beginning of the period to the disposal date. There is usually also a gain (or loss) on disposal.

The tax effect of the discontinued segment's operating income (or loss) is not included in income tax expense ($63,000 in Exhibit 14–5 ❸); rather, it is added or deducted in the discontinued operations part of the income statement ④.

Income Tax   Both the operating income (or loss) and the gain (or loss) on disposal are shown net of tax. This is because income tax is such a significant component of continuing operations and discontinued operations that investors and analysts need to know the tax effects. Operating losses and losses on disposal generate tax benefits because they reduce net income and thus reduce the amount of tax that needs to be paid.

Assume income and gains are taxed at the 35 percent rate. They would be reported as follows:

Discontinued operations	
Operating income $60,000, less income tax, $21,000	$39,000
Gain on disposal, $10,000 less income tax, $3,500	6,500
	$45,500

This presentation appears in Exhibit 14–5. An alternate presentation is shown in this chapter's Summary Problem on page 788.

If the transactions for discontinued operations have not been completed at the company's year end, the gain (or loss) may have to be estimated. To be conservative, the estimated net loss should be recorded in the accounts at year end while an estimated net gain would not be recognized until it was realized.

Discontinued operations are common in business. General Motors decided to stop producing the Saturn line of vehicles, and Molson Coors Brewing Company sold part of its interest in Cervejarias Kaiser, a Brazilian brewing company.

It is important that the assets, liabilities, and operations of the segment can be clearly identified as separate from those of other operations of the company. The notes to the financial statements should disclose fully the nature of the discontinued operations and other relevant information about the discontinued operations, such as revenue to the date of discontinuance.

Earnings per Share (EPS)

For many corporations, the final segment of a corporate income statement presents the company's earnings per share. **Earnings per share (EPS)** is the amount of a company's net income per outstanding common share. While ASPE does not require that corporations disclose EPS figures on the income statement or in a note to the financial statements, many corporations do provide this information because investors and financial analysts sometimes use it to assess a corporation's profitability. EPS is also widely reported in the financial press, so it is important to know how it is calculated and how it is used. Basic EPS is computed as follows:

$$\text{Earnings per share} = \frac{\text{Net income} - \text{Preferred dividends}}{\substack{\text{Weighted average number of} \\ \text{common shares outstanding*}}}$$

* How to calculate the *weighted average number of common shares outstanding* is illustrated below. If there is no change in the number of shares outstanding during the period, then use the total number of common shares outstanding.

If showing a higher EPS is a good thing, what prevents companies from buying back shares just to make the EPS look better? Nothing, really! This is why financial analysis is never done by looking at only one calculation. Prudent investors will look at many different factors when considering where to invest funds.

Just as the corporation lists separately its different sources of income from continuing operations and discontinued operations, it should list separately the EPS figure for income before discontinued operations and net income for the period to emphasize the significance of discontinued operations to a company's overall results.

Consider the income statement of KLR Technology Inc. shown in Exhibit 14–5; in 2020 it had 60,000 common shares outstanding. Income from continuing operations was $117,000 and income from discontinued operations net of tax was $45,500. KLR Technology Inc. could present the following EPS information:

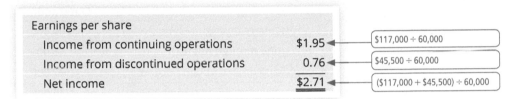

Earnings per share		
Income from continuing operations	$1.95	$117,000 ÷ 60,000
Income from discontinued operations	0.76	$45,500 ÷ 60,000
Net income	$2.71	($117,000 + $45,500) ÷ 60,000

Weighted Average Number of Common Shares Outstanding   Computing EPS is straightforward if the number of common shares outstanding does not change over the entire accounting period. For many corporations, however, this figure varies as the company issues new shares and repurchases its own shares over the course of the year. Consider a corporation that had 100,000 shares outstanding from January through November then purchased 60,000 of its own shares. This company's EPS would be misleadingly high if computed using 40,000 (100,000 − 60,000) shares. To make EPS as meaningful as possible, corporations use the weighted average number of common shares outstanding during the period.

Let's assume the following figures for IMC Corporation. From January through May 2020, the company had 240,000 common shares outstanding; from June through August, 200,000 shares; and from September through December, 210,000 shares. We compute the weighted average by considering the outstanding shares per month as a fraction of the year:

Remember that this is a *weighted* average and not a *simple* average. If you calculated the simple average [(240,000 + 200,000 + 210,000) ÷ 3], you would get an answer of 216,667, which is incorrect. The correct answer is 220,000, as shown to the right, because it reflects the fact that there are different amounts of shares held for different lengths of time.

	A	B	C	D	E	F
1	Number of Common Shares Outstanding		Fraction of Year			Weighted Average Number of Common Shares Outstanding
2	240,000	×	$5/12$	(January through May)	=	100,000
3	200,000	×	$3/12$	(June through August)	=	50,000
4	210,000	×	$4/12$	(September through December)	=	70,000
5	Weighted average number of common shares outstanding during 2020				=	220,000

The 220,000 weighted average number of shares would be divided into net income to compute the corporation's EPS.

A quick way to calculate the effect of an x% stock dividend or a 2-for-1 split would be to do the weighted average calculation and then when you get your answer multiply it by the 1.10 factor for a 10% dividend or x2 for a stock split.

Stock Dividends and Stock Splits The calculation of weighted average number of common shares outstanding becomes complicated when there have been stock dividends or stock splits during the year. The number of shares outstanding during the year are restated to reflect the stock dividend or stock split *as if it had occurred at the beginning of the year.*

To illustrate, let's extend the IMC Corporation example above by assuming a stock dividend of 10 percent was effective on September 1. The effect of the 10 percent stock dividend is a multiplier of 1.10 for the period January to August to restate the number of outstanding shares as if the stock dividend had occurred at the beginning of the year. The number of outstanding shares for September to December already reflects the 10 percent stock dividend, so the effect is a multiplier of 1.00 for those months. We compute the weighted average by considering the outstanding shares per month as a fraction of the year:

		A	B	C	D	E	F	G	H
1		Number of Common Shares Outstanding		Effect of Stock Dividend		Fraction of Year			Weighted Average Number of Common Shares Outstanding
2		240,000	×	1.10	×	5/12	(January through May)	=	110,000
3		200,000	×	1.10	×	3/12	(June through August)	=	55,000
4		231,000	×	1.00	×	4/12	(September through December)	=	77,000
5		Weighted average number of common shares outstanding during 2020						=	242,000

This recalculates shares the rest of the year as if also 10% higher.

Amount includes the 10 percent stock dividend on 210,000 shares.

The 242,000 weighted average number of common shares outstanding would be divided into net income to compute the corporation's EPS.

To illustrate the results of a stock split, change the IMC Corporation example above by assuming a 2-for-1 stock split on September 1, 2020, instead of the 10 percent stock dividend shown above. The effect of the 2-for-1 stock split is 2.00, which doubles the number of shares for the period January to August to restate the number of outstanding shares as if the stock split had occurred at the beginning of the year. The number of outstanding shares for September to December already reflects the 2-for-1 stock split, so the effect is 1.00 for those months. Again, we compute the weighted average by considering the outstanding shares per month as a fraction of the year:

		A	B	C	D	E	F	G	H
1		Number of Common Shares Outstanding		Effect of Stock Split		Fraction of Year			Weighted Average Number of Common Shares Outstanding
2		240,000	×	2.00	×	5/12	(January through May)	=	200,000
3		200,000	×	2.00	×	3/12	(June through August)	=	100,000
4		420,000	×	1.00	×	4/12	(September through December)	=	140,000
5		Weighted average number of common shares outstanding during 2020						=	440,000

This recalculates shares the rest of the year as if doubled.

Amount includes the 2-for-1 stock split of the 210,000 shares.

The 440,000 weighted average number of common shares outstanding would be divided into net income to compute the corporation's EPS.

Preferred Dividends Holders of preferred shares have no claim to the business's income beyond the stated preferred dividend. Even though preferred shares have no claims, preferred dividends do affect the EPS figure. Preferred dividends declared in the year are deducted from income to more accurately reflect what is left to be shared by the common shareholders. There is an exception to this rule if there are cumulative preferred shares. For cumulative preferred shares, the annual dividend is deducted in the formula even if it has not been declared.

Dividends in arrears are not used in the EPS calculation. Only current dividends *declared* or the annual amount of cumulative preferred dividends (even if not declared) are deducted from net income.

If KLR Technology Ltd. (from Exhibit 14–5) had 10,000 cumulative preferred shares outstanding, each with a $1.50 dividend, the annual preferred dividend would be $15,000 (10,000 × $1.50). The $15,000 would be subtracted from income, resulting in the following EPS computations:

Earnings per common share		
Income from continuing operations	$1.70	($117,000 − $15,000) ÷ 60,000
Income from discontinued operations	0.76	$45,000 ÷ 60,000
Net income	$2.46	($162,500 − $15,000) ÷ 60,000

Dilution   Some corporations make their bonds or preferred shares more attractive to investors by offering **conversion privileges**, which permit the holder to convert the bond or preferred shares into some specified number of common shares. If in fact the bonds or preferred shares are converted into common shares, then the EPS will be diluted (reduced) because more common shares are divided into net income. Because convertible bonds or convertible preferred shares can be traded for common shares, the common shareholders want to know the amount of the decrease in EPS that would occur if conversion took place. To provide this information, corporations with convertible bonds or convertible preferred shares outstanding present two sets of EPS amounts:

- EPS (**basic EPS**).
- EPS based on outstanding common shares plus the number of additional common shares that would arise from conversion of the convertible bonds and convertible preferred shares into common shares (**fully diluted EPS**). Fully diluted EPS is always lower than basic EPS.

The topic of dilution can be complex and is covered more fully in intermediate accounting texts.

Price–Earnings Ratio   EPS is one of the most widely used accounting figures. By dividing the market price of a company's share by its EPS, we compute a statistic called the **price–earnings ratio** or *price-to-earnings ratio*.

$$\text{Price–earnings ratio} = \frac{\text{Market price per common share}}{\text{Earnings per share}}$$

Calculated as (Net income − Preferred dividends) ÷ Weighted average number of common shares outstanding

Several websites as well as the business press, such as the *Globe and Mail Report on Business,* report the price–earnings ratios (listed as P/E) daily for companies listed on stock exchanges. The price–earnings ratio is explored more fully in Chapter 18.

Try It!

5. On September 1, 2020, Acme Equipment Corp. sells its division that manufactures mobile homes. The assets are sold at a taxable gain of $1,700,000. The loss from operations for the year up to the date of sale was $960,000. The tax rate is 30 percent. How would you present the loss for the year and the sale of the division on the income statement for the year ended December 31, 2020?
6. The net income of Hart Corp. amounted to $3,750,000 for the year ended December 31, 2020. Hart Corp. had 200,000 $9.00 cumulative preferred shares throughout the year, and 310,000 common shares at the end of the year. At January 1, 2020, Hart Corp. had 270,000 common shares outstanding and issued 40,000 common shares on April 1. Calculate Hart Corp.'s EPS.

Solutions appear at the end of this chapter and on **MyLab Accounting**

Statement of Retained Earnings

LO ④

How do we prepare a statement of retained earnings and a statement of shareholders' equity?

Retained earnings may be a significant portion of a corporation's shareholders' equity. It is so important that some corporations prepare a separate financial statement outlining the major changes in this equity account. The statement of retained earnings for KLR Technology Inc. appears in Exhibit 14–6.

EXHIBIT 14–6 | Statement of Retained Earnings

KLR TECHNOLOGY INC. Statement of Retained Earnings For the Year Ended December 31, 2020	
Retained earnings, January 1, 2020	$260,000
Net income for 2020	162,500
	422,500
Less: Dividends for 2020	42,000
Retained earnings, December 31, 2020	$380,500

Some companies report income and retained earnings on a single statement. Exhibit 14–7 illustrates how KLR Technology Inc. would combine its income statement and its statement of retained earnings.

EXHIBIT 14–7 | Statement of Income and Retained Earnings

	KLR TECHNOLOGY INC. Statement of Income and Retained Earnings For the Year Ended December 31, 2020	
Income statement	Sales revenue	$1,000,000
	Cost of goods sold	480,000
	Gross margin	520,000
	Operating expenses (listed individually)	362,000
Statement of Retained Earnings	Net income for 2020	162,500
	Retained earnings, January 1, 2020	260,000
		422,500
	Less: Dividends for 2020	42,000
	Retained earnings, December 31, 2020	$ 380,500
60,000 shares outstanding and no preferred dividends declared or cumulative	Earnings per common share	
	Income from continuing operations	$1.95
	Income from discontinued operations	0.76
	Net income	$2.71

Statement of Shareholders' Equity

In addition to the balance sheet and income statement, corporations that follow APSE *may* prepare a **statement of shareholders' equity**, or simply a **statement of equity**, to present changes in all components of equity, much as the statement of owner's equity presents information on changes in the equity of a proprietorship. The statement of shareholders' equity for KLR Technology Inc. appears in Exhibit 14–8, with some additional explanations.

EXHIBIT 14–8 | Statement of Shareholders' Equity

KLR TECHNOLOGY INC.
Statement of Shareholders' Equity
For the Year Ended December 31, 2020

	Common Shares	Contributed Surplus— Share Repurchases	Retained Earnings	Total Shareholders' Equity
Balance, December 31, 2019	$360,000	$ 0	$260,000	$620,000
Issuance of shares	100,000			100,000
Net income			162,500	162,500
Cash dividends			(42,000)	(42,000)
Repurchase of common shares	(40,000)	10,000		(30,000)
Balance, December 31, 2020	$420,000	$10,000	$380,500	$810,500

Annotations:
- Begins with the previous year's shareholders' equity balances. Showing the date as January 1, 2020 is also acceptable.
- Sales and repurchases of shares during the year may affect contributed capital.
- The year's income increases the Retained Earnings balance.
- Dividends decrease Retained Earnings.
- This information is from the statement of retained earnings in Exhibit 14–6.

Variations in Reporting Shareholders' Equity

Accountants sometimes report shareholders' equity in ways that differ from our examples. We use a detailed format in this book to help you learn the components of shareholders' equity. Companies assume that investors and creditors understand the details.

An important skill you will learn in this book is how to be comfortable with the information presented in the financial statements of actual companies as it sometimes differs from the examples used for teaching. In Exhibit 14–9, we present a side-by-side comparison of our teaching format and a format adapted from the 2017 annual report of Canadian Tire Corporation, Limited.

EXHIBIT 14–9 | Formats for Reporting Shareholders' Equity*

Textbook Format		Real-World Format	
Shareholders' Equity ($ amounts in millions)		**Equity ($ amounts in millions)**	
Contributed capital			
Preferred shares, 100,000,000 authorized, 63,066,561 issued and outstanding ❹	$ 0.2		
		Share capital (Note 25) ❶ ❷	$ 615.7
Common shares, 3,423,366 authorized, issued, and outstanding	615.5		
Contributed surplus	2.9	Contributed surplus	2.9
		Accumulated other comprehensive income loss	(37.5)
Retained earnings	4,131.8	Retained earnings	4,169.3
Total shareholders' equity	$4,750.4	Equity attributable to owners of the Company ❸	$4,750.4

Note 25: Share Capital (adapted) Authorized
3,423,366 Common Shares
100,000,000 Class A Non-Voting Shares
Issued
3,423,366 Common Shares
63,066,561 Class A Non-Voting Shares

*ASPE and IFRS suggest the presentation of comparative data; in order to simplify the illustration, data are presented for 2017 only.

❶ Canadian Tire uses the heading Share Capital instead of Contributed Capital.
❷ Some companies combine all classes of contributed capital into a single line item and provide specifics in the notes to the financial statements.
❸ Often total shareholders' equity is not specifically labelled using that term.
❹ If this were a statement for a private enterprise following ASPE, the number of authorized shares would not need to be disclosed.

Restrictions on Retained Earnings

To ensure that corporations maintain a minimum level of shareholders' equity for the protection of creditors, incorporating acts restrict the amount of its own shares that a corporation may repurchase and the amount of dividends that can be declared. In addition, companies may voluntarily create reserves, or *appropriations*. Companies report their restrictions in notes to the financial statements.

Appropriations of Retained Earnings

Appropriations are restrictions of retained earnings that are recorded by formal journal entries. A corporation may appropriate—that is, segregate in a separate account—a portion of retained earnings for a specific use. For example, the board of directors may appropriate part of retained earnings for expanding a manufacturing plant. A debit to Retained Earnings and a credit to a separate account—Retained Earnings Restricted for Plant Expansion—records the appropriation. Appropriated Retained Earnings is normally reported directly above the regular Retained Earnings account, with a footnote where the appropriation is more fully described. *Retained earnings appropriations are rare.* Presentation of this information on the balance sheet may take this form:

Shareholders' Equity		
Total contributed capital		$325,000
Retained earnings		
Appropriated for plant expansion	$125,000	
Unappropriated	50,000	
Total retained earnings		175,000
Total shareholders' equity		$500,000

Or the retained earnings could be shown with a notation that refers the reader to the notes for more details:

Shareholders' Equity	
Total contributed capital	$325,000
Retained earnings (Note X)	175,000
Total shareholders' equity	$500,000

Note X: The board of directors appropriated part of Retained Earnings to expand a manufacturing plant.

Limits on Dividends and Share Repurchases

Cash dividends and repurchases of shares require a cash payment. In fact, repurchases of shares are returns of their investment to the shareholders. These outlays decrease assets, so the corporation has fewer resources to pay liabilities. A bank may agree to lend $500,000 only if the borrowing corporation limits dividend payments and repurchases of its shares. A corporation might agree to restrict dividends as a condition for receiving a loan in order to get a lower interest rate.

This type of restriction on the payment of dividends is more often seen, as shown in the following note:

> **Restriction on Dividends:** Certain terms of the Company's preferred shares and debt instruments could restrict the Company's ability to declare dividends on preferred and common shares. At year end, such terms did not restrict or alter the company's ability to declare dividends.

Try It!

7. Complete the following statement of shareholders' equity by calculating the missing amounts a, b, c, and d.

CHECKPOINT INDUSTRIES INC.
Statement of Shareholders' Equity
For the Year Ended April 30, 2020

	Common Shares	Contributed Surplus—Share Repurchases	Retained Earnings	Total Share-holders' Equity
Balance, April 30, 2019	$260,000	$ 0	(a)	$360,000
Issuance of shares	100,000			100,000
Net income			62,500	(c)
Cash dividends			(22,000)	(22,000)
Repurchase of common shares	(60,000)	(b)		(50,000)
Balance, April 30, 2020	$300,000	$10,000	$140,500	(d)

Changing Financial Statements

LO ⑤

How do we record or report errors or changes?

The consistency principle is an important concept in accounting. But what if situations change and information on financial statements needs to be reported differently? Management might feel a different accounting method would provide better information to investors. Perhaps an error was made. Depending on the reason for the change, there are two ways this should be handled—with either *retrospective* treatment (looking back) or *prospective* treatment (looking forward).

Errors

What happens when a company makes an error in recording revenues or expenses? Detecting the error in the period in which it occurs allows the company to make a correction before preparing that period's financial statements. But failure to detect the error until a later period means that the business will have reported an incorrect amount of income on its income statement. After the revenue and expense accounts are closed, the Retained Earnings account will absorb the effect of the error, and its balance will be wrong until the error is corrected.

The **prior-period adjustment** to correct the error includes a debit or credit to Retained Earnings for the error amount and a debit or credit to the asset or liability account that was misstated.

Assume that Paquette Corporation recorded the closing inventory balance for 2019 as $30,000. When the inventory records were checked, it was discovered that the correct amount was $40,000. This error resulted in overstating 2019 expenses

Canopy Growth Corporation (listed on the Toronto Stock Exchange as "WEED") restated their 2016 loss of $16.7 million to a loss of $7.6 million in 2017.

by $10,000 and understating net income by $10,000. The entry to record this error correction in 2020 is as follows:

Jun. 19	Inventory	10,000	
	Retained Earnings		10,000
	Correction of prior years' error in recording closing inventory in 2019.		

The credit to Retained Earnings adjusts its account balance to reflect the understated income in 2019. If Cost of Goods Sold were credited in 2020 when the correcting entry was recorded, income in 2020 would be overstated. The journal entry properly locates the adjustment in the period prior to 2020 (i.e., to 2019, when the error occurred). This is an example of **retrospective** treatment because numbers from the prior year are restated to reflect the correction of the error. However, instead of restating prior financial statements, the opening balance of Retained Earnings is adjusted for the error.

The error correction would appear on the statement of retained earnings as shown below, or on the statement of shareholders' equity in the Retained Earnings section (shown in the Summary Problem for Your Review on page 788):

PAQUETTE CORPORATION Statement of Retained Earnings For the Year Ended December 31, 2020	
Retained earnings, January 1, 2020, as originally reported	$390,000
Adjustment to correct error in recording closing inventory in 2019	10,000
Retained earnings, January 1, 2020, as adjusted	400,000
Net income for 2020	114,000
	514,000
Less: Dividends for 2020	41,000
Retained earnings balance, December 31, 2020	$473,000

Change in Accounting Policy

The accounting framework principle of consistency (introduced in Chapter 6) reminds us that changes in policy should not happen too often.

A change in accounting policy should be applied *retrospectively*; in other words, prior periods should be restated to reflect the change. This would be done by restating any prior periods' comparative data provided in the current year's financial statements (not by reprinting the financial statements or annual reports from prior years). In addition, the facts of the restatement should be disclosed in the notes. An example would be a change in amortization method from straight line to units of production when the change results in the provision of more relevant information for users. The effect of the change on prior periods' results would appear as an item on the statement of retained earnings or on the statement of shareholders' equity in the Retained Earnings section, the same way an error would.

Change in Circumstances

Companies must make estimates about many items on the financial statements, such as the amount of warranties or bad debts, inventory obsolescence, or the useful life of assets for amortization. If these estimates need to change to better reflect a change in circumstances based on new information, then the changes are made to the current year and all future financial statements. This **prospective** treatment is in response to new information and is done to make the information more useful. There is no change to past financial statements because the estimates at that time were correct based on what was known at that time.

Try It!

8. Identify whether each of the following independent cases is a correction of an error, a change in policy, or a change in estimate, *and* indicate whether there should be retrospective or prospective changes to the financial statements of CP Industries Inc. for three unrelated situations.

Situation	Change in estimate	Change in policy	Error	Retrospective Statement	Prospective Statement
A. Accountants felt it provided better information for readers and changed to use the units-of-production method of amortization for its vehicles rather than the straight-line method that had been used so far.					
B. Management decided that its equipment would last three years longer than it had originally anticipated.					
C. During 2020, the accountant discovered that a supplies invoice in the amount of $16,500 had not been recorded in 2019.					

Solutions appear at the end of this chapter and on **MyLab Accounting**

Why It's Done This Way

In this chapter you were introduced to new features presented on most corporate income statements, specifically the separation of income from continuing and discontinued operations, and earnings per share calculations. As we have seen in earlier chapters, the multi-step income statement is designed to communicate *useful* information to interested users to help them assess the success of the company—this is the objective of the accounting framework. The multi-step income statement approach is a useful tool for users for the *relevance* and *comparability* features of the information contained in the statement, as well as the format of the statement.

Users of the financial statements want to assess the future profitability of the company and will use the income statement to achieve that objective. Users are also interested in assessing management's *stewardship* of the company. *Stewardship* is the concept of how well management uses the company's assets to meet company objectives such as earning a profit, serving specific markets, treating employees fairly, minimizing risks that face the company, and providing a good return to shareholders. Conveniently, the corporate multi-step income statement allows both objectives to be achieved. Future profitability can be estimated by studying the income from continuing operations, the ongoing operations that should continue into the future. Reporting unusual or infrequent activities separately on the income statement as part of ongoing operations helps users adjust their estimates of future profitability even more.

LO (6)

What is the impact of IFRS on the income statement and the statement of shareholders' equity?

ASPE	IFRS
The statements are less complex and require fewer disclosures because it is assumed that private corporation shareholders and lenders can get access to the information they need directly from the corporation.	Typically, shareholders and lenders need more information (disclosure) because they do not have access to this information any other way.
Does not require that an accounting policy change only be made under specific circumstances.	May only change an accounting policy if it meets the criteria of providing more *relevant* or *reliable* information.
When there is a retrospective restatement of information, the change is reported by restating any prior periods' comparative data in the current financial statements.	When there is a retrospective restatement of information, a statement of financial position must be prepared for the earliest period in which the accounting policy change resulted in a restated balance or a reclassified item.
Section 1506 of the *CPA Canada Handbook* for ASPE does not allow corporations to be exempt from restating financial information retroactively.	In International Accounting Standard (IAS) 8, a corporation may be exempt from restating financial information retroactively if it is *impractical* to do so.
EPS information is not required on the income statement. However, many private corporations do provide EPS information for current and potential investors.	IFRS requires companies to disclose EPS information on the income statement. It must be shown separately for both basic and diluted amounts, and results from continuing and discontinued operations must be shown separately, even if the results are negative.
Companies may prepare a statement of shareholders' equity.	Companies prepare a statement of changes in equity rather than a statement of retained earnings. The statement of changes in equity is similar to the statement of shareholders' equity described in this chapter.
Companies are not required to report **other comprehensive income**. Other comprehensive income arises from a number of sources, including unrealized gains and losses on certain classes of investment securities due in part to the use of fair value measurement.	Corporations are required to report *other comprehensive income*. May choose to prepare an income statement and a separate statement of comprehensive income, or combine this information into one statement. Exhibit 14–11 shows how the same information can be presented two different ways for the same company. Notice that the amount of income tax is shown separately for each component.

EXHIBIT 14-11 | Examples of a Consolidated Statement of Earnings and Comprehensive Income, and a Statement of Comprehensive Income

WEEKEE INDUSTRIES LIMITED
Consolidated Statement of Earnings and Comprehensive Income
For the Years Ended March 31, 2020 and 2019

	2020	2019
Profit before income tax	$ 799,500	$ 705,600
Income tax expense	239,850	211,680
Profit from continuing operations	559,650	493,920
Discontinued operations		
Profit (loss) from discontinued operation net of income tax	38,000	
Profit	597,650	493,920
Other comprehensive income		
Foreign currency translation differences		
for foreign operations, net of income tax	8,000	2,000
Net change in fair value of available-for-sale		
financial assets, net of income tax	9,250	7,500
Other comprehensive income for the period, net of income tax	17,250	9,500
Comprehensive income	$ 614,900	$ 503,420

WEEKEE INDUSTRIES LIMITED
Consolidated Statement of Earnings and Comprehensive Income
For the Years Ended March 31, 2020 and 2019

	2020	2019
Continuing operations		
Revenue	$1,650,000	$1,400,000
Cost of sales	750,000	600,000
Gross profit	900,000	800,000
Administrative expenses	50,000	45,000
Distribution expenses	30,000	27,000
Research and development expenses	15,000	13,000
Other expenses	5,000	9,000
Results from operating activities	800,000	706,000
Finance income	1,000	800
Finance costs	(1,500)	(1,200)
Net finance costs	(500)	(400)
Profit before income tax	799,500	705,600
Income tax expense	239,850	211,680
Profit from continuing operations	559,650	493,920
Discontinued operations		
Profit (loss) from discontinued operation, net of income tax	38,000	
Profit for the period	597,650	493,920
Other comprehensive income		
Foreign currency translation differences		
for foreign operations, net of income tax	8,000	2,000
Net change in fair value of available-for-sale		
financial assets, net of income tax	9,250	7,500
Other comprehensive income for the period, net of income tax	17,250	9,500
Total comprehensive income for the period	$ 614,900	$ 503,420
Earnings per share		
Basic earnings per share	$ 3.15	$ 2.58
Earnings per share from continuing operations	$ 2.87	$ 2.53

Note: Earnings per share is presented as part of the income statement if the income statement is separate from the statement of comprehensive income.

Expense presentation by nature would include depreciation, transportation costs, and advertising, whereas by function these would be shown on the income statement as administrative costs, distribution costs, and selling costs.

Summary Problem for Your Review

The following information was taken from the ledger of Kajal Exports Ltd. at December 31, 2020:

Loss on sale of discontinued operations	$ 20,000
Prior year error—credit to Retained Earnings	5,000
Gain on sale of property	61,000
Income tax expense, continuing operations	42,000
Income tax expense, discontinued operations-operating income	10,500
Income tax savings, discontinued operations-loss on sale	(7,000)
Total dividends	19,000
Retained earnings, January 1, 2020, as originally reported	108,000
Selling expenses	78,000
Common shares, 40,000 shares issued and outstanding	125,000
Sales revenue	620,000
Interest expense	30,000
Cost of goods sold	380,000
Operating income, discontinued operations	30,000
Loss due to lawsuit	11,000
General expenses	62,000
Preferred shares, $4.00, cumulative, 1,000 shares issued and outstanding	50,000

Required

Prepare a single-step income statement first, then a statement of retained earnings, then a statement of shareholders' equity for Kajal Exports Ltd. for the year ended December 31, 2020. Include the EPS presentation and show computations. List expenses in alphabetical order. Assume no changes in the share accounts during the year, and assume a 35 percent tax rate.

SOLUTION

KAJAL EXPORTS LTD.
Income Statement
For the Year Ended December 31, 2020

Revenue and gains			
Sales revenue			620,000
Gain on sale of property			61,000
Total revenues and gains			681,000
Expenses and losses			
Cost of goods sold		$380,000	
General expenses		62,000	
Income tax expense		42,000	
Interest expense		30,000	
Loss due to lawsuit		11,000	
Selling expenses		78,000	
Total expenses and losses			603,000
Income from continuing operations			78,000
Discontinued operations			
Operating income	$ 30,000		
Less income tax expense	(10,500)	19,500	
Loss on sale of discontinued operations	(20,000)		
Less income tax saving	7,000	(13,000)	6,500
Net income			$ 84,500
Earnings per share			
Income from continuing operations			$ 1.85
Income from discontinued operations			0.16
Net income			$ 2.01

Earnings per share = $\dfrac{\text{Net income} - \text{Preferred dividends}}{\text{Weighted average number of common shares outstanding}}$

A single-step income statement shows cost of goods sold as an expense and does not show the calculation for gross profit. In addition, gains and losses are shown as part of income from continuing operations and not as a separate section. A multi-step version is illustrated in Exhibit 14–5 on page 775.

Expenses include all normal operating costs related to the revenue reported. Income tax expense is included here.

Discontinued operations are reported net of income tax of 35 percent. Exhibit 14–5 on page 775 shows an alternative layout for this section.

Preferred dividends:
1,000 × $4.00 = $40,000
[($78,000 − $4,000) ÷ 40,000 shares]
($6,500 ÷ 40,000 shares)
[($84,500 − $4,000) ÷ 40,000 shares]

KAJAL EXPORTS LTD.
Statement of Retained Earnings
For the Year Ended December 31, 2020

Retained earnings, January 1, 2020, as originally reported	$108,000
Correction of prior year error—credit	5,000
Retained earnings, January 1, 2020, as adjusted	113,000
Net income for current year	84,500
	197,500
Less: Dividends for 2020	19,000
Retained earnings, December 31, 2020	$178,500

Prior period adjustments must be disclosed in a separate line in the statement of retained earnings.

The Retained Earnings column of the statement of shareholders' equity contains the same information as the statement of retained earnings created earlier.

KAJAL EXPORTS LTD.
Statement of Shareholders' Equity
For the Year Ended December 31, 2020

	Common Shares	Preferred Shares	Retained Earnings	Total Share-holders' Equity
Balance, January 1, 2020	$125,000	$50,000	$108,000	$283,000
Adjustment to correct error			5,000	5,000
Net income			84,500	84,500
Cash dividends			(19,000)	(19,000)
Balance, December 31, 2020	$125,000	$50,000	$178,500	$353,500

Using December 31, 2019, as the date is also acceptable practice.

Summary

Learning Objectives

(1) Account for stock dividends and stock splits Pg. 765

How do we account for stock dividends and stock splits?

- *Stock dividends*, or *share dividends*, are distributions of the corporation's own shares to its shareholders. At the date of declaration, the following journal entry would be made:

Date	Retained Earnings	Market value ($)	
	Common Stock Dividend Distributable		Market value ($)

- *Stock dividends* have the following effects:

  ↓ Retained Earnings ↑ Common Shares Total Shareholders' Equity is unchanged by a stock dividend

- *Stock splits* do not change any account balances.

(2) Account for repurchased shares Pg. 769

Why are shares repurchased, and how do we account for them?

- *Repurchased shares* are the corporation's own shares that have been issued and reacquired by the corporation.

Repurchase at average issue price:

Date	Account Titles and Explanations	Debit	Credit
	Common Shares	Number repurchased × Average issue price per share	
	Cash		Number repurchased × Price paid per share

Repurchase below average issue price:

Date	Account Titles and Explanations	Debit	Credit
	Common Shares	Number repurchased × Average issue price per share	
	Contributed Surplus— Share Repurchase		Difference between Cash and Common Shares amounts
	Cash		Number repurchased × Price paid per share

Repurchase above average issue price:

Date	Account Titles and Explanations	Debit	Credit
	Common Shares	Number repurchased × Average issue price per share	
	Contributed Surplus— Share Repurchase	Use up the credit balance in this account first	
	Retained Earnings	The amount of any remaining difference (the "plug" amount)	
	Cash		Number repurchased × Price paid per share

③ Prepare a detailed corporate income statement Pg. 774

How do we prepare a corporate income statement?
- The corporate *income statement* lists separately the various sources of income—*income from continuing operations* (which includes unusual gains and losses) and *discontinued operations*—as well as related *income tax expense*.
- The bottom line of the income statement reports *net income* or *net loss* for the period. *Earnings per share* figures may also appear on the income statement.
- Earnings per share is calculated as follows:

$$\text{Earnings per share} = \frac{\text{Net income} - \text{Preferred dividends}}{\text{Weighted average number of common shares outstanding}}$$

④ Prepare a statement of retained earnings and a statement of shareholders' equity Pg. 780

How do we prepare a statement of retained earnings and a statement of shareholders' equity?
- A corporation must prepare a statement of retained earnings, which reports the changes in the Retained Earnings account, including prior period adjustments, net income or net loss, and dividends paid. This statement may be combined with the income statement.
- Corporations may prepare a statement of shareholders' equity, which reports the changes in all the shareholders' equity accounts, including sales and repurchases of a corporation's own shares, cash and stock dividends paid, and net income or loss.

⑤ Account for errors and changes in accounting policy and circumstances Pg. 783

How do we record or report errors or changes?
- Retrospective: Restate prior periods to reflect the change. Required for errors and changes in accounting policies.
- Prospective: Change only current and future years for a change when there is a change in estimates to reflect a change in circumstances.

⑥ Identify the impact of IFRS on the income statement and the statement of shareholders' equity Pg. 786

What is the impact of IFRS on the income statement and statement of shareholders' equity?
- Companies that report under IFRS must present EPS information on their income statement and must report comprehensive income in a statement of comprehensive income.
- Under IFRS, the statement of shareholders' equity is called the statement of changes in equity. No statement of retained earnings is prepared.

Key Terms for the chapter are shown next and are in the **Glossary** at the back of the book. **Similar Terms** are shown after **Key Terms**.

KEY TERMS

Appropriations   Restriction of retained earnings that is recorded by a formal journal entry *(p. 782)*.

Basic EPS   Earnings per share calculated using the number of outstanding common shares *(p. 779)*.

Capitalized retained earnings   Retained earnings that are not available for distribution. Stock dividends result in retained earnings being moved to contributed capital *(p. 765)*.

Consolidation   A decrease in the number of shares outstanding by a fixed ratio. Also called a *reverse split (p. 768)*.

Conversion privileges   Shareholders with this right may exchange specified bonds or shares into a stated number of common shares *(p. 779)*.

Earnings per share (EPS)   The amount of a company's net income per outstanding common share *(p. 776)*.

Fully diluted EPS   Earnings per share calculated using the number of outstanding common shares plus the number of additional common shares that would arise from conversion of convertible bonds and convertible preferred shares into common shares *(p. 779)*.

Insider trading   According to the Canada Business Corporations Act, the purchase/sale of a security by someone who knows information not known by the general public that might affect the price of that security *(p. 773)*.

Memorandum entry   A journal entry without debits and credits *(p. 768)*.

Other comprehensive income   Income that arises from a number of sources, including unrealized gains and losses on certain classes of investment securities due in part to the use of fair value measurement *(p. 786)*.

Price–earnings ratio (or price-to-earnings ratio, or P/E) The market price of a common share divided by the company's earnings per share. Measures the value that the stock market places on $1 of a company's earnings (p. 779).

Prior-period adjustment A correction to Retained Earnings for an error in an earlier period (p. 783).

Prospective In the future. For example, changes in accounting estimates are reflected in future financial statements, *not* in past financial statements (p. 784).

Repurchase shares When a corporation purchases its own shares that it issued previously (p. 769).

Retrospective In the past. For example, changes in accounting policies are reflected in past financial statement figures as if those policies had always been in place (p. 784).

Reverse split Another name for a share *consolidation* (p. 768).

Segment of the business A significant part of a company (p. 776).

Share dividend Another name for a *stock dividend* (p. 765).

Statement of equity Another name for *statement of shareholders' equity* (p. 780).

Statement of shareholders' equity Presents changes in all components of equity. Also called *statement of equity* (p. 780).

Stock dividend A proportional distribution by a corporation of its own shares to its shareholders. Also called a *share dividend* (p. 765).

Stock split An increase in the number of authorized and outstanding shares coupled with a proportionate reduction in the book value of each share (p. 767).

Treasury shares When a corporation repurchases its own shares and holds the shares in its treasury for resale (p. 770).

SIMILAR TERMS

Consolidation	Reverse split
Income Statement	Statement of Earnings
Price–earnings ratio	Price-to-earnings ratio; P/E ratio
Shareholders' equity	Stockholders' equity (US term)
Statement of shareholders' equity	Statement of equity; Statement of changes in equity
Stock dividend	Share dividend

SELF-STUDY QUESTIONS

Test your understanding of the chapter by marking the best answer for each of the following questions:

1. A corporation has total shareholders' equity of $100,000, including Retained Earnings of $48,000. The Cash balance is $50,000. The maximum cash dividend the company can declare and pay is (p. 764)
   a. $48,000
   b. $50,000
   c. $98,000
   d. $100,000

2. A stock dividend, or share dividend, (p. 765)
   a. Decreases shareholders' equity
   b. Decreases assets
   c. Leaves total shareholders' equity unchanged
   d. Does none of the above

3. Wing Corp. has 10,000 common shares outstanding. The shares were issued at $20.00 per share, and now their market value is $40.00 per share. Wing's board of directors declares and distributes a common stock dividend of one share for every 10 held. Which of the following entries shows the full effect of declaration and distribution of the dividend? (p. 766)

a.	Retained Earnings	40,000	
	Common Stock Dividend Distributable		40,000
b.	Retained Earnings	20,000	
	Common Shares		20,000
c.	Retained Earnings	20,000	
	Cash		20,000
d.	Retained Earnings	40,000	
	Common Shares		40,000

4. Roam Inc. declared and distributed a 50 percent stock dividend. Which of the following stock splits would have the same effect on the number of Roam shares outstanding? (p. 767)
   a. 2-for-1
   b. 3-for-2
   c. 4-for-3
   d. 5-for-4

5. Deer Lake Outfitters Ltd. purchased 10,000 of its common shares that had been issued at $1.50 per share, paying $7.00 per share. This transaction (p. 771)
   a. Has no effect on company assets
   b. Has no effect on shareholders' equity
   c. Decreases shareholders' equity by $15,000
   d. Decreases shareholders' equity by $70,000

6. Which of the following items is not reported on the income statement? (p. 774)
   a. Issue price of shares
   b. Unusual gains and losses
   c. Income tax expense
   d. Earnings per share

7. The income statement item that is likely to be most useful for predicting income from year to year is (p. 774)
   a. Unusual items
   b. Discontinued operations
   c. Income from continuing operations
   d. Net income

8. In computing earnings per share (EPS), dividends on cumulative preferred shares are (p. 778)
   a. Added because they represent earnings to the preferred shareholders
   b. Subtracted because they represent earnings to the preferred shareholders
   c. Ignored because they do not pertain to the common shares
   d. Reported separately on the income statement

9. A restriction of retained earnings (p. 782)
   a. Has no effect on total retained earnings
   b. Reduces retained earnings available for the declaration of dividends
   c. Is usually reported by a note
   d. Does all of the above

10. Which of the following financial statements is not required under ASPE? (p. 786)
    a. Statement of retained earnings
    b. Statement of income
    c. Statement of shareholders' equity
    d. Statement of financial position

Assignment Material

MyLab Accounting   Make the grade with MyLab Accounting: The Starters, Exercises, and Problems can be found on MyLab. You can practise them as often as you want, and most feature step-by-step guided instructions to help you find the right answer.

QUESTIONS

1. Identify the two main sections of shareholders' equity and explain how they differ.

2. Identify the account debited and the account credited from the last closing entry a corporation makes each year. What is the purpose of this entry?

3. Hoc Automotive Ltd. reported a Cash balance of $2 million and a Retained Earnings balance of $12 million. Explain how Hoc Automotive Ltd. can have so much more retained earnings than cash. In your answer, identify the nature of retained earnings and state how it ties to cash.

4. Give two reasons why a corporation might distribute a stock dividend.

5. A friend of yours receives a stock dividend on an investment. She believes stock dividends are the same as cash dividends. Explain why the two are not the same.

6. Poly Panels Inc. declares a stock dividend on June 21 and reports Stock Dividend Payable as a liability on the June 30 balance sheet. Is this correct? Give your reason.

7. What value is normally assigned to shares issued as a stock dividend?

8. Explain the similarity and difference between a 100 percent stock dividend and a 2-for-1 stock split to the corporation issuing the stock dividend and the stock split.

9. Give three reasons why a corporation may repurchase its own shares.

10. What effect does the repurchase and cancellation of common shares have on the (a) assets, (b) authorized shares, and (c) issued and outstanding shares of the corporation?

11. Are there any cases when a company does not cancel its repurchased shares? If so, what are they?

12. Why do creditors wish to restrict a corporation's payment of cash dividends and repurchases of the corporation's shares?

13. Why is it necessary to use the *weighted* average number of common shares in the earnings per share calculation rather than the average number of common shares?

14. What is the earnings per share of Jasmine Corp., which had net income of $48,750 and a weighted average number of common shares of 15,000?

15. Why is it important for a corporation to report income from continuing operations separately from discontinued operations?

16. Give four examples of gains and losses that are unusual and reported separately in the continuing operations section of the income statement.

17. What information is recorded on the statement of shareholders' equity?

18. What are two ways to report a retained earnings restriction? Which way is more common?

19. What is a prior-period adjustment?

20. For errors made in prior periods, what account do all corrections affect? On what financial statement are these corrections reported?

STARTERS

①
Interpreting retained earnings

S14–1 The Retained Earnings account has the following transactions for the fiscal year shown in a T-account format:

Retained Earnings	
	150,000
20,000	X
	220,000

1. What does X represent?
2. How much is X?
3. What does the amount of $20,000 represent?

①
Recording a stock dividend

1. Dr Retained Earnings, $36,000

S14–2 Snowist Corp. has 10,000 common shares outstanding. Snowist distributes a 20 percent stock dividend when the market value of its shares is $18.00 per share.
1. Journalize Snowist's declaration of the stock dividend on September 30, 2020, and the distribution of the stock dividend on October 30, 2020. Explanations are not required.
2. What is the overall effect of the stock dividend on Snowist's total assets? On total shareholders' equity?

①
Comparing and contrasting cash dividends and stock dividends

S14–3 Compare and contrast the accounting for cash dividends and stock dividends. In the space provided, insert either "Cash dividends," "Stock dividends," or "Both cash dividends and stock dividends" to complete each of the following statements:
a. _____ decrease Retained Earnings.
b. _____ have no effect on a liability.
c. _____ increase contributed capital by the same amount that they decrease retained earnings.
d. _____ decrease both total assets and total shareholders' equity, resulting in a decrease in the size of the company.

①
Accounting for a stock split

1. Total shareholders' equity, $332,000

S14–4 Jurgen's Farms Inc. recently reported the following shareholders' equity on its balance sheet:

Common shares, 250,000 shares authorized, 55,000 shares issued and outstanding	$121,500
Retained earnings	210,500
Total shareholders' equity	$332,000

Suppose Jurgen's Farms split its common shares 2 for 1 to decrease the market price of its shares. The company's shares were trading at $83.00 immediately before the split.

1. Prepare the shareholders' equity section of Jurgen's Farms Inc.'s balance sheet after the stock split on June 30, 2020.
2. Which account balances changed after the stock split? Which account balances remain unchanged?

S14-5 Happy Valley Potato Corp. issued 100,000 common shares at $12.00 per share. Later, when the market price was $15.00 per share, the company distributed a 10 percent stock dividend. Then Happy Valley Potato Corp. repurchased 500 shares at $20.00 per share. What is the balance in the Common Shares account after these transactions?

① ②
Stock dividend and repurchase

S14-6 Toluca Inc. repurchased 1,000 common shares, paying cash of $12.00 per share on April 16, 2020. The shares were originally issued for $5.00 per share. Journalize the transaction. An explanation is not required.

②
Accounting for the repurchase of common shares

S14-7 Justice Inc. began 2020 with the following account balances:

⑦
Share repurchase entries
March 30, $87,500

Common shares, 150,000 shares authorized, 75,000 issued	$2,175,000
Retained earnings	820,000

Record the journal entries for the following transactions:

Jan.	10	Repurchased 7,500 of its own shares for $31 per share.
Feb.	20	Sold 4,000 of the repurchased shares for $32 per share.
Mar.	30	Sold the remaining repurchased shares for $25 per share.

S14-8 List the major parts of a multi-step corporate income statement for Star Pilates Trainers Inc. for the year ended December 31, 2020. Include all the major parts of the income statement, starting with net sales revenue and ending with net income (net loss). Remember to separate continuing operations from discontinued operations. You may ignore dollar amounts and earnings per share.

③
Preparing a corporate income statement

S14-9 Answer these questions about a corporate income statement:
1. How do you measure gross margin?
2. What is the title of those items that are unusual, infrequent, and are outside the company's core business activities?
3. Which income number is the best predictor of future net income?
4. What does *EPS* abbreviate?

③
Explaining the items on a complex corporate income statement

S14-10 CS Rentals Ltd.'s accounting records include the following items, listed in no particular order, at December 31, 2020:

③
Preparing a corporate income statement
Net income, $21,080

Other gains (losses)	$(12,500)	Net sales revenue	$100,000
Cost of goods sold	35,000	Operating expenses	30,000
Gain on discontinued operations	8,500	Accounts receivable	9,500

Income tax of 32 percent applies to all items.
Prepare CS Rentals Ltd.'s multi-step income statement for the year ended December 31, 2020. Use a one-column format. Omit earnings per share.

S14-11 Return to the CS Rentals Ltd. data in S14-10. CS Rentals had 10,000 common shares outstanding on January 1, 2020. CS Rentals declared and paid preferred dividends of $1,500 during 2020. In addition, CS Rentals paid a 20 percent common stock dividend on June 30.

Show how CS Rentals Ltd. reported EPS data on its 2020 income statement. Round to the nearest cent.

③
Reporting earnings per share
EPS for net income, $1.63

S14–12 Figero Inc. has $390,000 of income in 2020. During that same time it declared preferred dividends in the amount of $12,500. The following activities affecting common shares occurred during the year:

Jan. 1   120,000 common shares were outstanding
Aug. 1   Sold 35,000 common shares
Sep. 1   Issued a 10 percent common stock dividend

1. Calculate the weighted average number of common shares outstanding during the year.

2. Calculate earnings per share. Round to the nearest cent.

S14–13 The net income of Valente Inc. amounted to $3,750,000 for the year ended December 31, 2020. There were 200,000, $9.00 cumulative preferred shares throughout the year. At January 1, 2020, Valente Inc. had 270,000 common shares outstanding and issued 40,000 common shares on April 1. Then, on October 1, there was a 3-for-1 stock split of the common shares. Calculate Valente Inc.'s EPS.

S14–14 York Inc. had Retained Earnings of $60,000 at its fiscal year end on October 31, 2019. At that time, it had $75,000 in common shares and $20,000 in $2 preferred shares. During 2020, the company earned net income of $155,000 and declared dividends of $17,000. Additional common shares were sold in 2020 for $25,000. Complete York Inc.'s statement of shareholders' equity for the year ended October 31, 2020.

	YORK INC. Statement of Shareholders' Equity For the Year Ended October 31, 2020			
	Common Shares	**Preferred Shares**	**Retained Earnings**	**Total Shareholders' Equity**
Balance, October 31, 2019				
Balance October 31, 2020				

S14–15 Sharp Inc. ended 2019 with $20,000 in common shares, $15,000 in $0.50 preferred shares and retained earnings of $49,500. During 2020, no shares were sold or repurchased, the business earned net income of $50,000 and it paid cash dividends in the amount of $15,000. Create Sharp's statement of shareholders' equity for the year ended December 31, 2020.

S14–16 BLT Corporation's agreement with its bank lender restricts BLT's dividend payments. Why would a bank lender restrict a corporation's dividend payments and share repurchases?

S14–17 Taylor Corporation discovered in 2019 that it had incorrectly recorded in 2018 a cash payment of $70,000 for utilities expense. The correct amount of the utilities expense was $35,000.

1. Determine the effect of the error on the accounting equation in 2018.

2. How should this error be reported in the 2019 financial statements?

S14–18 Tamarack Research Inc. (TRI) ended 2019 with Retained Earnings of $37,500. During 2020 TRI earned net income of $50,000 and paid cash dividends of $15,000. Also during 2020 TRI got a $12,000 tax refund from the Canada Revenue Agency. A tax audit revealed that TRI paid too much income tax in 2018 in error.

Prepare TRI's statement of retained earnings for the year ended December 31, 2020, to report the correction of the prior period error.

S14-19 For each of the following situations, indicate whether there is a change in estimate (due to circumstances), a change of policy, or an error by inserting a check mark in the correct box. Then indicate if the correction needs to be applied retrospectively (change past statement information) or prospectively (only future statements will be affected) by checking the correct box in the right two columns.

⑤
Describing accounting changes

	Change in Estimate	Change in Policy	Error	Retrospective Statement	Prospective Statement
A switch from the weighted-average method of inventory to the FIFO method to reflect more accurate information.					
Based on new information, management decided the welding equipment will last 12 years and not the original estimate of 10 years.					
Missing expense invoices were found after the financial statements were finalized.					

S14-20 According to the information in this chapter, companies reporting under IFRS are required to report two types of information in their financial statements that are not required for companies reporting under ASPE. Describe each type of information and the financial statement on which it is reported.

⑥
Reporting under IFRS

S14-21 Companies reporting under ASPE, as described in the chapter, sometimes create a statement of shareholders' equity. What is the name of a similar statement for companies reporting under IFRS?

⑥
Comparing IFRS and ASPE

S14-22 Prepare a simple statement of comprehensive income for Yoshi Corporation using the following information:

- For the year ended June 30, 2020
- Loss for the year is $25,000
- Gain on equity investments is $60,000
- Tax rate is 25 percent

⑥
Preparing a statement of comprehensive income
Comprehensive income, $20,000

EXERCISES

E14-1 The shareholders' equity for Queen's Windows Inc. on June 30, 2020 (end of the company's fiscal year), follows:

①
Journalizing a stock dividend and reporting shareholders' equity
2. Total shareholders' equity, $680,000

Common shares, 800,000 shares authorized, 80,000 shares issued and outstanding	$300,000
Retained earnings	380,000
Total shareholders' equity	$680,000

On August 8, 2020, the company declared a 20 percent stock dividend. On that date, the market price of the common shares was $12.00 per share. Queen's Windows Inc. issued the dividend shares on August 31, 2020.

Required

1. Journalize the declaration and distribution of the stock dividend.
2. Prepare the shareholders' equity section of the balance sheet after the stock dividend distribution.

◉ **E14–2** Nest Corp. reports the following transactions for 2020:

Jan.	27	Sold 30,000 common shares for $10 per share.
Feb.	1	Sold 6,000 shares of $1.50, noncumulative, preferred shares for $70 per share.
Oct.	13	Declared a 10 percent stock dividend on the common shares. The current market price of the common shares is $12 per share. There are 90,000 common shares outstanding on October 13.
Nov.	16	Distributed the stock dividend declared on October 13.
Dec.	11	Declared the annual dividend required on the preferred shares and a $0.35 per share dividend on the common shares. There are 20,000 preferred shares outstanding at this time.

Required Prepare journal entries for the above transactions. Explanations are not required.

◐ **E14–3** Coolmatt Travel Ltd. is authorized to issue 500,000 common shares. As of December 31, 2019, the company had issued 70,000 shares at $7.50 per share and its Retained Earnings balance was $255,000. During 2020, the following transactions took place:

Jun.	10	Declared a 10 percent stock dividend using the market value of $4.00 per share.
Jul.	20	Distributed the stock dividend.
Aug.	5	Declared a $0.45 per share cash dividend. Date of record is August 21.
Sep.	15	Paid the cash dividend declared on August 5.

Required

1. Journalize the declaration and distribution of the stock dividend.
2. Journalize the declaration and payment of the cash dividend.
3. Prepare the shareholders' equity section of the balance sheet on August 5, 2020.

E14–4 Halifax Metal Products Ltd. reported the following shareholders' equity at October 31, 2020:

Common shares, unlimited shares authorized, 60,000 shares issued and outstanding	$150,000
Retained earnings	450,000
Total shareholders' equity	$600,000

On November 14, 2020, Halifax Metal Products Ltd. split its common shares 2 for 1.

Required

1. Make the memorandum entry to record the stock split.
2. Prepare the shareholders' equity section of the balance sheet immediately after the split.

E14–5 Examine Halifax Metal Products Ltd.'s shareholders' equity information in E14–4. Suppose that on November 14, 2020, Halifax Metal Products Ltd. consolidated its common shares 1 for 2 to increase the market price of its shares that were trading at $6.00 on October 31, 2020.

Required

1. Make the memorandum entry to record the share consolidation.
2. Prepare the shareholders' equity section of Halifax Metal Products Ltd.'s balance sheet immediately after the share consolidation.
3. What would you expect the market price to be, approximately, after the reverse split?

E14-6 Usurp Corp., an Internet service provider, has prospered during the past seven years, and recently the company's share price increased to $244.00. Usurp's management wishes to decrease the share price to the range of $116.00 to $124.00, which will be attractive to more investors.

① Using a stock split or a stock dividend to decrease the market price of a share

Required

1. Should the company issue a 100 percent stock dividend or split the stock? Why?
2. If you propose a stock split, state the split ratio that will accomplish the company's objective. Show your computations.

E14-7 Identify the effects of these transactions on shareholders' equity by completing the following table.

① ② Effects of share issuance, dividends, and share repurchase transactions

Independent Transactions	Impact on Shareholders' Equity		
	Increased (indicate amount)	Decreased (indicate amount)	No effect
a. A 10 percent stock dividend. Before the dividend, 400,000 common shares were outstanding; market value was $7.50 at the time of the dividend.			
b. A 2-for-1 stock split. Prior to the split, 50,000 common shares were outstanding.			
c. Repurchase of 5,000 common shares at $7.00 per share. The average issue price of these shares was $5.00.			
d. Sale of 2,000 repurchased common shares for $6.50 per share.			

E14-8 Journalize the following transactions that Flip Corp. conducted during 2020:

② Journalizing share repurchase transactions

April 8 contributed surplus, $2,500

Feb. 7   Issued 10,000 common shares at $15.00 per share.

Apr. 8   Repurchased 2,500 common shares at $13.00 per share. The average issue price of the shares was $14.00.

Jun. 2   Repurchased 2,000 common shares at $18.00 per share. The average issue price of the shares was $14.00.

E14-9 Yeong Ltd. reported the following shareholders' equity information on March 26, 2020:

Journalizing repurchase of company shares and reporting shareholders' equity

1. Total shareholders' equity, $877,500

Common shares, unlimited shares authorized, 140,000 shares issued and outstanding	$420,000
Retained earnings	475,000
Total shareholders' equity	$895,000

On May 3, 2020, the company repurchased and cancelled 5,000 common shares at $3.50 per share.

Required

1. Journalize the May 3 transaction.
2. Prepare the shareholders' equity section of the balance sheet at May 31, 2020.
3. How many common shares are outstanding after the share repurchase?

②
Accounting for the repurchase of preferred shares

(b) Reduced by $4,384 million

E14–10

Shareholders' Equity ($ amounts in millions) Adapted from a corporation's annual report	
Contributed capital	
Preferred shares (Note 15)*	$ 4,384
Common shares (Note 16)**	8,432
Retained earnings	24,662
Accumulated other comprehensive income (loss)	(4,718)
	$32,760

*Note 15: Preferred Shares (adapted) Authorized
An unlimited number of Preferred Shares without nominal or par value.
Issued and fully paid
Preferred shares   175,345,767 shares
**Note 16: Common Shares (adapted) Authorized
An unlimited number of Common Shares without nominal or par value.
Issued and fully paid
Common shares   1,088,972,173

Suppose the corporation repurchased its preferred shares. What would be the amount of the reduction of the company's total shareholders' equity if the cost to repurchase the preferred shares was (a) $5,000 million? (b) $4,384 million? (c) $4,000 million?

③
Preparing a single-step income statement

Net income, $61,230

E14–11 The following accounts are from Mizuko Limited's general ledger. All data are shown before tax.

Sales revenue	$306,000	Cost of goods sold	$199,000
Interest revenue	13,000	Loss on discontinued	
Interest expense	4,500	operations	10,000
Gain on sale of vehicle	19,000	Operating expenses	46,000

Required

Prepare a single-step income statement for the year ended December 31, 2020. Omit earnings per share. List expenses in alphabetical order. Use an income tax rate of 22 percent. (This format is presented in the Summary Problem on page 788. Use a two-column layout.)

③
Preparing a multi-step income statement

Net income, $32,500

E14–12 The ledger of Paint Supplies Inc. contains the following information for operations for the year ended September 30, 2020:

Sales revenue	$350,000
Gain on discontinued operations	18,750
Operating expenses (excluding income tax)	67,500
Income tax expense, operating income	10,000
Other loss	22,500
Cost of goods sold	230,000
Income tax expense, gain on discontinued operations	6,250

Required

1. Prepare a multi-step income statement for the year ended September 30, 2020. Omit earnings per share. Use a one-column layout.
2. Was 2020 a good year or a bad year for Paint Supplies Inc.? Explain your answer in terms of the outlook for 2021.

E14–13 Zelda Solutions Inc. earned net income of $152,000 in 2020. The general ledger reveals the following figures:

③
Computing earnings per share
EPS = $1.46

Preferred shares, $1.50, 10,000 authorized, 4,000 shares issued and outstanding	$ 50,000
Common shares, unlimited shares authorized, 100,000 shares issued and outstanding	300,000

Required Compute Zelda Solutions Inc.'s EPS for 2020, assuming no changes in the share accounts during the year.

E14–14 LeDuc Construction Ltd. had 60,000 common shares and 20,000, $0.75 cumulative preferred shares outstanding on December 31, 2019. On April 30, 2020, the company issued 6,000 additional common shares and split the common shares 2 for 1 on December 1, 2020. There were no other share issuances and no share repurchases during the year ended December 31, 2020. Income for the year from continuing operations was $70,000, and loss on discontinued operations (net of income tax) was $4,000.

③
Computing earnings per share
EPS for net income, $0.40

Required Compute and report LeDuc Construction Ltd.'s EPS amounts for the year ended December 31, 2020 in a partial income statement.

E14–15 Pacific Hotels Inc. had Retained Earnings of $250.0 million at the beginning of 2020. The company showed these figures at December 31, 2020:

④
Preparing a statement of retained earnings
Retained earnings, Dec. 31, 2020, $275.0 million

	($ millions)
Net income	$75.0
Cash dividends—Preferred	1.5
Common	44.5
Debit to retained earnings due to repurchase of preferred shares	4.0

Required Prepare the statement of retained earnings for Pacific Hotels Inc. for the year ended December 31, 2020.

E14–16 Kalios Corp. reported the following shareholders' equity information for the year ended October 31, 2019:

④
Preparing a statement of shareholders' equity
Total shareholders' equity, Dec. 31, 2020, $2,352,000

Common shares, 400,000 shares authorized, 140,000 shares issued and outstanding	$1,400,000
Retained earnings	672,000
Total shareholders' equity	$2,072,000

During 2020, Kalios Corp. completed these transactions and events:

Mar.	6	Declared and issued a 10 percent stock dividend. At the time, their common shares were quoted at a market price of $11.50 per share.
May.	12	Sold 1,000 common shares for $12.50 per share.
Aug.	22	Sold 1,000 common shares to employees at $10.00 per share.
Oct.	15	Declared cash dividends of $140,000
Oct.	31	Paid cash dividends declared on October 15.
Oct.	31	Net income for the year was $397,500.

Required Prepare Kalios Corp.'s statement of shareholders' equity for 2020.

E14–17 The shareholders' equity of Inspiration Management Corp. as of January 1, 2020, follows:

Contributed capital	
Preferred shares, $3, noncumulative 20,000 shares authorized, 4,000 shares issued and outstanding	$ 200,000
Common shares, unlimited shares authorized, 200,000 shares issued and outstanding	2,000,000
Total contributed capital	2,200,000
Retained earnings	626,900
Total shareholders' equity	$2,826,900

Inspiration Management Corp. completed the following transactions during 2020:

Feb. 6   Declared the required annual cash dividend on preferred shares and a $0.20 per share cash dividend on the common shares.

26   Paid the cash dividend that was declared on February 6.

Jun. 4   Purchased 6,000 of its own common shares for $15.25 per share.

Jul. 5   Distributed a 2-for-1 stock split on the common shares.

The net loss for the year was $78,000.

Required   Prepare the shareholders' equity section of the balance sheet of Inspiration Management Corp. as of December 31, 2020. Do not prepare journal entries for the above transactions.

E14–18 Ji-hyuk Corp.'s agreement for the issuance of long-term debt requires the restriction of $150,000 of the company's Retained Earnings balance. Total Retained Earnings is $337,500, and total contributed capital is $250,000.

Required   Show how to report shareholders' equity (including retained earnings) on Ji-hyuk Corp.'s balance sheet at December 31, 2020, assuming:

1. The restriction is disclosed in a note. Write the note.

2. The company appropriates retained earnings in the amount of the restriction and includes no note in its statements.

E14–19 As Bali Imports Inc. was finalizing its 2020 statements, it discovered that an accounting error caused the net income of 2019 to be understated by $10 million. Retained earnings at December 31, 2019, as previously reported, stood at $324 million. Net income for 2020 was $88 million, and 2020 dividends were $48 million.

Required

1. What impact will this prior-period error have on Bali Imports' 2020 income statement?

2. What is the impact on the 2019 financial statements?

E14–20 Given the following information, prepare League Products Ltd.'s statement of retained earnings for the year ended December 31, 2020:

- An inventory error caused net income of the prior year to be overstated by $50,000.
- Retained Earnings at January 1, 2020, as previously reported, stood at $2,408,000.
- Net income for the year ended December 31, 2020, was $448,000.
- Dividends during 2020 were $61,000.

SERIAL EXERCISE

E14–21 *The Serial Exercise involves a company that will be revisited throughout relevant chapters in Volume 1 and Volume 2. You can complete the Serial Exercises using MyLab Accounting.*

This exercise continues the Canyon Canoe company situation from Chapters 12 and 13. Students do not have to complete prior exercises in order to complete this question.

In 2022, Amber Wilson, owner of Canyon Canoe Company, started a new company that will be operated as a corporation, Outdoor Equipment Incorporated (OEI). This company sells outdoor clothing and equipment. The articles of incorporation for OEI authorized the company to issue 500,000 preferred shares that pay a dividend of $4.00 per year and 1,000,000 common shares.

Margin notes

④ Prepare the shareholders' equity section of a balance sheet

④ Reporting a retained earnings restriction

a. Total shareholders' equity, $587,500

⑤ Explain the impact of a prior-period error

④⑤ Preparing a statement of retained earnings with a correction of a prior period error

Retained earnings, Dec. 31, 2020, $2,745,000

② Journalizing and reporting share sale and repurchase transactions

2. Common Shares ending balance, $208,792

At January 1, 2023, the 2,000 preferred shares had a balance of $70,000, the 50,000 common shares had a balance of $200,000, and the retained earnings balance was $402,000.

In January 2023, OEI has the following transactions related to its common shares:

Jan. 3   The company sold 1,000 of its common shares for $8.00 per share to a small number of people who believed in the company's potential for profit.

      20   The company repurchased 100 of its common shares for $10.00 per share from a shareholder who was having financial difficulties.

      30   The company sold 100 common shares for $12.00 per share.

Required

1. Journalize the entries related to the transactions.
2. Calculate the ending balance in the Common Shares account.
3. Prepare the statement of shareholders' equity for January 31, 2023. Assume that net income for the period was $67,500.

CHALLENGE EXERCISES

E14–22 Scopis Ltd. reported its shareholders' equity as shown below:

②

Analyzing stock split and share repurchase transactions

5. b. Common Shares outstanding, 13,000

Shareholders' Equity	
Contributed capital	
Preferred shares, $1.00, 10,000 shares authorized, none issued and outstanding	$ 0
Common shares, 100,000 shares authorized, 14,000 shares issued and outstanding	70,000
Retained earnings	84,000
Total shareholders' equity	$154,000

Required

1. What was the average issue price per common share?
2. Journalize the issuance of 1,200 common shares at $8.00 per share on January 10.
3. How many Scopis Ltd. common shares are now outstanding?
4. On March 8, Scopis Ltd. splits its common shares 3 for 1. How many common shares would be outstanding after the split?
5. Ignore the prior transactions and return to the Scopis Ltd. shareholders' equity information in Requirement 1, which shows 14,000 common shares issued.

   a. Journalize the following share repurchase transactions by Scopis Ltd.:

   Mar.   8   Scopis Ltd. repurchases 500 of its own shares at $16.00 per share.

   Aug. 19   Scopis Ltd. repurchases 500 of its own shares at $4.00 per share.

   b. How many Scopis Ltd. common shares would be outstanding after the transactions in part (a) take place?

E14–23 Tillay Environmental Products Inc. (TEPI) began 2020 with 1.6 million common shares issued and outstanding for $4.0 million. Beginning Retained Earnings was $4.5 million. On February 26, 2020, TEPI issued 100,000 common shares at $3.50 per share. On November 16, 2020, when the market price was $5.00 per share, the board of directors declared a 10 percent stock dividend, which was distributed on December 20, 2020. Net income for the year was $550,000.

①④

Recording a stock dividend and preparing a statement of retained earnings

2. Retained Earnings, Dec. 31, 2020, $4,200,000

Required

1. Make the journal entries for the issuance of shares for cash and for the 10 percent stock dividend.
2. Prepare the company's statement of retained earnings for the year ended December 31, 2020.

BEYOND THE NUMBERS

② ③

Reporting special items

BN14–1

The following accounting issues have arisen at Tri-City Computers Corp.:

1. An investor noted that the market price of shares seemed to decline after the date of record for a cash dividend. Why do you think that would be the case?

2. Corporations sometimes repurchase their own shares. When asked why, Tri-City Computers Corp.'s management responded that the shares were undervalued. What advantage would Tri-City Computers Corp. gain by repurchasing its own shares under these circumstances?

3. Tri-City Computers Corp. earned a significant profit in the year ended June 30, 2020, because land that it held was expropriated for a low-rental housing project. The company proposes to treat the sale of land to the government as operating revenue. Why do you think Tri-City Computers Corp. is proposing such treatment? Is this treatment appropriate?

ETHICAL ISSUE

EI14–1

Sparkly Gold Mine Ltd. is a gold mine in northern Ontario. In February 2020, company geologists discovered a new vein of gold-bearing ore that tripled the company's reserves. After this discovery, but prior to disclosing the new vein to the public, top managers of the company quietly bought most of the outstanding Sparkly Gold Mine Ltd. shares for themselves personally. After the announcement of the discovery, Sparkly Gold Mine Ltd.'s share price increased from $4.00 to $30.00.

Required

1. Did Sparkly Gold Mine Ltd. managers behave ethically? Explain your answer.

2. Who was helped and who was harmed by management's action?

PROBLEMS (GROUP A)

①

Using a stock split to fight off a takeover of the corporation

P14–1A Skiptrace Software Inc. is positioned ideally in the manufacturing and distribution sectors. It is the only company providing highly developed inventory tracking software. The company does a brisk business with companies such as Home Hardware and Roots. Skiptrace Software Inc.'s success has made the company a prime target for a takeover. Against the wishes of Skiptrace Software Inc.'s board of directors, an investment group is attempting to buy 55 percent of Skiptrace Software Inc.'s outstanding shares. Board members are convinced that the investment group would sell off the most desirable pieces of the business and leave little of value.

At the most recent board meeting, several suggestions were advanced to fight off the hostile takeover bid. One suggestion was to increase the shares outstanding by splitting the company's shares 2 for 1.

Required As a significant shareholder of Skiptrace Software Inc., write a short memo to the board advising how a stock split would affect the investor group's attempt to take over Skiptrace Software Inc. Include in your memo a discussion of the effect that the stock split would have on assets, liabilities, and total shareholders' equity; that is, the split's effect on the size of the corporation.

① ②

Journalizing shareholders' equity transactions

Sep. 19 Common Shares, $360,000

P14–2A Western Wireless Inc. completed the following selected transactions during the year 2020:

May	19	Declared a cash dividend on the $8.50 preferred shares (3,000 shares outstanding). Declared a $2.00 per share dividend on the 100,000 common shares outstanding. The date of record was June 2, and the payment date was June 25.
Jun.	25	Paid the cash dividends.
Jul.	7	Split the company's 100,000 common shares 2 for 1; one new common share is issued for each old share held.
Aug.	29	Declared a 5 percent stock dividend on the common shares to holders of record on September 8, with distribution set for September 19. The market value was $36.00 per common share.
Sep.	19	Issued the stock dividend shares.
Nov.	6	Repurchased 5,000 of the company's own common shares at $40.00 per share. They had an average issue price of $28.00 per share.

Required Record the transactions from the previous page in the general journal.

P14–3A Nepal Grocery Inc.'s balance sheet showed the following account information at November 30, 2019; 250,000 common shares authorized, with 75,000 shares issued, a Common Shares balance of $187,500, and the Retained Earnings account had a credit balance of $150,000. During 2020, the company completed the following selected transactions:

Journalizing dividend and share-repurchase transactions, reporting shareholders' equity

2. Retained earnings, $283,000

Mar. 15   Repurchased 10,000 of the company's own common shares at $2.75 per share.

Apr. 29   Declared a 5 percent stock dividend on the 65,000 outstanding common shares to holders of record on May 2, with distribution set for May 16. The market value of Nepal's common shares was $6.00 per share.

May 16   Issued the stock dividend shares.

Nov. 19   Split the common shares 2 for 1 by issuing one new share for each old share held on December 30, 2020.

30   Earned net income of $155,000 during the year.

Required

1. Record the transactions in the general journal. Explanations are not required.

2. Prepare the shareholders' equity section of the balance sheet at November 30, 2020.

3. Calculate the average issue price per share on November 30, 2020. Assume no shares were issued or repurchased after November 19, 2020.

P14–4A The Stahl Metalworks Corp. general ledger contained the following information at September 30, 2020:

Preparing a single-step income statement

EPS Net income, $0.29

Cost of goods sold	$157,500
Loss on sale of property	17,500
Sales returns	3,500
Income tax expense, continuing operations	12,769
Income tax saving, discontinued segment—operating loss	(1,800)
Income tax expense, discontinued segment—gain on sale	600
Gain on sale of discontinued segment	1,750
Interest expense	4,250
General expenses	42,000
Interest revenue	1,750
Preferred shares, $1.00, 15,000 shares authorized, 7,500 shares issued and outstanding	93,750
Retained earnings, October 1, 2019	30,500
Selling expenses	50,750
Common shares, 50,000 shares authorized, issued, and outstanding	165,000
Sales revenue	315,000
Dividends	11,000
Operating loss, discontinued segment	5,250
Loss on insurance settlement	4,000

Required

1. Prepare a single-step income statement, including earnings per share, for Stahl Metalworks Corp. for the fiscal year ended September 30, 2020. List expenses from highest to lowest amount.

2. Evaluate income for the year ended September 30, 2020, in terms of the outlook for the 2021 fiscal year. Assume 2020 was a typical year and that Stahl Metalworks Corp.'s managers hoped to earn income from continuing operations equal to 10 percent of net sales.

① ② ④
Accounting for stock dividends, stock splits, share transactions, and preparing the statement of shareholders' equity

2. Total shareholders' equity, $1,069,750

P14–5A Timpano Communication Inc. reported the following shareholders' equity information on December 31, 2019:

Contributed capital	
Preferred shares, $2.00, cumulative (1 year in arrears), liquidation price of $20, 100,000 shares authorized, 15,000 shares issued and outstanding	$240,000
Common shares, unlimited number of shares authorized, 25,000 shares issued and outstanding	200,000
Total contributed capital	440,000
Retained earnings	512,000
Total shareholders' equity	$952,000

The following transactions took place during 2020:

Jan.	14	Declared a $90,000 cash dividend, payable on March 1 to the shareholders of record on February 1. Indicate the amount payable to each class of shareholder.
Feb.	28	Issued 10,000 common shares for $6.00 per share.
Mar.	1	Paid the cash dividend declared on January 14.
Apr.	1	Declared a 10 percent stock dividend on the common shares, distributable on May 2 to the shareholders of record on April 15. The market value of the shares was $6.40 per share.
May	2	Distributed the stock dividend declared on April 1.
Jul.	4	Repurchased 3,000 of the company's own common shares at $7.00 per share.
Sep.	2	Issued 2,500 common shares for $7.50 per share.
Nov.	2	Split the common shares 2 for 1.
Dec.	31	Reported net income of $150,000. Closed the Income Summary account.

Required

1. Record the transactions in the general journal. Explanations are not required.
2. Prepare the statement of shareholders' equity for the year ended December 31, 2020.

① ② ③ ④
Journalizing dividend and stock repurchase transactions; reporting shareholders' equity; calculating earnings per share

3. EPS = 1.98

P14–6A The balance sheet of Augen Vision Ltd. at December 31, 2019, reported the following shareholders' equity information:

Common shares, 200,000 shares authorized, 50,000 shares issued and outstanding	$745,500
Retained earnings	250,000
Total shareholders' equity	$995,500

During 2020, Augen Vision Ltd. completed the following selected transactions:

Apr.	29	Declared a 10 percent stock dividend on the common shares. The market value of Augen Vision Ltd.'s common shares was $15.00 per share. The record date was May 20, with distribution set for June 3.
Jun.	3	Issued the stock dividend shares.
Jul.	29	Repurchased 5,000 of the company's own common shares at $13.50 per share.
Nov.	1	Sold 1,000 common shares for $16.50 per share.
	25	Declared a $0.25 per share dividend on the common shares outstanding. The date of record was December 16, and the payment date was January 6, 2021.
Dec.	31	Closed the $105,000 credit balance of Income Summary to Retained Earnings.

Required

1. Record the transactions in the general journal.
2. Prepare a statement of shareholders' equity at December 31, 2020.
3. Calculate earnings per share at December 31, 2020. (Hint: Use issue dates in your calculations.)

P14–7A The capital structure of Renault Marketing Inc. at December 31, 2019, included 50,000, $0.50 preferred shares and 74,000 common shares. The 50,000 preferred shares were issued in 2009. Common shares outstanding during 2020 were 74,000 January through April and 80,000 May through September. A 20 percent stock dividend was paid on October 1. Income from continuing operations during 2020 was $122,000. The company discontinued a segment of the business at a gain (net of tax) of $9,250. The Renault Marketing Inc. board of directors restricts $125,000 of retained earnings for contingencies.

③④
Computing earnings per share and reporting a retained earnings restriction
1. EPS for net income, $1.14

Required

1. Compute and report Renault Marketing Inc.'s earnings per share at the end of 2020. Income of $122,000 is net of income tax.

2. Show two ways of reporting Renault Marketing Inc.'s retained earnings restriction. Retained Earnings at December 31, 2019, was $145,500, and total contributed capital at December 31, 2020, is $375,000. The company declared dividends of $49,500 in 2020.

P14–8A Muriel Thomas, accountant for Duchlorol Ltd., was injured in a hiking accident. Another employee prepared the income statement shown on the next page for the fiscal year ended December 31, 2020.

The individual amounts listed on the income statement are correct. However, some accounts are reported incorrectly, and others do not belong on the income statement at all. Also, income tax (30 percent) has not been applied to all appropriate figures. Duchlorol Ltd. issued 64,000 common shares in 2012 and has not issued or repurchased common shares since that time. The Retained Earnings balance, as originally reported at December 31, 2019, was $242,500. There were no preferred shares outstanding at December 31, 2020.

③④⑤
Preparing a corrected combined statement of income and retained earnings
EPS on net income, $$0.69

Required Prepare a corrected combined statement of income and retained earnings for the year ended December 31, 2020; include earnings per share. Prepare the income statement portion in single-step format. Use a two-column layout. Report expenses from largest to smallest.

DUCHLOROL LTD. Income Statement 2020		
Revenue and gains		
Sales		$295,000
Proceeds from sale of preferred shares		66,000
Gain on repurchase of preferred shares (issued for $76,000; repurchased for $66,500)		9,500
Total revenues and gains		370,500
Expenses and losses		
Cost of goods sold	$ 83,000	
Selling expenses	54,000	
General expenses	58,500	
Sales returns	7,500	
Dividends	5,500	
Sales discounts	4,500	
Income tax expense	29,200	
Total expenses and losses		242,200
Income from operations		128,300
Other gains and losses		
Loss on sale of discontinued operations	$ (2,500)	
Flood loss	(15,000)	
Operating loss on discontinued segment	(7,000)	
Correction for 2019 due to an inventory error	(2,000)	
Total other losses		(26,500)
Net income		$101,800
Earnings per share		$ 1.59

① ③ ④ ⑤

Accounting for stock dividends, stock splits, and errors from a prior period; preparing a combined statement of income and retained earnings; calculating earnings per share

2. Net income, $730,600

P14–9A Assured Collision Repair Inc. reported the following shareholders' equity information on December 31, 2019:

Contributed capital	
Preferred shares, $2.50, convertible to common on a 2-for-1 basis, 100,000 shares authorized, 50,000 shares issued and outstanding	$1,500,000
Common shares, unlimited number of shares authorized, 150,000 shares issued and outstanding	1,500,000
Total contributed capital	3,000,000
Retained earnings	1,200,000
Total shareholders' equity	$4,200,000

The following information is also available for the year ended December 31, 2020:

Sales for the year	$3,150,000
Cost of goods sold	1,290,000
Operating expenses	792,000
Income from discontinued operations	132,000
Loss on sale of discontinued operations	76,000

Required

1. Record the following transactions in the general journal. Explanations are not required.

Feb. 1 Declared a cash dividend of $275,000, payable on March 1 to the shareholders of record on February 15. Indicate the amount payable to each class of shareholder.

Mar. 1 Paid the cash dividend declared on February 1.

May 2 Declared a 20 percent stock dividend on the common shares, distributable on July 4 to the shareholders of record on June 15. The market value of the shares was $11.00 per share.

Jul. 4 Distributed the common shares dividend declared on May 2.

Aug. 8 The company discovered that amortization expense recorded in 2018 was understated in error by $30,000. (Ignore any tax consequences.)

Dec. 31 Close only the Income Summary account, assuming the company pays taxes at the rate of 35 percent.

2. Prepare a combined statement of income and retained earnings for the year ended December 31, 2020. Use a three-column format to break out the information for discontinued operations. Include earnings per share information. For purposes of the earnings per share calculation, the weighted average number of common shares is 180,000.

PROBLEMS (GROUP B)

P14–1B Fundybay Corporation is positioned ideally in its industry. Located in Nova Scotia, Fundybay Corporation is the only company with a reliable record for its locally managed transport company. The company does a brisk business with local corporations. Fundybay Corporation's recent success has made the company a prime target for a takeover. An investment group from Halifax is attempting to buy 51 percent of the company's outstanding shares against the wishes of Fundybay Corporation's board of directors. Board members are convinced that the Halifax investors would sell off the most desirable pieces of the business and leave little of value.

At the most recent board meeting, several suggestions were advanced to fight off the hostile takeover bid. The suggestion with the most promise is to repurchase and cancel a huge quantity of shares. Fundybay Corporation has the cash to carry out this plan.

Required

1. As a significant shareholder of Fundybay Corporation, write a memorandum to explain to the board how the repurchase and cancellation of shares might make it more difficult for the Halifax group to take over Fundybay Corporation. Include in your memo a discussion of the effect that repurchasing shares would have on shares outstanding and on the size of the corporation.

2. Suppose Fundybay Corporation management is successful in fighting off the takeover bid and later issues shares at prices greater than the purchase price. Explain what effect the sale of these shares will have on assets, shareholders' equity, and net income.

P14–2B RMA Corporation Inc. completed the following selected transactions during 2020:

①②
Journalizing shareholders' equity transactions

Mar.	4	Declared a cash dividend on the 30,000, $1.40 preferred shares. Declared a $0.20 per share cash dividend on the 40,000 common shares outstanding. The date of record was March 15, and the payment date was March 28.
	28	Paid the cash dividends.
Apr.	20	Declared a 15 percent stock dividend on the common shares to holders of record on April 29, with distribution set for May 31. The market value of the common shares was $14.00 per share.
May	31	Issued the stock dividend shares.
Jun.	17	Repurchased 3,000 shares of the company's own common shares at $11.00 per share; average issue price was $8.00 per share.
Nov.	14	Issued 1,000 common shares for $9.50 per share.

Required Record the transactions in the general journal.

P14–3B The balance sheet of Investtech Inc. at December 31, 2019, reported 2,000,000 common shares authorized with 250,000 shares issued at an average price of $4.00 each and a Retained Earnings balance of $800,000. During 2020, the company completed the following selected transactions:

①②③
Journalizing dividend and share-repurchase transactions, reporting shareholders' equity

Feb.	15	Repurchased 20,000 of the company's own common shares at $4.00 per share.
Mar.	8	Sold 8,000 common shares for $4.25 per share.
Sep.	28	Declared a 5 percent stock dividend on the 238,000 outstanding common shares to holders of record on October 15, with distribution set for October 31. The market value of Investtech Inc. common shares was $4.50 per share.
Oct.	31	Issued the stock dividend shares.
Nov.	5	Consolidated the common shares 1 for 2 (reverse split); one new common share was issued for every two existing shares held. Prior to the split, the corporation had 249,900 shares issued and outstanding.
Dec.	31	Earned net income of $230,000 during the year.

Required

1. Record the transactions in the general journal. Explanations are not required.

2. Prepare the shareholders' equity section of the balance sheet at December 31, 2020.

3. Calculate the average issue price per common share on December 31, 2020.

P14–4B Sintra Flights Inc. shows the following financial information at August 31, 2020:

General expenses..	$ 220,000
Loss on sale of discontinued segment..	18,000
Cost of goods sold...	570,000
Income tax expense—continuing operations...	35,500
Income tax expense, discontinued segment—operating income..............	2,000
Income tax saving, discontinued segment—loss on sale	(4,500)
Interest expense...	27,000
Gain on settlement of lawsuit...	27,000
Sales returns..	23,000
Contributed surplus from repurchase of preferred shares	18,000
Sales discounts..	7,000
Sales revenue	1,000,000
Operating income, discontinued segment...	8,000
Loss on sale of property, plant, and equipment	5,000
Dividends on preferred shares..	12,500
Preferred shares, $0.50, cumulative, 50,000 shares authorized, 25,000 shares issued and outstanding..	350,000
Dividends on common shares...	25,000
Retained earnings, September 1, 2019...	197,000
Selling expenses...	33,000
Common shares, unlimited shares authorized, 40,000 shares issued and outstanding...	433,000

Required

1. Prepare a single-step income statement, including earnings per share, for Sintra Flights Inc. for the fiscal year ended August 31, 2020. List expenses from highest to lowest amount.

2. Evaluate income for the year ended August 31, 2020, in terms of the outlook for the 2021 fiscal year. Assume 2020 was a typical year and that Sintra Flights's managers hoped to earn income from continuing operations equal to 12 percent of net sales.

①②④
Accounting for stock
dividends, stock splits,
share transactions, and
preparing the statement of
shareholders' equity

P14–5B Orillia Outfitters Ltd. reported the following shareholders' equity information on January 1, 2020:

Contributed capital	
Preferred shares, $0.75, cumulative (1 year in arrears), liquidation price of $5.00, 50,000 shares authorized, 15,000 shares issued and outstanding	$150,000
Common shares, unlimited number of shares authorized, 25,000 shares issued and outstanding	125,000
Total contributed capital	275,000
Retained earnings	220,000
Total shareholders' equity	$495,000

The following transactions took place during 2020:

Jan.	28	Declared a $25,000 cash dividend, payable on March 1 to the shareholders of record on February 15. Indicate the amount payable to each class of shareholder.
Feb.	25	Issued 10,000 common shares for $7.00 per share.
Mar.	1	Paid the cash dividend declared on January 28.
Apr.	4	Declared a 10 percent stock dividend on the common shares, distributable on May 15 to the shareholders of record on April 15. The market value of the shares was $8.00 per share.
May	15	Distributed the stock dividend declared on April 4.

Jul.	6	Repurchased 10,000 of the company's own common shares at $8.50 per share.
Sep.	3	Issued 5,000 common shares for $8.50 per share.
Nov.	2	Split the common shares 2 for 1.
Dec.	31	Reported net income of $100,000. Closed the Income Summary account.

Required

1. Record the transactions in the general journal. Explanations are not required.
2. Prepare the statement of shareholders' equity for the year ended December 31, 2020.

P14–6B The balance sheet of Toronto Exports Inc. at December 31, 2019, presented the following shareholders' equity information:

①②③④
Journalizing dividends
and stock repurchase
transactions; reporting
shareholders' equity

Common shares, 3,000,000 shares authorized, 500,000 shares issued and outstanding	$2,955,000
Retained earnings	1,820,000
Total shareholders' equity	$4,775,000

During 2020, Toronto Exports Inc. completed the following selected transactions:

Mar.	29	Declared a 10 percent stock dividend on the common shares. The market value of Toronto Exports Inc. common shares was $5.00 per share. The record date was April 20, with distribution set for May 29.
May	29	Issued the stock dividend shares.
Jul.	30	Repurchased 30,000 of the company's own common shares at $5.00 per share.
Oct.	4	Sold 20,000 common shares for $7.50 per share.
Dec.	27	Declared a $0.20 per share dividend on the common shares outstanding. The date of record was January 17, 2021, and the payment date was January 31, 2021.
	31	Closed the $875,000 net income to Retained Earnings.

Required

1. Record the transactions in the general journal.
2. Prepare the statement of shareholders' equity for the year ended December 31, 2020.
3. Calculate earnings per share at December 31, 2020. (Hint: Use issue dates in your calculations.)

P14–7B The capital structure of Redding Design Ltd. at December 31, 2019, included 15,000 $1 preferred shares and 420,000 common shares. Common shares outstanding during 2020 were 330,000 in January through March; 348,000 during April; 385,000 May through September; and 420,000 during October through December. Income from continuing operations during 2020 was $446,000. The company discontinued a segment of the business at a gain of $61,500. The board of directors of Redding Design Ltd. has restricted $82,500 of retained earnings for expansion of the company's office facilities.

③④
Computing earnings per
share and reporting a
retained earnings restriction

Required

1. Compute and report Redding Design Ltd.'s earnings per share at the end of 2020. Income and loss amounts are net of income tax.
2. Show two ways of reporting Redding Design Ltd.'s retained earnings restriction. Retained Earnings at December 31, 2019, was $172,000, and total contributed capital at December 31, 2020, is $575,000. Redding Design Ltd. declared cash dividends of $250,000 during 2020.

P14–8B Thomas Wong, accountant for APB Bikes Ltd., was injured in a biking accident. Another employee prepared the income statement shown on the next page for the fiscal year ended September 30, 2020.

③④⑤
Preparing a corrected
combined statement of
income and retained earnings

The individual amounts listed on the income statement are correct. However, some accounts are reported incorrectly, and others do not belong on the income statement at all. Also, income tax (25 percent) has not been applied to all appropriate figures. APB Bikes Ltd. issued 30,000 common shares in 2012 and has not issued or repurchased common shares since that date. The Retained Earnings balance, as originally reported at September 30, 2019, was $660,000. There were no preferred shares outstanding at September 30, 2020.

Required Prepare a corrected combined statement of income and retained earnings for fiscal year 2020; include earnings per share. Prepare the income statement portion in single-step format. Use a two-column layout. Report expenses from largest to smallest.

APB BIKES LTD. Income Statement September 30, 2020		
Revenues and gains		
Sales		$1,000,000
Gain on repurchase of preferred shares (issued for $60,000; repurchased for $48,000)		12,000
Total revenues and gains		1,012,000
Expenses and losses		
Cost of goods sold	$478,000	
Selling expenses	133,000	
General expenses	60,000	
Sales returns	13,000	
Correction of an error from a prior period—understated income tax for 2019 due to error	10,000	
Dividends	14,000	
Sales discounts	18,000	
Income tax expense	98,700	
Total expenses and losses		824,700
Income from operations		187,300
Other gains and losses		
Operating income on discontinued segment	16,000	
Loss on sale of discontinued operations	(32,000)	
Total other gains and losses		(16,000)
Net income		$ 171,300
Earnings per share		$ 5. 71

①③④⑤
Accounting for stock dividends, stock splits, and prior period adjustments; preparing a combined statement of income and retained earnings; calculating earnings per share

P14–9B Sarnia Hardware Ltd. reported the following shareholders' equity on December 31, 2019:

Contributed capital	
Preferred shares, $0.50 cumulative, convertible to common on a 2-for-1 basis, 50,000 shares authorized, 20,000 shares issued and outstanding	$ 55,000
Common shares, unlimited number of shares authorized, 50,000 shares issued and outstanding	62,500
Total contributed capital	117,500
Retained earnings	110,000
Total shareholders' equity	$227,500

The following information is available for the year ended December 31, 2020:

Sales for the year	$212,500
Cost of goods sold..	95,000
Operating expenses..	65,000
Income from discontinued operations....................................	4,000
Loss on sale of discontinued operations................................	2,500

Required

1. Record the following transactions in the general journal. Explanations are not required.

Mar. 7   Declared a cash dividend of $12,500, payable on April 1 to the shareholders of record on March 15. Indicate the amount payable to each class of shareholder.

Apr. 1   Paid the cash dividend declared on March 7.

Jun. 6   Declared a 5 percent stock dividend on the common shares, distributable on August 5 to the shareholders of record on July 4. The market value of the shares was $1.50 per share.

Aug. 5   Distributed the common shares dividend declared on June 6.

Sep. 15   Received notification from the Canada Revenue Agency that Sarnia Hardware Ltd. had made an error in filing its 2019 taxes. The reassessment showed that the company had reported and overpaid $4,000 in taxes.

Dec. 31   Close the Income Summary account, assuming the income tax on all types of income is 40 percent.

2. Prepare a combined multi-step statement of income and retained earnings for the year ended December 31, 2020. Use a three-column format to break out the information for discontinued operations. Include earnings per share information.

CHALLENGE PROBLEM

P14–1C Assume Watawa Inc., a private corporation with a small number of shareholders, had issued 20,000 common shares at incorporation at a price of $22.00 each. The book value per share was $34.00 at the most recent year end. The company has been paying an annual dividend of $1.56 per share. Recently, the company had offered to repurchase 3,000 shares at $28.00 per share.

    You and a friend bought 100 shares each when the shares were issued. Your friend wonders whether she should sell her shares back to Watawa Inc. since the company was offering 27 percent more than she had paid.

Required   Analyze the information provided to help your friend decide whether or not she should sell her shares back to the company.

②
Explaining the effects of a share repurchase

Extending Your Knowledge

DECISION PROBLEMS

(1)

Analyzing cash dividends and stock dividends

2. 2018 dividends, $20,000; 2020 dividends, $16,500

DP14–1

In 2018, you purchased 10,000 common shares of your friend's company, Kingston Technologies Inc., at a market price of $25.00 per share. On December 31, 2020, the company reported the following information about their shareholders' equity:

Common shares, 200,000 shares issued and outstanding	$2,000,000
Retained earnings	1,200,000
Total shareholders' equity	$3,200,000

In the past, Kingston Technologies Inc. has paid an annual cash dividend of $2.00 per share. In 2019, despite a large Retained Earnings balance, the board of directors wanted to conserve cash for expansion and did not pay a cash dividend but distributed a 10 percent stock dividend. During 2020, the company's cash position improved, so the board declared and paid a cash dividend of $1.50 per share.

Required

1. How did the stock dividend affect your proportionate ownership in the company? Explain.
2. What amount of cash dividends did you receive in 2018? What amount of cash dividends did you receive in 2020? Would you expect the dividend per share to remain unchanged between 2018 and 2020?
3. Immediately after the stock dividend was distributed, the market value of Kingston Technologies Inc. shares decreased from $25.00 per share to $22.72 per share. Does this represent a loss to you? Explain.
4. Suppose Kingston Technologies Inc. announces at the time of the stock dividend that the company will continue to pay the annual $2.00 cash dividend per share, even after the stock dividend. Would you expect the market price of the shares to decrease in 2019 to $22.72 per share as in Requirement 3 above? Explain.

FINANCIAL STATEMENT CASES

(3)(4)(6)

Corporate income statement and earnings per share

FSC14–1

Use the Indigo Books & Music Inc. financial statements that appear in Appendix A at the end of this book and on MyLab Accounting to answer the following questions:

1. Does Indigo use a single-step or multi-step income statement?
2. What does Indigo call their income statement? Is it separate from, or combined with, the comprehensive income?
3. Indigo's basic earnings per share at April 1, 2017, was $0.79 per share. For purposes of this calculation, what was the weighted average number of shares outstanding? Where did you find this information?

(2)(3)(4)(6)

Understanding financial statements and the effects of reporting under IFRS

FSC14–2

Use the TELUS Corporation 2016 financial statements that appear on MyLab Accounting to answer the following questions:

1. Which income statement format—single-step or multi-step—does TELUS's consolidated statement of income more closely resemble and how do you know?
2. What was TELUS's earnings per share in 2016? Did this increase or decrease from 2015?
3. Did the company declare dividends in fiscal 2016? If so, how much were they? And where is this information shown?

IFRS MINI-CASE

The IFRS Mini-Case is now available online at **MyLab Accounting** in Chapter Resources.

Try It! Solutions for Chapter 14

1. a.

Jul. 15	Retained Earnings	12,800	
	Common Stock Dividend Distributable		12,800
	To declare a 10 percent common stock dividend. (16,000 × 0.10 × $8)		

Aug. 31	Common Stock Dividend Distributable	12,800	
	Common Shares		12,800
	To issue common shares in a stock dividend.		

b. The accounting equation for this transaction shows that a stock dividend does not affect assets, liabilities, or total shareholders' equity.

Assets	=	Liabilities	+	Shareholders' Equity	
0	=	0	−	12,800	Retained earnings
0	=	0	+	12,800	Common shares

c. On July 15, Beachcomber would only issue an announcement or press release. On August 31, there would be a memorandum journal entry only, such as: Distributed one new common share for each old share previously outstanding. This increased the number of common shares issued from 16,000 to 32,000.

d. The only effect of the 2-for-1 stock split on shareholders' equity would be to change the number of outstanding shares, in this case from 16,000 to 32,000 common shares. It would also double the number of authorized shares, if the number is not unlimited.

2. Average price per share = 900,000 ÷ 150,000 = $6

20,000 shares × $6.00 = $120,000

20,000 shares × $4.50 = $90,000

Mar. 1	Common shares	120,000	
	Contributed Surplus—Share Repurchase		30,000
	Cash		90,000

3. 20,000 shares × $8.25 = $165,000

Mar. 1	Common Shares	120,000	
	Retained Earnings	45,000	
	Cash		165,000

4.

Shareholders' Equity	
Contributed capital	
Common shares, 400,000 shares authorized, 130,000 shares issued and outstanding	$ 780,000
Retained earnings	$ 655,000
Total shareholders' equity	$1,435,000

5. In the Discontinued Operations section of the income statement, you would list two items:

Operating loss, $960,000, less income tax savings, $288,000	$ (672,000)
Gain on disposal, $1,700,000 less income tax, $510,000	1,190,000
	$ 518,000

6. To calculate Hart Corp.'s EPS, first calculate the weighted average number of common shares outstanding during the year:

	A	B	C	D
1	Weighted average number of common shares:			
2	For January to March	270,000 × $^{3}/_{12}$ =	67,500	
3	For April to December	310,000 × $^{9}/_{12}$ =	232,500	
4			300,000	shares

$$EPS = [\$3{,}750{,}000 - (200{,}000 \times \$9)] \div 300{,}000 \text{ shares}$$
$$= (\$3{,}750{,}000 - \$1{,}800{,}000) \div 300{,}000$$
$$= \$6.50$$

7.

CHECKPOINT INDUSTRIES INC.
Statement of Shareholders' Equity
For the Year Ended April 30, 2020

	Common Shares	Contributed Surplus— Share Repurchases	Retained Earnings	Total Shareholders' Equity
Balance, April 30, 2019	$ 260,000	$ 0	$100,000 (a)	$360,000
Issuance of shares	100,000			100,000
Net income			62,500	62,500 (c)
Cash dividends			(22,000)	(22,000)
Repurchase of common shares	(60,000)	10,000 (b)		(50,000)
Balance, April 30, 2020	$ 300,000	$ 10,000	$140,500	$450,500 (d)

8.

	Change in estimate	Change in policy	Error	Retrospective Statement	Prospective Statement
A.		✓		✓	
B.	✓				✓
C.			✓	✓	

15 Long-Term Liabilities

CONNECTING CHAPTER 15

LEARNING OBJECTIVES

① Define bonds payable and the types of bonds

What are bonds?

Bonds: An Introduction, page 820
  Types of Bonds

② Determine the price of a bond, and account for basic bond transactions

How do we account for the sale of a bond?

Bonds, page 822
  Present Value
  Bond Interest Rates
Issuing Bonds to Borrow Money, page 824
  Issuing Bonds at Par Value
  Issuing Bonds and Notes between Interest Dates
  Issuing Bonds at a Discount
  Issuing Bonds at a Premium

③ Amortize a bond discount and premium by the straight-line amortization method and the effective-interest amortization method

How do we allocate a bond discount or premium over the life of a bond?

Amortization of a Bond Discount and a Bond Premium, page 829
  Straight-Line Method
  Effective-Interest Method
Adjusting Entries for Interest Expense, page 836
  Adjusting Entries Using the Straight-Line Method
  Adjusting Entries Using the Effective-Interest Method

④ Account for retirement and conversion of bonds

How do we account for changes in a bond issue?

Retirement of Bonds, page 839
Convertible Bonds and Notes, page 840

⑤ Show the advantages and disadvantages of borrowing

How do we decide whether to issue debt versus equity?

Advantages and Disadvantages of Issuing Bonds versus Shares, page 841

⑥ Account for other long-term liabilities

How do we account for other long-term liabilities?

Mortgages and Other Long-Term Liabilities, page 842
  Mortgages: An Introduction
  Balance Sheet Presentation of Long-Term Liabilities
  Other Long-Term Liabilities

⑦ Account for operating leases and for assets acquired through a capital lease

How do we account for leases?

Lease Liabilities, page 844
  Operating Leases
  Capital Leases

⑧ Identify the effects of IFRS on long-term liabilities

How does IFRS affect long-term liabilities?

The Effects of IFRS on Long-Term Liabilities, page 848

Ⓐ1 Compute the future value of an investment

How do we find the future value of an investment?

Future Value, page 873
  Future Value Tables
  Future Value of an Annuity

Ⓐ2 Compute the present value of a single future amount and the present value of an annuity

How do we find the present value of an investment?

Time Value of Money: Future Value and Present Value, page 873
Future Value, page 873
Present Value, page 876
  Present Value Tables
  Present Value of an Annuity
  Present Value of Bonds Payable

The **Summary** for Chapter 15 appears on pages 851–852.
Key Terms with definitions for this chapter's material appear on pages 852–853.

CPA competencies

This text covers material outlined in **Section 1: Financial Reporting of the CPA Competency Map**. The Learning Objectives for each chapter have been aligned with the CPA Competency Map to ensure the best coverage possible.

1.1.2 Evaluates the appropriateness of the basis of financial reporting

1.2.2 Evaluates treatment for routine transactions

5.1.1 Evaluates the entity's financial state

Hero Images/Getty Images

Kind Animations Inc. specializes in creating animated feature films for children. Founders Steve Lasseter and Lee Bird started the studio when they were still in school. The corporation plans to expand its existing operations by building a new studio that will produce short movies and TV specials. In order to fund this expansion, the corporation is considering several options. One option is for the corporation to issue additional shares to raise the necessary cash. Another option is for the corporation to take on additional debt. As majority shareholders, Steve and Lee have expressed their concern over issuing additional shares of stock, fearing that the additional shares will decrease their ownership percentage in the corporation and possibly allow others to gain control of the business. Due to these concerns, the corporation has decided that the best option would be to explore ways to secure the cash needed for expansion by taking on additional debt.

Kind Animations is currently evaluating different types of long-term liability options such as long-term notes payable and mortgages payable. These debts will most likely be secured by the studio building and will offer a reasonable interest rate and time period for repayment. In addition, Kind Animations is also considering a special type of long-term liability, called a *bond payable*. Bonds payable are issued on a bond market and typically provides a larger cash inflow and longer time for repayment than notes payable and mortgages payable do. Each of these long-term liabilities is unique and offers advantages and disadvantages that Kind Animations needs to consider before it can begin the expansion.

This chapter discusses the third way to finance a company—borrowing money on long-term liabilities. Recall from Chapter 4 that **long-term liabilities** are debts due to be paid in more than a year or more than one of the entity's operating cycles if an operating cycle is greater than one year. Examples include bonds and debentures payable, long-term notes payable, and lease liabilities. The chapter appendix provides an optional background on present and future value calculations used in the valuation of long-term liabilities.

In Chapter 11 we saw how to account for short-term notes payable. There is a lot of similarity between accounting for short-term notes payable and long-term notes payable.

> The three ways to finance a company are through contributed capital (investing or selling shares), profitable operations (retained earnings), and borrowing money (long-term liabilities).

Bonds: An Introduction

LO ①

What are bonds?

Large companies, such as McDonald's Corporation, Canadian National Railway Company (CN), and WestJet Airlines Ltd., cannot borrow billions of dollars from a single lender because no lender will risk lending that much money to a single company. Even for smaller companies it may be impossible to borrow all they need from a bank.

How, then, do large corporations borrow a huge amount of money? They may issue bonds to the public. A **bond** is a formal arrangement between the issuer of the bond and the holder of the bond. The bondholder (the person or company that buys the bond) lends a fixed amount of money to the issuer. The issuer, such as Kind Animations Inc., promises to pay the fixed amount at some future date and to pay regular payments of interest to the bondholder over the life of the bond. The details of the formal arrangement are contained in the **bond indenture** or offering circular. A bond is a debt of the company that issued the bond. **Bonds payable** are groups of notes payable issued to multiple lenders, called bondholders. Most investments, including bonds, are made using a licensed dealer who receives a commission or fee on the purchase.

Purchasers of bonds may receive a bond certificate, which shows the name of the company that borrowed the money, exactly like a note payable. Exhibit 15–1 shows a bond certificate issued by Kind Animations Inc. (with legal details in the middle omitted). The certificate also states the **principal value**, which is the amount that the company has borrowed from the bondholder. The bond's principal amount is also called the bond's **maturity value**, **par value**, or **face value**. The issuing company must pay each bondholder the principal amount at a specific future date, called the **maturity date**, which also appears on the certificate. Today transactions are completed electronically, thereby reducing the need for paper shares or certificates.

EXHIBIT 15–1 | Bond Certificate

Bondholders lend their money to earn interest. The bond certificate states the **coupon rate**, which is the interest rate that the issuer will pay the bondholder and the dates that the interest payments are due (generally twice a year).

For example, if Kind Animations Inc. issues a five-year, 9% bond at a face value of $100,000 on January 1, 2018, and makes 10 semi-annual interest payments of $4,500 ($100,000 $\times$ 0.09 $\times$ 6/12), the cash flow for the bond is as follows:

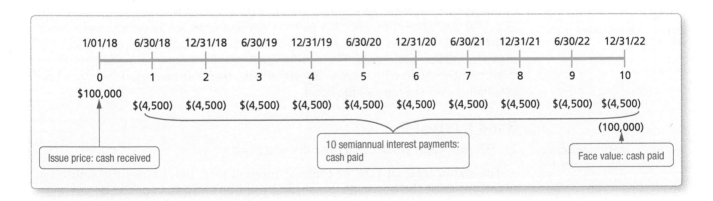

Types of Bonds

There are various types of bonds, which are summarized in Exhibit 15–2.

The discussion in this chapter will generally refer simply to *bonds,* since secured bonds and debentures (unsecured bonds) are treated essentially the same way for accounting purposes.

A debenture is an unsecured bond and, therefore, is riskier than a bond, which is secured.

EXHIBIT 15–2 | Types of Bonds

Type of Bond	Explanation
Term bonds	Bonds that all mature at the same time. For example, a $10,000 bond will return $10,000 at the end of the term.
Serial bonds	Bonds that mature in instalments at regular intervals. For example, a $500,000, five-year serial bond may mature in $100,000 annual instalments over a five-year period.
Secured bonds	Bonds that give the bondholder the right to take specified assets of the issuer (called collateral) if the issuer *defaults*, that is, fails to pay principal or interest. Details of the collateral must be provided in the notes to the financial statements.
Debentures	Unsecured bonds that are backed only by the good faith of the issuer. The bond shown in Exhibit 15–1 is a debenture because there are no rights to specific assets given in the first paragraph on the bond.
Bearer bonds	Bonds payable to the person that has possession of them. They are also called **unregistered bonds**.

Try It!

1. Refer to the bond certificate illustrated in Exhibit 15–1 and answer the following questions:
   a. What is the name of the corporation issuing the bond?
   b. What is the face value of the bond?
   c. What is the maturity date of the bond?
   d. What is the name of the bondholder?
   e. What is the stated interest rate the issuer will pay the bondholder?

Solutions appear at the end of this chapter and on **MyLab Accounting**

Bonds

LO ②

How do we account for the sale of a bond?

Bonds are sold at their *market price*, which is the amount that investors are willing to pay at any given time. Market price is calculated as the bond's present value, which equals the present value of the principal payment plus the present value of the cash interest payments. The cash interest payments can be made once every three months (quarterly), once every six months (semi-annually), or once per year (annually) over the term of the bond.

Bond Interest Rates

Because market interest rates fluctuate daily, the stated or contract interest rate will seldom equal the market interest rate on the date the bonds are sold.

Two interest rates work to set the price of a bond:

- The **stated interest rate**, or **contract interest rate**, determines the amount of cash interest the borrower pays—and the investor receives—each year. The stated interest rate is printed on the bond and is set by the bond contract. It may be fixed or adjustable. If the rate is fixed, it does not change during the life of the bond. For example, Kind Animations Inc.'s bonds have a stated interest rate of 9 percent (Exhibit 15–1). Thus, Kind Animations pays $9,000 of interest annually on each $100,000 bond. Each semi-annual interest payment is $4,500 ($100,000 × 0.09 × 1/2).

- The **market interest rate**, or **effective interest rate**, is the rate that investors demand for lending their money. The market interest rate changes constantly.

Bond Prices

A company may issue bonds with a stated interest rate that differs from the prevailing market interest rate. Kind Animations Inc. may issue its 9 percent bonds when the market rate for bonds issued by companies with a similar level of risk has risen to 10 percent. Will the Kind Animations bonds attract investors in this market? No, because investors can earn 10 percent on other bonds with a similar level of risk. In order to receive a 10 percent return on their investment, investors will purchase Kind Animations bonds only at a price less than the maturity value. The difference between the lower price and the bonds' maturity value is a **discount**. Conversely, if the market interest rate is 8 percent, Kind Animations' 9 percent bonds will be so attractive that investors will pay more than the maturity value for them. The difference between the higher price and the maturity value is a **premium**.

Exhibit 15–3 shows how the stated interest rate and the market interest rate interact to determine the issue price, or selling price, of a bond.

> A bond can be issued at any price agreed upon by the issuer and the bondholders. The issue price of a bond does not affect the required payment at maturity. In all cases, the issuer must pay the maturity value of the bonds when they mature.

> Bonds sell at a *premium* if the market rate drops below the stated (contract) rate. Bonds sell at a *discount* if the market rate rises above the stated rate.

EXHIBIT 15–3 | How the Stated Interest Rate and the Market Interest Rate Interact to Determine the Issue Price of a Bond

Example: Bond with a Stated (Contract) Interest Rate of 9%

Bond's Stated Interest Rate		Market Interest Rate		Issue Price of the Bond
9%	=	9%	→	Maturity value (face or par value)
9%	<	10%	→	Discount (price below maturity value)
9%	>	8%	→	Premium (price above maturity value)

After a bond is issued, investors may buy and sell it through bond markets. The bond market in Canada is called the **over-the-counter (OTC) market**. It is a network of investment dealers who trade bonds issued by the Government of Canada and Crown corporations, the provinces, municipalities, regions, and corporations.

Bond prices are quoted at a percentage of their maturity value, using 100 as a base. For example:

- A $1,000 bond quoted at 100 is bought or sold for 100 percent of par value ($1,000 × 1.000).
- A $1,000 bond quoted at 101.5 has a price of $1,015 ($1,000 × 1.015).
- A $1,000 bond quoted at 98.5 has a price of $985 ($1,000 × 0.985).

Exhibit 15–4 contains actual price information for a TELUS Corporation bond, as quoted on the website canadianfixedincome.ca on December 22, 2017.

EXHIBIT 15–4 | TELUS Bond Price

Bonds	Coupon	Eff. Maturity	Price	Yield
TELUS Corporation	2.350	Mar. 28, 2022	99.04	2.59

- 2.35% interest rate stated on the bond
- Date when the $1,000 bond will be paid back
- Quoted or **bid price** is $990.40 for each $1,000 bond
- Interest rate that an investor will receive, based on a compounding period of one year is 2.59%

Bonds sell at a premium or a discount when the interest rate that will be paid on the bond is different from the interest rate available to investors elsewhere in the market at the time of the bond issuance. As a bond nears maturity, its market price moves toward its maturity value. On the maturity date, the market value of a bond equals exactly its maturity value because the company that issued the bond pays that amount to retire the bond.

Present Value[1]

A dollar received today is worth more than a dollar received in the future. Why? Because you can invest today's dollar and earn income from it. Likewise, deferring any payment until later gives your money a period of time to grow. Money earns income over time, a concept called the *time value of money*. Let's examine how the time value of money affects the pricing of bonds.

Assume a $1,000 bond reaches maturity three years from today and carries no interest. Would you pay $1,000 to purchase this bond? No, because paying $1,000 today to receive the same amount in the future provides you with no income on the investment. You would not be taking advantage of the time value of money. Just how much should you pay today to receive $1,000 at the end of three years? The answer is some amount less than $1,000. The diagram below shows the relationship between a bond's price (present value) and its maturity amount (future value).

> You should be able to invest today's money (present value) so that its value will increase (future value). The difference between present value and future value is interest earned.
>
> Present Value
> + Interest Earned
> ─────────────
> = Future Value

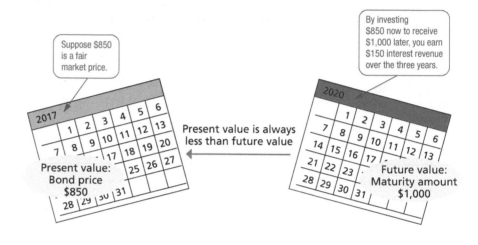

The exact **present value** of any future amount depends on the following:

1. The amount of the future payment (or receipt)
2. The length of time from the date of the investment to the date when the future amount is to be received (or paid)
3. The interest rate during the period

> When you buy a bond, you are really "buying" two future cash flows: principal and interest payments. The principal is a single sum received at maturity, and the interest payments are a series of receipts received each period until maturity.

Unlike the example above, most bonds have interest payments. So how do we come up with a price of 101.5 or 98.5? We apply the same math but also consider the value of the interim interest payments.

We show how to compute present value in this chapter's appendix. You need to be aware of the present value concept in the discussion of bonds that follows. If your instructor so directs you, please study the appendix now.

Issuing Bonds to Borrow Money

The basic journal entry to record the issuance of bonds debits Cash and credits Bonds Payable. The company may issue bonds for three different bond prices which we look at in turn:

- At *par* value
- At a *discount*
- At a *premium*

---

[1] The appendix for this chapter covers present value in more detail.

Issuing Bonds at Par Value

We begin with the simplest case: issuing bonds at par (maturity) value.

Suppose that UVW Corporation has $100 million in 6 percent bonds that mature in 10 years. Assume that UVW Corporation issued these bonds at par on January 2, 2020. The issuance entry is as follows:

2020			
Jan. 2	Cash	100,000,000	
	Bonds Payable		100,000,000
	To issue 6%, 10-year bonds at par.		

UVW Corporation, the borrower, makes this one-time entry to record the receipt of cash and issuance of bonds. Afterward, investors buy and sell the bonds through the bond markets, in a similar way to buying and selling shares through the stock market. Many of these transactions can be completed online. The buy-and-sell transactions between investors do not involve the company that issued the bonds. The company does not keep records of these transactions, except for the names and addresses of the bondholders. (This information is needed for mailing the interest and principal payments. The company may also have bondholder account information so that interest and principal payments can be directly deposited into bondholders' bank or investment accounts.)

Interest payments for these bonds occur each January 2 and July 2. UVW Corporation's entry to record the first semi-annual interest payment is:

Amount of interest = Principal × Rate × Time

2020			
Jul. 2	Interest Expense	3,000,000	
	Cash		3,000,000
	To pay semi-annual interest on bonds payable ($100,000,000 × 0.06 × 6/12).		

Each semi-annual interest payment follows this same pattern.
At maturity, UVW Corporation will record payment of the bonds as follows:

2030			
Jan. 2	Bonds Payable	100,000,000	
	Cash		100,000,000
	To pay bonds payable at maturity.		

Issuing Bonds and Notes between Interest Dates

The previous example of UVW Corporation's bond transactions are straightforward because the company issued the bonds on an interest payment date (January 2). However, corporations often issue bonds between interest dates.

Suppose Manitoba Hydro issues $200 million of 5 percent bonds due June 15, 2026. These bonds are dated June 15, 2020, and carry the price "100 plus accrued interest." An investor purchasing the bonds after the bond date must pay market value *plus accrued interest*. The issuing company will pay the full semi-annual interest amount to the bondholder at the next interest payment date. Companies do not split semi-annual interest payments among two or more investors who happen to hold the bonds during a six-month interest period since the record keeping for this would be difficult.

Assume that Manitoba Hydro sells $100,000 of its bonds on July 15, 2020, one month after the bond date of June 15. Also assume that the market price of the bonds on July 15 is the face value when issuing these bonds. Manitoba Hydro receives one month's accrued interest in addition to the bond's face value, as shown in the following timeline:

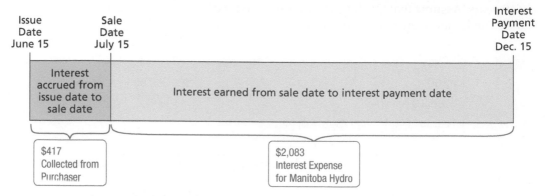

Manitoba Hydro's entry to record the issuance of the bonds payable is:

2020			
Jul. 15	Cash	100,417	
	Bonds Payable		100,000
	Interest Payable		417
	To issue 5%, 10-year bonds at par, one month after the original issue date. Interest payable is $417 ($100,000 × 0.05 × 1/12).		

Manitoba Hydro has collected one month's interest in advance. On December 15, 2020, Manitoba Hydro's entry to record the first semi-annual interest payment on this $100,000 is:

2020			
Dec. 15	Interest Expense	2,083	
	Interest Payable	417	
	Cash		2,500
	To pay semi-annual interest on bonds payable. Interest expense is $2,083 ($100,000 × 0.05 × 5/12); cash paid is $2,500 ($100,000 × 0.05 × 6/12).		

When an investor sells bonds or debentures to another investor between interest dates, the price is always "plus accrued interest." Suppose you hold a bond for two months of a semi-annual interest period and sell the bonds to another investor before you receive your interest. The person who buys the bonds will receive your two months of interest on the next specified interest date. Thus, you must collect your share of the interest from the buyer when you sell your investment, which happens when the price is "plus accrued interest."

The debit to Interest Payable eliminates the credit balance in that account from July 15. Manitoba Hydro has now paid that liability.

Note that Manitoba Hydro pays a full six months' interest on December 15. After subtracting the one month's accrued interest received at the time of issuing the bond, Manitoba Hydro has recorded interest expense for five months ($2,083). This interest expense is the correct amount for the five months that the bonds have been outstanding.

If Manitoba Hydro prepared financial statements immediately after December 15, 2020, it would report nothing on the balance sheet, because Interest Payable is $0, and would report Interest Expense of $2,083 on the income statement.

Issuing Bonds at a Discount

We know that market conditions may force a company like UVW Corporation to accept a discount price for its bonds. Suppose UVW Corporation issues $1,000,000 of its 6 percent, 10-year bonds when the market interest rate is 6.27 percent. As a result, the market price of the bonds drops to a rounded factor of 98.00, which means 98 percent of face or par value. To simplify the example we use a factor; however, a more accurate calculation of the bond price is in the margin. UVW Corporation receives $980,000 ($1,000,000 × 0.98) at issuance and makes the following journal entry:

2020			
Jan. 2	Cash	980,000	
	Discount on Bonds Payable	20,000	
	Bonds Payable		1,000,000
	To issue 6%, 10-year bonds at a discount.		

Using a financial calculator, the price would be $980,163.82 based on entering the following using a BAII Plus financial calculator:

$1,000,000 = **FV**
20 (or 10 yrs × periods) = **N**
3.135 or (6.27/2) = **I/Y**
$30,000 = **PMT**
($1,000,000 × .06/2 periods)
Then **CPT** **PV** = $980,163.82
Then $980,163.82/$1,000,000
× 100 = 98 (rounded)

Periods = payments/year

After posting, the bond accounts have the following balances:

Main Account: Bonds Payable	Contra Account: Discount on Bonds Payable
1,000,000	20,000

Bond carrying value = $980,000

Reporting Discount on Bonds Payable Discount on Bonds Payable is a contra account to Bonds Payable. Bonds Payable *minus* the discount gives the book value, or carrying value, of the bonds. The relationship between Bonds Payable and the Discount account is similar to the relationships between Equipment and Accumulated Amortization, and between Accounts Receivable and Allowance for Doubtful Accounts. Thus, UVW Corporation's liability is $980,000, which is the amount the company borrowed. UVW Corporation's balance sheet immediately after issuance of the bonds reports the following:

Long-term liabilities		
Bonds payable, 6%, due 2030	$1,000,000	
Less: Discount on bonds payable	20,000	$980,000

If UVW Corporation were to pay off the bonds immediately (an unlikely occurrence), the company's required outlay would be $980,000 because the market price of the bonds is $980,000.

Interest Expense on Bonds Issued at a Discount We saw earlier that a bond's stated interest rate may differ from the market interest rate. Suppose the market rate is 6.27 percent when UVW Corporation issues its 6 percent bonds. The 0.27 percent interest rate difference creates the $20,000 discount on the bonds. UVW Corporation borrows $980,000 cash but must pay $1,000,000 cash when the bonds mature 10 years later. What happens to the $20,000 balance of the discount account over the life of the bond issue?

The cash flow of the UVW bond, as payable to the bondholder, is shown below:

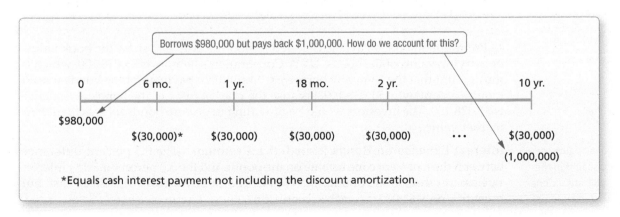

*Equals cash interest payment not including the discount amortization.

The $20,000 is in reality an additional interest expense to the issuing company. That amount is a cost—beyond the stated interest rate—that the business pays for borrowing the investors' money. The discount has the effect of raising the interest expense on the bonds to the market interest rate of 6.27 percent.

The discount amount is an interest expense not paid until the bond matures. However, the borrower—the bond issuer—benefits from the use of the investors' money each accounting period over the full term of the bond issue. The matching objective directs the business to match an expense against its revenues on a period-by-period basis, so the discount is allocated to Interest Expense through amortization for each accounting period over the life of the bonds. We will examine this in more detail shortly.

Issuing Bonds at a Premium

To illustrate issuing bonds at a premium, let's change the UVW Corporation example. Assume that the market interest rate is 5.5 percent when the company issues its 6 percent, 10-year bonds. These 6 percent bonds are attractive in a 5.5 percent market, so investors will pay a premium price to acquire them. We can use a factor again for simplicity and round the price to 103.81 so that UVW Corporation receives $1,038,100 cash upon issuance ($1,000,000 × 1.0381). The entry is as follows:

2020			
Jan. 2	Cash	1,038,100	
	Bonds Payable		1,000,000
	Premium on Bonds Payable		38,100
	To issue 6%, 10-year bonds at a premium.		

Using a financial calculator, the price would be $1,038,068.13, based on

$1,000,000 = **FV**
20 = **N**
2.75 = **I/Y**
$30,000 = **PMT**
CPT **PV**

The difference between $1,038,068.13 and $1,038,100 (which is $31.87) is due to rounding.

After posting, the bond accounts have the following balances:

Main Account: Bonds Payable		Companion Account: Premium on Bonds Payable	
	1,000,000		38,100

Bond carrying value = $1,038,100

Reporting Premium on Bonds Payable   UVW Corporation's balance sheet immediately after issuance of the bonds reports the following:

Long-term liabilities		
Bonds payable, 6%, due 2030	$1,000,000	
Premium on bonds payable	38,100	$1,038,100

Premium on Bonds Payable is added to Bonds Payable to show the book value, or carrying value, of the bonds. UVW Corporation's liability is $1,038,100, which is the amount that the company borrowed. Immediate payment of the bonds would require an outlay of $1,038,100, because the market price of the bonds at issuance is $1,038,100. The investors would be unwilling to give up bonds for less than their market value.

In addition to including the premium or discount in the selling price, all transactions also include accrued interest.

Interest Expense on Bonds Issued at a Premium   The 0.5 percent difference between the 6 percent contract rate on the bonds and the 5.5 percent market interest rate creates the $38,100 premium. UVW Corporation borrows $1,038,100 cash but must pay only $1,000,000 cash at maturity:

The cash flow of the UVW bond, payable to the bondholder, is shown below:

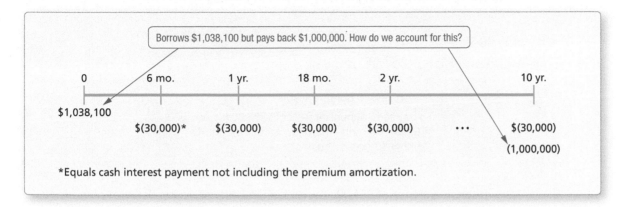

We treat the premium as a reduction of interest expense to UVW Corporation. The premium reduces UVW Corporation's cost of borrowing the money and reduces the company's interest expense to an effective interest rate of 5.5 percent, the market rate. We account for the premium much as we handled the discount. We amortize the bond premium as a *decrease* in interest expense over the life of the bonds.

Try It!

2. In each of the following situations, will the bonds sell at par, at a premium, or at a discount?
   a. 4 percent bonds sold when the market rate is 4.5 percent
   b. 4 percent bonds sold when the market rate is 3.8 percent
   c. 3.5 percent bonds sold when the market rate is 3.5 percent

3. Sunwood Insurance Corp. issued $1,000,000 of 3.75 percent, 10-year bonds at the market price of 99.00. Record the journal entry for the issuance of the bonds on April 1. Include an explanation.

4. Parksville Insurance Corp. issued $1,000,000 of 3.75 percent, 10-year bonds at the market price of 101.50. Record the journal entry for the issuance of the bonds on May 6. Include an explanation.

Solutions appear at the end of this chapter and on **MyLab Accounting**

Amortization of a Bond Discount and a Bond Premium

There are two methods for amortizing a bond discount and a bond premium: the straight-line method and the effective-interest method. Each of these will be discussed in turn.

LO ③

How do we allocate a bond discount or premium over the life of a bond?

Straight-Line Method

We can amortize a bond discount or a bond premium by dividing the discount or premium into equal amounts for each interest period. This method is called **straight-line amortization**. The calculations are similar to what we saw for assets in Chapters 3 and 10: divide the balance by the number of periods.

Straight-Line Amortization of a Bond Discount In our UVW Corporation example on page 827, the beginning discount is $20,000 and there are 20 semi-annual interest periods during the bonds' 10-year life. Therefore, 1/20 of the $20,000 bond discount ($20,000 ÷ 20 = $1,000) is amortized each interest period. UVW Corporation's semi-annual interest entry on July 2, 2020, is as follows:

2020			
Jul. 2	Interest Expense	31,000	
	Cash		30,000
	Discount on Bonds Payable		1,000
	To pay semi-annual interest of $30,000 ($1,000,000 × 0.06 × $^6/_{12}$) and amortize discount on bonds payable, $1,000 ($20,000 ÷ 20).[2]		

Interest expense of $31,000 for each six-month period is the sum of:

- The stated interest ($30,000), which is paid in cash
- *Plus* the amortization of the discount ($1,000)

Discount on Bonds Payable has a debit balance. Therefore, we credit the Discount account to amortize (reduce) its balance. Since Discount on Bonds Payable is a contra account, each reduction in its balance increases the book value or carrying value of Bonds Payable. At July 2, immediately after amortizing the bond discount the balance sheet would report the following:

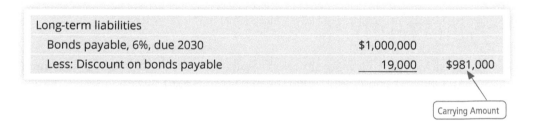

Long-term liabilities		
Bonds payable, 6%, due 2030	$1,000,000	
Less: Discount on bonds payable	19,000	$981,000

Carrying Amount

Twenty amortization entries (semi-annual journal entries for 10 years) will decrease the discount balance to zero, which means that the Bonds Payable book or carrying value will have increased by $20,000 up to its face value of $1,000,000 by the maturity date. The entry to pay the bonds at maturity is:

2030			
Jan. 2	Bonds Payable	1,000,000	
	Cash		1,000,000
	To pay the bonds payable at maturity.		

---

[2]Some accountants may record the payment of interest and the amortization of the discount in two separate entries, as follows (both approaches are equally correct):

2020			
Jul. 2	Interest Expense	30,000	
	Cash		30,000
	Paid semi-annual interest ($1,000,000 × 0.06 × $^6/_{12}$).		
2	Interest Expense	1,000	
	Discount on Bonds Payable		1,000
	Amortized discount on bonds payable ($20,000 ÷ 20).		

Straight-Line Amortization of a Bond Premium   In our UVW Corporation example on page 828, the beginning premium is $38,100 and there are 20 semi-annual interest periods during the bonds' 10-year life. Therefore, 1/20 of the $38,100 ($1,905) of bond premium is amortized each interest period. UVW Corporation's semi-annual interest entry on July 2, 2020, is as follows:

2020			
Jul. 2	Interest Expense	28,095	
	Premium on Bonds Payable	1,905	
	Cash		30,000
	To pay semi-annual interest ($1,000,000 × 0.06 × $\frac{6}{12}$) and amortize premium on bonds payable ($38,100 ÷ 20).[3]		

Interest expense of $28,095 is

- The stated interest ($30,000), which is paid in cash
- *Minus* the amortization of the premium ($1,905)

The debit to Premium on Bonds Payable reduces its normal balance, which is a credit.

At July 2, 2020, immediately after amortizing the bond premium, the bonds have a carrying amount of:

Long-term liabilities		
Bonds payable, 6%, due 2030	$1,000,000	
Premium on bonds payable	36,195	$1,036,195 ◄— 1,000,000 + ($38,100 − $1,905)

At January 2, 2021, after the interest payment has been recorded, the bond's carrying amount will be:

Long-term liabilities		
Bonds payable, 6%, due 2030	$1,000,000	
Premium on bonds payable	34,290	$1,034,290 ◄— $1,000,000 + ($38,100 − $1,905 − $1,905) Or $1,000,000 + ($36,195 − $1,905)

At maturity on January 2, 2030, the bond premium will have been fully amortized and the bonds' carrying amount will be $1,000,000. The journal entry to pay the bond at maturity is the same as if there were a discount or if it were issued at par.

---

[3] The payment of interest and the amortization of the bond premium can be recorded in two separate entries as follows:

2020			
Jul. 2	Interest Expense	30,000	
	Cash		30,000
	Paid semi-annual interest. ($1,000,000 × 0.06 × $\frac{6}{12}$).		
2	Premium on Bonds Payable	1,905	
	Interest Expense		1,905
	Amortized premium on bonds payable by reducing interest expense. ($38,100 ÷ 20).		

When bonds sell at a premium, we collect additional cash when they are sold. However, to amortize this amount, we reduce Interest Expense rather than set up a revenue account.

Effective-Interest Method

The amount of cash paid each semi-annual interest period is calculated with the formula Interest paid = Face value × (Stated rate ÷ 2). This amount does not change over the term of the bond.

The straight-line amortization method has a theoretical weakness. Each period's amortization amount for a premium or discount is the same dollar amount over the life of the bonds. However, over that time the bonds' carrying value continues to increase (with a discount) or decrease (with a premium). Thus the fixed dollar amount of amortization changes as a percentage of the bonds' carrying value, making it appear that the bond issuer's interest rate changes over time. This appearance is misleading because in fact the issuer locked in a fixed interest rate when the bonds were issued. The stated interest *rate* on the bonds does not change.

Effective-interest amortization keeps each interest expense amount at the same percentage of the bonds' carrying value or book value for every interest payment over the bonds' life. The total amount of bond discount or bond premium amortized over the life of the bonds is the same under both methods. International Financial Reporting Standards (IFRS) specify that the effective-interest method should be used because it does a better job of matching the interest expense to the revenue earned. However, the straight-line method is popular because of its simplicity, and in practice, if there is no material difference, then the cost–benefit constraint results in companies using straight-line amortization. Accounting Standards for Private Enterprises (ASPE) allows both methods of amortization.

Effective-Interest Method of Amortizing a Bond Discount

Assume that on January 2, 2020, UVW Corporation issues $1,000,000 of 5 percent bonds at a time when the market rate of interest is 6 percent. Also assume that these bonds mature in five years and pay interest semi-annually, so there are 10 semi-annual interest payments. The issue price of the bonds is $957,349.[4] The discount on these bonds is $42,651 ($1,000,000 – $957,349). Exhibit 15–5 illustrates amortization of the discount by the effective-interest method.

Recall that we want to present interest expense amounts over the full life of the bonds at a fixed percentage of the bonds' carrying value. The 3 percent rate—the effective-interest rate (6 ÷ 2)—*is* that percentage. We have calculated the cost of the money borrowed by the bond issuer—the interest expense—as a constant percentage of the carrying value of the bonds. The *dollar amount* of interest expense varies from period to period, but the interest percentage applied to the carrying value remains the same.

The *accounts* debited and credited under the effective-interest amortization method and the straight-line method are the same. Only the *amounts* differ. We may take the amortization *amounts* directly from the table in Exhibit 15–5. We assume that the first interest payment occurs on July 2 and use the appropriate amounts from Exhibit 15–5, reading across the line for the first interest payment date:

Jul. 2	Interest Expense	28,720	
	Discount on Bonds Payable		3,720
	Cash		25,000
	To pay semi-annual interest (Column B) and amortize discount (Column D) on bonds payable.		

---

[4]We show how to compute this amount in the appendix for this chapter. The calculation shown here was made with a calculator. In the appendix, the amount is computed using the present value tables that appear in the appendix.

EXHIBIT 15–5 | Effective-Interest Method of Amortizing a Bond Discount

	A	B	C	D	E	F
1	**Bond Data:**					
2	**Maturity value:**		$1,000,000			
3	**Stated interest rate:**		5%			
4	**Semi-annual interest:**		2.5%			
5	**Market interest rate:**		6%	Annual		
6			3%	Semi-annual		
7						
8	**Semi-annual Interest Period**	**Interest Payment (2.5% of Maturity Value)**	**Interest Expense (3% of Preceding F)**	**Discount Amortization (C – B)**	**Unamortized Discount Account Balance (Preceding E – Current D)**	**Bond Carrying Amount ($1,000,000 – E)**
9	Issue Date				$42,651	$ 957,349*
10	1	$25,000	$28,720	$3,720	38,931	961,069
11	2	25,000	28,832	3,832	35,099	964,901
12	3	25,000	28,947	3,947	31,152	968,848
13	4	25,000	29,065	4,065	27,087	972,913
14	5	25,000	29,187	4,187	22,900	977,100
15	6	25,000	29,313	4,313	18,587	981,413
16	7	25,000	29,442	4,442	14,145	985,855
17	8	25,000	29,576	4,576	9,569	990,431
18	9	25,000	29,713	4,713	4,856	995,144
19	10	25,000	29,856	4,856	0	1,000,000
	*Minor differences because of the effect of rounding.					

$1,000,000 = FV
10 = N
6/2 = I/Y
$25,000 = PMT
CPT PV = Issue price
– $957,349

$1,000,000 = FV
10 = N
6/2 = I/Y
$25,000 = PMT

CPT PV
2nd PV (AMORT)
(for period 1 and first row of table) Five amounts will show in the screen using the up arrows: ⇑P1 = 1, INT = $28,720, PRN = $ – 3,720, BAL = $ – 961,069, P2 = 1
Note: Each time you hit the up arrow on the calculator a corresponding amount will appear on the calculator screen.

Notes

Column B The semi-annual interest payments are constant because they are fixed by the stated interest rate and the bonds' maturity value (the orange horizontal line labeled Interest payment in Exhibit 15–6, Panel A, on page 834; this number is manually calculated).
$25,000 = $1,000,000 × 0.025

Column C Calculate the interest expense each period by multiplying the preceding period's bond carrying amount by the market interest rate for the period. The effect of this *effective-interest rate* determines the interest expense each period. The amount of interest expense each period increases as the effective-interest rate, a constant, is applied to the increasing bond carrying amount (F) (the green line labeled Interest expense in Exhibit 15–6, Panel A).

Column D The excess of each interest expense amount (C) over each interest payment amount (B) is the discount amortization for the period (the shaded amount in Exhibit 15–6, Panel A).

Column E The unamortized discount balance decreases by the amount of amortization for the period (D), from $42,651 at the bonds' issue date to zero at their maturity (the shaded amount in Exhibit 15–6, Panel B). The balance of the discount plus the bonds' carrying amount equals the bonds' maturity value at all times; this is manually calculated.

Column F The bonds' carrying amount increases from $957,349 at issuance to $1,000,000 at maturity (the blue line labeled Bond carrying amount in Exhibit 15–6, Panel B).

Panel A of Exhibit 15–6 shows the interest expense over the life of bonds issued at a discount. Notice that the amortization of the bond discount slowly increases the interest expense (the green line labeled Interest expense). Panel B shows how the carrying amount of the bonds rises to the maturity date. The notes at the bottom of Exhibit 15–5 explain the amounts and lines in Exhibit 15–6.

EXHIBIT 15–6 | Interest Expense and Bond Carrying Amount Both Increase for Bonds Issued at a Discount

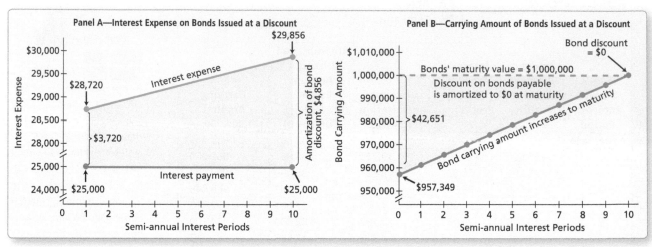

Effective-Interest Method of Amortizing a Bond Premium Let's modify the UVW Corporation example to illustrate the effective-interest method of amortizing a bond premium. Assume that on April 30 UVW Corporation issues $1,000,000 of five-year, 5 percent bonds that pay interest semi-annually. If the bonds are issued when the market interest rate is 4 percent, their issue price is $1,044,913.[5] The premium on these bonds is $44,913, and Exhibit 15–7 illustrates amortization of the premium by the effective-interest method.

Assuming that the first interest payment occurs on October 31, we read across the line in Exhibit 15–7 for the first interest payment date and pick up the appropriate amounts.

Oct. 31	Interest Expense	20,898	
	Premium on Bonds Payable	4,102	
	Cash		25,000
	To pay semi-annual interest (column B) and amortize premium (column D) on bonds payable.		

Panel A of Exhibit 15–8 shows the interest expense over the life of the bonds issued at a premium and how it decreases over time (green line). Panel B shows how the carrying amount of the bonds decreases to maturity. The notes at the bottom of Exhibit 15–7 explain the amounts and lines in Exhibit 15–8.

Does the method of amortizing a bond premium or discount affect the amount of cash interest paid on a bond? No. The amortization method for a bond premium or discount has *no effect* on the amount of cash interest paid on a bond. The amount of cash interest paid depends on the contract interest rate stated on the bond. That interest rate, and the amount of cash interest paid, are fixed and therefore remain constant over the life of the bond. To see this, examine Column B of Exhibits 15–5 and 15–7.

---

[5] Again, we compute the present value of the bonds using a calculator. In the appendix for this chapter, the amount is computed using present value tables.

EXHIBIT 15-7 | Effective-Interest Method of Amortizing a Bond Premium

	A	B	C	D	E	F
1	**Bond Data:**					
2	**Maturity value:**		$1,000,000			
3	**Stated interest rate:**		5%			
4	**Semi-annual interest:**		2.5%			
5	**Market interest rate:**		4%	**Annual**		
6			2%	**Semi-annual**		
7						
8	**Semi-annual Interest Period**	**Interest Payment (2.5% of Maturity Value)**	**Interest Expense (2% of Preceding F)**	**Premium Amortization (B − C)**	**Unamortized Premium Account Balance (Preceding E − Current D)**	**Bond Carrying Amount ($1,000,000 + E)**
9	Issue Date				$44,913	$1,044,913
10	1	$25,000	$20,898	$4,102	40,811	1,040,811
11	2	25,000	20,816	4,184	36,627	1,036,627
12	3	25,000	20,733	4,267	32,360	1,032,360
13	4	25,000	20,647	4,353	28,007	1,028,007
14	5	25,000	20,560	4,440	23,567	1,023,567
15	6	25,000	20,471	4,529	19,038	1,019,038
16	7	25,000	20,381	4,619	14,419	1,014,419
17	8	25,000	20,288	4,712	9,707	1,009,707
18	9	25,000	20,194	4,806	4,901	1,004,901
19	10	25,000	20,099	4,901	0	1,000,000

$1,000,000 = **FV**

10 = **N**

4/2 = **I/Y**

$25,000 = **PMT**

CPT **PV** = Issue price − $1,044,913

2nd **PV** (AMORT) #1 (for period 1 and first row of table) Five amounts will show in the screen using the up arrows: ⇑P1 = 1, INT = $20,898, PRN = $4,102, BAL = $ − 1,040,811, P2 = 1 Note: Each time you hit the up arrow on the calculator a corresponding amount will appear on the calculator screen.

Notes:

Column B	The semi-annual interest payments are a constant amount fixed by the stated interest rate and the bonds' maturity value (the orange horizontal line labeled Interest payment in Exhibit 15–8, Panel A, on page 836).
Column C	Calculate the interest expense each period by multiplying the preceding period's bond carrying amount by the effective-interest rate. The amount of interest expense decreases each period as the bond carrying amount decreases (the green line labeled Interest expense in Exhibit 15–8, Panel A).
Column D	The excess of each interest payment (B) over the period's interest expense (C) is the premium amortization for the period (the shaded area in Exhibit 15–8, Panel A).
Column E	The premium balance decreases by the amount of amortization for the period (D) from $44,913 at issuance to zero at maturity (the shaded area in Exhibit 15–9, Panel B). The bonds' carrying amount minus the premium balance equals the bonds' maturity value.
Column F	The bonds' carrying value decreases from $1,044,913 at issuance to $1,000,000 at maturity (the blue line labeled Bond carrying amount in Exhibit 15–8, Panel B)

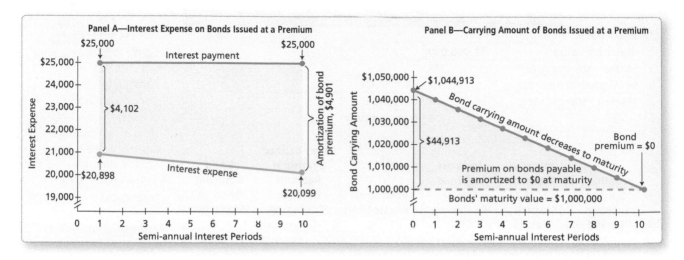

Adjusting Entries for Interest Expense

Chapter 3 introduced adjusting entries to accrue expenses. We are now adding a bond discount or premium amortization entry to the interest accrual entry.

Companies issue bonds when they need cash. The interest payments seldom occur on the end of the company's fiscal year. Nevertheless, interest expense must be accrued at the end of the period to measure net income accurately. The accrual entry may often be complicated by the need to amortize a discount or a premium for only a partial interest period.

Adjusting Entries Using the Straight-Line Method

Suppose Kind Animations Inc issues $50,000,000 of 8 percent, 10-year bonds at a $200,000 discount on October 1, 2020, for another expansion. Assume that interest payments occur on March 31 and September 30 each year. If December 31 is its year-end, Kind Animations records interest for the three-month period (October, November, and December) as follows:

2020			
Dec. 31	Interest Expense	1,005,000	
	Interest Payable		1,000,000
	Discount on Bonds Payable		5,000
	To accrue three months' interest payable ($50,000,000 $\times$ 0.08 $\times$ $^3/_{12}$) and amortize the discount on bonds payable for three months ($200,000 $\div$ 10 $\times$ $^3/_{12}$).		

Interest Payable is credited for the three months of cash interest that have accrued since September 30. Discount on Bonds Payable is credited for three months of amortization.

The Kind Animations balance sheet at December 31, 2020, reports Interest Payable of $1,000,000 as a current liability. Bonds Payable appears as a long-term liability, presented as follows:

Long-term liabilities		
Bonds payable, 8%, due 2030	$50,000,000	
Less: Discount on bonds payable	195,000	$49,805,000

Observe that the balance of Discount on Bonds Payable decreases by $5,000. The bonds' carrying value increases by the same amount. The bonds' carrying value continues to increase over their 10-year life, reaching $50,000,000 at maturity when the discount will be fully amortized.

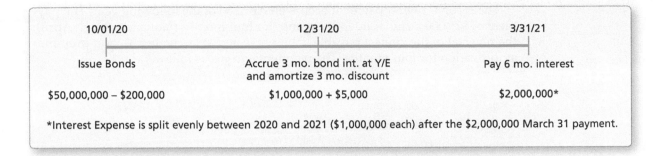

*Interest Expense is split evenly between 2020 and 2021 ($1,000,000 each) after the $2,000,000 March 31 payment.

The next semi-annual interest payment occurs on March 31, 2021, as follows:

2021			
Mar. 31	Interest Expense	1,005,000	
	Interest Payable	1,000,000	
	Cash		2,000,000
	Discount on Bonds Payable		5,000
	To pay semi-annual interest ($2,000,000 = $50,000,000 × 0.08 × $^6/_{12}$), of which $1,000,000 was accrued, and amortize three months' discount on bonds payable ($200,000 ÷ 10 × $^3/_{12}$).		

Amortization of a premium over a partial interest period is similar except that the account Premium on Bonds Payable is debited.

Adjusting Entries Using the Effective-Interest Method

At year-end, it is necessary to make an adjusting entry for accrued interest and amortization of the bond premium for a partial period. In our example using the effective-interest method of amortizing a premium on page 834, the last interest payment occurred on October 31. The adjustment for November and December must cover two months, or one-third of a semi-annual period.

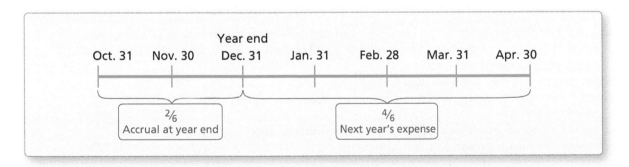

The entry, with amounts drawn from interest period 2 (line 11) in Exhibit 15–7 on page 835, is:

Dec. 31	Interest Expense	6,939	
	Premium on Bonds Payable	1,395	
	Interest Payable		8,334
	To accrue two months' interest expense ($20,816 × $^2/_6$), amortize the premium on bonds payable for two months ($4,184 × $^2/_6$), and record interest payable ($25,000 × $^2/_6$).		

The second interest payment occurs on April 30 of the following year. The payment of $25,000 includes interest expense for four months (January through April), the reversal of the interest payable liability created at December 31, and premium amortization for four months. The payment entry is as follows:

Apr. 30	Interest Expense	13,877	
	Interest Payable	8,334	
	Premium on Bonds Payable	2,789	
	Cash		25,000
	To record semi-annual interest for four months ($13,877 = $20,816 × ⁴⁄₆), reverse interest payable accrual ($8,334), amortize the premium on bonds payable for four months ($4,184 × ⁴⁄₆), and make the cash interest payment of $25,000.		

	A	B	C	D	E	F
1		Accrued for Nov-Dec (2/6 months)		Expense for Jan-Apr (4/6 months)		From line 11 in Exhibit 15-7
2	Total interest expense	$6,939	+	$13,877	=	$20,816
3	Total premium on bonds payable	$1,395	+	$ 2,789	=	$4,184
4	Total cash paid					$25,000

If these bonds had been issued at a discount, procedures for these interest entries would be the same except that Discount on Bonds Payable would be credited.

Try It!

5. Assume that Ontario Hydro has 6 percent, 10-year bonds that mature on May 1, 2030. Further, assume that $10,000,000 of the bonds are issued at 94.00 on May 1, 2020, and that Ontario Hydro pays interest each April 30 and October 31.
   a. Record issuance of the bonds on May 1, 2020.
   b. Record the interest payment and straight-line amortization of the premium or discount on October 31, 2020.
   c. Accrue interest and amortize the premium or discount on December 31, 2020.
   d. Show how the company would report the bonds on the balance sheet at December 31, 2020.
   e. Record the interest payment on April 30, 2021.

6. Refer to the example of the bonds issued at a premium illustrated in Exhibit 15–7. Use the data in Exhibit 15–7 to accrue two months of interest and amortize the bond premium at the end of the second year assuming that it ends on December 31, 2021 (4th interest period, line 13). Then record the April 30, 2022, payment of interest.

7. Refer to Exhibits 15–5 and 15–7 to answer the following questions:
   a. Will the periodic amount of interest expense increase or decrease over the life of a bond issued at a *discount* under the effective-interest amortization method?
   b. Will the periodic amount of interest expense increase or decrease for a bond issued at a *premium*? Assume the effective-interest method of amortizing the premium.

Solutions appear at the end of this chapter and on **MyLab Accounting**

Retirement of Bonds

Normally companies wait until maturity to pay off, or retire, their bonds payable. All the bond discount or premium has been amortized, and the retirement entry debits Bonds Payable and credits Cash for the bonds' maturity value, as we saw earlier. But companies sometimes retire their bonds prior to maturity. The main reason for retiring bonds early is to relieve the pressure of making interest payments. Interest rates fluctuate. The company may be able to borrow at a lower interest rate and use the proceeds from new bonds to pay off the old bonds, which bear a higher rate.

Redeemable bonds are bonds that give the purchaser the option of retiring them at a stated dollar amount prior to maturity. Others are **callable bonds**, which means that the company may *call* or pay off those bonds at a specified price whenever it so chooses normally to take advantage of lower interest rates. The call price is usually a few percentage points above the face value or par, to make the bonds attractive to lenders. An alternative to calling the bonds is to purchase them in the open market at their current market price. When bonds are retired early—whether the bonds are redeemed, called, or purchased in the open market—the same steps are followed:

LO (4)

How do we account for changes in a bond issue?

Callable bonds may be paid off at the corporation's option. The bondholder does not have the choice of refusing and must surrender the bond for retirement.

① Record a partial-period amortization of the premium or discount if the date is other than an interest payment date.

② Write off the portion of the premium or discount that relates to the portion of bonds being retired.

③ Calculate any gain or loss on retirement and record this amount in the retirement journal entry.

If bonds are retired at a date other than an interest payment date, any interest owing would be paid.

Suppose XYZ Corporation has $10,000,000 of bonds outstanding with an unamortized discount of $40,000. Lower interest rates in the market may convince management to retire these bonds on June 30, immediately after an interest date. Assume that the bonds are callable at 103.00. If the market price of the bonds is 99.50, will XYZ Corporation call the bonds or purchase them in the open market? The market price is lower than the call price, so the market price is the better choice. Retiring the bonds at 99.50 results in a gain of $10,000, computed as follows:

① (no partial-period amortization in this case)	
Face value of bonds being retired	$10,000,000
Unamortized discount ②	40,000
Book value, or carrying value	9,960,000
Face value × factor ($10,000,000 × 0.9950) or market price paid to retire the bonds	9,950,000
Gain on retirement of bonds ③	$ 10,000

The following entry records retirement of these bonds, which happens to be immediately after an interest date:

Jun. 30	Bonds Payable	10,000,000	
	Discount on Bonds Payable		40,000
	Cash		9,950,000
	Gain on Retirement of Bonds Payable		10,000
	To retire bonds payable before maturity.		

After posting, the bond accounts have zero balances.

Bonds Payable		Discount on Bonds Payable	
Retirement 10,000,000	Prior bal. 10,000,000	Prior bal. 40,000	Retirement 40,000

The double underline signals that the account balance is zero.

The entry removes the bonds payable and the related discount from the accounts and records a gain on retirement. Of course, any existing premium would be removed with a debit to the Premium on Bonds Payable account.

If XYZ Corporation had retired only half of these bonds, the accountant would remove half of the discount or premium. Likewise, if the price paid to retire the bonds exceeded their carrying value, the retirement entry would record a loss with a debit to the account Loss on Retirement of Bonds. ASPE requires that gains and losses on early retirement of debt that are both abnormal in size and unusual be reported separately as a line item on the income statement before the line items for income tax and discontinued operations.

Convertible Bonds and Notes

Corporations often add incentives or *sweeteners* to their bonds—features to make the bonds more attractive to potential investors. Many corporate bonds, debentures, and notes payable have the feature of being convertible into the common shares of the issuing company at the option of the investor. These bonds and notes, called **convertible bonds** (or **convertible notes**), combine the safety of assured receipts of principal and interest on the bonds with the opportunity for large gains on the shares. The conversion feature is so attractive that investors usually accept a lower stated interest rate than they would on nonconvertible bonds. The lower interest rate benefits the issuer. Convertible bonds are recorded like any other debt at issuance.

If the market price of the issuing company's shares gets high enough, the bondholders will convert the bonds into shares. The corporation records conversion by debiting the bond accounts and crediting the shareholders' equity accounts. Normally, the carrying value of the bonds becomes the book value of the newly issued shares, and *no gain or loss is recorded*.

Assume that XYZ Corporation bondholders converted $100,000 of XYZ Corporation bonds into 20,000 common shares on May 1, 2020. The bonds were issued at par. XYZ Corporation's entry to record the conversion would be:

May 1	Bonds Payable	100,000	
	Common Shares		100,000
	To record conversion of $100,000 bonds outstanding into 20,000 common shares.		

If there were any discount or premium, they would be removed at this time.

Try It!

8. Suppose Bunzell Corporation has $5,000,000 of bonds outstanding with an unamortized premium of $30,000. The call price is 105.00. To reduce interest payments, the company retires half of the bonds at the 100.50 market price. Calculate the gain or loss on retirement, and record the retirement immediately after an interest date (June 30).

9. Suppose Bunzell Corporation has $5,000,000 of bonds outstanding with an unamortized premium of $30,000. The bonds are convertible. Assume bondholders converted half of the bonds into 1,000,000 common shares on September 1, 2020. Record the conversion of these bonds into common shares.

Solutions appear at the end of this chapter and on **MyLab Accounting**

Advantages and Disadvantages of Issuing Bonds Versus Shares

Businesses acquire assets in different ways. Management may decide to purchase or to lease equipment. If management decides to purchase, the money to pay for the asset may be financed by the business's retained earnings, a note payable, a share issue, or a bond issue. Let's look at what businesses need to consider when comparing equity versus debt choices:

LO ⑤

How do we decide whether to issue debt versus equity?

Shares (Equity)	Bonds (and other debt)
Shares represent *ownership* (equity) of the corporation. Each shareholder is an owner.	Bonds represent a *debt* (liability) of the corporation. Each bondholder is a creditor with no voting rights. Share ownership is not diluted, and there is no loss of control of the corporation.
The corporation is *not* obligated to repay the amount invested by the shareholders. This is less risky for the corporation in case it does not have money to pay dividends in bad years.	The corporation *must* repay the bonds at maturity.
The corporation may or may not pay dividends on the shares. The flexibility to decide means that cash can be preserved until needed.	The corporation *must* pay interest on the bonds.
Dividends are *not* an expense and are not tax deductible by the corporation.	Interest is a tax-deductible expense of the corporation. This may help the corporation report higher earnings per share.
Raises capital without increasing debt and adversely affecting some key ratios	Can create greater returns for shareholders if leveraged profitably.

Exhibit 15–9 illustrates the earnings-per-share advantage of borrowing. Recall from Chapter 14 that earnings per share (EPS) is a company's net income per common share outstanding. Let's return to the company in the opening vignette and assume that Kind Animations Inc. has net income of $600,000 and 200,000 common shares outstanding before a new project. The company needs $1,000,000 for expansion, and management is considering two financing plans:

- Plan 1 is to issue $1,000,000 of 10 percent bonds.
- Plan 2 is to issue 100,000 common shares for $1,000,000.

Steve and Lee, the management of Kind Animations, believe that the new cash can be invested in operations to earn income of $300,000 before interest and taxes.

The EPS amount is higher if the company borrows (Plan 1). The business earns more on the investment ($120,000) than the interest it pays on the bonds ($100,000). Earning more income than the cost of borrowing increases the earnings for common shareholders and is called **trading on the equity**. It is widely used in business to increase earnings per common share.

Spreadsheets are useful in evaluating financing alternatives such as issuing common shares, preferred shares, or bonds. This assessment is often called "what if" analysis—for instance, "What if we finance with common shares?" The answers to "what if" questions can be modelled on a spreadsheet to project the company's financial statements over the next few years.

EXHIBIT 15–9 | Earnings-per-Share Advantage of Borrowing versus Issuing Shares

	Plan 1: Borrow $1,000,000 at 10%	Plan 2: Issue $1,000,000 of Common Shares
Net income after interest and income tax, before expansion	$600,000	$600,000
Project income before interest and income tax	300,000	300,000
Less: Interest expense ($1,000,000 × 0.10)	100,000	0
Project income before income tax	200,000	300,000
Less: Income tax expense (40%)	80,000	120,000
Project net income	120,000	180,000
Total company net income	$720,000	$780,000
Earnings per share including expansion:		
Plan 1 ($720,000 ÷ 200,000 shares)	$ 3.60	
Plan 2 ($780,000 ÷ 300,000 shares)		$ 2.60

Try It!

10. If trading on the equity can improve EPS, how might it be to the corporation's *disadvantage* to finance with debt?

Solutions appear at the end of this chapter and on **MyLab Accounting**

ETHICS Should additional debt be issued?

Phillip Mader is president and majority shareholder of Knightly Corporation. Phillip owns 54 percent of the shares in the corporation. The corporation is in dire need of additional cash inflow in order to maintain operations. Phillip is urging the board of directors to issue additional debt even though he knows that the corporation already has a substantial amount of debt. Phillip is well aware that by issuing additional debt, the corporation's debt to equity ratio will increase significantly. He believes this will negatively affect the corporation's credit rating and will further limit the company's ability to borrow at low interest rates in the future. If the corporation doesn't issue additional debt, it will be forced to issue shares in order to obtain the necessary funds. Phillip does not have the ability to purchase any of the additional shares of stock, and he knows that he will lose his majority shareholder status. What should Phillip do? What would you do?

Solution

Phillip's overall ethical responsibility lies with the good of the company over what is best for him. In urging the corporation to issue additional debt, he is putting his needs and desires above the best interests of the corporation and other shareholders. Phillip is aware that by issuing additional debt the corporation will be negatively affected. He should urge the board to issue shares—even though he will not gain personally from the situation.

Mortgages and Other Long-Term Liabilities

Mortgages: An Introduction

How do we account for other long-term liabilities?

A **mortgage** is a *loan secured* by *real property* using a *mortgage note*. The mortgage is repaid in equal monthly instalments. A portion of each payment represents interest on the unpaid balance of the loan and the remainder reduces the principal, or the outstanding balance of the loan. Such payments are known as **blended payments**. The principal and interest portions of each mortgage payment can be calculated and presented in a *mortgage instalment payment schedule,* also called a *mortgage amortization schedule.* Exhibit 15–10 illustrates a partial mortgage instalment payment schedule for a 10-year, 5 percent, $200,000 mortgage obtained on October 1, 2020, with monthly blended payments of $2,121. All amounts are rounded to the nearest dollar.

The total interest paid on a mortgage can be shocking; paying off a mortgage early can reduce the total interest substantially.

EXHIBIT 15–10 | Partial Mortgage Amortization Schedule

	A	B	C	D	E	F
1	Mortgage Instalment Payment Schedule (partial)					
2	Blended Mortgage Payments					
3	Period	Beginning Balance	Blended Monthly Payment	Interest Expense	Principal Payment	Ending Balance
4	Oct. 1, 2020					$200,000
5	Nov. 1, 2020	$200,000	$2,121	$833	$1,288	198,712
6	Dec. 1, 2020	198,712	2,121	828	1,293	197,419
7	Jan. 1, 2021	197,419	2,121	823	1,298	196,121
...	...	...	...	...	...	...

Payment (C) − interest (D)
= $2,121 − $833 = $1,288

Beginning balance (B) − principal payment (E)
= $200,000 − $1,288 = $198,712

Beginning balance (B) × interest rate × time (one month)
= $200,000 × 0.05 × 1/12 = $833

The blended mortgage payment ($2,121 in Column C) is a blend of both interest and principal. Notice how the reduction in principal (Column E) increases each month so that more of the principal is paid off as the mortgage note matures.

Journal Entry for Mortgage Payments   On November 1, 2020, the journal entry to record the first monthly payment on this $200,000 mortgage is:

2020			
Nov. 1	Interest Expense	833	
	Mortgage Payable	1,288	
	Cash		2,121
	To pay monthly mortgage loan and record interest portion of the blended payment.		

Some mortgages and long-term loans do not require blended payments of a fixed amount every month. Rather, they specify that a fixed amount of principal is repaid every month with interest paid on the balance. Fixed principal payments would ensure that the principal reduction is the constant while the interest and payment amount would change based on a reduced principal base.

Balance Sheet Presentation of Long-Term Liabilities

Long-term liabilities are divided into their current and long-term portions for reporting on the balance sheet. For each long-term liability, the portion that is due to be paid within the next year is classified as a current liability and is shown on the balance sheet as the liability "Current portion of long-term debt." The long-term debt is reduced by the same amount so that only the portion of the debt due to be paid in more than a year is listed as a long-term liability on the balance sheet.

The current and long-term portions of mortgage loans are reported on the balance sheet. In the mortgage instalment payment schedule above, the mortgage balance in column G represents the total mortgage debt, and this amount is divided into the current portion of the debt due in one year and the long-term portion due after one year. On December 31, 2020, the current portion of the mortgage is classified as a current liability, as well as the interest on the mortgage that has accrued since the December 1, 2020, payment. Using the amounts for the blended mortgage payments shown, the liabilities section of the balance sheet on December 31, 2020, would appear as follows:

Liabilities	
Current liabilities	
Current portion of mortgage*	$ 25,452
Long-term debt	
Mortgage**	$171,967

*Calculated as 12 × $2,121 for simplicity. If the mortgage instalment payment schedule were extended to show all the payments in 2021, you would add the 12 principal payments for the year from the schedule to calculate the current portion of the mortgage.

**Calculated as $197,419 − $25,452, which is the mortgage balance at December 31, 2020, (from column F) less the current portion of the mortgage shown as a current liability on the balance sheet.

Other Long-Term Liabilities

> Shareholder loans are liabilities that can appear on the financial statements as either short-term or long-term liabilities. These are loans made by the owners to the company either with or without terms of repayment.

Other long-term liabilities shown on published balance sheets would include **shareholder loans**, pension obligations, deferred compensation plans, and future income taxes. These topics will be left for more advanced accounting courses.

11. Suppose Austin Metal purchases land and a building for $200,000 on October 1, 2020. Austin obtains a mortgage at an annual rate of 5 percent and will make monthly payments for 10 years. Using the instalment payment schedule in this section on page 843, journalize the entry for the second mortgage payment, which is made on December 1, 2020.

Solutions appear at the end of this chapter and on MyLab Accounting

Lease Liabilities

LO ⑦

How do we account for leases?

A **lease** is an agreement in which the asset user (**lessee**) agrees to make regular, periodic payments to the property owner (**lessor**) in exchange for the exclusive use of the asset. Leasing is the way the lessee avoids having to make the large initial cash down payment that purchase agreements require. From the lessor's perspective, there are two categories of leases, operating and capital, with capital leases further divided into two kinds: *sales-type leases,* in which the lessor is usually a manufacturer or dealer, and *direct financing leases,* in which the lessor is usually not a manufacturer or dealer but provides financing. This text will consider the broader term, *capital lease* (or finance lease), and not the kinds of capital leases.

Operating Leases

Operating leases are usually short-term or cancellable. Many apartment leases and most short-term car rental agreements extend for a year or less. These operating leases give the lessee the right to use the asset but provide the lessee with no continuing rights to the asset. The lessor retains the usual risks and rewards of owning the leased asset. To account for an operating lease, the lessee makes the following journal entry for a $2,000 lease payment:

Jan. 1	Lease Expense (or Rent Expense)	2,000	
	Cash		2,000
	To record operating lease payment.		

The lessee's books report neither the leased asset nor any lease liability (except perhaps a prepaid rent amount or a rent accrual at the end of the period). However, the future lease payments for each of the next five years should be given in the notes to the financial statements. The nature of the **provisions**, or lease commitments, should also be stated in the notes.

Capital Leases

Many businesses use capital leasing to finance the acquisition of some assets. A capital lease is long-term, noncancellable financing that is a form of debt.

How do you distinguish a capital lease from an operating lease? Section 3065 of the *CPA Canada Handbook*, Part II, Accounting Standards for Private Enterprises, defines a **capital lease** as one that substantially transfers all the benefits and risks incident to ownership of the property to the lessee. The section goes on to suggest that a lease is a capital lease from the perspective of the lessee if one or more of the following conditions are present at the beginning of the lease:

1. There is reasonable assurance that the lessee will obtain ownership of the leased asset at the end of the lease term.
2. The lease term is of such a length that the lessee will obtain almost all (usually 75 percent or more) of the benefits from the use of the leased asset over its life.
3. The lessor will both recover the original investment and earn a return on that investment from the lease.

And both of the following are present:

1. The credit risk associated with the lease is normal.
2. The amounts of any unreimbursable costs to the lessor are estimable.

Accounting for a Capital Lease Accounting for a capital lease is much like accounting for a purchase. The lessee enters the asset into its accounts and records a lease liability at the beginning of the lease term. Thus, the lessee capitalizes the asset on its own financial statements even though the lessee may never take legal title to the property.

How does a lessee compute the cost of an asset acquired through a capital lease? Consider that the lessee gets the use of the asset but does *not* pay for the leased asset in full at the beginning of the lease. A capital lease is, therefore, similar to borrowing money to purchase the leased asset. The lessee must record the leased asset at the present value of the lease liability.

The cost of the asset to the lessee is the sum of any payment made at the beginning of the lease period plus the present value of the future lease payments. The lease payments are equal amounts occurring at regular intervals—that is, they are annuity payments.

Consider a 20-year building lease signed by Sierra Wireless, Inc. The lease starts on January 2, 2020, and requires 20 annual payments of $20,000 each, with the first payment due immediately. The building is estimated to last 25 years. Sierra will not be taking title to the building at the end of the 20 years. If the interest rate in the lease is 10 percent, then the present value of the 19 future payments is $167,298 (see the margin for the calculation of this amount). Sierra's cost of the building is $187,298 (the sum of the initial payment, $20,000, plus the present value of the future payments, $167,298).

This lease meets the second condition for a capital lease given above: The arrangement is similar to purchasing the building on an instalment plan. In an instalment purchase, Sierra would debit Building and credit Cash and Instalment Note Payable. The company would then pay interest and principal on the note payable and record amortization on the building. Accounting for a capital lease follows this same pattern—debit an asset, credit Cash, and credit a payable for the future lease payments—as shown next.

> With apartments, the lease period is typically one year, so you likely do not consume the apartment's usefulness by the end of the lease and you likely will not obtain ownership of the building at the end of the lease. Therefore, an apartment lease is an operating lease.

> To compute the present value of the lease asset using a financial calculator, ensure that the **BGN** key is on, then enter:
> **PMT** = $20,000
> **I/Y** = 10%
> **N** = 20
> **FV** = 0
> This gives PV of $ – 187,298 (negative numbers indicate the direction of cash flow; in this case, cash is flowing out). If using the tables, use ($20,000 × PV of annuity at 10 percent for 19 periods, or 8.365 from Exhibit 15A –7 = $167,300 + $20,000 initial payment = $187,300). The $2 difference is due to rounding in the tables.

Sierra records the building at cost, which is the sum of the $20,000 initial payment plus the present value of the 19 future lease payments of $20,000 each, or $187,298.[6] The company credits Cash for the initial payment and credits Lease Liability for the present value of the future lease payments. At the beginning of the lease term, Sierra Wireless makes the following entry:

2020			
Jan. 2	Building under Capital Lease	187,298	
	Cash		20,000
	Capital Lease Liability		167,298
	To lease a building ($20,000 + $167,298) and make the first annual lease payment on the capital lease ($20,000).		

Sierra's lease liability at January 2, 2020, is for 19 payments of $20,000 each on January 2, 2021, to January 2, 2039. However, included in those payments is interest calculated at 10 percent. The lease liability is as follows:

Cash payments January 2, 2021, to January 2, 2039 (19 × $20,000)	$380,000
Interest embedded in the lease payments	212,702
Present value of future lease payments	$167,298

If Sierra Wireless were to record the liability at $380,000, it would also have to record the interest included in that amount as a contra amount. Most companies net the interest against the cash payments and show the liability as the net amount (principal).

Because Sierra has capitalized the building, the company records amortization (using the straight-line method). Even though the building has an expected life of 25 years, it is amortized over the lease term of 20 years because the lessee has the use of the building only for that period. No residual value normally enters into the amortization computation because the lessee will have no residual asset when the building is returned to the lessor at the expiration of the lease. Therefore, the annual amortization entry is:

For an operating lease, the lessor, not the lessee, records the amortization expense on the leased asset. For a capital lease, the lessee records the amortization expense.

2020			
Dec. 31	Amortization Expense	9,365	
	Accumulated Amortization—Building under Capital Lease		9,365
	To record amortization on leased building of $9,365 ($187,298 ÷ 20).		

Note that a lessee, such as Sierra, might obtain ownership of the leased asset at the end of the lease term. In such a situation, the lessee would amortize the leased asset over its useful life instead of over the term of the lease. At year-end, Sierra must also accrue interest on the lease liability. Interest expense is computed by multiplying the lease liability by the interest rate on the lease. The following entry credits Capital Lease Liability (not Interest Payable) for this interest accrual:

---

[6]The appendix to this chapter explains present value.

2020			
Dec. 31	Interest Expense	16,730	
	Capital Lease Liability		16,730
	To accrue interest on the lease liability ($167,298 × 0.10, rounded).		

To distinguish between assets that an entity owns and assets it only has a right to use, information about assets acquired through capital leases must be disclosed separately from all other long-term assets. This information includes leased assets' costs, amortization, and interest expense. For the previous example, the partial balance sheet at December 31, 2020, reports the following:

Next payment due on Jan. 2, 2021

Assets			Liabilities	
Property, plant, and equipment			Current liabilities	
Building under capital lease	$187,298		Lease liability	$ 20,000
Less: Accumulated amortization	9,365	$177,933	Long-term liabilities	
			Lease liability	164,028*

*$164,028 = [Beginning balance ($167,298) + Interest accrual ($16,730) – Current portion ($20,000)]

In addition, the lessee must report the minimum capital lease payments for the next five years in the notes to the financial statements.

The lease liability is split into current and long-term portions because the next payment ($20,000) is a current liability and the remainder is long-term. The January 2, 2021, lease payment is recorded as follows:

2021			
Jan. 2	Lease Liability	20,000	
	Cash		20,000
	To make second annual lease payment on building.		

Try It!

12. Bedrock Construction Inc. acquired equipment under a capital lease that requires six annual lease payments of $30,000. The first payment is due when the lease begins on January 2, 2020. Future payments are due on January 2 of each year of the lease term. The interest rate in the lease is 12 percent and the present value of the five future lease payments is $108,143. Journalize (a) the acquisition of the equipment, (b) the amortization for 2020, (c) the accrued interest at December 31, 2020, and (d) the second lease payment on January 2, 2021.

Solutions appear at the end of this chapter and on **MyLab Accounting**

EXHIBIT 15–11 | The Effects of IFRS On Long-Term Liabilities

LO 8

How does IFRS affect long-term liabilities?

ASPE	IFRS
Allows either straight-line amortization or the effective-interest method for bond premium/discount calculations.	Requires the use of the effective-interest method for bond premium/discount calculations.
Companies are not required to recalculate the fair value of their bond debt every year. This is because, typically, there are not as many bondholders in a private corporation and those bondholders have access to information directly from the owners and managers of the company.	Companies can fairly value their bonds at the end of each fiscal period, which means they recalculate the present value of the bonds each year.
Operating leases are permitted.	IFRS 16 (effective January 2019) interprets virtually all leases as capital (finance) leases.

Why It's Done This Way

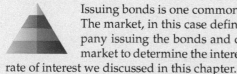

Issuing bonds is one common way of raising capital to fund existing or new operations and projects. The market, in this case defined as the creditors who purchase the bonds, assess the risk of the company issuing the bonds and compare the bond interest rate with other investments available in the market to determine the interest rate they must earn when they purchase the bonds. This is the market rate of interest we discussed in this chapter.

The action of the market in determining the market rate of interest for bonds leads to either the creation of a discount or a premium, the accounting for which you have also studied in this chapter. Since bondholders are always reassessing the risk of their investments, the market rate of interest can change daily. How is this constantly changing market rate of interest reflected in a company's financial statements? Under IFRS, companies can fairly value their bonds at the end of each fiscal period, which means they recalculate the present value of the bonds each year. This annual update to fair value is consistent with the characteristics of *relevance* and *reliability* in the accounting framework described in Chapter 1. Using the current rate of interest to calculate the fair value of bond debt is relevant information to the users of the financial statements. Since the rate of interest is determined by market forces, it is also reliable. Under ASPE, companies are not required to recalculate the fair value of their bond debt every year.

Under both ASPE and IFRS, details of the corporation's various bond issues must be disclosed in the notes to the financial statements, as described by the *recognition* and *measurement criteria* in the framework. Thus, the valuation of bonds and disclosure of bond information in the financial statements *communicate useful information to interested users*—this is the objective of the accounting framework.

Summary Problem for Your Review

Astoria Inc. has outstanding an issue of 8 percent convertible bonds that mature in 2030. Suppose the bonds were issued October 1, 2020, and pay interest each April 1 and October 1.

Required

1. Complete the following effective-interest amortization table through October 1, 2022. Round all amount to the nearest whole dollar.

    Bond data: Maturity value—$2,000,000
    Contract interest rate—8%
    Interest paid—4% semi-annually, $80,000 ($2,000,000 × 0.04)
    Market interest rate at time of issue—9% annually, 4.5% semi-annually
    Issue proceeds—$1,869,921

	A	B	C	D	E	F
1	Semi-annual Interest Period	Interest Payment (4% of Maturity Value)	Interest Expense (4.5% of Preceding F)	Discount Amortization (C – B)	Unamortized Discount Account Balance (Preceding E – Current D)	Bond Carrying Amount ($2,000,000 – E)
2	Oct. 1, 2020					
3	Apr. 1, 2021					
4	Oct. 1, 2021					
5	Apr. 1, 2022					
6	Oct. 1, 2022					

2. Using the amortization table, record the following transactions:
    a. Issuance of the bonds on October 1, 2020.
    b. Accrual of interest and amortization of discount on December 31, 2020.
    c. Payment of interest and amortization of discount on April 1, 2021.
    d. Conversion of one-third of the bonds payable into common shares on October 2, 2022.
    e. Retirement of two-thirds of the bonds payable on October 2, 2022. Purchase price of the bonds was 102.00.

SOLUTION

Requirement 1

	A	B	C	D	E	F
1	Semi-annual Interest Period	Interest Payment (4% of Maturity Value)	Interest Expense (4.5% of Preceding F)	Discount Amortization (C − B)	Unamortized Discount Account Balance (Preceding E − Current D)	Bond Carrying Amount ($2,000,000 − E)
2	Oct. 1, 2020				$130,079	$1,869,921
3	Apr. 1, 2021	$80,000	$84,146	$4,146	125,933	1,874,067
4	Oct. 1, 2021	80,000	84,333	4,333	121,600	1,878,400
5	Apr. 1, 2021	80,000	84,528	4,528	117,072	1,882,928
6	Oct. 1, 2022	80,000	84,732	4,732	112,340	1,887,660

The semi-annual interest payment is the same each period.

Calculated as $1,869,921 \times 0.045 = \$84,146.$

Money received on issue

Requirement 2

The bonds were issued for less than $2,000,000, reflecting a discount. Use the amounts from columns E and F for Oct. 1, 2020, from the amortization table.

a.

2020			
Oct. 1	Cash	1,869,921	
	Discount on Bonds Payable	130,079	
	Bonds Payable		2,000,000
	To issue 8%, 10-year bonds at a discount.		

The accrued interest is calculated, and the bond discount is amortized. Use $3/6$ of the amounts from columns B, C, and D for Apr. 1, 2021.

b.

Dec. 31	Interest Expense	42,073	
	Discount on Bonds Payable		2,073
	Interest Payable		40,000
	To accrue interest expense for three months ($84,146 \times 3/6$) and amortize bond discount for three months ($4,146 \times 3/6$), and record payable for three months ($80,000 \times 3/6$).		

The semi-annual interest payment is made ($80,000 from Column B). Only the January–March 2021 interest expense is recorded, since the October–December interest expense was already recorded in Requirement 2b. The same is true for the discount on bonds payable. Reverse Interest Payable from Requirement 2b, since cash is paid now.

c.

2021			
Apr. 1	Interest Expense	42,073	
	Interest Payable	40,000	
	Discount on Bonds Payable		2,073
	Cash		80,000
	To pay semi-annual interest, part of which was accrued on December 31, 2020, and amortize three months' discount on bonds payable ($4,146 \times 3/6$).		

d.

2022			
Oct. 2	Bonds Payable	666,667	
	Discount on Bonds Payable		37,447
	Common Shares		629,220
	To record conversion of $^1/_3$ of the bonds payable ($2,000,000 × $^1/_3$). Remove $^1/_3$ of the discount ($112,340 × $^1/_3$).		

When converting bonds to common shares, retire the full amount of the bonds ($^1/_3$ × $2,000,000) and the discount account balance ($^1/_3$ × $112,340) from column E for Oct. 1, 2022).

e.

Oct. 2	Bonds Payable	1,333,333	
	Loss on Retirement of Bonds	101,560	
	Discount on Bonds Payable		74,893
	Cash		1,360,000
	To retire remaining bonds payable ($2,000,000 × $^2/_3$) and discount ($112,340 × $^2/_3$) before maturity. Cash paid ($2,000,000 × $^2/_3$ × 1.02).		

The cash paid on retirement was $102 for every $100 of bonds. Use $^2/_3$ of the amount from column E for Oct. 1, 2022, to calculate Discount on Bonds Payable. The loss on retirement reflects the excess of the book value over the cash received and is the "plug" figure in the journal entry calculated as $1,333,333 − $74,893 −$1,360,000 = $101,560 debit.

Summary

Learning Objectives

① Define bonds payable and the types of bonds   Pg. 820

What are bonds?
- A corporation may borrow money by issuing long-term notes and bonds.
- Bondholders are the people or companies that lend the money to the bond or note issuer.
- A bond indenture or contract specifies the maturity value of the bonds, the stated interest rate, and the dates for paying interest and principal.
- Bonds may be secured (e.g., a mortgage) or unsecured (e.g., a debenture). Bonds and debentures are accounted for similarly.

② Determine the price of a bond, and account for basic bond transactions   Pg. 822

How do we account for the sale of a bond?
- An investor will pay a price for a bond equal to the present value of the bond principal plus the present value of the stream of bond interest receipts.
- Market interest rates fluctuate and may differ from the stated rate on a bond.
- Bonds are traded through organized markets, such as the over-the-counter market.
- Bonds are typically divided into $1,000 units. Their prices are quoted at the price per $100 bond.
- If a bond's stated rate exceeds the market rate, the bond sells at a premium.
- A bond with a stated rate below the market rate sells at a discount.
- Money earns income over time, a fact that gives rise to the present value concept.
- Accrued interest may be factored into the purchase if the bond is sold between interest dates.

③ Amortize a bond discount and premium by the straight-line amortization method and the effective-interest amortization method   Pg. 829

How do we allocate a bond discount or premium over the life of a bond?
- Straight-line amortization allocates an *equal dollar amount* of premium or discount to each interest period.
- The effective-interest method of amortization allocates a different dollar amount of premium or discount to each interest period because it allocates a *constant percentage* of premium or discount to each interest period. The market rate at the time of issuance is multiplied by the bonds' carrying amount to determine the interest expense for each period and to compute the amount of discount or premium amortization.

④ Account for retirement and conversion of bonds Pg. 839

How do we account for changes in a bond issue?
- Companies may retire their bonds payable before maturity.
- Redeemable bonds are bonds that give the purchaser the option of retiring the bonds at a stated dollar amount prior to maturity.
- Callable bonds give the borrower the right to pay off the bonds at a specified call price; otherwise, the company may purchase the bonds in the open market.
- Convertible bonds and notes give the investor the privilege of trading the bonds in for shares of the issuing corporation. The carrying amount of the bonds becomes the book value of the newly issued shares.

⑤ Show the advantages and disadvantages of borrowing Pg. 841

How do we decide whether to issue debt versus equity?
- A key advantage of raising money by borrowing versus issuing shares is that interest expense on debt is tax deductible. Thus, borrowing is less costly than issuing shares.
- If the company can earn more income than the cost of borrowing, EPS will increase.
- Borrowing's disadvantages result from the fact that the company must repay the loan and its interest, unlike issuing shares, where dividends do not have to be declared and paid.

⑥ Account for other long-term liabilities Pg. 842

How do we account for other long-term liabilities?
- A mortgage is a loan secured by real property using a mortgage note. The mortgage is repaid in equal monthly instalments.
- A portion of each payment represents interest on the unpaid balance of the loan and the remainder reduces the principal, or the outstanding balance of the loan.
- Amounts due within a year are reported as "current portion of long-term debt".

⑦ Account for operating leases and for assets acquired through a capital lease Pg. 844

How do we account for leases?
- A lease is an agreement between the lessor who owns an item and rents it to the lessee who has the use of the item.
- In an operating lease, the lessor retains the usual risks and rights of owning the asset.
- A capital lease is long-term, non-cancellable, and similar to an instalment purchase of the leased asset. In a capital lease, the lessee capitalizes and amortizes the leased asset and reports a lease liability on its balance sheet.

⑧ Identify the effects of IFRS on long-term liabilities Pg. 848

How does IFRS affect long-term liabilities?
- Under ASPE, liabilities for bond indebtedness are reported at amortized cost. Under IFRS, the liability may be reported at amortized cost or fair value.
- Under IFRS, companies are required to disclose more lease information than under ASPE.

Key Terms for the chapter are shown next and are in the **Glossary** at the back of the book. **Similar Terms** are shown after **Key Terms**.

KEY TERMS

Bearer bonds Bonds payable to the person that has possession of them. Also called *unregistered bonds* (p. 822).

Bid price The highest price that a buyer is willing to pay for a bond (p. 823).

Blended payments Payments that are a constant amount, and the amount of interest and principal that are applied to the loan change with each payment (p. 842).

Bond A formal agreement in which a lender loans money to a borrower who agrees to repay the money loaned at a future date and agrees to pay interest regularly over the life of the bond (p. 820).

Bond indenture The contract that specifies the maturity value of the bonds, the stated (contract) interest rate, and the dates for paying interest and principal (p. 820).

Bonds payable Groups of notes payable (bonds) issued to multiple lenders called bondholders (p. 820).

Callable bonds Bonds that the issuer may call or pay off at a specified price whenever the issuer wants (p. 839).

Capital lease A lease agreement that substantially transfers all the benefits and risks of ownership from the lessor to the lessee (p. 845).

Contract interest rate The interest rate that determines the amount of cash interest the borrower pays and the investor receives each year. Also called the *stated interest rate* (p. 822).

Convertible bond Bonds that may be converted into the common shares of the issuing company at the option of the investor (p. 840).

Convertible note Notes that may be converted into the common shares of the issuing company at the option of the investor (p. 840).

Coupon rate The contractual rate of interest that the issuer must pay the bondholders (p. 821).

Debentures Unsecured bonds, backed only by the good faith of the issuer (p. 822).

Discount The amount of a bond's issue price under its maturity (par) value; also called bond discount (p. 823).

Effective-interest amortization An amortization method in which a different amount of bond discount or premium is written off through interest expense each year (or period) of the bond's life. The amount of amortization expense is the same percentage of a bond's carrying value for every period over a bond's life (p. 832).

Effective interest rate The interest rate that investors demand in order to loan their money. Also called the *market interest rate* (p. 822).

Face value Another name for the principal or maturity value of a bond (p. 820).

Lease An agreement in which the tenant (lessee) agrees to make rent payments to the property owner (lessor) in exchange for the exclusive use of the asset (p. 844).

Lessee The tenant, or user of the asset, in a lease agreement (p. 844).

Lessor The property owner in a lease agreement (p. 844).

Long-term liabilities Debts due to be paid in more than a year or more than one of the entity's operating cycles if an operating cycle is greater than one year (p. 820).

Market interest rate The interest rate that investors demand in order to loan their money. Also called the *effective interest rate* (p. 822).

Maturity date The date on which the borrower must pay the principal amount to the lender (p. 820).

Maturity value The amount a company is required to pay back to the lender at the end of the term of the bond. Also another name for a bond's *principal value* or *face value* (p. 820).

Mortgage The borrower's promise to transfer the legal title to certain assets to the lender if the debt is not paid on schedule. A mortgage is a special type of *secured bond* (p. 842).

Operating lease Usually a short-term or cancellable rental agreement (p. 844).

Over-the-counter (OTC) market The decentralized market where bonds are traded between dealers. Unlike the stock market, there isn't a central bond exchange where transaction prices are posted for all to see (p. 823).

Par value Another name for the *principal or maturity value* of a bond (p. 820).

Premium The excess of a bond's issue price over its maturity (par) value; also called *bond premium* (p. 823).

Present value The amount a person would invest now to receive a greater amount at a future date (p. 824).

Principal value The amount a company borrows from a bondholder. Also called the bond's *maturity value*, par value, or *face value* (p. 820).

Provisions Accounts that represent a liability of one entity to another entity (p. 845).

Redeemable bonds Bonds that give the purchaser the option of retiring them at a stated dollar amount prior to maturity (p. 839).

Secured bonds Bonds that give the bondholder the right to take specified assets of the issuer if the issuer fails to pay principal or interest (p. 822).

Serial bonds Bonds that mature in instalments over a period of time (p. 822).

Shareholder loans Loans that are obtained from the owner either in the form of cash or in kind. This amount can be shown as a liability or as a receivable on the balance sheet, depending on whether the balance is a credit or a debit (p. 844).

Stated interest rate The interest rate that determines the amount of cash interest the borrower pays and the investor receives each year. Also called the *contract interest rate* (p. 822).

Straight-line amortization Allocating a bond discount or a bond premium to expense by dividing the discount or premium into equal amounts for each interest period (p. 829).

Term bonds Bonds that all mature at the same time for a particular issue (p. 822).

Trading on the equity Earning more income on borrowed money than the related expense, thereby increasing the earnings for the owners of the business (p. 841).

Unregistered bonds Another name for *bearer bonds* (p. 822).

Yield The interest rate that an investor will receive based on a compounding period of one year (p. 823).

SIMILAR TERMS

Bond	Secured bond; Mortgage bond
Bond principal	Maturity value; Face value; Par value; Principal value
Capital lease liability	Obligation under capital lease
Debenture	Unsecured bond
Finance lease	capital lease
Mortgage instalment payment schedule	Mortgage amortization schedule
Market interest rate	Effective interest rate
Operating lease	Short-term lease; Short-term rental
Retire the bond	Pay back the balance (principal value)
Stated interest rate	Contract interest rate; Indenture rate

SELF-STUDY QUESTIONS

Test your understanding of the chapter by marking the best answer for each of the following questions:

1. Which type of bond is unsecured? *(p. 822)*
   a. Serial bond
   b. Common bond
   c. Debenture bond
   d. Mortgage bond

2. How much will an investor pay for a $200,000 bond priced at 102.5? *(p. 823)*
   a. $200,000   c. $205,000
   b. $204,000   d. $202,500

3. A bond with a stated interest rate of 5 percent is issued when the market interest rate is 5.25 percent. This bond will sell at *(p. 826)*
   a. Par value
   b. A discount
   c. A premium
   d. A price minus accrued interest

4. Lite Corp. has $1,000,000 of 10-year bonds payable outstanding. These bonds had a discount of $80,000 at issuance, which was five years ago. The company uses the straight-line amortization method. The carrying amount or balance of the Lite Corp. bonds payable is *(p. 827)*
   a. $920,000
   b. $960,000
   c. $1,000,000
   d. $1,040,000

5. DRK Ltd. issued its 8 percent bonds payable at a price of $880,000 (maturity value is $1,000,000). The market interest rate was 10 percent when DRK Ltd. issued its bonds. The company uses the effective-interest method for the bonds. Interest expense for the first year is *(p. 832)*
   a. $70,400
   b. $80,000
   c. $88,000
   d. $100,000

6. Bonds payable with a face value of $1,800,000 and a balance or carrying value of $1,728,000 are retired before their scheduled maturity with a cash outlay of $1,752,000. Which of the following entries correctly records this bond retirement? *(p. 839)*

a.

Bonds Payable	1,800,000	
Discount on Bonds Payable	72,000	
Cash		1,752,000
Gain on Retirement of Bonds Payable		120,000

b.

Bonds Payable	1,800,000	
Loss on Retirement of Bonds Payable	24,000	
Discount on Bonds Payable		72,000
Cash		1,752,000

c.

Bonds Payable	1,800,000	
Discount on Bonds Payable		36,000
Cash		1,752,000
Gain on Retirement of Bonds Payable		12,000

d.

Bonds Payable	1,728,000	
Discount on Bonds Payable	72,000	
Gain on Retirement of Bonds Payable		48,000
Cash		1,752,000

7. Sassy Ltd. has $3,450,000 of debt outstanding at year-end, of which $990,000 is due in one year. What will this company report on its year-end balance sheet? *(p. 843)*
   a. Long-term debt of $3,450,000
   b. Current liability of $990,000 and long-term debt of $3,450,000
   c. Current liability of $990,000 and long-term debt of $2,460,000
   d. None of the above

8. An advantage of financing operations with debt versus shares is *(p. 841)*
   a. The tax deductibility of interest expense on debt
   b. The legal requirement to pay interest and principal
   c. Lower interest payments compared to dividend payments
   d. All of the above

9. Which of the following statements is true for mortgages with blended payments? *(p. 842)*
   a. Payments include an increasing amount of interest and a decreasing amount of principal over the life of the mortgage.
   b. Payments include an increasing amount of principal and a decreasing amount of interest over the life of the mortgage.
   c. Payments include an equal amount of principal and interest for every period over the life of the mortgage.
   d. The total cost of the asset secured by a mortgage is equal to the present value of the mortgage.

10. In a capital lease, the lessee records *(p. 845)*
   a. A leased asset and a lease liability
   b. Amortization on the leased asset
   c. Interest on the lease liability
   d. All of the above

Answers to Self-Study Questions

1. c   2. c [$200,000 × 1.025 = $205,000]   3. b   4. b   5. c   6. b   7. c   8. a
9. b   10. d

Assignment Material

MyLab Accounting Make the grade with MyLab Accounting: The Starters, Exercises, and Problems can be found on MyLab. You can practise them as often as you want, and most feature step-by-step guided instructions to help you find the right answer.

QUESTIONS

1. How do bonds payable differ from a note payable?

2. Compute the price to the nearest dollar for the following bonds with a face value of $10,000:
   a. 93.00   b. 101.375   c. 100.00

3. In which of the following situations will bonds sell at par? At a premium? At a discount?
   a. 3 percent bonds sold when the market rate is 3 percent
   b. 3 percent bonds sold when the market rate is 4 percent
   c. 3 percent bonds sold when the market rate is 2 percent

4. Identify the accounts using journal entries to debit and credit for transactions (a) to issue bonds at *par*, (b) to pay interest, (c) to accrue interest at year-end, and (d) to pay off bonds at maturity.

5. What type of account is Discount on Bonds Payable?

6. Identify the accounts using journal entries to debit and credit for transactions (a) to issue bonds at a *discount*, (b) to pay interest, (c) to accrue interest at year-end, and (d) to pay off bonds at maturity.

7. Identify the accounts using journal entries to debit and credit for transactions (a) to issue bonds at a *premium*, (b) to pay interest, (c) to accrue interest at year-end, and (d) to pay off bonds at maturity.

8. Consider bonds issued at a discount. Which is greater, the cash interest paid per period or the amount of interest expense?

9. How does the straight-line method of amortizing a bond discount (or premium) differ from the effective-interest method?

10. Bonds payable with a maturity value of $200,000 are callable at 102.50. Their market price is 101.25. If you are the issuer of these bonds, how much will you pay to retire them before maturity?

11. Why are convertible bonds attractive to investors? Why are they popular with borrowers?

12. Silver Corp. has $156 million of bonds outstanding at December 31, 2020. Of the total, $26 million are due in 2021 and the balance in 2022 and beyond. How would Silver Corp. report its bonds payable on its 2020 balance sheet?

13. Contrast the effects of a company of issuing bonds versus issuing shares.

14. What is an amortization schedule?

15. What are blended mortgage payments?

16. Describe how each portion of a blended mortgage payment changes over the life of the mortgage.

17. Identify the accounts a lessee debits and credits when making operating lease payments.

18. What characteristics distinguish a capital lease from an operating lease?

19. A business signs a capital lease for the use of a building. What accounts are debited and credited (a) to begin the lease term and make the first lease payment, (b) to record amortization, (c) to accrue interest on the lease liability, and (d) to make the second lease payment? The lease payments are made on the first day of the fiscal year.

20. Show how a lessee reports on the balance sheet any leased equipment and the related lease liability under a capital lease.

STARTERS

① Bond terms and definitions

S15–1 Match the following bond terms by entering in the blank space the letter of the phrase that best describes each term.

_____ Bond indenture   _____ Convertible bonds

_____ Secured bonds   _____ Bearer bonds

_____ Debentures   _____ Serial bonds

_____ Maturity date   _____ Coupon rate

_____ Contract interest rate   _____ Maturity value

a. Principal is payable to the person that has possession of the bonds

b. When the borrower must pay the principal amount to the lender

c. Matures in instalments over a period of time

d. Unsecured bond backed only by the good faith of the issuer

e. Contract agreed to between the issuer of the bonds and the purchaser

f. The contractual rate of interest that the issuer must pay the bondholders (another name for contract interest rate)

g. Assets of the issuer are provided as collateral

h. May be exchanged for the company's common shares.

i. Interest rate that determines the amount of cash interest the borrower pays and the investor receives each year

j. The amount the company borrows from the bondholder

② Pricing bonds

c. $92,600

S15–2 Compute the price of the following 4 percent bonds of Quebec Telecom:

a. $100,000 issued at 98.5

b. $100,000 issued at 102.5

c. $100,000 issued at 92.6

② Maturity value of a bond

S15–3 For which bond in S15–2 will Quebec Telecom have to pay the most at maturity? Explain your answer.

② Journalizing basic bond payable transactions

b. Interest expense, $8,125

S15–4 Neko Inc. issued a $500,000, 3.25 percent, 10-year bond payable on January 1, 2020. Journalize the following transactions for Neko Inc. assuming that the business has a December 31 fiscal year-end.

a. Issuance of the bond at par on January 1, 2020.

b. Payment of semi-annual interest on July 1, 2020. (Round to the nearest dollar.)

c. January 1, 2030. Payment of the bonds payable at maturity.

② Determining bonds payable amounts

c. Interest $30,000

S15–5 ICS Finance Corp. borrowed money by issuing $1,000,000 of 6 percent bonds payable at 98.5.

a. How much cash did ICS receive when it issued the bonds payable?

b. How much must ICS pay back at maturity?

c. How much cash interest will ICS pay every six months?

② Bond interest rates

S15–6 A 7 percent, 10-year bond was issued at a price of 93. Was the market interest rate per annum at the date of issuance closer to 6 percent, 7 percent, or 8 percent? Explain.

② Issuing bonds payable and accruing interest

b. Interest expense, $10,500

√S15–7 Sanjer Limited issued $700,000 of 6 percent, 10-year bonds payable on October 1, 2020, at par value. Sanjer's accounting year ends on December 31. Journalize the following transactions. Include an explanation for each entry.

a. Issuance of the bonds on October 1, 2020.

b. Accrual of interest expense on December 31, 2020.

c. Payment of the first semi-annual interest amount on April 1, 2021.

② Issuing bonds payable between interest dates and then paying the interest

b. Interest expense, $7,500

√ S15–8 Yankee Corp. sold $750,000 of 6 percent, 10-year bonds at par value on May 1, 2020, four months after the bond's original issue date of January 1, 2020. Journalize the following transactions. Include an explanation for each entry.

a. Issuance of the bonds payable on May 1, 2020.

b. Payment of the first semi-annual interest amount on July 1, 2020.

S15-9 Stat Inc. issued a $500,000, 4 percent, 5-year bond payable at a price of 95 on January 1, 2020. Journalize the following transactions for Stat Inc. Include an explanation for each entry. Stat uses the straight-line method to amortize the bond discount.

   a. Issuance of the bond payable on January 1, 2020.

   b. Payment of semi-annual interest and amortization of bond discount on July 1, 2020.

② ③
Issuing bonds payable at a discount, paying interest, and amortizing a discount by the straight-line method
b. Interest expense, $12,500

S15-10 Island Corp. issued a $400,000, 7 percent, 10-year bond payable at a price of 106 on January 1, 2020. Journalize the following transactions for Island Corp. Include an explanation for each entry. Island uses the straight-line method to amortize the premium.

   a. Issuance of the bond payable on January 1, 2020.

   b. Payment of semi-annual interest and amortization of bond premium on July 1, 2020.

② ③
Issuing bonds payable at a premium, paying interest, and amortizing a premium by the straight-line method
b. Interest expense, $12,800

✓S15-11 Marlies Inc. issued $1,500,000 of 6 percent, 10-year bonds payable and received cash proceeds of $1,393,407 on March 31, 2020. The market interest rate at the date of issuance was 7 percent, and the bonds pay interest semi-annually.

   a. Did the bonds sell at a premium or a discount?

   b. Prepare an effective-interest amortization table for the bond discount through the first two interest payments. Use Exhibit 15–5 (or the question below) as a guide, and round amounts to the nearest dollar.

   c. Record Marlies Inc.'s issuance of the bonds on March 31, 2020, and payment of the first semi-annual interest amount and amortization of the bond discount on September 30, 2020. Explanations are not required.

   d. If we were to amortize the bond discount using the straight-line method instead of the effective-interest method, record the first interest amortization entry.

③
Issuing bonds payable and amortizing a discount by the effective-interest method
c. Interest expense, $48,769

✓S15-12 Moe Jones Inc. issued $400,000 of 8 percent, 10-year bonds payable at a price of 114.88 on May 31, 2020. The market interest rate at the date of issuance was 6 percent, and the Moe Jones Inc. bonds pay interest semi-annually.

   The effective-interest amortization table for the bond premium is presented here for the first two interest periods:

③
Issuing bonds payable and amortizing a premium by the effective-interest method
c. Interest expense, $13,651

	A	B	C	D	E	F
	End of Semi-annual Interest Period	Interest Payment (4% of Maturity Value)	Interest Expense (3% of Preceding Bond Carrying Amount (F))	Premium Amortization (B – C)	Unamortized Premium Account Balance (Previous E – Current D)	Bond Carrying Amount ($400,000 + E)
1						
2	May 31, 2020				$59,520	$459,520
3	Nov. 30, 2020	$16,000	$13,786	$2,214	57,306	457,306
4	May 31, 2021	16,000	13,719	2,281	55,025	455,025
5						
6						

   a. How much cash did Moe Jones Inc. receive upon issuance of the bonds payable?

   b. Continue the effective-interest amortization table for the bond premium for the next two interest payments. Round amounts to the nearest dollar.

   c. Record issuance of the bonds on May 31, 2020, and payment of the third semi-annual interest amount and amortization of the bond premium on November 30, 2021. Explanations are not required.

S15-13 On January 1, 2020, Nanke Inc. issued $500,000 of 9 percent, five-year bonds payable at 104. Nanke has extra cash and wishes to retire all the bonds payable on January 1, 2021, immediately after making the second semi-annual interest payment. Nanke uses the straight-line method of amortization. To retire the bonds, Nanke pays the market price of 97.

   a. What is Nanke's carrying amount of the bonds payable on the retirement date?

   b. How much cash must Nanke pay to retire the bonds payable?

   c. Compute Nanke's gain or loss on the retirement of the bonds payable.

④
Accounting for the retirement of bonds payable
c. Gain, $31,000

④

Accounting for the conversion of bonds payable

b. Common shares, $3,030,000

S15–14 Junior Incorporated has $3,000,000 of convertible bonds payable outstanding, with a bond premium of $30,000 also on the books. The bondholders have notified Junior Incorporated that they wish to convert the bonds into shares on April 15. Specifically, the bonds may be converted into 400,000 of Junior's common shares.

a. What is Junior's carrying amount of its convertible bonds payable prior to the conversion?

b. Journalize Junior's conversion of the bonds payable into common shares. No explanation is required.

⑤

Comparison of financing plans

EPS Plan 1, $3.54

S15–15 Suppose Zen Corporation has net income of $600,000 and 200,000 common shares outstanding before a new project. The company needs $1,000,000 for expansion, and management is considering two financing plans:

- Plan 1 is to issue $1,000,000 of 12 percent bonds.
- Plan 2 is to issue 50,000 common shares for $1,000,000.

Zen Corporation management believes the new cash can be invested in operations to earn income of $300,000 before interest and taxes. Given the corporation's tax rate of 40 percent, which is the better plan? Why?

⑤

Earnings-per-share effects of financing with bonds versus shares

EPS: Plan A, $3.78

S15–16 T&T Marina needs to raise $2 million to expand. T&T's president is considering two plans:

- Plan A: Issue $2,000,000 of 8 percent bonds payable to borrow the money
- Plan B: Issue 100,000 common shares at $20.00 per share

Before any new financing, T&T expects to earn net income of $600,000, and the company already has 200,000 common shares outstanding. T&T believes the expansion will increase income before interest and income tax by $400,000. The income tax rate is 35 percent.

Prepare an analysis similar to Exhibit 15–9, on page 842, to determine which plan is likely to result in higher earnings per share. Which financing plan would you recommend?

⑥

Reporting liabilities

Total current liabilities, $38,500

S15–17 Talon Inc. includes the following selected accounts in its general ledger at December 31, 2020:

Notes Payable, Long-term	$160,000	Accounts Payable	$ 26,000
Bonds Payable	100,000	Discount on Bonds Payable	3,000
Interest Payable (due next year)	500	Mortgage Payable (payments are $1,000 per month)	100,000

Prepare the liabilities section of Talon Inc.'s balance sheet at December 31, 2020, to show how the company would report these items.

⑥

Applying mortgage concepts to a loan

√**S15–18** You qualified for a student loan in the amount of $10,000. Once you graduate, you are required to repay this loan over 10 years at a rate of interest of 4 percent. The monthly interest and principal repayments are calculated like a mortgage. The following table illustrates the first four payments beginning December 1, 2020:

	A	B	C	D	E	F
1			Student Loan Payments			
2	Period	Beginning Balance	Blended Monthly Loan Payment	Interest Expense	Principal Payment	Ending Balance
3	Nov. 1, 2020					$10,000.00
4	Dec. 1, 2020	$10,000.00	$101.25	$33.33	$67.92	9,932.08
5	Jan. 1, 2021	9,932.08	101.25	33.11	68.14	9,863.94
6	Feb. 1, 2021	9,863.94	101.25	32.88	68.37	9,795.57
7	Mar. 1, 2021	9,795.57	101.25	32.65	68.60	9,726.97

GIVEN

Using the information from the table, record the journal entry for the January 1, 2021, loan payment.

S15–19 On January 1, 2020, Thames Company purchases a vehicle and signs a six-year loan for $60,000 at 4 percent. Their accountant started the following table:

⑥
Account for long-term notes payable
b. Current portion, $11,760

	A	B	C	D	E	F
1	**Period**	**Beginning Balance**	**Blended Monthly Payment**	**Interest Expense**	**Principal Payment**	**Ending Balance**
2	Jan. 1, 2020					60,000.00
3	Jan. 31, 2020					
4	Feb. 29, 2020					
5	Mar. 31, 2020					
6	Apr. 30, 2020					
7	May 31, 2020					
8	Jun. 30, 2020					

a. Complete the partial amortization schedule assuming they will make a blended monthly payment of $980. Round all amounts to two decimal places.

b. At the end of 2020, what amount would be shown on the balance sheet for the current portion of the loan?

S15–20 Cotton Corp. agrees to lease a store in a mall and open a t-shirt shop. On January 2, 2020, the company pays a nonrefundable $20,000 deposit to secure the store and agrees to a lease amount of $10,000 per month for two years. Journalize the initial lease deposit, the first monthly lease payment, and the December 31 year-end adjustment of the $20,000 deposit. Explanations are not required. Would Cotton Corp. report the lease information in the notes to the financial statements? Why or why not?

⑦
Reporting lease liabilities

S15–21 Briefly answer the following questions:
a. When accounting for bonds, what is the primary difference between ASPE and IFRS?
b. When accounting for leases, what is the primary difference between ASPE and IFRS?

⑧
Difference between ASPE and IFRS

EXERCISES

E15–1 WestJet Airlines Ltd. needs to raise some funds to finance the purchase of a fleet of energy-efficient aircraft to replace the current fleet of aging planes. WestJet is planning on issuing bonds to finance this proposal. You are the CFO of WestJet. What would be the best type of bond to issue? As an investor, what would be the best type of bond to purchase in this case?

①
Bond types

E15–2 Tyler Corp. is planning to issue long-term bonds payable to borrow for a major expansion. The chief executive officer, Robert Tyler, asks your advice on some related matters:
a. At what type of bond price will Tyler have total interest expense equal to the cash interest payments?
b. Under which type of bond price will Tyler's total interest expense be greater than the cash interest payments?
c. The stated interest rate on the bonds is 3 percent, and the market interest rate is 4 percent. What type of price can Tyler expect for the bonds?
d. Tyler could raise the stated interest rate on the bonds to 5 percent (market rate is 4 percent). In that case, what type of price can Tyler expect for the bonds?

②
Determining whether the bond price will be at par, at a discount, or at a premium

E15–3 Oceanfront Developers Inc. issues $2,000,000 of 5 percent, semi-annual, 20-year bonds dated March 31.

Required Record (a) the issuance of bonds at par on March 31 and (b) the next semi-annual interest payment on September 30.

②
Issuing bonds and paying interest
b. Interest expense, $50,000

②

Calculating bond proceeds when sale is between interest dates

②

Journalizing bond issue between interest dates

②③

Issuing bonds; paying and accruing interest

b. Interest expense, $150,000

②③

Issuing bonds; paying and accruing interest

b. Interest expense, $125,000

②③

Issuing bonds, paying and accruing interest, and amortizing a discount by the straight-line method

b. Interest expense, $90,000

②③

Issuing bonds, paying and earning interest, and amortizing a premium by the straight-line method

c. Interest expense, $49,375

③

Debt payment and preparing a discount amortization schedule using a spreadsheet

Interest expense, Dec. 31, 2020 $377,255

E15–4 Arubi Inc. issued $7,000,000 of 15-year, 3 percent bonds on April 30. If the bonds were sold on July 31, how much cash would Arubi Inc. receive upon issuance of the bonds?

E15–5 Refer to the data for Arubi Inc. in E15–4. Journalize the sale of the bonds on July 31 and the first semi-annual interest payment on October 31. No explanations are required.

E15–6 On February 1, Lasquiti Logistics Inc. issues 20-year, 3 percent bonds payable with a maturity value of $10,000,000. The bonds sell at par and pay interest on January 31 and July 31.

Required Record (a) the issuance of the bonds on February 1, (b) the semi-annual interest payment on July 31, and (c) the interest accrual on December 31.

E15–7 Saturna Corp. issues 20-year, 6 percent bonds with a maturity value of $5,000,000 on April 30. The bonds sell at par and pay interest on March 31 and September 30.

Required Record (a) the issuance of the bonds on April 30, (b) the payment of interest on September 30, and (c) the accrual of interest on December 31.

E15–8 On April 1, Avalon Inc. issued 20-year, 3.5 percent bonds with a maturity value of $5,000,000. The bonds sell at 98.00 and pay interest on September 30 and March 31. Avalon Inc. amortizes bond discounts by the straight-line method.

Required Record (a) the issuance of the bonds on April 1, (b) the semi-annual interest payment on September 30, and (c) the interest accrual on December 31.

E15–9 Vindaloo Corp. issues a new set of 8 percent, 20-year bonds in the amount of $1,500,000 on February 1, 2020. The bonds sell at 102.00 and pay interest on January 31 and July 31.

Required Record (a) the issuance of the bonds on February 1, (b) the payment of interest on July 31, (c) the accrual of interest on December 31, and (d) the payment of interest on January 31, 2021. Assume Vindaloo Corp. amortizes the premium by the straight-line method.

E15–10 On January 2, 2020, Omni Industries Inc. issued $4,000,000 of 8.5 percent, 5-year bonds when the market interest rate was 10 percent. Omni Industries pays interest annually on December 31. The issue price of the bonds was $3,772,553.

Required Create a spreadsheet (either on paper or using software) to complete a schedule to amortize the discount on these bonds. Use the effective-interest method of amortization. Round to the nearest dollar, and format your answer as follows:

	A	B	C	D	E	F
1		8.5%	10%		Unamortized	Bond
2		Interest	Interest	Discount	Discount	Carrying
3	Date	Payment	Expense	Amortization	Balance	Amount
4						
5	Jan. 2, 2020				$227,447	$3,772,553
6	Dec. 31, 2020	$	$	$	$	$
7	Dec. 31, 2021					
8	Dec. 31, 2022					
9	Dec. 31, 2023					
10	Dec. 31, 2024					

=4,000,000*0.085 =F5*0.10 =C6−B6 =E5−D6 =F5+D6

E15–11 On September 30, 2020, when the market interest rate is 6 percent, Jammer Ltd. issues $8,000,000 of 8 percent, 20-year bonds for $9,849,182. The bonds pay interest on March 31 and September 30.

③
Preparing an effective-interest amortization table; recording interest accrual and payment and the related premium amortization

2. Premium on bonds payable, Dec. 31, $12,262

Required

1. Prepare an amortization table for the first four semi-annual interest periods. Follow the format of Panel B in Exhibit 15–7 on page 835. Jammer Ltd. amortizes a bond premium by the effective-interest method.

2. Record the issuance of the bonds on September 30, 2020, the accrual of interest at December 31, 2020, and the semi-annual interest payment on March 31, 2021.

E15–12 Bingo Ltd. is authorized to issue $6,000,000 of 5 percent, 10-year bonds. On January 2, 2020, when the market interest rate is 6 percent, the company issues $4,800,000 of the bonds and receives cash of $4,442,941. Interest is paid on June 30 and December 31 each year.

③
Preparing an effective-interest amortization table; recording interest payments and the related discount amortization

3. Discount, $301,059

Required

1. Prepare an amortization table for the first four semi-annual interest periods. Follow the format of Panel B in Exhibit 15–5 on page 833. Bingo Ltd. amortizes bond discounts by the effective-interest method.

2. Record the issue of the bonds on January 2, the first semi-annual interest payment on June 30, and the second payment on December 31.

3. Show the balance sheet presentation of the bond on the date of issue and on December 31, 2021.

E15–13 Gravity Inc. issued $10,000,000 of 7 percent, 20-year bonds at a premium. The bonds are retired prior to maturity at 102. The book value of the bonds is $10,453,000 at this time. Gravity Inc. amortizes bond premiums using the effective-interest method.

④
Account for the retirement of bonds

Required

1. Was the contract rate on the bonds at the time of issuance greater or less than the market rate of interest? Explain.

2. Prepare the journal entry to record the retirement of the bonds on May 6.

3. Assume that the bonds were redeemed at maturity. Would the total cash interest paid be different if the company used the straight-line method of amortization of premiums? Explain.

E15–14 Weisbrod Management Inc. issued 8 percent bonds with a maturity value of $6,000,000 for $5,762,618 on October 1, 2020, when the market rate of interest was 9 percent. These bonds mature on October 1, 2025, and are callable at 102.00. Weisbrod Management Inc. pays interest each April 1 and October 1. On October 1, 2021, when the bonds' market price is 103.00, Weisbrod Management Inc. retires the bonds in the most economical way available.

④
Recording retirement of bonds payable

Loss on retirement, $319,615

Required Record the payment of interest and the amortization of the bond discount at October 1, 2021; also record the retirement of the bonds on that date. Weisbrod Management Inc. uses the effective-interest method to amortize the bond discount.

E15–15 Saint Martin Inc. issued $300,000 of 12 percent, 10-year bonds on July 1, 2019. Interest payments dates are January 2 and July 1. The issue price was $293,400. The bonds are convertible into common shares at the rate of 15 common shares for each $1,000 bond. The market price of Saint Martin Inc. common shares has risen steadily over the last two years, and on July 1, 2021, half of the bonds are converted into common shares after the interest payment entry has been recorded.

④
Account for retirement and conversion of bonds

Required

1. Compute the balance in the premium or discount account on the date of conversion. Saint Martin Inc. uses the straight-line method of amortization.

2. Prepare the entry to convert half of the bonds into common shares.

E15–16 Healthcare Providers Ltd. issued $7,500,000 of 8.5 percent, 15-year convertible bonds payable on July 1, 2020, at a price of 97.0. Each $1,000 face amount of bonds is convertible into 80 common shares. On December 31, 2021, bondholders exercised their right to convert the bonds into common shares.

④
Recording conversion of bonds payable

4. 600,000 shares

Required

1. What would cause the bondholders to convert their bonds into common shares?
2. Without making journal entries, compute the carrying amount of the bonds payable at December 31, 2021. Healthcare Providers Ltd. uses the straight-line method to amortize a bond premium or discount on an annual basis.
3. All amortization has been recorded properly. Journalize the conversion transaction at December 31, 2021.
4. How many common shares were received by the bondholders?

④
Recording early retirement and conversion of bonds payable

2. $385,000 of common shares

E15–17 Pasteis Ltd. reported the following balances at September 30, 2020:

Long-term liabilities		
Convertible bonds payable, 9%, due September 30, 2026	$1,600,000	
Discount on bonds payable	60,000	$1,540,000

Required

1. Record the retirement of one-half of the bonds on October 1, 2020, at the call price of 103.00.
2. Record the conversion of one-fourth (of the original $1,600,000) of the bonds into 20,000 common shares of Pasteis Ltd. on October 1, 2020.

⑤
Analyzing alternative plans for raising money

EPS: Plan A, $5.78

E15–18 Pudong Transport Ltd. is considering two plans for raising $4,000,000 to expand operations. Plan A is to borrow at 9 percent, and Plan B is to issue 400,000 common shares. Before any new financing, Pudong Transport Ltd. has net income after interest and income tax of $2,000,000 and 400,000 common shares outstanding. Management believes the company can use the new funds to earn income of $840,000 per year before interest and taxes. The income tax rate is 35 percent.

Required Analyze Pudong Transport Ltd.'s situation to determine which plan will result in higher earnings per share. Use Exhibit 15–9 on page 842 as a guide.

⑤
Earnings-per-share effects of financing with bonds versus shares

EPS: Plan A, $4.12

E15–19 Knutsen Financial Services Ltd. needs to raise $3,000,000 to expand company operations. Knutsen's president is considering two options:

- Plan A: $3,000,000 of 4 percent bonds payable to borrow the money
- Plan B: 300,000 common shares at $10.00 per share

Before any new financing, Knutsen Financial Services Ltd. expects to earn net income of $900,000, and the company already has 300,000 common shares outstanding. The president believes the expansion will increase income before interest and income tax by $600,000. The company's income tax rate is 30 percent.

Required Prepare an analysis similar to Exhibit 15–9 on page 842, to determine which plan is likely to result in the higher earnings per share. Which financing plan would you recommend for Knutsen Financial Services Ltd.? Give your reasons.

⑥
Recording mortgage liabilities

E15–20 Spirit World Corp. borrowed $500,000 in the form of a mortgage on January 1, 2020, to finance the purchase of a small warehouse. The mortgage rate is 5 percent, the term is 20 years, and semi-annual payments of $19,918 are made on January 1 and July 1. The following chart shows the first five mortgage payments:

	A	B	C	D	E	F
1	Semi-annual Interest Period	Beginning Balance	Blended Payment	Interest Expense 2.5%	Principal Payment	Ending Balance
2	Jan. 1, 2020					$500,000
3	Jul. 1, 2020	$500,000	$19,918	$12,500	$7,418	492,582
4	Jan. 1, 2021	492,582	19,918	12,315	7,603	484,979
5	Jul. 1, 2021	484,979	19,918	12,124	7,794	477,185
6	Jan. 1, 2022	477,185	19,918	11,930	7,988	469,197
7	Jul. 1, 2022	469,197	19,918	11,730	8,188	461,009

Required Journalize the establishment of the mortgage and the first mortgage payment made on July 1, 2020.

E15-21 The chief accounting officer of Giffen Productions Ltd. is considering how to report long-term notes at March 31, 2020. The company's financial accountant has assembled the following information about their long-term notes payable:

③ ⑥
Reporting long-term debt on the balance sheet

Note 5: Long-Term Debt	
Total	$2,400,000
Less: Current portion	300,000
Less: Unamortized discount	16,000
Long-term debt	$2,084,000

None of the unamortized discount relates to the current portion of long-term debt. Show how Giffen Productions Ltd.'s balance sheet would report these liabilities.

E15-22 A lease agreement for equipment requires Granger Transport Ltd. to make 10 annual payments of $40,000, with the first payment due on January 2, 2020, the date of the inception of the lease.

⑦
Journalizing capital lease and operating lease transactions

2. Dec. 31, 2020, amortization expense, $27,036

Required

1. Journalize the following lessee transactions assuming that it is a capital lease:

2020

Jan. 2 Beginning of lease term and first annual payment. The present value of the nine future lease payments at 10 percent is $230,361.

Dec. 31 Amortization of equipment (10 percent).

  31 Interest expense on lease liability.

2021

Jan. 2 Second annual lease payment.

2. Assume now that this is an operating lease. Journalize the January 2, 2020, lease payment.

E15-23 Booth Ice Huts Inc. includes the following selected accounts in its general ledger at December 31, 2020:

⑦
Reporting liabilities, including capital lease obligations

Total liabilities $1,600,000

Bonds Payable	$1,020,000
Equipment under Capital Lease	350,000
Notes Payable, Long-term	200,000
Current Portion of Bonds Payable	162,000
Capital Lease Liability (long-term)	136,000
Accounts Payable	57,000
Interest Payable (due March 1, 2021)	31,000
Discount on Bonds Payable (all long-term)	18,000
Current Obligation under Capital Lease	12,000

Required Prepare the liabilities section of Booth Ice Huts Inc.'s balance sheet at December 31, 2020, to show how the company would report these items.

SERIAL EXERCISE

E15-24 *The Serial Exercise involves a company that will be revisited throughout relevant chapters in Volume 1 and Volume 2. You can complete the Serial Exercises using MyLab Accounting.*

② ③ ⑥
Determine the price of bond and account for basic bond transactions, amortize a bond discount or premium using the straight-line method, account for other long-term liabilities

June 30
Discount on Bonds Payable, $127

This exercise continues recordkeeping for the Canyon Canoe Company. Students do not have to complete prior exercises in order to answer this question.

Canyon Canoe Company is considering raising additional capital for further expansion. The company wants to finance a new business venture into guided trips down the Amazon River in South America. Additionally, the company wants to add another building on its land to offer more services for local customers.

Canyon Canoe Company plans to raise the capital by issuing $210,000 of 7.5 percent, six-year bonds on January 2, 2023. The bonds pay interest semi-annually on June 30 and December 31. The company receives $208,476 when the bonds are issued.

The company also issues a mortgage payable for $450,000 on January 2, 2023. The proceeds from the mortgage will be used to construct the new building. The mortgage requires annual payments of $45,000 plus interest for 10 years, payable on December 31. The mortgage interest rate is 8 percent.

Required

1. Will the bonds issue at face value, a premium, or a discount?

2. Record the following transactions. Include dates and round to the nearest dollar. Omit explanations.

   a. Cash received from the bond issue.

   b. Cash received from the mortgage payable.

   c. Semi-annual bond interest payments for 2023. Amortize the premium or discount using the straight-line amortization method.

   d. Payment on the mortgage payable for 2023.

5. Calculate the total interest expense incurred in 2023.

CHALLENGE EXERCISES

②③
Analyzing bond transactions
2. Interest payment, $9,000,000

E15–25 The (partial) advertisement below appeared in a newspaper:

This announcement appears as a matter of record only.

Millar Corporation, Inc.

$100,000,000

9% Series E Secured Debentures due May 16, 2025

guaranteed by

Millar Corporation and Company, Limited Parternship

Lévesque Beaubein Geoffrion Inc.		**Nesbitt Burns Inc.**
Richardson Greenshields of Canada Limited	**Toronto Dominion Securites Inc.**	**Wood Gundy Inc.**

Pearson Education

Interest is payable on November 16 and May 16.

Required   Answer these questions about Millar Corporation's secured debentures (bonds):

1. Suppose investors purchased these securities at 98.50 on May 16, 2020. Describe the transaction in detail, indicating who received cash, who paid cash, and how much.

2. Compute the annual cash interest payment on the Millar Corporation bonds.

3. Prepare an effective-interest amortization table for Millar Corporation's first two payments, on November 16, 2020, and May 16, 2021. Assume the market rate at the date of issuance was 9.2 percent.

4. Compute Millar Corporation's interest expense for the first full year ended May 16, 2021, under the effective-interest amortization method.

5. Another company's issue of unsecured bonds for $20,000,000 was issued the same day; it bore an interest rate of 12 percent. Why was the rate so much higher for this issue than for the Millar Corporation issue?

BEYOND THE NUMBERS

BN15–1

② ⑥
Questions about long-term debt

The following questions are not related to each other.

1. IMAX Corporation obtains the use of most of its theatre properties through leases. IMAX Corporation prefers operating leases over capital leases. Why is this a good idea? Consider IMAX Corporation's debt ratio.

2. IMAX Corporation likes to borrow for longer periods when interest rates are low and for shorter periods when interest rates are high. Why is this a good business strategy?

3. Suppose IMAX Corporation needs to borrow $2,000,000 to open new theatres. The company can borrow $2,000,000 by issuing 8 percent, 20-year bonds at a price of 96. How much will IMAX Corporation actually be borrowing under this arrangement? How much must the company repay at maturity?

ETHICAL ISSUE

EI15–1

Cavell Products Inc., a manufacturer of electronic devices, borrowed heavily between the years 2013 and 2017 to exploit the advantage of financing operations with debt. At first, Cavell Products was able to earn operating income much higher than its interest expense and was therefore quite profitable. However, when the business cycle turned down, Cavell Products' debt burden pushed the company to the brink of bankruptcy. Operating income was less than interest expense.

Required   Is it unethical for managers to commit a company to a high level of debt? Or is it just risky? Who could be hurt by a company's taking on too much debt? Discuss.

PROBLEMS (GROUP A)

P15–1A Danny's Hamburgers issued 6 percent, 10-year bonds payable at 90 on December 31, 2018. At December 31, 2020, Danny reported the bonds payable amortized on the straight-line basis as follows:

① ②
Analyze and journalize bond transactions.
2. Discount $3,000

Long-term liabilities		
Bonds payable	$ 600,000	
Less: Discount on bonds payable	48,000	$ 552,000

Danny's pays semi-annual interest each June 30 and December 31.

Required

1. Answer the following questions about Danny's bonds payable:
    a. What is the maturity value of the bonds?
    b. What is the carrying amount of the bonds at December 31, 2020?
    c. What is the semi-annual cash interest payment on the bonds?
    d. How much interest expense should the company record each year?
2. Record the June 30, 2020, semi-annual interest payment and amortization of discount.

P15–2A The board of directors of Jeter Production Co. Ltd. authorizes the issuance of 4 percent, 10-year bonds with a maturity value of $12,000,000. The semi-annual interest dates are May 31 and November 30. The bonds are issued through an underwriter on June 30, 2020, at par plus accrued interest from June 1, 2020. Jeter's year-end is December 31.

② ③
Journalizing bond transactions at par including accruals and interim sales, and reporting bonds payable
1. a. Interest payable, $40,000

Required

1. Journalize the following transactions:
    a. Issuance of the bonds on June 30, 2020.
    b. Payment of interest on November 30, 2020.
    c. Accrual of interest on December 31, 2020.
    d. Payment of interest on May 31, 2021.

2. Report interest payable and bonds payable as they would appear on the Jeter Production Co. Ltd. balance sheet at December 31, 2020.

3. Why do we need to accrue interest on June 30 and again on December 31, twice in 2020?

 Issuing bonds at a discount, amortizing by the straight-line method, and reporting bonds payable on the balance sheet

4. Total liabilities, $4,997,917

P15–3A On March 1, 2020, Gill Management Ltd. issues 8.5 percent, 20-year bonds payable with a maturity value of $5,000,000. The bonds pay interest on February 28 and August 31. Gill Management Ltd. amortizes premiums and discounts by the straight-line method.

Required

1. If the market interest rate is 7.5 percent when Gill Management issues its bonds, will the bonds be priced at par, at a premium, or at a discount? Explain.

2. If the market interest rate is 9 percent when Gill Management issues its bonds, will the bonds be priced at par, at a premium, or at a discount? Explain.

3. Assume the issue price of the bonds is 97.00. Journalize the following bond transactions:

   a. Issuance of the bonds on March 1, 2020.

   b. Payment of interest and amortization of the discount on August 31, 2020.

   c. Accrual of interest and amortization of the discount on December 31, 2020, Gill Management's year-end.

   d. Payment of interest and amortization of the discount on February 28, 2021.

4. Report interest payable and bonds payable as they would appear on the Gill Management Ltd.'s balance sheet at December 31, 2020.

 Analyzing a company's bonds, amortizing by the effective-interest method, and journalizing transactions

4. $1,790,455

P15–4A Assume that the notes to Echo Valley Ltd.'s financial statements reported the following data about their $2,000,000 debentures on September 30, 2020:

NOTE E: LONG-TERM DEBT	
5 percent debentures due 2033, net of unamortized discount of $223,162 (effective interest rate of 6.0 percent)	$1,776,838

Echo Valley Ltd. amortizes the discount by the effective-interest method. Round all calculated amounts to the nearest whole dollar.

Required

1. Answer the following questions about Echo Valley's long-term liabilities:

   a. What is the maturity value of the 5 percent debentures?

   b. What is the carrying amount of the 5 percent debentures at September 30, 2020? 2021?

   c. What are Echo Valley's annual cash interest payments on these debentures?

2. Prepare an amortization table through September 30, 2022. Echo Valley pays interest annually on September 30.

3. Record the September 30, 2022, interest payments.

4. What is Echo Valley's carrying amount of the debentures at September 30, 2022, immediately after the interest payment?

 Issuing convertible bonds at a premium, amortizing by the effective-interest method, retiring bonds early, converting bonds, and reporting the bonds payable on the balance sheet

3. Total, $1,065,275

P15–5A On December 31, 2020, Praga Ltd. issues 6 percent, 10-year convertible bonds with a maturity value of $6,000,000. The semi-annual interest dates are June 30 and December 31. The market interest rate is 5 percent and the issue price of the bonds is 107.79458.

Required

1. Prepare an effective-interest-method amortization table for the first four semi-annual interest periods. Round all amounts to the nearest whole dollar.

2. Journalize the following transactions:

   a. Issuance of the bonds on December 31, 2020. Credit Convertible Bonds Payable.

   b. Payment of interest on June 30, 2021.

   c. Payment of interest on December 31, 2021.

d. Retirement of bonds with maturity value of $3,000,000 on July 2, 2022. Praga pays the call price of 104.00.

e. Conversion by the bondholders on July 2, 2022, of bonds with maturity value of $2,000,000 into 40,000 of Praga Ltd. common shares.

3. Prepare the balance sheet presentation of the bonds payable that are outstanding at December 31, 2022.

P15–6A Two businesses must consider how to raise $10,000,000.

⑤

Financing operations with debt or with shares

Blackburn Inc. is in the midst of its most successful period since it began operations 48 years ago. For each of the past 10 years, net income and earnings per share have increased by 15 percent. The outlook for the future is equally bright, with new markets opening up and competitors unable to manufacture products of Blackburn Inc.'s quality. Blackburn Inc. is planning a large-scale expansion and would like to purchase equipment. The bank is reluctant to lend any more funds to this company as the lending rules have become stricter.

Sage Consulting Limited has fallen on hard times. Net income has remained flat for five of the last six years, even falling by 10 percent from last year's level of profits. Top management has experienced unusual turnover, and the company lacks strong leadership. To become competitive again, Sage Consulting Limited desperately needs $10,000,000 for expansion.

Required

1. Propose a plan for each company to raise the needed cash. Which company should borrow? Which company should issue shares? Consider the advantages and disadvantages of raising money by borrowing and by issuing shares, and discuss them in your answer.

2. How will what you have learned in this chapter help you manage a business?

P15–7A Domaine Wines Ltd. issued an $800,000, five-year, 6 percent mortgage note payable on December 31, 2020, to help finance a new warehouse. The terms of the mortgage provide for semi-annual blended payments of $93,784 on June 30 and December 31 of each year.

⑥

Accounting for a mortgage

1. Dec. 31, 2022, balance, $508,049

Required

1. Prepare a mortgage instalment payment schedule for the first two years of this mortgage. Round all amounts to the nearest whole dollar.

2. Record the issuance of the mortgage note payable on December 31, 2020.

3. Report the mortgage payable on the December 31, 2020, balance sheet. Use the principal reduction to calculate the current portion.

4. Journalize the first two instalment payments on June 30, 2021, and December 31, 2021.

P15–8A Journalize the following transactions of Applewood Corp.:

② ⑦

Journalizing bonds payable and capital lease transactions

Jan. 2, 2020, discount, $150,000

2020

Jan. 2 Issued 7 percent, 10-year bonds with a maturity value of $5,000,000. The bonds were sold at 97.00.

Jan. 2 Signed a five-year capital lease on equipment. The agreement requires annual lease payments of $400,000, with the first payment due immediately. The present value of the five lease payments is $1,724,851 (8 percent is the interest rate).

Jul. 2 Paid semi-annual interest and amortized the discount by the straight-line method on the 7 percent bonds.

Dec. 31 Accrued semi-annual interest expense and amortized the discount by the straight-line method on the 7 percent bonds.

31 Recorded amortization on the leased equipment using the straight-line method.

31 Accrued interest expense at 8 percent on the lease liability.

2030

Jan. 2 Paid the 7 percent bonds at maturity. (Ignore the final interest payment.)

P15–9A The accounting records of Cryptocurrency Managers Inc. include the following items:

Capital Lease Liability,		Mortgage Payable,	
Long-term	$538,000	Long-term	$ 501,000
Bonds Payable, Long-term	960,000	Building Acquired under	
Premium on Bonds Payable	78,000	Capital Lease	800,000
Interest Expense	300,000	Bonds Payable,	
Interest Payable	98,820	Current Portion	96,000
Interest Revenue	61,800	Accumulated Amortization,	
Capital Lease Liability,		Building	448,000
Current	74,000	Mortgage Payable,	
		Current	201,000

Required Show how these items would be reported on the Cryptocurrency Managers Inc. balance sheet, including headings for property, plant, and equipment, current liabilities, and long-term liabilities. Note disclosures are not required. The premium on bonds payable must be split between the current and long-term portions of the bonds payable.

PROBLEMS (GROUP B)

P15–1B Johnny's Hamburgers issued 8%, 10-year bonds payable at 85 on December 31, 2018. At December 31, 2020, Johnny reported the bonds payable amortized on the straight-line basis as follows:

Long-term Liabilities:		
Bonds Payable	$300,000	
Less: Discount on Bonds Payable	36,000	$264,000

Johnny pays semi-annual interest each June 30 and December 31.

Required

1. Answer the following questions about Johnny's bonds payable:
   a. What is the maturity value of the bonds?
   b. What is the carrying amount of the bonds at December 31, 2020?
   c. What is the semi-annual cash interest payment on the bonds?
   d. How much interest expense should the company record each year?
2. Record the June 30, 2020, semi-annual interest payment and amortization of discount.

② ③
Journalizing bond
transactions at par including
accruals and interim sales,
and reporting bonds payable

P15–2B The board of directors of Farrell Communications Ltd. authorizes the issuance of 6 percent, 20-year bonds with a maturity value of $10,000,000. The semi-annual interest dates are March 31 and September 30. The bonds are issued through an underwriter on April 30, 2020, at par plus accrued interest. Farrell's year-end is December 31.

Required

1. Journalize the following transactions:
   a. Issuance of the bonds on April 30, 2020.
   b. Payment of interest on September 30, 2020.
   c. Accrual of interest on December 31, 2020.
   d. Payment of interest on March 31, 2021.
2. Report interest payable and bonds payable as they would appear on the Farrell Communications Ltd. balance sheet at December 31, 2020.
3. Why do we need to accrue interest on April 30 and again on December 31, twice in 2020?

② ③
Issuing bonds at a premium,
amortizing by the straight-line
method, and reporting bonds
payable on the balance sheet

P15–3B On April 1, 2020, Sora Inc. issues 7 percent, 10-year bonds payable with a maturity value of $3,000,000. The bonds pay interest on March 31 and September 30, and Sora Inc. amortizes premiums and discounts by the straight-line method.

Required

1. If the market interest rate is 9 percent when Sora Inc. issues its bonds, will the bonds be priced at par, at a premium, or at a discount? Explain.

2. If the market interest rate is 5 percent when Sora Inc. issues its bonds, will the bonds be priced at par, at a premium, or at a discount? Explain.

3. Assume the issue price of the bonds is 103.00. Journalize the following bonds payable transactions:

   a. Issuance of the bonds on April 1, 2020.

   b. Payment of interest and amortization of the premium on September 30, 2020.

   c. Accrual of interest and amortization of the premium on December 31, 2020, the year-end.

   d. Payment of interest and amortization of the premium on March 31, 2021.

4. Report interest payable and bonds payable as they would appear on the Sora Inc. balance sheet at December 31, 2020.

P15–4B The notes to Shaolin Biotech Inc.'s financial statements recently reported the following data on June 30, 2020, the company's year-end:

Analyzing a company's bonds, amortizing by the effective-interest method, and journalizing transactions

NOTE 4: INDEBTEDNESS	
Long-term debt at June 30, 2020, included the following:	
6.00 percent debentures due June 30, 2039, with an effective interest rate of 7.00 percent, net of unamortized discount of $206,712	$1,793,288
Other indebtedness with an interest rate of 5.00 percent, due $408,000 in 2024 and $392,000 in 2025	800,000

Assume Shaolin Biotech Inc. amortizes the discount by the effective-interest method.

Required

1. Answer the following questions about Shaolin Biotech's long-term liabilities:

   a. What is the maturity value of the 6 percent debentures?

   b. What are Shaolin Biotech's annual cash interest payments on the 6 percent debentures?

   c. What is the carrying amount of the 6 percent debentures at June 30, 2020? 2021?

   d. How many years remain in the life of the 6 percent debentures?

2. Prepare an amortization table through June 30, 2023, for the 6 percent debentures. Round all amounts to the nearest dollar, and assume Shaolin Biotech pays interest annually on June 30.

3. Record the June 30, 2022 and 2023, interest payments on the 6 percent debentures.

4. There is no premium or discount on the other indebtedness. Assuming annual interest is paid on June 30 each year, record Shaolin Biotech Inc.'s June 30, 2021, interest payment on the other indebtedness.

P15–5B On December 31, 2020, Sierra Corp. issues 4 percent, 10-year convertible bonds with a maturity value of $4,500,000. The semi-annual interest dates are June 30 and December 31. The market interest rate is 5 percent, and the issue price of the bonds is 92.2054. Sierra Corp. amortizes bond premium and discount by the effective-interest method.

Issuing convertible bonds at a discount, amortizing by the effective-interest method, retiring bonds early, converting bonds, and reporting bonds payable on the balance sheet

Required

1. Prepare an effective-interest method amortization table for the first four semi-annual interest periods.

2. Journalize the following transactions:

   a. Issuance of the bonds on December 31, 2020. Credit Convertible Bonds Payable.

   b. Payment of interest on June 30, 2021.

   c. Payment of interest on December 31, 2021.

   d. Retirement of the bonds with a maturity value of $200,000 on July 2, 2022. Sierra Corp. purchases the bonds at 96.00 in the open market.

e. Conversion by the bondholders on July 2, 2022, of bonds with a maturity value of $400,000 into 5,000 Sierra Corp. common shares.

3. Prepare the balance sheet presentation of the bonds payable that are outstanding at December 31, 2022.

⑤
Financing operations with debt or with shares

P15–6B Marketing studies have shown that consumers prefer upscale restaurants, and recent trends in industry sales have supported the research. To capitalize on this trend, Orca Ltd. is embarking on a massive expansion. Plans call for opening five new restaurants within the next 18 months. Each restaurant is scheduled to be 30 percent larger than the company's existing restaurants, furnished more elaborately, with more extensive menus. Management estimates that company operations will provide $15 million of the cash needed for the expansion, and Orca also owns the existing waterfront property that the head office is located on. Orca Ltd. must raise the remaining $15 million from outsiders since the bank has tightened up lending. The board of directors is considering obtaining the $15 million either through borrowing or by issuing common shares.

Required Write a memo to company management. Discuss the advantages and disadvantages of borrowing and of issuing common shares to raise the needed cash. Use the following format for your memo:

Date:	
To:	Management of Orca Ltd.
From:	Student Name
Subject:	Advantages and disadvantages of borrowing and issuing shares to raise $15 million for expansion
Advantages and disadvantages of borrowing:	
Advantages and disadvantages of issuing shares:	

⑥
Accounting for a mortgage

P15–7B Werstirener Brewing Ltd. issued a $600,000, five-year, 6 percent mortgage note payable on December 31, 2020, to help finance a new distribution centre. The terms of the mortgage provide for semi-annual blended payments of $70,338 due June 30 and December 31 of each year.

Required

1. Prepare a mortgage instalment payment schedule for the first two years of this mortgage. Round all amounts to the nearest whole dollar.

2. Record the issuance of the mortgage note payable on December 31, 2020.

3. Report the mortgage payable on the December 31, 2020, balance sheet. Use the principal reduction when calculating the current portion.

4. Journalize the first two instalment payments on June 30, 2021, and December 31, 2021.

② ⑦
Journalizing bonds payable using the straight-line method and capital lease transactions

P15–8B Journalize the following transactions of Fayuz Communications Inc.:

2020

Jan. 2 Issued $8,000,000 of 7 percent, 10-year bonds payable at 97.00.

2 Signed a five-year capital lease on machinery. The agreement requires annual lease payments of $80,000, with the first payment due immediately. The present value of the five lease payments is $333,589, using a market rate of 10 percent.

Jul. 2 Paid semi-annual interest and amortized the discount by the straight-line method on the 7 percent bonds payable.

Dec. 31 Accrued semi-annual interest expense and amortized the discount by the straight-line method on the 7 percent bonds.

31 Recorded amortization on the leased machinery using the straight-line method.

31 Accrued interest expense at 10 percent on the lease liability.

2030

Jan. 2 Paid the 7 percent bonds at maturity. (Ignore the final interest payment.)

P15–9B The accounting records of Arthur Curry Associates Inc. include the following items:

(7)

Reporting liabilities on the balance sheet

Equipment Acquired under Capital Lease......................	$591,000	Mortgage Payable— Long-term............................	238,000
Bonds Payable—Current Portion	225,000	Accumulated Amortization— Equipment...........................	123,000
Capital Lease Liability— Long-term...........................	162,000	Capital Lease Liability— Current..................................	64,000
Discount on Bonds Payable— Long-term...........................	21,000	Mortgage Note Payable— Current..................................	69,000
Interest Revenue....................	15,000	Bonds Payable— Long-term............................	900,000
Interest Payable	84,000	Interest Expense	$171,000

Required Show how these items would be reported on the Arthur Curry Associates Inc. balance sheet, including headings for property, plant, and equipment, current liabilities, and long-term liabilities. Note disclosures are not required. The premium on bonds payable must be split between the current and long-term portions of the bonds payable.

CHALLENGE PROBLEMS

P15–1C You have just inherited $50,000 and have decided to buy shares. You have narrowed your choice down to QT Logistics Inc. and Next Systems Ltd. You carefully read each company's annual report to determine which company's shares you should buy. Your research indicates that the two companies are very similar. QT Logistics Inc.'s annual report states "The Company has financed its growth through long- and short-term borrowing," while the Next report contains the statement "The Company has financed its growth out of earnings retained in the business."

(5)

Evaluating alternative methods of financing growth

QT's shares are trading at $25.00, while Next's shares are trading at $13.00. You wonder if that is because QT has been paying an annual dividend of $2.00 per share while Next has been paying a dividend of $1.10.

You recall that the morning newspaper had an article about the economy that predicted that interest rates were expected to rise and stay at a much higher rate than at present for the next two to three years.

Required Explain which shares you would buy and indicate why you have selected them.

P15–2C Castlegar Systems Inc. had the following information available on bonds payable outstanding at December 31, 2020, its year-end:

(3) (7)

Amortizing a bond premium by the effective-interest method; accounting for lease transactions

- $5,000,000—Bonds Payable, 9 percent, interest paid on April 2 and October 2. The bonds had been issued on April 2, 2020, for $5,131,053 when the market rate of interest was 8 percent, and are due April 2, 2023.

The following transactions took place after December 31, 2020:

2021

Jan. 2 Castelgar Systems Inc. signed a lease to rent a warehouse for expansion of its operations. The lease is five years with an option to renew and calls for annual payments of $50,000 per year payable on January 2. Castelgar Systems gave a cheque for the first year upon signing the contract.

2 Castelgar Systems Inc. signed a lease for equipment. The lease is for 10 years with payments of $40,000 per year payable on January 2 (the first year's payment was made at the signing). At the end of the lease the equipment will become the property of Castelgar Systems. The future payments on the lease have a present value (at 10 percent) of $270,361. The equipment has a 10-year useful life and 10 percent residual value.

Apr. 2 Paid the interest on the bonds payable and amortized the premium using the effective-interest method. Assume half of the interest expense, amortization of the bond premium, and interest payable had been accrued properly on December 31, 2020.

Oct.	2	Paid the interest on the bonds payable and amortized the premium using the effective-interest method.
Dec.	31	Recorded any adjustments required at the end of the year for the bonds payable and the lease(s).
2022		
Jan.	2	Made the annual payments on the leases.
Apr.	2	Paid the interest on the bonds payable and amortized the premium using the effective-interest method.

Required

1. For the bonds issued on April 2, 2020, prepare an amortization schedule for the three-year life of the bonds. Round all amounts to the nearest whole dollar.
2. Record the general journal entries for the 2021 and 2022 transactions.
3. Show the liabilities section of the balance sheet on December 31, 2022.

Extending Your Knowledge

DECISION PROBLEMS

Analyzing alternative ways of raising $10,000,000

1. EPS: Plan A, $10.66

DP15–1

Business is going well for Valley Forest Products Inc. The board of directors of this family-owned company believes that the company could earn an additional $9,000,000 in income before interest and taxes by expanding into new markets. However, the $30,000,000 that the business needs for growth cannot be raised within the family. The directors, who strongly wish to retain family control of Valley Forest Products Inc., must consider issuing securities to outsiders. They are considering three financing plans:

- Plan A is to borrow at 8 percent.
- Plan B is to issue 300,000 common shares.
- Plan C is to issue 300,000 nonvoting, $7.50 cumulative preferred shares.

The company presently has net income before tax of $18,000,000 and has 1,500,000 common shares outstanding. The income tax rate is 35 percent.

Required

1. Prepare an analysis similar to Exhibit 15–9 to determine which plan will result in the highest earnings per common share.
2. Recommend one plan to the board of directors. Give your reasons.

FINANCIAL STATEMENT CASES

⑥ ⑦

Long-term debt

FSC15–1

The Indigo Books and Music Inc. financial statements that appear in Appendix A at the end of this book and on MyLab Accounting provide details about the company's long-term debt. Use the data to answer the following questions:

1. How much did Indigo report in long-term debt during the fiscal year ended April 1, 2017?
2. What type of long-term debt is listed on the balance sheet at April 1, 2017? See Note 21.
3. Under Note 3, Basis of Preparation, how does Indigo decide how to account for leases?
4. Is equipment that is leased shown as PPE in 2017?

FSC15–2

Long-term debt

TELUS Corporation's income statement and balance sheet on MyLab Accounting provide details about the company's long-term debt and equity. Use the data to answer the following questions:

1. List the long-term liability amounts at December 31, 2016 and 2015.

2. Where is detailed lease information shown in the annual report? Which of their leases are operating leases?

3. How much financing cost did TELUS record on the income statement for 2016 and 2015?

Chapter 15 Appendix

TIME VALUE OF MONEY: FUTURE VALUE AND PRESENT VALUE

The following discussion of future value lays the foundation for present value but is not essential. For the valuation of long-term liabilities, some instructors may wish to begin on page 876.

The phrase *time value of money* refers to the fact that money earns interest over time. Interest is the cost of using money. To borrowers, interest is the expense of renting money. To lenders, interest is the revenue earned from lending. When funds are used for a period of time, we must recognize the interest. Otherwise, we overlook an important part of the transaction. Suppose you invest $4,545 in corporate bonds that pay interest of 10 percent each year. After one year the value of your investment has grown to $5,000. The difference between your original investment ($4,545) and the future value of the investment ($5,000) is the amount of interest revenue you will earn during the year ($455). If you ignored the interest, you would fail to account for the interest revenue you have earned. Interest becomes more important as the time period lengthens because the amount of interest depends on the span of time the money is invested.

Let's consider a second example, but from the borrower's perspective. Suppose you purchase a machine for your business. The cash price of the machine is $8,000, but you cannot pay cash now. To finance the purchase, you sign an $8,000 note payable. The note requires you to pay the $8,000 plus 10 percent interest one year from the date of purchase. Is your cost of the machine $8,000, or is it $8,800 [$8,000 plus interest of $800 ($8,000 × 0.10)]? The cost is $8,000. The additional $800 is interest expense and not part of the cost of the machine, although interest expense is certainly a part of the decision of whether or not to purchase the machine.

FUTURE VALUE

The main application of future value *in this book* is to calculate the accumulated balance of an investment at a future date. In our first example, the investment earned 10 percent per year. After one year, $4,545 grew to $5,000, as shown in the timeline in Exhibit 15A–1.

LO (A1)
How do we find the future value of an investment?

EXHIBIT 15A–1 | Future Value

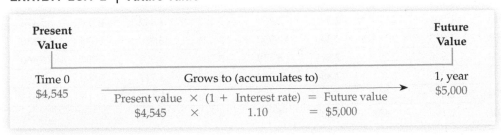

If the money were invested for five years, you would have to perform five such calculations. You would also have to consider the compound interest that your investment is earning. *Compound interest* is the interest you earn not only on your principal amount but also the interest you receive on the interest you have already earned. Most business applications include compound interest. The table below shows the interest revenue earned each year at 10 percent:

	A	B	C
1	**End of Year**	**Interest**	**Future Value**
2	0	—	$4,545
3	1	$4,545 × 0.10 = $455	5,000
4	2	5,000 × 0.10 = 500	5,500
5	3	5,500 × 0.10 = 550	6,050
6	4	6,050 × 0.10 = 605	6,655
7	5	6,655 × 0.10 = 666	7,321

Earning 10 percent, a $4,545 investment grows to $5,000 at the end of one year, to $5,500 at the end of two years, and so on. Throughout this discussion we round off to the nearest dollar to keep the numbers simple, although calculations like these are usually rounded to the nearest cent.

Future Value Tables

The formula for future value is
$$FV = PV(1 + i)^n$$
where
FV = future value
PV = present value
i = interest rate per period
n = number of compounding periods

The process of computing a future value is called *accumulating* or *compounding* because the future value is *more* than the present value. Mathematical tables ease the computational burden. You can also use financial calculators and functions in spreadsheet programs to calculate future value. (In the real world, calculators are used rather than tables—we use tables here to demonstrate the concepts.) Exhibit 15A–2, Future Value of $1, gives the future value for a single sum (a present value), $1, invested to earn a particular interest rate for a specific number of periods. Future value depends on three factors: (1) the amount of the investment, (2) the length of time between investment and future accumulation, and (3) the interest rate.

EXHIBIT 15A–2 | Future Value of $1

Future Value of $1

Periods	2%	3%	4%	5%	6%	7%	8%	9%	10%	12%
1	1.020	1.030	1.040	1.050	1.060	1.070	1.080	1.090	1.100	1.120
2	1.040	1.061	1.082	1.103	1.124	1.145	1.166	1.188	1.210	1.254
3	1.061	1.093	1.125	1.158	1.191	1.225	1.260	1.295	1.331	1.405
4	1.082	1.126	1.170	1.216	1.262	1.311	1.360	1.412	1.464	1.574
5	1.104	1.159	1.217	1.276	1.338	1.403	1.469	1.539	1.611	1.762
6	1.126	1.194	1.265	1.340	1.419	1.501	1.587	1.677	1.772	1.974
7	1.149	1.230	1.316	1.407	1.504	1.606	1.714	1.828	1.949	2.211
8	1.172	1.267	1.369	1.477	1.594	1.718	1.851	1.993	2.144	2.476
9	1.195	1.305	1.423	1.551	1.689	1.838	1.999	2.172	2.358	2.773
10	1.219	1.344	1.480	1.629	1.791	1.967	2.159	2.367	2.594	3.106
11	1.243	1.384	1.539	1.710	1.898	2.105	2.332	2.580	2.853	3.479
12	1.268	1.426	1.601	1.796	2.012	2.252	2.518	2.813	3.138	3.896
13	1.294	1.469	1.665	1.886	2.133	2.410	2.720	3.066	3.452	4.363
14	1.319	1.513	1.732	1.980	2.261	2.579	2.937	3.342	3.797	4.887
15	1.346	1.558	1.801	2.079	2.397	2.759	3.172	3.642	4.177	5.474
16	1.373	1.605	1.873	2.183	2.540	2.952	3.426	3.970	4.595	6.130
17	1.400	1.653	1.948	2.292	2.693	3.159	3.700	4.328	5.054	6.866
18	1.428	1.702	2.026	2.407	2.854	3.380	3.996	4.717	5.560	7.690
19	1.457	1.754	2.107	2.527	3.026	3.617	4.316	5.142	6.116	8.613
20	1.486	1.806	2.191	2.653	3.207	3.870	4.661	5.604	6.727	9.646

The heading in Exhibit 15A–2 states $1. Future value tables and present value tables are based on $1 because unity (the value 1) is so easy to work with. Observe the Periods column and the Interest Rate columns 2% through 12%. In business applications, interest rates are usually assumed to be for the annual period of one year unless specified otherwise. In fact, an interest rate can be stated for any period, such as 3 percent per quarter or 5 percent for a six-month period. The length of the period is arbitrary. For example, an investment may promise a return (income) of 3 percent per quarter for two quarters (six months). In that case you would be working with 3 percent interest for two periods. It would be incorrect to use 6 percent for one period because the interest is 3 percent compounded quarterly, and that amount differs somewhat from 6 percent compounded semi-annually. Take care in studying future value and present value problems to align the interest rate with the appropriate number of periods.

Remember that the number of periods is the number of compounding periods. It is not the number of years, unless the compounding period happens to be an annual period.

Let's use Exhibit 15A–2. The future value of $1.00 invested at 4 percent for one year is $1.04 ($1.00 × 1.040, which appears at the junction under the 4% column and across from 1 in the Periods column). The figure 1.040 includes both the principal (1.000) and the compound interest for one period (0.040).

Suppose you deposit $5,000 in a savings account that pays annual interest of 4 percent. The account balance at the end of the year will be $5,200. To compute the future value of $5,000 at 4 percent for one year, multiply $5,000 by 1.040 to get $5,200. Now suppose you invest in a 10-year, 6 percent certificate of deposit (CD). What will be the future value of the CD at maturity? To compute the future value of $5,000 at 6 percent for 10 periods, multiply $5,000 by 1.791 (from Exhibit 15A–2) to get $8,955. This future value of $8,955 indicates that $5,000 earning 6 percent interest compounded annually grows to $8,955 at the end of 10 years. In this way, you can find any present amount's future value at a particular future date. Future value is especially helpful for computing the amount of cash you will have on hand for some purpose in the future.

Future Value of an Annuity

In the preceding example, we made an investment of a single amount. Other investments, called annuities, include multiple payments of an equal periodic amount at fixed intervals over the duration of the investment. Consider a family investing for a child's education. The Dietrichs can invest $4,000 annually to accumulate a college fund for 15-year-old Helen. The investment can earn 7 percent annually until Helen turns 18—a three-year investment. How much will be available for Helen on the date of the last investment? Exhibit 15A–3 shows the accumulation—a total future value of $12,860.

EXHIBIT 15A–3 | Future Value of an Annuity

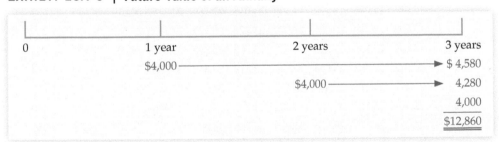

The first $4,000 invested by the Dietrichs grows to $4,580 over the investment period. The second $4,000 invested grows to $4,280, and the third $4,000 invested stays at $4,000 because it has no time to earn interest. The sum of the three future values ($4,580 + $4,280 + $4,000) is the future value of the annuity ($12,860), which can be computed as follows:

	A	B	C	D	E
1	End of Year	Annual Investment	Interest	Increase for the Year	Future Value of Annuity
2	0	—	—	—	$ 0
3	1	$4,000	—	$4,000	4,000
4	2	4,000	$280 ($4,000 × 0.07)	$4,280	8,280
5	3	4,000	$580 ($8,280 × 0.07)	4,580	12,860

The formula for the future value of an annuity is

$$S_n = R\left[(1 + i)^{(n-1)}/i\right]$$

where

S_n = future value of a simple annuity

R = the periodic payment (rent)

i = interest rate per period

n = number of periodic payments

As with the future value of $1 (a lump sum), mathematical tables ease the strain of calculating annuities. Exhibit 15A–4, Future Value of Annuity of $1, gives the future value of a series of investments, each of equal amount, at regular intervals.

What is the future value of an annuity of three investments of $1 each that earn 7 percent? The answer, 3.215 can be found in the 7% column and across from 3 in the Periods column of Exhibit 15A–4. This amount can be used to compute the future value of the investment for Helen's education, as follows:

Amount of each periodic investment		Future value of annuity of $1 (Exhibit 15A–4)		Future value of investment
$4,000	×	3.215	=	$12,860

EXHIBIT 15A–4 | Future Value of Annuity of $1

Periods	2%	3%	4%	5%	6%	7%	8%	9%	10%	12%
1	1.000	1.000	1.000	1.000	1.000	1.000	1.000	1.000	1.000	1.000
2	2.020	2.030	2.040	2.050	2.060	2.070	2.080	2.090	2.100	2.120
3	3.060	3.091	3.122	3.153	3.184	3.215	3.246	3.278	3.310	3.374
4	4.122	4.184	4.246	4.310	4.375	4.440	4.506	4.573	4.641	4.779
5	5.204	5.309	5.416	5.526	5.637	5.751	5.867	5.985	6.105	6.353
6	6.308	6.468	6.633	6.802	6.975	7.153	7.336	7.523	7.716	8.115
7	7.434	7.663	7.898	8.142	8.394	8.654	8.923	9.200	9.487	10.089
8	8.583	8.892	9.214	9.549	9.897	10.260	10.637	11.028	11.436	12.300
9	9.755	10.159	10.583	11.027	11.491	11.978	12.488	13.021	13.579	14.776
10	10.950	11.464	12.006	12.578	13.181	13.816	14.487	15.193	15.937	17.549
11	12.169	12.808	13.486	14.207	14.972	15.784	16.645	17.560	18.531	20.655
12	13.412	14.192	15.026	15.917	16.870	17.888	18.977	20.141	21.384	24.133
13	14.680	15.618	16.627	17.713	18.882	20.141	21.495	22.953	24.523	28.029
14	15.974	17.086	18.292	19.599	21.015	22.550	24.215	26.019	27.975	32.393
15	17.293	18.599	20.024	21.579	23.276	25.129	27.152	29.361	31.772	37.280
16	18.639	20.157	21.825	23.657	25.673	27.888	30.324	33.003	35.950	42.753
17	20.012	21.762	23.698	25.840	28.213	30.840	33.750	36.974	40.545	48.884
18	21.412	23.414	25.645	28.132	30.906	33.999	37.450	41.301	45.599	55.750
19	22.841	25.117	27.671	30.539	33.760	37.379	41.446	46.018	51.159	63.440
20	24.297	26.870	29.778	33.066	36.786	40.995	45.762	51.160	57.275	72.053

This one-step calculation is much easier than computing the future value of each annual investment and then summing the individual future values. In this way, you can compute the future value of any investment consisting of equal periodic amounts at regular intervals. Businesses make periodic investments to accumulate funds for equipment replacement and other uses—an application of the future value of an annuity.

PRESENT VALUE

LO A2

How do we find the present value of an investment?

Often a person knows a future amount and needs to know the related present value. Recall Exhibit 15A–1, in which present value and future value are on opposite ends of the same timeline. Suppose an investment promises to pay you $5,000 at the *end* of one year. How much would you pay *now* to acquire this investment? You would be willing to pay the present value of the $5,000, which is a future amount.

Present value also depends on three factors: (1) the amount of payment (or receipt), (2) the length of time between investment and future receipt (or payment), and (3) the interest rate. The process of computing a present value is called *discounting* because the present value is *less* than the future value.

In our investment example, the future receipt is $5,000. The investment period is one year. Assume that you demand an annual interest rate of 10 percent on your investment. With all three factors specified, you can compute the present value of $5,000 at 10 percent for one year:

$$\text{Present value of \$5,000 at 10 percent for one year}$$
$$= \frac{\text{Future value}}{1 + \text{Interest rate}} = \frac{\$5,000}{1.10} = \$4,545$$

By turning the problem around, we verify the present value computation:

	A	B
1	Amount invested (present value)	$4,545
2	Expected earnings ($4,545 × 0.10)	455
3	Amount to be received one year from now (future value)	$5,000

This example illustrates that present value and future value are based on the same equation:

$$\text{Present value} \times (1 + \text{Interest rate}) = \text{Future value}$$
$$\text{Present value} = \frac{\text{Future value}}{1 + \text{Interest rate}}$$

The formula for present value is
$PV = FV \div (1 + i)^n$
where
PV = present value
FV = future value
i = interest rate per period
n = number of compounding periods

If the $5,000 is to be received two years from now, you will pay only $4,132 for the investment, as shown in Exhibit 15A–5.

EXHIBIT 15A–5 | Two-Year Investment

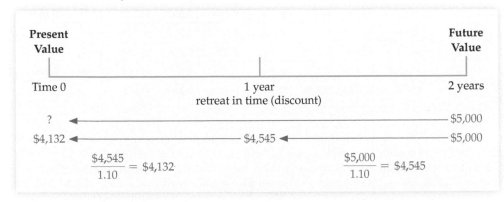

By turning the data around, we verify that $4,132 accumulates to $5,000 at 10 percent for two years:

	A	B
1	Amount invested (present value)	$4,132
2	Expected earnings for first year ($4,132 × 0.10)	413
3	Amount invested after one year	4,545
4	Expected earnings for second year ($4,545 × 0.10)	455
5	Amount to be received two years from now (future value)	$5,000

Notice that earnings for the first year are $413 but the earnings for the second year are $455—this demonstrates the power of compounding. The $42 increase from $413 to $455 comes from earning interest on the interest as well as on the principal.

You would pay $4,132—the present value of $5,000—to receive the $5,000 future amount at the end of two years at 10 percent per year. The $868 difference between the amount invested ($4,132) and the amount to be received ($5,000) is the return on the investment, the sum of the two interest receipts: $413 + $455 = $868.

Present Value Tables

We have shown the simple formula for computing present value. However, calculating present value "by hand" for investments spanning many years presents too many opportunities for arithmetical errors and it is too much work. Present value tables ease our work and allow us to see at a glance the relationship between time (in the Periods column) and each interest rate. (In the real world, calculators and computers are used rather than tables—we use tables here to demonstrate the concepts.) Let's re-examine our examples of present value by using Exhibit 15A–6: Present Value of $1.

EXHIBIT 15A–6 | Present Value of $1

Periods	2%	3%	4%	5%	6%	7%	8%	10%	12%
1	0.980	0.971	0.962	0.952	0.943	0.935	0.926	0.909	0.893
2	0.961	0.943	0.925	0.907	0.890	0.873	0.857	0.826	0.797
3	0.942	0.915	0.889	0.864	0.840	0.816	0.794	0.751	0.712
4	0.924	0.889	0.855	0.823	0.792	0.763	0.735	0.683	0.636
5	0.906	0.863	0.822	0.784	0.747	0.713	0.681	0.621	0.567
6	0.888	0.838	0.790	0.746	0.705	0.666	0.630	0.564	0.507
7	0.871	0.813	0.760	0.711	0.665	0.623	0.583	0.513	0.452
8	0.854	0.789	0.731	0.677	0.627	0.582	0.540	0.467	0.404
9	0.837	0.766	0.703	0.645	0.592	0.544	0.500	0.424	0.361
10	0.820	0.744	0.676	0.614	0.558	0.508	0.463	0.386	0.322
11	0.804	0.722	0.650	0.585	0.527	0.475	0.429	0.350	0.287
12	0.789	0.701	0.625	0.557	0.497	0.444	0.397	0.319	0.257
13	0.773	0.681	0.601	0.530	0.469	0.415	0.368	0.290	0.229
14	0.758	0.661	0.577	0.505	0.442	0.388	0.340	0.263	0.205
15	0.743	0.642	0.555	0.481	0.417	0.362	0.315	0.239	0.183
16	0.728	0.623	0.534	0.458	0.394	0.339	0.292	0.218	0.163
17	0.714	0.605	0.513	0.436	0.371	0.317	0.270	0.198	0.146
18	0.700	0.587	0.494	0.416	0.350	0.296	0.250	0.180	0.130
19	0.686	0.570	0.475	0.396	0.331	0.277	0.232	0.164	0.116
20	0.673	0.554	0.456	0.377	0.312	0.258	0.215	0.149	0.104

Present value payments are assumed to be at the beginning of the year, and future value receipts are assumed to be at the end of the year.

For the 10 percent investment for one year, we find the junction under 10% and across from 1 in the Period column. The table figure of 0.909 is computed as follows: $1 \div 1.10 = 0.909$. This work has been done for us, and only the present values are given in the table. The heading in Exhibit 15A–6 states present value for $1. To calculate present value for $5,000, we multiply 0.909 by $5,000. The result is $4,545, which matches the result we obtained by hand.

For the two-year investment, we read down the 10% column and across the Period 2 row. We multiply 0.826 (computed as $0.909 \div 1.10 = 0.826$) by $5,000 and get $4,130, which confirms our earlier computation of $4,132 (the difference is due to rounding in the present value table). Using the table, we can compute the present value of any single future amount.

While we focus on tables in this text, you can also use financial calculators and functions in spreadsheet programs to calculate present value.

Present Value of an Annuity

Lotteries that pay the winner $1,000 a week for life are an example of an annuity, an equal periodic amount ($1,000) received at a fixed interval (each year for life).

Return to the investment example beginning on the previous page. That investment provided the investor with only a single future receipt ($5,000 at the end of two years). Annuity investments provide multiple receipts of an equal amount at fixed intervals over the investment's duration.

Consider an investment that promises *annual* cash receipts of $10,000 to be received at the end of each of three years. Assume that you demand a 12 percent return on your investment. What is the investment's present value? What would you pay today to acquire the investment? The investment spans three periods, and you would pay the sum of three present values. The computation is as follows:

The formula for the present value of an annuity is

$$A_n = R[(1 - (1 + i)^{-n})/i]$$

where

A_n = present value of a simple annuity

R = the periodic payment (rent)

i = interest rate per period

n = number of periodic payments

	A	B	C	D	E
		Annual Cash Receipt		Present Value of $1 at 12% (Exhibit 15A–6)	Present Value of Annual Cash Receipt
1	Year				
2	1	$10,000	×	0.893	$ 8,930
3	2	10,000	×	0.797	7,970
4	3	10,000	×	0.712	7,120
5	Total present value of investment				$24,020

The present value of this annuity is $24,020. By paying this amount today, you will receive $10,000 at the end of each of three years while earning 12 percent on your investment.

The example illustrates repetitive computations of the three future amounts, a time-consuming process. One way to ease the computational burden is to add the three present values of $1 (0.893 + 0.797 + 0.712) and multiply their sum (2.402) by the annual cash receipt ($10,000) to obtain the present value of the annuity ($10,000 × 2.402 = $24,020).

An easier approach is to use a present value of an annuity table. Exhibit 15A–7 shows the present value of $1 to be received periodically for a given number of periods. The present value of a three-period annuity at 12 percent is 2.402 (the junction of the Period 3 row and the 12% column). Thus, $10,000 received annually at the end of each of three years, discounted at 12 percent, is $24,020 ($10,000 × 2.402), which is the present value.

EXHIBIT 15A–7 | Present Value of Annuity of $1

Periods	2%	3%	4%	5%	6%	7%	8%	10%	12%
1	0.980	0.971	0.962	0.952	0.943	0.935	0.926	0.909	0.893
2	1.942	1.914	1.886	1.859	1.833	1.808	1.783	1.736	1.690
3	2.884	2.829	2.775	2.723	2.673	2.624	2.577	2.487	2.402
4	3.808	3.717	3.630	3.546	3.465	3.387	3.312	3.170	3.037
5	4.714	4.580	4.452	4.329	4.212	4.100	3.993	3.791	3.605
6	5.601	5.417	5.242	5.076	4.917	4.767	4.623	4.355	4.111
7	6.472	6.230	6.002	5.786	5.582	5.389	5.206	4.868	4.564
8	7.326	7.020	6.733	6.463	6.210	5.971	5.747	5.335	4.968
9	8.162	7.786	7.435	7.108	6.802	6.515	6.247	5.759	5.328
10	8.983	8.530	8.111	7.722	7.360	7.024	6.710	6.145	5.650
11	9.787	9.253	8.760	8.306	7.887	7.499	7.139	6.495	5.938
12	10.575	9.954	9.385	8.863	8.384	7.943	7.536	6.814	6.194
13	11.348	10.635	9.986	9.394	8.853	8.358	7.904	7.103	6.424
14	12.106	11.296	10.563	9.899	9.295	8.745	8.244	7.367	6.628
15	12.849	11.938	11.118	10.380	9.712	9.108	8.559	7.606	6.811
16	13.578	12.561	11.652	10.838	10.106	9.447	8.851	7.824	6.974
17	14.292	13.166	12.166	11.274	10.477	9.763	9.122	8.022	7.120
18	14.992	13.754	12.659	11.690	10.828	10.059	9.372	8.201	7.250
19	15.679	14.324	13.134	12.085	11.158	10.336	9.604	8.365	7.366
20	16.351	14.878	13.590	12.462	11.470	10.594	9.818	8.514	7.469

Using a financial calculator:*

FV = −1,000,000

PMT = −25,000

I = 3

N = 10

CPT PV = 957,348 .99

* Financial calculator keys and results may differ from those shown. Financial calculator results will also differ from those obtained with tables because of the rounding in present value and future value tables.

Present Value of Bonds Payable

The present value of a bond—its market price—is the present value of the future principal amount at maturity plus the present value of the future contract interest payments. The principal is a single amount to be paid at maturity. The interest is an annuity because it occurs periodically.

Let's compute the present value of 5 percent, five-year bonds of UVW Corporation. The face value of the bonds is $1,000,000, and they pay 2.5 percent contract (cash) interest semi-annually. At issuance the market interest rate is 6 percent, but it is computed at 3 percent semi-annually. Therefore, the effective-interest rate for each of the 10 semi-annual periods is 3 percent. We use 3 percent in computing the present value of the maturity and of the interest. The market price of these bonds is $957,250, as follows:

	A	B	C	D
1		Effective annual interest rate ÷ 2	Number of semi-annual interest payments	
2	PV of principal			
3	$1,000,000 × **PV of single amount** at ($1,000,000 × 0.744—Exhibit 15A–6)	3%	for 10 periods	$744,000
4	PV of interest			
5	($1,000,000 × 0.025) × **PV of annuity** at ($25,000 × 8.530—Exhibit 15A–7)	3%	for 10 periods	213,250
6	PV (market price) of bonds			$957,250

The market price of the UVW Corporation bonds shows a discount because the contract interest rate on the bonds (5 percent) is less than the market interest rate (6 percent). We discuss these bonds in more detail on page 822.

Let's consider a premium price for the UVW Corporation bonds. Assume that UVW Corporation issues $1,000,000 of 5 percent bonds when the market interest rate is 4 percent at issuance. The effective-interest rate is 2 percent for each of the 10 semi-annual periods.

	A	B	C	D
1		Effective annual interest rate ÷ 2	Number of semi-annual interest payments	
2	PV of principal:			
3	$1,000,000 × **PV of single amount** at ($1,000,000 × 0.820—Exhibit 15A–6)	2%	for 10 periods	$ 820,000
4	PV of interest:			
5	($1,000,000 × 0.025) × **PV of annuity** at ($25,000 × 8.983—Exhibit 15A–7)	2%	for 10 periods	224,575
6	PV (market price) of bonds			$1,044,575

We discuss accounting for bonds on page 825.

Many calculators, websites, and spreadsheet software packages can quickly and accurately perform present value calculations for bonds and leases.

APPENDIX PROBLEMS

(A1)
Computing the future value of an investment

2. At 6%, $56,370

P15A–1

For each situation, compute the required amount using the tables in this appendix.

1. Summit Enterprises Ltd. is budgeting for the acquisition of land over the next several years. The company can invest $800,000 at 9 percent. How much cash will Summit Enterprises Ltd. have for land acquisitions at the end of five years? At the end of six years?

2. Alton Associates Inc. is planning to invest $10,000 each year for five years. The company's investment advisor believes that Alton Associates Inc. can earn 6 percent interest without taking on too much risk. What will be the value of Alton's investment on the date of the last deposit if Alton can earn 6 percent? If Alton can earn 8 percent?

P15A–2

For each situation, compute the required amount using the tables in this appendix.

Relating the future and present values of an investment

1. $16,080,000

Required

1. XS Technologies Inc.'s operations are generating excess cash that will be invested in a special fund. During 2020, XS Technologies invests $12,000,000 in the fund for a planned advertising campaign for a new product to be released six years later, in 2026. If XS Technologies's investments can earn 5 percent each year, how much cash will the company have for the advertising campaign in 2026?

2. XS Technologies Inc. will need $20 million to advertise a new product in 2026. How much must XS Technologies invest in 2020 to have the cash available for the advertising campaign? XS Technologies's investments can earn 5 percent annually.

3. Explain the relationship between your answers to (1) and (2).

P15A–3

Determine the present value of the following notes and bonds using the tables in this appendix (notes are accounted for in the same way as bonds):

Computing the present values of various notes and bonds

3. $254,280
4. $200,040

Required

1. $100,000, five-year note payable with a contract interest rate of 9 percent, paid annually. The market interest rate at issuance is 10 percent.

2. Ten-year bonds payable with a maturity value of $200,000 and a contract interest rate of 12 percent, paid semi-annually. The market rate of interest is 10 percent at issuance.

3. Same bonds payable as in Requirement 2, but the market interest rate is 8 percent.

4. Same bonds payable as in Requirement 2, but the market interest rate is 12 percent.

P15A–4

On December 31, 2020, when the market interest rate is 8 percent, Churchill Land Corporation issues $600,000 of 10-year, 7.25 percent bonds payable. The bonds pay interest semi-annually.

Computing a bond's present value; recording its issuance at a discount and interest payments

1. $569,183

Required

1. Determine the present value of the bonds at issuance using the tables in this appendix.

2. Assume that the bonds are issued at the price computed in Requirement 1. Prepare an effective-interest method amortization table for the first two semi-annual interest periods.

3. Using the amortization table prepared in Requirement 2, journalize the issuance of the bonds and the first two interest payments.

P15A–5

Ontario Children's Choir needs a fleet of vans to transport the children to singing engagements throughout Ontario. Ford offers the vehicles for a single payment of $120,000 due at the end of four years. Toyota prices a similar fleet of vans for four annual payments of $28,000 each. Ontario Children's Choir could borrow the funds at 6 percent, so this is the appropriate interest rate. Which company should get the business, Ford or Toyota? Base your decision on present value and give your reason.

Deciding between two payment plans

IFRS MINI-CASE

The IFRS Mini-Case is now available online at **MyLab Accounting** in Chapter Resources.

Try It! Solutions for Chapter 15

1. a. Kind Animations Inc.
   b. $100,000.00
   c. Dec. 31, 2022
   d. John Doe
   e. 9% per year; the frequency of interest payments is not shown in Exhibit 15–1, but interest is typically paid twice a year (4.5% every 6 months).

2. a. At a discount
   b. At a premium
   c. At par

3.

Apr. 1	Cash	990,000	
	Discount on Bonds Payable	10,000	
	Bonds Payable		1,000,000
	To issue 3.75%, 10-year bonds at a discount. Cash received was $990,000 ($1,000,000 × 0.99).		

4.

May 6	Cash	1,015,000	
	Bonds Payable		1,000,000
	Premium on Bonds Payable		15,000
	To issue 3.75%, 10-year bonds at a premium. Cash received was $1,015,000 ($1,000,000 × 101.50).		

5. a. Compare the bond issue date (May 1, 2020) to the bonds' interest payment dates (April 30 and October 31). If time has passed between the interest payment date and the issue date, then include interest for this time in the amount paid for the bonds. In this case, no time has passed from April 30 to May 1, so no interest needs to be calculated. Also, determine whether there is a premium or a discount. Since bonds were issued at 94.00, which is less than 100.00, there is a discount.

2020			
May 1	Cash	9,400,000	
	Discount on Bonds Payable	600,000	
	Bonds Payable		10,000,000
	Issued 6 percent, 10-year bonds at a discount ($10,000,000 × 0.94).		

   b. Since the six-month period of May 1 to October 31, 2020, occurs before year-end, no accruals or partial amortization are necessary on October 31.

Oct. 31	Interest Expense	330,000	
	Cash		300,000
	Discount on Bonds Payable		30,000
	Paid semi-annual interest ($10,000,000 × 0.06 × $6/12$) and amortized discount ($600,000 ÷ 20).		

   c. Calculate the time period from the last interest payment (October 31, 2020) to the year-end (December 31, 2020). Accrue interest and amortize the premium or discount for this time period (2 months).

Dec. 31	Interest Expense	110,000	
	Discount on Bonds Payable		10,000
	Interest Payable		100,000
	Accrued interest ($10,000,000 × 0.06 × $2/12$) and amortized bond discount for two of the six months ($600,000 ÷ 20 × $2/6$).		

   d. Make sure all amortization of the bond discount is reflected in Discount on Bonds Payable, including the accrual calculated in part (c). Then subtract the discount from Bonds Payable to show the net liability for bonds payable.

Long-term liabilities		
Bonds payable, 6%, due 2030	$10,000,000	
Discount on bonds payable*	560,000	$9,440,000

   * ($600,000 − $30,000 − $10,000)

   e. The cash payment of interest is always the same: Bonds payable × Stated rate × Time. Reverse the year-end accrual (Interest Payable amount), then calculate interest and amortization of the discount or premium for the period January 1 to April 30, 2021.

2021			
Apr. 30	Interest Expense	220,000	
	Interest Payable	100,000	
	Cash		300,000
	Discount on Bonds Payable		20,000
	Paid semi-annual interest ($10,000,000 × 0.06 × $6/12$), part of which was accrued ($100,000), and amortized four of the six months discount ($600,000 ÷ 20 × $4/6$).		

Here are some suggestions for checking your solutions. While you don't have to follow these procedures for every problem, you can use them to check your solutions for reasonableness as well as accuracy.

On April 30, 2021, the bonds have been outstanding for one year. After the entries have been recorded, the account balances should show the results of one year's cash interest payments and one year's bond discount amortization.

Fact 1 Cash interest payments should be $600,000 ($10,000,000 × 0.06).

Accuracy check Two credits to Cash of $300,000 each = $600,000. Cash payments are correct.

Fact 2 Discount amortization should be $60,000 ($600,000 ÷ 20 semi-annual periods × 2 semi-annual periods in 1 year).

Accuracy check Three debits to Discount on Bonds Payable ($30,000 + $10,000 + $20,000 = $60,000). Discount amortization is correct.

Fact 3 Also, we can check the accuracy of interest expense recorded during the year ended December 31, 2020.

The bonds in this problem will be outstanding for a total of 10 years, or 120 (that is, 10 × 12) months. During 2020, the bonds are outstanding for 8 months (May through December).

Interest expense for 8 months *equals* payment of cash interest for 8 months plus discount amortization for 8 months.

Interest expense should therefore be ($10,000,000 × 0.06 × 8/12 = $400,000) plus [($600,000/120) × 8 = $40,000] or ($400,000 + $40,000 = $440,000).

Accuracy check: Two debits to Interest Expense ($330,000 + $110,000) = $440,000. Interest expense for 2020 is correct.

6.

2021			
Dec. 31	Interest Expense	6,882	
	Premium on Bonds Payable	1,451	
	Interest Payable		8,333
	To accrue two months' interest expense ($20,647 × 2/6), amortize premium on bonds payable for two months ($4,353 × 2/6), and record interest payable ($25,000 × 2/6).		

2022			
Apr. 30	Interest Expense	13,765	
	Interest Payable	8,333	
	Premium on Bonds Payable	2,902	
	Cash		25,000
	To pay semi-annual interest ($20,647 × 4/6), some of which was accrued, and amortize premium on bonds payable for four months ($4,353 × 4/6).		

7. a. The periodic amount of interest expense *increases* because the carrying amount of the bond *increases* toward maturity value. To see this, refer to columns B and E of Exhibit 15–5. The upward-sloping line in Exhibit 15–6, Panel A, illustrates the increasing amount of interest expense.

b. The periodic amount of interest expense *decreases* because the carrying amount of the bond *decreases* toward maturity value. To see this, study columns B and E of Exhibit 15–7. The downward-sloping line in Exhibit 15–8, Panel A, illustrates the decreasing amount of interest expense.

8. Calculation of the gain or loss on retirement:

Face value of bonds being retired ($5,000,000 × 1/2)	$2,500,000
Unamortized premium ($30,000 × 1/2)	15,000
Book value, or carrying value	2,515,000
Market price paid to retire the bonds ($2,500,000 × 1.0050)	2,512,500
Gain on retirement of bonds	$ 2,500

The journal entry to record the retirement:

Jun. 30	Bonds Payable	2,500,000	
	Premium on Bonds Payable	15,000	
	Cash		2,512,500
	Gain on retirement of bonds		2,500
	To retire bonds payable before maturity.		

9.

Sep. 1	Bonds Payable	2,500,000	
	Premium on Bonds Payable	15,000	
	Common Shares		2,515,000
	To record conversion of $2,515,000 of bonds outstanding into 1,000,000 common shares.		

10. While trading on the equity can improve EPS, it might be to the corporation's *disadvantage* to finance with debt. This is because the corporation would suffer (1) if the interest rate on its debt is greater than the rate of earnings from that money and (2) if the company borrows so much that it cannot meet interest and principal payments.

11.

2020			
Dec. 1	Interest Expense	828	
	Mortgage Payable	1,293	
	Cash		2,121
	To pay monthly mortgage loan and record interest portion.		

12.

a.

2020			
Jan. 2	Equipment	138,143	
	Cash		30,000
	Capital Lease Liability		108,143
	To lease equipment and make the first annual lease payment on a capital lease. (Equipment = $30,000 + $108,143 = $138,143).		

(If using a financial calculator: Remember to set payment to "bgn".

PMT = $30,000, **N** = 6,

I = 12 **FV** = 0,

CPT **PV** = $−138,143.29).

b. | Dec. 31 | Amortization Expense | 23,024 | |
| | | Accumulated Amortization—Leased Equipment | | 23,024 |
| | | To record amortization on leased equipment ($138,143 ÷ 6) | | |

c. | Dec. 31 | Interest Expense | 12,977 | |
| | | Capital Lease Liability | | 12,977 |
| | | To accrue interest expense on the capital lease liability ($108,143 × 0.12). | | |

d. | 2021 | | | |
Jan. 2	Capital Lease Liability	30,000	
	Cash		30,000
	To make second annual lease payment on equipment.		

16 Investments and International Operations

CONNECTING CHAPTER 16

LEARNING OBJECTIVES

1 **Account for short-term investments**

How do we account for short-term investments?

Share Investments, page 888
- Share Prices
- Investors and Investees
- Classifying Investments

Accounting for Short-Term Investments, page 890
- Share (Equity) Investments
- Reporting Short-Term Equity Investments
- Reporting Short-Term Bond (Debt) Investments

2 **Account for long-term share investments**

How do we account for long-term share investments when we own few shares?

Long-Term Equity Investments without Significant Influence, page 894

3 **Use the equity method to account for investments**

What is the equity method, and how do we use it?

Long-Term Share Investments with Significant Influence, page 896

4 **Describe and create consolidated financial statements**

How do we perform a simple consolidation?

Long-Term Share Investments Accounted for by the Consolidation Method, page 898

Consolidated Financial Statements, page 899
- Consolidated Balance Sheet—Parent Owns All Subsidiary's Shares

- Parent Buys Subsidiary's Shares and Pays for Goodwill
- Consolidated Balance Sheet—Parent Owns Less than 100 Percent of Subsidiary's Shares
- Income of a Consolidated Entity
- Summary of Long-Term Equity Investments

5 **Account for investments in bonds**

How do we record investments in bonds?

Investments in Bonds, page 906
- Short-Term Investments in Bonds
- Long-Term Investments in Bonds

6 **Account for foreign-currency transactions**

How do we record transactions in foreign currencies?

Foreign-Currency Transactions, page 910
- Foreign Currencies and Foreign-Currency Exchange Rates
- Foreign-Currency Transactions
- Payables in a Foreign Currency
- Receivables in a Foreign Currency
- Minimizing Risk

7 **Identify the impact of IFRS on accounting for investments and international transactions**

How does IFRS apply to investments and international transactions?

The Impact of IFRS on Accounting for Investments and International Transactions, page 915

The **Summary** for Chapter 16 appears on pages 918–919.

Key Terms with definitions for this chapter's material appears on pages 919–920.

CPA competencies

This text covers material outlined in **Section 1: Financial Reporting of the CPA Competency Map**. The Learning Objectives for each chapter have been aligned with the CPA Competency Map to ensure the best coverage possible.

1.1.2 Evaluates the appropriateness of the basis of financial reporting

1.2.2 Evaluates treatment for routine transactions

1.2.3 Evaluates treatment for non-routine transactions

Bloomberg/Getty Images

S hopify Inc. is an Ottawa company that has been listed on the Toronto Stock Exchange under the symbol SHOP since its initial public offering (IPO) in May 2015. Shopify provides entrepreneurs with an online storefront and all the tools to manage their business—from social media and design to inventory and order management, payment, and shipping—as well as all the reporting and data functions needed to operate. There are over half a million small and medium-sized businesses who conduct their businesses through Shopify.

As an investment, shareholders in Shopify had a great year in 2018. It was the third top performer on the Toronto Stock Exchange. Shopify's share price increased by over 500 percent from its IPO in 2015 until late in 2018.

Just like individuals invest in businesses to earn a return on their investment, a corporation can invest in other businesses. Shopify owns nine other corporations (subsidiaries), in four countries, whose results are combined into the corporation's *consolidated* financial statements. Most of these investments are held as part of a long-term strategy for the company rather than for short-term financial gain. The reporting for these investments is different depending on why they are held and how long management intends to own them. The first part of this chapter will explore investments in other companies.

Operating an international business is complex. Running operations and providing services in multiple countries means transacting in different currencies. These transactions add another set of operational challenges to the business model. Shopify's income statement for the year ended December 31, 2017, showed a $1,312,000 US foreign exchange gain. In 2015, there was a $1,234,000 US loss. This chapter will also address how foreign-currency transactions are recorded.

Throughout this course, you have become increasingly familiar with the financial statements of companies such as Shopify Inc., Dollarama Inc., and TELUS Corporation. This chapter continues to examine the real world of accounting by discussing investments and international operations.

Share Investments

Share Prices

LO ①

How do we account for short-term investments?

Investors can purchase shares directly from the issuing company or from other investors who wish to sell their shares. Investors buy more shares in transactions with other investors than in purchases directly from the issuing company. Each share is issued only once, but it may be traded among investors multiple times thereafter. People and businesses buy shares from and sell shares to each other in markets, such as the Toronto Stock Exchange (TSX) and the TSX Venture Exchange. Recall that share ownership is transferable. Investors trade (buy and sell) millions of shares each day. Brokers like RBC Dominion Securities and CIBC Investor Services Inc. handle share transactions for a commission. Individuals may also choose to do the trading themselves using discount trading/brokerage accounts to reduce transaction costs. Exhibit 16–1 presents information for the common shares of several Canadian companies listed on the TSX.

EXHIBIT 16–1 | Share Price Information for Three Canadian Companies

| 52 Weeks | | Trading | | Daily | Daily | Cls or | | P/E |
High	Low	Symbol	Stock	High	Low	Latest	Volume	Ratio
56.67	30.70	DOL	Dollarama Inc	32.01	31.18	31.67	927.36K	19.4
49.15	43.88	T	TELUS Corporation	45.43	45.04	45.20	872.10K	18.0
232.65	126.06	SHOP	Shopify Inc.	185.45	176.58	182.02	351.14K	n/a

Source: Data from Toronto Stock Exchange: tmxmoney.com, retrieved January 1, 2018.

Companies listed on stock exchanges have their name and type of shares shown in short form on many reports. WestJet Airlines Ltd.'s shares are shown under WJA or WJA.A depending on the class of shares.

A broker (or website) may "quote a share price," which refers to the current market price per share. Exhibit 16–1 shows Shopify Inc. common shares traded at $182.02 on December 29, 2018. At some point during the previous 52 weeks, Shopify common shares reached a high of $232.65 and, at some other point, a low of $126.06 per share. The TSX website continually updates this information while the stock market is open and then provides a summary at the end of each trading day. From this information, we also learn that over 351,000 shares of Shopify stock were traded that day. The P/E ratio (ratio of the share price to earnings per share) is not applicable because the business does not currently have positive earnings.

Investors and Investees

A person or a company that owns shares in a corporation is an *investor*. The corporation that issued the shares is the *investee*. If you own common shares of Shopify, you are an investor and Shopify is the investee.

Why do individuals and corporations invest in shares? You would probably make an investment to earn dividend revenue and to sell the shares at a higher price than you paid for them. Corporations and investment companies such as pension funds, mutual funds, insurance companies, bank trust departments, and other investment-related corporations buy shares for this same reason.

Many companies invest in shares for a second reason: to influence or to control another company that is in a related line of business. Kinross Gold Corporation holds 100 percent of the shares of a Canadian company called Underworld Resources Inc., which means Kinross can exert complete control over the affairs of that company. It owns 25 percent, or one-fourth, of Compañía Minera Casale (Chile). While Kinross doesn't own all the shares of the Chilean company, it owns "enough" to influence the decisions of its management and, therefore, it reports in the notes to the financial statements that it has influence over the affairs of that company.

The term **significant influence** is used when a company participates in the decision making of another company without having full control over it. Somewhere in the range of 20 to 50 percent of the ownership of the company is usually sufficient for this to be the case. An investor holding more than 50 percent of the outstanding common shares has controlling interest in the investee. Determining the amount of influence requires the use of professional judgment. This is necessary because different accounting methods apply to different types of investments.

Classifying Investments

Investments are assets to the investor. Equity investments are reported on the balance sheet as current or long-term based on the length of time management *intends* to own them. Investments in the shares of other businesses are called equity investments because some share of the ownership is purchased.

Exhibit 16–2 provides an example of the presentation of the investment accounts on the balance sheet.

> Management *intent* is the key determinant about whether an investment is categorized as long-term or short-term.

EXHIBIT 16–2 | Reporting Investments on the Balance Sheet

Current assets		
Cash	$x	
Short-term investments	x	
Accounts receivable	x	
Inventories	x	
Prepaid expenses	x	
Total current assets		$x
Long-term investments (or simply **Investments**)—**Note X**		x
Property, plant, and equipment		x

Note X—Long-Term Investments
Details of the long-term investments in shares where there is no significant influence, long-term investments in shares where there is significant influence, and long-term investments in bonds would be given in this note.

> We report assets in order of their liquidity, starting with cash. Short-term investments are shown as current assets, while long-term investments and investments subject to significant influence are reported as long-term assets. Notice that these long-term investments are reported before property, plant, and equipment, and that there is no subtitle for long-term assets like there is for current assets.

> "Long-term" is not often used in the account title. It is assumed that unless it is specifically labelled as short-term, it is long-term.

Short-Term Investments

- **Short-term investments** may also be described as *marketable securities* or *temporary investments*.

- They may include **treasury bills, certificates of deposit**, and **money market funds**, as well as shares and bonds of other companies.

- Short-term investments are **actively traded**, with the primary objective being to make a profit from changes in short-term market values.
- They must be liquid (readily convertible to cash).

Long-Term Investments

- An investment in the equity of a company that is *not* a short-term investment is categorized as a *long-term investment.*

Long-term investments are those investments the investor intends to convert to cash in more than one year.

Investments in debt instruments of other companies, such as notes and bonds, can be either short-term or long-term investments. These will be discussed separately in this chapter.

Investments vary in how they are reported, depending on the purpose of the investment and thus the percentage of voting interest acquired. Each of the types and their related accounting method is introduced on the following pages and summarized in Exhibit 16–3.

EXHIBIT 16–3 | Types of Equity Investments and Primary* Accounting Methods under ASPE

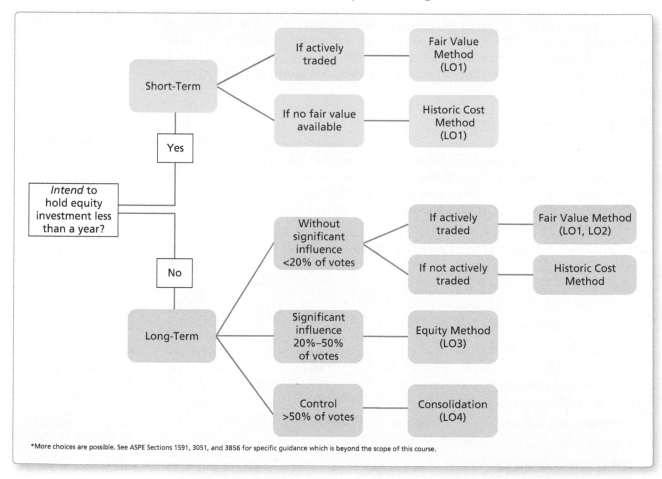

*More choices are possible. See ASPE Sections 1591, 3051, and 3856 for specific guidance which is beyond the scope of this course.

Accounting for Short-Term Investments

The **fair value method**, or **market value method**, is used to account for short-term investments in shares. If there is an available market price for the investment, the historic cost is used only as the initial amount for recording investments and as the basis for measuring gains and losses on their sale. These investments are reported on the balance sheet at their fair values. (If there is not an available market price for the investment, it is recorded and reported on the balance sheet at historic cost.)

Share (Equity) Investments

Let's work through an example to show how share transactions are recorded and the share information is reported on the financial statements.

Investment All investments are recorded initially at cost. Cost is the price paid for the shares. Section 3856 of Part II of the *CPA Canada Handbook* states that brokerage commissions and other transaction costs are expensed.

Unless otherwise stated, we assume all short-term investments in this chapter have an available market price.

Suppose that Elk Valley Ltd. purchases 1,000 common shares of the 687,000 outstanding shares from Finning International Inc. at the market price of $16.00 per share and pays a $500 commission. Elk Valley Ltd. intends to sell this investment within one year or less and, therefore, classifies it as a short-term investment. Elk Valley Ltd.'s entry to record the investment is as follows:

Aug. 22	Short-Term Investments	16,000	
	Brokerage Commissions Expense	500	
	Cash		16,500
	Purchased 1,000 common shares of Finning International Inc. at $16.00 per share plus commission of $500.		

Carrying Value: 1,000 × $16.00 = $16,000

Cash Dividend Assume Elk Valley Ltd. receives a $0.25 per share cash dividend on the Finning shares. Elk Valley Ltd.'s entry to record receipt of the dividends is:

Oct. 14	Cash	250	
	Dividend Revenue		250
	Received $0.25 per share cash dividend (1,000 × $0.25) on Finning International Inc. common shares.		

Dividends do not accrue with the passage of time (as interest does). An investor makes no accrual entry for dividend revenue at year-end in anticipation of a dividend declaration. However, if a dividend declaration does occur before year-end, say, on December 28, the investor *may* debit Dividend Receivable and credit Dividend Revenue on that date. The investor would then report this receivable and the revenue in the December 31 financial statements. Receipt of the cash dividend in January would be recorded by a debit to Cash and a credit to Dividend Receivable. The more common practice, however, is to record the dividend as income when it is received.

Stock Dividend Receipt of a stock dividend does not require a formal journal entry. As we have seen, a stock dividend increases the number of shares held by the investor but does not affect the total cost of the investment. The *cost per share* of the share investment therefore decreases. The investor usually makes a memorandum entry of the number of stock dividend shares received and the new cost per share.

Assume that Elk Valley Ltd. receives a 10 percent stock dividend on its 1,000 share investment in Finning International Inc. that cost $16,000. Elk Valley Ltd. would make a memorandum entry like this:

Receipts of stock dividends and stock splits are recorded in a memorandum entry. However, for income tax purposes a stock dividend is considered income received by the investor, and tax must be paid on this deemed income.

| Nov. 22 | Received 100 Finning International Inc. common shares in a 10 percent stock dividend. New cost per share is $14.55 ($16,000 ÷ 1,100 shares). |

Gain or Loss on Sale Prior to Adjustments to Fair Value

Any gain or loss on the sale of the investment is the difference between the sale proceeds and the **carrying value** of the investment.

Assume that Elk Valley Ltd. sells 400 shares of Finning International Inc. for $20.00 per share, less a $300 brokerage commission. The entry to record the sale is:

$$(400 \times \$20) - \$300$$

Dec. 18	Cash	7,700	
	Brokerage Commissions Expense	300	
	Short-Term Investments		5,820
	Gain on Sale of Investment		2,180
	Sold 400 common shares of Finning International Inc.		

Number of shares sold times new cost from Nov. 22: 400 × $14.55

The carrying value per share of the investment ($14.55) is based on the total number of shares held, including those received as a stock dividend.

Reporting Short-Term Equity Investments

ASPE requires that equity investments where there is no significant influence be reported at their fair value, or current market value, at year-end. There is no significant influence in this case because Elk Valley owns only a small percentage of the total outstanding shares of Finning International Inc. (Elk Valley owns only 700 of Finning's total of 755,700 common shares after the stock dividend, which is less than $\frac{1}{10}$ of 1 percent of Finning's shares.) Any gain or loss is recorded as an unrealized gain or loss in the non-operating section of the company's income statement under "Other gains and losses."

Unrealized Gain on Fair Value Adjustment In our previous example, Elk Valley Ltd. had purchased 1,000 shares of Finning International Inc. for $16.00 per share. Ignoring the stock dividend and the December 18 sale, assume that the fair value of the shares at the December 31 year-end had increased to $18.00 per share. Elk Valley Ltd. must adjust the value of the short-term investment to $18,000 (1,000 shares × $18.00) from its carrying value of $16,000, which is an increase of $2,000.

To record this adjustment, a Fair Value Valuation Allowance account is created, which is a **companion account** to the Short-Term Investments or Long-Term Investments account:

> Fair Value Valuation Allowance is a companion account to the main Investments account. We have seen companion accounts before. The Allowance for Doubtful Accounts is a companion account to Accounts Receivable. The companion account may or not be a contra account.

Dec. 31	Fair Value Valuation Allowance	2,000	
	Unrealized Gain on Fair Value Adjustment		2,000
	Adjusted Finning International Inc. investment to fair value.		

Unrealized means that the gain or loss resulted from a change in fair value, not from a sale of the investment. A gain or loss on the sale of an investment is said to be *realized* when the company receives cash.

Elk Valley Ltd.'s balance sheet would report short-term investments, and its income statement would report the increase in the short-term investment as follows:

> The amount presented here includes $16,000 for the Short-Term Investments account balance plus $2,000 for the companion Fair Value Valuation Allowance account balance.

Balance Sheet (partial)	
Current Assets	
Cash	$ xxx
Short-term investments, at fair value	18,000
Accounts receivable,	
net of allowance of $x	xxx

Income Statement (partial)	
Other gains and losses	
Unrealized gain on short-term investments	$2,000
Income before income taxes	xxx
Income tax expense	x
Net income (or net loss)	$ xx

Unrealized Loss on Fair Value Adjustment *Now assume instead* that the Finning International Inc. shares decreased, in value, and at the December 31 year-end Elk Valley Ltd.'s investment in the Finning shares is worth $13,000 ($3,000 less than the carrying value of $16,000). The following journal entry is recorded to decrease the short-term investment's value by $3,000:

Dec. 31	Unrealized Loss on Fair Value Adjustment	3,000	
	Fair Value Valuation Allowance		3,000
	Adjusted Finning International Inc. investment to fair value.		

Elk Valley Ltd.'s balance sheet would report short-term investments, and its income statement would report the decrease in the short-term investments, as follows:

> The amount presented here includes $16,000 for the Short-Term Investments account balance less $3,000 for the companion Fair Value Valuation Allowance account balance.

Balance Sheet (partial)		
Current Assets		
Cash	$	xxx
Short-term investments, at fair value		13,000
Accounts receivable,		
net of allowance of $x		xxx

Income Statement (partial)	
Other gains and losses	
Unrealized loss on short-term investments	$3,000
Income before income taxes	xxx
Income tax expense	x
Net income (or net loss)	$ xx

Selling a Short-Term Equity Investment When a company sells an equity investment, the gain or loss on the sale is the difference between the sale proceeds and the last carrying amount.

We now continue the previous loss example. If Elk Valley Ltd. sells the Finning International Inc. shares after year-end for $12,000, Elk Valley Ltd. would record the sale and the $1,000 loss ($12,000 selling price − $13,000 carrying value) as follows:

Jan. 19	Cash	12,000	
	Loss on Sale of Short-Term Investments	1,000	
	Fair Value Valuation Allowance	3,000	
	Short-Term Investments		16,000
	Sold Finning International Inc. shares at a loss.		

These entries remove the fair value of the investment from the books.

Companies would normally account for each investment separately, which can be done quite easily with computerized record keeping.

Elk Valley Ltd.'s income statement would report the *realized* loss on the sale of the short-term investment in the "Other gains and losses" section.

Unrealized gains/losses occur when investments are adjusted to fair value. Realized gains/losses occur when investments are sold.

Reporting Short-Term Bond (Debt) Investments

The fair value method is used to account for short-term investments in bonds. Like shares, short-term bond investments are valued at fair value, or market value. Premiums or discounts are not amortized as the intent is to hold the bonds for only a short period.

Try It!

1. Calculate the price per share immediately after each of the following actions. This is a short-term investment and the investor does not have a significant influence on the investee.
   a. 1,000 shares were purchased for $18,700 plus brokerage commission of $300.
   b. The shares were split 2 for 1 one month later.
   c. The shares' total market value at year-end was $16,000.
   d. All the shares were sold after year-end for $20,000 plus brokerage commission of $250.
2. Levon Ltd. completed the following investment transactions during 2019 and 2020. Journalize the transactions, providing explanations.

2019

Sep. 30   Purchased 1,200 of the 50,000 outstanding common shares of Betam Ltd. at a price of $36.00 per share, intending to sell the investment within the next year. Brokerage commissions were $125.

Dec. 21   Received a cash dividend of $0.09 per share on the Betam Ltd. shares.

　　31   At Levon Ltd.'s year-end, adjusted the investment to its fair value of $33.50 per share.

2020

Apr. 13   Sold the Betam Ltd. shares for $31.00 per share. Brokerage commissions were $120.

Solutions appear at the end of this chapter and on **MyLab Accounting**

Long-Term Equity Investments Without Significant Influence

LO ②

How do we account for long-term share investments when we own few shares?

Investments are always long-term unless specifically stated otherwise, so the term "long-term" does not need to be in the account title. It is shown in this text just for clarity.

An investor may make a long-term investment in the shares of another corporation where the purpose is similar to that of short-term investing—the investor will hold the investment to earn dividend revenue or make a profit from selling the investment at a higher price than its purchase price. In such a situation, the investor will generally hold less than 20 percent of the voting interest of the investee and would normally play no important role in the investee's operations. They would normally account for the investment using the *fair value method* (*market value method*), if the market value for the shares of the investee is readily available, and at cost if there is no market price available. *This is the same treatment as for short-term equity investments.*

Investment   Suppose Elm Corporation purchases 1,000 common shares of Molson Coors Brewing Company at the market price of $48.00 per share plus a brokerage commission of $1,000. Elm plans to hold these shares for longer than a year and classifies them as a long-term investment. Elm's entry to record the investment is:

Feb. 23	Long-Term Investments	48,000	
	Brokerage Commission Expense	1,000	
	Cash		49,000
	Purchased 1,000 common shares of Molson Coors Brewing Company at $48 per share.		

Cash Dividend   Assume that Elm receives a $1.00 per share cash dividend on the Molson Coors Brewing Company shares. Elm's entry for receipt of the dividend is:

Jul. 14	Cash	1,000	
	Dividend Revenue		1,000
	Received dividend on the Molson Coors Brewing Company shares (1,000 × $1.00).		

Reporting Long-Term Investments at Fair Value Reporting at fair value requires an adjustment to current market value on the balance sheet date. Assume that the fair value of Elm's investment in Molson Coors Brewing Company shares has increased to $50,000 on December 31, its year-end. In this case, Elm makes the following adjustment:

Dec. 31	Fair Value Valuation Allowance	2,000	
	Unrealized Gain on Fair Value Adjustment		2,000
	Adjusted long-term investment to $50,000 fair value ($50,000 − $48,000).		

The balance sheet would report the investment at the fair (market) value of $50,000.

Long-Term Investments	Fair Value Valuation Allowance
48,000	2,000

Investment carrying amount = Market value of $50,000

Here the Fair Value Valuation Allowance account has a debit balance because the investment has increased in value. If the investment's value declines, the allowance is credited. In that case, the investment carrying amount is cost *minus* the allowance. Fair Value Valuation Allowance with a credit balance becomes a contra account.

The other side of the December 31 adjusting journal entry credits Unrealized Gain on Fair Value Adjustment. If the investment declines, the company debits Unrealized Loss on Fair Value Adjustment.

Selling a Long-Term Investment Where There Is No Significant Influence The sale of a long-term investment where there is no significant influence usually results in a *realized* gain or loss. Suppose Elm Corporation sells its investment in the Molson Coors Brewing Company shares for $52,000 during the next year, with brokerage commissions of $1,050. Elm would record the sale as follows:

Apr. 16	Cash	50,950		$52,000 − $1,050 = $50,950 cash received
	Brokerage Commissions Expense	1,050		
	Gain on Sale of Long-Term Investment		2,000	
	Long-Term Investments		48,000	These two accounts are closed since the asset is no longer owned.
	Fair Value Valuation Allowance		2,000	
	Sold Molson Coors Brewing Company shares at a gain.			

Elm Corporation would report the Gain on Sale of Long-Term Investment as an "Other gain or loss" in the non-operating section of the income statement.

Long-Term Share Investments with Significant Influence

LO ③

What is the equity method, and how do we use it?

An investor may make an investment in the investee by purchasing from 20 to 50 percent of the investee's voting shares. In this case, the investor will likely be able to exert a *significant influence* over the investee and how the investee operates the business. Such an investor can likely affect the investee's decisions on dividend policy, product lines, sources of supply, and other important matters. We often use the **equity method for investments** to account for investments in which the investor can significantly influence the decisions of the investee.

An investor who holds 20 percent of a company's shares can usually influence some decisions of the board of directors and gain influence in company decisions. With more than 50 percent ownership (majority ownership), the investor can usually control the affairs of the company.

The ability to influence matters more than the actual percentage of ownership. In certain circumstances, an investor with less than a 20 percent holding may still exert significant influence if there are many other shareholders who all own a small number of shares. In another case, a shareholder with a larger holding, such as a 30 percent holding, may exert no significant influence if another shareholder owns 51 percent of the shares and thus has control of the corporation.

Initial Investment   Investments accounted for by the equity method are recorded initially at cost. Suppose Saturna Corp. pays $4,000,000 for 30 percent of the common shares of Galiano Corporation on January 6, 2020. Brokerage commissions are $5,000. Saturna Corp.'s entry to record the purchase of this investment is as follows:

Jan. 6	Investment in Galiano Corporation Common Shares	4,000,000	
	Brokerage Commissions Expense	5,000	
	Cash		4,005,000
	To purchase a 30% investment in Galiano Corporation common shares.		

Share of Income/Loss   Under the equity method, Saturna Corp., as the investor, records its share of the investee's net income (loss) as revenue (or loss) from post-acquisition earnings. If Galiano Corporation reports net income of $1,000,000 for the year, Saturna Corp. records 30 percent of this amount as an increase in the investment account and as equity method investment revenue, as follows:

Dec. 31	Investment in Galiano Corporation Common Shares	300,000	
	Equity Method Investment Revenue		300,000
	To record 30% of Galiano Corporation net income, $300,000 ($1,000,000 × 0.30).		

Equity Method Investment Revenue is specifically identified separately from other revenue. It is put into its own account for the same reason that we distinguish Sales Revenue from Service Revenue —to get better management information from the financial statements.

The investor increases the Investment (asset) account and records Investment Revenue when the investee reports income because of the close relationship between the two companies. As the investee's shareholders' equity increases, so does the value of the investment on the books of the investor.

Equity Method Investment in Galiano Corp.

Original cost	Share of losses
Share of income	Share of dividends
Balance	

Share of Dividends   Saturna Corp. records its cash dividends received from Galiano Corporation. Assuming Galiano Corporation declares and pays a cash dividend of $600,000, Saturna Corp. receives 30 percent of this dividend, recording it as follows:

Dec. 31	Cash	180,000	
	Investment in Galiano Corporation Common Shares		180,000
	To record receipt of 30% of Galiano Corporation cash dividend, $180,000 ($600,000 × 0.30).		

Observe that the Investment account is credited for the receipt of a dividend on an equity method investment. Why? It is because the dividend decreases the investee's shareholders' equity, so it also reduces the investor's investment. In effect, the investor received cash for this portion of the investment.

After the above entries are posted, Saturna Corp.'s Investment account reflects its equity in the net assets of Galiano Corporation (also known as its *carrying value*):

Investment in Galiano Corporation Common Shares

2020					
Jan. 6	Purchase	4,000,000			
Dec. 31	Net income	300,000	Dec. 31	Dividends	180,000
Dec. 31	Balance	4,120,000			

Gain or Loss on the Sale of an Equity Method Investment   The gain or loss on sale is measured as the difference between the sale proceeds and the carrying value of the investment.

If next year Saturna Corp. sold $1/10$ of its' Galiano Corporation common shares for $400,000 with brokerage commission fees of $500, the transaction would be recorded as follows:

2021			
Feb. 13	Cash	399,500	
	Brokerage Commissions Expense	500	
	Loss on Sale of Investment	12,000	
	Investment in Galiano Corporation Common Shares		412,000
	Sold $1/10$ of investment in Galiano Corporation common shares at a loss of $12,000 [$400,000 − ($4,120,000 × $1/10$)]		

This account is reported in the non-operating section of the income statement.

Companies with investments accounted for by the equity method often refer to the investee as an **affiliated company**. The account titles Investments in Affiliated Companies or Investments Subject to Significant Influence also refer to investments that are accounted for by the equity method.

Write-downs   Sometimes a company must write-down an investment accounted for by the equity method because of what is expected to be a permanent decline in the value of the asset. These **write-downs** are rare. The 2017 annual report from Shaw Communications explained its other losses to include

A write-down means there was a credit (decrease) to the asset account and a debit to an expense account, which reduces profit on the income statement.

> a net $82 million provision in respect of the Company's investment in shomi which announced a wind down of operations during the first quarter. In the prior year, the category also includes a write-down of $54 in respect of the Company's investment in shomi, a write-down of $20 in respect of a private portfolio investment and asset write-downs of $16.[1]

Try It!

4. Investor Ltd. paid $140,000 to acquire 40 percent of the common shares of Investee Ltd. on January 1. The investment is subject to significant influence. At the end of the first year (on December 31), Investee Ltd.'s net income was $180,000, and Investee Ltd. declared and paid cash dividends of $140,000. Journalize Investor Ltd.'s (a) purchase of the investment, (b) share of Investee Ltd.'s net income, (c) receipt of dividends from Investee Ltd., and (d) sale of all the Investee Ltd. shares for $160,000.

Solutions appear at the end of this chapter and on **MyLab Accounting**

Long-Term Share Investments Accounted for by the Consolidation Method

LO (4)

How do we perform a simple consolidation?

A **controlling interest** (or **majority interest**) is normally the ownership of more than 50 percent of the investee's voting shares. Such an investment enables the investor to elect a majority of the investee's board of directors and so control the investee. In such a situation, the investor is called the **parent company** and the investee company is called the **subsidiary**. The financial statements of subsidiaries are normally *consolidated* with those of the parent. For example, Galen Weston and other shareholders own George Weston Limited. In turn, that company owns 46 percent of Loblaw Companies Limited and 100 percent of Weston Foods, as shown in Exhibit 16–4. It can be said that George Weston Limited has control over both Loblaw Companies Limited and Weston Foods.

Why have subsidiaries? Why not have the corporation take the form of a single legal entity? Subsidiaries may limit the parent's liabilities in a risky venture; may make mergers, acquisitions, and sales easier; and may ease expansion into foreign countries. For example, George Weston Limited sold off Neilson Dairy to Saputo Inc. for $465 million and purchased ACE Bakery for $110 million. These deals would have been much more complex if they were all part of one big company.

Consolidation accounting is a method of combining the financial statements of two or more companies that are controlled by the same owners. This method implements the entity concept by reporting a single set of financial statements for the consolidated entity, which carries the name of the parent company.

ASPE allows parent companies to account for their subsidiaries using the equity method or the cost method if the cost of providing **consolidated financial statements**

---

[1] 2017 Annual Report, Shaw Communications.

EXHIBIT 16–4 | **Partial Ownership Structure of George Weston Limited, 2016**

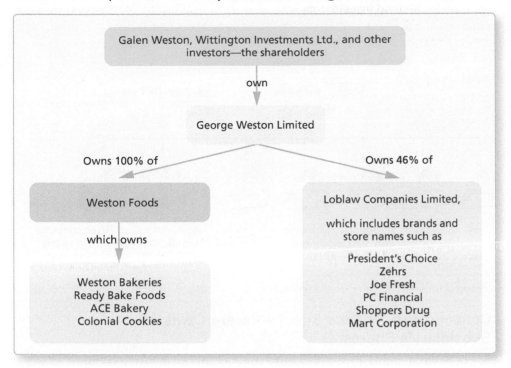

is greater than the benefits for users who are able to gain access to financial information directly from the parent company. However, the *CPA Canada Handbook* emphasizes consolidation for companies with controlling interest, so we focus on consolidation accounting in such situations. The next section in this chapter will focus on how to do this.

Consolidated Financial Statements

Many published financial reports include consolidated statements. To understand the statements you are likely to encounter, you need to know the basic concepts underlying consolidation accounting.

Consolidated statements combine the balance sheets, income statements, and other financial statements of the parent company with those of the subsidiaries into an overall set as if the parent and its subsidiaries were a single entity. The goal is to provide a better perspective on operations than could be obtained by examining the separate reports of each of the individual companies. The assets, liabilities, revenues, and expenses of each subsidiary are added to the parent's accounts. The consolidated financial statements present the combined account balances. For example, the balance in the Cash account of Loblaw Companies Limited is added to the balance in the George Weston Limited Cash account, and the sum of the two amounts is presented as a single amount in the consolidated balance sheet of George Weston Limited. Loblaw Companies Limited and the names of all other George Weston Limited subsidiaries do not appear in the statement titles. But the names of the subsidiary companies are listed in the notes that accompany the parent company's annual report.

Exhibit 16–5, on the next page, shows a corporate structure where the parent corporation owns controlling interests in five subsidiary companies and equity method investments in two other investee companies.

The *CPA Canada Handbook* provides guidance about how to record transactions and present financial information. It is not exclusively a book of rules. There are often alternatives from which companies need to choose based on what provides the best information to readers of financial statements at the most reasonable cost. In this case, there is an emphasis (or recommendation) to consolidate when there is controlling interest, but it is not the only choice.

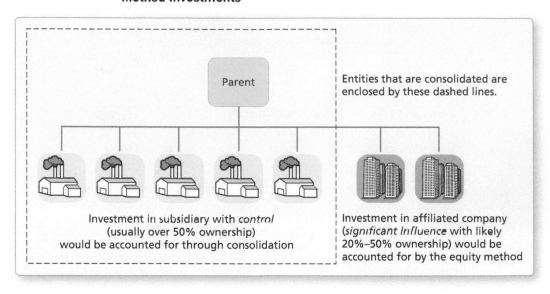

Consolidated Balance Sheet—Parent Owns All Subsidiary's Shares

Buying shares is not the only way to purchase a company. It is also possible to buy the assets, but this alternative is covered in advanced courses.

Suppose that Parent Corporation purchased all the outstanding common shares of Subsidiary Corporation at its book value of $1,200,000 on June 14. In addition, Parent Corporation loaned Subsidiary Corporation $640,000 on June 30. The $1,200,000 is paid to the *former* owners (the shareholders) of Subsidiary Corporation as private investors. The $1,200,000 *is not* an addition to the existing assets and shareholders' equity of Subsidiary Corporation. That is, the books of Subsidiary Corporation are completely unaffected by Parent Corporation's initial investment and Parent's subsequent accounting for that investment. Subsidiary Corporation is not dissolved. It lives on as a separate legal entity but with a new owner, Parent Corporation.

	Parent Corporation Books		
June 14	Investment in Subsidiary Corporation	1,200,000	
	Cash		1,200,000
June 30	Notes Receivable from Subsidiary Corp.	640,000	
	Cash		640,000

	Subsidiary Corporation Books		
June 14	No entry		
June 30	Cash	640,000	
	Notes Payable to Parent Corp.		640,000

Each legal entity has its individual set of books. The consolidated entity does not keep a separate set of books. Instead, a worksheet is used to prepare the consolidated statements. A major concern in consolidation accounting is this: *Do not double count—that is, do not include the same item twice.*

Each subsidiary company keeps its own set of books and pays its own taxes, just as the parent company does; however, for reporting purposes, the parent and subsidiary companies are treated as one economic unit when they are consolidated. Intercompany transactions must be eliminated.

Companies may prepare a consolidated balance sheet immediately after acquisition. The consolidated balance sheet shows all the assets and liabilities of the parent and the subsidiary. The Investment in Subsidiary account on the parent's books represents all the assets and liabilities of Subsidiary Corporation. The consolidated statements cannot show both the investment account and the amounts for the subsidiary's assets and liabilities. Doing so would count the same net resources twice. To avoid this double counting, we eliminate ❶ the $1,200,000 Investment in Subsidiary Corporation on the parent's books and the $1,200,000 shareholders' equity on the subsidiary's books ($800,000 Common Shares and $400,000 Retained Earnings), and ❷ the intercompany $640,000 note.

EXHIBIT 16–6 | Worksheet for Consolidated Balance Sheet—Parent Corporation Owns All Subsidiary Corporation's Shares

	Parent Corporation	Subsidiary Corporation	Eliminations Debit	Eliminations Credit	Consolidated Amounts
Assets					
Cash	96,000	144,000			240,000
Notes receivable from Subsidiary Corp.	640,000	—		❷ 640,000	—
Inventory	832,000	728,000			1,560,000
Investment in Subsidiary Corp.	1,200,000	—		❶1,200,000	—
Other assets	1,744,000	1,104,000			2,848,000
Total assets	4,512,000	1,976,000			4,648,000
Liabilities and Shareholders' Equity					
Accounts payable	344,000	136,000			480,000
Notes payable	1,520,000	640,000	❷ 640,000		1,520,000
Common shares	1,408,000	800,000	❶ 800,000		1,408,000
Retained earnings	1,240,000	400,000	❶ 400,000		1,240,000
Total liabilities and shareholders' equity	4,512,000	1,976,000	1,840,000	1,840,000	4,648,000

> Notice that in the consolidation worksheet there are no dollar signs. That is because this is an internal working document and not a formal financial statement, and because all amounts are stated in dollars.

Explanation of Elimination-Entry ❶ (Ownership) Exhibit 16–6 shows the *worksheet* for consolidating the balance sheet. (Notice that this is a much different sort of worksheet than what was shown in Chapter 4!) Consider the elimination entry for the parent–subsidiary ownership accounts, which are intercompany accounts. Entry ❶ credits the parent's Investment account to eliminate its debit balance. It also eliminates the subsidiary's shareholders' equity accounts by debiting Common Shares for $800,000 and Retained Earnings for $400,000. The resulting consolidated balance sheet reports no Investment in Subsidiary Corporation account, and the Common Shares and Retained Earnings are those of Parent Corporation only. The consolidated amounts are in the final column of the consolidation worksheet. Another way of stating this is to say that the subsidiary's equity is the parent company's investment balance—which represents the same resource. Therefore, including them both would amount to double counting.

Explanation of Elimination-Entry ❷ (Intercompany Transactions) Parent Corporation loaned $640,000 to Subsidiary Corporation. Therefore, Parent Corporation's balance sheet includes a $640,000 note receivable, and Subsidiary Corporation's balance sheet reports a note payable for this amount. This loan was entirely within the consolidated entity and so must be eliminated. Entry ❷ in Exhibit 16–6 accomplishes this. The $640,000 credit in the elimination column of the worksheet offsets Parent Corporation's debit balance in Notes Receivable from Subsidiary Corporation. After this worksheet entry, the consolidated amount for notes receivable is zero and the resulting consolidated amount for notes payable is the amount owed to those outside the consolidated entity.

Parent Buys Subsidiary's Shares and Pays for Goodwill

A company may acquire a controlling interest in a subsidiary by paying a price above the fair value of the subsidiary's net assets (assets minus liabilities), which we assume is equal to the book value of the subsidiary's shareholders' equity. This excess is called *goodwill*. Accounting for goodwill was introduced in Chapter 10 on page 572.

The subsidiary does not record goodwill; only the purchaser does. The goodwill is shown as a separate line of the worksheet in the process of consolidating the parent and subsidiary financial statements.

EXHIBIT 16–7 | Worksheet for Consolidated Balance Sheet—Par Corporation Owns All Sub Corporation's Shares and Paid for Goodwill

	Par Corporation	Sub Corporation	Eliminations Debit	Eliminations Credit	Consolidated Amounts
Assets					
Cash	880,000	100,000			980,000
Inventory	500,000	1,500,000			2,000,000
Investment in Sub Corp.	2,700,000	—		2,700,000	—
Goodwill	—	—	420,000		420,000
Other assets	816,000	785,000			1,601,000
Total assets	4,896,000	2,385,000			5,001,000
Liabilities and Shareholders' Equity					
Accounts payable	426,000	25,000			451,000
Notes payable	1,000,000	80,000			1,080,000
Common shares	1,280,000	1,200,000	1,200,000		1,280,000
Retained earnings	2,190,000	1,080,000	1,080,000		2,190,000
Total liabilities and shareholders' equity	4,896,000	2,385,000	2,700,000	2,700,000	5,001,000

Let's look at a new example in Exhibit 16–7. Suppose Par Corporation paid $2,700,000 to acquire 100 percent of the common shares of Sub Corporation, which had Common Shares of $1,200,000 and Retained Earnings of $1,080,000. Par's payment included $420,000 for goodwill ($2,700,000 − $1,200,000 − $1,080,000 = $420,000).[2]

Assume that Par Corporation recorded the purchase on December 31 as follows:

Dec. 31	Investment in Sub Corporation	2,700,000	
	Cash		2,700,000

The entry to eliminate Par Corporation's Investment account against Sub Corporation's equity accounts is:

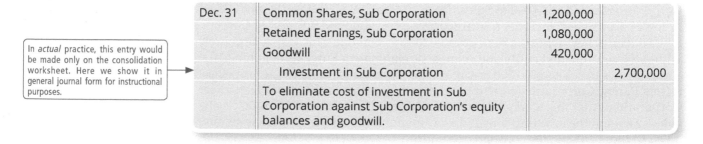

Dec. 31	Common Shares, Sub Corporation	1,200,000	
	Retained Earnings, Sub Corporation	1,080,000	
	Goodwill	420,000	
	Investment in Sub Corporation		2,700,000
	To eliminate cost of investment in Sub Corporation against Sub Corporation's equity balances and goodwill.		

In actual practice, this entry would be made only on the consolidation worksheet. Here we show it in general journal form for instructional purposes.

The asset Goodwill is reported as a separate line item on the consolidated balance sheet. For example, Shopify Inc.'s December 31, 2017, consolidated balance sheet includes goodwill of $21,317,000 as a separate line item in the non-current assets section of the balance sheet.

---

[2] For simplicity, we are assuming the fair market value of the subsidiary's net assets (Assets–Liabilities) equals the book value of the company's shareholders' equity. Advanced courses consider other situations.

Consolidated Balance Sheet—Parent Owns Less than 100 Percent of Subsidiary's Shares

When a parent company owns more than 50 percent (a majority) of the subsidiary's shares but less than 100 percent of them, a new category of balance sheet account, called *non-controlling interest,* must appear on the consolidated balance sheet. Suppose P Ltd. buys 75 percent of S Ltd.'s common shares. The non-controlling interest is the remaining 25 percent of S Ltd.'s equity. Thus, **non-controlling interest** (sometimes called **minority interest**) is the subsidiary's equity that is held by shareholders other than the parent company.

Assume P Ltd. buys 75 percent of S Ltd.'s common shares for $1,440,000 and there is no goodwill. Also, P Ltd. owes $600,000 on a note payable to S Ltd. P Ltd. would record this purchase on December 31 as follows:

| Dec. 31 | Investment in S. Ltd | 1,440,000 | |
| | Cash | | 1,440,000 |

Exhibit 16–8 is the consolidation worksheet for this example.

- Entry ❶ eliminates P Ltd.'s Investment balance of $1,440,000 against the $1,920,000 shareholders' equity of S Ltd. Observe that all of S Ltd.'s equity is eliminated even though P Ltd. holds only 75 percent of S Ltd.'s shares. The remaining 25 percent interest in S Ltd.'s equity is credited to Non-controlling Interest ($1,920,000 × 0.25 = $480,000). Thus, entry ❶ *reclassifies* 25 percent of S Ltd.'s equity as non-controlling interest.

- Entry ❷ eliminates S Ltd.'s $600,000 note receivable against P Ltd.'s note payable of the same amount. The consolidated amount of notes payable ($504,000) is the amount that S Ltd. owes to outsiders.

The balance sheet elimination entry requires, at most, these steps:
- *Eliminate intercompany receivables and payables.*
- *Eliminate the shareholders' equity accounts of the subsidiary against investment in subsidiary.*
- *Record goodwill.*
- *Record non-controlling interest.*

EXHIBIT 16–8 | Worksheet for Consolidated Balance Sheet: Parent (P Ltd.) Owns Less than 100 Percent of Subsidiary's (S Ltd.'s) Shares

	P Ltd.	S Ltd.	Eliminations Debit	Eliminations Credit	Consolidated Amounts
Assets					
Cash	396,000	216,000			612,000
Notes receivable from P Ltd.	—	600,000		❷ 600,000	—
Accounts receivable, net	648,000	468,000			1,116,000
Inventory	1,104,000	792,000			1,896,000
Investment in S Ltd.	1,440,000	—		❶ 1,440,000	—
Property, plant, and equipment, net	2,760,000	1,476,000			4,236,000
Total assets	6,348,000	3,552,000			7,860,000
Liabilities and Shareholders' Equity					
Accounts payable	1,692,000	1,128,000			2,820,000
Notes payable	600,000	504,000	❷ 600,000		504,000
Non-controlling interest	—	—		❶ 480,000	480,000
Common shares	2,040,000	1,200,000	❶ 1,200,000		2,040,000
Retained earnings	2,016,000	720,000	❶ 720,000		2,016,000
Total liabilities and shareholders' equity	6,348,000	3,552,000	2,520,000	2,520,000	7,860,000

The consolidated balance sheet of P Ltd., shown in Exhibit 16–9, is based on the worksheet of Exhibit 16–8.

EXHIBIT 16–9 | Consolidated Balance Sheet of P Ltd.

P LTD. Balance Sheet December 31, 2020		
Assets		
Current assets		
Cash	$ 612,000	
Accounts receivable, net	1,116,000	
Inventory	1,896,000	
Total current assets		$3,624,000
Property, plant, and equipment, net		4,236,000
Total assets		$7,860,000
Liabilities		
Current liabilities		
Accounts payable		$2,820,000
Long-term liabilities		
Notes payable		504,000
Total liabilities		3,324,000
Non-controlling interest		480,000
Shareholders' equity		
Common shares	$2,040,000	
Retained earnings	2,016,000	
Total shareholders' equity		4,056,000
Total liabilities and shareholders' equity		$7,860,000

> Even though the *CPA Canada Handbook* does not stipulate where to include non-controlling interest, common practice is to list it as a liability between liabilities and shareholders' equity, as shown here.

Income of a Consolidated Entity

The income of a consolidated entity is the net income of the parent plus the parent's proportion of the subsidiaries' net income. Suppose Mega-Parent Inc. owns all the shares of Subsidiary S-1 Inc. and 60 percent of the shares of Subsidiary S-2 Inc. During the year just ended, Mega-Parent Inc. earned net income of $1,980,000, Subsidiary S-1 Inc. earned $900,000, and Subsidiary S-2 Inc. had a net loss of $600,000. Mega-Parent Inc. would report net income of $2,520,000, computed as follows:

	A	B	C	D
1		**Net Income**	**Mega-Parent Inc.**	**Mega-Parent Inc.**
2		**(Net Loss)**	**Shareholders' Ownership**	**Net Income (Net Loss)**
3	Mega-Parent Inc.	$1,980,000	100%	$1,980,000
4	Subsidiary S-1 Inc.	900,000	100	900,000
5	Subsidiary S-2 Inc.	(600,000)	60	(360,000)
6	Consolidated net income			$2,520,000

The parent's net income is the same amount that would be recorded under the equity method. However, the equity method stops short of reporting the investee's assets and liabilities on the parent balance sheet because, with an investment in the range of 20 to 50 percent, the investor owns less than a controlling interest in the investee company.

The procedures for preparation of a consolidated income statement are similar to those outlined for the balance sheet, but it is discussed in an advanced accounting course.

Try It!

5. Parent Inc. paid $400,000 for all the common shares of Subsidiary Inc., and Parent Inc. owes Subsidiary Inc. $70,000 on a note payable. Assume the fair value of Subsidiary Inc.'s net assets is equal to book value. Complete the following consolidation worksheet:

	Parent Inc.	Subsidiary Inc.	Eliminations Debit	Eliminations Credit	Consolidated Amounts
Assets					
Cash	38,000	36,000			
Note receivable from Parent Inc.	—	70,000			
Investment in Subsidiary Inc.	400,000	—			
Goodwill	—	—			
Other assets	432,000	396,000			
Total assets	870,000	502,000			
Liabilities and Shareholders' Equity					
Accounts payable	60,000	42,000			
Notes payable	70,000	120,000			
Common shares	560,000	240,000			
Retained earnings	180,000	100,000			
Total liabilities and sh. equity	870,000	502,000			

Solutions appear at the end of this chapter and on **MyLab Accounting**

Summary of Long-Term Equity Investments

So far we have introduced several types of ownership and several methods for recording and reporting information. Exhibit 16–10 summarizes the accounting method and financial statement presentation used generally for share investments according to the percentage of the investor's ownership in the investee company.

EXHIBIT 16–10 | Summary of Accounting for Investments under ASPE

Type of Investment (% of votes)	Primary* Accounting Method	Financial Statement Effects	
		Balance Sheet	**Income Statement****
Short-Term			
No significant influence (<20%, actively traded)	Fair Value Method	Reported as a current asset using market value.	Report dividend income.
No significant influence (<20%, not actively traded)	Historic Cost Method	Reported as a current asset at cost.	Report dividend income.
Long-Term			
Without significant influence (<20%, actively traded)	Fair Value Method	Reported as a long-term asset using market value.	Report dividend income.
Without significant influence (<20%, not actively traded)	Historic Cost Method	Reported as a long-term asset at cost.	Report dividend income.
Significant influence (20–50%)	Equity Method	Investor's share of income (loss) is added to the asset balance. Dividends deducted from the asset balance.	Report investor's share of investee's net income (loss).
Control (>50%)	Consolidation	The balance sheets of the parent and subsidiary are combined.	The income statements of the parent and subsidiary are combined.

* Choices in the accounting method are possible for many types of investment and are beyond the scope of this chapter.

** Realized gains/losses are reported in the non-operating section of the income statement. Brokerage commission fees are expensed.

Why It's Done This Way

Investments in Bonds[3]

LO 5

How do we record investments in bonds?

Industrial and commercial companies invest far more in shares than they do in bonds. The major investors in bonds are financial institutions, such as pension plans, trust companies, and insurance companies.

We looked at bonds in Chapter 15, but at that time it was from the perspective of the issuer. In this chapter we will look at how the business *investor* records and reports the same transactions. The dollar amount of a bond transaction is the same for both, but the accounts debited and credited differ.

Issuing Corporation	Investor (Bondholder)
Bonds Payable ⟶	Investment in Bonds
Interest Expense ⟶	Interest Revenue

Short-Term Investments in Bonds

Short-term investments in bonds are rare, since the purpose of investing in bonds is to provide a stream of investment income over the life of the bonds, and bonds typically have a life that is longer than one year. We covered accounting for short-term bonds using the fair value method briefly on page 893. Therefore, we focus here on long-term investments in bonds.

Long-Term Investments in Bonds

The accounting treatment of long-term bond investments is typically referred to as the **amortized cost method**, which involves the following journal entries:

① Long-term bond investments are recorded at cost, which includes the purchase price and brokerage commission fees.

② The accountant records interest and amortization on the cash interest dates.

③ At year-end, interest receivable and the related amortization is accrued.

The discount or premium is amortized to account more precisely for interest revenue over the period the bonds will be held. The journal entries would be:

Discount:	Investment in Bonds	XXX	
	Interest Revenue		XXX
Premium:	Interest Revenue	XXX	
	Investment in Bonds		XXX

---

[3]Section 3856 of Part II of the *CPA Canada Handbook* addresses financial instruments. Much of the discussion is beyond the scope of this text and is covered in advanced accounting courses.

④ Long-term investments in bonds are reported at their *amortized cost*, which determines the carrying amount.

⑤ At maturity, the investor will receive the face value of the bonds.

Consider the following scenario to illustrate accounting for a bond investment:

- $100,000 of 6 percent Xpress Trucking Ltd. bonds were purchased on April 1, 2020, at a price of 98 (98 percent of par value)
- Interest dates are April 1 and October 1
- Bonds mature on April 1, 2024 (outstanding for 48 months)
- Brokerage charges are $800 and are added to the cost
- Purchaser's year-end is December 31
- Use the straight-line method of amortization for the premium or discount. It is calculated the same way as it is calculated for bonds payable in Chapter 15 on pages 829–831.

The transactions for the bond investment are recorded as follows:

① Purchase at Cost   The $100,000, 6 percent bond was purchased at a price of 98. Brokerage costs are not expensed; they are added to the cost of the bond.

2020			
Apr. 1	Investment in Bonds	98,800	
	Cash		98,800
	To purchase long-term bond investment ($100,000 × 0.98) + $800 brokerage fee.		

② Amortization of Discount/Premium   The amortization of the discount or the premium on a bond investment affects Interest Revenue and the carrying amount of the bonds in the same way as for the company that issued the bonds. The entries bring the investment balance to the bond's face value on the maturity date and record the correct amount of interest revenue each period. Recall that in Exhibit 15–6 we looked at bond discounts from the perspective of the seller. Exhibit 16–11 shows a similar amortization of the discount except from the perspective of the purchaser in this Xpress Trucking Ltd. example.

EXHIBIT 16–11 | Amortization of a Bond Discount by a Purchaser

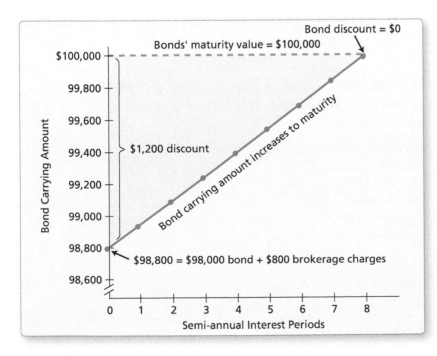

At the first interest date, the interest revenue and bond discount amortization must be recorded:[4]

The company purchasing the bonds can amortize the discount or premium using the straight-line or effective interest amortization method.

Oct. 1	Cash	3,000	
	Interest Revenue		3,000
	To receive semi-annual interest ($100,000 × 0.06 × $\frac{6}{12}$)		
1	Investment in Bonds	150	
	Interest Revenue		150
	To amortize discount on bond investment for six months ([($100,000 − $98,800) ÷ 48] × 6).		

❸ Year-end Accrual At year-end, interest revenue must be accrued. The amortization of the bond discount is also recorded at this time.

Dec. 31	Interest Receivable	1,500	
	Interest Revenue		1,500
	To accrue interest revenue for three months		
	($100,000 × 0.06 × $\frac{3}{12}$)		
31	Investment in Bonds	75	
	Interest Revenue		75
	To amortize discount on bond investment for three months ([($100,000 − $98,800) ÷ 48] × 3).		

---

[4] Companies sometimes record the investment at par value and the premium or discount in a separate account. If so, the journal entries would be

Apr. 1	Investment in Bonds	100,000	
	Discount on Investment in Bonds		1,200
	Cash		98,800
Oct. 1	Discount on Investment in Bonds	150	
	Interest Revenue		150
	Cash	3,000	
	Interest Revenue		3,000

④ Reporting Long-Term Investments in Bonds If we assume that the bond's market price is 102 at December 31, 2020, the year-end financial statements report the following effects of this long-term investment in bonds, where $99,025 = $98,800 + $150 + 75:

Balance Sheet (partial) December 31, 2020	
Current assets	
Interest receivable	$ 1,500
Total current assets	X,XXX
Investments in bonds—Note 6	99,025

Note 6: Investment in Bonds
Investments in bonds are reported at their amortized cost. At December 31, 2020, the current market value of the investments in bonds was $102,000.

Income statement (partial, multi-step) For the Year Ended December 31, 2020	
Other revenues	
Interest revenue	$4,725

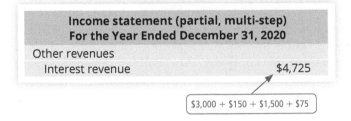
$3,000 + $150 + $1,500 + $75

⑤ Maturity At maturity, the following journal entry would record the return of the face value of the bond. Interest revenue would be reported separately as shown in ②.

2024			
Apr. 1	Cash	$100,000	
	Investment in Bonds		$100,000
	To collect face value of the bond at maturity.		

Write-down If the market value of a long-term bond investment declines below cost and the decline is considered to be other than temporary (thus it is an impairment), the investment should be *written down to market*. Suppose the market price for the bonds at December 31, 2020, was 97 (instead of the 102 noted in ④). The journal entry to write-down the investment would be:

2020			
Dec. 31	Impairment Loss	2,025	
	Investment in Bonds		2,025
	To record reduction in bond value not considered to be temporary ($99,025 book value − $97,000).		

If there is a subsequent improvement in the value, it is possible to reverse the adjustment and increase the book value of the investment to its amortized cost.

Try It!

6. Cana Corp. purchased $50,000 of 4 percent bonds from Xylomax Inc. on June 1, 2020. It paid $46,490 and intends to hold the bonds for three years or more. There were no brokerage commission fees. Interest is paid semi-annually on December 1 and June 1. Using the partial amortization schedule below, prepare the journal entries for June 1, 2020, and December 1, 2020. (Refer to Chapter 15 for information on the effective-interest method.)

	A	B	C	D	E	F
1	Annual Interest Period	Interest Received 4.00%	Period Interest Revenue (market rate)	Discount Amortization	Unamortized Discount Balance	Bond Carrying Value
2	Jun. 1, 2020				$3,510	$46,490
3	Dec. 1, 2020	$1,000	$1,395	$395	3,115	46,885
4	Jun. 1, 2021	1,000	1,407	407	2,708	47,292

Solutions appear at the end of this chapter and on **MyLab Accounting**

Foreign-Currency Transactions

LO ⑥

How do we record transactions in foreign currencies?

Accounting for business activities across national boundaries makes up the field of *international accounting*. Did you know that Shopify reports all of its transactions in US dollars even though it is a Canadian company? And Bombardier earned more than 93 percent of revenues outside of Canada in 2016? It is common for Canadian companies to do a large part of their business abroad.

The economic environment varies from country to country. Canada may be booming while other countries may be depressed economically. International accounting must deal with such differences.

Foreign Currencies and Foreign-Currency Exchange Rates

When companies engage in business transactions across national borders, there are no rules about which currency should be used. The choice of currency is just one of many business management decisions to be made. Assume BlackBerry sells 1,000 of its BlackBerry wireless devices to a US retailer. Will BlackBerry receive Canadian dollars or US dollars? If the transaction takes place in Canadian dollars, the US retailer must buy Canadian dollars to pay BlackBerry in Canadian currency. If the transaction takes place in US dollars, BlackBerry will receive US dollars and then exchange them for the Canadian dollars they need to pay their Canadian employees. In either case, a step has been added to the transaction: One company must convert domestic currency into foreign currency, or the other company must convert foreign currency into domestic currency.

The price of one nation's currency can be stated in terms of another country's monetary unit. The price of a foreign currency is called the **foreign-currency exchange rate**. In Exhibit 16–12, the Canadian dollar value of a Japanese yen is $0.01114. This means that one Japanese yen could be bought for approximately one cent. Other currencies, are also listed in Exhibit 16–12.

EXHIBIT 16–12 | Currency Exchange Rates

Notice that the exchange rates are quoted to at least 5 decimal places in Exhibit 16–12. When using exchange rates in calculations, do not round calculations until the last step when you round to the nearest cent.

Country	Monetary Unit	Cost in Canadian Dollars	Country	Monetary Unit	Cost in Canadian Dollars
United States	Dollar ($)	$1.25506	Britain	Pound (£)	$ 1.69323
European Union	Euro (€)	1.50339	n/a	Bitcoin (฿)	17,989.60000
Japan	Yen (¥)	0.01114	Denmark	Krone (kr)	0.20188

Source: Based on OANDA.com, Currency Converter. © 2018 OANDA Corporation.

We use the exchange rate to convert the price of an item stated in one currency to its price in a second currency. We call this conversion a **translation**. Suppose an item costs 200 euros. To compute its cost in dollars, we multiply the amount in euros by the conversion rate: 200 euros × $1.50339 = $300.68.

To aid the flow of international business, a market exists for foreign currencies. Traders buy and sell Canadian dollars, US dollars, euros, and other currencies in the same way that they buy and sell other commodities such as beef, corn, cotton, and automobiles. And just as supply and demand cause the prices of these other commodities to shift, so supply and demand for a particular currency cause exchange rates to fluctuate daily—even minute by minute. When the demand for a nation's currency exceeds the supply of that currency, its exchange rate rises. When supply exceeds demand, the currency's exchange rate falls.

Currencies are often described in the financial press as "strong" or "weak." What do these terms mean? The exchange rate of a **strong currency** is rising relative to other nations' currencies. The exchange rate of a **weak currency** is falling relative to other currencies.

The relationship between the Canadian and US dollar over the long term looks like this:

March 2001	exchange rate was $1 US = $1.5480 Canadian
January 2018	exchange rate was $1 US = $1.2551 Canadian

Based on this limited information, we would come to the conclusion that it has taken *fewer* Canadian dollars to buy a US dollar over time. In other words, during this particular period the Canadian dollar appreciated or gained strength over the US dollar.

Exchange rates can rise and fall dramatically within a short period. Exhibit 16–13 shows how the US dollar has had periods in which it is falling and then rising. Buying goods in US dollars in May 2017 when the exchange rate was 1.3751 and paying for them in September 2017 when the rate was 1.2107 makes money for the Canadian company because the exchange rate has decreased, which means each US dollar costs less. Buying goods in September 2017 and paying for them at any time later that year cost money for a Canadian company because the exchange rate has increased—each US dollar costs more.

A Canadian dollar at $1.3751 in April 2017 made travel to the United States less attractive to Canadians than when the US dollar was at $0.9858 in January 2013.

EXHIBIT 16–13 | Canadian–US Dollar Exchange Rates for January 2017 to January 2018

Source: Yahoo! Finance

Foreign-Currency Transactions

When a Canadian company transacts business with a foreign company, the transaction price can be stated either in Canadian dollars or in the national currency of the other company or in any other currency that is stipulated by contract. This adds risk to the transactions because, as we just saw, exchange rates fluctuate over time.

Shopify Inc. wrote in the Management Discussion and Analysis section of its third quarter report on October 31, 2017, that a 10 percent strengthening of the Canadian dollar against the US dollar would result in a loss of over $14 million for the nine months ended September 30, 2017.

So how is this exchange information used on a daily basis? First we will look at how to record transactions when foreign currencies are exchanged, and then we will look briefly at ways to minimize foreign-exchange risk.

Payables in a Foreign Currency

If the transaction price is stated in units of the foreign currency, the Canadian company encounters two accounting steps. First, the transaction price must be translated into Canadian dollars for recording in the accounting records. Second, these transactions usually cause the Canadian company to experience a **foreign-currency transaction gain** or **foreign-currency transaction loss**. This type of gain or loss occurs when the exchange rate changes between the date of the purchase or sale on account and the date of the subsequent payment or receipt of cash.

If a company purchases products from a supplier in another country, Accounts Payable is created. It is recorded at the exchange rate in effect at the time of the transaction. Later, when the company pays the invoice, the exchange rate has almost certainly changed. Accounts Payable is debited for the amount recorded earlier, and Cash is credited for the amount paid at the current exchange rate. A debit difference is a loss, and a credit difference is a gain.

> For an accounts payable transaction, there is a *loss* if the exchange rate has moved *higher* in the period between the purchase and the payment. There is a *gain* if the exchange rate has moved *lower*.

Purchase Date Suppose on December 13, 2019, The Petit Parfum Boutique in Barrie imports Shalimar perfume from a French supplier at a price of 75,000 euros (which can also be shown as €75,000). If the exchange rate is $1.56 per euro, the boutique records this credit purchase as follows:

2019			
Dec. 13	Inventory	117,000	
	Accounts Payable		117,000
	To record a purchase on account (€75,000 × $1.56 per euro).		

The boutique translates the euro price of the merchandise (€75,000) into Canadian dollars ($117,000) for recording the purchase and the related account payable.

If the boutique were to pay this account immediately (which is unlikely in most business scenarios), the boutique would debit Accounts Payable and credit Cash for $117,000. Suppose, however, that the credit terms specify payment within 60 days and suppose as well that the Boutique's year-end is January 31, 2020. It is almost certain that the exchange rate for the euro will be different on the year-end and payment dates.

Year-End On January 31, 2020, the payable must be reported at its current dollar value. Suppose the exchange rate at January 31, 2020, has changed to $1.57 per euro. The boutique's payable would be $117,750 (€75,000 × $1.57 per euro), which is $750 higher than the amount of the payable recorded originally. The entry to record this change in the euro exchange rate at year-end is:

2020			
Jan. 31	Foreign-Currency Transaction Loss	750	
	Accounts Payable		750
	To record the change in the exchange rate of the euro at year-end [€75,000 × ($1.57 − $1.56)].		

Payment Date On February 2, 2020, when the boutique pays this debt, suppose the exchange rate has changed to $1.58 per euro. The boutique's payment entry is:

Feb. 2	Accounts Payable	117,750	
	Foreign-Currency Transaction Loss	750	
	Cash		118,500
	To record payment of the account for a credit purchase. (Cash paid is €75,000 × $1.58.)		

> $117,000 purchase + $750 year-end exchange rate change

The boutique has a loss because the company has settled the debt with more dollars than the adjusted accounts payable balance. If on the payment date the exchange rate of the euro was less than $1.56, the boutique would have paid fewer dollars than the $117,750 year-end valuation of the payable. The company would have recorded a gain on the transaction as a credit to Foreign-Currency Transaction Gain.

Receivables in a Foreign Currency

International sales on account may also be measured in foreign currency.

Sale Date Suppose the boutique sells some products to an American customer on January 30, 2020. The total sales price of the products is US$140,000, and the exchange rate is $1.04. The boutique's sale entry is:

Jan. 30	Accounts Receivable	145,600	
	Sales Revenue		145,600
	To record a sale on account (US$140,000 × $1.04).		

Collection Date Assume the boutique collects from the American customer on March 2, 2020, when the exchange rate has fallen to $1.02. The boutique receives fewer Canadian dollars than the recorded amount of the receivable and so experiences a foreign-currency transaction loss. The collection entry is:

Mar. 2	Cash	142,800	
	Foreign-Currency Transaction Loss	2,800	
	Accounts Receivable		145,600
	To record collection of a receivable.		
	(Cash received is US$140,000 × $1.02).		

If the exchange rate had increased by the time the payment was received, this would have resulted in more cash than the amount of the receivable. The company would have recorded a credit to Foreign-Currency Transaction Gain.

When a subsidiary prepares financial statements in a currency other than Canadian dollars, the subsidiary must translate the financial statements into Canadian dollars for the consolidated financial statements at the exchange rate in effect on the date of the financial statements. ASPE Section 1651 provides more specific guidance.

Foreign-currency transaction gains and losses are combined for each accounting period. The net amount of gain or loss can be reported as Other Revenue and Expense on the income statement.

Year-End Adjustment   In addition, the year-end balance for accounts receivable must be updated to show any foreign currency amounts at the exchange rate in effect on the date of the financial statements. The gain or loss would be recorded to the same accounts as shown above.

Minimizing Risk

One way for Canadian companies to avoid foreign-currency transaction losses is to insist that international transactions be settled in Canadian dollars. This requirement puts the burden of currency translation on the foreign party. However, such a strategy may alienate customers and decrease sales, or it may cause customers to demand unreasonable credit terms to compensate for the risk they would need to take in the transaction.

Hedging   Another way for a company to protect itself from the effects of fluctuating foreign-currency exchange rates is by hedging. **Hedging** means protecting oneself from losing money in one transaction by engaging in a **counterbalancing transaction**—a second, related transaction to offset the risk of the first one. Such an arrangement can be set up using one of several tactics—this example assumes that the company has a roughly equal amount of receivables and payables in different currencies.

Let's go back to the boutique example for a moment. If the company sold goods online to be paid for in Mexican pesos, it would expect to receive a fixed number of pesos in the future. If the peso is losing value, the Canadian company would expect the pesos to be worth fewer dollars than the amount of the receivable—an expected loss situation. However, since the boutique will accumulate payables stated in a different foreign currency—the euro, in this case—losses on the receipt of pesos may be approximately offset by gains on the payment of euros to the French supplier.

There are other strategies available for managing risk—**futures contracts**, **forward contracts**, and **currency options**, to name a few—but they are outside the scope of this text and will be covered in more advanced accounting and finance courses.

Try It!

7. In each of the following situations, determine whether the Canadian company will experience a foreign-currency transaction gain or loss, and explain why:
   a. A Canadian company purchased car parts from a German supplier at a price of 200,000 euros. On the date of the credit purchase, the exchange rate of the euro was $1.0891. On the payment date, the exchange rate of the euro is $1.0723. The payment is in euros.
   b. A Canadian company sold merchandise to a Danish company at a price of 500,000 kroner. On the date of the credit sale, the exchange rate of the krone was $0.20962. On the day the payment is received in kroner, the exchange rate of the krone is $0.21325.
   c. A Canadian company purchased electronics from a Japanese supplier at a price of 1,200,000 yen. On the date of the credit purchase, the exchange rate of the yen was $0.01172. On the payment date, the exchange rate of the yen is $0.01221. The payment is in yen.
   d. A Canadian company sold merchandise to a US company at a price of US$15,000. On the date of the credit sale, the exchange rate of the US dollar was $1.0891. On the day the payment is received in US dollars, the exchange rate of the US dollar is $1.0624.

Solutions appear at the end of this chapter and on **MyLab Accounting**

LO (7)

How does IFRS apply to investments and international transactions?

ASPE	IFRS
Equity Investments **No Significant Influence (non-strategic investments)**	
Report using fair value or cost (if fair value is too difficult or costly to obtain).	Most **financial instruments** must be measured at fair value (market value).
Gains and losses are reported under Net Income.	Gains and losses are reported under either Net Income or Other Comprehensive Income depending on specifics outside of the scope of this text.
Where there is Significant Influence (strategic investments)	
Use the cost or equity method.	Only the equity method may be used.
Significant influence depends on the situation rather than a specific percentage.	Significant influence is a **rebuttable presumption**. It is *presumed* that if an investor holds, directly or indirectly, 20 percent or more of the voting power of the investee, it has significant influence, unless it can be clearly demonstrated that this is not the case.
Reversal of impairment losses is not permitted over the original cost.	Reversals of impairment losses are permitted and it is possible to increase the asset above its cost.
Where there is Control (majority interest)	
The parent company may choose to consolidate its subsidiaries' financial results.	The parent company must consolidate its subsidiaries' financial results.
There is no guidance about where to report minority interest on the balance sheet.	Minority interest must be presented within the equity section, but separate from the parent's shareholders' equity.
Investments in Debt Instruments	
Short-term investments in bonds The standards are converged. Both suggest that these investments are measured and reported at fair value. (Use the cost method if no market price is available.)	
Long-Term Investments in Bonds	
Amortized cost method uses either straight-line amortization or the effective-interest-rate method.	Must use the effective-interest-rate method.
Foreign-Currency Translation Gains and Losses	
Usually reported as Other Revenue and Expense.	Included in Other Comprehensive Income.
Hedging	
There are fewer categories of transactions that qualify as hedging relationships.	General cash flow hedges and fair value hedges are reported.

Summary Problem for Your Review

Problem 1

The January 31, 2020, year-end balance sheet of Shijie Corp. included an Investment in Bran Ltd. account in the amount of $10,000,000. The balance in the Short-Term Investments account for several small investments in other companies was $86,000. Suppose the company completed the following investment transactions:

2020

Feb.	1	Purchased 3,000 common shares as another investment to be included in the Short-Term Investments account, paying $25.00 per share plus brokerage commission of $400.
Feb.	2	Purchased additional common shares in Bran Ltd. at a cost of $1,750,000. Commissions on the purchase were $30,000. Shijie Corp. now owns 31 percent of Bran Ltd.'s equity. Shijie does not have control over Bran Ltd.
Sep.	15	Received the semi-annual cash dividend of $0.15 per share on the short-term investment purchased April 8.
Oct.	16	Sold 750 shares of the short-term investment purchased on April 8 for $28.00 per share, less brokerage commission of $300.
Dec.	1	Received a cash dividend of $150,000 from Bran Ltd.

2021

Jan.	31	Bran Ltd. reported total net income for the year of $2,100,000. Assume that the short-term investment's book value is the same as their market value at this date.

Required

a. Record the transactions in the general journal of Shijie Corp.

b. What are the balances in the Investments accounts at January 31, 2021?

Problem 2

Journalize the following transactions of Canada Corp.:

2019

Nov.	16	Purchased equipment on account for US$40,000 when the exchange rate was $1.07 per US dollar.
	27	Sold merchandise on account to a Swiss company for 700,000 Swiss francs. Each Swiss franc is worth $0.81. Ignore the inventory and cost of goods sold accounts.
Dec.	22	Paid the US company when the US dollar's exchange rate was $1.05.
	31	Adjusted for the change in the exchange rate of the Swiss franc. Its current exchange rate is $0.80. Ignore the inventory and cost of goods sold accounts.

2020

Jan.	4	Collected from the Swiss company. The exchange rate is $0.82.

SOLUTIONS

Problem 1

Requirement 1a

2020			
Feb. 1	Short-Term Investments	75,000	
	Brokerage Commissions Expense	400	
	Cash		75,400
	Purchased 3,000 shares at $25.00 plus commission of $400.		
Feb. 2	Investment in Bran Ltd. Common Shares	1,750,000	
	Brokerage Commissions Expense	30,000	
	Cash		1,780,000
	Purchased additional shares of Bran Ltd.		
Sep.15	Cash	450	
	Dividend Revenue		450
	Received $0.15 per share cash dividend on short-term investment (3,000 × $0.15).		
Oct. 16	Cash	20,700	
	Brokerage Commissions Expense	300	
	Gain on Sale of Short-Term Investment		2,250
	Short-Term Investments		18,750
	Sold 750 shares of a short-term investment purchased Apr. 8. ($75,000 × 750/3,000 shares).		
Dec. 1	Cash	150,000	
	Investment in Bran Ltd. Common Shares		150,000
	Received cash dividends from Bran Ltd.		
2021			
Jan. 31	Investment in Bran Ltd. Common Shares	651,000	
	Equity Method Investment Revenue		651,000
	To record proportion of Bran Ltd.'s net income ($2,100,000 × 0.31).		

Brokerage commissions are expensed and not capitalized.

Dividend and interest income on short-term investments are reported as revenue.

Selling price = $20,700 ((750 × $28) − $300)
Investment = $18,750 (750 × $25)
Gain = $2,250

Requirement 1b

Investment in Bran Ltd.

2020						
Feb.	1	Balance	10,000,000			
Feb.	2	Purchase	1,750,000	Dec. 1	Dividends	150,000
2021						
Jan.	31	Net income	651,000			
Jan.	31	Balance	12,251,000			

Short-Term Investments

2020						
Feb.	1	Balance	86,000			
Feb.	1	Purchase	75,000	Oct. 16	Sale	18,750
2021						
Jan.	31	Balance	142,250			

These short-term investments are classified as short-term because of management's intention is to sell them within the year. If this does not happen but management still intends to sell them soon, then they remain listed as short-term.

Problem 2

Entries for transactions stated in foreign currencies:

2019			
Nov. 16	Equipment	42,800	
	Accounts Payable		42,800
	To record a purchase on credit ($40,000 \times \$1.07$).		
27	Accounts Receivable	567,000	
	Sales Revenue		567,000
	To record a sale on account ($700,000 \times \$0.81$).		
Dec. 22	Accounts Payable	42,800	
	Cash		42,000
	Foreign-Currency Transaction Gain		800
	To record payment of a credit purchase ($40,000 \times \$1.05$).		
31	Foreign-Currency Transaction Loss	7,000	
	Accounts Receivable		7,000
	Year-end exchange rate adjustment $[700,000 \times (\$0.81 - \$0.80)]$.		
2020			
Jan. 4	Cash	574,000	
	Accounts Receivable		560,000
	Foreign-Currency Transaction Gain		14,000
	Collection of account receivable $= (700,000 \times \$0.82)$ Accounts Receivable $= (\$567,000 - \$7,000)$ Gain $= [700,000 \times (\$0.82 - \$0.80)]$		

Always use the exchange rates in effect on the date of a transaction. When journalizing the payment or receipt for a foreign-currency transaction, calculate the cash payment or receipt amount first.

Cash payment	>	Payable	→ F-C transaction loss
Cash payment	<	Payable	→ F-C transaction gain
Cash receipt	>	Receivable	→ F-C transaction gain
Cash receipt	<	Receivable	→ F-C transaction loss

Summary

Learning Objectives

① Account for short-term investments Pg. 888

How do we account for short-term investments?

- Use the fair value (market value) method:
  - Change in value at year-end is an unrealized gain or loss in the non-operating section of the income statement under "Other gains and losses."
  - Dividends and interest are recorded as income.
  - Brokerage commission fees are expensed.

② Account for long-term share investments Pg. 894

How do we account for long-term share investments when we own few shares?
- The fair value (market value) method is used when there is "no significant influence" over the corporation whose shares are owned.
- This typically occurs when less than 20 percent of shares are owned.

③ Use the equity method to account for investments   Pg. 896

What is the equity method, and how do we use it?
- Use when there is "significant influence" or ownership of about 20 to 50 percent of the shares.
- Investee income is recorded by the investor by debiting the Investment account and crediting the Equity Method Investment Revenue account.
- The investor records the receipt of dividends from the investee by crediting the Investment account.

④ Describe and create consolidated financial statements
Pg. 898

How do we perform a simple consolidation?
- Ownership of more than 50 percent of the voting shares—*consolidation* method must be used.
- Parent has "control" over the subsidiary.
- The subsidiary's financial statements are included in the consolidated statements of the parent company.
- Two features of consolidation accounting are:
  1. Addition of the parent and subsidiary accounts to prepare the parent's consolidated statements, and
  2. Elimination of intercompany items.
- When a parent owns less than 100 percent of the subsidiary's shares, the portion owned by outside investors is called a non-controlling interest.

⑤ Account for investments in bonds   Pg. 906

How do we record investments in bonds?
- Long-term investments in bonds are *recorded at cost.* Fees are capitalized.
- Bonds are reported at their *amortized cost,* which means the discount or premium is amortized to account more precisely for interest revenue over the period the bonds will be held.
- At maturity the investor will receive the face value of the bonds.

⑥ Account for foreign-currency transactions   Pg. 910

How do we record transactions in foreign currencies?
- Foreign-currency transaction gains:
  - When a company receives foreign currency worth *more* in Canadian dollars than the amount of the receivable recorded earlier.
  - When a company pays foreign currency that costs *less* in Canadian dollars than the amount of the payable recorded earlier.
- Foreign-currency transaction losses:
  - When a company receives foreign currency worth *less* in Canadian dollars than the amount of the receivable recorded earlier.
  - When a company pays foreign currency that costs *more* in Canadian dollars than the amount of the payable recorded earlier.

⑦ Identify the impact of IFRS on accounting for investments and international transactions   Pg. 915

How does IFRS apply to investments and international transactions?
- In general, IFRS and ASPE require the same or similar treatment of investments and foreign-currency transactions.
- In many cases, ASPE allows companies more options for accounting for their investments.

Key Terms for the chapter are shown next and are in the **Glossary** at the back of the book. **Similar Terms** are shown after **Key Terms**.

KEY TERMS

Actively traded   Financial instruments that are easily bought or sold because there are a lot of them in the market and it is easy to find someone who is willing to engage in a transaction (p. 890).

Affiliated company   An investment in a company in which there is significant influence and 20 to 50 percent ownership. These investments are accounted for using the equity method (p. 898).

Amortized cost method   To account for long-term bond investments, the discount or premium is amortized to more accurately reflect the interest revenue. These bonds are reported at their amortized cost (p. 906).

Carrying value   The amount at which an asset is reported on the balance sheet (p. 892).

Certificate of deposit   A secure form of investment with a fixed interest rate and term. Unlike a bank account, they must be held to maturity (p. 889).

Companion account   An account that is typically paired up with another account (p. 892).

Consolidated financial statements   Financial statements of the parent company plus those of majority-owned subsidiaries as if the combination were a single legal entity (p. 898).

Controlling interest Ownership of more than 50 percent of an investee company's voting shares. Also called *majority interest* (p. 898).

Counterbalancing transaction Engaging in a second transaction to offset the risk of the first transaction (p. 914).

Currency options A contract that can be purchased to guarantee the right to a future exchange rate (p. 914).

Equity method for investments The method used to account for investments in which the investor generally has 20 to 50 percent of the investor's voting shares and can significantly influence the decisions of the investee. The investment account is debited for ownership in the investee's net income and credited for ownership in the investee's dividends (p. 896).

Fair value method The method of accounting for shares held as short-term investments that values them at their fair, or market, value on the year-end balance sheet date. Any gain or loss resulting from the change in fair value is recognized in net income for the period in which it arises, and fair value becomes the new carrying value of the shares. Also called the *market value method* (p. 890).

Financial instrument A contract that creates an asset for one party and a liability or equity for another (p. 915).

Foreign-currency exchange rate The measure of one currency against another currency (p. 910).

Foreign-currency transaction gain The gain that occurs when a cash payment is less than the related account payable or a cash receipt is greater than the related account receivable due to a change in exchange rate between the transaction date and the payment date (p. 912).

Foreign-currency transaction loss The loss that occurs when a cash payment is greater than the related account payable or a cash receipt is less than the related account receivable due to a change in exchange rate between the transaction date and the payment date (p. 912).

Forward contract An agreement to purchase at a specified future date and price (p. 914).

Futures contract A contract that can be purchased to guarantee the right to a product at a specified price in the future (p. 914).

Hedging A way to protect oneself from losing money in a foreign-currency transaction by engaging in a counterbalancing foreign-currency transaction (p. 914).

Long-term investments Investments that a company intends to hold for more than one year (p. 890).

Majority interest Another name for *controlling interest* (p. 898).

Market value method Another name for the *fair value method* of accounting for short-term investments in shares (p. 890).

Minority interest Another name for *non-controlling interest* (p. 903).

Money market fund An investment product generally considered safe because it invests in short-term debt securities, such as certificates of deposit (p. 889).

Non-controlling interest A subsidiary company's equity that is held by shareholders other than the parent company. Also called *minority interest* (p. 903).

Parent company An investor company that generally owns more than 50 percent of the voting shares of a subsidiary company (p. 898).

Rebuttable assumption A conclusion that something is true unless proven that it isn't (p. 915).

Segmented information Financial information presented in the notes to the financial statements either by industry or by geography (p. 906).

Short-term investments Investments that management intends to hold for less than one year (p. 889).

Significant influence When a company participates in the decision making of another company without having full control over it (p. 889).

Strong currency A currency that is rising relative to other nations' currencies (p. 911).

Subsidiary An investee company in which a parent company owns more than 50 percent of the voting shares (p. 898).

Translation Another term for a currency conversion or foreign-currency exchange (p. 911).

Treasury bills A short-term debt obligation issued by a government (p. 889).

Weak currency A currency that is falling relative to other nations' currencies (p. 911).

Write-down An accounting entry to recognize the decrease in the value of an asset by debiting an expense account and crediting the asset account (p. 898).

SIMILAR TERMS

CD	Certificates of deposit
Controlling interest	Majority interest
Fair value method	Market value method
Minority interest	Non-controlling interest
Short-term investments	Marketable securities; Temporary investments
Translation	Foreign-currency conversion
Trade shares	Buy/sell shares

SELF-STUDY QUESTIONS

Test your understanding of the chapter by marking the best answer for each of the following questions:

1. Short-term investments are reported on the balance sheet (p. 890)
   a. Immediately after inventory
   b. Immediately after accounts receivable
   c. Immediately after cash
   d. Immediately after current assets

2. APR Inc. distributes a stock dividend. An investor who owns APR Inc. shares as a short-term investment should (p. 891)
   a. Debit Short-Term Investments and credit Dividend Revenue for the book value of the shares received in the dividend distribution
   b. Debit Short-Term Investments and credit Dividend Revenue for the market value of the shares received in the dividend distribution
   c. Debit Cash and credit Short-Term Investments for the market value of the shares received in the dividend distribution
   d. Make a memorandum entry to record the new cost per share of APR Inc. shares held

3. Mulgarvey Corporation owns 30 percent of the voting shares of Turner Inc. Turner Inc. reports net income of $200,000 and declares and pays cash dividends of $80,000. Which method should Mulgarvey Corporation use to account for this investment? (p. 896)
   a. Cost   c. Fair value
   b. Equity   d. Consolidation

4. Refer to the facts of the preceding question. What effect do Turner Inc.'s income and dividends have on Mulgarvey Corporation's net income? (p. 897)
   a. Increase of $24,000   c. Increase of $60,000
   b. Increase of $36,000   d. Increase of $84,000

5. In applying the consolidation method, elimination entries are (p. 899)
   a. Necessary
   b. Required only when the parent has a receivable from or a payable to the subsidiary
   c. Required only when there is a minority interest
   d. Required only for the preparation of the consolidated balance sheet

6. Parent Corp. reports net income of $200,000. Sub A Ltd., of which Parent Corp. owns 90 percent, reports net income of $80,000, and Sub B Ltd., of which Parent Corp. owns 60 percent, reports net income of $100,000. What is Parent Corp.'s consolidated net income? (p. 904)
   a. $200,000   c. $335,000
   b. $332,000   d. $380,000

7. If the market value of a long-term bond decreases below cost and it is expected to be a permanent impairment, what account is used for the expense of the write-down? (p. 909)
   a. Bond Write-down Expense
   b. Loss on Investment
   c. Impairment Loss
   d. Bond Impairment

8. On May 16, the exchange rate of the euro was $1.50. On May 20, the exchange rate was $1.52. Which of the following statements is true? (p. 910)
   a. The Canadian dollar has risen against the euro.
   b. The Canadian dollar has fallen against the euro.
   c. The Canadian dollar is stronger than the euro.
   d. The Canadian dollar and the euro are equally strong.

9. A strong Canadian dollar encourages (p. 911)
   a. Travel to Canada by foreigners
   b. Purchase of Canadian goods by foreigners
   c. Canadians to save dollars
   d. Canadians to travel abroad

10. Canadian Furniture Inc. purchased dining room suites from an English supplier at a price of 400,000 British pounds sterling. On the date of the credit purchase, the exchange rate of the British pound was $1.75. On the payment date, the exchange rate of the pound is $1.77. If payment is in pounds, Canadian Furniture experiences (p. 912)
    a. A foreign-currency transaction gain of $8,000
    b. A foreign-currency transaction loss of $8,000
    c. Neither a transaction gain nor loss because the debt is paid in Canadian dollars
    d. None of the above

> *Answers to Self-Study Questions*
> 1. c   2. d   3. b   4. c ($200,000 × 0.30 = $60,000; dividends have no effect on investor net income under the equity method)   5. a   6. b [$200,000 + ($80,000 × 0.90) + ($100,000 × 0.60) = $332,000]
> 7. c   8. b   9. d   10. b [400,000 × ($1.77 − $1.75) = $8,000; a loss since cash payment > payable]

Assignment Material

QUESTIONS

1. If a company buys the shares of another company as an investment, what is the investor's cost of 200 Shopify Inc. common shares at $101.50 with a brokerage commission of $75?

2. What distinguishes a short-term investment in shares from a long-term investment in shares?

3. Give an example of two debt instruments.

4. What is an equity investment?

5. At the end of a fiscal period, all equity investments that are traded on public stock exchanges must be revalued on the balance sheet to their market value. Does this policy provide better information for the investor? Explain.

6. How does an investor record the receipt of a cash dividend on an investment accounted for by the fair value method? How does this investor record receipt of a stock dividend?

7. An investor paid $30,000 for 1,000 common shares and later that same year received a 10 percent stock dividend. Compute the gain or loss on sale of 500 common shares for $15,000 before year-end.

8. When is an investment accounted for by the equity method? Outline how to apply the equity method. Include in your answer how to record the purchase of the investment, the investor's proportion of the investee's net income, and receipt of a cash dividend from the investee. Indicate how a gain or loss on the sale of the investment would be measured.

9. Identify three transactions that cause changes to an equity method investment account.

10. Why are intercompany items eliminated from consolidated financial statements? Name two intercompany items that are eliminated.

11. Name the account that expresses the excess of cost of an investment over the fair market value of the subsidiary's net assets. What type of account is this, and where in the financial statements is it reported?

12. Where is non-controlling interest reported on the balance sheet?

13. How would you measure the net income of a parent company with three subsidiaries? Assume that two subsidiaries are wholly owned (100 percent) and that the parent owns 60 percent of the third subsidiary.

14. Weel Soo purchases Canadian Utilities Inc. bonds as a long-term investment. Suppose the face amount of the bonds is $300,000 and the purchase price is 101.30. The bonds pay interest at the stated annual rate of 8 percent. How much did Soo pay for the bonds? How much principal will Soo collect at maturity?

15. The purchase date of the bond investment in the preceding question was August 1, 2020. The bonds pay semiannual interest on January 31 and July 31. How much interest will Soo earn during the year ended December 31, 2020?

16. Mentacos Inc. purchased inventory from a French company, agreeing to pay 150,000 euros. On the purchase date, the euro was quoted at $1.55. When Mentacos Inc. paid the debt, the price of a euro was $1.57. What account does Mentacos Inc. debit for the $3,000 difference between the cost of the inventory and the amount of cash paid?

17. A credit purchase denominated in pesos, followed by weakness in the peso results in a foreign-currency gain or loss for a Canadian business?

18. When a Canadian business completes a credit sale denominated in pesos but then there is a weakness in the dollar, does this result in a foreign-currency gain or loss for the business?

19. What is the main difference between IFRS and ASPE for short-term investments?

20. What is the main difference between IFRS and ASPE for investments in subsidiaries?

STARTERS

S16–1 Compute the cost of each of the following short-term investments that would be reported on the balance sheet. Round all answers to the nearest dollar.

 a. 550 shares of Grey Ltd. at $16.50 per share. Brokerage commission fees were $175.

 b. 600 shares of Red Corp. at $74 per share. Red Corp. pays a cash dividend of $0.66 per year. Brokerage commission fees were $550.

 c. 1,000 shares of White Inc. at $55.10 per share. Brokerage commission fees were $560.

 d. 70 shares of Tangerine Ltd. at $35.50 per share. Brokerage commission fees were $250.

① Computing the cost of an investment in shares

a. $9,075
b. $44,400

S16–2 Journalize Consumer Evaluation Ltd.'s investment transactions. Explanations are not required.

① Accounting for a short-term investment

Dec. 31 unrealized gain, $4,000

2019

Dec. 6   Purchased 1,000 shares of Georgian Reports Inc. at a price of $41.00 per share, intending to sell the investment within three months. Brokerage commission fees were $350.

     23   Received a cash dividend of $1.10 per share on the Georgian Reports Inc. shares.

     31   Adjusted the investment to its fair value of $45.00 per share.

2020

Jan. 27   Sold the Georgian Reports Inc. shares for $46.00 per share, less brokerage commission fees of $370.

S16–3 All Corp. completed the following investment transactions during 2019 and 2020:

① Accounting for a short-term investment

2. Jan. 16, 2020, loss on sale, $3,750

2019

Dec. 12   Purchased 1,500 shares of Blackmore Ltd. at a price of $62.00 per share, intending to sell the investment within the next year. Brokerage commission fees were $510.

     21   Received a cash dividend of $0.48 per share on the Blackmore Ltd. shares.

     31   Adjusted the investment to its fair value of $61.50 per share.

2020

Jan. 16   Sold the Blackmore Ltd. shares for $59.00 per share, less brokerage commissions of $490.

 1. Classify All Corp.'s investment as short-term or long-term.

 2. Journalize All Corp.'s investment transactions. Explanations are not required.

S16–4 Baines Corp. purchased 1,000 common shares in each of three companies:

 a. Investment in Cullen Corp. to be sold within the next 9 to 12 months.

 b. Investment in Gerson Canada Ltd. to be sold within the next 90 days.

 c. Investment in Arnold Ltd. to be sold within the next two years.

Classify each investment as a current asset or a long-term asset. None of these investments is subject to significant influence.

①② Classifying investments as short-term or long-term

S16–5 At what amount should the following investment portfolio be reported on the December 31 year-end balance sheet? All the investments are less than 5 percent of the investee's shares. Prepare one adjusting journal entry for the portfolio rather than making separate journal entries.

② Year-end adjustment to market value

Unrealized loss, $5,000

Shares	Carrying Value	Fair Value (Market value)
All Seasons Hotels	$88,000	$97,000
Tent Manufacturing Corp.	140,000	124,000
East End Grocers Inc.	74,000	76,000

②

Measuring gain or loss on the sale of a share investment after receiving a stock dividend

2. Loss on sale, $6,200

S16–6 Gerber Ltd. buys 2,000 of the 100,000 shares of Efron Inc., paying $35.00 per share. Suppose Efron distributes a 10 percent stock dividend. Later the same year, Gerber Ltd. sells the Efron shares for $29.00 per share. Disregard commissions on the purchase and sale.

1. Compute Gerber Ltd.'s new cost per share after receiving the stock dividend.

2. Compute Gerber Ltd.'s gain or loss on the sale of this long-term investment.

②

Accounting for a long-term investment's unrealized gain or loss

1. Dec. 31, 2020, unrealized gain, $9,750

S16–7 Marsland Inc. completed these long-term investment transactions during 2020. Disregard commissions.

Jan. 14	Purchased 1,000 shares of Crew Ltd., paying $41.00 per share.
Aug. 22	Received a cash dividend of $3.28 per share on the Crew Ltd. shares.
Dec. 31	Adjusted the Crew Ltd. investment to its current fair value of $50,750.

1. Journalize Marsland's investment transactions. Explanations are not required. Marsland Inc. exerts no significant influence on Crew Ltd. and intends to hold the investment indefinitely.

2. What value is reported for the investment on Marsland's balance sheet at December 31, 2020?

②

Accounting for the sale of a long-term investment

1. Gain on sale, $3,250

S16–8 Use the data given in S16–7. On August 4, 2021, Marsland Inc. sold its investment in Crew Ltd. for $54.00 per share.

1. Journalize the sale, excluding any brokerage commission expense. No explanation is required.

2. How does the gain or loss that you recorded differ from the gain or loss that was recorded at December 31, 2020 (in S16–7)?

③

Accounting for a 40 percent investment in another company

3. Bal. $5,400,000

S16–9 On January 6, 2020, Ling Corp. paid $5,000,000 for its 40 percent investment in True World Inc. Assume that on December 31 that same year, True World earned net income of $1,800,000 and paid cash dividends of $800,000.

1. What method should Ling Corp. use to account for the investment in True World Inc.? Give your reason.

2. Journalize these three transactions on the books of Ling Corp. Include an explanation for each entry. Ignore any brokerage commission expenses.

3. Post to the Investment in True World Inc. Common Shares T-account. What is its balance after all the transactions are posted?

③

Accounting for an investment with significant influence

S16–10 On March 1, 2019, Brrr Inc. paid $1,000,000 to acquire a 35 percent investment in Mint Ltd. After one year, Mint Ltd. reported net income of $250,000 for the first year and declared and paid cash dividends of $55,000. Record the following entries in Brrr's general journal:

1. The purchase of the investment (excluding any brokerage commission fees).

2. Brrr's proportion of Mint Ltd.'s net income on February 29, 2020.

3. Receipt of the cash dividends on March 1, 2020.

④

Understanding consolidated financial statements

S16–11 Answer these questions about consolidation accounting:

1. Define "parent company." Define "subsidiary."

2. Which company's name appears on the consolidated financial statements? How much of the subsidiary's shares must the parent own before reporting consolidated statements?

3. How do consolidated financial statements differ from the financial statements of a single company?

④

Reading consolidated financial statements

S16–12 Answer these questions about consolidated financial statements:

1. Why does consolidated shareholders' equity (contributed capital + retained earnings) exclude the equity of a subsidiary corporation?

2. Suppose A Ltd. owns 90 percent of B Ltd. What are the remaining 10 percent of B Ltd.'s shares called, and where do they appear, if at all, in A Ltd.'s consolidated financial statements?

3. Suppose C Ltd. paid $2,000,000 to acquire D Ltd., whose shareholders' equity (which has the same fair value as net assets) totalled $1,400,000. What is the

$600,000 excess called? Which company reports the excess? Where in the consolidated financial statements is the excess reported?

S16–13 Heinz Ltd. owns vast amounts of corporate bonds. Suppose the company buys $1,000,000 of Kuzawa Corporation bonds on January 2, 2020, at a price of 97. The Kuzawa bonds pay cash interest at the annual rate of 6 percent and mature on December 31, 2024.

⑤
Working with a bond investment
3. Annual interest revenue, $66,000

1. How much did Heinz Ltd. pay to purchase the bond investment? How much will Heinz Ltd. collect when the bond investment matures?

2. How much cash interest will Heinz Ltd. receive each year from Kuzawa Corporation?

3. Compute Heinz Ltd.'s annual interest revenue on this bond investment. Use the straight-line method to amortize the discount on the investment.

S16–14 Return to S16–3, the Heinz Ltd. investment in Kuzawa Corporation bonds. Journalize the following transactions on Heinz Ltd.'s books, along with an explanation:

⑤
Recording bond investment transactions
h. Cash interest received, $60,000

1. Purchase of the bond investment on January 2, 2020. As Heinz Ltd. expects to hold the investment to maturity, it is classified as a long-term investment.

2. Receipt of the annual cash interest on December 31, 2020.

3. Amortization of the discount on December 31, 2020.

4. Collection of the investment's face value at its maturity date on December 31, 2024. (Assume that the interest and amortization of discount for 2024 have already been recorded, so you may ignore these entries.)

S16–15 On April 30, 2020, Cana Corp. paid 97.50 for 4 percent bonds of Starr Limited as an investment. Maturity value of the bonds is $100,000 at October 31, 2025; they pay interest on April 30 and October 31. Cana Corp.'s year-end is December 31. Cana Corp. plans to hold the bonds until they mature. Using the straight-line method of amortizing the discount, journalize all transactions on the Starr bonds for 2020 in Cana's records. Round all amounts to the nearest dollar.

⑤
Recording and reporting bond investments
Dec. 31 accrued revenue, $667

S16–16 Shyster Originals Corp. purchased US$10,000 of American maple syrup to sell in Canada. At the time of the June 2 purchase, the exchange rate was 1.3504. When the payment was made on July 28, the exchange rate was 1.2447. Journalize both transactions.

⑥
Accounting for purchase transactions stated in a foreign currency
Gain, $1,057

S16–17 Suppose Fleetstar Ltd. sells athletic shoes to a German company on March 14. Fleetstar agrees to accept 2,000,000 euros. On the date of sale, the euro is quoted at $1.56. Fleetstar collects half the receivable on April 19, when the euro is worth $1.55. Then, on May 10, when the price of the euro is $1.58, Fleetstar collects the final amount.

⑥
Accounting for sales transactions stated in a foreign currency
Net foreign-currency gain, $10,000

a. Journalize these three transactions for Fleetstar; include an explanation.

b. Overall, did Fleetstar have a net foreign-currency gain or loss?

S16–18 Fill in the blanks to indicate how investments are reported under IFRS:

⑦
IFRS reporting of investments

a. Financial instruments are measured at _____.

b. Significant influence is a rebuttable assumption. It is presumed if an investor holds (directly or indirectly) _____ or more of the votes.

c. Minority interest is shown on the balance sheet _____ but separate from the parent's _____.

d. Short-term investments in bonds are measured and reported at _____.

e. Long-term investments in bonds are amortized using the _____.

EXERCISES

①
Accounting for a short-term investment

June 14, 2021, gain on sale, $3,900

E16–1 Journalize the following investment transactions of Russell Corp.:

2020

Nov. 6   Purchased 1,200 common shares of Aveda Corporation at $78.00 per share, with brokerage commission of $500. The shares will be sold early in 2021.

30   Received a cash dividend of $3.85 per share on the Aveda Corporation investment.

Dec. 31   The share price for Aveda Corporation's common shares was $76.25 on December 31, 2020, which is Russell Corp.'s year-end.

2021

Jun. 14   Sold the Aveda Corporation shares for $79.50 per share. Brokerage commissions were $400.

①
Reporting investments at fair value

E16–2 Shopify Inc. reported the following (adapted) information in its 2016 balance sheet:

Current assets	(in thousands of US dollars)
Cash and cash equivalents	$ 84,013
Marketable securities	308,401

Assume that the carrying value (and cost) of Shopify's short-term investments is $303,901,000 prior to the year-end adjustment to fair value.

Required

1. Write a brief note to identify the method used to report short-term investments and to disclose cost and fair value.

2. Show the journal entry that would have been made by Shopify if you determine that a journal entry was needed at year-end.

①
Accounting for a short-term investment

Jan. 20, 2021, gain on sale, $2,000

E16–3 Suppose Ryerson Corp. completed the following investment transactions in 2020 and 2021:

2020

Nov. 6   Purchased 2,000 McGill Corporation common shares for $60,000. Ryerson plans to sell the shares in the near future to meet its operating cash flow requirements. Brokerage commissions on the purchase were $800.

30   Received a quarterly cash dividend of $1.50 per share on the McGill Corporation shares.

Dec. 31   Current fair value of the McGill common shares is $62,000. This is year-end for Ryerson Corp.

2021

Jan. 20   Sold the McGill Corporation shares for $64,000, less brokerage commissions on the sale of $900.

Required

1. Make the entries to record Ryerson Corp.'s investment transactions. Explanations are not required.

2. Show how Ryerson Corp. would report its investment in the McGill Corporation shares on the balance sheet at December 31, 2020.

①②
Classifying equity investments

E16–4 Cummins Corp. reports its annual financial results on June 30 each year. Cummins Corp. purchased 1,000 shares in each of three companies. Classify each investment as a short-term or long-term investment.

a. Investment to be sold within the next 9 to 12 months.

b. Investment to be sold within the next 90 days.

c. Investment to be sold within the next two years.

E16–5 Journalize the following investment transactions of Vantage Inc.:

Aug. 6 Purchased 900 Rhodes Corporation common shares as a long-term investment, paying $90.00 per share. Vantage Inc. exerts no significant influence on Rhodes Corporation. Brokerage commissions on the purchase were $900.

Sep. 12 Received cash dividends of $1.60 per share on the Rhodes Corporation investment.

Nov. 23 Received 90 Rhodes Corporation common shares in a 10 percent stock dividend.

Dec. 4 Unexpectedly sold all the Rhodes Corporation shares for $88.00 per share, less brokerage commissions on the sale of $750.

② Journalizing transactions for a long-term investment
Dec. 4, gain on sale, $6,120

E16–6 Kinross Gold Corp. paid $12,000,000 to acquire a 40 percent investment in Minecraft Ltd. Further, assume Minecraft Ltd. reported net income of $1,780,000 for the first year and declared and paid cash dividends of $650,000. Record the following entries in Kinross's general journal:

Jan. 2 Purchase of the investment. Disregard brokerage commissions on the purchase.

Dec. 31 Kinross's proportion of Minecraft Ltd.'s net income.

Dec. 31 Receipt of the cash dividends.

③ Journalizing transactions under the equity method

E16–7 Using the information from E16–6, calculate the balance in the Investment in Minecraft Ltd. Common Shares account. Assume that after all the above transactions took place, Kinross Gold Corp. sold its entire investment in Minecraft Ltd. common shares for $13,200,000 cash. Journalize the sale of the investment on December 31. Disregard brokerage commissions on sale.

③ Recording equity method transactions in the accounts
Gain on sale, $748,000

E16–8 Markle Inc. paid $760,000 for a 35 percent investment in the common shares of Harry Systems Inc. For the first year, Harry Systems Inc. reported net income of $360,000 and at year-end declared and paid cash dividends of $105,000. On the balance sheet date, the fair value of Markle Inc.'s investment in Harry Systems Inc. shares was $780,000.

②③ Applying the appropriate accounting method for investments
2. Year-end carrying value $849,250

Required

1. Which method is appropriate for Markle Inc. to use in accounting for its investment in Harry Systems Inc.? Why?

2. Show everything that Markle Inc. would report for the investment and any investment revenue in its year-end financial statements.

3. What role does the fair value of the investment play in this situation?

④ Completing a consolidation worksheet with 100 percent ownership
Total consolidated assets, $7,932,000

E16–9 Penfold Ltd. owns all the common shares of Simmons Ltd. Prepare a consolidation worksheet using the following information. Assume that the fair value of the assets and liabilities of Simmons Ltd. are equal to their book values.

	Penfold Ltd.	Simmons Ltd.	Eliminations Debit	Eliminations Credit	Consolidated Amounts
Assets					
Cash	225,000	55,000			
Accounts receivable, net	360,000	264,000			
Note receivable from Simmons Ltd	76,000	—			
Inventory	258,000	159,000			
Investment in Simmons Ltd	2,350,000	—			
Property, plant, and equipment, net	3,590,000	2,900,000			
Total assets	6,859,000	3,378,000			
Liabilities and Shareholders' Equity					
Accounts payable	357,000	180,000			
Notes payable	462,000	759,000			
Other liabilities	78,000	210,000			
Common shares	1,980,000	670,000			
Retained earnings	3,982,000	1,559,000			
Total liabilities and shareholders' equity	6,859,000	3,378,000			

E16–10 Peanut Holdings Ltd. owns an 80 percent interest in Snoop Inc. Prepare a consolidation worksheet using the information below. Assume that the fair values of Snoop Inc.'s assets and liabilities are equal to their book values.

	Peanut Holdings Ltd.	Snoop Inc.	Eliminations Debit	Eliminations Credit	Consolidated Amounts
Assets					
Cash	96,000	36,000			
Accounts receivable, net	210,000	144,000			
Note receivable from Snoop Inc.	60,000	—			
Inventory	246,000	216,000			
Investment in Snoop Inc.	228,000	—			
Property, plant, and equipment, net	720,000	312,000			
Other assets	48,000	42,000			
Total assets	1,608,000	750,000			
Liabilities and Shareholders' Equity					
Accounts payable	108,000	66,000			
Notes payable	120,000	96,000			
Other liabilities	204,000	324,000			
Non-controlling interest	—	—			
Common shares	780,000	204,000			
Retained earnings	396,000	60,000			
Total liabilities and shareholders' equity	1,608,000	750,000			

E16–11 G Holdings Ltd. has a large investment in corporate bonds. Suppose G Holdings Ltd. buys $6,000,000 of CN Railway bonds at a price of 98. The CN Railway bonds pay cash interest at the annual rate of 2.5 percent and mature in 10 years. G Holdings Ltd. plans to hold the bonds until maturity.

Required

1. How much did G Holdings Ltd. pay to purchase the bond investment? How much will G Holdings Ltd. collect when the bond investment matures?
2. How much cash interest will G Holdings Ltd. receive each year from CN Railway?
3. Will G Holdings Ltd.'s annual interest revenue on the bond investment be more or less than the amount of cash interest received each year? Give your reason.
4. Compute G Holdings Ltd.'s annual interest on this bond investment. Use the straight-line method to amortize the discount on the investment.

E16–12 On March 31, 2020, Kingpin Corp. paid 98.25 for 4 percent bonds of Claim Limited as an investment. The maturity value of the bonds is $100,000 at September 30, 2024; they pay interest on March 31 and September 30. At December 31, 2020, the bonds' market value is 99.25. The company plans to hold the bonds until they mature.

Required

1. How should Kingpin Corp. account for the bonds?
2. Using the straight-line method of amortizing the discount, journalize all transactions on the bonds for 2020.
3. Show how the investment would be reported by Kingpin Corp. on the balance sheet at December 31, 2020.

E16–13 On May 1, 2020, Auto Corp. purchased a five-year, 4.5 percent bond. It intends to hold the bond until it matures. The market rate on the purchase date was 5.2 percent. Interest is paid annually each April 30. Information about the bond appears in the table below. Journalize the purchase and the April 30, 2021, entries.

⑤
Recording bond investment transactions using the effective-interest method

	A	B	C	D	E	F
1	Annual Interest Period	Interest Received 4.50%	Period Interest Revenue	Discount Amort.	Unamortized Discount Balance	Bond Carrying Value
2	May 1, 2020				$30,100	$ 969,900
3	April 30, 2021	$ 45,000	$ 50,435	$ 5,435	24,665	975,335
4	April 30, 2022	45,000	50,717	5,717	18,948	981,052
5	April 30, 2023	45,000	51,015	6,015	12,933	987,067
6	April 30, 2024	45,000	51,327	6,327	6,606	993,394
7	April 30, 2025	45,000	51,606	6,606	0	1,000,000
8	Total	$225,000	$255,100	$30,100		

E16–14 Suppose Zed Ltd. sells lumber to a British company on May 16. Zed agrees to accept 80,000 British pounds sterling. On the date of sale, the pound is quoted at $1.7831. Zed collects half the receivable on June 19, when the pound is worth $1.7614. Then, on July 16, when the price of the pound is $1.7792, Zed collects the final amount.

⑥
Calculating foreign-currency gain/loss

2. Loss of $1,024

Required

1. Journalize these three transactions for Zed; include an explanation. Round final amounts to the nearest whole dollar.
2. Overall, did Zed have a net foreign-currency gain or loss?

E16–15 Journalize the following foreign-currency transactions for Queensway Import Inc.:

⑥
Journalizing foreign-currency transactions

Jan. 14, 2021 gain $3,200

2020

Nov. 17   Purchased goods on account from a Japanese company. The price was 500,000¥, and the exchange rate of the yen was $0.0117. Assume Queensway uses the perpetual method of inventory so purchases are reported directly in the Inventory account.

Dec. 16   Paid the Japanese supplier when the exchange rate was $0.0120.

     19   Sold merchandise on account to a French company at a price of €80,000. The exchange rate for euros was $1.57 (ignore the inventory and cost of goods sold here).

     31   Adjusted for the decrease in the value of the euro, which had an exchange rate of $1.54. Kingsway Import Inc.'s year-end is December 31.

2021

Jan. 14   Collected from the French company. The exchange rate was $1.58.

E16–16 Indicate the appropriate financial reporting standard by completing each sentence with either "ASPE" or "IFRS" in the blank.

①②③⑤⑦
Differences between ASPE and IFRS

a. Gains and losses may be recorded under "other comprehensive income" under _____.

b. Equity investments with no significant influence can only be recorded at cost under _____.

c. Equity investments with over 20 percent ownership must be treated as having significant influence unless proven otherwise under _____.

d. When there is significant influence, impairment loss reversals are permitted under _____, and it is possible to increase the asset value above its cost.

e. For long-term investments in bonds, the straight-line amortization method is not allowed under _____.

SERIAL EXERCISE

② ③ ④ ⑤

Accounting for short-term investments, long-term investments with significant influence, and for investments in bonds

Dec. 31: 2. Adobe $1,040

E16–17 *The Serial Exercise involves a company that will be revisited throughout relevant chapters in Volume 1 and Volume 2. You can complete the Serial Exercises using MyLab Accounting.*

This exercise continues recordkeeping for the Canyon Canoe Company from Chapter 15. Students do not need to have completed prior exercises in order to answer this exercise.

Amber Wilson is pleased with the growth of the business and has decided to invest its temporary excess cash in a brokerage account. The company had the following securities transactions in 2024.

Jul.	1	Purchased 8,000 shares in Adobe Outdoor Adventure Company for $3 per share. Canyon Canoe Company does not have significant influence over Adobe. Canyon plans to hold these shares for longer than a year and should record them in an account called Long-Term Investments.
	7	Purchased 35 percent of the shares of Bison Backpacks Inc. consisting of 43,750 shares (out of a total of 125,000 shares) for $5 per share. Canyon Canoe Company has significant influence over Bison.
	10	Purchased a bond at par from Camelot Canoes with a face value of $80,000. Canyon Canoe intends to hold the bond to maturity. The bond pays interest semi-annually on June 30 and December 31. Ignore the 10 days of accrued interest.
Sep.	30	Received dividends of $0.15 per share from Adobe.
Nov.	1	Received dividends of $0.30 per share from Bison.
Dec.	31	Received an interest payment of $3,200 from Camelot Canoes.
	31	Bison Backpacks reported net income of $30,000 for the year.
	31	Adjusted the Adobe shares for a market value of $2.98 per share.

Required

1. Journalize the transactions including any entries, if required, at December 31, 2024.

2. Determine the effect on Canyon Canoe Company's net income for the year for each of the three investments.

CHALLENGE EXERCISES

③

Analyzing long-term investments

2020 dividends, $840

E16–18 Kagit Inc. is a paper products company based just outside of Vancouver. Suppose Kagit's financial statements reported the following items for affiliated companies whose shares Kagit owns in various percentages between 20 and 50 percent:

	(In thousands of dollars)	
	2020	**2019**
Balance Sheet (adapted)		
Equity method investments	$6,950	$6,800
Cash Flow Statement		
Increase in equity method investments	350	330
Income Statement		
Equity earnings in affiliates	640	510

Assume there were no sales of equity method investments during 2019 or 2020.

Required Prepare a T-Account for Equity Method Investments to determine the amount of dividends Kagit Inc. received from investee companies during 2020. The company's year-end is December 31. Show your calculations.

BEYOND THE NUMBERS

BN16–1

4

Analyzing long-term investments

Sophie Bu inherited some investments, and she has received the annual reports of the companies in which the funds are invested. The financial statements of the companies are puzzling to Sophie, and she asks you the following questions:

1. The companies label their financial statements as *consolidated* balance sheet, *consolidated* income statement, and so on. What are consolidated financial statements?

2. Notes to the statements indicate that "certain intercompany transactions, loans, and other accounts have been eliminated in preparing the consolidated financial statements." Why does a company eliminate transactions, loans, and accounts? Sophie states that she thought a transaction was a transaction and that a loan obligated a company to pay real money. She wonders if the company is juggling the books to defraud the Canada Revenue Agency.

3. The balance sheet lists the asset Goodwill. What is goodwill? Does this mean that the company's shares have increased in value?

Required   Respond to each of Sophie Bu's questions.

ETHICAL ISSUE

EI16–1

Woods Inc. owns 18 percent of the voting shares of Lo Foods Ltd. The remainder of the Lo Foods Ltd. shares are held by numerous investors with small holdings. Susan Shearer, president of Woods Inc. and a member of Lo Foods Ltd.'s board of directors, heavily influences Lo Foods Ltd.'s policies.

Under the fair value method of accounting for investments, Woods Inc.'s net income increases when it receives dividends from Lo Foods Ltd. Woods Inc. pays Ms. Shearer, as president, a bonus computed as a percentage of Woods Inc.'s net income. Therefore, Shearer can control her personal bonus to a certain extent by influencing Lo Foods Ltd.'s dividends.

Woods Inc. has a bad year in 2020, and corporate income is low. Shearer uses her power to have Lo Foods Ltd. pay a large cash dividend. This action requires Lo Foods Ltd. to borrow a substantial sum one month later to pay operating costs.

Required

1. In getting Lo Foods Ltd. to pay the large cash dividend, is Shearer acting within her authority as a member of the Lo Foods Ltd. board of directors? Are Shearer's actions ethical? Whom can her actions harm?

2. Discuss how using the equity method of accounting for investments would decrease Shearer's potential for manipulating her bonus.

PROBLEMS (GROUP A)

P16–1A Oliver Corp. owns numerous investments in the shares of other companies. Assume Oliver Corp. completed the following investment transactions:

1 2 3

Journalizing transactions under the fair value and equity methods

Dec. 31 Loss, $2,000

2020

Jan.	1	Purchased 12,000 common shares (total issued and outstanding common shares, 50,000) of Canadian Parts Corp. at a cost of $950,000. Brokerage commissions on the purchase were $20,000.
Jan.	2	Purchased an additional 2,000 Canadian Parts Corp. common shares at a cost of $162,000. Brokerage commissions on the purchase were $1,500.
Sep.	15	Received semi-annual cash dividend of $3.20 per share on the Canadian Parts Corp. investment.
Oct.	12	Purchased 1,000 Sharma Ltd. common shares as a short-term investment, paying $33.00 per share plus brokerage commission of $1,000.
Dec.	14	Received semi-annual cash dividend of $1.50 per share on the Sharma Ltd. investment.
	31	Received annual report from Canadian Parts Corp. Net income for the year was $800,000. Of this amount, Oliver Corp.'s proportion is 28 percent. The current market value for 1,000 Sharma Ltd. shares is $31,000.

2021

Feb.	6	Sold 2,000 Canadian Parts Corp. shares for cash of $168,500, less brokerage commissions of $1,550.

Required Record the transactions in the general journal of Oliver Corp.; the company's year-end is December 31.

① ② ③

Applying the fair value method and the equity method

2. Dec. 31 balance, $3,405,000

P16–2A The balance sheet of Northern Developments Corp. at the start of the year included these balances:

Short-term investments	$ 250,000
Investments in significantly influenced and other companies	2,500,000

Assume the company completed the following investment transactions during 2020:

Mar.	3	Purchased 8,000 common shares as a short-term investment, paying $25.00 per share plus brokerage commission of $500.
	4	Purchased additional shares in a company that is significantly influenced by Northern Developments Corp. at a cost of $600,000 plus brokerage commission of $4,500.
May	14	Received semi-annual cash dividend of $1.70 per share on the short-term investment purchased March 3.
Jun.	15	Received cash dividend of $55,000 from a significantly influenced company.
Aug.	28	Sold the short-term investment (purchased on March 3) for $24.00 per share, less brokerage commission of $500.
Oct.	24	Purchased other short-term investments for $275,000, plus brokerage commission of $400.
Dec.	15	Received cash dividend of $30,000 from a significantly influenced company.
	31	Received annual reports from significantly influenced companies. Their total net income for the year was $1,300,000. Of this amount, Northern Developments Corp.'s proportion is 30 percent.

Required

1. Record the transactions in the general journal of Northern Developments Corp.

2. Post entries to the Investments in Significantly Influenced and Other Companies T-account, and determine its balance at December 31, 2020.

3. Post entries to the Short-Term Investments T-account and determine its balance at December 31, 2020.

4. Assuming the market value of the short-term investment portfolio is $510,000 at December 31, 2020, show how Northern Developments Corp. would report short-term investments and investments in significantly influenced and other companies on the December 31, 2020, balance sheet. Use the following format:

Current assets	
Cash	$XXX
Short-term investments, at fair value	[ ]
Accounts receivable (net)	XXX
⌇	⌇
Total current assets	XXX
Investments in significantly influenced and other companies	[ ]

① ② ③

Compare accounting methods as share ownership percentage varies

Option 1 year-end balance in the investments account, $108,000

P16–3A Niall Holdings is deciding on how to account for their potential investment in BF Ltd. The accounting for equity investments changes with the amount of shares held. Niall Holdings knows that BF Ltd. has a total of 30,000 shares outstanding. Managers at Niall Holdings need a brief comparison of the two options they are considering to show how they should record the transaction and balances if Niall owns different amounts of BF Ltd. shares as a long-term investment.

Answer the following questions for each option:

	Option 1: purchase 3,600 shares	Option 2: purchase 11,400 shares
Which accounting method should be used for this long-term investment?		
Journal entry to record purchase of shares at $27 each. Ignore brokerage commissions.		
Journal entry to recognize share of $25,000 in dividends declared and paid.		
Journal entry to recognize $50,000 in net income declared by BF Ltd.		
Journal entry to recognize the year-end market value of $30 per share.		
What is the balance in the Investments account at year-end?		

P16–4A Pluto Corp. paid $750,000 to acquire all the common shares of Saturn Inc., and Saturn Inc. owes Pluto Corp. $170,000 on a note payable. The fair market value of Saturn Inc.'s net assets equalled the book value. Immediately after the purchase on May 31, 2020, the two companies' balance sheets were as follows:

④
Preparing a consolidated balance sheet; goodwill; no non-controlling interest

Total consolidated assets, $2,420,000

	Pluto Corp.	Saturn Inc.	Eliminations Debit	Eliminations Credit	Consolidated Amounts
Assets					
Cash	60,000	100,000			
Accounts receivable, net	210,000	150,000			
Note receivable from Saturn Inc.	170,000	—			
Inventory	300,000	440,000			
Investment in Saturn Inc.	750,000	—			
Property, plant, and equipment, net	600,000	500,000			
Total assets	2,090,000	1,190,000			
Liabilities and Shareholders' Equity					
Accounts payable	250,000	40,000			
Notes payable	400,000	210,000			
Note payable to Pluto Corp.	—	170,000			
Other liabilities	156,000	80,000			
Common shares	800,000	500,000			
Retained earnings	484,000	190,000			
Total liabilities and shareholders' equity	2,090,000	1,190,000			

Required Prepare the consolidation worksheet.

P16–5A On July 18, 2020, Patrone Holdings Ltd. paid $1,920,000 to purchase 90 percent of the common shares of Smirnoff Inc., and Smirnoff Inc. owes Patrone Holdings Ltd. $240,000 on a note payable. All historical cost amounts are equal to their fair market value on July 18, 2020. Immediately after the purchase, the two companies' balance sheets were as follows:

④
Preparing a consolidated balance sheet with goodwill and non-controlling interest

Total consolidated assets, $8,299,600

	Patrone Holdings Ltd.	Smirnoff Inc.	Eliminations		Consolidated Amounts
			Debit	Credit	
Assets					
Cash	200,000	340,000			
Accounts receivable, net	720,000	480,000			
Note receivable from Smirnoff Inc.	240,000	—			
Inventory	1,480,000	920,000			
Investment in Smirnoff Inc.	1,920,000	—			
Property, plant, and equipment, net	2,190,000	1,540,000			
Goodwill	—	—			
Total assets	6,750,000	3,280,000			
Liabilities and Shareholders' Equity					
Accounts payable	1,060,000	680,000			
Notes payable	1,680,000	320,000			
Note payable to Patrone Holdings Ltd.	—	240,000			
Other liabilities	260,000	384,000			
Common shares	1,540,000	1,060,000			
Retained earnings	2,210,000	596,000			
Total liabilities and shareholders' equity	6,750,000	3,280,000			

Required Prepare the consolidation worksheet.

⑤

Accounting for a long-term bond investment purchased at a premium, using straight line amortization

2. Carrying value, $1,019,500

P16–6A Financial institutions such as insurance companies and pension plans hold large quantities of bond investments. Suppose Sun Life Insurance Company purchases $1,000,000 of 3.00 percent bonds of Hydro-Québec at 102.00 on July 1, 2020. These bonds pay interest on January 1 and July 1 each year. They mature on July 1, 2040. At December 31, 2020, the market price of the bonds is 101.00. Sun Life plans to hold these bonds to maturity.

Required

1. Journalize Sun Life's purchase of the bonds as a long-term investment in bonds on July 1, 2020. Disregard brokerage commissions.
2. Journalize the accrual of interest revenue and amortization of the premium for six months at December 31, 2020. Assume the straight-line method is appropriate for amortizing the premium.
3. Calculate the carrying value of the Hydro-Québec bonds at December 31, 2020.

⑤

Computing the cost of a bond investment and journalizing its transactions using the effective-interest method of amortizing a discount

Dec. 31, 2021, total interest revenue, $19,496

P16–7A On December 31, 2020, when the market interest rate is 6 percent, an investor purchases $700,000 of Solar Ltd. 10-year, 5 percent bonds at issuance for $647,929. Interest is paid semi-annually. Assume that the investor plans to hold the investment to maturity.

Required

1. Prepare a schedule for amortizing the discount on the bond investment through December 31, 2021. The investor uses the effective-interest amortization method. Use Try It! 6 on page 910 as a guide to create the schedule.
2. Journalize the purchase on December 31, 2020, the first semi-annual interest receipt on June 30, 2021, and the year-end interest receipt on December 31, 2021.

①⑤

Accounting for short-term investments using the fair value method and long-term investments in bonds

Dec. 31, 2020, fair value valuation allowance, $107,727

P16–8A Sparta Investments Ltd. had the following short-term investments in marketable securities at fair value at December 31, 2019:

Alberta Energy Co.	$310,000
Finning Ltd.	180,000
Canadian National Railway	285,000
Total short-term investments	$775,000

Sparta Investments Ltd. had the following investment transactions during 2020:

Jan. 5   Purchased 5,000 shares (2 percent) of HHN Ltd. as a short-term investment. The shares were purchased at $51.00 and the brokerage commission was $500.

     31   HHN Ltd. reported net income of $7,000,000 and declared a cash dividend of $2,100,000.

Feb. 15   Received $42,000 from HHN Ltd. as a cash dividend.

Apr. 1   Purchased $400,000 (face value) of bonds at 99 as a long-term investment. The bonds pay 5 percent interest (2.5 percent semi-annually) on October 1 and April 1. Sparta Investments Ltd. plans to hold the bonds until maturity in two years. The company uses the straight-line method to amortize the discount.

Aug. 31   Received a 10 percent stock dividend from HHN Ltd.

Oct. 1   Received the interest on the bonds.

Nov. 1   HHN Ltd. declared and distributed a 2-for-1 stock split.

Dec. 15   Sold 4,000 shares of HHN Ltd. for $28.00 per share. The brokerage commission was $1,500.

     31   Recorded the adjustment for accrued interest on the bonds.

     31   The fair values of the investments were as follows:

Alberta Energy Co.	$ 280,000
Finning Ltd.	187,000
Canadian National Railway	290,000
HHN Ltd	288,000
Total short-term investments	$1,045,000

Required Prepare the general journal entries required to record the transactions of 2020.

P16–9A Freedom Electronics Inc. completed the following transactions:

2020

Dec. 1   Sold machinery on account to a Japanese company for $45,000. The exchange rate of the Japanese yen is $0.0113, and the Japanese company agrees to pay in Canadian dollars.

     10   Purchased supplies on account from a US company at a price of US$125,000. The exchange rate of the US dollar is $1.06, and payment will be in US dollars.

     17   Sold machinery on account to an English firm for 220,000 British pounds. Payment will be in pounds, and the exchange rate of the pound is $1.61.

     22   Collected from the Japanese company. The exchange rate of the yen has not changed since December 1.

     31   Adjusted the accounts for changes in foreign-currency exchange rates. Current rates: US dollar, $1.10; British pound, $1.59.

2021

Jan. 18   Paid the US company. The exchange rate of the US dollar is $1.08.

     24   Collected from the English firm. The exchange rate of the British pound is $1.63.

Required

1. Record these transactions in Freedom Electronics' general journal, and show how to report the transaction gain or loss on the income statement for the fiscal year ended December 31, 2020. For simplicity, use Sales Revenue as the credit.

2. How will what you have learned in this problem help you structure international transactions?

⑥
Journalizing foreign-currency transactions and reporting the transaction gain or loss

1. Foreign-currency transaction loss at Dec. 31, 2020, $9,400

PROBLEMS (GROUP B)

① ② ③

Journalizing transactions
under the fair value and
equity methods

P16–1B Beauchesne Insurance Ltd. owns numerous investments in the shares of other companies. Assume Beauchesne Insurance Ltd. completed the following investment transactions:

2020

Jan.	1	Purchased 30,000 (total issued and outstanding common shares, 120,000) common shares of Earl Mfg. Ltd. at a cost of $2,550,000. Brokerage commissions on the purchase were $15,000.
Jan.	2	Purchased 6,000 additional Earl Mfg. Ltd. common shares at a cost of $88.00 per share. Brokerage commissions on the purchase were $400.
Aug.	9	Received the annual cash dividend of $2.00 per share on the Earl Mfg. Ltd. investment.
Oct.	16	Purchased 2,000 Excellence Ltd. common shares as a short-term investment, paying $63.00 per share plus brokerage commission of $500.
Nov.	30	Received the semi-annual cash dividend of $2.50 per share on the Excellence Ltd. investment.
Dec.	31	Received the annual report from Earl Mfg. Ltd. Net income for the year was $1,160,000. Of this amount, Beauchesne Insurance Ltd.'s proportion is 30 percent.
	31	The current market value of the Excellence Ltd. shares is $140,000.

2021

Jan.	14	Sold 5,000 Earl Mfg. Ltd. shares for $460,000, less brokerage commissions of $800.

Required Record the transactions in the general journal of Beauchesne Insurance Ltd. The company's year-end is December 31.

① ② ③

Applying the fair value method
and the equity method

P16–2B FT Corporation reported the following amounts on its balance sheet at the start of the year:

Short-term investments	$ 104,000
Investments—Associated Companies at Equity	15,000,000

Assume that FT Corporation completed the following investment transactions during 2020:

Mar.	2	Purchased 2,000 common shares as a short-term investment, paying $38.00 per share plus brokerage commission of $900.
	5	Purchased additional shares in an associated company at a cost of $1,600,000. Brokerage commissions on the purchase were $30,000.
Jul.	21	Received the semi-annual cash dividend of $1.50 per share on the short-term investment purchased March 2.
Aug.	17	Received a cash dividend of $160,000 from an associated company.
Oct.	16	Sold 1,100 shares of the short-term investment (purchased on March 2) for $36.00 per share, less brokerage commission of $600.
Nov.	8	Purchased short-term investments for $310,000, plus brokerage commission of $5,000.
	17	Received a cash dividend of $280,000 from an associated company.
Dec.	31	Received annual reports from associated companies. Their total net income for the year was $6,900,000. Of this amount, FT's proportion is 24 percent.

Required

1. Record the transactions in the general journal of FT Corporation.
2. Post entries to the Equity Investments T-account and determine its balance at December 31, 2020.
3. Post entries to the Short-Term Investments T-account and determine its balance at December 31, 2020.

4. Assuming the market value of the short-term investment portfolio is $425,000 at December 31, 2020, show how FT Corporation would report short-term investments and investments in associated companies on the ending balance sheet. (No journal entry is required.) Use the following format:

Current assets	
Cash	$XXX
Short-term investments, at fair value	☐
Accounts receivable (net)	XXX
∼	∼
Total current assets	XXX
Investments—Associated companies at equity	☐

P16–3B Soochow Corp. has a new accounting co-op student who heard that the accounting for equity investments changes with the amount of shares held. The student needs to know the accounting differences between two different scenarios and how Soochow Corp. should record the transaction and balances if it owns different amounts of Hughes Ltd. shares as a long-term investment. Hughes Ltd. has a total of 35,000 shares outstanding.

①②③
Compare accounting methods as share ownership percentage varies

Answer the following questions for each option:

	Option 1: 3,800 shares	Option 2: 11,900 shares
Which accounting method should be used for this long-term investment?		
Journal entry to record purchase of shares at $35 each. Ignore brokerage commissions.		
Journal entry to recognize share of $40,000 in dividends declared and paid.		
Journal entry to recognize $75,000 in net income declared by Hughes Ltd.		
Journal entry to recognize the year-end market value of $34 per share.		
What is the balance in the investments account at year-end?		

P16–4B Pisa Inc. paid $1,040,000 to acquire all the common shares of Sienna Ltd., and Sienna Ltd. owes Pisa Inc. $120,000 on a note payable. The fair market value of Sienna's net assets equalled the book value. Immediately after the purchase on June 30, 2020, the two companies' balance sheets were as shown below:

④
Preparing a consolidated balance sheet; goodwill, no non-controlling interest

	Pisa Inc.	Sienna Ltd.	Eliminations Debit	Eliminations Credit	Consolidated Amounts
Assets					
Cash	80,000	72,000			
Accounts receivable, net	288,000	144,000			
Note receivable from Sienna Ltd.	120,000	—			
Inventory	480,000	388,000			
Investment in Sienna Ltd.	1,040,000	—			
Property, plant, and equipment, net	608,000	720,000			
Total assets	2,616,000	1,324,000			
Liabilities and Shareholders' Equity					
Accounts payable	192,000	128,000			
Notes payable	588,000	224,000			
Note payable to Pisa Inc.	—	120,000			
Other liabilities	204,000	12,000			
Common shares	880,000	440,000			
Retained earnings	752,000	400,000			
Total liabilities and shareholders' equity	2,616,000	1,324,000			

Required Prepare the consolidation worksheet.

④

Preparing a consolidated balance sheet; goodwill with non-controlling interest

P16–5B On March 22, 2020, Pink Corp. paid $1,575,000 to purchase 70 percent of the common shares of Salmon Inc., and Pink Corp. owes Salmon Inc. $400,000 on a note payable. The fair market value of Salmon Inc.'s net assets equalled the book value. Immediately after the purchase, the two companies' balance sheets were as follows:

	Pink Corp.	Salmon Inc.	Eliminations Debits	Eliminations Credits	Consolidated Amounts
Assets					
Cash	570,000	150,000			
Accounts receivable, net	540,000	440,000			
Note receivable from Pink Corp.	—	400,000			
Inventory	750,000	540,000			
Investment in Salmon Inc.	1,575,000	—			
Property, plant, and equipment, net	1,797,000	1,520,000			
Total assets	5,232,000	3,050,000			
Liabilities and Shareholders' Equity					
Accounts payable	480,000	420,000			
Notes payable	1,077,000	270,000			
Note payable to Salmon Inc.	400,000	—			
Other liabilities	155,000	230,000			
Non-controlling interest	—	—			
Common shares	1,170,000	540,000			
Retained earnings	1,950,000	1,590,000			
Total liabilities and shareholders' equity	5,232,000	3,050,000			

Required Prepare the consolidation worksheet.

P16-6B Financial institutions such as insurance companies and pension plans hold large quantities of bond investments. Suppose Meridian Credit Union purchases $2,000,000 of 3.0 percent bonds of the Province of Manitoba at 105 on January 1, 2020. These bonds pay interest on January 1 and July 1 each year. They mature on January 1, 2030. Meridian plans to hold the bonds to maturity.

⑤ Accounting for a bond investment purchased at a premium, using straight line amortization

Required

1. Journalize Meridian's purchase of the bonds as a long-term investment on January 1, 2020. Disregard brokerage commissions.

2. Journalize the receipt of cash interest and amortization of premium on July 1, 2020. Assume the straight-line method is appropriate for amortizing the premium as there is no material difference from the effective-interest method

3. Record the accrual of interest revenue and amortization of premium at October 31, 2020, the fiscal year-end.

4. Calculate the book value of Meridian's investment in the Province of Manitoba bonds at October 31, 2020.

P16-7B On December 31, 2020, when the market interest rate is 6 percent, Elle Corporation purchases $5,000,000 of Belmont Products Inc.'s six-year, 5.5 percent bonds at issuance for $4,875,575. Interest is payable semi-annually. Elle Corporation plans to hold these bonds to maturity.

③ Computing the cost of a long-term bond investment and journalizing its transactions using the effective-interest method of amortizing a discount

Required

1. Prepare a schedule for amortizing the discount on the bond investment through December 31, 2021. Elle Corporation uses the effective-interest amortization method. Use Try It! 6 on page 910 as a guide to create the schedule.

2. Journalize the purchase on December 31, 2020, the first semi-annual interest receipt on June 30, 2021, and the year-end interest receipt on December 31, 2021.

P16-8B Portal Holdings Ltd. had the following short-term investments in marketable securities on December 31, 2019, at fair value and book value:

① ⑤ Accounting for short-term investments using the fair value method; investments in bonds

Canadian Utilities Limited	$310,000
TELUS Corporation	425,000
Talisman Energy Ltd.	160,000
Total short-term investments	$895,000

Portal Holdings Ltd. had the following investment transactions during 2020:

Jan.	5	Purchased 5,000 shares (2 percent) of Salmon Ltd. as a short-term investment. The shares were purchased at $50.00 and the brokerage commission was $300.
	31	Salmon Ltd. reported net income of $1,500,000 and declared a cash dividend of $900,000.
Feb.	15	Received $18,000 from Salmon Ltd. as a cash dividend.
Apr.	1	Purchased $300,000 (face value) of bonds at 100 as a long-term investment. The bonds pay 6 percent interest (3 percent semi-annually) on October 1 and April 1 and mature in two years.
Aug.	31	Received a 10 percent stock dividend from Salmon Ltd.
Oct.	1	Received the interest on the bonds.
Nov.	1	Salmon Ltd. declared and distributed a 2-for-1 stock split.
Dec.	15	Sold 3,300 shares (30%) of Salmon Ltd. at $48.00 and the brokerage commission was $200.
	31	Recorded the adjustment for accrued interest on the bonds.
	31	The fair values of the investments were as follows:

Canadian Utilities Limited	$ 290,000
TELUS Corporation	420,000
Salmon Ltd.	270,000
Talisman Energy Ltd.	175,000
Total short-term investments	$1,155,000

Required Prepare the general journal entries required to record the transactions of 2020.

⑥

Journalizing foreign-currency transactions and reporting the transaction gain or loss

P16–9B Suppose Custom Ice Cream Corporation completed the following transactions:

2020

Dec. 4   Sold product on account to a Mexican company for $110,000. The exchange rate of the Mexican peso was $0.078, and the customer agreed to pay in Canadian dollars.

     13   Purchased inventory on account from an American company at a price of US$240,000. The exchange rate of the US dollar was $1.05, and payment will be in US dollars. Assume that Custom uses a perpetual inventory system.

     20   Sold goods on account to an English retailer for £180,000. Payment will be in pounds, and the exchange rate of the pound was $1.66. Ignore the cost of goods sold and inventory entry.

     27   Collected from the Mexican company. The exchange rate of the Mexican peso was $0.075.

     31   Adjusted the accounts for changes in foreign-currency exchange rates in one compound entry. Year-end rates: US dollar, $1.07; British pound, $1.65.

2021

Jan. 21   Paid the American company. The exchange rate of the US dollar was $1.06.

Feb. 17   Collected from the English firm. The exchange rate of the British pound was $1.69.

Required

1. Record these transactions in Custom Ice Cream Corporation's general journal, and show how to report the transaction gain or loss on the income statement for the year ended December 31, 2020. No explanations are required.

2. How will what you have learned in this problem help you structure international transactions?

CHALLENGE PROBLEMS

①②③④

Accounting for ownership of shares in another company

P16–1C The text lists general rules for accounting for long-term investments in the voting shares of another corporation. However, the management of the investing company may decide that, in their judgment, the rules do not apply in a particular situation.

Required

1. Identify a situation where an investing company that owns less than 20 percent might believe that the equity method was appropriate.

2. Identify a situation where an investing company that owns between 20 and 50 percent might believe that the fair value method was appropriate.

3. Identify a situation where an investing company that owns more than 50 percent might believe that the fair value method was appropriate.

⑥

Accounting for foreign operations

P16–2C Canadian exporters are pleased when the Canadian dollar weakens against the US dollar, while the federal and provincial ministers of finance are likely not happy when this happens.

Required Explain why a weakening Canadian dollar makes Canadian exporters happy. Why would a weaker Canadian dollar make the finance ministers unhappy?

Extending Your Knowledge

DECISION PROBLEM

DP16–1

①②③

Understanding the fair value and equity methods of accounting for investments

Margaret Joyce is the owner of Trickle Music Holdings Ltd., a newly formed company whose year-end is December 31. The company made two investments during the first week of January 2020. Both investments are to be held for at least the next five years. Information about each of the investments follows:

a. Trickle Music Holdings Ltd. purchased 30 percent of the common shares of Old Times Ltd. for its book value of $600,000. During the year ended December 31, 2020, Old Times Ltd. earned $240,000 and paid a total dividend of $150,000.

b. Trickle Music Holdings Ltd. purchased 10 percent of the common shares of Mountain Music Inc. for its book value of $150,000. During the year ended December 31, 2020, Mountain Music Inc. paid Trickle Music Holdings Ltd. a dividend of $10,000. Mountain Music Inc. earned a profit of $225,000 for that period. The market value of Trickle Music Holdings Ltd.'s investment in Mountain Music Inc. was $204,000 at December 31, 2020.

   Joyce has come to you as her auditor to ask you how to account for the investments. Trickle Music Holdings Ltd. has never had such investments before. You attempt to explain the proper accounting to her by indicating that different accounting methods apply to different situations.

Required   Help Joyce understand by:

1. Describing the methods of accounting applicable to investments such as these.
2. Identifying which method should be used to account for the investments in Old Times Ltd. and Mountain Music Inc.

FINANCIAL STATEMENT CASES

FSC16–1

③④⑥⑦

Investments and foreign-currency transactions

Indigo Books & Music Inc.'s (Indigo's) financial statements appear in Appendix A at the end of this book and on MyLab Accounting.

Required

1. The financial statements are labelled "consolidated." What evidence can you find in the financial statements that reveals how Indigo accounts for its subsidiaries?
2. What business(es) is(are) included in the consolidated statements?
3. Does Indigo have any foreign-currency transactions? How do you know?
4. How much was the gain or loss on foreign-currency transactions in 2017?

FSC16–2

④⑥

Investments and foreign-currency transactions

The TELUS Corporation December 31, 2016, financial statements appear on MyLab Accounting. Access them to answer the following questions.

Required

1. What information can you find about TELUS Corporation's accounting policies on foreign-currency transactions in the Notes to the statements?
2. Using Note 1, identify two consolidated subsidiaries of TELUS Corporation as of December 31, 2016.

COMPREHENSIVE PROBLEM FOR PART 3

Comprehensive cases are available in MyLab, Chapter Resources.

4. Accounting for Corporate Transactions

1. a. $18.70 per share ($18,700 ÷ 1,000 shares; the brokerage commission is expensed, not included in the price per share)

   b. $9.35 per share ($18,700 ÷ 2,000 shares)

   c. $8.00 per share ($16,000 ÷ 2,000 shares)

   d. $10.00 per share ($20,000 ÷ 2,000 shares; the brokerage commission is expensed, not included in the price per share)

2.

2019			
Sep. 30	Short-Term Investments	43,200	
	Brokerage Commission Expense	125	
	Cash		43,325
	Purchased 1,200 common shares of Betam Ltd. at $36.00 per share (1,200 × $36.00 = $43,200) plus commission.		

Dec. 21	Cash	108	
	Dividend Revenue		108
	Received $0.09 per share cash dividend (1,200 × $0.09) on Betam Ltd. common shares.		

Dec. 31	Unrealized Loss on Fair Value Adjustment	3,000	
	Fair Value Valuation Allowance		3,000
	Adjusted Betam Ltd. investment to fair value [1,200 × ($36.00 − $33.50)].		

2020			
Apr. 13	Cash	37,080	
	Loss on Sale of Investment	3,000	
	Fair Value Valuation Allowance	3,000	
	Brokerage Commission Expense	120	
	Short-Term Investments		43,200
	Sold all the Betam Ltd. common shares held for $31.00 per share. Carrying value of the common shares sold was $40,200 ($43,200 − $3,000). Loss on sale was $3,000 (1,200 × $31.00 − $40,200).		

3.

2019			
Oct. 16	Long-Term Investments	450,000	
	Brokerage Commission Expense	425	
	Cash		450,425
	Purchased 10,000 common shares of Levell Inc. at $45.00 per share (10,000 × $45.00 = $450,000) plus commission of $425.		

Dec. 1	Cash	20,000	
	Dividend Revenue		20,000
	Received $2.00 per share cash dividend (10,000 × $2.00) on Levell Inc. common shares.		

Dec. 31	Fair Value Valuation Allowance	10,000	
	Unrealized Gain on Fair Value Adjustment		10,000
	Adjusted Levell Inc. investment to fair value [10,000 × ($46.00 − $45.00)].		

2020			
Feb. 15	Cash	244,740	
	Brokerage Commission Expense	260	
	Short-Term Investments		225,000
	Fair Value Valuation Allowance		5,000
	Gain on Sale of Investment		15,000
	Sold 5,000 of the Levell Inc. common shares held for $49.00 per share. Carrying value of the common shares sold was $230,000 [50% × ($450,000 + $10,000)]. Gain on sale was $15,000 (5,000 × $49.00 − $230,000).		

4. For a 40 percent equity method investment, the Investment in Investee Ltd. Common Shares account includes the cost of the investment +40% of the investee's net income −40% of the investee's cash dividends.

Remember that cash dividends received from an equity method investment are credited to Investment in Investee Ltd. Common Shares, *not to Dividend Revenue*.

a.	Jan. 1	Investment in Investee Ltd. Common Shares	140,000	
		Cash		140,000
		To purchase 40 percent investment in Investee Ltd. common shares.		

b.	Dec. 31	Investment in Investee Ltd. Common Shares	72,000	
		Equity Method Investment Revenue		72,000
		To record 40 percent of Investee Ltd. net income ($180,000 × 0.40).		

c.	Dec. 31	Cash	56,000	
		Investment in Investee Ltd. Common Shares		56,000
		To record receipt of 40 percent of Investee Ltd. cash dividend ($140,000 × 0.40).		

d.	Dec. 31	Cash	160,000	
		Investment in Investee Ltd. Common Shares		156,000
		Gain on Sale of Investment		4,000
		Sold investment in Investee Ltd. common shares ($140,000 + $72,000 − $56,000).		

5. ➊ Eliminate all parent-and-subsidiary intercompany transactions to avoid double counting items when consolidating.
➋ Check for goodwill by comparing the net assets purchased (represented by the subsidiary's shareholders' equity balance) with the amount paid. The completed worksheet appears below.

	Parent Inc.	Subsidiary Inc.	Eliminations Debit	Eliminations Credit	Consolidated Amounts
Assets					
Cash	38,000	36,000			74,000
Note receivable from Parent Inc.	—	70,000		➊ 70,000	—
Investment in Subsidiary Inc.	400,000	—		➋ 400,000	—
Goodwill	—	—	➋ 60,000*		60,000
Other assets	432,000	396,000			828,000
Total assets	870,000	502,000			962,000
Liabilities and Shareholders' Equity					
Accounts payable	60,000	42,000			102,000
Notes payable	70,000	120,000	➊ 70,000		120,000
Common shares	560,000	240,000	➋ 240,000		560,000
Retained earnings	180,000	100,000	➋ 100,000		180,000
Total liabilities and equity	870,000	502,000	470,000	470,000	962,000

*60,000 = 400,000 − (240,000 + 100,000)

6.

Jun. 1	Investment in Bonds	46,490	
	Cash		46,490
	To record purchase of bond held as a long-term investment.		

Dec. 1	Cash	1,000	
	Interest Revenue		1,000
	To record interest revenue for six months ($50,000 × 0.04 × 6/12)		

Dec. 1	Investment in Bonds	395	
	Interest Revenue		395
	To amortize bond discount using the effective-interest method according to the table provided.		

7. a. Foreign-currency transaction gain—the payment is made in fewer Canadian dollars than when the purchase was recorded.
b. Foreign-currency transaction gain—the payment is received in more Canadian dollars than when the sale was recorded.
c. Foreign-currency transaction loss—the payment is made in more Canadian dollars than when the purchase was recorded.
d. Foreign-currency transaction loss—the payment is received in fewer Canadian dollars than when the sale was recorded.

17

The Cash Flow Statement

CONNECTING CHAPTER 17

LEARNING OBJECTIVES

1 **Identify the purposes of the cash flow statement**

What is a cash flow statement?

The Cash Flow Statement: Basic Concepts, page 949
Purpose of the Cash Flow Statement, page 950
    Cash and Cash Equivalents

2 **Identify cash flows from operating, investing, and financing activities**

How is the cash flow statement set up?

Format of the Cash Flow Statement, page 952
Operating, Investing, and Financing Activities, page 952
    Discontinued Operations
    Interest and Dividends as Operating Activities
    Non-cash Investing and Financing Activities
Measuring Cash Adequacy: Free Cash Flow, page 955

3 **Prepare a cash flow statement by the indirect method**

What is the indirect method, and how is it used to prepare a cash flow statement?

The Cash Flow Statement: The Indirect Method, page 956
    Preparing the Operating Activities Section

4 **Compute the cash effects of investing and financing transactions**

What are the cash effects of different business transactions?

Computing Individual Amounts for the Cash Flow Statement, page 961
    Computing the Cash Amounts of Investing Activities
    Computing the Cash Amounts of Financing Activities

5 **Identify the impact of IFRS on the cash flow statement**

How does IFRS affect the cash flow statement?

The Impact of IFRS on the Cash Flow Statement, page 964

A1 **Prepare a cash flow statement by the direct method**

What is the direct method, and how is it used to prepare a cash flow statement?

The Cash Flow Statement: The Direct Method, page 969
    Cash Flows from Operating Activities
    Cash Flows from Investing Activities
    Cash Flows from Financing Activities
Calculating Amounts for the Operating Section of the Cash Flow Statement, page 975
    Computing the Cash Amounts of Operating Activities

The **Summary** for Chapter 17 appears on pages 968–969.
Key Terms with definitions for this chapter's material appears on page 986.

CPA competencies

This text covers material outlined in **Section 1: Financial Reporting of the CPA Competency Map.** The Learning Objectives for each chapter have been aligned with the CPA Competency Map to ensure the best coverage possible.

1.1.2 Evaluates the appropriateness of the basis of financial reporting

1.2.2 Evaluates treatment for routine transactions

1.3.1 Prepares financial statements

Cole Burston/CP Images

Corus Entertainment had a busy year ending in 2017 as it completed its $2.6 billion acquisition of Shaw Media Inc. to become Canada's leading English Canadian commercial television company. Corus's businesses include Global Television (one of its 15 televisions channels), Corus Radio (with 39 stations), and the new Cooking Channel (Canada). Its Kids Can Press won Children's North American Publisher of the Year, and Corus Studios' and Nelvana's original content plays in over 100 countries. Operating a growing company like this requires significant amounts of cash.

Corus earned $224 million of net income for the year, but the cash and equivalents accounts increased by only $22 million, so where did the cash go? Why wouldn't the balances increase by the full $224 million? There's nothing to worry about. Corus paid down debt, expanded, paid dividends to shareholders, added new equipment, and improved buildings. All of that used up cash. They were still left with a respectable increase in their cash balance.

The company's Message to Shareholders in the 2017 Annual Report stated, "Our intense focus on free cash flow enabled us to reach our deleveraging target of 3.5 times net debt to segment profit one quarter earlier than anticipated. In fact, we delivered $293 million in free cash flow this year, above our expectations."

Managers, lenders, and investors have a financial report available to explain these changes. It is called a *cash flow statement*. Cash is the lifeblood of a business. Tracking it and making sure there is enough of it is an important part of a company's success. Companies who forget to ensure there is sufficient cash to pay bills as they come due will not remain in business.

Chapter 1 we briefly introduced you to the cash flow statement as a required financial statement. Like the other two major financial reports—the income statement and the balance sheet—the cash flow statement enables investors and creditors to make informed decisions about a company. The income statement might present one picture of the company (e.g., relatively high income), while the cash flow statement might present a different picture (e.g., not enough cash). This example underscores the challenge of financial analysis: A company's signals may point in different directions. Astute investors and creditors know what to look for, and increasingly they are focusing on cash flows because a company that does not have cash to pay its bills won't remain in business even if it is profitable.

Let's start by looking at an example before discussing how to create this statement. Exhibit 17–1 shows Corus Entertainment Inc.'s 2017 cash flow statement. They call it a "statement of cash flows," and that is fine too. For now, just get a sense of the layout and what information it provides.

EXHIBIT 17–1 | Corus Entertainment Inc.'s 2017 Cash Flow Statement—Adapted*

CORUS ENTERTAINMENT INC.
Consolidated Statement of Cash Flows
For the Year Ended August 31, 2017

It covers the same period of time as the income statement.

(in thousands of Canadian dollars)	2017	2016
OPERATING ACTIVITIES		
Net income for the year	224,089	143,561
Adjustments to reconcile net income to cash provided by operating activities:		
Amortization of program rights	510,716	313,300
Amortization of film investments	23,958	22,690
Depreciation and amortization	91,750	73,969
Deferred income taxes (recovery)	17,109	(22,554)
Intangible and other assets impairment (recovery)	5,250	(822)
...	...	...
Other	(508,804)	(373,146)
Cash flow from operations	364,067	156,998
Net change in non-cash working capital balances related to operations	(65,934)	43,229
Cash provided by operating activities	298,133	200,227
INVESTING ACTIVITIES		
Additions to property, plant, and equipment	(26,989)	(22,550)
Net proceeds from disposition	----	209,474
Business combinations, net of acquired cash	3,000	(1,827,452)
Proceeds from disposition of non-controlling interest	5,250	----
Proceeds from disposition of investment	4,122	1,684
Net cash flows for intangibles, investments, and other assets	(6,291)	(19,583)
Cash used in investing activities	(20,908)	(1,658,427)
FINANCING ACTIVITIES		
Increase (decrease) in bank loans	(110,706)	1,959,209
Issuance of shares under stock option plan	154	----
Dividends paid	(106,062)	(89,702)
Dividends paid to non-controlling interest	(35,026)	(19,824)
...	...	...
Other	(3,247)	(357,542)
Cash provided by (used in) financing activities	(254,887)	1,492,141
Net change in cash and cash equivalents during the year	22,338	33,941
Cash and cash equivalents, beginning of the year	71,363	37,422
Cash and cash equivalents, end of the year	93,701	71,363

Brackets indicate an outflow of funds

There are four sections to a cash flow statement:
• Operating
• Investing
• Financing
• Cash reconciliation

Overall increase in cash

A helpful feature of the cash flow statement is that the change in cash during the year at the bottom of the statement acts like a "check figure." You balance to amount of cash at the end of the year.

*Adapted to combine some more complex issues into "Other" so you can focus on the main points. Also removed references to "notes" since you will not be reviewing them at this time. Students wanting to see the full document can look it up online.

The results seem positive overall because Corus has made decisions that will improve cash flows. Exhibit 17–1 shows that Corus ended 2017 with a positive cash and equivalents balance in the amount of $93,701,000, an increase of $22,338,000 from the previous year. Positive operating cash flows left money to add property, plant, and equipment, pay off loans, and pay dividends to shareholders. Positive cash flow from operations is a positive signal about any company because operations should be the main source of cash.

The Cash Flow Statement: Basic Concepts

LO ①

What is a cash flow statement?

The balance sheet reports a company's cash balance at the end of the period. By comparing the beginning and ending balance sheets, you can tell whether cash increased or decreased during the period. However, the balance sheet does not indicate *why* the cash balance changed. The income statement reports revenues, expenses, and net income (or net loss)—clues about the sources and uses of cash—but it does not tell *why* cash increased or decreased. To discover more about the changes in cash, we need another financial statement: the cash flow statement.

Exhibit 17–2 illustrates the relationships among the balance sheet, the income statement, and the cash flow statement, and the time periods covered by each.

The **cash flow statement** reports the entity's **cash flows**—cash receipts and cash payments—during the period.

- It shows where cash came from (sources of funds) and how cash was spent (uses of funds).
- It reports why cash increased or decreased during the period.
- It covers a period of time and is dated "For the Month Ended xxxx" or "For the Year Ended xxxx," the same as the income statement.

EXHIBIT 17–2 | Timing of the Financial Statements

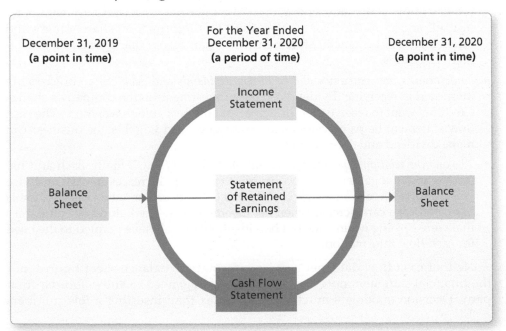

The end of the day on December 31 of this year is considered to be the same as the beginning of the day on January 1 of next year.

Exhibit 17–3 shows the Cash T-account and some of the types of transactions that affect its balance during a period.

EXHIBIT 17–3 | Some Transactions that Affect the Cash Account

Cash (and cash equivalents)

Increases	Decreases
Beginning cash balance	Payments to suppliers
Collections from customers	Payments to employees
Interest received on notes	Payments for income tax
Issuance of shares	Payments for assets
Issuance of bonds	Loan to another company
Receipt of dividends	Payment of dividends
	Repayment of a bank loan
	Repayment of long-term loans
Ending cash balance	

Purpose of the Cash Flow Statement

Cash flows are important to a company's survival. A business must operate profitably to be a going concern. Information about accrual-based net income is found on the income statement. However, a business must have cash to pay suppliers, employees, and so on. A cash shortage is usually the most pressing problem of a struggling organization. Abundant cash allows a company to expand, invest in research and development, and hire the best employees.

How then do investors (and their representatives, financial analysts) and creditors use cash flow information for decision making?

- *To predict future cash flows.* It takes cash to pay the bills or take advantage of opportunities. In many cases, past cash receipts and cash payments help predict future cash flows.

- *To evaluate management decisions.* Wise decisions lead to profits and strong cash flows. Unwise decisions often bring bankruptcy. One of the areas that the cash flow statement reports on is the investments a company is making in itself and in outside companies. With this information, shareholders and other interested financial statement users can assess management's investment decisions.

- *To determine the company's ability to pay dividends and debts.* Shareholders are interested in receiving dividends on their investments in the company's shares. Creditors want to receive their principal and interest amounts on time. The cash flow statement helps investors and creditors predict whether the business can make dividend and debt payments.

- *To show the relationship between net income and cash flow.* Usually, cash and net income move together. High profits tend to lead to increases in cash and vice versa. However, a company's cash balance can decrease when net income is high, and cash can increase when net income is low. The failures of companies that were earning net income but had insufficient cash have pointed to the need for cash flow information.

Neither cash flow data, net income information, balance sheet figures, nor the financial statement notes tell investors all they need to know about a company. Decision making is much more complex than inserting a few numbers into a simple formula. To decide whether to invest in a company's shares, investors analyze

- A company's financial statements
- Articles in the financial press
- Data about the company's industry
- Predictions about the world and local economy

In evaluating a loan request, a bank loan officer may interview a company's top managers to decide whether they are trustworthy and whether their projections for the future of the company are reasonable. Both investors and creditors are interested mainly in a company's future. They want to make predictions about a company's future net income and future cash flows.

It has been said that cash flow data help to spot losers better than winners. This is often true. When a company's business is booming, profits are high and cash flows are usually improving. In almost all cases, a negative cash flow from operations warrants investigation. A cash downturn in a *single* year is not necessarily a danger signal. But negative cash flows for two or more *consecutive* years may lead to bankruptcy. Without cash flow from operations, a business simply cannot survive.

You may ask, "Can't the business raise money by issuing shares or by borrowing?" The answer is often no, because if operations cannot generate enough cash, then investors will not buy the company's shares, and bankers will not lend it money. *Over the long run, if a company cannot generate cash from operations it is doomed.*

Cash and Cash Equivalents

The cash flow statement does not just explain the change in cash in the bank accounts. The report analyzes the change in *cash and cash equivalents*.

On the financial statements, *Cash* has a broader meaning than just cash on hand and cash in the bank. It includes **cash equivalents** (introduced in Chapter 8), which are highly liquid short-term investments convertible into cash with little delay. Because their liquidity is one reason for holding these investments, they are treated as cash. Examples of cash equivalents are investments in money market funds and investments in Government of Canada Treasury bills. Note 6 from the Indigo Books & Music 2017 annual report in Exhibit 17–4 shows an example of cash and cash equivalents. Businesses invest their extra cash in these types of liquid assets to earn interest income or to satisfy credit obligations. Throughout this chapter, the term *cash* refers to cash and cash equivalents.

EXHIBIT 17–4 | Indigo's Note about Its Cash and Cash Equivalents (2017)

6. CASH AND CASH EQUIVALENTS
Cash and cash equivalents consist of the following:

(thousands of Canadian dollars)	April 1, 2017	April 2, 2016
Cash	63,872	102,862
Restricted cash	1,343	3,460
Cash equivalents	65,223	110,166
Cash and cash equivalents	130,438	216,488

Restricted cash represents cash pledged as collateral for letter of credit obligations issued to support the Company's purchases of offshore merchandise.

Try It!

Format of the Cash Flow Statement

LO ②

How is the cash flow statement set up?

There are two ways to format operating activities on the cash flow statement. Both explain the change in cash for the period. The only part of the report which differs is the explanations within the operating activities section.

- The **indirect method**, which reconciles net income to net cash provided by operating activities. This is the more commonly used format and the method used by Corus Entertainment Inc. in Exhibit 17–1. Learning Objective 3 shows how to prepare the operating section of the statement using this method. Many businesses prefer this method because it shows a clearer relationship between net income and cash flows.

- The **direct method**, which reports all the cash receipts and all the cash payments from operating activities. Accounting standards for private enterprises (ASPE) *encourages* the presentation of information in a cash flow statement using the direct method (*CPA Canada Handbook*, paragraph 1540.21). However, accounting systems often don't produce the cash flow data easily so the calculations and presentation of the operating section using the direct method is shown in the Appendix to this chapter.

Just because the direct method is in the Appendix does not mean it is not important! Many argue that this method provides better information for users because it does a better job of showing the individual cash flows from operating activities.

Operating, Investing, and Financing Activities

A business engages in three basic categories of business activities:

- **Operating activities**
- **Investing activities**
- **Financing activities**

The cash flow statement has a section for each category of cash flows. Exhibit 17–5 outlines what each section reports.

EXHIBIT 17–5 | Sections of the Cash Flow Statement

Operating Activities . . .	• Create revenues, expenses, gains, and losses • Affect net income on the income statement • Affect current assets and current liabilities on the balance sheet • Are the most important category of cash flows because they reflect the day-to-day operations that determine the future of an organization
Investing Activities . . .	• Increase and decrease long-term assets, such as computers, software, land, buildings, and equipment, and purchases and sales of these long-term assets • Include purchases and sales of long-term share investments • Include long-term note receivable in the form of loans to others as well as the collection of long-term loans • Are the next most important category of cash flows after operating activities
Financing Activities . . .	• Increase and decrease long-term liabilities and owners' equity • Include issuing shares, paying dividends, and repurchasing a company's own shares • Include borrowing money and paying off loans • Are the least important of all the activities because what a company invests in is usually more important than how the company finances the investment

> Once the business is up and running, *operations* are the most important activity, followed by *investing activities* and *financing activities*. Investing activities are generally more important than *financing activities* because what a company invests in is usually more important than *how* the company finances the investment.

Exhibit 17–6 also shows the relationships among operating, investing, and financing cash flows and where the information comes from on the balance sheet.

EXHIBIT 17–6 | Operating, Investing, and Financing Cash Flows and the Balance Sheet Accounts

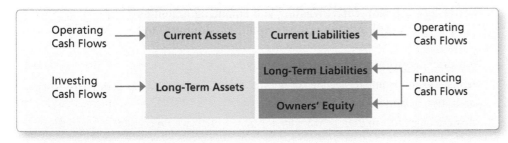

> Notice that the term *investing* is used differently than you may be used to. This is not about the Investments account but rather changes in long-term assets held by the business.

As you can see, operating cash flows affect the current accounts. Investing cash flows affect the long-term assets. Financing cash flows affect long-term liabilities and owners' equity.

Discontinued Operations

Just as discontinued operations are shown separately on the income statement, so they are also shown separately on the cash flow statement. The cash inflow or outflow resulting from discontinued operations should be shown as part of operating, investing, or financing activities, as appropriate. Look back at Exhibit 17–1 to see how Corus Entertainment reported their sale (proceeds from disposition) under investing activities and removed the effect of the gain on net income under operating activities. To see more details about these transactions, look at the notes to the statements found online in the original annual report.

Interest and Dividends as Operating Activities

Under ASPE, cash receipts of interest and dividends are included as operating activities because they affect the computation of net income and are received on a regular basis. Interest revenue and dividend revenue (from investments without significant influence) increase net income, and interest expense decreases income. Therefore, cash receipts of interest and dividends and cash payments of interest are reported as operating activities on the cash flow statement.

In contrast, dividend payments are reported as a financing activity. This is because they do not enter into the computation of net income but rather are payments to the entity's shareholders, who finance the business by purchasing its shares.

Non-cash Investing and Financing Activities

Non-cash investing and financing activities are reported in the notes to the financial statements.

Companies make investments that do not require cash. For example, they may issue a note payable to buy land, or they may pay off a loan by issuing shares. So far, our examples did not include these transactions.

Suppose Dunbar Ltd. issued common shares with a stated value of $730,000 to acquire a warehouse on January 1. Dunbar Ltd. would make this journal entry:

| Jan. 1 | Warehouse | 730,000 | |
| | Common Shares | | 730,000 |

Since this transaction has no net effect on the cash flow statement, Paragraph 1540.48 in Part II of the *CPA Canada Handbook* requires that non-cash investing and financing activities be disclosed elsewhere in the financial statements in a way that provides all the relevant information about these investing and financing activities. Exhibit 17–7 illustrates an example of a note that would fulfil this requirement.

EXHIBIT 17–7 | Non-cash Investing and Financing Activities (All Amounts Assumed for Illustration Only)

Non-cash investing and financing activities	(in thousands)
Acquisition of building by issuing common shares	$ 730
Acquisition of land by issuing note payable	172
Payment of long-term debt by transferring investments to the creditor	250
Acquisition of equipment by issuing short-term note payable	89
Total non-cash investing and financing activities	$1,241

When there is a cash component to a transaction, it is appropriate to show only the net effect of the transaction on the cash flow statement. For example, if the purchase of the building had been for common shares of $700,000 and for cash of $30,000, it would be appropriate to show only the net effect on cash of $30,000 and the other components of the transaction in the notes to the financial statements.

Measuring Cash Adequacy: Free Cash Flow

Some investors want to know how much cash a company can "free up" for new opportunities. **Free cash flow** is the amount of cash available from operations after paying for planned investments in long-term assets. Free cash flow can be computed as follows:

Free cash flow =	Net cash provided by operating activities	−	Cash payments for investments in property, plant, equipment, and other long-term assets

There are many ways to calculate free cash flow so don't be surprised to see other definitions. This is the one used for this text.

Corus Entertainment's 2017 Annual Report says that free cash flow "measures the Company's ability to repay debt, finance strategic business acquisitions and investments, pay dividends, and repurchase shares" (page 38). Corus has $292.7 million of free cash flow in 2017, as can be seen in Exhibit 17–8.

EXHIBIT 17–8 | Corus Entertainment's Calculation of Free Cash Flow (2017)

(thousands of Canadian dollars)	2017
Cash provided by (used in):	
Operating activities	298,133
Investing activities(1)	(5,473)
Free cash flow	292,660

(1) Adapted – Net cash payments for capital assets

Try It!

3. Identify each of the following transactions as either an operating activity (O), an investing activity (I), a financing activity (F), or an activity that is not reported on a cash flow statement (N).

_____ Payment of cash dividend

_____ Decrease in inventory

_____ Cash purchase of land

_____ Payment of long-term note payable

_____ Amortization of building

_____ Accrual of interest expense

Solutions appear at the end of this chapter and on **MyLab Accounting**

Having seen the contents of the cash flow statement, we can turn to the accounting framework described in Chapter 1 to understand why the cash flow statement is one of the required financial statements for all companies.

The accounting framework states the objective of financial reporting is to communicate financial information that is *useful* in evaluating investment decisions and in assessing the success of a company. Two characteristics that make statements useful are *relevance* and *reliability*.

Relevance Many investors feel that the cash flow statement provides the most relevant information of all of the financial statements. Why? While the income statement provides information about how much income was earned during the period, it does not state clearly how much cash was generated by the company. The income statement uses accruals to match revenues and expenses and reports them in the proper time period in which they were earned or incurred. However, the cash generated by a company and the use of that cash in the business are a significant predictor of future financial performance. We make the cash flow statement even more relevant and informative by classifying the cash flows as coming from operating, investing, or financing activities.

Reliability The cash flow statement is reliable since it deals only with cash transactions and, typically, cash transactions are easy to verify. There are no accrual assumptions to assess when dealing with cash transactions.

The Cash Flow Statement: The Indirect Method

LO ③

What is the indirect method, and how is it used to prepare a cash flow statement?

The indirect method of reporting cash flows from operating activities is a reconciliation from net income to net cash inflow (or outflow) from operating activities. It is a conversion of accrual-based net income to the cash-based net income, which shows how the company's net income is related to net cash flows from operating activities.

This method shows the link between net income and cash flows from operations better than the direct method. The main drawback of the indirect method is that it does not report the detailed operating cash flows—collections from customers and other cash receipts, payments to suppliers, payments to employees, and payments for interest and taxes. The vast majority of Canadian (and US) companies use the indirect method.

Dunbar Ltd.'s income statement and balance sheet are shown here as Exhibits 17–9 and 17–10. The income statement net income or net loss is the starting point for the creation of the cash flow statement. Net income, amortization expense, and gains or losses on the sale of long-term assets are key balances to be used in the creation of the cash flow statement.

EXHIBIT 17–9 | Income Statement

The two methods (direct and indirect) of preparing the cash flow statement affect only the operating activities section of the statement. No difference exists for investing activities or financing activities.

DUNBAR LTD. Income Statement For the Year Ended December 31, 2020 (amounts in thousands)		
Revenues and gains		
Sales revenue	$682	
Interest revenue	29	
Dividend revenue	22	
❸ Gain on sale of property, plant, and equipment	19	
Total revenues and gains		$752
Expenses		
Cost of goods sold	360	

DUNBAR LTD. Income Statement For the Year Ended December 31, 2020 (amounts in thousands)		
Salaries expense	134	
❷ Amortization expense	43	
Other operating expenses	41	
Interest expense	38	
Total expenses		616
Net income before income taxes		136
Income tax expense		36
❶ Net income		$100

In addition to the income statement balances, the cash flow statement also reports the changes in balance sheet accounts. So first calculate the difference (increase/decrease) in each account balance as shown in Exhibit 17–10. Then identify what part of the cash flow statement is impacted by the account.

EXHIBIT 17–10 | Balance Sheet Comparing December 31, 2020 and 2019 Balances

DUNBAR LTD. Balance Sheet December 31, 2020 and 2019 (amounts in thousands)				
Assets	**2020**	**2019**	**Increase (Decrease)**	Changes in the following:
Current assets				
❿ Cash	$ 57	$ 101	$ (44)	
❹ Accounts receivable	224	192	32	
❹ Interest receivable	8	3	5	
❹ Inventory	323	330	(7)	Current assets—Operating
❹ Prepaid expenses	18	17	1	
❻ Long-term receivable from another company	26	—	26	Noncurrent assets—Investing
❺ Property, plant, and equipment, net of amortization	1,087	525	562	
Total	$1,743	$1,168	$575	
Liabilities				
Current liabilities				
❹ Accounts payable	$ 220	$ 137	$ 83	
❹ Salaries payable	6	12	(6)	Current liabilities—Operating but current portion of long-term debt—Financing
❹ Accrued liabilities	5	7	(2)	
❼ Long-term debt	384	185	199	Most long-term liabilities and contributed capital—Financing
Shareholders' Equity				
❽ Common shares	861	619	242	
❾ Retained earnings	267	208	59	Change due to net income—Operating and change due to dividends—Financing
Total	$1,743	$1,168	$575	

Other data from the 2020 financial records needed for the creation of a cash flow statement:

❺ acquisitions of property, plant, and equipment, $735,000, and sold equipment costing $155,000 (accumulated amortization, $25,000)

❻ issued new loans to customers, $26,000

⑦ issued long-term debt, $226,000

⑧ issues new common shares, $242,000

Exhibit 17–11 is Dunbar Ltd.'s cash flow statement prepared by the indirect method. The items identified with numbers in circles are keyed to their explanations and additional assumptions/information provided, which are discussed below.

EXHIBIT 17–11 | Cash Flow Statement (Indirect Method for Operating Activities)

DUNBAR LTD.
Cash Flow Statement
For the Year Ended December 31, 2020
(amounts in thousands)

Cash flows from operating activities		
① Net income		$100
Add (subtract) items that affect net income and cash flow differently:		
② Amortization expense	$143	
③ Gain on sale of property, plant, and equipment	(19)	
④ Increase in accounts receivable	(32)	
④ Increase in interest receivable	(5)	
④ Decrease in inventory	7	
④ Increase in prepaid expenses	(1)	
④ Increase in accounts payable	83	
④ Decrease in salaries payable	(6)	
④ Decrease in accrued liabilities	(2)	68
Net cash inflow from operating activities		168
Cash flows from investing activities		
⑤ Acquisition of property, plant, and equipment	(735)	
⑥ Loan to another company	(26)	
⑤ Cash received from selling property, plant, and equipment	149	
Net cash outflow from investing activities		(612)
Cash flows from financing activities		
⑧ Cash received from issuing common shares	242	
⑦ Cash received from issuing long-term debt	226	
⑦ Payment of long-term debt	(27)	
⑨ Payment of dividends	(41)	
Net cash inflow from financing activities		400
Net increase (decrease) in cash and cash equivalents		(44)
⑩ Cash and cash equivalents at beginning of 2020		101
⑩ Cash and cash equivalents at end of 2020		$ 57

The "at beginning of 2020" could also be written as "December 31, 2019" or "January 1, 2020".

The "at end of 2020" could also be written as "December 31, 2020"

Preparing the Operating Activities Section

① The indirect method cash flow statement begins with accrual-basis net income from the income statement. Additions and subtractions follow. These are labelled "Add (subtract) items that affect net income and cash flow differently." Refer to Exhibits 17–9, 17–10, and 17–11 to see the amounts explained here.

② Amortization Expenses These expenses are added back to net income to compute cash flow from operations. Let's see why.

Amortization was originally recorded as follows:

Dec. 31	Amortization Expense	43,000	
	Accumulated Amortization		43,000

This entry neither debits nor credits Cash because amortization has no cash effect. However, amortization expense is deducted from revenues to compute income. Therefore, in going from net income to cash flows from operations, we add amortization back to net income. The add back cancels the earlier deduction.

The following example should help clarify this practice. Suppose a company had only two transactions during the period: a $5,000 cash sale and amortization expense of $1,000. Net income is $4,000 ($5,000 − $1,000). But cash flow from operations is $5,000. To go from net income ($4,000) to cash flow ($5,000), we must add back the amortization amount of $1,000.

> Other adjustments commonly made to net income are for amortization of bond premium/discount and equity method revenue.

③ Gains and Losses on the Sale of Assets Sales of property, plant, and equipment and of intangible assets are investing activities on the cash flow statement. Gains and losses are bookkeeping amounts that we track on the income statement. Starting with net income, we *subtract the gain*, which removes the gain's earlier effect on income—in effect, this moves the amount out of net income so we can record the cash flow in the investing section (item ⑤).

A loss on the sale of property, plant, and equipment and of intangible assets is also an adjustment to net income on the cash flow statement. A loss is *added back* to income to compute cash flow from operations.

④ Changes in the Current Asset and Current Liability Accounts Most current assets and current liabilities result from operating activities. Changes in the current accounts are reported as adjustments to net income on the cash flow statement. The following rules apply and are summarized in Exhibit 17–12:

- **An increase in a current asset other than cash is subtracted from net income to compute cash flow from operations.** Suppose a company makes a sale. Income is increased by the sale amount. However, collection of less than the full amount increases Accounts Receivable. For example, Exhibit 17–10 reports that Dunbar Ltd.'s Accounts Receivable increased by $32,000 during 2020. To compute the impact of revenue on Dunbar Ltd.'s cash flows, we must subtract the $32,000 increase in Accounts Receivable from net income in Exhibit 17–11. The reason is this: We have *not* collected this $32,000 in cash. The same logic applies to the other current assets. If they increase during the period, subtract the increase from net income.

- **A decrease in a current asset other than cash is added to net income.** Suppose Dunbar Ltd.'s Accounts Receivable balance decreased by $8,000 during the period. Cash receipts cause Accounts Receivable to decrease and Cash to increase, so decreases in Accounts Receivable and the other current assets are *added* to net income.

- **A decrease in a current liability is subtracted from net income.** The payment of a current liability decreases both Cash and the current liability, so decreases in current liabilities are subtracted from net income. For example, in Exhibit 17–11, the $2,000 decrease in Accrued Liabilities is *subtracted* from net income to compute net cash inflow from operating activities.

- **An increase in a current liability is added to net income.** Dunbar Ltd.'s Accounts Payable increased during the year. This increase can occur only if cash is not spent to pay this liability, which means that cash payments are less than the related expense. As a result, we have more cash on hand. Thus, increases in current liabilities are *added* to net income.

> The additions and subtractions of current assets and current liabilities in the operating section are not inflows and outflows of cash. They are adjustments to net income to convert it to the cash basis.

Exhibit 17–12 summarizes the adjustments needed to convert net income to net cash inflow (or net cash outflow) from operating activities by the indirect method.

EXHIBIT 17–12 | Indirect Method of Determining Cash Flows from Operating Activities

Item	Adjustment on Statement of Cash Flows (+ increase, − decrease)
Amortization, Depletion, and Depreciation Expense	+
Gains on Disposal of Long-term Assets	−
Losses on Disposal of Long-term Assets	+
Increases in Current Assets	−
Decreases in Current Assets	+
Increases in Current Liabilities	+
Decreases in Current Liabilities	−

Or you can try to remember it this way?

Impact of Change in Account on Cash Flow Statement	Current Assets	Current Liabilities
Increase	−	+
Decrease	+	−

To convert net income from accrual basis to cash basis:

- Expenses with no cash effects, such as accruals, are added back to net income on the cash flow statement.
- Revenues that do not provide cash, such as accrued income, are subtracted from net income.
- Items are either added or subtracted by calculating differences in current assets and current liabilities between the opening and closing amounts.

Try It!

4. The information listed below is taken from the financial statements of Swank Incorporated for the year ended December 31, 2020, when net income is $150. All amounts are in thousands of dollars:

	Dec. 31, 2020	Jan. 1, 2020
Cash	$45	$15
Accounts Receivable	12	18
Inventory	66	48
Accounts Payable	20	9
Salaries Payable	24	39

Compute cash flow from operating activities using the indirect method.

5. Examine Dunbar Ltd.'s cash flow statement, Exhibit 17–11, and answer these questions:
   a. Does Dunbar Ltd. appear to be growing or shrinking? How can you tell?
   b. Where did most of Dunbar Ltd.'s cash for expansion come from?
   c. Suppose Accounts Receivable decreased by $80,000 (instead of increasing by $32,000) during the current year. What would Dunbar Ltd.'s cash flow from operating activities be?

Solutions appear at the end of this chapter and on MyLab Accounting

Computing Individual Amounts for the Cash Flow Statement

How do we compute the amounts for the investing and financing sections of the cash flow statement? We use the income statement and *changes* in the related balance sheet accounts. The adjustment process for both the direct and indirect methods follows a T-account approach, which is illustrated in the next section.

Computing the Cash Amounts of Investing Activities

Investing activities affect long-term asset accounts, such as Property, Plant, and Equipment, intangible assets, Investments, and Notes Receivable. Cash flows from investing activities can be computed by analyzing these accounts. The income statement and beginning and ending balance sheets provide the data.

④ **Acquisitions and Sales of Tangible and Intangible Assets** Companies keep separate accounts for Land, Buildings, Equipment, and other tangible and intangible assets. Here we combine these accounts into a single total for computing the cash flows from acquisitions and sales of these assets. Also, we often subtract accumulated amortization from the assets' cost and work with a *net* figure for property, plant, and equipment and amortizable intangible assets, which is the book value.

Observe that Dunbar Ltd.'s balance sheet (Exhibit 17–10) reports beginning property, plant, and equipment, net of amortization, of $525,000 and an ending net amount of $1,087,000. The income statement in Exhibit 17–9 shows amortization of $43,000 and a $19,000 gain on the sale of property, plant, and equipment. Assume that the accounting records state that the acquisitions are $735,000. How much are the proceeds from the sale of property, plant, and equipment?

Learning to analyze T-accounts is one of the most useful accounting skills you will acquire. It will enable you to measure the cash effects of a wide variety of transactions.

Changes in asset accounts, other than those used to compute cash flow from operating activities, are investing activities. An increase in an asset represents a cash outflow; a decrease in an asset represents a cash inflow.

Property, Plant, and Equipment (net*)

Beginning balance (net)	525,000	Accumulated Amortization	43,000
Acquisitions	735,000	Book value of assets sold	130,000
Ending balance (net)	1,087,000		

*Accumulated amortization is subtracted

First, we must compute the book value of property, plant, and equipment sold as fol lows:

Property, Plant, and Equipment, Net

Beginning balance	+ Acquisitions	− Accumulated Amortization	− Book value of assets sold	= Ending balance
$525,000	+ $735,000	− $43,000	− X	= $1,087,000
			−X	= $1,087,000 − $525,000 − $735,000 + $43,000
			X	= $130,000

Now we can compute the proceeds from the sale of property, plant, and equipment as follows:

Sale proceeds	=	Book value of assets sold	+	Gain	−	Loss
	=	$130,000	+	$19,000	−	$0
	=	$149,000				

If we assume that the accounting records show that the equipment cost $155,000 and had accumulated amortization of $25,000, the journal entry for the sale would have looked like this:

Dec. 31	Cash	$149,000	
	Accumulated Amortization Old Asset	25,000	
	Old Asset Original Cost		155,000
	Gain on the Sale of Old Asset		$ 19,000

Book value
= $130,000 ($155,000 − $25,000)

Normally, when an asset is sold the asset account is decreased by the asset's original cost, not the selling price. Proceeds from the sale of an asset need not equal the asset's book value.

Book value + Gain = Proceeds

Book value − Loss = Proceeds

The book value information comes from the balance sheet; the gain or loss comes from the income statement.

If the sale had resulted in a loss of $6,000, the sale proceeds would be $124,000 ($130,000 − $6,000) and the cash flow statement would report $124,000 as a cash receipt from this investing activity.

⑥ Acquisitions and Sales of Long-Term Investments and Long-Term Loans (Receivables) and Loan Collections The cash amounts of long-term investment and loan transactions can be computed in the manner illustrated for property, plant, and equipment and intangible assets. Investments are easier to analyze because there is no amortization to account for, as shown by the following T-account:

Investments

Beginning balance*	XXX		
Purchases**	XXX	Cost of investments sold	XXX
Ending balance*	XXX		

* From the balance sheet
** From the accounting records, used to create the cash flow statement

Long-Term Investments (amounts assumed for illustration only)

Beginning balance	+ Purchases	−	Cost of investments sold	= Ending balance
$200,000	+ $100,000	−	X	= $280,000
			− X	= $280,000 − $200,000 − $100,000
			X	= $20,000

Sale proceeds	=	Cost of investments sold	+ Gain	− Loss
	=	$20,000	+ $6,000	− $0
	=	$26,000		

Assume that the accounting records of Dunbar Ltd. show that there was $26,000 of new loans made to customers. New loans made increase the receivable and decrease the amount of cash. Collections decrease the receivable and increase the amount of cash for Dunbar Ltd., as follows:

Loans and Notes Receivable (Long-Term)

Beginning balance	0		
New loans made	26,000	Collections	0
Ending balance	26,000		

Loans and Notes Receivable

Beginning balance	+ New loans made	−	Collections	= Ending balance
$ 0	+ $26,000	−	X	= $26,000
			−X	= $26,000 − $0 − $20,000
			X	= $0

Computing the Cash Amounts of Financing Activities

Financing activities affect the long-term liability and shareholders' equity accounts. To compute the cash flow amounts, analyze these accounts as follows:

❼ Issuances and Payments of Long-Term Debt Notes Payable, Bonds Payable, and Long-Term Debt accounts are related to borrowing, a financing activity. Their balances come from the balance sheet. If either the amount of new issuances or the amount of the payments is known, the other amount can be computed.

Assume that the accounting records identified that new debt issuances for Dunbar Ltd totalled $226,000. Debt payments are computed from the Long-Term Debt T-account, using amounts from Dunbar Ltd.'s balance sheet, Exhibit 17–10:

Changes in liability and shareholders' equity accounts, other than those used to compute cash flow from operating activities, are financing activities.

Long-Term Debt

		Beginning balance	185,000
Payments	27,000	Issuance of new debt	226,000
		Ending balance	384,000

Long-Term Debt

Beginning balance	+	Issuance of new debt	−	Payments of debt	=	Ending balance
$185,000	+	$226,000	−	X	=	$384,000
				$-X$	=	$384,000 - $185,000 - $226,000
				X	=	$27,000

The $27,000 payment of debt is reported in the financing section of Exhibit 17–11.

❽ Issuances and Repurchases of Shares These financing activities are computed from the various share accounts. It is convenient to work with a single summary account for shares. Using data from Exhibit 17-10 and the assumption that the accounting records identified the issuance of $242,000 worth of new shares, we have the following:

Common Shares

		Beginning balance	619,000
Retirements of shares	0	Issuance of new shares	242,000
		Ending balance	861,000

Common Shares

Beginning balance	+	Issuance of new share	−	Retirements of shares	=	Ending balance
$619,000	+	$242,000	−	X	=	$861,000
				$-X$	=	$861,000 - $619,000 - $242,000
				X	=	$0

When there is no change in an account for retirements, no amount is shown in the cash flow statement.

❾ Dividend Payments If the amount of the dividends is not given elsewhere (e.g., in a statement of retained earnings), it can be computed as follows:

First, we must compute dividend declarations by analyzing Retained Earnings:

How are you able to tell by referring to the balance sheet if the amount of dividends paid is different from the dividends declared? If there is not a Dividends Payable account (or there is no change in the Dividends Payable account), then the dividends declared are equal to the dividends paid. Remember, only dividends *paid* appear on the cash flow statement, not dividends *declared*.

Retained Earnings

		Beginning balance	208,000
Dividend declaration	41,000	Net income	100,000
		Ending balance	267,000

Then we can solve for dividend payments with the Dividends Payable account:

Dividends Payable

		Beginning balance	0
Dividend payments	41,000	Dividend declaration	41,000
		Ending balance	0

In this book, assume that all declared dividends are paid unless expressly told to the contrary.

Dunbar Ltd. has no Dividends Payable account balance, so dividend payments are the same as declarations.

The following computations show how to figure out Dunbar Ltd.'s dividend payments:

Retained Earnings						
Beginning balance	+	Net income	−	Dividend declarations	=	Ending balance
$208,000	+	$100,000	−	X	=	$267,000
				−X	=	$267,000 − $208,000 − $100,000
				X	=	$41,000

The *payment* of cash dividends, not the *declaration,* appears as a cash outflow on the cash flow statement in the financing activities section.

❿ Reconcile Cash and Cash Equivalents Dunbar's $44,000 decrease in cash explains the balance sheet cash decreasing from $101,000 in 2019 to $57,000 in 2020.

Try It!

6. Bolin Corp. reported the following (amounts in thousands):

Retirement of Bolin Corp. preferred shares	$ 90
Sale of bonds issued by Blue Ltd.	224
Purchase of land	316
Sale of Bolin Corp. common shares	210
Collection of long-term note receivable	126
Payment of dividends	300

What is Bolin Corp.'s net change in cash from investing activities?

7. Refer to the Bolin Corp. data in the previous question. What is Bolin Corp.'s net change in cash from financing activities?

Solutions appear at the end of this chapter and on **MyLab Accounting**

LO ⑤

How does IFRS affect the cash flow statement?

EXHIBIT 17–13 | The Impact of IFRS on the Cash Flow Statement

ASPE	IFRS
Interest paid or received and dividend income that goes through net income are considered operating activities. Dividends paid are financing activities.	Interest and dividends need to be reported consistently from period to period as operating, investing, or financing activities.

While both ASPE and IFRS permit both the direct and indirect method, the *CPA Canada Handbook* section for ASPE encourages the use of the direct method. Once a company chooses a method for its accounting policy, it must apply the policy consistently to all similar transactions.

Summary Problem for Your Review

The Bella Corporation reported the following income statement for 2020 and comparative balance sheet for 2020 and 2019, along with transaction data for 2020:

BELLA CORPORATION Comparative Balance Sheet December 31, 2020 and 2019			
Assets	**2020**	**2019**	**Increase (Decrease)**
Current assets			
Cash	$ 22,000	$ 3,000	$19,000
Accounts receivable	22,000	23,000	(1,000)
Inventory	35,000	34,000	1,000
Property, Plant, and Equipment			
Equipment	153,200	97,200	56,000
Less: Accum. amortization-equiment	27,200	25,200	2,000
Total assets	$205,000	$132,000	$73,000
Liabilities			
Current liabilities			
Accounts payable	$ 35,000	$ 26,000	$ 9,000
Accrued liabilities	7,000	9,000	(2,000)
Income tax payable	10,000	10,000	0
Long-term liabilities			
Bonds payable	84,000	53,000	31,000
Total liabilities	136,000	98,000	38,000
Shareholders' Equity			
Common shares	42,000	15,000	27,000
Retained earnings	27,000	19,000	8,000
Total shareholders' equity	69,000	34,000	35,000
Total liabilities and shareholders' equity	$205,000	$132,000	$73,000

BELLA CORPORATION
Income Statement
For the Year Ended December 31, 2020

Sales revenue		$662,000
Cost of goods sold		560,000
Gross profit		102,000
Operating expenses		
Salaries expense	$46,000	
Amortization expense–equipment	10,000	
Rent expense	2,000	
Total operating expenses		58,000
Operating income		44,000
Other revenues and (expenses)		
Loss on disposal of equipment	(2,000)	
Total other revenues and (expenses)		(2,000)
Net income before income taxes		42,000
Income tax expense		16,000
Net income		$ 26,000

Transaction data for 2020 from other accounting records

Cash paid for purchase of equipment	$140,000
Cash payment of dividends	18,000
Issuance of common shares to retire bonds payable	13,000
Issuance of bonds payable to borrow cash	44,000
Cash receipt from issuance of common shares	14,000
Cash receipt from sale of equipment (cost, $84,000; accumulated amortization, $8,000)	74,000

Prepare Bella Corporation's cash flow statement for the year ended December 31, 2020. Format cash flows from operating activities by the indirect method.

SOLUTION

<table>
<tr><td colspan="3">BELLA CORPORATION
Statement of Cash Flows
For the Year Ended December 31, 2020</td></tr>
<tr><td colspan="3">Cash flows from operating activities</td></tr>
<tr><td>Net Income</td><td></td><td>$26,000</td></tr>
<tr><td>Add (subtract) items that affect net income and cash
flow differently:</td><td></td><td></td></tr>
<tr><td>Amortization expense–equipment</td><td>$ 10,000</td><td></td></tr>
<tr><td>Loss on disposal of equipment</td><td>2,000</td><td></td></tr>
<tr><td>Decrease in accounts receivable</td><td>1,000</td><td></td></tr>
<tr><td>Increase in inventory</td><td>(1,000)</td><td></td></tr>
<tr><td>Increase in accounts payable</td><td>9,000</td><td></td></tr>
<tr><td>Decrease in accrued liabilities</td><td>(2,000)</td><td>19,000</td></tr>
<tr><td>Net cash inflow from operating activities</td><td></td><td>45,000</td></tr>
<tr><td colspan="3">Cash flows from investing activities</td></tr>
<tr><td>Cash payment for acquisition of equipment</td><td>(140,000)</td><td></td></tr>
<tr><td>Cash receipt from disposal of equipment</td><td>74,000</td><td></td></tr>
<tr><td>Net cash outflow from investing activities</td><td></td><td>(66,000)</td></tr>
<tr><td colspan="3">Cash flows from financing activities</td></tr>
<tr><td>Cash receipt from issuance of bonds payable</td><td>44,000</td><td></td></tr>
<tr><td>Cash receipt from issuance of common shares</td><td>19,000</td><td></td></tr>
<tr><td>Cash payment for purchase of preferred shares</td><td>(5,000)</td><td></td></tr>
<tr><td>Cash payment of dividends</td><td>(18,000)</td><td></td></tr>
<tr><td>Net cash inflow from financing activities</td><td></td><td>40,000</td></tr>
<tr><td>Net increase in cash</td><td></td><td>19,000</td></tr>
<tr><td>Cash balance, January 1, 2020</td><td></td><td>3,000</td></tr>
<tr><td>Cash balance, December 31, 2020</td><td></td><td>$22,000</td></tr>
<tr><td colspan="3">Non-cash investing and financing activities</td></tr>
<tr><td>Issuance of common shares to retire bonds payable</td><td></td><td>$13,000</td></tr>
<tr><td>Total non-cash investing and financing activities</td><td></td><td>$13,000</td></tr>
</table>

The title must include the name of the company, "Cash Flow Statement," and the specific period of time covered.

For the indirect method, always begin with accrual-basis net income from the income statement.

Add back non-cash items: amortization and losses; deduct gains

Reflect changes in current assets and liabilities as follows:
Current asset increases—deduct
Current asset decreases—add
Current liability increases—add
Current liability decreases—deduct

For cash flows from investing activities, look for activities that have a cash impact on long-term asset accounts. Brackets indicate cash outflows (purchases).

For cash flows from financing activities, look for activities that have a cash impact on short-term debt (or note) accounts, long-term liability accounts, and equity accounts. Brackets indicate cash outflows.

The end result should equal the year-end balance sheet amount of cash and cash equivalents. If it does not, there is an error in the cash flow statement.

Relevant T-accounts:

Equipment

Dec. 31, 2019	97,200		
Acquisitions	140,000	Disposals	84,000
Dec. 31, 2020	153,200		

Accumulated Amortization—Equipment

		Dec. 31, 2019	25,200
Disposals	8,000	Amort. exp.	10,000
		Dec. 31, 2020	27,200

Bonds Payable

		Dec. 31, 2019	53,000
Retirement	13,000	Issuance	44,000
		Dec. 31, 2020	84,000

Common Shares

		Dec. 31, 2019	15,000
		Issuance	13,000
Retirement	0	Issuance	14,000
		Dec. 31, 2020	42,000

Retained Earnings

		Dec. 31, 2019	19,000
Dividends	18,000	Net Income	26,000
		Dec. 31, 2020	27,000

Summary

Learning Objectives

① Identify the purposes of the cash flow statement   Pg. 949

What is a cash flow statement?
- The *cash flow statement* reports *why* cash increased or decreased during the period.
- It is a required financial statement and it gives a different view of the business from that given by accrual-basis statements.
- The cash flow statement aids in the prediction of future cash flows and evaluation of management decisions.
- Cash includes cash on hand, cash in the bank, and *cash equivalents,* such as liquid short-term investments.

② Identify cash flows from operating, investing, and financing activities   Pg. 952

How is the cash flow statement set up?
- The cash flow statement reports *operating activities, investing activities,* and *financing activities.*
- Operating activities create revenues and expenses in the entity's major line of business.
- Investing activities affect the long-term assets.
- Financing activities include the cash obtained from investors and creditors to launch and sustain the business.
- The statement must agree with the change in cash reported on the comparative balance sheet.
- In addition, *non-cash investing* and *financing activities* are reported either in the notes to the financial statements or in a separate section.

> Free cash flow = Net cash provided by operating activities − Cash payments for investments in property, plant, equipment, and other long-term assets

③ Prepare a cash flow statement by the indirect method   Pg. 956

What is the indirect method, and how is it used to prepare a cash flow statement?
- The *indirect method* starts with net income and reconciles net income to cash flow from operations.

(4) Compute the cash effects of investing and financing transactions   Pg. 961

What are the cash effects of different business transactions?
- The analysis of T-accounts aids in the computation of the cash effects of business transactions.

(5) Identify the impact of IFRS on the cash flow statement   Pg. 964

How does IFRS affect the cash flow statement?
- Under IFRS, the receipt of interest and dividends may be recorded as either operating, investing, or financing activities, while the payment of interest and dividends may be recorded as either operating or financing activities.
- Once the company chooses an accounting policy, however, it must apply the policy consistently to all transactions of a similar nature.

(A1) Prepare a cash flow statement by the direct method   Pg. 969

What is the direct method, and how is it used to prepare a cash flow statement?
- Examples of items that the *direct method* reports include collections from customers and receipts of interest and dividends minus cash payments to suppliers, payments to employees, and payments for interest and income taxes.
- Investing cash flows and financing cash flows are unaffected by the method used to report operating activities.

Key Terms for the chapter are shown next and are in the **Glossary** at the back of the book. **Similar Terms** are shown after **Key Terms.**

Chapter 17 Appendix

THE CASH FLOW STATEMENT: THE DIRECT METHOD

We have already illustrated the preparation of the cash flow from operating activities using the indirect method. In this appendix we will examine the direct method. To use the direct method, a company must be able to access information on cash inflows and cash outflows. Exhibit 17A–1 gives an overview of the process of converting from accrual-basis income to the cash basis for the cash flow statement.

LO (A1)

What is the direct method, and how is it used to prepare a cash flow statement?

EXHIBIT 17A–1 | Converting from the Accrual Basis to the Cash Basis for the Cash Flow Statement

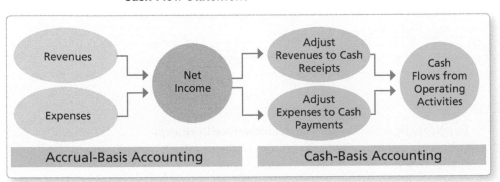

There are two ways questions are presented for students to solve/prepare the cash flow statement. The first is to start with two years of financial statements and find the cash transactions by explaining the changes in the balances from the first year to the next. The other way is to start with the results of such a comparison. Let's first see how to prepare the cash flow statement using the second method.

Suppose Dunbar Ltd. has assembled the summary of 2020 transactions in Exhibit 17A–2. These transactions give data for both the income statement and the cash flow statement. Some transactions affect one statement, some the other. Sales, for example, are reported on the income statement, but cash collections appear on the cash flow statement. Other transactions, such as the cash receipt of dividend revenue, affect both. *The cash flow statement reports only those transactions with cash effects.*

EXHIBIT 17A–2 | Summary of Dunbar Ltd.'s 2020 Transactions

Operating Activities:

1. Sales on account, $682,000
2. Collections of accounts receivable and cash sales, $650,000
3. Interest revenue on notes receivable, $29,000
4. Collection of interest receivable, $24,000
5. Cash receipt of dividend revenue on investments in shares, $22,000
6. Cost of goods sold, $360,000
7. Purchases of inventory on credit, $353,000
8. Salaries expense, $134,000
9. Payments of salaries, $140,000
10. Payments to suppliers for inventory, $270,000, and operating expenses, $44,000
11. Amortization expense, $43,000
12. Other operating expense, $41,000
13. Interest expense and payments, $38,000
14. Income tax expense and payments, $36,000

Investing Activities:

15. Cash payments to acquire property, plant, and equipment, $735,000
16. Loan to another company, $26,000
17. Cash receipts from sale of property, plant, and equipment $149,000, including a $19,000 gain

Financing Activities:

18. Cash receipts from issuing common shares, $242,000
19. Cash receipts from issuing a long-term note payable, $226,000
20. Payment of long-term debt, $27,000
21. Declaration and payment of cash dividends, $41,000

Note that cash collections from customers are not the same as sales. Cash collections from customers could include collections from sales that were made last year (beginning accounts receivable) but not credit sales from the current year that have not yet been collected (ending accounts receivable).

To prepare the cash flow statement, follow these three steps:

1. Identify the activities that increased cash or decreased cash—those items in blue in Exhibit 17A–2.

2. Classify each transaction as an operating activity, an investing activity, or a financing activity.

3. Identify the cash effect (increase or decrease) of each transaction.

Exhibit 17A–3 shows the cash flow statement created using the information provided. Note that the subtotals match Exhibit 17–11. Details about how amounts were calculated follow the exhibit.

EXHIBIT 17A–3 | Cash Flow Statement (Direct Method for Operating Activities)

DUNBAR LTD.
Cash Flow Statement
For the Year Ended December 31, 2020
(amounts in thousands)

Cash flows from operating activities		
Receipts		
Collections from customers	$650	
Interest received on note receivable	24	
Dividends received on investments in shares	22	
Total cash receipts		$696
Payments		
To employees	(140)	
To suppliers for inventory	(270)	
To suppliers for operating expenses	(44)	
For interest	(38)	
For income tax	(36)	
Total cash payments		(528)
Net cash inflow from operating activities		168
Cash flows from investing activities		
Acquisition of property, plant, and equipment	(735)	
Loan to another company	(26)	
Cash received from selling property, plant, and equipment	149	
Net cash outflow from investing activities		(612)
Cash flows from financing activities		
Cash received from issuing common shares	242	
Cash received from issuing long-term note payable	226	
Payment of long-term debt*	(27)	
Payment of dividends	(41)	
Net cash inflow from financing activities		400
Net increase (decrease) in cash and cash equivalents		(44)
Cash and cash equivalents at beginning of 2020		101
Cash and cash equivalents at end of 2020		$ 57

> Both the indirect and direct methods will balance to the same net cash inflow from operating activities—$168,000—and will reconcile to the same total cash change of $(44,000).

*This would also include the current portion of long-term debt payable, which is NIL in this case.

Cash Flows from Operating Activities

Operating cash flows are listed first because they are the most important source of cash for most businesses. The failure of operations to generate the bulk of cash inflows for an extended period may signal trouble for a company. Exhibit 17A–3 shows that Dunbar Ltd. is sound; its operating activities generated the greatest amount of cash, $696,000 in operating receipts. Dunbar's cash flows from operating activities section from the exhibit is repeated here for reference. Refer to it as we organize the operating activities into receipts and payments based on the operating transactions shown in Exhibit 17A–2. We will go through it line by line.

From 17A-2	Cash flows from operating activities	(in thousands)	
	Receipts		
2	Collections from customers	$650	
4	Interest received on notes receivable	24	
5	Dividends received on investments in shares	22	
	Total cash receipts		$696
	Payments		
9	To employees	(140)	
10	To suppliers for inventory	(270)	
10	To suppliers for operating expenses	(44)	
13	For interest	(38)	
14	For income tax	(36)	
	Total cash payments		(528)
	Net cash inflow from operating activities		$168

2 Cash Collections from Customers   Cash sales bring in cash immediately. Credit sales bring in cash later, when cash is collected. "Collections from customers" include both cash sales and collections of accounts receivable from credit sales—$650,000.

4 Cash Receipts of Interest   Interest revenue is earned on notes receivable. The income statement reports interest revenue. As time passes, interest revenue accrues, but *cash* interest is received only on specific dates. Only the cash receipts of interest appear on the cash flow statement—$24,000.

5 Cash Receipts of Dividends   Dividends are earned on share investments. Dividend revenue is ordinarily recorded on the income statement when cash is received (for non-equity accounted investments). This cash receipt is reported on the cash flow statement—$22,000. (Dividends *received* are part of operating activities, but dividends *paid* are a financing activity.)

   These cash receipts add to the total cash receipts of $696,000.

9 Cash Payments to Employees   Salaries, wages, commissions, and other forms of employee compensation require payments to employees. Accrued amounts are excluded because they have not yet been paid. The income statement reports the expense, including accrued amounts. The cash flow statement reports only the cash payments—$140,000.

10 Cash Payments to Suppliers   Payments to suppliers include all cash payments for inventory and most operating expenses, but not for interest, income taxes, and employee compensation expenses. *Suppliers* are entities that provide the business with its inventory and essential services. For example, a clothing store's payments to Gildan Activewear Inc., Nygård International, and Stanfield's Ltd. are payments to suppliers. Other suppliers provide advertising, utilities, and other services. Payments to suppliers *exclude* payments to employees, payments for interest, and payments for income taxes because these are separate categories of operating cash payments. Dunbar Ltd.'s payments to suppliers are $270,000 for inventory and $44,000 for operating expenses.

11 Amortization Expense   This expense is not listed on the cash flow statement because it does not affect cash. Amortization is recorded by debiting the expense and crediting Accumulated Amortization (there is no debit or credit to the Cash account).

Using the direct method, cash receipts from issuing shares are *a financing activity.* Payment of dividends is also considered *a financing activity.* Cash receipts from and payments of short- or long-term borrowing are *financing activities.* But interest expense on these borrowings is considered an *operating activity.*

13 & 14 Cash Payments for Interest Expense and Income Tax Expense   These cash payments are reported separately from the other expenses. In the Dunbar Ltd. example, interest and income tax expenses equal the cash payments. The cash flow statement reports the cash payments for interest of $38,000 and income tax of $36,000.

   Therefore, the same amount appears on the income statement and the cash flow statement. In practice, this is rarely the case. Year-end accruals and other transactions usually cause the expense and cash payment amounts to differ.

Cash Flows from Investing Activities

Investing activities are important because a company's investments determine its future. Purchases of tangible assets such as property, plant, and equipment, as well as intangible assets such as patents, indicate the company is expanding, which is usually a good sign about the company. Low levels of investing activity over a lengthy period mean the business is not replenishing its property, plant, and equipment or intangible assets. Knowing the cash flows from investing activities helps investors and creditors evaluate the direction that managers are charting for the business.

Dunbar's cash flows from investing activities shown on the statement in Exhibit 17A–3 is repeated here for reference. Refer to it as we go through this section line by line.

From 17A–2	Cash flows from investing activities		
15	Acquisition of property, plant, and equipment	$(735)	
16	Loan to another company	(26)	
17	Cash received from selling property, plant, and equipment	149	
	Net cash outflow from investing activities		$(612)

15 & 16 Cash Payments for Property, Plant, and Equipment and Intangible Assets, Investments, and Loans to Other Companies All these cash payments acquire a long-term asset. The first investing activity reported by Dunbar Ltd. on its cash flow statement is the purchase of property, plant, and equipment and intangible assets, such as land, buildings, equipment, and patents, for $735,000. The second transaction is a $26,000 loan; Dunbar Ltd. obtained a long-term note receivable. These are investing activities because the company is mainly investing in assets for business use rather than for resale. The other typical transaction in this category, which is not shown for Dunbar Ltd., is a purchase of long-term investments. Long-term notes or investments are assets with future economic value and serve to support the strategic initiatives of the business.

17 Cash Received from the Sale of Property, Plant, and Equipment and Intangible Assets, Investments, and the Collection of Loans These transactions are the opposite of making acquisitions of property, plant, and equipment or intangible assets, investments, and loans. They are cash receipts from investment transactions.

The sale of the property, plant, and equipment and intangible assets needs explanation. The cash flow statement reports that Dunbar Ltd. received $149,000 cash on the sale of these assets. The income statement shows a $19,000 gain on this transaction. What is the appropriate amount to show on the cash flow statement? It is $149,000, the cash received from the sale.

If we assume Dunbar Ltd. sold equipment that cost $155,000 and had accumulated amortization of $25,000, the following journal entry would record the sale:

> Any time Cash is debited in a journal entry, it must appear on the cash flow statement as a cash inflow. Likewise, a credit signals an outflow. To think this through, make journal entries but do not post them as they are merely a way to help you understand the cash effect of the transaction.

Dec. 31	Cash	149,000	
	Accumulated Amortization	25,000	
	Equipment		155,000
	Gain on Sale of Equipment (from income statement)		19,000

Book value
= $130,000 ($155,000 − $25,000)

The book value of the asset sold and the gain are not reported on the cash flow statement. Only the *cash proceeds* of $149,000 are reported on the cash flow statement.

Because a gain occurred, you may wonder why this cash receipt is not reported as part of operations. Operations consist of buying and selling merchandise or rendering services to earn revenue. Investing activities are the acquisition and disposition of assets used in operations. Therefore, the cash received from the sale of property, plant, and equipment and intangible assets and the sale of investments should be viewed as cash inflows from investing activities. Any gain or loss on the sale is not cash, but rather an accounting amount based on the asset's book value in the accounting records.

Investors and creditors are often critical of a company that sells large amounts of its property, plant, and equipment and intangible assets. Such sales may signal an emergency need for cash and negative news. But selling property, plant, and equipment or intangible assets may be positive news if the company is selling an unprofitable division or a useless property, plant, and equipment asset. Whether sales of property, plant, and equipment or intangible assets are positive news or negative news, they should be evaluated in light of a company's overall picture.

Cash Flows from Financing Activities

Readers of the financial statements want to know how the entity obtains its financing. Cash flows from financing activities include several specific items. The majority are related to obtaining money from investors and lenders and paying them back.

Dunbar's cash flows from financing activities shown in the statement in Exhibit 17A–3 is repeated here for reference. Refer to it as we go through this section line by line.

From 17A–2	Cash flows from financing activities	
18	Cash received from issuing common shares	$242
19	Cash received from issuing long-term note payable	226
20	Payment of long-term debt	(27)
21	Payment of dividends	(41)
	Net cash inflow from financing activities	$400

18 & 19 Cash Received from Issuing Shares and Debt Issuing shares (preferred and common) and debt are two common ways to finance operations. Dunbar Ltd. issued common shares for cash of $242,000 and long-term note payable for cash of $226,000.

20 Payment of Debt and Repurchases of the Company's Own Shares The payment of debt decreases Cash, which is the opposite of borrowing money. Dunbar Ltd. reports debt payments of $27,000. Other transactions in this category are repurchases of the company's shares.

21 Payment of Cash Dividends The payment of cash dividends decreases Cash and is therefore reported as a cash payment. Dunbar Ltd.'s $41,000 payment is an example. A dividend in another form—such as a stock dividend—has no effect on Cash and either is *not* reported on the cash flow statement or is reported in the non-cash financing and investing footnote section described earlier in this chapter.

Try It!

8. Identify each of the following transactions as either an operating activity (O), an investing activity (I), a financing activity (F), or an activity that is not reported on a cash flow statement (N). Assume the direct method is used to report cash flows from operating activities.

_____ Payment of income taxes

_____ Issuance of preferred shares

_____ Payment of employee salaries

_____ Collections of accounts receivable

_____ Payment for a delivery truck

_____ Repayment of a long-term bank loan (principal only)

_____ Receipt of loan interest

_____ Payment of accounts payable

9. Suppose Markham Corp. sold land at a $3 million gain. The land cost Markham Corp. $2 million when it was purchased in 1995. What amount will Markham Corp. report as an investing activity on the cash flow statement?

Solutions appear at the end of this chapter and on **MyLab Accounting**

CALCULATING AMOUNTS FOR THE OPERATING SECTION OF THE CASH FLOW STATEMENT

Let's practise this same analysis but this time using the income statement and the comparative balance sheets to calculate the amounts needed to create the cash flow statement.

The following explanations use Dunbar Ltd.'s income statement in Exhibit 17A–4, comparative balance sheet in Exhibit 17A–5, and cash flow statement in Exhibit 17A–6. (Exhibits 17A–4, 17A–5, and 17A–6 are repeats of Exhibits 17–9, 17–10 and 17–3, respectively, for your convenience). Now let's compute the cash flows from operating activities.

Learning Objective 4 provides more information on calculating amounts for investing and financing activities.

EXHIBIT 17A–4 | Income Statement

DUNBAR LTD. Income Statement For the Year Ended December 31, 2020 (amounts in thousands)		
Revenues and gains		
Sales revenue	$682	
Interest revenue	29	
Dividend revenue	22	
Gain on sale of property, plant, and equipment	19	
Total revenues and gains		$752
Expenses		
Cost of goods sold	360	
Salaries expense	134	
Amortization expense	43	
Other operating expenses	41	
Interest expense	38	
Total expenses		616
Net income before income taxes		136
Income tax expense		36
Net income		$100

DUNBAR LTD.
Balance Sheet
December 31, 2020 and 2019
(amounts in thousands)

Assets	2020	2019	Increase (Decrease)	Changes in the following:
Current assets				
Cash	$ 57	$ 101	$ (44)	
Accounts receivable	224	192	32	
Interest receivable	8	3	5	Current assets—*Operating*
Inventory	323	330	(7)	
Prepaid expenses	18	17	1	
Long-term receivable from another company	26	—	26	Noncurrent assets—*Investing*
Property, plant, and equipment, net of amortization	1,087	525	562	
Total assets	$1,743	$1,168	$ 575	
Liabilities				
Current liabilities				
Accounts payable	$ 220	$ 137	$ 83	Current liabilities—*Operating* and
Salaries payable	6	12	(6)	change in current portion of long-
Accrued liabilities	5	7	(2)	term debt—*Financing*
Long-term debt	384	185	199	Most long-term liabilities and
Shareholders' Equity				contributed capital—*Financing*
Common shares	861	619	242	
Retained earnings	267	208	59	Change due to net income— *Operating* and change due to
Total liabilities and shareholders' equity	$1,743	$1,168	$ 575	dividends—*Financing*

EXHIBIT 17A–6 | Cash Flow Statement (Direct Method for Operating Activities)

DUNBAR LTD. Cash Flow Statement For the Year Ended December 31, 2020 (amounts in thousands)		
Cash flows from operating activities		
Receipts		
Collections from customers	$650	
Interest received on notes receivable	24	
Dividends received on investments in shares	22	
Total cash receipts		$696
Payments		
To employees	(140)	
To suppliers for inventory	(270)	
To suppliers for operating expenses	(44)	
For interest	(38)	
For income tax	(36)	
Total cash payments		(528)
Net cash inflow from operating activities		168
Cash flows from investing activities		
Acquisition of property, plant, and equipment	(735)	
Loan to another company	(26)	
Cash received from selling property, plant, and equipment	149	
Net cash outflow from investing activities		(612)
Cash flows from financing activities		
Cash received from issuing common shares	242	
Cash received from issuing long-term debt	226	
Payment of long-term debt*	(27)	
Payment of dividends	(41)	
Net cash inflow from financing activities		400
Net increase (decrease) in cash and cash equivalents		(44)
Cash and cash equivalents at beginning of 2020		101
Cash and cash equivalents at end of 2020		$ 57

*This would also include the current portion of long-term debt payable, which is NIL in this case.

Exhibit 17A–6 shows that Dunbar Ltd.'s net cash inflow from operating activities is $168,000. A large positive cash inflow from operations is a good sign about a company. The acquisition of long-term assets dominates Dunbar Ltd.'s investing activities, which produce a net cash outflow of $612,000. Financing activities of Dunbar Ltd. brought in net cash receipts of $400,000. One thing to watch among financing activities is whether the business is borrowing heavily. Excessive borrowing has been the downfall of many companies. Each of these categories of activities—operating, investing, and financing—includes both cash receipts and cash payments, as shown in Exhibit 17A–7. The exhibit lists the more common cash receipts and cash payments that appear on the cash flow statement.

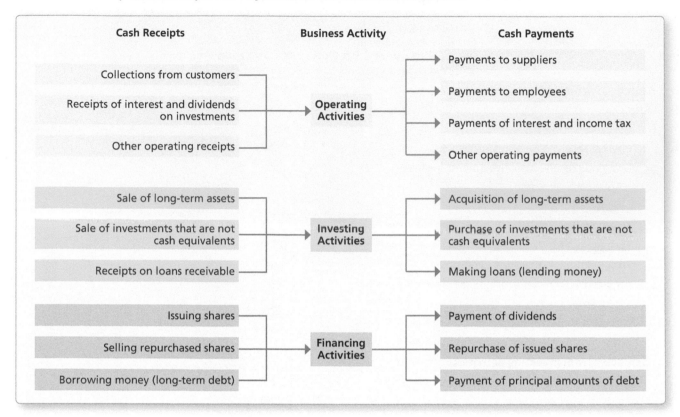

How do we compute the amounts for the cash flow statement? We use the income statement and *changes* in the related balance sheet accounts. For the *operating* cash flow amounts, the adjustment process follows this basic approach:

A *decrease* in Accounts Receivable indicates that cash collections were greater than sales. The decrease is *added* to Sales. An *increase* in Accounts Receivable indicates that cash collections were less than sales. The increase is *deducted* from Sales.

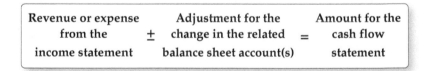

| Revenue or expense from the income statement | ± | Adjustment for the change in the related balance sheet account(s) | = | Amount for the cash flow statement |

This is called the *T-account approach,* and it will be illustrated in the next section, "Computing the Cash Amounts of Operating Activities." Learning to analyze T-accounts is one of the most useful accounting skills you will acquire. It will enable you to measure the cash effects of a wide variety of transactions.

Computing the Cash Amounts of Operating Activities

See Exhibit 17A–8 for a checklist of accounts and calculations for each of the following:

EXHIBIT 17A–8 | Direct Method of Determining Cash Flows from Operating Activities

	From the Income Statement (Exhibit 17A–4)	From the Balance Sheet (Exhibit 17A–5)
CASH RECEIPTS		
From customers	Sales Revenue	+ Decrease in Accounts Receivable – Increase in Accounts Receivable
Of interest	Interest Revenue	+ Decrease in Interest Receivable – Increase in Interest Receivable
Of dividends	Dividend Revenue	+ Decrease in Dividends Receivable – Increase in Dividends Receivable
CASH PAYMENTS		
To suppliers of inventory	Cost of Goods Sold	+ Increase in Inventory + Decrease in Accounts Payable – Decrease in Inventory – Increase in Accounts Payable
To suppliers of other items	Operating Expense	+ Increase in Prepaids + Decrease in Accrued Liabilities – Decrease in Prepaids – Increase in Accrued Liabilities
To employees	Salaries Expense	+ Decrease in Salaries Payable – Increase in Salaries Payable
For interest	Interest Expense	+ Decrease in Interest Payable – Increase in Interest Payable
For income tax	Income Tax Expense	+ Decrease in Income Tax Payable – Increase in Income Tax Payable

This exhibit was created from a suggestion made by Barbara Gerrity.

Cash Collections from Customers   Collections can be computed by converting sales revenue (an accrual-basis amount) to the cash basis. Dunbar Ltd.'s income statement (Exhibit 17A–4) reports sales of $682,000. Exhibit 17A–5 shows that Accounts Receivable increased from $192,000 at the beginning of the year to $224,000 at year-end, a $32,000 increase. Based on those amounts, cash collections equals $650,000, as shown in the Accounts Receivable T-account:

Accounts Receivable					Cash	
Beginning balance	192,000				650,000	
Sales	682,000	Collections	650,000			
Ending balance	224,000					

Another explanation: Accounts Receivable increased by $32,000, so Dunbar Ltd. must have received $32,000 less cash than sales revenue for the period. ($682,000 – $32,000 = $650,000)

The following equation shows another way to compute cash collections from customers:

Accounts Receivable				
Beginning balance	**+ Sales**	**– Collections**	**= Ending balance**	
$192,000	+ $682,000	– X	= $224,000	
		– X	= $224,000 – $192,000 – $682,000	
		X	= $650,000	

Remember that each account contains four basic elements:

Beginning Balance
+ Increases
– Decreases
————————
= Ending Balance

Apply this relationship to Accounts Receivable for Dunbar Ltd.

Compute collections:

Beg. A/R	$192,000
+ Sales	682,000
– Collections*	?
= Ending Balance	$224,000

*Collections = $650,000

A decrease in Accounts Receivable would mean that the company received more cash than the amount of sales revenue.

All collections of receivables are computed in the same way. In our example, Dunbar Ltd.'s income statement, Exhibit 17A–4, reports interest revenue of $29,000. Interest Receivable's balance in Exhibit 17A–5 increased $5,000. Cash receipts of interest must be $24,000 (Interest Revenue of $29,000 minus the $5,000 increase in Interest Receivable).

Payments to Suppliers   This computation includes two parts, payments for inventory related to cost of goods sold and payments for operating expenses.

Payments for inventory are computed by converting cost of goods sold to the cash basis. We must analyze the Inventory and Accounts Payable accounts. To "analyze" an account means to explain each amount in the account. The computation of Dunbar Ltd.'s cash payments for inventory is given by this analysis of the T-accounts (again, we are using Exhibits 17A–4 and 17A–5 for our numbers):

Inventory				Accounts Payable		
Beg. Inventory 330,000	COGS	360,000		Payments for inventory 270,000	Beg. bal.	137,000
Purchases 353,000					Purchases	353,000
End. Inventory 323,000					End. bal.	220,000

The first equation details the activity in the Inventory account to compute purchases, as follows:

Inventory

Beginning inventory	+	Purchases	−	Cost of goods sold	=	Ending inventory
$330,000	+	X	−	$360,000	=	$323,000
		X			=	$323,000 − $330,000 + $360,000
		X			=	$353,000

The COGS calculation requires two adjustments. The adjustment for inventory gives the amount of purchases; the adjustment for accounts payable gives the payments for inventory.

Now we can insert the purchases figure into accounts payable to compute the amount of cash paid for inventory, as follows:

Accounts Payable

Beginning balance	+	Purchases	−	Payments for inventory	=	Ending balance
$137,000	+	$353,000	−	X	=	$220,000
				−X	=	$220,000 − $137,000 − $353,000
				X	=	$270,000

Beginning and ending inventory amounts come from the balance sheet, and cost of goods sold comes from the income statement.

Payments for inventory appear in the Accounts Payable account, but we must first work through the Inventory account to calculate payments to suppliers of inventory.

Payments to Employees   Companies keep separate accounts for salaries, wages, and other forms of employee compensation. It is convenient to combine all compensation amounts into one account for presentation purposes. Dunbar Ltd.'s calculation adjusts Salaries Expense for the change in Salaries Payable, as shown in the following T-account:

Salaries Payable			
		Beginning balance	12,000
Payments to employees	140,000	Salaries expense	134,000
		Ending balance	6,000

Salaries Payable							
Beginning balance	+	Salaries expense	−	Payments	=	Ending balance	
$12,000	+	$134,000	−	X	=	$6,000	
				−X	=	$6,000 − $12,000 − $134,000	
				X	=	$140,000	

Remember: Exhibit 17A–8 summarizes these sorts of computations.

Payments for Operating Expenses   Payments for operating expenses is similar to payments to employees, but in this case there are two items affecting operating expenses that makes the calculation of the cash paid more difficult. Payments for operating expenses other than interest and income tax can be computed as "plug figures," or differences, by analyzing Prepaid Expenses and Accrued Liabilities, as follows for Dunbar Ltd. (again, all numbers are taken from Exhibits 17A–4 and 17A–5). The assumption here is that all prepaid items, such as rent, insurance, and advertising, or all accrued liabilities, such as entertainment, telephone, and utilities, flow through the one Operating Expenses account.

The question is, how much cash did Dunbar pay for operating expenses? An assumption is made regarding operating expenses in the following example. It assumes that all the prepaid expenses at the beginning of the year ($17,000) expired during the year and were adjusted in the current year by crediting the Prepaid Expenses account ❶ and debiting the applicable expense. We know that accrued expenses ❷ during the year were and we can assume that they were paid in the current year $5,000 and we can assume that they were paid in the current year, so we have enough data to determine how much cash was paid out for these operating expenses combined ($44,000).

Increases and decreases in other payables (Salaries Payable, Interest Payable, and Income Tax Payable) are treated in the same way as increases and decreases in Accounts Payable and Accrued Liabilities. A *decrease* in the payable indicates that payments for salaries/interest/income taxes were greater than the expense. The decrease is *added* to the expense. An *increase* in the payable indicates that payments for salaries/interest/income taxes were less than the expense. The increase is *deducted* from the expense.

Prepaid Expenses

Beg. bal.	17,000	❶ Expiration of prepaid expense	17,000
Payments	18,000		
End. bal.	18,000		

Accrued Liabilities

Payments	7,000	Beg. bal.	7,000
		❷ Accrual of expense at year-end	5,000
		End. bal.	5,000

Operating Expenses (Other than Salaries, Wages, and Amortization)

❷ Accrual of expense at year-end	5,000	
❶ Expiration of prepaid expense	17,000	
Payments	19,000	
End. bal.	41,000	

Total payments for operating expenses = **$44,000**

$18,000 + $7,000 + $19,000 = **$44,000**

The following equations show another way to calculate payments for operating expenses:

Prepaid Expenses

Beginning balance	+	Payments	−	Expiration of prepaid expense	=	Ending balance
$17,000	+	X	−	$17,000	=	$18,000
		X			=	$18,000 − $17,000 + $17,000
		X			=	$18,000

Accrued Liabilities

Beginning balance	+	Accrual of expense at year-end	−	Payments	=	Ending balance
$7,000	+	$5,000	−	X	=	$5,000
				−X	=	$5,000 − $7,000 − $5,000
				X	=	$7,000

Chapter 17 The Cash Flow Statement   981

Operating Expenses

Accrual of expense at year-end		Expiration of prepaid expense		Payments		Ending balance
$5,000	+	$17,000	+	X	=	$41,000
				X	=	$41,000 − $5,000 − $17,000
				X	=	$19,000

The expense total for operating expenses is $41,000. Once we remove the prepaid expirations and the expense accruals, the remaining balance must be the cash payments for expenses.

Payments of Interest and Income Tax In our example, the expense and payment amount is the same for interest and income tax. Therefore, no analysis is required to determine the payment amount—we can use the expense amounts on the income statement for the cash flow statement. However, if the expense and the payment differ, the payment can be computed by analyzing the related liability or prepayment account. The payment computation follows the pattern illustrated for payments to employees.

Exhibit 17A–8 shows a short checklist about how to compute operating cash flows under the direct method.

Try It!

9. Pardellies Limited reported the following amounts at year-end:

	December 31,	
	2020	**2019**
Current assets		
Cash and cash equivalents	$38,000	$ 6,000
Accounts receivable	44,000	46,000
Inventories	68,000	62,000
Prepaid expenses	2,000	6,000
Current liabilities		
Note payable (for inventory purchases)	$22,000	$14,000
Accounts payable	48,000	38,000
Accrued liabilities	14,000	18,000
Income and other taxes payable	22,000	20,000

- Sales totalled $240,000 and all sales were on credit.
- Assume the change in Accounts Payable is due to inventory.
- Cost of goods sold was $140,000.
- Income tax expense for 2020 was $20,000.
- Prepaid expenses of $8,000 expired during 2020.

Compute the following information for the company for 2020:
  a. Collections from customers.
  b. Payments for inventory.
  c. Payments for income taxes.
  d. Payments for prepaid expenses.

Solutions appear at the end of this chapter and on **MyLab Accounting**

Summary Problem For Your Review

Matheson Corporation's accounting records include the information shown below for the year ended December 31, 2020. Prepare Matheson Corporation's income statement and cash flow statement for the year ended December 31, 2020. Follow the cash flow statement format of Exhibit 17A–3, using the direct method for operating cash flows, and follow the single-step format for the income statement (grouping all revenues together and all expenses together, as shown in Exhibit 17A–4). Net income is $61,000.

a. Salaries expense, $290,000

b. Amortization expense on property, plant, and equipment, $104,000

c. Cash received from issuing common shares, $87,000

d. Declaration and payment of cash dividends, $62,000

e. Collection of interest on notes receivable, $20,000

f. Payments of salaries, $308,000

g. Collections from credit customers, $1,030,000

h. Loan to another company, $118,000

i. Cash received from selling property, plant, and equipment, $50,000, including a $3,000 loss

j. Payments to suppliers, $893,000

k. Income tax expense and payments, $45,000

l. Credit sales, $1,005,000

m. Cash sales, $258,000

n. Interest revenue, $22,000

o. Cash received from issuing short-term debt, $106,000

p. Payments of long-term debt, $160,000

q. Interest expense and payments, $31,000

r. Loan collections, $143,000

s. Cash received from selling investments, $61,000, including a $36,000 gain

t. Purchase of inventory on credit, $832,000

u. Dividends received in cash on investments in shares, $8,000

v. Cash payments to acquire property, plant, and equipment, $232,000

w. Cost of goods sold, $795,000

x. Cash balance:

December 31, 2019—$230,000
December 31, 2020—$144,000

Note that, for simplicity, uncollectible accounts have been ignored.

SOLUTION

To create the income statement, select revenues, expenses, gains, and losses from the list of items (a) to (x). Items can be listed in order of declining balances or in alphabetical order. Income tax expense is almost always shown separately, as the last item before net income.

Item (reference letter)	MATHESON CORPORATION Income Statement For the Year Ended December 31, 2020 (amounts in thousands)		
	Revenue and gains		
l, m	Sales revenue ($1,005 + $258)	$1,263	
s	Gain on sale of investments	36	
n	Interest revenue	22	
u	Dividend revenue	8	
	Total revenues and gains		$1,329
	Expenses and losses		
w	Cost of goods sold	795	
a	Salary expense	290	
b	Amortization expense	104	
q	Interest expense	31	
i	Loss on sale of property, plant, and equipment	3	
	Total expenses		1,223
	Net income before income tax		106
k	Income tax expense		45
	Net income		$ 61

- Operating activities: Activities that have a cash impact on revenues (cash receipts) and expenses (cash payments).
- Investing activities: Activitiesthat have a cash impact on long-term asset accounts.
- Financing activities: Activities that have a cash impact on short-term debt accounts, long-term liability accounts, and equity accounts.

Item (reference letter)	MATHESON CORPORATION Cash Flow Statement For the Year Ended December 31, 2020 (amounts in thousands)		
	Cash flows from operating activities		
	Receipts		
g, m	Collections from customers ($1,030 + $258)	$1,288	
e	Interest received on notes receivable	20	
u	Dividends received on investments in shares	8	
	Total cash receipts		$ 1,316
	Payments		
j	To suppliers	(893)	
f	To employees	(308)	
q	For interest	(31)	
k	For income tax	(45)	
	Total cash payments		(1,277)
	Net cash inflow from operating activities		39
	Cash flows from investing activities		
v	Acquisition of property, plant, and equipment	$ (232)	
h	Loan to another company	(118)	
s	Cash received from sale of investments	61	
i	Cash received from sale of property, plant, and equipment	50	
r	Collection of loans	143	
	Net cash outflow from investing activities		(96)
	Cash flows from financing activities		
o	Cash received from issuing short-term debt	106	
c	Cash received from issuing common shares	87	
p	Payments of long-term debt	(160)	
d	Dividends declared and paid	(62)	
	Net cash outflow from financing activities		(29)
	Net decrease in cash		(86)
x	Cash balance at beginning of 2020		230
x	Cash balance at end of 2020		$ 144

Compare to Cash account

KEY TERMS

Cash equivalents   Highly liquid short-term investments that can be converted into cash with little delay *(p. 951)*.

Cash flows   Cash receipts and cash payments (disbursements) *(p. 949)*.

Cash flow statement   Reports cash receipts and cash payments classified according to the entity's major activities: operating, investing, and financing *(p. 949)*.

Direct method   The format of the operating activities section of the cash flow statement that shows cash receipts from and cash payments for operating activities *(p. 952)*.

Financing activities   Activities that increase or decrease long-term liabilities and equity; a section of the cash flow statement *(p. 953)*.

Free cash flow   The amount of cash available from operations after paying for investments in plant, equipment, and other long-term assets *(p. 955)*.

Indirect method   The format of the operating activities section of the cash flow statement that starts with net income and shows the reconciliation from net income to operating cash flows. Also called the *reconciliation method (p. 952)*.

Investing activities   Activities that increase and decrease the long-term assets available to the business; a section of the cash flow statement *(p. 952)*.

Operating activities   Activities that create revenue or expense in the entity's major line of business; a section of the cash flow statement *(p. 952)*.

SIMILAR TERMS

Cash flows	Cash receipts and cash payments
Cash flow statement	Statement of cash flows
Cash payments	Disbursements, uses of funds
Cash receipts	Proceeds, sources of funds
Indirect method	Reconciliation method

SELF-STUDY QUESTIONS

Test your understanding of the chapter by marking the correct answer for each of the following questions:

1. The income statement and the balance sheet *(p. 949)*
   a. Report the cash effects of transactions
   b. Fail to report why cash changed during the period
   c. Report the sources and uses of cash during the period
   d. Are divided into operating, investing, and financing activities

2. The purpose of the cash flow statement is to *(p. 950)*
   a. Predict future cash flows
   b. Evaluate management decisions
   c. Determine the ability to pay liabilities and dividends
   d. Do all of the above

3. A successful company's major source of cash should be *(p. 953)*
   a. Operating activities
   b. Investing activities
   c. Financing activities
   d. A combination of the above

4. Dividends paid to shareholders are usually reported on the cash flow statement as a(n) *(p. 953)*
   a. Operating activity
   b. Investing activity
   c. Financing activity
   d. Combination of the above

5. Tancredi Ltd. sold a long-term investment for $50,000; the selling price included a loss of $2,500. The cash flow from investing activities will show *(p. 953)*
   a. An increase of $50,000
   b. An increase of $47,500
   c. A decrease of $52,500
   d. None of the above

6. Herdsman Corp. borrowed $100,000, issued common shares for $40,000, and paid dividends of $30,000. What was Herdsman Corp.'s net cash inflow (outflow) from financing activities? *(p. 953)*
   a. $0
   b. $110,000
   c. $(30,000)
   d. $140,000

7. In preparing a cash flow statement by the indirect method, the accountant will treat an increase in inventory as a(n) (p. 959)

   a. Increase in investment cash flows
   b. Decrease in investment cash flows
   c. Decrease in operating cash flows
   d. Increase in operating cash flows

8. Net income is $40,000, and amortization is $12,000. In addition, the sale of property, plant, and equipment generated an $8,000 gain. Current assets other than cash increased by $12,000, and current liabilities increased by $16,000. What was the amount of cash flow from operations using the indirect method? (p. 958)

   a. $64,000
   b. $48,000
   c. $40,000
   d. $72,000

9. Which of the following appears as a line on a cash flow statement prepared by the direct method? (p. 971)

   a. Amortization expense
   b. Decrease in accounts receivable
   c. Loss on sale of property, plant, and equipment and intangible assets
   d. Cash payments to suppliers

10. Falcon Lake Copy Centre had accounts receivable of $40,000 at the beginning of the year and $50,000 at year-end. Revenue for the year totalled $150,000. How much cash did Falcon Lake Copy Centre collect from customers? (p. 979)

   a. $160,000
   b. $190,000
   c. $200,000
   d. $140,000

Assignment Material

MyLab Accounting   Make the grade with MyLab Accounting: The Starters, Exercises, and Problems can be found on MyLab. You can practise them as often as you want, and most feature step-by-step guided instructions to help you find the right answer

QUESTIONS

1. What information does the cash flow statement report that is not shown on the balance sheet, the income statement, or the statement of retained earnings?

2. Identify four purposes of the cash flow statement.

3. Identify and briefly describe the three types of activities that are reported on the cash flow statement.

4. How is the cash flow statement dated and why?

5. What is the check figure for the cash flow statement? In other words, which figure do you check to make sure you've done your work correctly? Where is it obtained, and how is it used?

6. What is the most important cash flow category on the cash flow statement for most successful companies?

7. How can cash decrease during a year when income is high? How can cash increase when income is low? How can investors and creditors learn these facts about the company?

8. How should issuance of a note payable to purchase land be reported in the financial statements? Identify three other transactions that fall into this same category.

9. What is free cash flow, and how is it calculated?

10. Which format of the cash flow statement gives a clearer description of the individual cash flows from operating activities? Which format better shows the relationship between net income and operating cash flow?

11. Why is amortization expense added to net income in the operating activities section of the cash flow statement when using the indirect method?

12. If current assets other than cash increase, what is the effect on cash? What about a decrease?

13. If current liabilities increase, what is the effect on cash? What about a decrease in current liabilities?

14. Aggasiz Corporation earned net income of $90,000 and had amortization expense of $24,000. Also, non-cash current assets decreased by $18,000, and current liabilities decreased by $12,000. Using the indirect method, what was Aggasiz Corporation's net cash flow from operating activities?

15. An investment that cost $150,000 was sold for $160,000, resulting in a $10,000 gain. Show how to report this transaction on a cash flow statement prepared by the indirect method.

16. Trail Corporation's beginning property, plant, and equipment balance, net of accumulated amortization, was $200,000, and the ending amount was $180,000. Trail Corporation recorded amortization of $35,000 and sold property, plant, and equipment with a book value of $10,000. How much cash did Trail Corporation pay to purchase property, plant, and equipment during the period? Where on the cash flow statement should Trail Corporation report this item?

*17. Summarize the major cash receipts and cash payments in the three categories of activities that appear on the cash flow statement prepared by the direct method.

*18. Fort Inc. prepares its cash flow statement using the *direct* method for operating activities. Identify the section of Fort Inc.'s cash flow statement where the results of each of the following transactions will appear. If the transaction does not appear on the cash flow statement, give the reason.

a. Cash	14,000	
Note Payable, Long-Term		14,000
b. Salaries Payable	7,300	
Cash		7,300
c. Cash	28,400	
Sales Revenue		28,400
d. Amortization Expense	6,500	
Patent		6,500
e. Accounts Payable	1,400	
Cash		1,400

*19. Winford Distributing Corp. collected cash of $102,000 from customers and $8,000 interest on notes receivable. Cash payments included $28,000 to employees, $18,000 to suppliers, $11,000 as dividends to shareholders, and $10,000 as a long-term loan to another company. How much was Winford Distributing Corp.'s net cash inflow from operating activities using the direct method?

*20. Nelson Inc. recorded salaries expense of $54,000 during a year when the balance of Salaries Payable decreased from $8,000 to $2,000. How much cash did Nelson Inc. pay to employees during the year? Where on the cash flow statement should Nelson Inc. report this item?

*21. What is the difference between the direct method and the indirect method of reporting investing activities and financing activities?

*22. Why is amortization expense *not* reported on a cash flow statement that reports operating activities by the direct method?

*These Questions cover Chapter 17 Appendix topics.

STARTERS

① Purposes of the cash flow statement

S17–1 Describe how the cash flow statement helps investors and creditors perform each of the following functions:

1. Predict future cash flows
2. Evaluate management decisions
3. Predict the ability to make debt payments to lenders and pay dividends to shareholders
4. Show the relationship of net income to cash flow

① Classifying cash flow items

S17–2 Answer these questions about the cash flow statement:

a. List the categories of cash flows in order of importance.
b. What is the "check figure" for the cash flow statement? Where do you get this check figure?
c. What is the first dollar amount to report for the direct method?
d. What is the first dollar amount to report for the indirect method?

① Using a cash flow statement

S17–3 Which company shown below is likely a start-up company rather than an established company? Give reasons for your answer.

	Company X	Company Y
Cash inflow (outflow)—operating activities	$ (10,000)	$50,000
Cash inflow (outflow)—investing activities	(100,000)	30,000
Cash inflow (outflow)—financing activities	80,000	(20,000)
Income (loss) for the year	20,000	20,000

② Free cash flow
Free cash flow, $56,000

S17–4 Latham Company expects the following for 2020:

• Net cash inflow from operating activities of $120,000
• Net cash inflow from financing activities of $48,000
• Net cash outflow from investing activities of $64,000 (no sales of long-term assets)

How much free cash flow does Latham Company expect for 2020?

S17–5 Boost Plus Inc. reported the following data for 2020:

③
Computing cash flows from operating activities—indirect method

Net cash inflow, $61,000

Income Statement	
Net income	$63,000
Amortization expense	10,000
Balance sheet	
Increase in Accounts receivable	7,000
Decrease in Accounts payable	5,000

Compute Boost Plus Inc.'s net cash inflow (outflow) from operating activities using the *indirect* method.

S17–6 Apple Distillery Inc. accountants have assembled the following data for the year ended June 30, 2020:

③
Computing operating cash flows—indirect method

Net cash inflow, $70,000

Payment of dividends	$12,000	Net income	$100,000
Cash receipt from issuance of common shares...............................	40,000	Purchase of equipment,..............	80,000
		Decrease in current liabilities ..	10,000
Increase in current assets other than cash	60,000	Payment of note payable...........	60,000
		Cash receipt from sale of land	120,000
Repurchase of Apple Distillery shares.....	10,000	Amortization expense	40,000

Prepare the *operating* activities section of Apple Distillery Inc.'s cash flow statement for the year ended June 30, 2020. Apple Distillery uses the *indirect* method for operating cash flows.

S17–7 Prepare the operating section of Preston Media Corporation's 2020 cash flow statement using the *indirect* method.

③
Preparing the operating section of the cash flow statement—indirect method

Net cash inflow, $29,000

Use the comparative balance sheet provided and the following selected fiscal 2020 income statement information:

- Net income, $19,000
- Amortization expense, $11,000

PRESTON MEDIA CORPORATION Balance Sheet March 31, 2020 and 2019		
Assets	**2020**	**2019**
Current assets		
Cash	$ 5,000	$ 3,900
Accounts receivable	9,600	5,100
Company vehicle	105,350	84,350
Less: Accumulated amortization—company vehicle	29,350	18,350
Total assets	$90,600	$75,000
Liabilities		
Current liabilities		
Accounts payable	$8,000	$ 4,500
Long-term liabilities		
Notes payable	9,000	12,000
Total liabilities	17,000	16,500
Shareholders' Equity		
Common shares	27,000	23,000
Retained earnings	46,600	35,500
Total shareholders' equity	73,600	58,500
Total liabilities and shareholders' equity	$90,600	$75,000

S17–8 Which of the following amounts are reported on the cash flow statement? Indicate the section where they are reported.

Equipment

Beginning Balance	$100,000			
Jul. 1	200,000	Jul. 15		$50,000
Aug. 1	57,000			
Ending balance	$307,000			

July 1 and July 15 were cash transactions.

August 1 was a purchase with a long-term note.

S17–9 Techno Toys Ltd. had the following comparative balance sheet:

TECHNO TOYS LTD.
Balance Sheet
December 31, 2020 and 2019

Assets	2020	2019	Liabilities	2020	2019
Current assets			Current liabilities		
Cash	$ 57,000	$ 48,000	Accounts payable	$ 141,000	$ 126,000
Accounts receivable	162,000	144,000	Salaries payable	69,000	63,000
Inventory	240,000	232,000	Accrued liabilities	24,000	33,000
Prepaid expenses	9,000	6,000	Long-term notes payable	198,000	204,000
Long-term investments	225,000	270,000	**Shareholders' Equity**		
			Common shares	120,000	111,000
Property, plant, and equipment, net	675,000	575,000	Retained earnings	816,000	738,000
Total assets	$1,368,000	$1,275,000	Total liab. and shareholders' equity	$1,368,000	$1,275,000

Compute the following:

a. New borrowing or payment of long-term note payable, with Techno having only one long-term note payable transaction during the year.

b. Issuance of common shares, with Techno having only one common share transaction during the year.

c. Payment of cash dividends. Net income for the year ended December 31, 2020, was $120,000.

S17–10 KS Media Corporation had the following income statement and balance sheet for 2020:

KS MEDIA CORPORATION
Income Statement
For the Year Ended December 31, 2020

Service revenue	$120,000
Amortization expense	9,000
Other expenses	81,000
Net income	$ 30,000

KS MEDIA CORPORATION Balance Sheet December 31, 2020 and 2019						
Assets	**2020**	**2019**	**Liabilities**		**2020**	**2019**
Current assets			Current liabilities			
Cash	$ 7,500	$ 6,000	Accounts payable		$ 12,000	$ 9,000
Accounts receivable	15,000	9,000	Long-term notes payable		15,000	18,000
Equipment, net	112,500	105,000	**Shareholders' equity**			
			Common shares		33,000	30,000
			Retained earnings		75,000	63,000
Total assets	$135,000	$120,000	Total liabilities and shareholders' equity		$135,000	$120,000

Compute the following for KS during 2020:

a. Acquisition of equipment. KS sold no equipment during the year.

b. Payment of a long-term note payable. During the year, KS issued a $7,500 note payable.

S17–11 Werstiner Corporation is preparing its cash flow statement by the *indirect* method. The company has the following items for you to consider in preparing the statement. Identify each item by where it is shown on the statement and indicate if it is shown as a positive (+) or negative (−) amount. (For example, an increase in Investments (which represents a decrease in cash) is shown as I–.)

④

Identifying items for reporting cash flows from operations— indirect method

a. O +

j. O −

- Operating activity (O)
- Investing activity (I)
- Financing activity (F)
- Activity that is not used to prepare the cash flow statement (N)

Answer by placing the appropriate symbol in the blank space.

_____ a. Loss on sale of land
_____ b. Amortization expense
_____ c. Increase in inventory
_____ d. Decrease in accounts receivable
_____ e. Purchase of equipment

_____ f. Increase in accounts payable
_____ g. Payment of dividends
_____ h. Decrease in accrued liabilities
_____ i. Issuance of common shares
_____ j. Gain on sale of building

S17–12 Sunshine Ice Cream Shops earned net income of $98,000, which included amortization of $16,500. Sunshine's paid $132,000 for a building and borrowed $66,000 on a long-term note payable. How much did Sunshine's cash balance increase or decrease during the year?

④

Computing a cash increase or decrease—indirect method

Increased by $48,500

S17–13 Apple Distillery Inc. accountants have assembled the following data for the year ended June 30, 2020:

④

Preparing a cash flow statement—indirect method

Net increase in cash, $68,000

Payment of dividends $12,000
Cash receipt from issuance of common shares.................................. 40,000
Increase in current assets other than cash 60,000
Repurchase of Apple Distillery shares.... 10,000

Net income $100,000
Purchase of equipment.............. 80,000
Decrease in current liabilities ... 10,000
Payment of note payable........... 60,000
Cash receipt from sale of land... 120,000
Amortization expense 40,000

Use the data in S17-6 (and your answer if you completed that question) to prepare Apple Distillery Inc.'s cash flow statement for the year ended June 30, 2020. The business uses the *indirect* method for operating activities. Complete only the first three sections and omit the reconciliation of cash.

S17–14

1. Under IFRS, what options does an entity have for classifying cash inflows from interest and dividends on the statement of cash flows? How does this differ from ASPE?

2. Under IFRS, what options does an entity have for classifying cash payments of interest and dividends on the statement of cash flows? How does this differ from ASPE?

*S17–15 Napanee Resources Inc. has assembled the following data for the year ended June 30, 2020:

Payment of dividends	$ 12,000
Cash received from issuing shares	40,000
Collections from customers	400,000
Cash received from sale of land	120,000
Payments to suppliers	220,000
Purchase of equipment	80,000
Payments to employees	140,000
Payment of note payable	60,000

Prepare only the *operating* activities section of Napanee's cash flow statement for the year ended June 30, 2020. Napanee uses the *direct* method for operating cash flows.

*S17–16 Graviton Medics Ltd. reports the following partial balance sheet information:

GRAVITON MEDICS LTD. Balance Sheet (partial) January 31, 2020 and 2019						
Assets	**2020**	**2019**	**Liabilities**		**2020**	**2019**
Current assets			Current liabilities			
Cash	$ 57,000	$ 48,000	Accounts payable	$ 141,000	$ 126,000
Accounts receivable	162,000	144,000	Salaries payable		69,000	63,000
Inventory	240,000	232,000	Accrued liabilities		24,000	33,000
Prepaid expenses	9,000	6,000				

Compute the following for Graviton Medics Ltd.:

a. Collections from customers during fiscal 2020. Sales totalled $420,000.

b. Payments for inventory during fiscal 2020, assuming the change in Accounts Payable is due to inventory. Cost of goods sold was $240,000.

*S17–17 Memmot Health Labs Inc. began 2020 with cash of $65,000. During the year, Memmot earned service revenue of $650,000 and collected $660,000 from customers. Expenses for the year totalled $470,000, of which Memmot paid $460,000 in cash to suppliers and employees. Memmot also paid $150,000 to purchase equipment and paid a cash dividend of $40,000 to its shareholders during 2020.

Prepare the company's cash flow statement for the year ended December 31, 2020. Format operating activities by the *direct* method.

*S17–18 Use the data in S17–15 (and your answer if you completed that question) to prepare Napanee Resources Inc.'s cash flow statement for the year ended June 30, 2020. Napanee uses the *direct* method for operating activities. Complete only the first three sections and omit the reconciliation of cash.

---

*These Starters cover Chapter 17 Appendix topics.

EXERCISES

E17–1   Hazelton Properties Ltd., a real estate developer, has experienced 10 years of growth in net income. Nevertheless, the business is facing bankruptcy. Creditors are calling all Hazelton Properties Ltd.'s outstanding loans for immediate payment, and the cash is simply not available. Where did Hazelton Properties Ltd. go wrong? Managers placed too much emphasis on net income and gave too little attention to cash flows.

① Identifying the purposes of the cash flow statement

Required   Write a brief explaination of the purpose of the cash flow statement for Hazelton Properties Ltd.'s managers.

E17–2   Suppose Whiteshell Inc.'s cash flow statement showed a net cash outflow from operations of $6,000,000.

① Using a cash flow statement

Required

1. Suggest possible reasons for the cash outflow from operations.
2. What is the main danger signal this situation reveals?
3. Suppose Whiteshell Inc. has two more years with the cash flows mentioned above. What is likely to happen to the company?

E17–3   Identify each of the following transactions as an operating activity (O), an investing activity (I), a financing activity (F), or a transaction that is not reported on the cash flow statement (N). For each cash flow, indicate whether the item increases (+) or decreases (−) cash. Assume the *indirect* method is used to report cash flows from operating activities. It is possible to answer more than one section.

② Identifying activities for the cash flow statement

a. O +
e. F +

Activity	Section	(+)/(−) Cash	Transactions
a.		_____	Amortization of equipment
b.		_____	Sale of long-term investment at a loss
c.		_____	Payment of cash dividend
d.		_____	Increase in inventory
e.		_____	Issuance of preferred shares for cash
f.		_____	Prepaid expenses decreased during the year
g.		_____	Accrual of salaries expense
h.		_____	Issuance of long-term note payable to borrow cash
i.		_____	Cash sale of land
j.		_____	Payment of long-term debt

E17–4   Consider three independent cases for the cash flow data of Ontario Home Products Corporation:

② Interpreting a cash flow statement—indirect method

	Case A	Case B	Case C
Cash flows from operating activities			
Net income	$120,000	$ 12,000	$ 120,000
Amortization expense	44,000	44,000	44,000
Increase in current assets	(4,000)	(28,000)	(76,000)
Decrease in current liabilities	0	(32,000)	(24,000)
	160,000	(4,000)	64,000
Cash flows from investing activities			
Acquisition of property, plant, and equipment	$(364,000)	$(364,000)	$(364,000)
Sales of property, plant, and equipment	16,000	16,000	388,000
	(348,000)	(348,000)	24,000
Cash flows from financing activities			
New borrowing	200,000	516,000	64,000
Payment of debt	(36,000)	(116,000)	(84,000)
	164,000	400,000	(20,000)
Net increase (decrease) in cash	$ (24,000)	$ 48,000	$ 68,000

Required For each case, identify from the cash flow statement the primary method that Ontario Home Products Corporation used to generate the cash to acquire new property, plant, and equipment.

②

Interpreting cash flow
statements—indirect method

E17–5 Refer to the data in E17–4 for Ontario Home Products Corporation. Which case indicates the best financial position? Give the reasons for your answer by analyzing each case.

③

Computing cash flows from
operating activities—indirect
method

Cash outflows from operating
activities, $(24,000)

E17–6 The accounting records of TaiRong Corporation reveal the following at its year-end July 31, 2020:

Acquisition of land	$ 444,000	Loss on sale of land	$ 60,000
Amortization	156,000	Net income	288,000
Cash sales	108,000	Payment of accounts payable	576,000
Collection of accounts receivable	1,116,000	Payment of dividends	84,000
Collection of dividend revenue	108,000	Payment of income tax	96,000
Decrease in current liabilities	276,000	Payment of interest	192,000
Increase in current assets other than cash	252,000	Payment of salaries	432,000

Required

1. Compute cash flows from operating activities by the *indirect* method.
2. Evaluate TaiRong Corporation's operating cash flows as being either strong or weak.

③

Computing net income using
cash flows from operating
activities—indirect method

E17–7 Innisfil Ice Hunt Rentals Inc. reported a net cash flow from operating activities of $40,625 on its cash flow statement for the year ended December 31, 2020. The following information was reported in the Cash Flows from Operating Activities section of the cash flow statement, which uses the *indirect* method:

Decrease in legal fees payable	$1,000
Increase in prepaid expenses	400
Amortization	3,350
Loss on sale of equipment	1,500
Increase in accounts payable	600
Decrease in inventory	2,175
Increase in trade accounts receivable	2,000

Required Determine the net income reported by Innisfil Ice Hunt Rentals Inc. for the year ended December 31, 2020. Hint: complete the operating section of the cash flow statement and then solve for net income.

③

Computing cash flows from
operating activities—indirect
method

Net cash inflow from operating
activities, $16,000

E17–8 The records of Vintage Colour Engraving reveal the following:

Net income	$36,000	Amortization expense	$5,000
Revenue	53,000	Decrease in current liabilities	19,000
Loss on sale of land	4,000	Increase in current assets other than cash	10,000
Acquisition of land	35,000		

Compute net cash flows from operating activities by the *indirect* method for the year ended April 30, 2020.

E17–9 Hip Dance Academy Ltd.'s year-end is February 28. The accounting records at March 31, 2020, include the selected accounts shown below.

Cash

Mar. 1	75,000	Dividend	24,000
Collections	126,000	Payments	138,000
Mar. 31	39,000		

Accounts Receivable

Mar. 1	54,000		
Sales	228,000	Collections	126,000
Mar. 31	156,000		

Shoe Inventory

Mar. 1	57,000		
Purchases	111,000	Cost of sales	108,000
Mar. 31	60,000		

Music Equipment

Mar. 1	279,000	
Mar. 31	279,000	

Accumulated Amortization—Music Equipment

		Mar. 1	78,000
		Amortization	9,000
		Mar. 31	87,000

Accounts Payable

		Mar. 1	42,000
Payments	96,000	Purchases	111,000
		Mar. 31	57,000

Accrued Liabilities

		Mar. 1	27,000
Payments	42,000	Expenses	33,000
		Mar. 31	18,000

Retained Earnings

Quarterly		Mar. 1	192,000
dividend	24,000	Net income	69,000
		Mar. 31	237,000

Required

1. Compute Hip Dance Academy Ltd.'s net cash inflow or outflow from operating activities during the month ended March 31, 2020. Use the *indirect* method.

2. Does the business have trouble collecting receivables or selling inventory? How can you tell?

E17–10 Compute the following items for the cash flow statement:

a.		
	Beginning Retained Earnings	$ 120,000
	Ending Retained Earnings	160,000
	Net income for the period	150,000
	Stock dividends	65,000
	Cash dividend payments	?

b.		
	Beginning Property, Plant, and Equipment	$320,000 net
	Ending Property, Plant, and Equipment	365,000 net
	Amortization for the period	36,000
	Acquisitions of new property, plant, and equipment	104,000

Property, plant, and equipment was sold at an $8,000 loss. What was the amount of the cash receipt from the sale?

E17–11 Indicate whether or not each of the items below would be shown on a cash flow statement with operating activities reported using the *indirect* method. Indicate whether the adjustment is added to, is deducted from, or has no effect on the cash flow statement. If the transaction affects the cash flow statement, state whether it relates to operating activities, investing activities, or financing activities. Provide the reason for your answer.

a. The payment of interest on long-term debt.

b. The declaration and distribution of a common stock dividend.

c. A decrease in accounts payable.

d. The sale of office equipment for its book value.

e. The borrowing of funds for future expansion through the sale of bonds.

f. A gain on the sale of property, plant, and equipment.

g. The purchase of equipment in exchange for common shares.

h. Amortization expense—buildings.

i. A decrease in merchandise inventory.

j. An increase in prepaid expenses.

k. Amortization of the premium on bonds payable.

l. An investment in a money market fund.

m. The receipt of interest on long-term investments.

n. The purchase of office equipment.

o. Receiving funds for future expansion through the sale of common shares.

p. Amortization of intangible assets.

②④

Classifying transactions for the cash flow statement

E17–12 Two transactions of LRT Logistics Inc. are recorded as follows:

a.	Cash	80,000	
	Accumulated Amortization—Computer Equipment	830,000	
	Computer Equipment		870,000
	Gain on Sale of Computer Equipment		40,000

b.	Land	2,900,000	
	Cash		1,300,000
	Note Payable		1,600,000

Required Indicate where, how, and in what amount to report these transactions on the cash flow statement and accompanying schedule of non-cash investing and financing activities. Are they cash receipts or payments? LRT Logistics Inc. reports cash flows from operating activities by the *indirect* method.

②③④

Preparing the cash flow statement by the indirect method

Net cash flow from operating, $288,000; investing, $(182,000); financing, $(86,000)

E17–13 The income statement of Flashpoint Consulting Ltd. is shown here:

FLASHPOINT CONSULTING LTD. Income Statement For the Year Ended September 30, 2020		
Revenues		
Consulting revenue		$548,000
Expenses		
Salaries expense	$296,000	
Amortization expense	58,000	
Rent expense	14,000	
Office supplies expense	16,000	
Insurance expense	4,000	
Interest expense	4,000	
Income tax expense	36,000	428,000
Net income		$120,000

Additional data during fiscal year 2020 includes:

a. Acquisition of computer equipment was $232,000. Of this amount, $202,000 was paid in cash and $30,000 by signing a long-term note payable. Flashpoint Consulting Ltd. sold no computer equipment during fiscal year 2020.

b. Cash received from sale of land, $20,000.

c. Cash received from issuance of common shares, $84,000.

d. Payment of long-term note payable, $40,000.

e. Payment of dividends, $130,000.

f. Change in cash balance, $?

g. From the comparative balance sheet at September 30:

	A	B	C	D
1		2020	2019	Increase/(Decrease)
2	Current assets			
3	Cash	$56,000	$ 36,000	
4	Accounts receivable	30,000	144,000	
5	Office supplies	18,000	6,000	
6	Prepaid expenses	10,000	10,000	
7	Current liabilities			
8	Accounts payable	$68,000	$ 56,000	
9	Accrued liabilities	38,000	42,000	

Required

1. Prepare Flashpoint Consulting Ltd.'s cash flow statement for the year ended September 30, 2020, using the *indirect* method.

2. Evaluate Flashpoint Consulting Ltd.'s cash flows for the year. In your evaluation, mention all three categories of cash flows and give the reason for your evaluation.

E17–14 Prepare the 2020 cash flow statement for Buragina Inc. using the *indirect* method to report cash flows from operating activities.

②③④

Preparing the cash flow statement by the indirect method

Transaction data for 2020

Net cash flow from operating, $180,000; investing, $(128,000); financing, $12,000

Amortization expense .... $ 40,000✓	Payment of cash dividends............ $ 72,000
Issuance of long-term note payable to borrow cash 28,000	Net income .... 104,000✓
Issuance of common shares for cash............................. 76,000	Purchase of long-term investment..................................... 32,000✓
Cash received from sale of building...................................... 296,000✓	Issuance of long-term note payable to purchase patent........ 148,000~non-cash
Repurchase of own shares 20,000	Issuance of common shares to retire $52,000 of bonds .... 52,000 -non-Cash
Loss on sale of building................... 8,000✓	
Purchase of equipment................... 392,000✓	

	A	B	C	D
1	**Selected balances at December 31**	**2020**	**2019**	**Increase/(Decrease)**
2	Current assets			
3	Cash and cash equivalents	$ 76,000	$ 12,000	
4	Accounts receivable	88,000	92,000	
5	Inventory	136,000	124,000	
6	Prepaid expenses	4,000	12,000	
7	Current liabilities			
8	Note payable (for inventory purchases)	$ 44,000	$ 28,000	
9	Accounts payable	96,000	76,000	
10	Accrued liabilities	28,000	36,000	
11	Income and other taxes payable	40,000	40,000	

*E17–15 Identify each of the following transactions as an operating activity (O), an investing activity (I), a financing activity (F), a non-cash investing and financing activity (NIF), or a transaction that is not reported on the cash flow statement (N). For each cash flow, indicate whether the item increases + or decreases − cash. Assume the direct method is used to report cash flows from operating activities.

	Activity	Section	(+)/(−) Cash	Transactions
a.			_____	Acquisition of a building by issuance of common shares
b.			_____	Issuance of common shares for cash
c.			_____	Payment of accounts payable
d.			_____	Acquisition of equipment by issuance of note payable
e.			_____	Purchase of long-term investment
f.			_____	Payment of wages to employees
g.			_____	Collection of cash interest
h.			_____	Distribution of stock dividend
i.			_____	Repurchase of common shares
j.			_____	Amortization of bond discount
k.			_____	Collection of accounts receivable

*E17–16 Use the information provided to prepare a cash flow statement for Northern Auto Repair Services using the *direct* method for December 31, 2020. Assume that the beginning balance of cash is $55,000. Identify by letter which entry matches the line item on the cash flow statement.

a.	Land	185,000	
	Cash		185,000
b.	Dividends Payable	40,000	
	Cash		40,000
c.	Furniture and Fixtures	43,000	
	Note Payable, Short-Term		43,000
d.	Salaries Expense	19,000	
	Cash		19,000
e.	Equipment	137,000	
	Cash		137,000
f.	Cash	125,000	
	Long-Term Investment in Bonds		125,000
g.	Cash	80,000	
	Bonds Payable		80,000
h.	Building	210,000	
	Note Payable, Long-Term		210,000
i.	Cash	85,000	
	Accounts Receivable		85,000
j.	Accounts Payable	39,000	
	Cash		39,000
k.	Cash	140,000	
	Common Shares		140,000
l.	Cash	8,000	
	Interest Revenue		8,000

*These Exercises cover Chapter 17 Appendix topics.

*E17–17 Compute the following items for the cash flow statement:

(A1)

Computing amounts for the cash flow statement—direct method

a. $104,000

a.	Beginning Accounts Receivable	$ 25,000
	Ending Accounts Receivable	21,000
	Credit sales for the period	100,000
	Cash collections	?

b.	Cost of goods sold	$ 80,000
	Beginning Inventory balance	20,000
	Ending Inventory balance	16,000
	Beginning Accounts Payable	12,000
	Ending Accounts Payable	8,000
	Cash payments for inventory	?

*E17–18 The accounting records of The Olive Oil Company reveal the following for the month ended August 31, 2020:

(A1)

Computing cash flows from operating activities—direct method

Net cash inflow from operating activities, $60,000

Acquisition of land................................	$ 89,000	Loss on sale of land........................	$ 6,000
Amortization...	50,000	Net income	78,000
Cash sales	78,000	Payment of accounts payable.......	110,000
Collection of accounts receivable.......	186,000	Payment of dividends	25,000
Collection of dividend revenue.........	4,000	Payment of income tax.................	8,000
Decrease in current liabilities	52,000	Payment of interest	14,000
Increase in current assets other than cash	48,000	Payment of salaries and wages..	76,000

Required Compute cash flows from operating activities by the *direct* method.

*E17–19 Selected accounts of Homestead Bakery Inc. show the following:

(A1)

Identifying items for the cash flow statement—direct method

Accounts Receivable

Beginning balance	27,000	Cash receipts from customers	354,000
Service revenue	360,000		
Ending balance	33,000		

Land

Beginning balance	640,000		
Acquisitions paid with cash	81,000		
Ending balance	721,000		

Long-Term Debt

Payments	207,000	Beginning balance	819,000
		Issuance of debt for cash	249,000
		Ending balance	861,000

Required For each account, identify the item or items that should appear on a cash flow statement prepared by the *direct* method. Also, state each item's amount and where to report the item.

---

*These Exercises cover Chapter 17 Appendix topics.

*E17–20 Unbeweaveable Beauty Supply began 2020 with cash of $112,000. During the year, the company earned service revenue of $2,400,000 and collected $2,360,000 from clients. Expenses for the year totalled $1,760,000, of which the company paid $1,640,000 in cash to employees and $60,000 in cash for supplies. Unbeweaveable Beauty Supply also paid $480,000 to purchase computer equipment and paid a cash dividend of $80,000 to its shareholders during 2020.

Required

1. Compute net income for the year.
2. Determine the cash balance at the end of the year.
3. Prepare the company's cash flow statement for the year. Format operating activities by the *direct* method.

②④Ⓐ1

Preparing a cash flow
statement—direct method

Net cash from
operating, $288,000;
investing, $(182,000);
financing, $(86,000)

*E17–21 The 2020 income statement and some additional data for Flashpoint Consulting Ltd. follow:

FLASHPOINT CONSULTING LTD.		
Income Statement		
For the Year Ended September 30, 2020		
Revenues		
Consulting revenue		$548,000
Expenses		
Salaries expense	$296,000	
Amortization expense	58,000	
Rent expense	14,000	
Office supplies expense	16,000	
Insurance expense	4,000	
Interest expense	4,000	
Income tax expense	36,000	428,000
Net income		$120,000

Additional data:

a. Collections from clients were $114,000 more than revenues.
b. Increase in cash balance, $20,000.
c. Payments to employees are $8,000 less than salaries expense.
d. Interest expense and income tax expense equal their cash amounts.
e. Acquisition of computer equipment is $232,000. Of this amount, $202,000 was paid in cash and $30,000 by signing a long-term note payable.
f. Cash received from sale of land, $20,000.
g. Cash received from issuance of common shares, $84,000.
h. Payment of long-term note payable, $40,000.
i. Payment of cash dividends, $130,000.
j. Payments for rent and insurance were equal to expense.
k. Payment for office supplies was $12,000 more than expense.
l. Beginning cash balance; $36,000, ending cash balance; $56,000.

Required

1. Prepare Flashpoint Consulting Ltd.'s cash flow statement by the *direct* method and the note to the financial statements giving the summary of non-cash investing and financing activities.
2. Evaluate Flashpoint's cash flow for the year. Mention all three categories of cash flows and the reason for your evaluation.

---

*These Exercises cover Chapter 17 Appendix topics.

*E17–22 The income statement and additional data of Ahn Photography Ltd. follow:

② ④ ⑤ Ⓐ①

Preparing the cash flow statement under IFRS—direct method

Net cash flow from operating, $47,000; investing, $(45,500); financing, $3,500

AHN PHOTOGRAPHY LTD.
Income Statement
For the Year Ended December 31, 2020

Revenues		
Consulting revenue		$137,000
Expenses		
Salaries expense	$74,000	
Amortization expense	14,500	
Rent expense	6,000	
Office supplies expense	1,500	
Insurance expense	1,000	
Interest expense	1,000	
Income tax expense	9,000	107,000
Net income		$ 30,000

Additional data:

a. Collections from clients are $3,500 more than revenues.

b. Increase in cash balance, $5,000.

c. Payments to employees are $2,000 less than salaries expense.

d. Interest expense and income tax expense equal their cash amounts.

e. Acquisition of property, plant, and equipment is $58,000. Of this amount, $50,500 is paid in cash, $7,500 by signing a long-term note payable.

f. Cash received from sale of land, $5,000.

g. Cash received from issuance of common shares, $21,000.

h. Payment of long-term note payable, $10,000.

i. Payment of cash dividends, $7,500.

j. Payments for rent and insurance are equal to expense.

k. Payment for office supplies is $3,000 more than expense.

l. Opening cash balance, $8,000.

Required

1. Prepare Ahn Photography Ltd.'s cash flow statement by the *direct* method for operating activities and a note to the financial statements providing a summary of non-cash investing and financing activities.

2. Assume Ahn Photography Ltd. has adopted IFRS. What would be the difference in the cash flow statement using this framework?

---

*This Exercise covers Chapter 17 Appendix topics

SERIAL EXERCISE

② ③

Identify cash flows from operating, investing and financing activities, prepare a cash flow statement using the indirect method

Net cash inflow from operating activities, $441,092

E17–23 *The Serial Exercise involves a company that will be revisited throughout relevant chapters in Volume 1 and Volume 2. You can complete the Serial Exercises using MyLab Accounting.*

This exercise continues recordkeeping for the Canyon Canoe Company from Chapter 16. Students do not need to have completed prior exercises in order to answer this exercise.

Canyon Canoe Company's comparative balance sheet is shown below. Amounts for 2024 are assumed, but include several transactions from prior chapters.

CANYON CANOE COMPANY Comparative Balance Sheet December 31, 2023 and 2024		
Assets	**2024**	**2023**
Current assets		
Cash	$ 523,693	$ 12,125
Short-term investments, net	23,840	0
Accounts receivable, net	2,422	7,600
Inventory	355	0
Office supplies	60	165
Prepaid rent	0	2,000
Property, plant, and equipment		
Land	155,000	85,000
Building	610,000	35,000
Canoes	12,000	12,000
Office furniture and equipment	150,000	0
Less: Accum. amort. furn. and equip.	35,180	850
Total assets	$ 1,442,190	$153,040
Liabilities		
Current liabilities		
Accounts payable	$ 6,640	$ 3,670
Salaries payable	4,250	1,250
Note payable	15,000	0
Interest payable	350	50
Unearned revenue	500	350
Long-term liabilities		
Note payable	7,200	7,200
Mortgage payable	405,000	0
Bonds payable	210,000	0
Discount on bonds payable	(1,270)	0
Total liabilities	647,670	12,520
Shareholders' Equity		
Preferred shares	70,000	0
Common shares	336,000	136,000
Retained earnings	388,520	4,520
Total shareholders' equity	794,520	140,520
Total liabilities and shareholders' equity	$ 1,442,190	$153,040

Additional data follow:

1. The income statement for 2024 included the following items:
   a. Net income, $417,000.
   b. Amortization expense for the year, $34,330.
   c. Amortization of discount on the bonds payable, $254.
2. There were no disposals of property, plant, and equipment during the year. All acquisitions of property, plant, and equipment were for cash except the land, which was acquired by issuing preferred shares.

3. The company issued bonds payable with a face value of $210,000, receiving cash of $208,476.

4. All dividends were paid in cash.

5. The common shares were issued for cash.

6. The cash receipt from the note payable in 2024 is considered a financing activity because it does not relate to operations.

Required Prepare the statement of cash flows for the year ended December 31, 2024, using the *indirect* method.

CHALLENGE EXERCISES

E17–24 Nanotech Security Corp. is a company in British Columbia which specializes in globally recognized anti-counterfeiting products. Its consolidated cash flow statement for the years ended September 30, 2017 and 2016, is adapted and reproduced below:

①②
Analyzing an actual company's cash flow statement

NANOTECH SECURITY CORP. Consolidated Cash Flow Statement (adapted*) For the Years Ended September 30		
(In Canadian dollars)	**2017**	**2016**
Cash flows provided by (used in):		
Operating activities:		
Net loss from continuing operations	$ (3,853,853)	$(7,658,910)
Items not involving cash:		
Depreciation and amortization	2,917,883	3,077,997
Share-based compensation	921,198	661,786
Accretion of convertible debentures	589,858	80,825
Other	(27,570)	(27,570)
Deferred income taxes	—	(162,797)
Non-cash working capital changes (note 15(a))	(720,420)	371,023
	(172,904)	(3,657,646)
Discontinued operations (note 18):		
Net loss from discontinued operations	(900,279)	(170,895)
Depreciation	12,804	17,689
Items not involving cash	313,162	(91,976)
Cash used in operating activities	(747,217)	(3,902,828)
Investing activities:		
Purchase of property and equipment	(106,944)	(148,752)
Cash used in investing activities	(106,944)	(148,752)
Financing activities:		
Issuance of shares for options exercised	223,000	197,400
Proceeds on financing, net of costs (note 10(a))	12,486,784	—
Repayment of note payable (note 8)	(3,000,000)	—
Repayment of convertible debentures (note 9)	(1,370,000)	—
Proceeds on issuance of convertible debentures, net of costs	—	4,120,289
Cash provided by financing activities	8,339,784	4,317,689
Effect of foreign exchange on cash and cash equivalents	85,605	24,654
Increase in cash and cash equivalents	7,571,228	290,763
Cash and cash equivalents, beginning of year	3,312,691	3,021,928
Cash and cash equivalents, end of year	$10,883,919	$ 3,312,691

Working capital accounts are current assets and current liabilities. Because businesses have so many of these accounts, listing all the line by line changes in their reports would make them too long. It is common for real cash flow statements to summarize the total like this and include the details in the notes to the financial statements.

*Used with permission from Nanotech Security Corp.

1. Which format did Nanotech Security Corp. use for reporting cash flows from operating activities?
2. What was Nanotech Security's largest source of cash during the year ended September 30, 2017? During the previous year?
3. What was Nanotech Security's largest use of cash during the year ended September 30, 2017?
4. Which section—operating, investing, or financing—did Nanotech Security have the largest source of cash shown for 2017 and 2016? Comment on your findings.
5. During the year ended September 30, 2017, Nanotech Security has a large negative cash flow from operating activities. Does this mean Nanotech Security is expanding, downsizing, or remaining stable?
6. How is the business's cash balance doing overall?

BEYOND THE NUMBERS

①②
Using cash flow data to evaluate an investment

BN17–1

Your employer is looking to diversify into the baked goods industry. It is considering an investment in either Sweet Treats Ltd. or Cupcakes Inc. Both companies earn about the same net income and have similar financial positions, so your decision depends on their cash flow statements, summarized as follows:

	Sweet Treats Ltd.		Cupcakes Inc.	
Net cash inflows from operating activities		$ 90,000		$ 50,000
Net cash inflows (outflows) from investing activities				
Purchase of property, plant, and equipment	$(100,000)		$ (20,000)	
Sale of property, plant, and equipment	10,000	(90,000)	40,000	20,000
Net cash inflows (outflows) from financing activities				
Issuance of common shares	30,000		—	
Issuance of long-term debt	—		80,000	
Repayment of long-term debt	—	30,000	(120,000)	(40,000)
Net increase in cash		$ 30,000		$ 30,000

Based on their cash flows, which company looks better? Give your reasons.

ETHICAL ISSUE

EI17–1

Globex Travel Ltd. is experiencing a bad year. Net income is only $60,000. Also, two important clients are falling behind in their payments to Globex Travel Ltd., and the agency's accounts receivable are increasing dramatically. The company desperately needs a loan. The company's board of directors is considering ways to put the best face on the company's financial statements. The company's bank closely examines cash flow from operations. Aleksi Belland, a director, suggests reclassifying as long term the receivables from the slow-paying clients. He explains to the other members of the board that removing the $40,000 rise in accounts receivable will increase net cash inflow from operations. This approach will increase the company's cash balance and may help Globex Travel Ltd. get the loan.

Required

1. Using only the amounts given, compute net cash inflow from operations both without and with the reclassification of the receivables. Which reporting makes Globex Travel Ltd. look better?

2. Where else in Globex's cash flow statement will the reclassification of the receivable be reported? What cash flow effect will this item report? What effect would the reclassification have on overall cash flow from all activities?

3. Under what condition would the reclassification of the receivables be ethical? Unethical?

PROBLEMS (GROUP A)

P17–1A Managers of Sew It Seams Repairs are reviewing company performance for 2020. The income statement reports a 16 percent increase in net income, which is excellent. The balance sheet shows modest increases in assets, liabilities, and shareholders' equity. The assets with the largest increases are plant and equipment because the company is halfway through an expansion program. No other assets and no liabilities are increasing dramatically. A summarized version of the cash flow statement reports the following:

①
Using cash flow information to evaluate performance

Net cash inflow from operating activities	$ 1,240,000
Net cash outflow from Investing activities	(1,140,000)
Net cash inflow from financing activities	280,000
Increase in cash during 2020	$ 380,000

Required Write a memo to give top managers of Sew It Seams Repairs your assessment of 2020 and your outlook for the future. Focus on the information content of the cash flow data.

P17–2A Brentwood Bay Inc.'s comparative balance sheet at September 30, 2020, is shown below:

②③
Preparing the operating section of the cash flow statement—indirect method

Net cash inflow, $243,600

BRENTWOOD BAY INC. Balance Sheet September 30, 2020 and 2019		
Assets	**2020**	**2019**
Current assets		
Cash	$ 194,800	$ 96,400
Accounts receivable	167,600	164,000
Interest receivable	16,400	11,200
Inventory	486,800	467,600
Prepaid expenses	34,400	37,200
Long-term investments	204,400	55,200
Plant and equipment, net	527,600	416,400
Land	188,400	297,200
Total assets	$1,820,400	$1,545,200
Liabilities		
Current liabilities		
Notes payable, short-term	$ 40,000	$ 0
Accounts payable	247,200	281,200
Income tax payable	47,200	46,400
Accrued liabilities	71,600	116,400
Interest payable	18,000	12,800
Salaries payable	6,000	4,400
Long-term note payable	492,000	525,600
Shareholders' Equity		
Common shares	543,600	336,000
Retained earnings	354,800	222,400
Total liabilities and shareholders' equity	$1,820,400	$1,545,200

Other information for the year ended September 30, 2020 that *may* be needed includes

a. Acquired equipment by issuing long-term note payable, $89,200, and paying $16,000 cash.

b. Paid long-term note payable, $122,800.

c. Received $207,600 cash for issuance of common shares.

d. Paid cash dividends, $217,200.

e. Acquired equipment by issuing short-term note payable, $40,000.

f. Net income, $349,600

g. Amortization expense, $34,000

h. Gain on sale of land, $43,600

Required

1. Prepare Brentwood Bay Inc.'s operating section of the cash flow statement for the year ended September 30, 2020, using the *indirect* method.

2. Describe how the *direct* method would differ from the partial statement you created in Requirement 1.

② ③ ④
Preparing the cash flow statement—indirect method
1. Net cash flow from operating, $666,000; investing, $(526,000); financing, $(249,000)

P17–3A The 2020 comparative balance sheet and income statement of Shock Electricity Inc. follow:

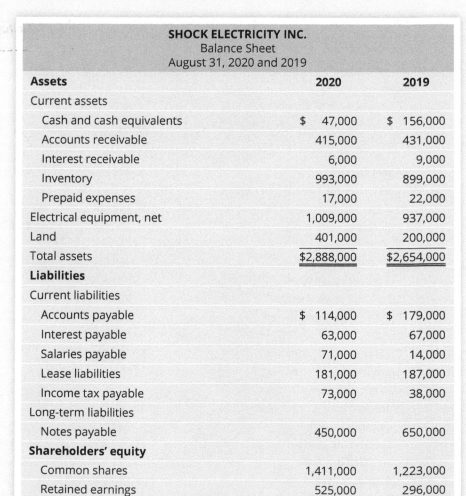

SHOCK ELECTRICITY INC. Balance Sheet August 31, 2020 and 2019		
Assets	**2020**	**2019**
Current assets		
Cash and cash equivalents	$ 47,000	$ 156,000
Accounts receivable	415,000	431,000
Interest receivable	6,000	9,000
Inventory	993,000	899,000
Prepaid expenses	17,000	22,000
Electrical equipment, net	1,009,000	937,000
Land	401,000	200,000
Total assets	$2,888,000	$2,654,000
Liabilities		
Current liabilities		
Accounts payable	$ 114,000	$ 179,000
Interest payable	63,000	67,000
Salaries payable	71,000	14,000
Lease liabilities	181,000	187,000
Income tax payable	73,000	38,000
Long-term liabilities		
Notes payable	450,000	650,000
Shareholders' equity		
Common shares	1,411,000	1,223,000
Retained earnings	525,000	296,000
Total liabilities and shareholders' equity	$2,888,000	$2,654,000

SHOCK ELECTRICITY INC.
Income Statement
For the Year Ended August 31, 2020

Revenues		
Sales revenue		$4,380,000
Interest revenue		17,000
Total revenues		4,397,000
Expenses		
Cost of goods sold	$1,952,000	
Salaries expense	814,000	
Amortization expense	253,000	
Other operating expenses	497,000	
Interest expense	246,000	
Income tax expense	169,000	
Total expenses		3,931,000
Net income		$ 466,000

Shock Electricity had no non-cash investing and financing transactions during 2020. During the year, there were no sales of land or electrical equipment, no issuances of notes payable, and no repurchase of common shares.

Required

1. Prepare the cash flow statement by the *indirect* method for 2020.
2. Evaluate the cash flow for this company.

P17–4A Accountants for Nature's Design Ltd. have assembled the following data for the year ended December 31, 2020:

② ③ ④
Preparing the cash flow statement—indirect method
Net cash flow from operating, $17,775; investing, $(21,575); financing, $4,150

	A	B	C	D	E
1			**2020**	**2019**	**Difference**
2	Current assets	Cash and cash equivalents	$ 9,050	$ 8,700	
3		Accounts receivable	17,025	18,425	
4		Inventory	29,625	24,125	
5		Prepaid expenses	800	525	
6	Current liabilities	Note payable (for inventory purchases)	7,575	9,200	
7		Accounts payable	18,025	16,875	
8		Income tax payable	1,475	1,950	
9		Accrued liabilities	12,075	5,800	

Transaction data for 2020:

Acquisition of building by issuing long-term note payable ...	$33,000	Issuance of common shares, class B, for cash	$14,050
Acquisition of farm equipment......	18,500	Net income	12,625
Acquisition of long-term investment.....................................	11,200	Payment of cash dividends.............	10,700
		Payment of long-term debt.............	16,950
Amortization expense	5,075	Retirement of bonds payable by issuing preferred shares.........	22,350
Collection of loan	2,575		
Gain on sale of investment	875	Sale of long-term investment for cash..	5,550
Issuance of long-term debt to borrow cash	17,750	Share dividends.................................	10,150

Required

1. Prepare Nature's Design Ltd.'s cash flow statement using the *indirect* method to report operating activities. Include a note regarding non-cash investing and financing activities.

2. Evaluate Nature's Design Ltd.'s cash flows for the year. Mention all three categories of cash flows, and give the reason for your evaluation.

P17–5A The financial statements for Zaibak Corp. for the year ended December 31, 2020, are as follows:

(2)(3)(4)
Using the financial statements to compute the cash effects of a wide variety of business transactions; preparing a cash flow statement by the indirect method

1. Net cash flow from operating, $586,000; investing, $(204,000); financing, $(430,000)

ZAIBAK CORP. Balance Sheet December 31, 2020 and 2019		
Assets	**2020**	**2019**
Cash	$ 10,000	$ 18,000
Investment in money market fund	0	40,000
Accounts receivable	189,000	175,000
Inventory	280,000	610,000
Prepaid expenses	30,000	23,000
Equipment	1,798,000	1,654,000
Less: Accumulated amortization	160,000	120,000
Investment	200,000	0
Goodwill	90,000	100,000
Total assets	$2,437,000	$2,500,000
Liabilities		
Accounts payable	$ 176,000	$ 120,000
Salaries payable	110,000	100,000
Loan payable	350,000	400,000
Total liabilities	636,000	620,000
Shareholders' equity		
Preferred shares	800,000	500,000
Common shares	500,000	500,000
Retained earnings	501,000	880,000
Total shareholders' equity	1,801,000	1,880,000
Total liabilities and shareholders' equity	$2,437,000	$2,500,000

ZAIBAK CORP. Income Statement For the Year Ended December 31, 2020		
Net sales		$1,600,000
Cost of goods sold		840,000
Gross margin		760,000
Operating expenses		
Selling expenses	$ 350,000	
Administrative expenses	230,000	
Interest expense	40,000	
Total operating expenses		620,000
Operating income		140,000
Income taxes		39,000
Net income		$ 101,000

Additional information:

a. The administrative expenses included the following:

   Amortization expense on equipment, $100,000. ✓
   Writedown of goodwill, $10,000. ✓

b. Sold equipment _for its book value._ The equipment cost $430,000 and had been *no gain or loss!*
   amortized for $60,000.

c. Purchased additional equipment in December for $574,000. ✓

d. Issued preferred shares for an investment purchase of $200,000.

e. Declared and paid cash dividends: preferred, $230,000; common, $250,000. ✓

f. Sold 20,000 preferred shares for $5.00 per share.

g. Paid $90,000 (of which $40,000 was interest) on the loans.

Required

1. Prepare a cash flow statement for Zaibak Corp. for the year ended December 31, 2020, using the *indirect* method. The investment in the money market fund is a cash equivalent.

2. Did the company improve its cash position in 2020? Give your reasons.

*P17–6A The 2020 comparative balance sheet and income statement of Shock Electricity Inc. follow:

Preparing the operating section of the cash flow statement—direct method

1. Net cash flow from operating, $666,000

SHOCK ELECTRICITY INC. Balance Sheet August 31, 2020 and 2019		
Assets	**2020**	**2019**
Current assets		
Cash and cash equivalents	$ 47,000	$ 156,000
Accounts receivable	415,000	431,000
Interest receivable	6,000	9,000
Inventory	993,000	899,000
Prepaid expenses	17,000	22,000
Electrical equipment, net	1,009,000	937,000
Land	401,000	200,000
Total assets	$2,888,000	$2,654,000
Liabilities		
Current liabilities		
Accounts payable	$ 114,000	$ 179,000
Interest payable	63,000	67,000
Salaries payable	71,000	14,000
Lease liabilities	181,000	187,000
Income tax payable	73,000	38,000
Long-term liabilities		
Notes payable	450,000	650,000
Shareholders' equity		
Common shares	1,411,000	1,223,000
Retained earnings	525,000	296,000
Total liabilities and shareholders' equity	$2,888,000	$2,654,000

---

*This Problem covers Chapter 17 Appendix topics.

SHOCK ELECTRICITY INC.		
Income Statement		
For the Year Ended August 31, 2020		
Revenues		
Sales revenue		$4,380,000
Interest revenue		17,000
Total revenues		4,397,000
Expenses		
Cost of goods sold	$1,952,000	
Salaries expense	814,000	
Amortization expense	253,000	
Other operating expenses*	497,000	
Interest expense	246,000	
Income tax expense	169,000	
Total expenses		3,931,000
Net income		$ 466,000

*Includes lease liability and prepaid expense.

Shock Electricity had no non-cash investing and financing transactions during 2020. During the year, there were no sales of land or plant and equipment, no issuances of notes payable, and no repurchase of common shares.

Required

1. Prepare the operating section of the 2020 cash flow statement, formatting by the *direct* method.

2. How would this look different if the indirect method were used for Requirement 1?

Preparing the cash flow statement—direct method

1. Net cash flow from operating, $(240,000); investing, $307,800; financing $401,200

*P17–7A Sawyer Products Ltd.'s accountants have developed the following data from the company's accounting records for the year ended July 31, 2020:

a. Salaries expense, $631,800.

b. Cash payments to purchase property, plant, and equipment, $1,035,000.

c. Proceeds from issuance of long-term debt, $264,600.

d. Payments of long-term debt, $142,800.

e. Proceeds from sale of property, plant, and equipment, $318,200.

f. Interest revenue, $72,600.

g. Cash receipt of dividend revenue on investments in shares, $56,200.

h. Payments to suppliers, $4,129,800.

i. Interest expense and payments, $226,800.

j. Cost of goods sold, $2,886,600.

k. Collection of interest revenue, $30,200.

l. Acquisition of equipment by issuing short-term note payable, $213,000.

m. Payment of salaries, $804,000.

n. Credit sales, $3,648,600.

o. Income tax expense and payments, $338,400.

p. Amortization expense, $309,600.

q. Collections on accounts receivable, $4,038,600.

r. Collection of long-term notes receivable, $486,400.

s. Proceeds from sale of investments, $538,200.

t. Payment of long-term debt by issuing common shares, $900,000.

*This Problem covers Chapter 17 Appendix topics.

u. Cash sales, $1,134,000.

v. Proceeds from issuance of common shares, $589,400.

w. Payment of cash dividends, $310,000.

x. Cash balance:

July 31, 2019—$654,800
July 31, 2020—$?

Required

1. Prepare Sawyer Products Ltd.'s cash flow statement for the year ended July 31, 2020, using the *direct* method for the operating activities section. Include a note to the financial statements giving a summary of non-cash investing and financing activities.

2. Evaluate 2020 in terms of cash flow. Give your reasons.

*P17–8A Brentwood Bay Inc.'s comparative balance sheet at September 30, 2020, and its 2020 income statement are shown below:

② ④ A1
Preparing the cash flow
statement—direct method

1. Net cash flow from
operating, $243,600;
investing, $(12,800);
financing, $(132,400)

BRENTWOOD BAY INC. Balance Sheet September 30, 2020 and 2019		
Assets	**2020**	**2019**
Current assets		
Cash	$ 194,800	$ 96,400
Accounts receivable	167,600	164,000
Interest receivable	16,400	11,200
Inventory	486,800	467,600
Prepaid expenses	34,400	37,200
Long-term investments	204,400	55,200
Plant and equipment, net	527,600	416,400
Land	188,400	297,200
Total assets	$1,820,400	$1,545,200
Liabilities		
Current liabilities		
Note payable, short-term	$ 40,000	$ 0
Accounts payable	247,200	281,200
Income tax payable	47,200	46,400
Accrued liabilities	71,600	116,400
Interest payable	18,000	12,800
Salaries payable	6,000	4,400
Long-term note payable	492,000	525,600
Shareholders' Equity		
Common shares	543,600	336,000
Retained earnings	354,800	222,400
Total liabilities and shareholders' equity	$1,820,400	$1,545,200

---

*This Problem covers Chapter 17 Appendix topics.

BRENTWOOD BAY INC.		
Income Statement		
For the Year Ended September 30, 2020		
Sales revenue		$1,468,400
Cost of goods sold		646,000
Gross margin		822,400
Operating expenses		
Amortization	$ 34,000	
Salaries	253,600	
Other	118,400	406,000
Operating income		416,400
Other revenues and expenses		
Revenues and gains		
Interest	39,200	
Gain on sale of land	43,600	82,800
		499,200
Interest expense		64,000
Income before income taxes		435,200
Income tax expense		85,600
Net income		$ 349,600

Other information for the year ended September 30, 2020:

a. Acquired equipment by issuing long-term note payable, $89,200, and paying $16,000 cash.

b. Paid long-term note payable, $122,800.

c. Received $207,600 cash for issuance of common shares.

d. Paid cash dividends, $217,200.

e. Acquired equipment by issuing short-term note payable, $40,000.

Required

1. Prepare Brentwood Bay Inc.'s cash flow statement for the year ended September 30, 2020, using the *direct* method to report operating activities.

2. Also prepare a note to the financial statements giving a summary of non-cash investing and financing activities. All current accounts, except short-term note payable, result from operating transactions.

②③④Ⓐ⒈
Preparing the cash flow statement—direct and indirect methods

1. Net cash flow from operating, $84,100; investing, $(51,500); financing, $(44,500)

*P17–9A To prepare the cash flow statement, accountants for West Boats Ltd. have summarized 2020 activity in two T-accounts as follows:

Cash

Beginning balance	87,100	Payments of operating expenses	46,100
Sale of common shares	80,800	Payment of long-term debt	78,900
Receipts of dividends	17,900	Repurchase of common shares	30,400
Sale of investments	28,400	Payment of income tax	6,000
Receipts of interest	22,200	Payments on accounts payable	101,600
Collections from customers	307,000	Payments of dividends	16,000
		Payments of salaries and wages	67,500
		Payments of interest	41,800
		Purchase of equipment	79,900
Ending balance	75,200		

Common Shares

Repurchase of common shares	30,400	Beginning balance	103,500
		Issuance for cash	80,800
		Issuance to acquire land	64,500
		Issuance to retire long-term debt	31,600
		Ending balance	250,000

*This Problem covers Chapter 17 Appendix topics.

West Boats Ltd.'s 2020 income statement and selected balance sheet data follow:

WEST BOATS LTD. Income Statement For the Year Ended October 31, 2020		
Revenues and gains		
Sales revenue		$317,000
Interest revenue		22,200
Dividend revenue		17,900
Gain on sale of investments		700
Total revenues and gains		357,800
Expenses		
Cost of goods sold	$103,600	
Salaries and wages expense	66,800	
Amortization expense	10,900	
Other operating expenses	44,700	
Interest expense	44,100	
Income tax expense	9,200	
Total expenses		279,300
Net income		$ 78,500

	A	B	C
1		**October 31, 2020, Balance Sheet Data**	**Increase/ (Decrease)**
2	Current assets	Cash and cash equivalents	$?
3		Accounts receivable	10,000
4		Inventory	5,700
5		Prepaid expenses	(1,900)
6	Long-term	Investments	(27,700)
7		Plant and equipment, net	69,000
8		Land	75,000
9	Current liabilities	Accounts payable	7,700
10		Interest payable	2,300
11		Salaries payable	(700)
12		Other accrued liabilities	(3,300)
13		Income tax payable	3,200
14		Long-term debt	(100,000)
15		Common shares	146,500
16		Retained earnings	62,500

Required

1. Prepare West Boats Ltd.'s cash flow statement for the year ended October 31, 2020, using the *direct* method to report operating activities. Also prepare a note to the financial statements summarizing the non-cash investing and financing activities.

2. Prepare a schedule showing cash flows from operating activities using the *indirect* method. All activity in the current accounts results from operations.

*P17–10A Asjid Analytics Ltd.'s accountants have developed the following data from the company's accounting records for the year ended December 31, 2020:

a. Salaries expense, $210,600.

b. Cash payments to purchase property, plant, and equipment, $345,000.

c. Proceeds from issuance of long-term debt, $88,200.

d. Payments of long-term debt, $37,600.

e. Proceeds from sale of property, plant, and equipment, $119,400.

f. Interest revenue, $24,200.

g. Cash receipt of dividend revenue on investments in shares, $5,400.

h. Payments to suppliers, $1,376,600.

i. Interest expense and payments, $75,600.

j. Cost of goods sold, $962,200.

k. Collection of interest revenue, $33,400.

l. Acquisition of equipment by issuing short-term note payable, $91,000.

m. Payment of salaries, $468,000.

n. Credit sales, $1,216,200.

o. Income tax expense and payments, $112,800.

p. Depreciation expense, $103,200.

q. Collections on accounts receivable, $1,346,200.

r. Collection of long-term notes receivable, $138,800.

s. Proceeds from sale of investments, $179,400.

t. Payment of long-term debt by issuing preferred shares, $400,000.

u. Cash sales, $578,000.

v. Proceeds from issuance of common shares, $209,800.

w. Payment of cash dividends, $100,000.

x. Cash balance:

   December 31, 2019—$151,600
   December 31, 2020—$?

Required

1. Prepare Asjid Analytics's cash flow statement for the year ended December 31, 2020, reporting operating activities by the *direct* method. Include a note to the financial statements providing a summary of non-cash investing and financing activities. Assume that the business has adopted IFRS and has elected to place all dividend and interest receipts and payments into operating activities.

2. Assume that Asjid Analytics Ltd. has adopted IFRS and has elected to classify cash inflows from interest and dividends as investing activities and cash outflows for the payment of interest and dividends as financing activities. How would this election change the balances in the three sections of the cash flow statement? Note the balances of each section and comment.

---

*This Problem covers Chapter 17 Appendix topics.

PROBLEMS (GROUP B)

P17–1B Top managers of the Deli Llama Food Truck Ltd. are reviewing company performance for 2020. The income statement reports a 20 percent increase in net income over 2019. However, most of the net income increase resulted from an unusual gain of $60,000 on the sale of equipment. The cash proceeds were $180,000. The balance sheet shows a large increase in receivables in their catering division. The cash flow statement, in summarized form, reports the following:

① Using cash flow information to evaluate performance

Net cash outflow from operating activities	$(330,000)
Net cash inflow from investing activities	300,000
Net cash inflow from financing activities	150,000
Increase in cash during 2020	$ 120,000

Required Write a memo to give the managers of the Deli Llama Food Truck Ltd. your assessment of 2020 operations and your outlook for the future. Focus on the information content of the cash flow data.

P17–2B Gariepy Wholesale Ltd.'s comparative balance sheet at December 31, 2020, and its 2020 income statement are as follows:

② ③ Preparing the operating section of the cash flow statement—indirect method

GARIEPY WHOLESALE LTD. Balance Sheet December 31, 2020 and 2019		
Assets	**2020**	**2019**
Current assets		
Cash	$ 188,000	$ 43,000
Accounts receivable	370,000	241,500
Interest receivable	14,500	18,000
Inventory	343,000	301,000
Prepaid expenses	18,500	14,000
Long-term investment	50,500	26,000
Plant and equipment, net	422,500	368,000
Land	212,000	480,000
Total assets	$1,619,000	$1,491,500
Liabilities		
Current liabilities		
Note payable, short-term	$ 67,000	$ 90,500
Accounts payable	234,500	201,500
Income tax payable	69,000	72,500
Accrued liabilities	41,000	48,500
Interest payable	18,500	14,500
Salaries payable	4,500	13,000
Long-term note payable	237,000	470,500
Shareholders' Equity		
Common shares	319,500	256,000
Retained earnings	628,000	324,500
Total liabilities and shareholders' equity	$1,619,000	$1,491,500

GARIEPY WHOLESALE LTD.
Income Statement
For the Year Ended December 31, 2020

Net sales		$1,327,000
Cost of goods sold		402,000
Gross margin		925,000
Operating expenses		
Salaries expense	$194,000	
Amortization expense	27,000	
Other expenses	210,000	431,000
Operating income		494,000
Other revenues and expenses		
Revenues and gains		
Interest revenue		53,000
Expenses and losses		
Interest expense	(30,500)	
Loss on sale of land	(33,500)	(64,000)
Income before income taxes		483,000
Income tax expense		49,500
Net income		$ 433,500

Other information for the year ended December 31, 2020 which *may* be useful includes:

a. Acquired equipment by issuing a long-term note payable, $76,500, and paying $5,000 cash.

b. Purchased a long-term investment for cash.

c. Received cash for issuance of common shares, $40,000.

d. Only cash dividends were issued during the year.

e. Paid short-term note payable by issuing common shares.

Required

1. Prepare Gariepy Wholesale Ltd.'s operating section of the cash flow statement for the year ended December 31, 2020, using the *indirect* method. All current accounts, except short-term note payable, result from operating transactions.

2. Describe how the *direct* method would differ from the partial statement you created in Requirement 1.

P17–3B The 2020 income statement and comparative balance sheet of Mandarin Design Ltd. follow:

② ③ ④
Preparing the cash flow
statement—indirect method
Σ×

MANDARIN DESIGN LTD.
Income Statement
For the Year Ended June 30, 2020

Revenues		
Sales revenue		$257,000
Interest revenue		13,600
Total revenues		270,600
Expenses		
Cost of goods sold	$76,600	
Salaries expense	27,800	
Amortization expense	4,000	
Other operating expenses	10,500	
Interest expense	16,600	
Income tax expense	27,800	
Total expenses		163,300
Net income		$107,300

MANDARIN DESIGN LTD.
Balance Sheet
June 30, 2020 and 2019

Assets	2020	2019
Current assets		
Cash and cash equivalents	$ 7,200	$ 6,300
Accounts receivable	31,600	26,900
Interest receivable	1,900	700
Inventory	33,600	57,200
Prepaid expenses	2,500	1,900
Plant and equipment, net	66,500	49,400
Land	103,000	54,000
Total assets	$246,300	$196,400
Liabilities		
Current liabilities		
Accounts payable	$ 31,400	$ 28,800
Interest payable	4,400	4,900
Salaries payable	3,100	6,600
Other accrued liabilities	13,700	16,000
Income tax payable	8,900	7,700
Long-term liabilities		
Notes payable	75,000	95,000
Shareholders' equity		
Common shares	68,300	34,700
Retained earnings	41,500	2,700
Total liabilities and shareholders' equity	$246,300	$196,400

Mandarin Design Ltd. had no non-cash financing and investing transactions during 2020. During the year, there were no sales of land or plant and equipment, and no issuances of notes payable.

Required

1. Prepare the 2020 cash flow statement by the *indirect* method.
2. Evaluate the cash flow for this company.

②③④
Preparing the cash flow
statement—indirect method

P17–4B GG's Coffee Ltd.'s accountants have assembled the following data for the year ended December 31, 2020:

	A	B	C	D	E
1			**2020**	**2019**	**Increase/ (Decrease)**
2	Current assets	Cash and cash equivalents	$ 75,500	$ 56,750	
3		Accounts receivable	174,250	155,500	
4		Inventory	271,500	212,500	
5		Prepaid expenses	13,250	10,250	
6	Current liabilities	Note payable (for inventory purchases)	56,500	45,750	
7		Accounts payable	132,250	139,500	
8		Income tax payable	96,500	41,750	
9		Accrued liabilities	38,750	68,000	

Transaction data for 2020:

Acquisition of building	$325,750	Issuance of long-term note payable to borrow cash	$ 36,000
Acquisition of land by issuing long-term note payable	237,500	Loss on sale of equipment	16,750
Acquisition of long-term investment	79,000	Net income	199,000
		Payment of cash dividends	90,750
Amortization expense	60,250	Repurchase and retirement of	
Collection of loan	71,750	common shares	85,750
Issuance of common shares for cash	123,000	Retirement of bonds payable by issuing common shares	157,500
Stock dividends	79,500	Sale of equipment for cash	145,000

Required

1. Prepare GG's Coffee Ltd.'s cash flow statement using the *indirect* method to report operating activities. Note any additional disclosures that are required.
2. Evaluate GG's Coffee Ltd.'s cash flows for the year. Mention all three categories of cash flows, and give the reason for your evaluation.

P17–5B Vaughan Sales Corp. prepared the financial statements for the year ended December 31 shown below:

②③④
Using the financial statements to compute the cash effects of a wide variety of business transactions; preparing a cash flow statement by the indirect method

VAUGHAN SALES CORP.
Income Statement
For the Year Ended December 31, 2020

Net sales		$267,000
Cost of goods sold		120,000
Gross margin		147,000
Operating expenses		
Selling expenses	$ 73,800	
Administrative expenses	43,500	
Interest expense	8,700	
Total operating expenses		126,000
Operating income		21,000
Income taxes		8,400
Net income		$ 12,600

VAUGHAN SALES CORP.
Balance Sheet
December 31, 2020 and 2019

Assets	2020	2019
Cash	$ 6,000	$ 27,600
Investments in money market funds	1,500	4,500
Accounts receivable	12,700	34,200
Inventory	45,900	107,815
Prepaid expenses	3,600	2,850
Equipment	285,600	235,535
Less: Accumulated amortization	24,000	15,000
Land	90,000	0
Goodwill	18,000	22,500
Total assets	$439,300	$420,000
Liabilities		
Accounts payable	$ 21,300	$ 22,500
Salaries payable	34,000	21,000
Loans payable	84,000	99,000
Total liabilities	139,300	142,500
Shareholders' equity		
Common shares	165,000	150,000
Retained earnings	135,000	127,500
Total shareholders' equity	300,000	277,500
Total liabilities and shareholders' equity	$439,300	$420,000

Additional information:

a. The administrative expenses included the following:

Amortization expense on equipment = $24,000
Writedown of goodwill = $4,500

b. Sold equipment for its net book value. The equipment cost $44,685 and had been amortized for $15,000.

c. Purchased additional equipment for $94,750.

d. Exchanged common shares for land valued at $90,000.

e. Declared and paid cash dividends on common shares, $5,100.

f. Repurchased common shares for $75,000.

g. Paid $23,700 (of which $8,700 was interest) on the loans.

Required

1. Prepare a cash flow statement for Vaughan Sales Corp. for the year ended December 31, 2020, using the *indirect* method. Consider the investments in money market funds to be a cash equivalent.

2. Comment on the results indicated by the cash flow statement you created.

② Ⓐ1
Preparing the operating
section of the cash flow
statement—direct method

*P17–6B The 2020 income statement and comparative balance sheet of Mandarin Design Ltd. follow:

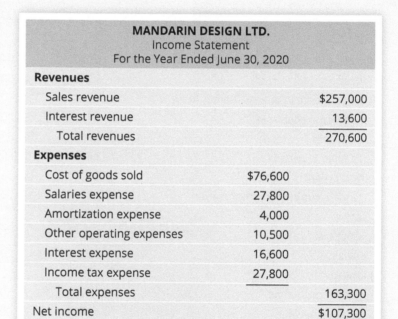

MANDARIN DESIGN LTD. Income Statement For the Year Ended June 30, 2020		
Revenues		
Sales revenue		$257,000
Interest revenue		13,600
Total revenues		270,600
Expenses		
Cost of goods sold	$76,600	
Salaries expense	27,800	
Amortization expense	4,000	
Other operating expenses	10,500	
Interest expense	16,600	
Income tax expense	27,800	
Total expenses		163,300
Net income		$107,300

---

*This Problem covers Chapter 17 Appendix topics.

MANDARIN DESIGN LTD.
Balance Sheet
June 30, 2020 and 2019

Assets	2020	2019
Current assets		
Cash and cash equivalents	$ 7,200	$ 6,300
Accounts receivable	31,600	26,900
Interest receivable	1,900	700
Inventory	33,600	57,200
Prepaid expenses	2,500	1,900
Plant and equipment, net	66,500	49,400
Land	103,000	54,000
Total assets	$246,300	$196,400
Liabilities		
Current liabilities		
Accounts payable	$ 31,400	$ 28,800
Interest payable	4,400	4,900
Salaries payable	3,100	6,600
Other accrued liabilities	13,700	16,000
Income tax payable	8,900	7,700
Long-term liabilities		
Note payable	75,000	95,000
Shareholders' equity		
Common shares	68,300	34,700
Retained earnings	41,500	2,700
Total liabilities and shareholders' equity	$246,300	$196,400

Mandarin Design Ltd. had no non-cash financing and investing transactions during 2020. During the year, there were no sales of land or plant and equipment, and no issuances of note payable.

Required

1. Prepare the operating section of the 2020 cash flow statement, using the *direct* method.
2. Evaluate net cash flows from operating activities compared to its net income.

*P17–7B Accountants for Direct Builders' Supply Ltd. have developed the following data from the company's accounting records for the year ended April 30, 2020:

a. Credit sales, $728,125.

b. Income tax expense and payments, $47,375.

c. Cash payments to acquire property, plant, and equipment, $49,250.

d. Cost of goods sold, $478,250.

e. Cash received from issuance of long-term debt, $85,000.

f. Payment of cash dividends, $80,500.

g. Collection of interest, $34,250.

h. Acquisition of equipment by issuing short-term note payable, $40,500.

i. Payment of salaries, $129,500.

j. Cash received from sale of property, plant, and equipment, $28,000, including an $8,500 loss.

k. Collections on accounts receivable, $578,250.

l. Interest revenue, $4,750.

②④Ⓐ1
Preparing the cash flow statement—direct method

---

*This Problem covers Chapter 17 Appendix topics.

m. Cash receipt of dividend revenue on investment in shares, $25,125.

n. Payments to suppliers, $460,625.

o. Cash sales, $214,875.

p. Amortization expense, $78,500.

q. Cash received from issuance of short-term debt, $69,500.

r. Payments of long-term debt, $62,500.

s. Interest expense and payments, $16,625.

t. Salaries expense, $119,125.

u. Collections of notes receivable, $35,000.

v. Cash received from sale of investments, $11,375, including $2,500 gain.

w. Payment of short-term note payable by issuing long-term note payable, $78,750.

x. Cash balance:

May 1, 2019—$99,125

April 30, 2020—$?

Required

1. Prepare Direct Builders' Supply Ltd.'s cash flow statement for the year ended April 30, 2020, using the *direct* method for the operating activities section. Include a note regarding the non-cash investing and financing activities.

2. Evaluate 2020 from a cash flow standpoint. Give your reasons.

② ④ Ⓐ1

Preparing the cash flow statement—direct method

*P17–8B Gariepy Wholesale Ltd.'s comparative balance sheet at December 31, 2020, and its 2020 income statement are as follows:

GARIEPY WHOLESALE LTD. Balance Sheet December 31, 2020 and 2019		
Assets	**2020**	**2019**
Current assets		
Cash	$ 188,000	$ 43,000
Accounts receivable	370,000	241,500
Interest receivable	14,500	18,000
Inventory	343,000	301,000
Prepaid expenses	18,500	14,000
Long-term investment	50,500	26,000
Plant and equipment, net	422,500	368,000
Land	212,000	480,000
Total assets	$1,619,000	$1,491,500
Liabilities		
Current liabilities		
Note payable, short-term	$ 67,000	$ 90,500
Accounts payable	234,500	201,500
Income tax payable	69,000	72,500
Accrued liabilities	41,000	48,500
Interest payable	18,500	14,500
Salaries payable	4,500	13,000
Long-term note payable	237,000	470,500
Shareholders' Equity		
Common shares	319,500	256,000
Retained earnings	628,000	324,500
Total liabilities and shareholders' equity	$1,619,000	$1,491,500

*This Problem covers Chapter 17 Appendix topics.

GARIEPY WHOLESALE LTD.
Income Statement
For the Year Ended December 31, 2020

Net sales		$1,327,000
Cost of goods sold		402,000
Gross margin		925,000
Operating expenses		
Salaries expense	$194,000	
Amortization expense	27,000	
Other expenses	210,000	431,000
Operating income		494,000
Other revenues and expenses		
Revenues and gains		
Interest revenue		53,000
Expenses and losses		
Interest expense	(30,500)	
Loss on sale of land	(33,500)	(64,000)
Income before income taxes		483,000
Income tax expense		49,500
Net income		$ 433,500

Other information for the year ended December 31, 2020:

a. Acquired equipment by issuing a long-term note payable, $76,500, and paying $5,000 cash.

b. Purchased a long-term investment for cash.

c. Received cash for issuance of common shares, $40,000.

d. Only cash dividends were issued during the year.

e. Paid short-term note payable by issuing common shares.

Required

1. Prepare the cash flow statement of Gariepy Wholesale Ltd. for the year ended December 31, 2020, using the *direct* method to report operating activities. All current accounts, except short-term note payable, result from operating transactions.

2. Prepare a note to the financial statements providing a summary of non-cash investing and financing activities.

*P17–9B To prepare the cash flow statement, accountants for Craftique Inc. have summarized activity for the year 2020 in two accounts as follows:

② ③ ④ Ⓐ1
Preparing the cash flow statement—direct and indirect methods

Cash

Beginning balance	64,320	Payments on accounts payable	447,720
Collection of loan	39,600	Payments of dividends	52,640
Sale of investment	31,440	Payments of salaries and wages	172,560
Receipts of interest	39,120	Payments of interest	56,280
Collections from customers	814,440	Purchase of equipment	37,680
Issuance of common shares	33,360	Payments of operating expenses	41,160
Receipts of dividends	25,400	Payment of long-term debt	73,560
		Repurchase of common shares	20,280
		Payment of income tax	22,680
Ending balance	123,120		

*This Problem covers Chapter 17 Appendix topics.

Common Shares

Repurchase of shares	20,280	Beginning balance	101,280
		Issuance for cash	33,360
		Issuance to acquire land	77,320
		Issuance to retire long-term debt	42,800
		Ending balance	234,480

Craftique Inc.'s income statement and selected balance sheet data follow:

CRAFTIQUE INC.
Income Statement
For the Year Ended December 31, 2020

Revenues		
Sales revenue		$847,560
Interest revenue		39,120
Dividend revenue		25,400
Total revenues		912,080
Expenses and losses		
Cost of goods sold	$420,720	
Salaries and wages expense	180,960	
Amortization expense	29,160	
Other operating expenses	52,920	
Interest expense	58,560	
Income tax expense	19,440	
Loss on sale of investments	3,720	
Total expenses		765,480
Net income		$146,600

	A	B	C
1		**Dec 31, 2020 Balance Sheet Data**	**Increase / (Decrease)**
2	Current assets	Cash and cash equivalents	$?
3		Accounts receivable	33,120
4		Inventory	(14,160)
5		Prepaid expenses	720
6	Long-term	Loan receivable	(39,600)
7		Long-term investments	(35,160)
8		Plant and equipment, net	8,520
9		Land	97,320
10	Current liabilities	Accounts payable	(41,160)
11		Interest payable	2,280
12		Salaries payable	8,400
13		Other accrued liabilities	12,480
14		Income tax payable	(3,240)
15	Long-term	Long-term debt	(96,360)
16	Shareholders' equity	Common shares	133,200
17		Retained earnings	93,960

Required

1. Prepare the cash flow statement of Craftique Inc. for the year ended December 31, 2020, using the *direct* method to report operating activities. Also prepare a note to the financial statements summarizing the non-cash investing and financing activities.

2. Prepare a schedule showing cash flows from operating activities using the *indirect* method. All activity in the current accounts results from operations.

*P17–10B Accountants for Grech Restaurant Supply Ltd. have developed the following data from the company's accounting records for the year ended December 31, 2020:

②④⑤Ⓐ1
Preparing the cash flow statement under IFRS—direct method

a. Credit sales, $291,950.

b. Income tax expense and payments, $18,950.

c. Cash payments to acquire property, plant, and equipment, $29,700.

d. Cost of goods sold, $191,300.

e. Cash received from issuance of long-term debt, $34,000.

f. Payment of cash dividends, $24,200.

g. Collection of interest, $13,700.

h. Acquisition of equipment by issuing short-term note payable, $18,200.

i. Payment of salaries, $43,800.

j. Cash received from sale of property, plant, and equipment, $11,200, including a $3,400 loss.

k. Collections on accounts receivable, $231,300.

l. Interest revenue, $1,900.

m. Cash receipt of dividend revenue on investment in shares, $2,050.

n. Payments to suppliers, $184,250.

o. Cash sales, $85,950.

p. Depreciation expense, $31,400.

q. Cash received from issuance of short-term debt, $29,800.

r. Payments of long-term debt, $25,000.

s. Interest expense and payments, $16,650.

t. Salaries expense, $47,650.

u. Collections of notes receivable, $24,000.

v. Cash received from sale of investments, $4,550, including $1,000 gain.

w. Payment of short-term note payable by issuing long-term note payable, $31,500.

x. Cash balance:

December 31, 2019—$39,650
December 31, 2020—$?

Required

1. Prepare Grech's cash flow statement for the year ended December 31, 2020, reporting operating activities by the *direct* method. Include a note to the financial statements providing a summary of non-cash investing and financing activities. Assume that the business has adopted IFRS and has elected to place all dividend and interest receipts and payments into operating activities.

2. Assume that Grech Restaurant Supply Ltd. has adopted IFRS and has elected to classify cash inflows from interest and dividends as investing activities and cash outflows for the payment of interest and dividends as financing activities. How would this election change the balances in the three sections of the cash flow statement? Note the balances in each section and comment.

---

*This Problem covers Chapter 17 Appendix topics.

CHALLENGE PROBLEMS

②③Ⓐ1

Distinguishing between the direct method and indirect method

P17–1C Both the Accounting Standards Board (AcSB) in Canada and the Financial Accounting Standards Board (FASB) in the United States prefer the direct method of preparing the operating activities section of the cash flow statement. Yet most companies use the indirect method when preparing their cash flow statement.

Required Discuss why you think companies use the indirect method when the direct method is preferred by the standard-setting bodies.

①②④

Accounting for non-cash financing and investing activities

P17–2C Initially, the *CPA Canada Handbook* did not require financial statements to include information about non-cash investing and financing activities. The financial statements reported only changes in working capital (defined as current assets less current liabilities), so transactions such as the use of long-term debt to purchase property, plant, and equipment or conversion of debt into equity were excluded.

Required Discuss the present *CPA Canada Handbook's* requirements with respect to disclosure of non-cash financing and investing decisions, and explain why you think the required disclosure does or does not benefit users.

Extending Your Knowledge

DECISION PROBLEM

①②③④

Preparing and using the cash flow statement to evaluate operations

1. Net cash flow from operating, $60,000; investing, $(66,500); financing, $(18,500)

DP17–1

The 2020 comparative income statement and the 2020 comparative balance sheet of Eclipse Golf Inc. (shown below) have just been distributed at a meeting of the company's board of directors.

    In discussing the company's results of operations and year-end financial position, the members of the board raise a fundamental question: Why is the cash balance so low? This question is especially puzzling to the board members because 2020 showed record profits. As the controller of the company, you must answer the question.

ECLIPSE GOLF INC. Income Statement For the Years Ended December 31, 2020 and 2019 (amounts in thousands)		
Revenues and gains	**2020**	**2019**
Sales revenue	$222.0	$155.0
Gain on sale of equipment (sale price, $17.5)	—	9.0
Total revenues and gains	222.0	164.0
Expenses and losses		
Cost of goods sold	110.5	81.0
Salaries expense	24.0	14.0
Amortization expense	28.5	16.5
Interest expense	6.5	10.0
Loss on sale of land (sale price, $30.5)	—	17.5
Total expenses and losses	169.5	139.0
Net income	$ 52.5	$ 25.0

ECLIPSE GOLF INC. Balance Sheet December 31, 2020 and 2019 (amounts in thousands)		
Assets	**2020**	**2019**
Cash	$ 6.5	$ 31.5
Accounts receivable, net	46.0	30.5
Inventory	97.0	90.5
Property, plant, and equipment, net	74.0	30.5
Patents, net	88.5	94.0
Total assets	$312.0	$277.0
Liabilities and Shareholders' Equity		
Note payable, short-term (for general borrowing)	$ 16.0	$ 50.5
Accounts payable	31.5	28.0
Accrued liabilities	6.0	8.5
Note payable, long-term	73.5	81.5
Common shares	74.5	30.5
Retained earnings	110.5	78.0
Total liabilities and shareholders' equity	$312.0	$277.0

Required

1. Prepare a cash flow statement for 2020 in the format that best shows the relationship between net income and operating cash flow. The company sold no capital assets or long-term investments and issued no note payable during 2020. The changes in all current accounts except short-term note payable arose from operations. There were no non-cash financing and investing transactions during the year. Show all amounts in thousands. Amortization expense on the patent was $5,500.

2. Answer the board members' question: Why is the cash balance so low? In explaining the business's cash flows, identify two significant cash receipts that occurred during 2019 but not in 2020. Also point out the two largest cash payments during 2020.

3. Considering net income and the company's cash flows during 2020, was it a good year or a bad year for Eclipse Golf Inc.? Give your reasons.

FINANCIAL STATEMENT CASES

FSC17–1

①②③④
Using the cash flow statement

Use the Indigo Books & Music Inc.'s Consolidated Statements of Cash Flow which appear in Appendix A at the end of this book and on MyLab Accounting to answer the following questions:

1. Which method does Indigo use to report net cash flows from operations? How can you tell?

2. Did Indigo improve its cash position in the year ended April 1, 2017? If so, by how much? If not, by how much did it decline?

3. By how much did Indigo's cash from operations increase or decrease in the year ended April 1, 2017 versus 2016? Why is it important for cash from operating activities to be a positive number?

4. What were the major investing activities during fiscal 2017? Financing activities?

5. Was Indigo expanding or contracting in fiscal 2017? Support your answer with specific references to the financial statements.

FSC17–2

Use the TELUS Corporation's Statements of Cash Flows found on MyLab Accounting to answer the following questions:

1. Which method does TELUS use to report net cash flows from operations? How can you tell?
2. Did TELUS improve its cash position in 2016? If so, by how much?
3. TELUS and many other companies report items differently in the operating section than the method illustrated or described in the chapter. Explain why this is the case.
4. Explain the cause for the large outflow in the investing section and discuss.
5. Was TELUS expanding, contracting, or holding steady in 2016?

IFRS MINI-CASE

The IFRS Mini-Case is now available online at **MyLab Accounting** in Chapter Resources.

Try It! Solutions for Chapter 17

1. a. The year ended August 31, 2017.
   b. Net income of $224,089,000.
   c. Additions to property, plant, and equipment in the amount of $26,989,000.
   d. Payment of bank loans in the amount of $110,706,000.
   e. $93,701,000.

2. − Payment of dividends
   + Issuance of shares
   − Payment to employees
   + Collections from customers
   − Payments for assets
   − Repayment of a bank loan
   + Issuance of bonds

3. F Payment of cash dividend
   O Decrease in inventory
   I Cash purchase of land
   F Payment of long-term note payable
   O Amortization of building
   O Accrual of interest expense

4. Computation of cash flow from operating activities using the indirect method (amounts in thousands):

Net income	$150
Add (subtract):	
Decrease in accounts receivable	6
Increase in inventory	(18)
Increase in accounts payable	11
Decrease in salaries payable	(15)
Cash flow from operating activities	$134

5. a. Dunbar Ltd. appears to be growing. The company acquired more property, plant, and equipment and intangible assets ($735,000) than it sold during the year ($149,000), and current assets changed very little.
   b. Most of the cash for expansion came from issuing common shares ($242,000) and from borrowing ($226,000). However, cash from the balance on January 1, 2020, and cash from operating activities could have been used for expansion too.
   c. Accounts Receivable ↓, Cash ↑
   Therefore, net cash inflow from operating activities would be $280,000 ($168,000 + $80,000 + $32,000).

6. Net change in cash from investing activities (amounts in thousands):

Sale of bonds issued by Blue Ltd.	$ 224
Purchase of land	(316)
Collection of long-term note receivable	126
Net cash inflow from investing activities	$ 34

7. Net change in cash from financing activities (amounts in thousands):

Retirement of Bolin Corp. preferred shares	$ (90)
Sale of Bolin Corp. common shares	210
Payment of dividends	(300)
Net cash outflow from financing activities	$(180)

8. O Payment of income taxes
   F Issuance of preferred shares
   O Payment of employee salaries
   O Collections of accounts receivable
   I Payment for a delivery truck
   F Repayment of a long-term bank loan (principal only)
   O Receipt of loan interest
   O Payment of accounts payable

9. Markham Corp. will report a cash receipt of $5 million (cost of $2 million plus the gain of $3 million).

10. a. Cash collections from customers:

Accounts Receivable

Beginning balance	+	Sales	−	Collections	=	Ending balance
$46,000	+	$240,000	−	X	=	$44,000
				−X	=	$44,000 − $46,000 − $240,000
				X	=	$242,000

b. Payments for inventory:

Inventory

Beginning balance	+	Purchases	−	Cost of goods sold	=	Ending balance
$62,000	+	X	−	$140,000	=	$68,000
				X	=	$68,000 − $62,000 + $140,000
				X	=	$146,000

Accounts and Note Payable

Beginning balance	+	Purchases	−	Payments for inventory	=	Ending balance
$52,000	+	$146,000	−	X	=	$70,000
				− X	=	$70,000 − $52,000 − $146,000
				X	=	$128,000

c. Payments for income taxes:

Income and Other Taxes Payable

Beginning balance	+	Income tax expense	−	Payments	=	Ending balance
$20,000	+	$20,000	−	X	=	$22,000
				−X	=	$22,000 − $20,000 − $20,000
				X	=	$18,000

d. Payments for prepaid expenses:

Prepaid Expenses

Beginning balance	+	Payments	−	Expiration of prepaid expenses	=	Ending balance
$6,000	+	X	−	$8,000	=	$2,000
				X	=	$2,000 − $6,000 + $8,000
				X	=	$4,000

18 Financial Statement Analysis

CONNECTING CHAPTER 18

LEARNING OBJECTIVES

1 Perform a horizontal analysis of financial statements

How do we compare several years of financial information?

Objectives of Financial Statement Analysis, page 1032
Methods of Analysis, page 1033
Horizontal Analysis, page 1033
Trend Percentages

2 Perform a vertical analysis of financial statements

What is vertical analysis, and how do we perform one?

Vertical Analysis, page 1037

3 Prepare and use common-size financial statements

What are common-size financial statements, and how do we use them?

Common-Size Statements, page 1040
Benchmarking

4 Compute the standard financial ratios

How do we compute standard financial ratios, and what do they mean?

Using Ratios to Make Decisions, page 1044
Measuring the Ability to Pay Current Liabilities (Liquidity)
Measuring the Ability to Sell Inventory and Collect Receivables (Efficiency)
Measuring the Ability to Pay Long-Term Debt (Solvency)
Measuring Profitability
Analyzing Shares as an Investment (Value)

Limitations of Financial Analysis, page 1055
Investor Decisions, page 1055
Annual Reports
Red Flags in Analyzing Financial Statements

5 Describe the impact of IFRS on financial statement analysis

What is the impact of IFRS on financial statement analysis?

The Impact of IFRS on Financial Statement Analysis, page 1058

The **Summary** for Chapter 18 appears on page 1061.
Key Terms with definitions for this chapter's material appears on page 1063.

CPA competencies

This text covers material outlined in **Section 1: Financial Reporting of the CPA Competency Map**. The Learning Objectives for each chapter have been aligned with the CPA Competency Map to ensure the best coverage possible.

1.1.2 Evaluates the appropriateness of the basis of financial reporting

1.4.4 Interprets financial reporting results for stakeholders (internal or external)

Patrick T. Fallon/Bloomberg/Getty Images

S pin Master Corp. is a Canadian-owned world-leading children's toy and entertainment company. Since 2015, it has traded on the Toronto Stock Exchange under the symbol TOY. It is known for creating the award-winning interactive Hatchimals, distributing Etch A Sketch and Meccano toys, and developing shows like *PAW Patrol* and *Rusty Rivets*.

Everyone wants to know, "How is the company doing?" There are a number of different ways to answer that question because there are a number of different tools to use when performing financial analysis.

- Investors and management of Spin Master compare the performance of the most recent period against prior periods. Financial results for two or more years are presented in annual reports for this reason.
- Investors like you can compare Spin Master's earnings to its number of shareholders to measure success against other companies in which you might invest. By comparing different amounts of earnings against different numbers of shareholders, *relative* performance is considered rather than just the total dollar amounts, which is another form of analysis.
- Investors and creditors compare Spin Master against its competitors in the same field of business and the industry in general.
- Managers might analyze inventory levels to see if they are too high so that operations managers can adjust production, marketing managers can see whether changes to advertising results in increased sales, and human resources managers can see if labour costs are in line with other companies in the industry.

So how is Spin Master doing? See for yourself. In this chapter, we will explore ratios and other forms of financial statement analysis for Spin Master and other companies.

As the opening vignette illustrates, managers rely on accounting information to make business decisions. Investors and creditors also rely on accounting information. Often they want to compare two or more similar companies. The way to compare companies of different sizes is to use *standard* measures. In earlier chapters, we have discussed financial ratios, such as the current ratio, inventory turnover, and return on shareholders' equity. These ratios are standard measures that enable investors to compare companies of similar sizes or different sizes, or companies that operate in the same or different industries. In this chapter, we discuss many of the basic ratios and related measures that managers use to run a company. Investors and lenders use the same tools to search for good investments and loan prospects. It is important to know how ratios are calculated to better understand and interpret the results of financial statement analysis.

Objectives of Financial Statement Analysis

Financial statement analysis focuses on techniques used by internal managers and by analysts external to the organization.

Investors who purchase a company's shares expect to receive dividends and hope the shares' value will increase. Creditors make loans with the expectation of receiving cash for the interest and principal. Both groups bear the risk they will not receive their expected returns. They use financial statement analysis to predict the amount of expected returns and assess the risks associated with those returns.

Creditors generally expect to receive specific fixed amounts and have the first claim on a company's assets if the company goes bankrupt, so they are most concerned with assessing short-term liquidity and long-term solvency. **Short-term liquidity** is an organization's ability to meet current payments as they become due. **Long-term solvency** is the ability to generate enough cash to pay long-term debts as they mature.

In contrast, *investors* are more concerned with profitability, dividends, and future share prices. Why? Because dividends and future share prices depend on profitable operations. Creditors also assess profitability because profitable operations are the company's prime source of cash to repay loans.

However, investors and creditors cannot evaluate a company by looking at only one year's data. This is one reason why most financial statements present results for at least two periods. This chapter illustrates some of the analytical tools for charting a company's progress over time.

Exhibit 18–1 shows graphical data taken from the 2016 annual report of Spin Master Corp. Management presents information this way to show how the company performed over a five-year period.

> When performing financial analysis, it is important to not look at only one period or one ratio. Think of financial analysis as solving a mystery, where one clue leads to another until a conclusion can be reached based on the clues fitting together.

EXHIBIT 18–1 | Financial Data from Spin Master Corp.'s 2016 Annual Report

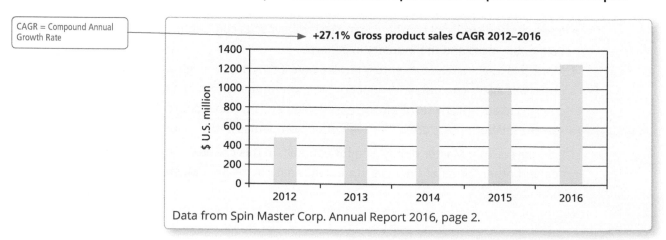

Data from Spin Master Corp. Annual Report 2016, page 2.

How can we decide what we really think about Spin Master's performance?

We can analyze a company's performance in different ways:

- From year to year
- Compared with a competing company
- Compared with the company's industry

Then we can better judge the company's current situation and try to predict what might happen in the near future.

Methods of Analysis

There are three main ways to analyze financial statements:

- Perform horizontal analysis to provide a year-to-year comparison of performance in different periods.
- Perform vertical analysis to compare different companies.
- Calculate and interpret financial ratios.

Horizontal Analysis

Many managerial decisions hinge on whether the numbers—revenues, expenses, and net income—are increasing or decreasing. Have revenues risen from last year? By how much? The fact that revenues may have risen by $20,000 may be interesting, but considered alone it is not very useful for decision making. Did $2,000,000 or $200,000 in revenues increase by $20,000? The *percentage change* in the net revenues over time is more useful because it shows the changes over time in *relative* terms. It is more useful to know that revenues increased by 20 percent than to know that revenues increased by $20,000.

The study of percentage changes in comparative statements is called **horizontal analysis**. Computing a percentage change in comparative statements requires three steps:

1 Lay out at least two periods of financial statement information side by side.

2 Compute the dollar amount of the change from the earlier period to the later period.

3 Divide the dollar amount of the change by the earlier-period amount and multiply by 100. We call the earlier period the *base period*.

Let's look at how horizontal analysis, which is illustrated for Spin Master Corp. in Exhibits 18–2 and 18–3, is done.

1 Organize financial information into a chart format, as shown here:

	A	B	C	D	E
1		(US dollar amounts in millions)		Increase (Decrease)	
2		2016	2015	Amount	Percent
3	Sales	$1,154.5	$879.4		
4	Cost of Sales	557.7	420.5		
5	Gross margin	596.8	458.9		

Spreadsheet programs like Excel are ideal for performing horizontal analysis.

It is important to consider both dollar changes and percentage changes in horizontal analysis. The dollar increase may be growing, but the percentage change may be growing less because the base is also changing at a different rate.

$$\frac{\$\text{ change}}{\text{Base year }\$} \times 100 = \%\text{ change}$$

❷ Compute the dollar amount of change in each account during the most recent year:

	A	B	C	D	E
1		(US dollar amounts in millions)		Increase (Decrease)	
2		2016	2015	Amount	Percent
3	Sales	$1,154.5	$879.4	$275.1	
4	Cost of sales	557.7	420.5	137.2	
5	Gross margin	596.8	458.9	137.9	

❸ Divide the dollar amount of change by the base-period amount and multiply by 100 to compute the percentage change during the later period. For sales, the calculation is as follows:

$$\text{Percentage change} = \frac{\text{Dollar amount of change}}{\text{Base year amount}} = \frac{\$275.1}{\$879.4} \times 100 = 31.3 \text{ percent}$$

	A	B	C	D	E
1		(US dollar amounts in millions)		Increase (Decrease)	
2		2016	2015	Amount	Percent
3	Sales	$1,154.5	$879.4	$275.1	31.3
4	Cost of sales	557.7	420.5	137.2	32.6
5	Gross margin	596.8	458.9	137.9	30.1

The comparative income statement for Spin Master Corp. shown in Exhibit 18–2 indicates that sales increased by $275.1 million, or 31.3 percent. The gross margin increased only 30.1 percent because the cost of goods sold (cost of sales) increased by more than the increase in sales.

EXHIBIT 18–2 | Comparative Income Statement—Horizontal Analysis

SPIN MASTER CORP.
Consolidated Statements of Income (adapted*)
For the Years Ended December 31, 2016, and December 31, 2015
(US dollar amounts in millions except per-share amounts)

	2016	2015	Increase (Decrease) Amount	Increase (Decrease) Percent
Sales	$1,154.5	$879.4	$275.1	31.3%
Cost of sales	557.7	420.5	137.2	32.6
Gross margin	596.8	458.9	137.9	30.1
Expenses				
Selling, marketing, distribution, and product development	243.7	183.8	59.9	32.6
Administrative expenses	201.0	195.9	5.1	2.6
Other, including foreign exchange loss and finance costs	14.2	(0.4)	14.6	
Income before income tax expense	137.9	79.6	58.3	73.2
Income tax expense	38.4	32.6	5.8	17.8
Net income	$ 99.5	47.0	$ 52.5	111.7
Earnings per share (basic and fully diluted)	$ 0.99	$ 0.48	$ 0.51	106.3

*Differences are due to rounding.

Note: Percentage changes are typically not computed for shifts from a negative amount to a positive amount, and vice versa.

Source: Spin Master Ltd. Annual consolidated financial statements. For the year of December 31, 2016, and December 31, 2015.

The comparative balance sheet in Exhibit 18–3 shows the changes between 2015 and 2016. Total assets increased by $365.1 million, or 94 percent, and total liabilities increased by $195.9 million, or 84.5 percent. These numbers are blue in Exhibit 18–3 for easy reference.

EXHIBIT 18–3 | Comparative Balance Sheet—Horizontal Analysis

SPIN MASTER CORP. Consolidated Balance Sheet (adapted*) December 31, 2016, and December 31, 2015 (US dollar amounts in millions)				
			Increase (Decrease)	
	2016	**2015**	**Amount**	**Percent**
Assets				
Current assets				
Cash	$ 99.4	$ 45.7	$ 53.7	117.5%
Accounts receivable	272.9	134.6	138.3	102.8
Inventory	79.9	49.1	30.8	62.7
Prepaid expenses	21.4	16.3	5.1	31.3
Total current assets*	473.6	245.8	227.8	92.7
Property, plant, and equipment	30.0	16.1	13.9	86.3
Intangible assets	130.4	62.4	68.0	109.0
Goodwill, and misc. advances and deferrals	119.4	64.0	55.4	86.6
Total assets	$753.4	$388.3	$365.1	94.0
Liabilities and Shareholders' Equity				
Current liabilities				
Accounts payable and accrued liabilities	206.8	134.7	72.1	53.5
Loans and provisions	190.1	20.3	169.8	836.5
Income taxes and interest payable	12.3	20.2	(7.9)	(39.1)
Total current liabilities	409.2	175.2	234.0	133.6
Non-current liabilities				
Loans and provisions	12.1	55.3	(43.2)	(78.1)
Other long-term liabilities	6.5	1.4	5.1	364.3
Total non-current liabilities	18.6	56.7	(38.1)	(67.2)
Total liabilities	427.8	231.9	195.9	84.5
Shareholders' equity				
Share capital	670.1	589.3	80.8	13.7
Accumulated deficit	(408.4)	(507.9)	99.5	(19.6)
Other**	64.0	75.0	(11.0)	(14.7)
Total shareholders' equity*	325.7	156.4	169.3	108.3
Total liabilities and shareholders' equity	$753.4	$388.3	$365.1	94.0

*Slight differences are due to rounding throughout the statement.

**Contributed surplus and cumulative translation accounts.

Source: Spin Master Ltd. Annual consolidated financial statements. For the year of December 31, 2016, and December 31, 2015.

There are no equal sign lines for the total in the Percent column. This column will never add up because a separate percentage has been calculated for each item.

Trend Percentages

Trend percentages are a form of horizontal analysis. Trends are important indicators of the direction a business is taking. To gain a realistic view of the company, it is often necessary to examine more than just a two- or three-year period. How have sales changed over a five-year period? What trend does gross margin show? These questions can be answered by analyzing trend percentages over a recent period, such as the most recent five years or ten years.

Trend percentages are computed by selecting a base year. The base-year amounts are set to 100 percent. The amounts for each following year are expressed as a percentage of the base amount. To compute trend percentages, divide each item for following years by the base-year amount and multiply by 100 to get the percentage.

$$\text{Trend \%} = \frac{\text{Any year \$}}{\text{Base year \$}} \times 100$$

Using the comparative data provided by Spin Master on page 2 of their 2016 annual report, we can create a summary chart to show sales and net income for the past four years:

	(Amounts in millions)			
	2016	**2015**	**2014**	**2013**
Gross Product Sales	$1,254.6	$982.7	$811.9	$576.9
Adjusted Net Income	120.1	98.6	66.3	22.9

The trend percentage for sales is computed by dividing the sales amount by the 2013 amount of $576.9 million (the base year). The same steps are done for the other accounts. The resulting trend percentages follow:

$1,254.6 ÷ 576.9 × 100 = 217.5%

	2016	**2015**	**2014**	**2013**
Gross Product Sales	217.5%	170.3%	140.7%	100%
Adjusted Net Income	524.5	430.6	289.5	100

Spin Master's sales have trended upward from 2013; 2016 sales are 217.5 percent of 2013 sales. Net income followed the same upward trend, from $22.9 million in 2013 to $120.1 million in 2016; 2016's net income was 524.5 percent of 2013's net income. This is a historic analysis and caution would be needed before projecting these trends into future periods.

Try It!

1. Perform a horizontal analysis of the comparative income statement of Winston Inc. Round to one decimal place for the percentage answers. State whether 2020 was a good year or a bad year and give your reasons.

WINSTON INC. Income Statement For the Years Ended December 31, 2020, and December 31, 2019				
			Increase (Decrease)	
	2020	2019	Amount	Percent
Net sales	$275,000	$225,000		
Expenses				
Cost of goods sold	194,000	165,000		
Engineering, selling, and admin. expenses	54,000	48,000		
Interest expense	5,000	5,000		
Income tax expense	9,000	3,000		
Other expense (income)	1,000	(1,000)		
Total expenses	263,000	220,000		
Net income	$ 12,000	$ 5,000		

2. Suppose Winston Inc. reported the following net sales and net income amounts:

	(in thousands)			
	2020	2019	2018	2017
Net sales	$275,000	$225,000	$210,000	$200,000
Net income	12,000	5,000	6,000	3,000

a. Show Winston Inc.'s trend percentages for net sales and net income. Use 2017 as the base year.
b. Which measure increased faster between 2017 and 2020?

Solutions appear at the end of this chapter and on MyLab Accounting

Vertical Analysis

As we have seen, horizontal analysis and trend percentages highlight changes in an item over time. However, no single technique provides a complete picture of a business. Another way to analyze a company is called *vertical analysis*.

Vertical analysis of a financial statement reveals the relationship of each statement item to a base, which represents 100 percent.

LO ②

What is a vertical analysis, and how do we perform one?

$$\text{Vertical analysis } \% = \frac{\text{Each account}}{\text{Base amount}^*} \times 100$$

*Base amount for an income statement is net sales. Base amount for a balance sheet is total assets.

For example, when an income statement for a merchandising company is subjected to vertical analysis, net sales is usually the base. Every other item on the income statement is then reported as a percentage of that base.

While horizontal analysis shows the relationship among numbers over several years, vertical analysis shows the relationship among numbers on the financial statements for the same year.

Suppose under normal conditions a company's gross margin is 40 percent of net sales. A drop in gross margin to 30 percent of net sales may cause the company to report a net loss on the income statement. Management, investors, and creditors view a large decline in gross margin with alarm. If analysis were performed using just dollar amounts, it is possible that this decline would be missed because an increase in sales and gross margin might not show the *relative* decline in the gross margin.

Exhibit 18–4 shows the vertical analysis of Spin Master Corp.'s income statement as a percentage of sales. Notice that the total sales dollars, cost of sales, and gross margin dollars *increased*, but the gross margin percentage *decreased* from 52.2 percent of sales in 2015 to 51.7 percent of sales in 2016. This tells us the same sort of information as horizontal analysis—that cost of sales rose and the gross margin decreased relative to sales. Now before you dismiss the half-percent difference as being a small number, this could be interpreted to say that had Spin Master maintained the same gross margin percentage in 2016 that it had in 2015, it would have earned $5,849,000 more gross profit than it did!

EXHIBIT 18–4 | Comparative Income Statement—Vertical Analysis

SPIN MASTER CORP. Consolidated Statements of Income (adapted*) For the Years Ended December 31, 2016 and December 31, 2015 (US dollar amounts in millions)				
	2016		**2015**	
	Amount	**Percent***	**Amount**	**Percent***
Sales	$1,154.5	100.0%	$879.4	100.0%
Cost of sales	557.7	48.3	420.5	47.8
Gross margin	596.8	51.7	458.9	52.2
Expenses				
Selling, marketing, distribution and product development	243.7	21.1	183.8	20.9
Administrative expenses	201.0	17.4	195.9	22.3
Other, including foreign exchange loss and finance costs	14.2	1.2	(0.4)	−0.1
Income before income tax expense	137.9	11.9	79.6	9.1
Income tax expense	38.4	3.3	32.6	3.7
Net income	$ 99.5	8.6	$ 47.0	5.3
Earnings per share (basic and fully diluted)	$ 0.99		$ 0.48	

*Amounts and percentages may not add up due to rounding.

Source: Spin Master Ltd. Annual consolidated financial statements. For the year of December 31, 2016, and December 31, 2015.

This gross margin percentage of sales shown in a vertical analysis is the same as what you learned in Chapter 6:
Gross margin percentage
= Gross margin ÷ Net sales revenue

The vertical analysis of Spin Master's balance sheet in Exhibit 18–5 shows that the business is holding less inventory *relative to the total assets of the company*. In 2015 the business held 12.6 percent of its total assets in inventory, but in 2016 it held 10.6 percent of assets in inventory. This sort of analysis cannot be seen by just looking at the dollar amounts. The dollar amounts of inventory increased, but the balance decreased relative to total assets.

EXHIBIT 18–5 | Comparative Balance Sheet—Vertical Analysis

SPIN MASTER CORP. Consolidated Balance Sheet (adapted*) December 31, 2016, and December 31, 2015 (US dollar amounts in thousands)	2016		2015	
	Amount	Percent*	Amount	Percent*
Assets				
Current assets				
Cash	$ 99.4	13.2%	$ 45.7	11.8%
Accounts receivable	272.9	36.2	134.6	34.7
Inventory	79.9	10.6	49.1	12.6
Prepaid expenses	21.4	2.8	16.3	4.2
Total current assets*	473.6	62.9	245.8	63.3
Property, plant, and equipment	30.0	4.0	16.1	4.2
Intangible assets	130.4	17.3	62.4	16.1
Goodwill, and misc. advances and deferrals	119.4	15.8	64.0	16.5
Total assets	$753.4	100.0%	$388.3	100.0%
Liabilities and Shareholders' Equity				
Current liabilities				
Accounts payable and accrued liabilities	206.8	27.5	134.7	34.7
Loans and provisions	190.1	25.2	20.3	5.2
Income taxes and interest payable	12.3	1.6	20.2	5.2
Total current liabilities	409.2	54.3	175.2	45.1
Non-current liabilities				
Loans and provisions	12.1	1.6	55.3	14.2
Other long-term liabilities	6.5	.9	1.4	.4
Total non-current liabilities	18.6	2.5	56.7	14.6
Total liabilities	427.8	56.8	231.9	59.7
Shareholders' equity				
Share capital	670.1	88.9	589.3	151.8
Accumulated deficit	(408.4)	(54.2)	(507.9)	(130.8)
Other	64.0	8.5	75.0	19.3
Total shareholders' equity*	325.7	43.2	156.4	40.3
Total liabilities and shareholders' equity	$753.4	100.0%	$388.3	100.0%

*Amounts and percentages may not add up due to rounding.

Source: Spin Master Ltd. Annual consolidated financial statements. For the year of December 31, 2016, and December 31, 2015.

To show the *relative* importance of each item on a financial statement, vertical analysis presents everything on that statement as a percentage of one total amount.

3. Refer to the Winston Inc. information in Try It! #1.
  a. Perform a vertical analysis of the comparative income statement by creating a report with the following headings:

WINSTON INC. Vertical Analysis of Comparative Income Statement For the Years Ended December 31, 2020 and 2019				
	2020		2019	
	Amount	Percent	Amount	Percent
Net sales				

  Round all percentages to one decimal place.
  b. Was 2020 a good year or a bad year? State your reasons.

Solutions appear at the end of this chapter and on **MyLab Accounting**

Common-Size Statements

LO ③

What are common-size financial statements, and how do we use them?

Horizontal analysis and vertical analysis provide useful data about a company. As we have seen, Spin Master appears to be a successful company. But the Spin Master data apply only to one business, so we might want to know—how do their results compare to other companies?

To compare one company to another we can use a common-size statement. A **common-size statement** reports only percentages—the same percentages that appear in a vertical analysis. For example, Spin Master's common-size income statement could be created by removing the dollar amounts from Exhibit 18–4 and presenting just the percentages.

A common-size statement is a form of vertical analysis used to facilitate comparison between different companies by making all amounts relative to some base amount.

On a common-size income statement, each item is expressed as a percentage of the net sales (or revenues) amount. Net sales is the *common size* to which we relate the statement's other amounts. On the balance sheet, the *common size* is total assets *or* the sum of total liabilities and shareholders' equity.

Common-size statements provide information that is useful for analyzing the changes in account balances over time irrespective of the dollar amounts. For example, look at Exhibit 18–6 to see a partial common-size balance sheet. Spin Master's total current assets increased from $245.8 million to $473.6 million, but percentage-wise it decreased from 63.3 percent of total assets in 2015 to 62.9 percent of total assets in 2016. If this decrease was not planned, this would be important information for management, telling them they have relatively less current assets.

A common-size statement also eases the comparison of different companies because their amounts are stated as percentages. If Spin Master's competitors held inventory that was 15 percent of their total assets, then Spin Masters might be holding too little.

EXHIBIT 18–6 | Common-Size Analysis of Current Assets

SPIN MASTER CORP. Partial Common-Size Balance Sheet December 31, 2016, and December 31, 2015		
	Percent of Total Assets	
	2016	**2015**
Current assets		
Cash	13.2%	11.8%
Accounts receivable	36.2	34.7
Inventory	10.6	12.6
Prepaid expenses	2.8	4.2
Total current assets	62.9	63.3

Source: Spin Master Ltd. Annual consolidated financial statements. For the year of December 31, 2016, and December 31, 2015.

Benchmarking

Benchmarking is the practice of comparing any part of a company's performance with that of other leading companies. There are two main types of benchmarks in financial statement analysis: against another company and against an industry average.

Benchmarking Against Another Company A company's financial statements show past results and help investors predict future performance. Still, that knowledge may be limited to that one company. We may learn that gross margin and net income have increased. This information is helpful, but it does not consider how other companies in the same industry have fared over the same period. Have competitors profited even more? Is there an industry-wide increase in net income? Managers, investors, creditors, and other interested parties need to know how one company compares with other companies in the same line of business.

We can look at Gildan Activewear Inc. and Canada Goose Holdings Inc. as an example. Investors wanting to hold shares of a business in a Canadian clothing manufacturer and retailer would compare them to see which one is more profitable. The different sizes of the companies would make a direct comparison very complex: Gildan's revenues for the year ended 2017 were about $2.5 billion, while Canada Goose's revenues were around $403 million. So how does Gildan's operating income of $371 million compare to Canada Goose's $40.5 million operating income? Exhibit 18–7 presents their common-size income statements. Gildan's operating income is 14 percent of revenues, while Canada Goose's operating income is 10 percent of revenues. From this analysis, we can see that Canada Goose is less profitable than Gildan when compared with the amount of revenues each earns.

	Gildan Activewear	Canada Goose
Revenues	100.00%	100.00%
Cost of sales	72.16%	47.48%
Gross margin	27.84%	52.52%
Selling, general, and administrative expense	13.01%	40.86%
Other income/expenses	0.45%	1.63%
Operating income	14.37%	10.03%

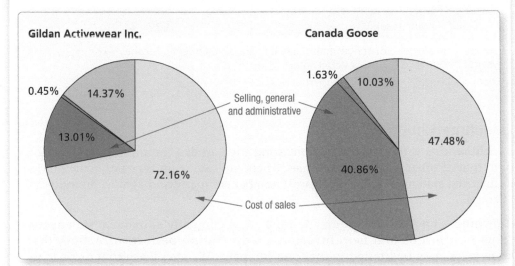

Source: Data from 2017 Third Quarter Shareholder Report. http://www.gildancorp.com/documents/Q3-Shareholder-Report-/Gildan-Q3-2017-Shareholder-Report.pdf

When the same information—the common-size income statement data—is presented in a graph, we can also notice other differences in the companies, such as the fact that Gildan spends relatively more making their products and less on overhead (selling, general, and administrative expenses) than does Canada Goose.

Benchmarking Against the Industry Average   The industry average can also serve as a useful benchmark for evaluating a company. The *RMA Annual Statement Studies,* published by the Risk Management Association, provides common-size statements for most industries. Benchmarks can also be found in industry-specific publications. For example, the National Automobile Dealers Association provides some industry averages for dealerships on its website.

Information Sources   Financial analysts draw their information from various sources:

- Annual and quarterly reports offer readers a good look at an individual business's operations. The SEDAR website (www.sedar.com) provides access to annual reports and other financial information for Canadian corporations.

- Publicly held companies must submit annual and quarterly reports to the provincial securities commission in each province where they are listed on a stock exchange (e.g., the Ontario Securities Commission for the Toronto Stock Exchange).
- Business publications such as the *National Post* and the *Globe and Mail*'s *Report on Business* carry information about individual companies and Canadian industries.
- Credit agencies, such as Dun & Bradstreet Canada, offer industry averages as part of their financial service.
- Online financial databases, such as LexisNexis, the *Financial Post*, Market Data, and Globe Investor, offer quarterly financial figures for hundreds of public corporations going back as far as 10 years.

Try It!

4. Refer to the vertical analysis of Winston Inc. performed in Try It! #3. Suppose Orisa Ltd. is a competitor of Winston Inc. in the same industry.
   a. Use the Orisa Ltd. information given below to create its common-size income statement. Round all results to one decimal place.
   b. How do the results of Winston Inc. compare with those of Orisa Ltd.?

ORISA LTD. Income Statement For the Year Ended December 31, 2020		Common Size Analysis	
		ORISA	WINSTON
Net sales	$580,000		
Expenses			
Cost of goods sold	395,000		
Engineering, selling, and administrative expenses	100,000		
Interest expense	30,000		
Income tax expense	23,000		
Other expense (income)	1,800		
Total expenses	549,800		
Net income	$ 30,200		

Solutions appear at the end of this chapter and on **MyLab Accounting**

Using Ratios to Make Decisions

LO 4

How do we compute standard financial ratios, and what do they mean?

An important part of financial analysis is the calculation and interpretation of ratios. A ratio is a useful way to show the relationship of one number to another. For example, if the balance sheet shows current assets of $100,000 and current liabilities of $25,000, the ratio of current assets to current liabilities is $100,000 to $25,000. We could simplify this numerical expression to the ratio of 4 to 1, which may also be written 4:1 and 4/1. Other acceptable ways of expressing this ratio include "Current assets are 400 percent of current liabilities," "The business has four dollars in current assets for every one dollar in current liabilities," or simply, "The current ratio is 4.0."

A manager, a lender, or a financial analyst may review any combination of ratios that are relevant to a particular decision. The ratios we discuss in this chapter may be classified as follows:

The definition of liquidity in this context is different than the definition you have learned previously.

- Measuring ability to pay current liabilities (short-term **liquidity**)
- Measuring ability to sell inventory and collect receivables (efficiency)
- Measuring ability to pay long-term debt (long-term solvency)
- Measuring profitability

Notice that there are many different ways to say the same thing!

- Analyzing shares as an investment (value)

All the ratios discussed in this chapter are summarized on page 1062, after the Summary. You may want to tab the ratios summary page for easy reference.

Exhibits 18–8 and 18–9 give the comparative income statement and balance sheet, respectively, of Blizzard Heating Inc. We will use this information to calculate several key ratios for the company.

EXHIBIT 18–8 | Comparative Income Statement

BLIZZARD HEATING INC. Income Statement For the Years Ended December 31, 2020 and 2019		
	2020	**2019**
Net sales	$858,000	$803,000
Cost of goods sold	513,000	509,000
Gross margin	345,000	294,000
Operating expenses		
Selling expenses	116,000	104,000
General expenses	118,000	123,000
Total operating expenses	234,000	227,000
Income from operations	111,000	67,000
Interest revenue	4,000	—
Less: interest expense	34,000	24,000
Income before income taxes	81,000	43,000
Income tax expense	33,000	17,000
Net income	$ 48,000	$ 26,000

EXHIBIT 18–9 | Comparative Balance Sheet

BLIZZARD HEATING INC. Balance Sheet December 31, 2020 and 2019		
Assets	**2020**	**2019**
Current assets		
Cash	$ 39,000	$ 42,000
Accounts receivable, net	114,000	85,000
Inventories	113,000	111,000
Prepaid expenses	6,000	8,000
Total current assets	272,000	246,000
Long-term investments	18,000	9,000
Property, plant, and equipment, net	507,000	399,000
Total assets	$797,000	$654,000
Liabilities		
Current liabilities		
Note payable	$ 42,000	$ 27,000
Accounts payable	83,000	78,000
Accrued liabilities	27,000	31,000
Total current liabilities	152,000	136,000
Long-term debt	289,00	198,000
Total liabilities	441,000	334,000
Shareholders' Equity		
Common shares	186,000	186,000
Retained earnings	170,000	134,000
Total shareholders' equity	356,000	320,000
Total liabilities and shareholders' equity	$797,000	$654,000

Measuring the Ability to Pay Current Liabilities (Liquidity)

Working capital is calculated as

> Working capital = Current assets − Current liabilities

Working capital measures the company's ability to meet short-term obligations with current assets. The working capital amount considered alone, however, does not give a complete picture of the entity's working capital position. Consider two companies with equal working capital:

	Blizzard Heating	Sunny AC Service
Current assets	$272,000	$570,000
Less: current liabilities	152,000	450,000
Working capital	$120,000	$120,000
Working capital as a percent of current liabilities	79%	27%

Both companies have working capital of $120,000, but Blizzard's working capital is almost as large as its current liabilities. Sunny AC Service's working capital, on the other hand, is less than one-third as large as its current liabilities. Which business has a better level of working capital? Blizzard, because relative to the level of current liabilities, there are more current assets with which to pay its obligations.

Two decision tools based on working capital data are the *current ratio* and the *acid-test ratio*.

Current Ratio

The current ratio measures the company's ability to pay current liabilities with current assets. So it should make sense that the result of the calculation of the current ratio should always be greater than 1. In other words, we need at least as much current assets as current liabilities, otherwise short-term payments cannot be made.

Current Ratio   The **current ratio** looks at total current assets compared to total current liabilities. We introduced the current ratio in Chapter 4.

The current ratio measures the company's ability to pay bills that are due to be paid in the coming year with items that can be turned into cash easily in the coming year. A high current ratio indicates a strong financial position and that the business has sufficient **liquid assets** to maintain normal business operations. Recall that

- Current assets consist of cash, short-term investments, net receivables, inventory, and prepaid expenses.
- Current liabilities include accounts payable, short-term note payable, unearned revenues, and all types of accrued liabilities.

The current ratio calculation for Blizzard for both years, and compared to the industry average is as follows:

$$\text{Current ratio} = \frac{\text{Current assets}}{\text{Current liabilities}}$$

2020	2019	Industry Avg.
$\dfrac{\$272,000}{\$152,000} = 1.79$	$\dfrac{\$246,000}{\$136,000} = 1.81$	1.68◄

The industry average for the home heating and air conditioning service industry.

What is an acceptable current ratio? The answer to this question depends on the nature of the business. The current ratio should generally exceed 1.0, while the norm for companies is around 1.50. In many industries a current ratio of 2.0 is considered very good. Blizzard's current ratio has declined from 2019 to 2020, but since it is still above the home heating and air conditioning service industry average, the result is "good."

We can look at the ratios for some real companies from a variety of industries:

Company	Current Ratio
BlackBerry Limited	5.19
Canadian Tire Corporation, Limited	1.93
Dollarama Inc.	2.43
Shopify Inc.	10.64

All ratios were accessed from Investing.com on January 1, 2018, and will change with market conditions.

Acid-Test Ratio   The **acid-test ratio** (or **quick ratio**) tells us whether the entity could pay all its current liabilities if they came due immediately. We saw in Chapter 9 that the higher the acid-test ratio, the better able the business is to pay its current liabilities. That is, *could the company pass this acid test?* To do so, the company would have to convert its most liquid assets to cash.

The acid-test ratio measures liquidity using fewer assets than the current ratio does. Inventory and prepaid expenses are *not* included in the acid-test computations because a business may not be able to convert them to cash immediately to pay current liabilities.

$$\text{Acid-test ratio} = \frac{\text{Cash} + \text{Short-term investment} + \text{Net current receivables}}{\text{Current liabilities}}$$

> Net current receivables includes accounts and notes receivable, net of allowances.

2020	2019	Industry Avg.
$\dfrac{\$39{,}000 + \$0 + \$114{,}000}{\$152{,}000} = 1.01$	$\dfrac{\$42{,}000 + \$0 + \$85{,}000}{\$136{,}000} = 0.93$	0.60

The company's acid-test ratio improved during 2020 and is better than the retail furniture industry average. An acid-test ratio of 0.90 to 1.00 is considered good in most industries. Note the range for the companies listed below is from a low of 0.40 to a high of 6.15.

Company	Acid-Test Ratio
BlackBerry Limited	5.17
Canadian Tire Corporation, Limited	1.46
Dollarama Inc.	0.40
Shopify Inc.	6.15

ETHICS Should the Debt be Reclassified?

Victor Brannon, senior accountant for Moose Corporation, was preparing the latest financial ratios. He knew that the ratios were watched carefully by Moose Corporation's lenders due to strict loan agreements that required the corporation to maintain a minimum current ratio of 1.5. Victor knew that the past quarter's financial ratios would not meet the lenders' requirements. His boss, Cara Romano, suggested that Victor classify a note payable due in 11 months as a long-term liability. What should Victor do? What would you do?

Solution

Liabilities are classified as current if they will be settled within one year or the operating cycle, whichever is longer. The classification between current and long-term is clear. Victor should not classify the note payable as a long-term liability. It should be classified as current even though the corporation will not meet the lenders' requirements.

Measuring the Ability to Sell Inventory and Collect Receivables (Efficiency)

The ability to sell inventory and collect receivables is fundamental to the business success of a merchandiser. (Recall the operating cycle—cash to inventory to receivables and back to cash—from Chapter 5.) This section discusses ratios that measure the ability to sell inventory and collect receivables.

Inventory Turnover Companies generally seek to achieve the quickest possible return on their investments. A return on an investment in inventory is no exception, because inventory is often a large investment for the business. The faster inventory sells, the sooner the business creates accounts receivable, and the sooner it collects cash. In addition, companies make a profit each time they sell inventory. The more often they sell inventory, the greater the total amount of profit.

Inventory turnover measures the number of times a company sells its average level of inventory during a year. A turnover of 6 means that the company sold its average level of inventory six times during the year (or every two months). Inventory turnover is also used as a measure of the efficiency of a company in managing its inventory. A high rate of turnover indicates ease in selling inventory; a low rate of turnover indicates slower sales and may indicate difficulty in selling. It could also indicate obsolete inventory or poor inventory management. We introduced inventory turnover in Chapter 5.

High turnover has been the recipe for success for companies like Walmart and Dollarama. Students who have taken a marketing course may recognize this pricing strategy—these are low-cost, high-volume retailers.

Of course, there is a relationship between turnover and the product; Dollarama will have a higher rate of turnover than a company such as Finning International Inc. of Vancouver, which sells heavy equipment.

A business also strives for the *most profitable* rate of inventory turnover, not necessarily the *highest* rate. Selling for too low of a price just to move the product quickly may not be as profitable as keeping it a little longer and getting a better price for the product.

To compute inventory turnover, we divide cost of goods sold by the average inventory for the period. We use the cost of goods sold—not sales—because both cost of goods sold and inventory are stated *at cost*. Sales at *retail* are not comparable to inventory at *cost*.

$$\text{Inventory turnover} = \frac{\text{Cost of goods sold}}{\text{Average inventory}}$$

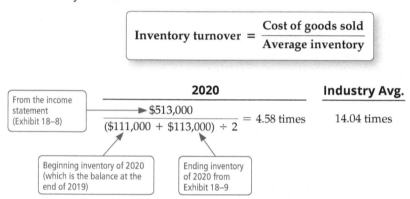

The example above uses the average of the beginning and ending inventory balance. If inventory levels vary greatly from month to month, compute the average by adding the 12 monthly balances and dividing this sum by 12. If inventory balances don't vary, then use the year-end balance rather than the average.

Inventory turnover varies widely with the nature of the business. Companies that remove natural gas from the ground hold their inventory for a very short period of time and have an average turnover of 30. Blizzard Heating Inc.'s turnover of 4.58 times a year is low for its industry, which has an average turnover of 14.04. Blizzard's low inventory turnover is an issue it needs to improve.

Days' Sales in Inventory   Another way to analyze inventory is to consider the number of days that inventory is held before it is sold. This is the same information as is calculated using the inventory turnover, but it provides another way of explaining the concept. The calculation for Blizzard for 2020 would be

$$\text{Days' Sales in Inventory} = \frac{365 \text{ days}}{\text{Inventory turnover}} = \frac{365 \text{ days}}{4.58} = 80 \text{ days}$$

It took the company approximately 80 days to sell all the items in inventory. Compared to competitors that hold their inventory for 26 days, Blizzard is significantly less efficient with its inventory management.

Accounts Receivable Turnover   **Accounts receivable turnover** measures the company's ability to collect cash from credit customers. It is also used as a measure of the efficiency of a company to manage its cash collections. The higher the ratio is, the faster the cash collections are. However, a receivable turnover that is too high may indicate that credit is too tight, causing the loss of sales to good customers.

Blizzard makes all sales on credit. (If a company makes both cash and credit sales, this ratio is best computed using only net *credit* sales. *Credit* means "on account"—it does not mean "using a credit card.")

$$\text{Accounts receivable turnover} = \frac{\text{Net credit sales}}{\text{Average net accounts receivable}}$$

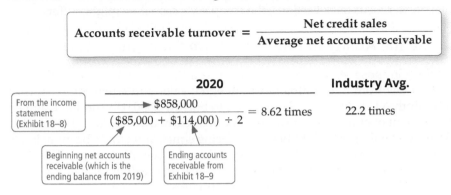

Net accounts receivable is computed by subtracting the allowance for doubtful accounts from the accounts receivable total.

The result indicates how many times during the year the average level of receivables was turned into cash. Blizzard's accounts receivable turnover of 8.62 times is much lower than the industry average. Why the difference? Blizzard Heating is a hometown store that sells to local people who tend to pay their bills over a period of time. Many larger home heating and cooling service providers sell their receivables to other companies called **factors**. This practice keeps receivables low and receivable turnover high. In return for receiving the cash sooner, companies that factor (sell) their receivables receive less than face value for the receivables.

If accounts receivable balances exhibit a seasonal pattern, compute the average net receivable using the 12 monthly balances added together and divided by 12. If receivable balances don't vary, then use the year-end balance rather than the average.

Days' Sales in Receivables   The **days' sales in receivables** ratio measures the ability to collect receivables and tells us how many days' credit sales remain in Accounts Receivable. Recall from Chapter 9 that days' sales in receivables indicates how many days it takes to collect the average level of receivables. To compute the ratio, we can follow a two-step process:

When a business's accounts receivable turnover is different from the industry average, look past the ratio before deciding if a result is "good" or "bad." In the case of Blizzard Heating, the industry average might be high due to the use of factors rather than faster collection. If this industry is dominated by large corporations, then the industry average is not a reasonable benchmark for a smaller business like Blizzard.

❶ One days' sales $= \dfrac{\text{Net sales}}{365 \text{ days}}$

❷ Day's sales in accounts receivable $= \dfrac{\text{Average net accounts receivable}}{\text{One day's sales}}$

	2020	**Industry Avg.**
❶	$\dfrac{\$858,000}{365 \text{ days}} = \$2,351$	
❷	$\dfrac{(\$85,000 + \$114,000) \div 2}{\$2,351} = 42 \text{ days}$	16 days

Days' sales in receivables and accounts receivables turnover both "say the same thing in a different way." Notice that when turnover is 8.62 times, that is $365 \div 8.62 = 42$ days!

Days' sales in receivables can also be computed in a single step:

$$[(\$85,000 + \$114,000) \div 2] \div (\$858,000 \div 365 \text{ days}) = 42 \text{ days}$$

Blizzard Heating's ratio tells us that 42 days' sales remained in average accounts receivable during the year, or that it takes 42 days to collect receivables. The company will increase its cash inflow if it can decrease this ratio. Ways to do this include offering discounts for early payments, tightening credit policies to disallow slow-paying customers, using more aggressive collection procedures, and selling receivables to factors. The days' sales in receivables is higher (worse) than the industry average because the company collects its own receivables. Other heating and air conditioning businesses may sell their receivables or carry fewer days' sales in receivables. Blizzard remains competitive because of the personal relationship with customers. Without a greater focus on collections, the company's cash flow might suffer.

Measuring the Ability to Pay Long-Term Debt (Solvency)

Debt Ratio Suppose you are a loan officer at a bank and you are evaluating loan applications from two companies with equal sales and equal total assets of $1,000,000. Both A Co. and B Co. have asked to borrow $500,000 and have agreed to repay the loan over a five-year period. A Co. already owes $900,000 to another bank. B Co. owes only $250,000. Other things being equal, you would be more likely to lend money to B Co. because B Co. owes less money than A Co. owes. This relationship between total liabilities and total assets—called the **debt ratio**—shows the proportion of the company's assets that it has financed with debt. We introduced the debt ratio in Chapter 4.

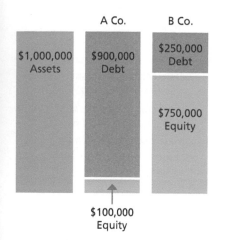

If the debt ratio for A Co. in the margin is calculated to be 0.90 ($900,000 ÷ $1,000,000) then debt has been used to finance most of the assets. A debt ratio of 0.25 for B Co. means that the company has borrowed to finance one-quarter of its assets; the owners have financed the other three-quarters of the assets. The higher the debt ratio is, the higher is the strain of paying interest each year and the principal amount at maturity, and the less likely a bank is to approve another loan.

What makes a corporation with a lot of debt a riskier loan prospect than one with a lot of equity? For a corporation with a lot of debt, interest on debt is contractual and must be paid. If interest on debt is not paid, creditors can force the company into bankruptcy. With equity, dividends are discretionary and do not have to be declared.

Creditors view a high debt ratio with caution. To help protect themselves, creditors generally charge higher interest rates on borrowings to companies with an already-high debt ratio.

Blizzard Heating Inc.'s debt ratios at the end of 2020 and 2019 are as follows:

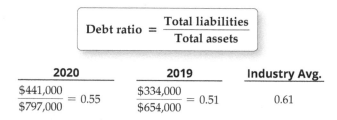

$$\text{Debt ratio} = \frac{\text{Total liabilities}}{\text{Total assets}}$$

2020	2019	Industry Avg.
$\dfrac{\$441,000}{\$797,000} = 0.55$	$\dfrac{\$334,000}{\$654,000} = 0.51$	0.61

Blizzard Heating expanded operations by financing the purchase of buildings and fixtures through borrowing, which is common. This expansion explains the company's increased debt ratio. Even after the increase in 2020, the company's debt is not very high. The average debt ratio for most industries ranges around 0.57 to 0.67. Blizzard's 0.55 debt ratio indicates a fairly low-risk debt position in comparison with the home heating and air conditioning industry average of 0.61.

One way of remembering this formula is the statement "If I go to Los Angeles (LA), I will be in debt."

$$\text{debt ratio} = \frac{L}{A}$$

Debt/Equity Ratio We can also analyze the A Co. and B Co. information presented in the margin of the previous section by comparing the amount of total liabilities to the amount of total equity in the **debt/equity ratio**. A Co. has a ratio of 9.0 ($900,000 ÷ $100,000), and B Co. has a ratio of 0.3 ($250,000 ÷ $750,000). A Co. uses more financing from outsiders than from shareholders.

The debt/equity (or debt-to-equity, or debt-equity) ratio measures financial **leverage**. Companies that finance operations with debt are said to *leverage* their positions. Some leverage is good. Leverage usually increases profitability because a company can earn more with the borrowed money than the interest it pays for the borrowed money. Leverage could have a negative impact on profitability. If revenues drop, debt and interest expense must still be paid. Therefore, leverage can have positive and negative effects on profits, increasing profits during good times but increasing risk during bad times because of higher fixed interest payments.

The higher the debt/equity ratio, the greater the company's financial risk.

Blizzard Heating's debt/equity ratios compared to the industry average are as follows:

$$\text{Debt/Equity ratio} = \frac{\text{Total liabilities}}{\text{Total equity}}$$

2020	2019	Industry Avg.
$\frac{\$441{,}000}{\$356{,}000} = 1.24$	$\frac{\$334{,}000}{\$320{,}000} = 1.04$	1.56

Blizzard Heating has increased the level of debt but is still below the industry average. This mirrors the result of the debt ratio.

Times-Interest-Earned Ratio   The debt ratio indicates nothing about the ability to pay interest expense. Analysts use a second ratio—the **times-interest-earned ratio**—to relate income to interest expense. This ratio is sometimes called the *interest coverage ratio*. It measures the number of times that operating income can cover interest expense. A high times-interest-earned ratio indicates ease in paying interest expense; a low value suggests difficulty.

$$\text{Times-interest-earned ratio} = \frac{\text{Income from operations}}{\text{Interest expense}}$$

2020	2019	Industry Avg.
$\frac{\$111{,}000}{\$34{,}000} = 3.26 \text{ times}$	$\frac{\$67{,}000}{\$24{,}000} = 2.79 \text{ times}$	2.00 times

The company's times-interest-earned ratio increased in 2020. This is a favourable sign about the company, especially since the company's liabilities rose substantially during the year. We can conclude that Blizzard Heating's new buildings and fixtures have earned more in operating income than they have cost the business in interest expense. The company's times-interest-earned ratio of 3.26 is much better than the 2.00 average for home heating and air conditioning service businesses. The norm for businesses falls in the range of 2.00 to 3.00 for many companies. Based on its debt ratio and times-interest-earned ratio, Blizzard Heating Inc. appears to have little difficulty **servicing its debt**, that is, paying its liabilities.

Measuring Profitability

We often hear that the fundamental goal of business is to earn a profit. This is not the only objective of a business. Managers attempt to meet the needs of shareholders, who require a sufficient return on their investment, and to support other goals related to corporate social responsibility—to earn money to spend for the greater good (to support charities or environmental causes, for example). And yes, we do look to see if a company has made "enough" money! Ratios that measure profitability are reported in the business press, by investment services, and in annual reports. We examine four profitability measures.

Return on Sales   In business, the term *return* is used broadly as a measure of profitability. Consider a ratio called the **return on sales** or *return on net sales*. (The word *net* is usually omitted for convenience, even though net sales is used to compute the ratio.) This ratio shows the percentage of each sales dollar earned as net income, or the amount of profit per dollar of sales.

It is also called the *rate of return on net sales, ROS, or profit margin.*

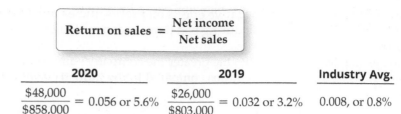

$$\text{Return on sales} = \frac{\text{Net income}}{\text{Net sales}}$$

2020	2019	Industry Avg.
$\dfrac{\$48,000}{\$858,000} = 0.056$ or 5.6%	$\dfrac{\$26,000}{\$803,000} = 0.032$ or 3.2%	0.008, or 0.8%

Companies strive for a high rate of return on sales. The higher the rate of return, the more each dollar of sales provides is profit. The increase in Blizzard Heating's return on sales is good. The company is more successful than the average home heating and air conditioning service company.

Return on Assets   The **return on assets** measures success in using assets to earn a profit. We first discussed rate of return on total assets in Chapter 13.

It is also called the rate of return on total assets, return on total assets, or ROA.

Two groups finance a company's assets. Creditors have lent money to the company, and they earn interest on this money. Shareholders have invested in shares, and their rate of return is the company's net income. The sum of interest expense and net income is thus the return to the two groups that have financed the company's assets.

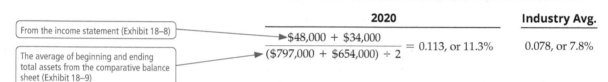

$$\text{Return on assets} = \frac{\text{Net Income} + \text{Interest expense}}{\text{Average total assets}}$$

From the income statement (Exhibit 18–8)

The average of beginning and ending total assets from the comparative balance sheet (Exhibit 18–9)

2020	Industry Avg.
$\dfrac{\$48,000 + \$34,000}{(\$797,000 + \$654,000) \div 2} = 0.113$, or 11.3%	0.078, or 7.8%

Compare Blizzard Heating's 11.3 percent rate of return on assets to the rates of some other Canadian companies, which range from −5.78 percent to 26.37 percent:

Company	Return on Assets
BlackBerry Ltd.	12.58%
Canadian Tire Corporation, Limited	5.03%
Dollarama Inc.	26.37%
Shopify Inc.	−5.78%

Return on Common Shareholders' Equity   A popular measure of profitability is the **return on common shareholders' equity**. We examined this ratio in Chapter 13.

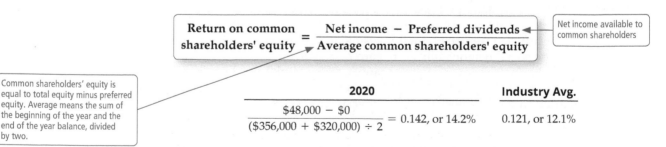

$$\frac{\text{Return on common}}{\text{shareholders' equity}} = \frac{\text{Net income} - \text{Preferred dividends}}{\text{Average common shareholders' equity}}$$

Net income available to common shareholders

Common shareholders' equity is equal to total equity minus preferred equity. Average means the sum of the beginning of the year and the end of the year balance, divided by two.

2020	Industry Avg.
$\dfrac{\$48,000 - \$0}{(\$356,000 + \$320,000) \div 2} = 0.142$, or 14.2%	0.121, or 12.1%

Observe that Blizzard Heating's return on equity, 14.2 percent, is higher than its return on assets, 11.3 percent. This difference results from borrowing from the bank and paying interest at a rate of 8 percent and then investing the funds to earn a higher rate, such as the firm's 14.2 percent return on shareholders' equity. This practice is called **trading on the equity**, or *using leverage.*

Compare Blizzard's rate of return on common shareholders' equity with rates of other companies:

It is also called the *rate of return on common shareholders' equity, return on equity*, or *ROE*. Return on shareholders' equity measures how much income is earned for every $1 invested by the *common* shareholders (both contributed capital and retained earnings).

Company	Return on Common Shareholders' Equity
BlackBerry Ltd.	21.22%
Canadian Tire Corporation, Limited	14.88%
Dollarama Inc.	543.25%
Shopify Inc.	−6.56%

Blizzard Heating is more profitable than one of these companies. A return on equity of 15 to 20 percent year after year is considered excellent in most industries.

Earnings per Common Share   Earnings per common share, or **earnings per share (EPS)**, is perhaps the most widely quoted of all financial statistics. It was introduced in Chapter 14. While Accounting Standards for Private Enterprises (ASPE) do not require that corporations disclose EPS figures on the income statement or in a note to the financial statements, many corporations do provide this information because investors and financial analysts use it to assess a corporation's profitability.

Earnings per share is computed by dividing net income available to common shareholders by the weighted average number of common shares outstanding during the year. Preferred dividends are subtracted from net income because the preferred shareholders have a prior claim to their dividends if they have been declared, or, if they have not been declared, if they are cumulative.

If the company has bonds or preferred shares that are convertible into common shares, the company must also disclose *fully diluted* earnings per share.

Blizzard Heating has no preferred shares outstanding and so has no preferred dividends. It had 10,000 common shares outstanding throughout both years:

$$\text{Earnings per common share (EPS)} = \frac{\text{Net income} - \text{Preferred dividends}}{\text{Weighted average number of common shares outstanding}}$$

2020
$$\frac{\$48,000 - \$0}{10,000} = \$4.80$$

2019
$$\frac{\$26,000 - \$0}{10,000} = \$2.60$$

Blizzard's EPS increased 85 percent from 2019 to 2020. (This is calculated as [$4.80 − $2.60] ÷ $2.60 = 85%). Its shareholders should not expect such a large increase in EPS every year. Most companies strive to increase EPS by 10 to 15 percent annually, and strong companies do so. However, even the most successful companies have an occasional bad year.

Analyzing Shares as an Investment (Value)

Investors purchase shares to earn a return on their investment from both gains from selling the shares at a price that is higher than the investors' purchase price, and dividends, the periodic distributions to shareholders. The ratios we examine in this section help analysts evaluate investments in shares.

Price–Earnings Ratio   The **price–earnings (P/E) ratio** is the relationship between the market price of a common share and the company's earnings per share. The ratio plays an important part in evaluating decisions to buy, hold, and sell shares. It indicates the market price of $1.00 of earnings. The market price can be obtained online from financial websites, the company website, or other news outlets. If earnings are negative, the P/E ratio is not applicable.

Chapter 18 Financial Statement Analysis **1053**

We will assume that the market price of Blizzard Heating's common shares were $50.00 at the end of 2020 and $35.00 at the end of 2019.

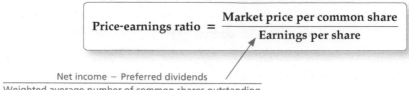

$$\text{Price-earnings ratio} = \frac{\text{Market price per common share}}{\text{Earnings per share}}$$

$$\frac{\text{Net income} - \text{Preferred dividends}}{\text{Weighted average number of common shares outstanding}}$$

2020	2019
$\dfrac{\$50.00}{\$4.80} = 10.4$	$\dfrac{\$35.00}{\$2.60} = 13.5$

Given Blizzard's 2020 P/E ratio of 10.4, we would say that the company's shares are "selling at 10.4 times earnings." The decline from the 2019 P/E ratio of 13.5 is a concern but not a cause for alarm because the market price of the shares is not under Blizzard's control. Net income is more controllable, and it increased during 2020.

Like most other ratios, P/E ratios vary from industry to industry. In January 2018, they ranged from 29.7 for Spin Master Ltd., to 12.3 for Corus Entertainment, to 14.6 for BlackBerry Limited.

Check to see how these companies are doing now!

The higher a share's P/E ratio, the higher its **downside risk**—the risk that the share's market price will fall. Some investors interpret a sharp increase in a share's P/E ratio as a signal to sell the shares.

Dividend Yield   The **dividend yield** is the ratio of dividends per share to the share's market price. It may be calculated for both preferred shares and common shares. This ratio measures the percentage of a share's market value that is returned annually as dividends. Preferred shareholders, who invest primarily to receive dividends, pay special attention to this ratio.

Blizzard Heating paid annual cash dividends of $1.20 per share in 2020 and $1.00 in 2019, and market prices of the company's common shares were $50.00 in 2020 and $35.00 in 2019, so the yields are:

$$\text{Dividend yield} = \frac{\text{Annual dividend per common (or preferred) share}}{\text{Market price per common (or preferred) share}}$$

2020	2019
$\dfrac{\$1.20}{\$50.00} = 0.024 \text{ or } 2.4\%$	$\dfrac{\$1.00}{\$35.00} = 0.029 \text{ or } 2.9\%$

Investors who buy Blizzard's common shares for $50.00 can expect to receive about 2.4 percent of their investment annually in the form of cash dividends. Dividend yields vary widely, from almost 5.0 percent for older, established firms (e.g., BCE Inc. at 4.63 percent) down to 0.71 percent for a growing company like Dollarama Inc. Blizzard's dividend yield places the company somewhere in the middle.

Book Value per Common Share   **Book value per common share** is common shareholders' equity divided by the number of common shares outstanding. Common shareholders' equity equals total shareholders' equity less preferred equity including cumulative preferred dividends.

Blizzard Heating has no preferred shares outstanding. Recall that 10,000 common shares were outstanding throughout 2019 and 2020.

Notice that the total of the numerator is common shareholders' equity

$$\text{Book value per common share} = \frac{\text{Total shareholders' equity} - \text{Preferred equity}}{\text{Number of common shares outstanding}}$$

2020	2019
$\dfrac{\$356,000 - \$0}{10,000} = \$35.60$	$\dfrac{\$320,000 - \$0}{10,000} = \$32.00$

Some experts argue that book value is not useful for investment analysis. Recall from Chapter 13 that book value depends on historical costs, while market value depends on investors' outlook for dividends and an increase in the share's market price. Book value bears no relationship to market value and provides little information beyond shareholders' equity reported on the balance sheet. However, some investors base their investment decisions on book value. For example, some investors rank shares on the basis of the ratio of market price to book value. To these investors, the lower the ratio, the lower the risk, and the more attractive the shares. These investors who focus on the balance sheet are called *value investors*, as contrasted with *growth investors*, who focus more on trends in a company's net income.

Limitations of Financial Analysis

Business decisions are made in a world of uncertainty. As useful as ratios may be, they do have limitations. When a physician reads a thermometer, 39°C indicates that something is wrong with the patient, but the temperature alone does not indicate what the problem is or how to cure it. The same is true of ratios.

In financial analysis, a sudden drop in a company's current ratio usually signals that *something* is wrong, but this change does not identify the problem or show how to correct it. The business manager and users of the financial statements must analyze the figures that go into the ratio to determine whether current assets have decreased, current liabilities have increased, or both. If current assets have dropped, is the problem a cash shortage? Are accounts receivable down? Are inventories too low? Is the condition temporary? This process can be shown in a figure:

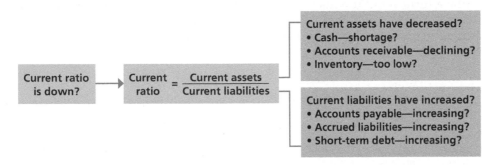

By analyzing the individual items that make up the ratio, managers can determine how to solve the problem and users of the financial statements can determine whether the company is a good investment or a credit risk. The managers and users of the financial statements must evaluate data on all ratios in the light of other information about the company and about its particular line of business, such as increased competition or seasonality or a slowdown in the economy.

Legislation, international affairs, competition, scandals, and many other factors can turn profits into losses, and vice versa. To be most useful, ratios should also be analyzed over a period of years to take into account a representative group of these factors. Any one year, or even any two years, may not be representative of the company's performance over the long term.

And finally, when comparing ratios across companies, remember to check how the ratio was calculated so you are sure you are actually comparing the same sort of information! There are no firm rules about what is included in a ratio nor how it is named. For example, the debt/equity ratio is sometimes referred to as the *debt ratio* even though in this book the two names refer to different ratios.

Investor Decisions

An **efficient capital market** is one in which the market prices reflect the impact of all information available to the public. Market efficiency means that managers cannot fool the market with accounting gimmicks. If the information is available, the market as a whole can translate accounting data into a "fair" price for the company's shares.

Suppose you are the president of CompSys Ltd. Reported earnings per share are $4.00 and the share price is $40.00—so the P/E ratio is 10. You believe the corporation's shares are underpriced in comparison with other companies in your industry. What if you are considering changing from accelerated to straight-line amortization to give the market a more accurate reflection of the company's value? The accounting change will increase earnings per share to $5.00. Will the shares then rise to $50.00? Probably not. The share price will likely remain at $40.00 because the market can understand that the change in amortization method, not improved operations, caused earnings to increase.

In an efficient market, the search for "underpriced" shares is fruitless unless the investor has relevant private information. Moreover, it is unlawful to invest based on *insider* information—information that is available only to corporate management.

Users of financial statements should be aware of potential problems in companies they might want to invest in or lend money to. Users of a company's financial statements should also consider the following additional information found in annual reports and should look for red flags when evaluating the company.

Annual Reports

Annual reports are one key place to get information about a corporation beyond the figures used for horizontal and vertical analyses and computing the standard ratios. The non-quantitative parts of the annual report may hold more important information than the financial statements. For example, the president's letter may describe a turnover of top managers. The management's discussion and analysis will reveal management's opinion of the year's results.

Annual reports usually contain the following sections:

President's Letter to the Shareholders	The president of the company gives their view of the year's results and outlines the direction top management is charting for the company. A shift in top management or a major change in the company's direction is important to investors. TELUS calls this the CEO Letter to Investors.
Management's Report to the Shareholders	There is a second letter written to the shareholders. Here management states that *all information in the annual report is the responsibility of management* and indicates which standards were followed in the preparation of the report. TELUS report also addresses how the board of directors ensures that internal controls are monitored.
Management's Discussion and Analysis (MD&A)	The people who know the most about a company are its executives. For this reason, the shareholders want to know what management thinks about the company's net income (or net loss), cash flows, and financial position. The MD&A section of the annual report discusses *why* net income was up or down, how the company invested the shareholders' money, and plans for future spending. Through the MD&A, investors may learn of the company's plan to discontinue a product line or to expand into new markets.
Independent Auditor's Report	The president's letter, the management letter, and the MD&A express the views of corporate insiders. The financial statements are also produced by the management of the company. These people naturally want to describe the company in a favourable light. Therefore, all the information coming from the company could be presented in a way to make the company look good.
	Investors are aware of the possibility for management bias in the financial statements. For this reason, the various provincial securities acts require that all financial statements of public corporations be audited by independent accountants. The auditors are not employees of the companies they audit, so they can be objective. After auditing the Shopify Inc. financial statements, Pricewaterhouse Coopers LLP, an international accounting firm, issued statements to provide an audit opinion that the statements present fairly the results of operations. They also verify they have reviewed managements' internal controls to determine they were likely effective.* This is how investors in Canada and other countries with a similar requirement for audits gain *assurance* that they can rely on a company's financial statements.

The Financial Statements	The financial statements consist of the balance sheet, income statement, statement of retained earnings, cash flow statement, and the *notes to the financial statements*, including a statement of significant accounting policies. Comparative information is provided for at least two years.
Other Information	Other financial and non-financial information about the company, such as information related to sustainability and environmental policies.

*The full scope of the audit report is more detailed than this. Accounting majors will address this topic in more advanced courses.

Red Flags in Financial Statements

Recent accounting scandals highlight the importance of *red flags* that may signal financial trouble. Watch out for the following conditions:

- Changes in sales, inventory, and receivables. Sales, receivables, and inventory generally move together. Increased sales lead to higher receivables and require more inventory to meet demand. Unusual increases in receivables without an increase in sales may indicate trouble.

- Earnings problems. Has net income decreased significantly for several years in a row? Has income turned into a loss? Most companies cannot survive consecutive annual losses.

- Decreased cash flow. Is cash flow from operations consistently lower than net income? Are the sales of property, plant, and equipment assets a major source of cash? If so, the company may face a cash shortage.

- Too much debt. How does the company's debt ratio compare with that of major competitors and with the industry average? If the debt ratio is too high, the company may be unable to pay its debts.

- Inability to collect receivables. Are days' sales in receivables growing faster than for other companies in the industry? A cash shortage may be looming.

- Build-up of inventories. Is inventory turnover too slow? If so, the company may be unable to sell goods, or it may be overstating inventory. Recall from the discussion on cost of goods sold that one of the easiest ways to overstate net income is to overstate ending inventory.

Why It's Done This Way

This final chapter of the book discusses the many ways in which a user of the financial statements can analyze results. As we have shown in previous chapters, the accounting framework has allowed us to develop financial statements that are *useful* to interested users.

For assessing the success of a company, however, the financial statements are a starting point. To evaluate the success of a company appropriately, we must perform a thorough analysis of the various aspects of the business. We also need to compare the performance of the company in the current year against the performance in previous years and against the performance of its competitors.

Try It!

5. For each of the following unrelated situations, use a check mark to indicate whether the change is generally positive for the company or negative.

Situation	Positive change	Negative change
A decrease in return on equity		
A decrease in days' sales in inventory		
An increase in the debt/equity ratio		
An increase in the acid-test ratio		
A decrease in receivables turnover		

6. Big Bend Picture Frames Inc. has asked you to determine whether the company's ability to pay its current liabilities and total liabilities has improved or deteriorated during 2020. To answer this question, you gather the following data:

	2020	2019
Cash	$ 50,000	$ 47,000
Short-term investments	27,000	—
Net receivables	128,000	124,000
Inventory	237,000	272,000
Total assets	480,000	490,000
Total current liabilities	295,000	202,000
Long-term note payable	44,000	56,000
Income from operations	170,000	168,000
Interest expense	46,000	33,000

Compute the following ratios for 2020 and 2019:

   a. Current ratio
   b. Acid-test ratio
   c. Debt ratio
   d. Times-interest-earned ratio
   e. Summarize the results of the above analysis of Big Bend Picture Frames Inc.'s ratios.

Solutions appear at the end of this chapter and on **MyLab Accounting**

EXHIBIT 18–10 | The Impact of IFRS on Financial Statement Analysis

LO ⑤

What is the impact of IFRS on financial statement analysis?

ASPE	IFRS
The procedures for performing financial analysis do not change because of the accounting standard being used. This is because financial analysis involves determining relationships between various components of the statements to assess the company's current position and to predict future performance.	
Dividend yield analysis may require an extra step because earnings per share is not required to be reported on the income statement and would need to be calculated before being used in the formula.	The calculation of dividend yield would be as shown in the chapter because earnings per share information must be reported on the income statement or statement of comprehensive income.
Accounting practices vary since some companies have choices about how to report information. Care must always be taken to read the notes to the financial statements.	

Summary Problem for Your Review

Bazinga Inc., which operates a chain of clothing stores, reported these figures:

BAZINGA INC. Five-Year Selected Financial Data For the Years Ended January 31 (Dollar amounts in thousands)					
	2020	2019	2018	2017	2016
Operating Results					
Net sales	$2,960	$2,519	$1,934	$1,587	$1,252
Cost of goods sold	1,856	1,496	1,188	1,007	814
Interest expense (net)	4	4	1	3	3
Income from operations	340	371	237	163	126
Income taxes	129	141	92	65	52
Net income	211	230	145	98	74
Cash dividends	44	41	30	23	18
Financial Position					
Merchandise inventory	366	314	247	243	193
Total assets	1,379	1,147	777	579	481
Working capital	355	236	579	129	434
Shareholders' equity	888	678	466	338	276
Current ratio	2.06	1.71	1.39	1.69	1.70
Average number of common shares outstanding (in thousands)	144	142	142	141	145

Required

Compute the following ratios for 2017 through 2020, and evaluate Bazinga Inc.'s operating results. Are operating results strong or weak? Did they improve or deteriorate during the four-year period?

1. Gross margin percentage (gross margin ÷ net sales revenue)
2. Return on sales (ROS)
3. Earnings per common share (EPS)
4. Inventory turnover
5. Times-interest-earned ratio
6. Return on common shareholders' equity (ROE)

SOLUTIONS

Remember to add the previous year's ending inventory balance and the current year's ending balance and divide by two when calculating average inventory in the inventory turnover ratio.

	2020	2019	2018	2017
1. Gross margin percentage	$\dfrac{\$2,960 - \$1,856}{\$2,960}$ $= 37.3\%$	$\dfrac{\$2,519 - \$1,496}{\$2,519}$ $= 40.6\%$	$\dfrac{\$1,934 - \$1,188}{\$1,934}$ $= 38.6\%$	$\dfrac{\$1,587 - \$1,007}{\$1,587}$ $= 36.5\%$
2. ROS	$\dfrac{\$211}{\$2,960} = 7.1\%$	$\dfrac{\$230}{\$2,519} = 9.1\%$	$\dfrac{\$145}{\$1,934} = 7.5\%$	$\dfrac{\$98}{\$1,587} = 6.2\%$
3. EPS	$\dfrac{\$211}{144} = \$1.47$	$\dfrac{\$230}{142} = \$1.62$	$\dfrac{\$145}{142} = \$1.02$	$\dfrac{\$98}{141} = \$0.70$
4. Inventory turnover	$\dfrac{\$1,856}{(\$366 + \$314) \div 2}$ $= 5.5 \text{ times}$	$\dfrac{\$1,496}{(\$314 + \$247) \div 2}$ $= 5.3 \text{ times}$	$\dfrac{\$1,188}{(\$247 + \$243) \div 2}$ $= 4.8 \text{ times}$	$\dfrac{\$1,007}{(\$243 + \$193) \div 2}$ $= 4.6 \text{ times}$
5. Times-interest-earned ratio	$\dfrac{\$340}{\$4} = 85 \text{ times}$	$\dfrac{\$371}{\$4} = 93 \text{ times}$	$\dfrac{\$237}{\$1} = 237 \text{ times}$	$\dfrac{\$163}{\$3} = 54 \text{ times}$
6. ROE	$\dfrac{\$211}{(\$888 + \$678) \div 2}$ $= 26.9\%$	$\dfrac{\$230}{(\$678 + \$466) \div 2}$ $= 40.2\%$	$\dfrac{\$145}{(\$466 + \$338) \div 2}$ $= 36.1\%$	$\dfrac{\$98}{(\$338 + \$276) \div 2}$ $= 31.9\%$

Add the previous year's shareholders' equity and current year's shareholder's equity and divide by two when calculating average shareholders' equity in the return on shareholders' equity.

For the six ratios calculated, think of the results as "the higher the ratio, the better." When these ratios increase each year, it is a positive trend and indicates good news.

Evaluation

During the first three years, Bazinga Inc's operating results were outstanding: Operating results improved, with all ratio values higher. The most recent year might be a concern. Results are lower than the previous year. It is too soon to know if this is a downward trend or an isolated bad year. Lenders and investors might be cautious based on the most recent results, even though many results are better than the base year.

Remember to evaluate all ratios along with other information about the company. One ratio will not tell the complete story.

Summary

Learning Objectives

(1) Perform a horizontal analysis of financial statements   Pg. 1033

How do we compare several years of financial information?
- *Horizontal analysis* is the study of percentage changes in financial statement items from one period to the next.
  - Calculate the dollar amount of the change from the base (earlier) period to the later period.
  - Divide the dollar amount of change by the base-period amount and multiply by 100.
- *Trend percentages* are a form of horizontal analysis.

(2) Perform a vertical analysis of financial statements   Pg. 1037

What is a vertical analysis, and how do we perform one?
- *Vertical analysis* shows the relationship of each statement item to a specified base, which is the 100 percent figure.
  - On an income statement, net sales (or revenues) is usually the base.
  - On a balance sheet, total assets is usually the base.

(3) Prepare and use common-size financial statements   Pg. 1040

What are common-size financial statements, and how do we use them?
- Common-size financial statements
  - Report only percentages, not dollar amounts
  - Ease the comparison of different companies
- *Benchmarking* is the practice of comparing a company's performance with that of other companies, usually in the same industry.

(4) Compute the standard financial ratios   Pg. 1044

How do we compute standard financial ratios, and what do they mean?
- A ratio expresses the relationship of one item to another.
- The financial ratios we discussed measure:
  - **Liquidity:** a company's ability to pay current liabilities (current ratio, acid-test ratio)
  - **Efficiency:** its ability to sell inventory and collect receivables (inventory turnover, days' sales in inventory accounts receivable turnover, days' sales in receivables)
  - **Solvency:** its ability to pay long-term debt (debt ratio, debt/equity ratio, times-interest-earned ratio)
  - **Profitability** (return on sales, return on assets, return on common shareholders' equity, earnings per common share)
  - **Value as an investment** (price–earnings ratio, dividend yield, book value per common share)
- The formulas for these ratios are listed on the next page.
- An average is calculated by adding up the amount at the start of the year and the end of the year and then dividing by two.

(5) Describe the impact of IFRS on financial statement analysis   Pg. 1058

What is the impact of IFRS on financial statement analysis?
- The procedures for analyzing the relationships among the reported numbers are the same. Analysts must read the notes to the financial statements to understand the reporting *choices* made by each corporation.

Key Terms for the chapter are shown next and are in the Glossary at the back of the book. **Similar Terms** are shown after **Key Terms**.

Ratios Used in Financial Statement Analysis

Name	Formula	Interpretation
Measuring the company's ability to pay current liabilities (liquidity):		
Current ratio	$\dfrac{\text{Current assets}}{\text{Current liabilities}}$	Measures ability to pay current liabilities with current assets.
Acid-test (quick) ratio	$\dfrac{\text{Cash + Short-term investments + Net current receivables}}{\text{Current liabilities}}$	Shows ability to pay all current liabilities if they come due immediately.
Measuring the company's ability to sell inventory and collect receivables (efficiency):		
Inventory turnover	$\dfrac{\text{Cost of goods sold}}{\text{Average inventory}}$	Indicates saleability of inventory—the number of times a company sells its average amount of inventory during a year.
Days' sales in inventory	$\dfrac{365 \text{ days}}{\text{Inventory turnover}}$	Measures the average number of days the inventory is held.
Accounts receivable turnover	$\dfrac{\text{Net credit sales}}{\text{Average net accounts receivable}}$	Measures ability to collect cash from credit customers.
Days' sales in receivables	**❶** One day's sales $= \dfrac{\text{Net sales}}{365 \text{ days}}$ **❷** $\dfrac{\text{Average net accounts receivable}}{\text{One day's sales}}$	Shows how many days' sales remain in Accounts Receivable—how many days it takes to collect the average level of receivables.
Measuring the company's ability to pay long-term debt (solvency):		
Debt ratio	$\dfrac{\text{Total liabilities}}{\text{Total assets}}$	Indicates the percentage of assets financed with debt.
Debt/equity ratio	$\dfrac{\text{Total liabilites}}{\text{Total equity}}$	Measures leverage and financial risk by evaluating the extent of debt obtained from outside sources.
Times-interest-earned ratio	$\dfrac{\text{Income from operations}}{\text{Interest expense}}$	Measures the number of times operating income can cover interest expense.
Measuring the company's profitability:		
Return on sales	$\dfrac{\text{Net income}}{\text{Net sales}}$	Shows the percentage of each sales dollar earned as net income.
Return on assets	$\dfrac{\text{Net income + Interest expense}}{\text{Average total assets}}$	Measures how profitably a company uses its assets.
Return on common shareholders' equity	$\dfrac{\text{Net income − Preferred dividends}}{\text{Average common shareholders' equity}}$	Gauges how much income is earned for each dollar invested by common shareholders.
Earnings per common share	$\dfrac{\text{Net income − Preferred dividends}}{\text{Weighted average number of common shares outstanding}}$	Gives the amount of earnings earned for each of the company's common shares.
Analyzing the company's shares as an investment (value):		
Price–earnings ratio	$\dfrac{\text{Market price per common share}}{\text{Earnings per share}}$	Indicates the market price of $1 of earnings.
Dividend yield	$\dfrac{\text{Annual dividends per common (or preferred) share}}{\text{Markets price per common (or preferred) share}}$	Shows the percentage of the market price of each share returned as dividends to shareholders each period.
Book value per common share	$\dfrac{\text{Total shareholders' equity − Preferred equity}}{\text{Number of common shares outstanding}}$	Indicates the recorded accounting amount for each common share outstanding.

KEY TERMS

Accounts receivable turnover Ratio of net credit sales to average net accounts receivable. Measures ability to collect cash from credit customers (p. 1048).

Acid-test ratio Ratio of the sum of cash plus short-term investments plus net current receivables to current liabilities. Tells whether the entity could pay all its current liabilities if they came due immediately. Also called the *quick ratio* (p. 1046).

Benchmarking Comparison of current performance with some standard. The standard often is the performance level of a leading outside organization or the industry average (p. 1041).

Book value per common share Common shareholders' equity divided by the number of common shares outstanding (p. 1054).

Common-size statement A financial statement that reports only percentages (no dollar amounts); a type of vertical analysis (p. 1040).

Current ratio Current assets divided by current liabilities. Measures the ability to pay current liabilities from current assets (p. 1046).

Days' sales in inventory 365 divided by inventory turnover indicates how many days of sales remain in inventory waiting to be sold (p. 1048).

Days' sales in receivables Ratio of average net accounts receivable to one day's sales. Indicates how many days' sales remain in Accounts Receivable awaiting collection (p. 1049).

Debt ratio Ratio of total liabilities to total assets. Gives the proportion of a company's assets that it has financed with debt (p. 1050).

Debt/equity ratio Ratio of total liabilities to total equity. Gives the proportion of debt financed by those outside the company (p. 1050).

Dividend yield Ratio of dividends per share to the share's market price per share. Tells the percentage of a share's market value that the company pays to shareholders as dividends (p. 1054).

Downside risk An estimate of the potential loss from a change in market conditions (p. 1054).

Earnings per share (EPS) The amount of a company's net income per outstanding common share (p. 1053).

Efficient capital market A market in which the market prices fully reflect the impact of all information available to the public (p. 1055).

Factors Companies that purchase other firms' accounts receivable at a discount. Receivables are sold so that the cash can be received more quickly (p. 1049).

Horizontal analysis The calculation and use of percentage changes in comparative financial statements (p. 1033).

Inventory turnover The ratio of cost of goods sold to average inventory. Measures the number of times a company sells its average level of inventory during a year (p. 1048).

Leverage The use of financial instruments to increase the potential return on investment by earning more income on borrowed money than the related expense, thereby increasing the earnings for the owners of the business. Another name for *trading on the equity* (p. 1050).

Liquid assets Assets that can be converted to cash quickly. Often they are financial instruments that can be sold without a discount (p. 1046).

Liquidity A company's ability to meet current payments as they come due (p. 1044).

Long-term solvency The ability to generate enough cash to pay long-term debts as they mature (p. 1032).

Price–earnings (P/E) ratio The market price of a common share divided by the company's earnings per share. Measures the value that the stock market places on $1 of a company's earnings (p. 1053).

Quick ratio Another name for the *acid-test ratio* (p. 1046).

Return on assets (ROA) The sum of net income plus interest expense divided by average total assets. This ratio measures the success a company has in using its assets to earn income for the people who finance the business. (p. 1052).

Return on common shareholders' equity (ROE) Net income minus preferred dividends divided by average common shareholders' equity. A measure of profitability (p. 1052).

Return on sales (ROS) Ratio of net income to net sales. A measure of profitability. (p. 1051).

Servicing its debt A phrase that means the repayment of principal and interest on loans or bonds (p. 1051).

Short-term liquidity Ability to meet current payments as they come due (p. 1032).

Times-interest-earned ratio Ratio of income from operations to interest expenses. Measures the number of times that operating income can cover interest expense. Also called the interest coverage ratio (p. 1051).

Trading on the equity Earning more income on borrowed money than the related expense, thereby increasing the earnings for the owners of the business. Also called *leverage* (p. 1052).

Vertical analysis Analysis of a financial statement that reveals the relationship of each statement item to a total, which is 100 percent (p. 1037).

Working capital Current assets minus current liabilities; measures a business's ability to meet its short-term obligations with its current assets (p. 1045).

SIMILAR TERMS

Acid-test ratio	Quick ratio
Debt-to-equity ratio	debt/equity ratio, debt–equity ratio, gearing ratio
EPS	Earnings per share
Leverage	Trading on the equity
P/E Ratio	Price–earnings ratio
Rate of return on common shareholders' equity	Return on common shareholders' equity; Return on equity; ROE
Rate of return on net sales	Return on sales; ROS; profit margin
Rate of return on total assets	Return on assets; ROA
ROA	Return on assets
ROE	Return on equity
ROS	Return on sales
Servicing its debt	Paying liabilities
Solvency	Long-term solvency
Times-interest-earned ratio	Interest coverage ratio

SELF-STUDY QUESTIONS

Test your understanding of the chapter by marking the correct answer for each of the following questions:

1. Net income for PJ Ltd. was $240,000 in 2018, $210,000 in 2019, and $252,000 in 2020. The change from 2019 to 2020 is a(n) (p. 1033)
   a. Increase of 5 percent
   b. Increase of 20 percent
   c. Decrease of 10 percent
   d. Decrease of 12.5 percent

2. Vertical analysis of a financial statement shows (p. 1037)
   a. Trend percentages
   b. The percentage change in an item from period to period
   c. The relationship of an item to a base amount on the statement
   d. Net income expressed as a percentage of shareholders' equity

3. Common-size statements are useful for comparing (p. 1040)
   a. Changes in the makeup of assets from period to period
   b. Different companies
   c. A company to its industry
   d. All of the above

4. Benchmarking allows a user of the financial statements of a company to (p. 1041)
   a. Compare the performance of the company against that of its key competitors
   b. Compare the performance of the company against best practices
   c. Compare the performance of the company against average performance
   d. Do all of the above

5. The following figures were taken from the 2020 balance sheet of Plateau Golf Academy Ltd. Cash is $10,000, net accounts receivable amount to $22,000, inventory is $55,000, prepaid expenses total $3,000, and current liabilities are $40,000. What is the acid-test ratio? (p. 1046)
   a. 0.25
   b. 0.80
   c. 2.18
   d. 2.25

6. Inventory turnover is computed by dividing (p. 1048)
   a. Sales revenue by average inventory
   b. Cost of goods sold by average inventory
   c. Credit sales by average inventory
   d. Average inventory by cost of goods sold

7. Garnet Motors Ltd. is experiencing a severe cash shortage because of its inability to collect accounts receivable. The decision tool most likely to help identify the appropriate corrective action is the (p. 1049)
   a. Acid-test ratio
   b. Inventory turnover
   c. Times-interest-earned ratio
   d. Days' sales in receivables

8. Which of the following is most likely to be true? (p. 1052)
   a. Return on common equity > return on total assets
   b. Return on total assets > return on common equity
   c. Return on total assets = return on common equity
   d. None of the above is true

9. How are financial ratios used in decision making? *(p. 1054)*
   a. They remove the uncertainty of the business environment.
   b. They give clear signals about the appropriate action to take.
   c. They can help identify the reasons for success and failure in business, but decision making requires information beyond the ratios.
   d. They are not useful because decision making is too complex.

10. What part of Indigo Books and Music's annual report is written by the company and could present a biased view of financial conditions and results? *(p. 1056)*
   a. Management's Responsibility for Financial Reporting
   b. MD&A
   c. Independent Auditor's Report
   d. Notes to consolidated financial statements

Answers to Self-Study Questions
1. b $252,000 − $210,000 = $42,000; $42,000 ÷ $210,000 = 0.20, or 20%   2. c   3. d   4. d
5. b ($10,000 + $22,000) ÷ $40,000 = 0.80   6. b   7. d   8. a   9. c   10. b

Assignment Material

MyLab Accounting   Make the grade with MyLab Accounting: The Starters, Exercises, and Problems can be found on MyLab. You can practise them as often as you want, and most feature step-by-step guided instructions to help you find the right answer.

QUESTIONS

1. Identify three groups of users of accounting information and the decisions they base on accounting data.

2. Briefly describe horizontal analysis. How do decision makers use this analytical tool?

3. What is vertical analysis, and what is its purpose?

4. What is the purpose of common-size statements?

5. What is benchmarking? Give an example of its use.

6. Identify two ratios used to measure a company's ability to pay current liabilities. Show how they are computed.

7. Why is the acid-test ratio given that name?

8. What does the inventory turnover ratio measure?

9. Suppose the days' sales in receivables ratio of Stratham Corp. increased from 33 days at January 1 to 45 days at December 31. Is this a good sign or a bad sign about the company? What might Stratham Corp.'s management do in response to this change?

10. Janner Inc.'s debt ratio has increased from 0.40 to 0.75. Identify a decision maker to whom this increase is important, and state how the increase affects this party's decisions about the company.

11. Which ratio measures the effect of debt on (a) financial position (the balance sheet) and (b) the company's ability to pay interest expense (the income statement)?

12. Freshie Ltd. is a chain of grocery stores, and Benjamin's Inc. is a furniture store. Which company is likely to have the higher (a) current ratio, (b) inventory turnover, (c) return on sales? Give your reasons.

13. Identify four ratios used to measure a company's profitability.

14. Recently, the price–earnings ratio of WestJet Airlines was 10.1 and the price–earnings ratio of Air Canada was 3.65. Which company did the stock market favour? Explain.

15. Recently, TransCanada Corporation paid cash dividends of $0.501 per share when the market price of the company's shares was $61.04 per share. What was the dividend yield on TransCanada's shares? What does dividend yield measure?

16. Hold all other factors constant and indicate whether each of the following situations generally signals good or bad news about a company. Explain your answer.
   a. Increase in return on sales
   b. Decrease in earnings per share
   c. Increase in current ratio
   d. Decrease in inventory turnover
   e. Increase in debt ratio

17. Explain how an investor might use book value per share in making an investment decision.

18. Describe how decision makers use ratio data. What are the limitations of ratios?

19. What is an annual report? Briefly describe some of the information found in an annual report.

20. Are there procedural differences when analyzing financial statements prepared under ASPE and financial statements prepared under IFRS? Why or why not?

STARTERS

①

Horizontal analysis of revenues and gross margin

2016 net sales increased 5.76%

S18-1 Air Canada reported the following income statement information:

	(in millions)		
	2016	**2015**	**2014**
Net sales	$14,667	$13,868	$13,272
Cost of sales	11,094	10,427	9,513

Perform a horizontal analysis of net sales, cost of sales, and gross margin, both in dollar amounts and in percentages, for 2016 and 2015. Show two decimal places in the percentage answers.

①

Trend analysis of revenues and net income

1. 2016 net sales, 111%

S18-2 Air Canada reported the following net sales and net income amounts:

	(in millions)		
	2016	**2015**	**2014**
Net sales	$14,667	$13,868	$13,272
Net income	876	303	100

1. Show Air Canada's trend percentages for net sales and net income. Use 2014 as the base year. Round the results to the nearest full percent.
2. Which measure increased at a higher rate in this period?

②

Vertical analysis of income statement

SG&A, 34.5%

S18-3 Use the following information to perform a vertical analysis and check if selling, general, and administrative (SG&A) expenses are in line with the industry average of 37 percent. Show all percentages rounded to one decimal place.

KONE CORP. Income Statement For the year ended November 30, 2020	
Net sales	$310,550
Cost of goods sold	148,800
Gross margin	161,750
Selling, general, and administrative expenses	107,150
Income from operations	54,600
Income tax expense	20,725
Net income	$ 33,875

②

Vertical analysis of assets

Cash and receivables are 29% of total assets

S18-4 Sporting Apparel Inc. reported the following amounts on its balance sheet at December 31, 2020:

	2020
Cash and receivables	$ 80,640
Inventory	56,840
Property, plant, and equipment, net	142,520
Total assets	$280,000

Perform a vertical analysis of the company's assets at the end of 2020. Round all percentages to the nearest whole percent.

S18-5 Compare HomePro Corp. and Away Inc.

③

Common-size income statements of two companies

Net income as % of sales: HomePro, 6.2%

	(Amounts in thousands)	
	HomePro Corp.	**Away Inc.**
Net sales	$18,978	$39,072
Cost of goods sold	11,570	28,202
Other expenses	6,228	8,994
Net income	$ 1,180	$ 1,876

1. Convert their income statements to common size. Round all percentages to one decimal place.
2. Which company earns more net income?
3. Which company's net income is a higher percentage of its net sales?

S18-6 Match each of the following terms with its description. Place the letter for the description in the blank beside the term.

① ② ④

Match terms with definitions

Terms	**Description**
_____ 1. Horizontal analysis	a. Ability to meet current payments as they come due.
_____ 2. Quick ratio	b. Ratio of cost of goods sold to average inventory.
_____ 3. Vertical analysis	c. Ratio of total liabilities to total assets.
_____ 4. Debt ratio	d. Ratio of the sum of cash plus short-term investments plus net current receivables to current liabilities.
_____ 5. Inventory turnover	e. Analysis of a financial statement that reveals the relationship of each statement item to a total, which is 100 percent.
_____ 6. Liquidity	f. Earning more income on borrowed money than the related expense, thereby increasing the earnings for the owners of the business.
_____ 7. Leverage	g. The use of percentage changes in comparative financial statements.

S18-7 For each of the following ratios, indicate whether it is a liquidity, efficiency, solvency, or profitability ratio by checking off the appropriate column:

④

What ratios evaluate

Ratio	Liquidity	Efficiency	Solvency	Profitability
Return on common shareholders' equity				
Inventory turnover				
Current ratio				
Debt/equity ratio				
Acid-test ratio				
Accounts receivable turnover				
Return on sales				

S18-8 For each of the following ratios, indicate with a check mark if a higher result is considered "good."

④

Understanding ratio results

_____ Current ratio   _____ Debt/equity ratio

_____ Accounts receivable turnover _____ Earnings per common share

_____ Return on assets   _____ Return on sales

_____ Book value per common share   _____ Days' sales in inventory

Use the following data for Starters 18–9 through 18–13. Bastion Computer Corp., a technology support company providing security for small businesses, reported these summarized figures (in millions):

BASTION COMPUTER CORP. Income Statement For the Year Ended December 31, 2020	
Net sales	$61.6
Cost of goods sold	42.4
Interest expense	0.6
All other expenses	15.0
Net income	$ 3.6

BASTION COMPUTER CORP.
Balance Sheet
December 31, 2020 and 2019

Assets	2020	2019	Liabilities and Equity	2020	2019
Cash	$ 2.8	$ 1.6	Total current liabilities	$ 8.8	$ 7.2
Short-term investments	0.4	0.5	Long-term liabilities	8.6	8.3
Accounts receivable	0.5	0.4	Total liabilities	17.4	15.5
Inventory	9.2	8.0			
Other current assets	0.8	0.6	Common shares	5.2	4.8
Total current assets	13.7	11.1	Retained earnings	15.7	11.8
All other assets	24.6	21.0	Total equity	20.9	16.6
Total assets	$38.3	$32.1	Total liabilities and equity	$38.3	$32.1

Round all answers for questions related to this company to two decimal places.

④
Evaluating a company's current ratio

2020 current ratio, 1.56

S18–9 Use the Bastion Computer Corp. balance sheet data given above.
1. Compute the company's current ratio and acid-test ratio at December 31, 2020 and 2019.
2. Did Bastion Computer Corp.'s ratios value improve, deteriorate, or hold steady during 2020?

④
Computing inventory turnover and days' sales in receivables

Inventory turnover, 4.93 times

S18–10 Use the Bastion Computer Corp. data to compute the following for 2020:
1. Inventory turnover.
2. Days' sales in receivables. All sales are made on account. Round interim dollar amounts in this calculation to three decimal places to get a more accurate answer.

④
Measuring ability to pay liabilities

Debt ratio, 0.45

S18–11 Use the financial statements of Bastion Computer Corp.
1. Compute the debt ratio and the debt/equity ratio at December 31, 2020.
2. Is Bastion Computer Corp.'s ability to pay its liabilities strong or weak? Explain your reasoning.

④
Measuring profitability

a. ROS, 5.84%

S18–12 Use the financial statements of Bastion Computer Corp.
1. Compute these profitability measures for 2020:
   a. Return on sales
   b. Return on assets; interest expense for 2020 was $0.6 million
   c. Return on common shareholders' equity
2. Are these rates of return strong or weak?

S18-13 Use the financial statements of Bastion Computer Corp., plus the following item (in millions):

Number of common shares outstanding 0.8

1. Compute earnings per share (EPS). Round the result to the nearest cent.
2. Compute the price–earnings ratio. The price of a Bastion Computer Corp. common share is $131.00.

④

Computing EPS and the price–earnings ratio

1. $4.50

S18-14 A summary of Pasmore Ltd.'s income statement appears as follows:

④

Using ratio data to reconstruct an income statement

Income tax expense, $158

PASMORE LTD. Income Statement For the Year Ended March 31, 2019	
Net sales	$3,600
Cost of goods sold	(A)
Selling and administrative expenses	855
Interest expenses	(B)
Other expenses	75
Income before taxes	500
Income tax expenses	(C)
Net income	$ (D)

Use the following ratio data to complete Pasmore Ltd.'s income statement:
a. Inventory turnover was 5.50 (beginning inventory was $395, ending inventory was $375).
b. Return on sales is 0.095, or 9.5 percent.

S18-15 A summary of Pasmore Ltd.'s balance sheet appears as follows:

④

Using ratio data to reconstruct a balance sheet

Total current assets, $735

PASMORE LTD. Balance Sheet March 31, 2019			
Assets		**Liabilities**	
Current assets			
Cash	$ 25	Total current liabilities	$1,050
Accounts receivable	(A)		
Inventories	375	Long-term note payable	(E)
Prepaid expenses	(B)	Other long-term liabilities	410
Total current assets	(C)		
Property, plant, and equipment, net	(D)		
Other assets	1,075	**Shareholders' equity**	1,200
Total assets	$3,400	Total liabilities and equity	$ (F)

Use the following ratio data to complete Pasmore Ltd.'s balance sheet:
a. Current ratio is 0.70.
b. Acid-test ratio is 0.30.

EXERCISES

①

Horizontal analysis of an income statement
2020 total expenses, increased 13.5%

E18–1 Prepare a horizontal analysis of the comparative income statement of Bright Tutoring Inc. Round percentage changes to the nearest one-tenth percent.

Why was the percentage increase in net income higher than that in total revenue during 2020?

BRIGHT TUTORING INC. Income Statement For the Years Ended December 31, 2020 and 2019		
	2020	**2019**
Net sales	$533,000	$465,000
Expenses		
Cost of goods sold	235,000	202,000
Selling and general expenses	140,000	135,000
Interest expense	10,000	6,000
Wages expense	51,000	41,000
Total expenses	436,000	384,000
Net income	$ 97,000	$ 81,000

①

Computing trend percentages
2020 net sales, increased 24.6%

E18–2 Compute trend percentages for Ceder Inc.'s net sales and net income for the following five-year period, using 2016 as the base year:

	2020	**2019**	**2018**	**2017**	**2016**
		(Amounts in thousands)			
Net sales	$1,625	$1,469	$1,375	$1,200	$1,304
Net income	149	131	100	82	105

Which measure grew more during the period, net sales or net income? By what percentage did net sales and net income grow from 2016 to 2020?

③

Vertical analysis of a balance sheet
Total liabilities, 45.8% of total assets

E18–3 As requested by Purposeful Products Inc., perform a vertical analysis of its balance sheet.

	A	B	C
1	**PURPOSEFUL PRODUCTS INC.** Vertical Analysis of Balance Sheet December 31, 2020		
2		**Amount**	**Percent**
3	**Assets**		
4	Total current assets	$219,000	
5	Property, plant, and equipment, net	267,000	
6	Other assets	40,000	
7	Total assets	$526,000	
8	**Liabilities**		
9	Total current liabilities	$ 85,000	
10	Long-term debt	156,000	
11	Total liabilities	241,000	
12	**Shareholders' Equity**		
13	Total shareholders' equity	285,000	
14	Total liabilities and shareholders' equity	$526,000	

③

Preparing a common-size
income statement

2020 interest expense, 1.9%

③

Common-size analysis of
assets

Cash and equiv. as % of total
assets: Bhagwan Inc., 4.1%; Bigwig
Ltd., 2.4%

E18–4 Prepare a comparative common-size income statement for Bright Tutoring Inc. using the 2020 and 2019 data found in E18–1. Round percentages to one-tenth of a percent.

E18–5 You are a bank loans officer trying to decide which of these two customers has more fixed assets than the other, *relative to their total assets*.

Assets (in millions of dollars)	Bhagwan Inc.	Bigwig Ltd.
Current assets		
Cash and equivalents	$ 462	$ 472
Short-term investments	—	804
Accounts receivable, net	2,898	882
Inventories	2,082	5,380
Other current assets	408	134
Total current assets	5,850	7,672
Property, plant, and equipment, net	4,960	11,280
Goodwill and other intangibles	206	226
Other assets	302	540
Total assets	$11,318	$19,718

Required

1. Prepare a common-size analysis to compare the asset composition of Bhagwan Inc. and Bigwig Ltd.
2. To which company are *current assets* more important?
3. Which company places more emphasis on its *property, plant, and equipment?*

① ④

Computing year-to-year
changes in working capital

2020 increase in working capital,
5.4%

E18–6 Compute the dollar change and the percentage change (rounded to one decimal place) in Juti Corp.'s working capital each year during 2019 and 2020. Is this trend favourable or unfavourable?

	2020	2019	2018
Total current assets	$92,250	$87,000	$78,750
Total current liabilities	37,200	34,750	42,500

④

Interpreting ratio results

ROE: +, +

E18–7 Compare the results of two years of ratios for Prince George Corp.

Ratio	2020	2019	1. Ratio Change + or −	Benchmark	2. Performance + or −
Current ratio	1.5	1.7		2	
Acid-test ratio	0.83	0.85		0.95	
Inventory turnover	8	7		10	
Accounts receivable turnover	12	14		13	
Debt ratio	0.3	0.2		0.7	
Times-interest-earned ratio	7	6		4	
Return on assets	0.06	0.04		0.05	
Return on common shareholders' equity	0.24	0.23		0.14	

1. Identify whether the change from 2019 to 2020 was good (+) or bad (−).
2. Assess whether the performance in 2020 is good (+) or bad (−) compared to the industry average presented in the benchmark column.

4

Computing liquidity and efficiency ratios

c. 3.30 ×

E18–8 The financial statements of Baca Bay Ltd. include the following items:

	A	B	C
1		**2020**	**2019**
2	**Balance sheet balances**		
3	Cash	$ 11,500	$ 14,500
4	Short-term investments	6,500	10,500
5	Net receivables	39,000	35,000
6	Inventory	45,500	38,500
7	Prepaid expenses	3,500	3,500
8	Total current assets	$106,000	$102,000
9	Total current liabilities	$ 69,000	$ 46,000
10	**Income statement balances**		
11	Net credit sales	$248,500	
12	Cost of goods sold	138,500	

Required   Compute the following ratios for 2020, showing results to two decimal places: (a) current ratio, (b) acid-test ratio, (c) inventory turnover, (d) days' sales in inventory, (e) accounts receivable turnover, and (f) days' sales in receivables. Hint for (f): hold interim amounts to three decimal places before rounding to two for the final answer.

4

Compute ratios and analyze a company

a. 2020, 2.04; 2019, 1.78

E18–9 The Hip Apple Pie Corporation has requested that you determine whether the company's ability to pay its current liabilities and long-term debt has improved or deteriorated during 2020. To answer this question, compute the following ratios for 2020 and 2019: (a) current ratio, (b) acid-test ratio, (c) debt ratio, (d) debt/equity ratio, and (e) times-interest-earned ratio. Summarize the results of your analysis in a paragraph explaining what the results of the calculations mean.

	2020	2019
Cash	$ 13,000	$ 25,500
Short-term investments	15,000	—
Net receivables	59,500	65,500
Inventory	125,000	135,000
Prepaid expenses	9,000	5,500
Total assets	275,000	260,000
Total current liabilities	108,500	130,000
Total liabilities	137,000	143,000
Income from operations	99,000	82,500
Interest expense	22,500	21,000

E18–10 Compute four ratios that measure the ability to earn profits for Elk Ranch Ltd., whose comparative income statement appears below. Additional data follow.

④

Analyzing profitability

EPS: 2020, $0.34; 2019, $0.71

ELK RANCH LTD. Income Statement For the Years Ended December 31, 2020 and 2019		
	2020	**2019**
Net sales	$195,000	$174,000
Cost of goods sold	101,500	91,750
Gross margin	93,500	82,250
Selling and general expenses	50,200	40,000
Income from operations	43,300	42,250
Interest expense	25,400	12,050
Income before income tax	17,900	30,200
Income tax expense	4,475	7,550
Net income	$ 13,425	$ 22,650

Additional data	2020	2019
a. Average total assets	$230,000	$222,000
b. Average common shareholders' equity	102,000	98,000
c. Preferred dividends	5,000	5,000
d. Number of common shares outstanding	25,000	25,000

Did the company's operating performance improve or deteriorate during 2020?

E18–11 Evaluate the common shares of Payment Software Inc. as an investment. Specifically, use the three share (value) ratios to determine whether the shares have increased or decreased in attractiveness during the past year. Round final answers to two decimal places.

④

Evaluating shares as an investment

Dividend yield: 2020, 3.93%; 2019, 3.34%

	2020	2019
Net income	$ 33,000	$ 27,000
Dividends (25% to preferred shareholders)	19,000	13,000
Common shareholders' equity at year-end (75,000 shares)	275,000	250,000
Preferred shareholders' equity at year-end	50,000	50,000
Market price per common share at year-end	$ 4.83	$ 3.89

E18–12 The following data are from the financial statements of Joachim's Equipment Manufacturing Ltd.:

② ③ ④

Using ratio data to reconstruct a company's balance sheet

Current liabilities, $13,999

Total liabilities.. $ 29,204
Preferred shares.. 0
Debt ratio... .55312%
Current ratio 1.75

Required Complete the following condensed balance sheet. Report amounts to the nearest dollar:

Current assets $24,498
Property, plant, and equipment .... $?
Less: Accumulated amortization .... 7,854 ?
Total assets.. $?
Current liabilities... $?
Long-term liabilities.. ?
Shareholders' equity .... ?
Total liabilities and shareholders' equity.......... $?

SERIAL EXERCISE

④
Compute the standard
financial ratios

Current ratio, Paddle Company,
2024, 3.01

E18–13 *The Serial Exercise involves a company that will be revisited throughout relevant chapters in Volume 1 and Volume 2. You can complete the Serial Exercise using MyLab Accounting.*

This exercise continues the Canyon Canoe Company situation from Chapter 17. Students do not have to complete prior exercise in order to answer this question.

The company wants to invest some of its excess cash in trading securities and is considering two investments, Paddle Company (PC) and Recreational Life Vests (RLV). The income statement, balance sheet, and other data for both companies follow for 2024 and 2023 as well as selected data for 2022:

	PADDLE COMPANY Comparative Financial Statements For the Years Ended December 31			**RECREATIONAL LIFE VESTS** Comparative Financial Statements For the Years Ended December 31		
Income Statement	**2024**	**2023**	**2022**	**2024**	**2023**	**2022**
Net sales revenue	$ 430,489	$ 425,410		$ 410,570	$ 383,870	
Cost of goods sold	258,756	256,797		299,110	280,190	
Gross margin	171,733	168,613		111,460	103,680	
Operating expenses	153,880	151,922		78,290	70,830	
Operating income	17,853	16,691		33,170	32,850	
Interest expense	865	788		2,780	2,980	
Income before income tax	16,988	15,903		30,390	29,870	
Income tax expense	5,137	4,809		8,780	8,630	
Net income	$ 11,851	$ 11,094		$ 21,610	$ 21,240	
Balance Sheet						
Assets						
Cash and cash equivalents	$ 69,159	$ 70,793		$ 65,730	$ 55,270	
Accounts receivable	44,798	44,452	$ 44,104	39,810	38,650	$ 36,460
Inventory	79,919	66,341	76,363	68,500	65,230	59,930
Other current assets	15,494	16,264		24,450	37,630	
Total current assets	209,370	197,850		198,490	196,780	
Long-term assets	89,834	90,776		116,760	116,270	
Total assets	$ 299,204	$ 288,626	$ 276,482	$ 315,250	$ 313,050	$310,640
Liabilities						
Current liabilities	$ 69,554	$ 60,232		$ 90,810	$ 90,010	
Long-term liabilities	31,682	29,936		96,310	105,890	
Total liabilities	101,236	90,168		187,120	195,900	
Shareholders' Equity						
Common shares	72,795	80,885		111,530	102,480	
Retained earnings	125,173	117,573		16,600	14,670	
Total shareholders' equity	197,968	198,458	197,668	128,130	117,150	103,840
Total liabilities and shareholder's equity	$ 299,204	$ 288,626		$ 315,250	$ 313,050	
Other Data						
Market price per share	$ 21.38	$ 33.82		$ 46.37	$ 51.64	
Annual dividend per share	0.32	0.30		0.53	0.45	
Weighted average number of shares outstanding	9,000	8,000		9,000	8,000	

Required

1. Using the financial statements given, compute the following ratios for both companies for 2024 and 2023. Assume all sales are credit sales. Round all ratios to two decimal places.

   a. Current ratio
   b. Inventory turnover
   c. Accounts receivable turnover
   d. Gross margin percentage
   e. Debt ratio
   f. Return on assets
   g. Return on common shareholders' equity
   h. Earnings per share
   i. Price-earnings ratio
   j. Dividend yield

2. Compare the companies' performance for 2024 and 2023. Make a recommendation to Canyon Canoe Company about investing in these companies. Which company would be a better investment, Paddle Company or Recreational Life Vests? Base your answer on ability to pay current liabilities, ability to sell merchandise and collect receivables, ability to pay long-term debt, profitability, and attractiveness as an investment.

CHALLENGE EXERCISES

E18–14 The following data are adapted from the financial statements of Pospisil Tennis Shops, Inc.:

④
Using ratios to reconstruct a balance sheet

Total current assets	$1,216,000
Accumulated amortization	2,000,000
Total liabilities	1,540,000
Preferred shares	0
Debt ratio	0.55
Current ratio	1.60

Required Prepare a condensed balance sheet as of December 31, 2019.

E18–15 Pria Developments Corp. is a Canadian real estate investment and development company looking to expand internationally. If growth in this market continues, they will need to make a one-time change to report using IFRS, but they want to evaluate what this might look like and what implications this might have for readers of the financial statements. For the year ended December 31, 2019, Pria Developments prepared two sets of financial statements—one in accordance with ASPE and the other in accordance with IFRS.

④ ⑤
Computing ratios under ASPE and IFRS

Current ratio:
1. (a) Under ASPE, 0.39
2. (a) Under IFRS, 0.62

Excerpts from Pria Development's financial statements appear below and on the following pages.

ASPE-Based Financial Statements:

PRIA DEVELOPMENTS CORP. Consolidated Balance Sheet ($ amounts in thousands)		
	December 31, 2019	**December 31, 2018**
Assets		
Current assets		
Cash	$ 16,359	$ 17,927
Receivables and other	138,397	78,845
Long-term assets		
Investment properties	3,310,317	2,939,960
Development properties	360,562	293,955
Long-term investments	40,086	39,562

PRIA DEVELOPMENTS CORP.
Consolidated Balance Sheet
($ amounts in thousands)

	December 31, 2019	December 31, 2018
Intangible assets	110,067	100,619
Goodwill		33,036
Restricted cash	25,969	27,704
Currency guarantee receivable	28,165	
	$4,029,922	$3,531,608
Liabilities		
Current liabilities		
Accounts payable and other liabilities	$ 268,796	$ 579,373
Construction financing	102,433	66,393
Liabilities of discontinued operations	28,903	28,903
Long-term liabilities		
Long-term debt	2,952,124	2,094,122
Future income taxes	129,097	110,578
Intangible liabilities	15,429	12,234
Derivative instrument liability	19,427	—
	3,516,209	2,891,603
Shareholders' equity	513,713	640,005
	$4,029,922	$3,531,608

PRIA DEVELOPMENTS CORP.
Consolidated Statement of Earnings (Loss)
For the Year Ended December 31
($ amounts in thousands)

	2019	2018
Property revenue	$309,579	$207,331
Sale of properties developed for resale	191,260	229,139
Dividend income and distributions	2,992	2,011
Gain on fair value increase in investments		938
Other income	1,849	3,857
Foreign exchange gain		18,305
Gain on derivative instrument		2,303
Gain on sale of assets	443	2,051
	506,123	465,935
Property operating expenses	84,421	45,173
Cost of sale of properties developed for resale	142,841	147,677
Interest on long-term debt	154,899	106,818
Interest and financing costs	11,916	13,053
Depreciation and amortization	62,860	39,278
General and administrative	23,956	11,051
Stock-based compensation	307	5,288
Foreign exchange loss	19,656	
Loss on derivative instruments	18,542	

PRIA DEVELOPMENTS CORP.
Consolidated Statement of Earnings (Loss)
For the Year Ended December 31
($ amounts in thousands)

	2019	2018
Goodwill impairment loss	63,456	
Loss on fair value decrease in investments	23,133	
	605,987	368,338
Earnings (loss) before income taxes	(99,864)	97,597
Total income taxes (recovery)	(3,781)	16,270
Net earnings (loss) from continuing operations	(96,083)	81,327
Net loss from discontinued operations		(2,159)
Net earnings (loss)	$ (96,083)	$ 79,168

IFRS-Based Financial Statements:

PRIA DEVELOPMENTS CORP.
Consolidated Balance Sheet
($ amounts in thousands)

	December 31, 2019	December 31, 2018
Assets		
Non-current assets		
Investment properties	$ 3,549,744	$ 3,304,880
Development properties	224,285	126,522
Currency guarantee receivable	28,165	
Goodwill		48,594
Investments	40,086	39,562
Restricted cash	25,969	27,704
	3,868,249	3,547,262
Current assets		
Cash	16,359	17,927
Construction properties being developed for resale	194,638	225,596
Receivables and other	65,390	26,694
	276,387	270,217
Total assets	$ 4,144,636	$ 3,817,479
Equity and Liabilities		
Total equity	$ 606,768	$ 886,271
Non-current liabilities		
Long-term debt	2,901,348	1,910,668
Derivatives	19,427	
Deferred tax liabilities	143,930	145,559
Other liabilities	29,727	28,602
	3,094,432	2,084,829
Current liabilities		
Accounts payable and other	255,585	561,122
Income taxes payable	5,739	6,507

PRIA DEVELOPMENTS CORP.
Consolidated Balance Sheet
($ amounts in thousands)

	December 31, 2019	December 31, 2018
Liabilities of discontinued operations	28,903	28,903
Construction financing	102,433	66,393
Current portion of long-term debt	50,776	183,454
	443,436	846,379
Total liabilities	3,537,868	2,931,208
Total equity and liabilities	$ 4,144,636	$ 3,817,479

PRIA DEVELOPMENTS CORP.
Consolidated Income Statement
For the Year Ended December 31
($ amounts in thousands)

	2019	2018
Property revenue	$ 310,466	$211,025
Sales of properties developed for resale	186,350	191,139
Total revenues	496,816	402,164
Property operating expenses	88,414	51,854
Cost of sale of properties developed for resale	143,131	131,677
	231,545	183,531
Gross income from operations	265,271	218,633
General and administrative	(23,956)	(11,051)
Stock-based compensation	(307)	(5,288)
Other income, net	1,849	3,857
Dividend income and distributions	2,992	2,011
Net adjustment to fair value of investment properties	(286,060)	55,757
Gain on sale of investment properties	443	924
Goodwill impairment loss	(48,594)	
Net adjustment to fair value of held-for-trading financial assets	(23,133)	938
Net adjustment to fair value of derivative financial instruments	(18,542)	2,303
Interest expense	(166,815)	(119,871)
Exchange differences, net	(19,656)	18,305
Income (loss) before income taxes	(316,508)	166,518
Total income taxes (recovery)	(39,855)	23,864
Net income (loss) from continuing operations	(276,653)	142,654
Net loss from discontinued operations		(2,159)
Net income (loss)	$(276,653)	$140,495

Notice that the presentation of the financial statements differs somewhat, as well as some of the recorded balances. These differences arise because ASPE and IFRS rules measure certain transactions differently. However, the focus of this question is the impact on ratios of using a different set of accounting rules. Investors need to understand that if two companies in the same industry are being compared, their results could be very different depending on whether IFRS or ASPE is used in the preparation of the financial information.

Required

1. Compute the following ratios for 2019 based on Pria Developments Corp.'s financial statements prepared in accordance with ASPE. Include both "interest on long-term debt" and "interest and financing costs" in your computations for part (d).

   a. Current ratio

   b. Acid-test ratio

   c. Debt ratio

   d. Return on assets

2. Compute the same ratios in Requirement 1 for 2019 based on Pria Developments Corp.'s IFRS financial statements.

BEYOND THE NUMBERS

BN18–1

Consider the following unrelated business situations:

1. Teresa Chan has asked you about the shares of a particular company. She finds them attractive because they have a high dividend yield relative to another company's shares that she is also considering. Explain to her the meaning of the ratio and the danger of making a decision based on it alone. Suggest other information (ratios) Teresa should consider as she makes the investment decision.

2. Saskatoon Plumbing Supplies Ltd.'s owners are concerned because the number of days' sales in receivables has increased over the previous two years. Explain why the ratio might have increased.

④ Understanding the components of accounting ratios

BN18–2

Moe Sahota is the controller of Forochar Ltd., whose year-end is December 31. Sahota prepares cheques for suppliers in December and posts them to the appropriate accounts in that month. However, he holds on to the cheques and mails them to the suppliers in January. What financial ratio(s) are most affected by the action? What is Sahota's purpose in undertaking the activity?

④ Taking unethical action to improve accounting ratios

ETHICAL ISSUE

EI18–1

Harrison Outfitters Inc.'s (HOI) long-term debt agreements make certain demands on the business. For example, HOI may not repurchase company shares in excess of the balance of Retained Earnings. Long-term debt may not exceed shareholders' equity, and the current ratio may not fall below 1.60. If HOI fails to meet these requirements, the company's lenders have the authority to take over management of the corporation.

Changes in consumer demand have made it hard for HOI to sell its products. Current liabilities have increased faster than current assets, causing the current ratio to fall to 1.45. Prior to releasing financial statements, HOI management is scrambling to improve the current ratio. The controller points out that an equity investment can be classified as either long-term or short-term, depending on management's intention. By deciding to convert an investment to cash within one year, HOI can classify the investment as short-term (a current asset). On the controller's recommendation, HOI's board of directors votes to reclassify the long-term equity investments as short-term equity investments.

Required

1. What effect will reclassifying the investment have on the current ratio? Is Harrison Outfitters Inc.'s financial position stronger as a result of reclassifying the investment?

2. Shortly after releasing the financial statements, sales improve and so, then, does the current ratio. As a result, HOI management decides not to sell the investments it had reclassified as short-term. Accordingly, the company reclassifies the investments as long-term. Has management behaved unethically? Give your reason.

PROBLEMS (GROUP A)

①

P18–1A Selected financial information for DMA Corp. for a six-year period follows:

A	B	C	D	E	F	G
1 (Amounts in thousands)	**2020**	**2019**	**2018**	**2017**	**2016**	**2015**
2						
3 Net sales	$1,806	$1,757	$1,606	$1,704	$1,638	$1,588
4 Net income	144	120	89	126	100	96
5 Ending common shareholders' equity	940	860	772	684	628	600

Required

1. Prepare a horizontal analysis to compare 2020 to 2019. Round percentages to two decimal places. Which accounts increased the most?

2. Compute trend percentages for 2016 through 2020, using 2015 as the base year. Round to the nearest whole percentage.

3. From the above data, what can we infer about expenses from 2015 through 2020? (Hint: Sales less net income will give amount of expenses. Compare the rate of growth in expenses to that of sales.)

P18–2A The president of Mackey Car Parts, Inc. has asked you to compare the company's profit performance and financial position with the averages for the industry. The accounting office has given you the company's income statement and balance sheet, as well as the industry average data for competitors:

<table>
<tr><td colspan="3" align="center">MACKEY CAR PARTS, INC.
Income Statement Compared with Industry Average
For the Year Ended December 31, 2020</td></tr>
<tr><td></td><td>Mackey Car Parts</td><td>Industry Average</td></tr>
<tr><td>Net sales</td><td>$778,000</td><td>100.0%</td></tr>
<tr><td>Cost of goods sold</td><td>522,816</td><td>65.8</td></tr>
<tr><td>Gross margin</td><td>255,184</td><td>34.2</td></tr>
<tr><td>Operating expenses</td><td>161,046</td><td>19.7</td></tr>
<tr><td>Operating income</td><td>94,138</td><td>14.5</td></tr>
<tr><td>Other expenses</td><td>4,668</td><td>0.4</td></tr>
<tr><td>Net income</td><td>$ 89,470</td><td>14.1%</td></tr>
</table>

① Trend percentages, return on common equity, and comparison with the industry

2. Net income, 2020, 150%

② Performing vertical analysis

1. Net income, 11.5%

MACKEY CAR PARTS, INC.
Balance Sheet Compared with Industry Average
December 31, 2020

	Mackey Car Parts	Industry Average
Current assets	$325,440	70.9%
Property, plant, and equipment	120,960	23.6
Intangible assets, net	8,640	0.8
Other assets	24,960	4.7
Total assets	$480,000	100.0%
Current liabilities	$222,720	48.1%
Long-term liabilities	107,520	16.6
Total liabilities	330,240	64.7
Shareholders' equity	149,760	35.3
Total liabilities and shareholders' equity	$480,000	100.0%

Required

1. Prepare a vertical analysis for Mackey for both its income statement and balance sheet. Round all answers to one decimal place.

2. Compare the company's gross margin percentage (gross margin as a percent of net sales) with the average for the industry. Comment on their investment in assets compared to the industry information shown.

P18–3A Computer Doctor Ltd. has asked for your help in comparing the company's profit performance and financial position with the computer services industry average. The manager has given you the company's income statement and balance sheet, and also the following industry average data for similar companies:

(2) (3)

Common-size statements, analysis of profitability and financial position compared against the industry

2020 current assets are 64.1% of total assets

COMPUTER DOCTOR LTD.
Income Statement
For the Year Ended December 31, 2020

	Computer Doctor Ltd.	Industry Average
Net sales	$425,625	100.0%
Cost of goods sold	250,375	53.2
Gross margin	175,250	46.8
Operating expenses	87,300	21.3
Operating income	87,950	25.5
Other expenses	20,500	5.2
Net income	$ 67,450	20.3%

COMPUTER DOCTOR LTD. Balance Sheet December 31, 2020		
	Computer Doctor Ltd.	Industry Average
Current assets	$162,750	62.5%
Property and equip., net	85,250	35.2
Other assets	6,000	2.3
Total assets	$254,000	100.0%
Current liabilities	$112,500	42.5%
Long-term liabilities	62,500	32.5
Shareholders' equity	79,000	25.0
Total liabilities and shareholders' equity	$254,000	100.0%

Required

1. Prepare a two-column common-size income statement and a two-column common-size balance sheet for Computer Doctor Ltd. The first column of each statement should present Computer Doctor Ltd.'s common-size statement, and the second column should show the industry averages. Round all answers to one decimal place.

2. For the profitability analysis, compare each of Computer Doctor Ltd.'s (a) ratio of gross margin to net sales, (b) ratio of operating income to net sales, and (c) ratio of net income to net sales. Compare these figures to the industry averages. Is Computer Doctor Ltd.'s profit performance better or worse than the industry average?

3. For the analysis of financial position, compare each of Computer Doctor Ltd.'s (a) ratio of current assets to total assets, and (b) ratio of shareholders' equity to total assets to the industry averages. Is Computer Doctor Ltd.'s financial position better or worse than the industry averages?

Effects of business transactions on selected ratios

1. Earnings per share, $2.70

P18–4A Financial statement data of MKR Dealer Supplies Ltd. include the following items:

Cash	$ 68,000
Accounts receivable, net	97,500
Inventories	129,000
Prepaid expenses	6,000
Total assets	625,000
Short-term note payable	39,000
Accounts payable	109,500
Accrued liabilities	27,000
Long-term liabilities	204,000
Net income	108,000
Number of common shares outstanding	40,000 shares

Required

1. Compute MKR Dealer Supplies Ltd.'s current ratio, debt ratio, and earnings per share.

2. Compute each of the three ratios after evaluating the effect of each transaction that follows. Consider each transaction *separately*.

   a. Purchased merchandise of $43,000 on account, debiting Inventory.

   b. Paid long-term liabilities, $40,000.

   c. Declared, but did not pay, a $60,000 cash dividend on common shares.

d. Borrowed $50,000 on a long-term note payable.

e. Issued 10,000 common shares at the beginning of the year, receiving cash of $140,000.

f. Received cash on account, $29,000.

g. Paid short-term note payable, $25,000.

Set up a table in the following format for your answers, showing all answers to two decimal places:

Transaction	Current Ratio	Debt Ratio	Earnings per Share

P18–5A Comparative financial statement data of Old Tyme Candies Corp. appear below:

④

Using ratios to evaluate a share investment

1. f. ROA 2020, 20.76%

OLD TYME CANDIES CORP. Income Statement For the Years Ended December 31, 2020 and 2019		
	2020	**2019**
Net sales	$311,850	$297,000
Cost of goods sold	148,850	147,000
Gross margin	163,000	150,000
Operating expenses	79,250	77,000
Income from operations	83,750	73,000
Interest expense	12,500	14,000
Income before income tax	71,250	59,000
Income tax expense	17,850	14,600
Net income	$ 53,400	$ 44,400

OLD TYME CANDIES CORP. Balance Sheet December 31, 2020 and 2019			
	2020	**2019**	**2018**
Current assets			
Cash	$ 27,500	$ 25,000	
Current receivables, net	67,500	62,500	$ 52,500
Inventories	127,500	117,500	95,000
Prepaid expenses	5,000	4,000	
Total current assets	227,500	209,000	
Property, plant, and equipment, net	100,500	98,000	
Total assets	$328,000	$307,000	295,500
Total current liabilities	$ 93,000	$100,725	
Long-term liabilities	117,500	127,500	
Total liabilities	210,500	228,225	
Preferred shares, $1.25	5,000	5,000	
Common shares	50,000	37,500	17,500
Retained earnings	62,500	36,275	25,000
Total liabilities and shareholders' equity	$328,000	$307,000	

(selected 2018 amounts given for calculation of ratios)

Other information:

- Market price of Old Tyme Candies Corp. common shares: $24.00 at December 31, 2020, and $12.00 at December 31, 2019.
- Common shares outstanding: 10,000 during 2020 and 7,500 during 2019.
- There are 1,000 preferred shares outstanding at December 31, 2020 and 2019. Preferred dividends were declared each year.
- All sales are on credit.

Required

1. Compute the following ratios for 2020 and 2019, rounding all answers to two decimal places:

    a. Current ratio

    b. Inventory turnover

    c. Accounts receivable turnover

    d. Debt/equity ratio

    e. Times-interest-earned ratio

    f. Return on assets

    g. Return on common shareholders' equity

    h. Earnings per common share

    i. Price–earnings ratio

    j. Book value per common share at year-end

2. Decide (a) whether Old Tyme Candies Corp.'s financial position improved or deteriorated during 2020, and (b) whether the investment attractiveness of its common shares appears to have increased or decreased.

④
Using ratio data to complete a set of financial statements

Net income, $4,954,000

P18–6A Incomplete versions of the comparative financial statements of Kayma Carpet Corp. follow (amounts in thousands):

KAYMA CARPET CORP. Income Statement For the Year Ended May 31, 2020	
Net sales	$ 30,718
Cost of goods sold	(a)
Gross margin	(b)
Selling and general expenses	9,654
Other expense (income)	1,130
Income before income tax	(c)
Income tax expense (25%)	(d)
Net income	$ (e)

KAYMA CARPET CORP. Balance Sheet May 31, 2020 and 2019		
Assets	**2020**	**2019**
Current assets		
Cash	$ (f)	$ 300
Short-term investments	1,852	1,630
Receivables, net	4,224	3,726
Inventories	1,300	1,046
Prepaid expenses	(g)	168
Total current assets	(h)	6,870
Property, plant, and equipment, net	22,354	19,248
Total assets	$ (i)	$26,118
Liabilities		
Current liabilities	$ 9,270	$ 7,434
Long-term liabilities	(j)	15,964
Total liabilities	(k)	23,398
Shareholders' Equity		
Common shareholders' equity	(l)	2,720
Total liabilities and shareholders' equity	$ (m)	$26,118

KAYMA CARPET CORP. Cash Flow Statement For the Year Ended May 31, 2020	
Net cash inflow from operating activities	$ 4,324
Net cash outflow from investing activities	(2,464)
Net cash outflow from financing activities	(1,130)
Net increase (decrease) in cash during 2020	$ (n)

Ratio data:
- Current ratio at May 31, 2020, is 0.9276.
- Inventory turnover for the year ended May 31, 2020, is 11.3620.
- Debt ratio at May 31, 2020, is 0.7521.

Required Complete the financial statements. Round all amounts to the nearest thousand dollars.

Hint: Start with the income statement, then complete the cash flow statement. Finish the balance sheet last.

P18–7A Assume you are purchasing an investment and have decided to invest in a company in the home renovation business. Suppose you have narrowed the choice to FixRight Ltd. and FastFix Inc. You have assembled the following selected data:

Selected income statement data for current year:

	FixRight Ltd.	FastFix Inc.
Net sales (all on credit)	$323,050	$231,875
Cost of goods sold	187,700	154,250
Income from operations	89,500	48,750
Interest expense	15,000	2,500
Net income	70,000	36,550

④

Using ratios to decide between two share investments

a. FixRight, 1.86; FastFix, 2.56

Selected balance sheet and market price data at end of current year:

	FixRight Ltd.	FastFix Inc.
Current assets		
Cash	$ 17,250	$ 18,500
Short-term investments	11,500	9,750
Current receivables, net	32,300	26,100
Inventories	60,950	55,775
Prepaid expenses	2,000	1,250
Total current assets	124,000	111,375
Total assets	225,000	169,000
Total current liabilities	66,750	43,500
Total liabilities	97,500	68,500
Preferred shares, $3.00 (250 shares)	12,500	
Common shares (4,000 shares)		15,000
Common shares (7,000 shares)	17,500	
Total shareholders' equity	127,500	100,500
Market price per common share	$ 10.00	$ 10.00

FixRight's preferred dividends are paid each year.

Selected balance sheet data at beginning of current year:

	FixRight Ltd.	FastFix Inc.
Current receivables, net	$ 30,250	$ 16,000
Inventories	52,500	52,500
Total assets	240,000	192,500
Preferred shareholders' equity, $3.00 (250 shares)	12,500	
Common shares (4,000 shares)		15,000
Common shares (7,000 shares)	17,500	
Total shareholders' equity	90,000	87,500

Your investment strategy is to purchase the shares of companies that have low price–earnings ratios but appear to be in good shape financially. Assume you have analyzed all other factors, and your decision depends on the results of the ratio analysis to be performed.

Required Compute the following ratios (rounded to two decimal places) for both companies for the current year and decide which company's shares better fits your investment strategy:

a. Current ratio

b. Acid-test ratio

c. Inventory turnover

d. Days' sales in inventory

e. Accounts receivable turnover

f. Days' sales in receivables

g. Debt ratio

h. Debt/equity ratio

i. Times-interest-earned ratio

j. Return on sales

k. Return on assets

l. Return on common shareholders' equity

m. Earnings per common share

n. Price–earnings ratio

o. Book value per common share

P18–8A Waterloo Chip Ltd.'s financial statements for the year ended December 31, 2020, are shown below:

① ② ④
Preparing a horizontal and vertical analysis of a financial statement, computing the standard financial ratios used for decision making, using ratios in decision making

3. a. 8.64

WATERLOO CHIP LTD. Income Statement For the Year Ended December 31, 2020		
Net sales		$945,000
Cost of goods sold		610,000
Gross margin		335,000
Operating expenses		
Selling expenses	$128,200	
Administrative expenses	78,000	
Interest expense	22,000	
Total operating expenses		228,200
Operating income		106,800
Income taxes (25%)		26,700
Net income		$ 80,100

WATERLOO CHIP LTD. Statement of Retained Earnings For the Year Ended December 31, 2020		
Retained earnings, January 1, 2020		$162,000
Add: net income for 2020		80,100
		242,100
Less dividends:		
Preferred	$25,000	
Common	9,000	34,000
Retained earnings, December 31, 2020		$208,100

WATERLOO CHIP LTD. Balance Sheet December 31, 2020 and 2019		
	2020	**2019**
Assets		
Cash	$ 92,000	$ 45,000
Accounts receivable	84,000	92,000
Inventory	102,000	118,000
Prepaid expenses	8,000	6,000
Property, plant, and equipment	498,000	474,000
Less: Accumulated amortization	106,000	70,000
Goodwill	40,000	40,000
Total assets	$718,000	$705,000

(Continued)

WATERLOO CHIP LTD. Balance Sheet December 31, 2020 and 2019		
	2020	**2019**
Liabilities		
Accounts payable	$ 30,100	$ 43,000
Note payable (due in 30 days)	3,000	10,000
Mortgage payable	68,800	130,000
Total liabilities	101,900	183,000
Shareholders' equity		
Preferred shares (1,250 shares, $20.00 callable at $210.00 per share)	$240,000	$240,000
Common shares		
(2020—12,000 shares; 2019—6,000 shares)	168,000	120,000
Retained earnings	208,100	162,000
Total shareholders' equity	616,100	522,000
Total liabilities and shareholders' equity	$718,000	$705,000

Required

1. Perform a horizontal analysis of the comparative balance sheets. Round all calculations to one decimal place. Comment on the analysis.

2. Perform a vertical analysis of the income statement. Round all calculations to one decimal place. The industry standards are gross margin of 35 percent and net income of 12 percent. Comment on the results

3. Calculate each of the following ratios for the year ended December 31, 2020. Round answers to two decimal places. The industry standards are provided in parentheses for some of the ratios.

    a. Current ratio (3.14)

    b. Acid-test ratio

    c. Inventory turnover

    d. Days' sales in inventory

    e. Accounts receivable turnover

    f. Days' sales in receivables

    g. Debt ratio (0.50)

    h. Debt/equity ratio

    i. Times-interest-earned ratio

    j. Return on sales

    k. Return on assets

    l. Return on common shareholders' equity

    m. Price–earnings ratio—the market price per share is $30.00 at year-end, when dividends were paid (5.00)

    n. Dividend yield (5.12%)

4. Comment on your calculations for Waterloo Chip Ltd. in Requirement 3. Include comments for those ratios for which industry standards were provided.

PROBLEMS (GROUP B)

P18–1B Selected financial information for Excelsior Limited for a six-year period follows:

①
Trend percentages, return on sales, and comparison with the industry

	A	B	C	D	E	F	G
1	(Amounts in thousands)	**2020**	**2019**	**2018**	**2017**	**2016**	**2015**
2							
3	Net sales	$804	$912	$662	$714	$616	$604
4	Net income	112	92	65	82	68	58
5	Total assets	654	610	522	470	462	410

Required

1. Prepare a horizontal analysis to compare 2020 to 2019. Round percentages to two decimal places. Which accounts increased the most?

2. Compute trend percentages for 2016 through 2020, using 2015 as the base year. Round to the nearest whole percentage.

3. From the above data, what can we infer about expenses from 2015 through 2020? (Hint: sales less net income will give amount of expenses. Compare the rate of growth in expenses to that of sales.)

4. Have total assets grown at the same rate as the growth in sales?

P18–2B The Western Farm Supplies Inc. chief executive officer (CEO) has asked you to compare the company's profit performance and financial position with the averages for the industry. The CEO has given you the company's income statement and balance sheet, as well as the industry average data for retailers:

②
Performing vertical analysis

WESTERN FARM SUPPLIES INC.
Income Statement Compared with Industry Average
For the Year Ended December 31, 2020

	Western Farm	Industry Average
Net sales	$782,000	100.0%
Cost of goods sold	528,632	65.8
Gross margin	253,368	34.2
Operating expenses	163,438	19.7
Operating income	89,930	14.5
Other expenses	4,692	0.4
Net income	$ 85,238	14.1%

WESTERN FARM SUPPLIES INC.
Balance Sheet Compared with Industry Average
December 31, 2020

	Western Farm	Industry Average
Current assets	$303,750	70.9%
Property, plant, and equipment	117,000	23.6
Intangible assets, net	5,850	0.8
Other assets	23,400	4.7
Total assets	$450,000	100.0%
Current liabilities	$208,800	48.1%
Long-term liabilities	102,600	16.6
Total liabilities	311,400	64.7
Shareholders' equity	138,600	35.3
Total liabilities and shareholders' equity	$450,000	100.0%

Required

1. Prepare a vertical analysis for Western for both its income statement and balance sheet. Round all answers to one decimal place.

2. Compare the company's gross margin percentage with the average for the industry. Comment on their investment in assets and the amount of current liabilities compared to the industry information shown.

② ③ ④
Common-size statements, analysis of profitability, and comparison with the industry

P18–3B Top managers of Tilt Windows Inc., a specialty fabricating company, have asked for your help in comparing the company's profit performance and financial position with the average for the window-making industry. The accountant has given you the company's income statement and balance sheet, and also the average data for their industry (amounts in millions):

TILT WINDOWS INC.
Income Statement
For the Year Ended December 31, 2020

	Tilt Windows	Industry Average
Net sales	$29.2	100.0%
Cost of goods sold	17.6	65.9
Gross margin	11.6	34.1
Operating expenses	8.4	28.1
Operating income	3.2	6.0
Other expenses	0.2	0.4
Net income	$ 3.0	5.6%

TILT WINDOWS INC.
Balance Sheet
December 31, 2020

	Tilt Windows	Industry Average
Current assets	$10.4	66.6%
Property, plant, equip., net	8.0	32.3
Other assets	0.2	1.1
Total assets	$18.6	100.0%
Current liabilities	$ 6.2	35.6%
Long-term liabilities	5.2	19.0
Shareholders' equity	7.2	45.4
Total liabilities and shareholders' equity	$18.6	100.0%

Required

1. Prepare a two-column common-size income statement and a two-column common-size balance sheet for Tilt Windows Inc. The first column of each statement should present Tilt Windows Inc.'s common-size statement, and the second column should show the industry averages. Round all answers to one decimal place.

2. For the profitability analysis, compare Tilt Windows Inc.'s (a) ratio of gross margin to net sales, (b) ratio of operating income (loss) to net sales, and (c) ratio of net income (loss) to net sales with the industry averages. Is Tilt Windows Inc.'s profit performance better or worse than the average for the industry?

3. For the analysis of financial position, compare Tilt Windows Inc.'s (a) ratio of current assets to total assets and (b) ratio of shareholders' equity to total assets with the industry averages. Is Tilt Windows Inc.'s financial position better or worse than the average for the industry?

P18–4B Financial statement data of Xi Supplies Inc. as at December 31, 2020, include the following items:

Effects of business transactions on selected ratios

Cash	$ 53,000
Accounts receivable, net	127,000
Inventories	251,000
Prepaid expenses	10,000
Total assets	922,000
Short-term note payable	80,000
Accounts payable	91,000
Accrued liabilities	64,000
Long-term liabilities	248,000
Net income	147,000
Number of common shares outstanding	44,000 shares

Required

1. Compute Xi Supplies Inc.'s current ratio, debt ratio, and earnings per share. Round all ratios to two decimal places.

2. Compute each of the three ratios after evaluating the effect of each transaction that follows. Consider each transaction *separately*.

   a. Borrowed $100,000 on a long-term note payable.

   b. Issued 12,000 common shares on January 2, 2021, receiving cash of $180,000.

   c. Received cash on account, $29,000.

   d. Paid short-term note payable, $50,000.

   e. Purchased merchandise costing $62,000 on account, debiting Inventory.

   f. Paid long-term liabilities, $15,000.

   g. Declared, but did not pay, a $40,000 cash dividend on the common shares.

Set up a table in the following format for your answers:

Transaction	Current Ratio	Debt Ratio	Earnings per Share

P18–5B Comparative financial statement data of Avenger Hardware Ltd. are as follows:

Using ratios to evaluate a share investment

AVENGER HARDWARE LTD. Income Statement For the Years Ended December 31, 2020 and 2019		
	2020	**2019**
Net sales	$351,500	$310,000
Cost of goods sold	201,000	155,000
Gross margin	150,500	155,000
Operating expenses	65,000	71,000
Income from operations	85,500	84,000
Interest expense	26,000	20,000
Income before income tax	59,500	64,000
Income tax expense	19,000	22,500
Net income	$ 40,500	$ 41,500

AVENGER HARDWARE LTD.			
Balance Sheet			
December 31, 2020 and 2019			
	2020	**2019**	**2018**
Current assets			
Cash	$ 21,000	$ 25,000	
Current receivables, net	116,000	80,500	$ 62,500
Inventories	149,000	137,000	86,000
Prepaid expenses	6,000	9,000	
Total current assets	292,000	251,500	
Property, plant, and equipment, net	154,500	143,500	
Total assets	$446,500	$395,000	351,500
Total current liabilities	$141,000	$138,500	
Long-term liabilities	114,500	121,000	
Total liabilities	255,500	259,500	
Preferred shares, $1.50	30,000	30,000	
Common shares	75,000	60,000	60,000
Retained earnings	86,000	45,500	19,000
Total liabilities and shareholders' equity	$446,500	$395,000	

(selected 2018 amounts given for computation of ratios)

Other information:

- Market price of Avenger Hardware Ltd. common shares: $19.00 at December 31, 2020, and $31.00 at December 31, 2019.
- Weighted-average number of common shares outstanding: 15,000 during 2020 and 12,000 during 2019.
- There are 2,000 preferred shares outstanding. Dividends were declared each year.
- All sales are on credit.

Required

1. Compute the following ratios for 2020 and 2019, rounding all answers to two decimal places:
   a. Current ratio
   b. Inventory turnover
   c. Accounts receivable turnover
   d. Debt/equity ratio
   e. Times-interest-earned ratio
   f. Return on assets
   g. Return on common shareholders' equity
   h. Earnings per common share
   i. Price–earnings ratio
   j. Book value per common share at year end
2. Decide (a) whether Avenger Hardware Ltd.'s ability to pay its debts and to sell inventory improved or deteriorated during 2020 and (b) whether the investment attractiveness of its common shares appears to have increased or decreased.

④
Using ratio data to complete a set of financial statements

P18–6B Incomplete and adapted versions of the financial statements of Beach Paradise Corp. follow (amounts in thousands).

Ratio data:

- Current ratio at December 31, 2020, is 0.7547.
- Inventory turnover for 2020 was 5.2840.
- Debt ratio at December 31, 2020, is 0.5906.

BEACH PARADISE CORP.
Income Statement
For the Year Ended December 31, 2020

Net sales	$32,548
Cost of goods sold	(a)
Gross margin	(b)
Selling and general expenses	13,624
Other expense (income)	480
Income before income tax	(c)
Income tax expense (35%)	(d)
Net income	$ (e)

BEACH PARADISE CORP
Cash Flow Statement
For the Year Ended December 31, 2020

Net cash inflow from operating activities	$16,640
Net cash outflow from investing activities	(2,420)
Net cash outflow from financing activities	(4,094)
Net increase (decrease) in cash during 2020	$ (n)

BEACH PARADISE CORP.
Balance Sheet
December 31, 2020 and 2019

	2020	2019
Assets		
Current assets		
Cash	$ (f)	$ 2,528
Short-term investments	1,702	1,702
Receivables, net	3,600	2,984
Inventories	2,428	2,196
Prepaid expenses	(g)	204
Total current assets	(h)	9,614
Property, plant, and equipment, net	19,632	17,336
Total assets	$ (i)	$26,950
Liabilities		
Current liabilities	$14,204	$11,684
Long-term liabilities	(j)	4,416
Total liabilities	(k)	16,100
Shareholders' Equity		
Common shareholders' equity	(l)	10,850
Total liabilities and shareholders' equity	$ (m)	$26,950

Required Complete the financial statements. Round all final amounts to the nearest thousand dollars.

Hint: Complete them in this order: income statement, then cash flow statement, and finally the balance sheet.

P18–7B Assume that you are purchasing shares in a company in the variety store and gas bar supply business. Suppose you have narrowed the choice to BFI Trading Ltd. and Lin Corp. and have assembled the following data:

Selected income statement data for the year ended December 31, 2020:

	BFI Trading Ltd.	Lin Corp.
Net sales (all on credit)	$1,060,000	$1,246,000
Cost of goods sold	602,000	722,000
Income from operations	186,000	202,000
Interest expense	40,000	10,000
Net income	82,000	124,000

Selected balance sheet and market price data for the year ended December 31, 2020:

	BFI Trading Ltd.	Lin Corp.
Current assets		
Cash	$ 134,000	$ 110,000
Short-term investments	0	24,000
Current receivables, net	312,000	392,000
Inventories	424,000	448,000
Prepaid expenses	24,000	28,000
Total current assets	894,000	1,002,000
Total assets	2,070,000	2,344,000
Total current liabilities	748,000	800,000
Total liabilities	1,444,000	1,508,000
Preferred shares, $10.00 (300 shares)	60,000	
Common shares (75,000 shares)		450,000
Common shares (10,000 shares)	100,000	
Total shareholders' equity	626,000	836,000
Market price per common share	$ 84.00	$ 55.00

BFI's preferred dividends are paid each year.

Selected balance sheet data at January 1, 2020:

	BFI Trading Ltd.	Lin Corp.
Current receivables, net	$ 330,000	$ 280,000
Inventories	448,000	470,000
Total assets	1,970,000	1,720,000
Preferred shareholders' equity, $10.00 (300 shares)	60,000	
Common shares (75,000 shares)		450,000
Common shares (10,000 shares)	100,000	
Total shareholders' equity	560,000	720,000

Your investment strategy is to purchase the shares of companies that have low price–earnings ratios but appear to be in good shape financially. Assume you have analyzed all other factors and your decision depends on the results of the ratio analysis to be performed.

Required Compute the following ratios (rounded to two decimal places) for both companies for the current year and decide which company's shares better fit your investment strategy:

a. Current ratio
b. Acid-test ratio
c. Inventory turnover
d. Days' sales in inventory
e. Accounts receivable turnover
f. Days' sales in receivables
g. Debt ratio
h. Debt/equity ratio

i. Times-interest-earned ratio
j. Return on sales
k. Return on assets
l. Return on common shareholders' equity
m. Earnings per common share
n. Price–earnings ratio
o. Book value per common share

P18–8B Cruz Burgers Inc.'s financial statements for the year ended December 31, 2020, are shown below:

① ② ④
Preparing a horizontal and vertical analysis of a financial statement, computing the standard financial ratios used for decision making, using ratios in decision making

CRUZ BURGERS INC. Balance Sheet December 31, 2020 and 2019		
	2020	**2019**
Assets		
Cash	$ 21,600	$ 15,600
Accounts receivable	33,050	21,000
Inventory	38,000	42,000
Prepaid expenses	1,000	1,500
Property, plant, and equipment	170,000	157,000
Less: Accumulated amortization	34,000	24,000
Goodwill	15,000	15,000
Total assets	$244,650	$228,100
Liabilities		
Accounts payable	$ 15,000	$ 18,500
Note payable (due in 30 days)	2,000	3,500
Mortgage payable	40,000	45,000
Total liabilities	57,000	67,000
Shareholders' equity		
Preferred shares (8,000 shares; $2.00, callable at $15.00 per share)	48,000	48,000
Common shares (2020—12,000 shares; 2019—8,000 shares)	81,000	65,000
Retained earnings	58,650	48,100
Total shareholders' equity	187,650	161,100
Total liabilities and shareholders' equity	$244,650	$228,100

CRUZ BURGERS INC.	
Income Statement	
For the Year Ended December 31, 2020	
Net sales	$330,000
Cost of goods sold	190,000
Gross margin	140,000
Operating expenses	
Selling expenses	40,000
Administrative expenses	23,000
Interest expense	6,000
Total operating expenses	69,000
Operating income	71,000
Income taxes (30%)	21,300
Net income	$ 49,700

CRUZ BURGERS INC.		
Statement of Retained Earnings		
For the Year Ended December 31, 2020		
Retained earnings, January 1, 2020		$48,100
Add: net income for 2020		49,700
		97,800
Less dividends:		
Preferred	$16,000	
Common	23,150	39,150
Retained earnings, December 31, 2020		$58,650

Required

1. Perform a horizontal analysis of the comparative balance sheets. Round all answers to one decimal place. Comment on the analysis.

2. Perform a vertical analysis of the income statement. Round all answers to one decimal place. The industry standards are a gross margin of 45 percent and net income of 15 percent. Comment on the analysis.

3. Calculate each of the following ratios for the year ended December 31, 2020. Round all answers to two decimal places. The industry standards are provided in parentheses for some of the ratios.

   a. Current ratio (2.17)
   b. Acid-test ratio
   c. Inventory turnover
   d. Days' sales in inventory
   e. Accounts receivable turnover
   f. Days' sales in receivables
   g. Debt ratio (0.47)
   h. Debt/equity ratio
   i. Times-interest-earned ratio

   j. Return on sales
   k. Return on assets
   l. Return on common shareholders' equity
   m. Price–earnings ratio—the market price per share is $9.00 at year-end, when dividends were paid (14.00)
   n. Dividend yield (4.15%)

4. Comment on your calculations for Cruz Burgers Inc. Include comments for those ratios for which industry standards were provided.

CHALLENGE PROBLEMS

P18–1C Recently, newspapers carried stories about a company that fired three top executives for management fraud. The three had been using dishonest accounting practices to overstate profits, including improperly recording assets on the company's balance sheet, overstating sales, and understating cost of goods sold by inflating inventory numbers. When inventory got out of line, the executives would debit property, plant, and equipment and credit inventory to further hide their fraud.

①

Using horizontal analysis to assess whether a company is using improper accounting practices

The company had been growing at a rapid pace, outdistancing its competitors. However, there were warning signals or "red flags" that revealed that all was not well with the company and that suggested that the books might have been "cooked" to report the rapid growth. For example, sales, which were almost all on credit, grew much faster than accounts receivable when these balances on the company's financial statements were compared with industry data. Inventory turnover was lower than that of competitors, while sales were unusually low relative to property, plant, and equipment. A final "red flag" was that management bonuses were tied to sales increases.

Required

1. Which items would be misstated in a horizontal analysis of the company's income statement? Which items would be misstated in a horizontal analysis of the company's balance sheet? Indicate the direction of the misstatement.

2. Why do you think the issue of management bonuses is considered a "red flag"?

P18–2C You are a senior staff member of a public accounting firm, and you have been asked by one of the firm's partners to discuss the impact of improper accounting practices on the financial statements of a company to new junior staff accountants. Using the information given in P18–1C, use the following questions to frame your comments to the new juniors.

④

Understanding the impact of improper accounting practices on the financial statements of a company

Required

1. Sales grew faster than receivables. Would this situation create an unusually high or unusually low accounts receivable turnover?

2. Why was the fact that sales grew faster than receivables relative to other companies in the industry a "red flag"?

3. Explain why inventory turnover was too low.

4. Why was the fact that inventory turnover was low relative to other companies a "red flag"?

5. Compare the company's receivables turnover with inventory turnover. Does the comparison suggest a "red flag"? If so, what is it?

Extending Your Knowledge

DECISION PROBLEMS

DP18–1

Suppose you manage WinterWorld Inc., a ski and snowboard store, which lost money during the past year. Before you can set the business on a successful course, you must first analyze the company and industry data for the current year in an effort to learn what is wrong. The data appear on the next page.

② ④

Identifying action to cut losses and establish profitability

Income Statement Data

	WinterWorld Inc.	Industry Average
Net sales	100.0%	100.0%
Cost of sales	(61.2)	(55.4)
Gross margin	38.8	44.6
Operating expense	(40.2)	(38.6)
Operating income (loss)	(1.4)	6.0
Interest expense	(3.1)	(1.2)
Other revenue	0.8	0.4
Income (loss) before income tax	(3.7)	5.2
Income tax (expense) saving	1.3	(1.8)
Net income (loss)	(2.4)%	3.4%

Balance Sheet Data

	WinterWorld Inc.	Industry Average
Cash and short-term investments	0.2%	8.0%
Accounts receivable	20.0	15.5
Inventory	67.1	57.5
Prepaid expenses	0.5	0.6
Total current assets	87.8	81.6
Property, plant, and equipment, net	10.2	14.4
Other assets	2.0	4.0
Total assets	100.0%	100.0%
Bank loan, 6%	18.0%	14.0%
Note payable, short-term, 8%	6.0	0.0
Accounts payable	18.2	22.3
Accrued liabilities	6.9	8.4
Total current liabilities	49.1	44.7
Long-term debt, 8%	16.0	14.0
Total liabilities	65.1	58.7
Common shareholders' equity	34.9	41.3
Total liabilities and shareholders' equity	100.0%	100.0%

Required On the basis of your analysis of these figures, suggest three courses of action WinterWorld Inc. should take to reduce its losses and establish profitable operations. Give your reasons for each suggestion.

FINANCIAL STATEMENT CASES

FSC18–1

Indigo Books & Music Inc.'s 2017 annual report included a Five Year Summary of Financial Information on page 60, with data for the fiscal years ended March 30, 2013, to April 1, 2017. Portions are reproduced below.

④ Measuring profitability and analyzing shares as an investment

For the years ended (millions of Canadian dollars, except share and per share data)	April 1, 2017	April 2, 2016	March 28, 2015	March 29, 2014	March 30, 2013
SELECTED STATEMENTS OF EARNINGS INFORMATION					
Revenues					
Superstores	702.1	695.3	625.2	607.2	615.2
Small format stores	140.7	140.2	127.8	127.4	137.6
Online	148.2	133.3	114.0	102.0	91.9
Other	28.8	25.4	28.4	31.1	34.1
Total revenues	1,019.8	994.2	895.4	867.7	878.8
Adjusted EBITDA[1]	52.2	43.1	20.5	0.1	28.5
Earnings (loss) before income taxes	29.0	22.1	(3.2)	(26.9)	4.2
Net earnings (loss)	20.9	28.6	(3.5)	(31)	4.3
Dividends per share	–	–	–	$ 0.33	$ 0.44
Net earnings (loss) per common share	$ 0.79	$ 1.10	$(0.14)	$(1.21)	$ 0.17
SELECTED BALANCE SHEET INFORMATION					
Working capital	248.1	217.9	198.7	189.7	224.3
Total assets	608.6	584.0	538.4	512.6	569.1
Long-term debt (including current portion)	–	0.1	0.2	0.8	1.5
Total equity	371.8	344.0	311.1	311.7	350.3
Weighted-average number of shares outstanding	26,84,775	25,949,068	25,722,640	25,601,260	25,529,035
Common shares outstanding at end of period	26,351,484	25,797,351	25,495,289	25,298,239	25,297,389

[1] Earnings before interest, taxes, depreciation, amortization, impairment, and equity investment. Also see "Non-IFRS Financial Measures."

Required

1. Using the Five Year Summary of Financial Information, perform a four-year trend analysis of
   a. Total revenues
   b. Earnings (loss) before income taxes
   c. Net earnings (loss) per common share

   Start with 2014 and end with 2017; use 2013 as the base year (100%). Do not calculate anything for losses. Round percentage answers to one decimal place.

2. Evaluate Indigo's profitability trend during this four-year period.

IFRS MINI-CASE

The IFRS Mini-Case is now available online at **MyLab Accounting** in Chapter Resources.

COMPREHENSIVE PROBLEM FOR PART 4

Comprehensive cases are available in Mylab, Chapter Resources.

5. Analyzing a Company for its Investment Potential

Try It! Solutions for Chapter 18

1. Large or unusual changes in $ or % should be investigated.

WINSTON INC.
Horizontal Analysis of Comparative Income Statement
For the Years Ended December 31, 2020 and 2019

	2020	2019	Increase (Decrease) Amount	Percent
Net sales	$275,000	$225,000	$50,000	22.2%
Expenses				
Cost of goods sold	194,000	165,000	29,000	17.6
Engineering, selling, and admin. expenses	54,000	48,000	6,000	12.5
Interest expense	5,000	5,000	—	—
Income tax expense	9,000	3,000	6,000	200.0
Other expense (income)	1,000	(1,000)	2,000	—*
Total expenses	263,000	220,000	43,000	19.5
Net income	$ 12,000	$ 5,000	$ 7,000	140.0%

*Percentage changes are typically not computed for shifts from a negative amount to a positive amount, and vice versa.

The net earnings increase of 140 percent occurred because the dollar amounts are quite small. Income tax expense increased 200 percent, which should be investigated.

The horizontal analysis shows that net sales increased 22.2 percent. This percentage increase was greater than the 19.5 percent increase in total expenses, resulting in a 140 percent increase in net income. This indicates 2020 was a good year.

2. a.

	(in thousands)			
	2020	**2019**	**2018**	**2017**
Net sales	138%	113%	105%	100%
Net income	400%	167%	200%	100%

b. Net income increased faster than net sales.

3. a.

WINSTON INC.
Vertical Analysis of Comparative Income Statement
For the Years Ended December 31, 2020 and 2019

	2020 Amount	Percent	2019 Amount	Percent
Net sales	$ 275,000	100.0%	$ 225,000	100.0%
Expenses				
Cost of goods sold	194,000	70.5	165,000	73.3
Engineering, selling, and admin expenses	54,000	19.6	48,000	21.3
Interest expense	5,000	1.8	5,000	2.2
Income tax expense	9,000	3.3	3,000	1.4*
Other expense (income)	1,000	0.4	(1,000)	(0.4)
Total expenses	263,000	95.6	220,000	97.8
Net income	$ 12,000	4.4%	$ 5,000	2.2%

*Number rounded up.

% of net sales = Each expense $
(and net income $) ÷ Net sales $

b. The vertical analysis shows decreases in the percentages of net sales consumed by
- Cost of goods sold (from 73.3 percent in 2019 to 70.5 percent in 2020)
- Engineering, selling, and administrative expenses (from 21.3 percent in 2019 to 19.6 percent in 2020).

These two items are Winston Inc.'s largest dollar expenses, so their percentage decreases are important positive changes.

In addition, the 2020 net income rose to 4.4 percent of sales, compared with 2.2 percent the preceding year. The analysis shows that 2020 was significantly better than 2019.

4. a.

Winston Inc. and Orisa Ltd. Common-Size Income Statements For the Year Ended December 31, 2020	ORISA LTD.	WINSTON INC.
Net sales	100.0%	100.0%
Expenses		
Cost of goods sold	68.1	70.5
Engineering, selling, and admin. expenses	17.2	19.6
Interest expense	5.2	1.8
Income tax expense	4.0	3.3
Other expense (income)	0.3	0.4
Total expenses	94.8	95.6
Net income	5.2%	4.4%

b. Winston Inc.'s results are similar to those of Orisa Ltd., although they are, in general, not quite as good. Winston's cost of goods sold and engineering, selling, and administrative expenses are slightly higher than Orisa's, perhaps reflecting efficiencies that Orisa might have from being a larger company (its sales are more than twice those of Winston's). Except for interest expense, Orisa's expenses as a proportion of net sales are not as great as Winston's. Orisa's net income percentage would have been almost double that of Winston if Orisa did not have such a high proportion of interest expenses. As a result of this benchmarking against a competitor, Winston should explore ways to further reduce its cost of goods sold and engineering, selling, and administrative expenses to improve its future performance.

5.

Situation	Positive change	Negative change
A decrease in return on equity		✓
A decrease in days' sales in inventory	✓	
An increase in the debt/equity ratio*		✓
An increase in acid-test ratio	✓	
A decrease in receivables turnover		✓

* This could also be a positive change depending on a company's situation. If there was too little debt then more might mean they can use leverage to their advantage.

6. a. Current ratio:

$$2020: \frac{\$50,000 + \$27,000 + \$128,000 + \$237,000}{\$295,000} = 1.50$$

$$2019: \frac{\$47,000 + \$124,000 + \$272,000}{\$202,000} = 2.19$$

b. Acid-test ratio:

$$2020: \frac{\$50,000 + \$27,000 + \$128,000}{\$295,000} = 0.69$$

$$2019: \frac{\$47,000 + \$124,000}{\$202,000} = 0.85$$

c. Debt ratio:

$$2020: \frac{\$295,000 + \$44,000}{\$480,000} = 0.71$$

$$2019: \frac{\$202,000 + \$56,000}{\$490,000} = 0.53$$

d. Times-interest-earned ratio:

$$2020: \frac{\$170,000}{\$46,000} = 3.70 \text{ times}$$

$$2019: \frac{\$168,000}{\$33,000} = 5.09 \text{ times}$$

e. Summary: The company's ability to pay its current liabilities has deteriorated based on the comparison of the current and acid-test ratios from 2020 to 2019. The ability to pay long-term debt has also deteriorated, as evidenced by the higher debt ratio and the lower times-interest-earned ratio in 2020 compared to 2019.

Appendix A

Portions of Indigo's 2017 Annual Report are reproduced here. The information here is needed to complete each chapter's Financial Statement Case 1. To download your own copy of the full annual report, please go to the Chapter Resources section of MyAccountingLab. In addition, the TELUS 2016 Annual Report is available there, which is needed to complete the Financial Statement Case 2 in each chapter.

"*A truly great book
should be read in youth,
again in maturity and
once more in old age,
as a fine building should
be seen by morning light,
at noon and by moonlight.*"

– ROBERTSON DAVIES

ANNUAL REPORT
FOR THE 52-WEEK PERIOD
ENDED APRIL 1, 2017

Management's Responsibility for Financial Reporting

Management of Indigo Books & Music Inc. (the "Company") is responsible for the preparation and integrity of the consolidated financial statements as well as the information contained in this report. The following consolidated financial statements of the Company have been prepared in accordance with International Financial Reporting Standards, which involve management's best judgments and estimates based on available information.

The Company's accounting procedures and related systems of internal control are designed to provide reasonable assurance that its assets are safeguarded and its financial records are reliable. In recognizing that the Company is responsible for both the integrity and objectivity of the consolidated financial statements, management is satisfied that the consolidated financial statements have been prepared according to and within reasonable limits of materiality and that the financial information throughout this report is consistent. The Board of Directors, along with the Company's management team, have reviewed and approved the consolidated financial statements and information contained within this report.

The Board of Directors monitors management's internal control and financial reporting responsibilities through an Audit Committee composed entirely of independent directors. This Committee meets regularly with senior management and the Company's internal and independent external auditors to discuss internal control, financial reporting, and audit matters. The Audit Committee also meets with the external auditors without the presence of management to discuss audit results.

Ernst & Young LLP, whose report follows, were appointed as independent auditors by a vote of the Company's shareholders to audit the consolidated financial statements.

Heather Reisman
Chair and Chief Executive Officer

R. Craig Loudon
Interim Chief Financial Officer

Independent Auditors' Report

To the Shareholders of Indigo Books & Music Inc.

We have audited the accompanying consolidated financial statements of Indigo Books & Music Inc., which comprise the consolidated balance sheets as at April 1, 2017 and April 2, 2016, and the consolidated statements of earnings and comprehensive earnings, changes in equity, and cash flows for the 52 week period ended April 1, 2017 and the 53 week period ended April 2, 2016, and a summary of significant accounting policies and other explanatory information.

Management's responsibility for the consolidated financial statements

Management is responsible for the preparation and fair presentation of these consolidated financial statements in accordance with International Financial Reporting Standards, and for such internal control as management determines is necessary to enable the preparation of consolidated financial statements that are free from material misstatement, whether due to fraud or error.

Auditors' responsibility

Our responsibility is to express an opinion on these consolidated financial statements based on our audits. We conducted our audits in accordance with Canadian generally accepted auditing standards. Those standards require that we comply with ethical requirements and plan and perform the audit to obtain reasonable assurance about whether the consolidated financial statements are free from material misstatement.

An audit involves performing procedures to obtain audit evidence about the amounts and disclosures in the consolidated financial statements. The procedures selected depend on the auditors' judgment, including the assessment of the risks of material misstatement of the consolidated financial statements, whether due to fraud or error. In making those risk assessments, the auditors consider internal control relevant to the entity's preparation and fair presentation of the consolidated financial statements in order to design audit procedures that are appropriate in the circumstances, but not for the purpose of expressing an opinion on the effectiveness of the entity's internal control. An audit also includes evaluating the appropriateness of accounting policies used and the reasonableness of accounting estimates made by management, as well as evaluating the overall presentation of the consolidated financial statements.

We believe that the audit evidence we have obtained in our audits is sufficient and appropriate to provide a basis for our audit opinion.

Opinion

In our opinion, the consolidated financial statements present fairly, in all material respects, the financial position of Indigo Books & Music Inc. as at April 1, 2017 and April 2, 2016, and its financial performance and its cash flows for the 52-week period ended April 1, 2017 and for the 53-week period ended April 2, 2016 in accordance with International Financial Reporting Standards

Ernst & Young LLP

Toronto, Canada
May 30, 2017

Chartered Professional Accountants
Licensed Public Accountants

Consolidated Balance Sheets

(thousands of Canadian dollars)	As at April 1, 2017	As at April 2, 2016
ASSETS		
Current		
Cash and cash equivalents (note 6)	130,438	216,488
Short-term investments (note 6)	100,000	–
Accounts receivable	7,448	7,663
Inventories (note 7)	231,576	217,788
Income taxes recoverable	–	25
Prepaid expenses	11,706	11,290
Derivative financial instruments (note 8)	266	–
Assets held for sale (note 11)	1,037	–
Total current assets	482,471	453,254
Property, plant, and equipment (note 9)	65,078	60,973
Intangible assets (note 10)	15,272	16,506
Equity investment (note 22)	1,800	1,421
Deferred tax assets (note 12)	43,981	51,836
Total assets	608,602	583,990
LIABILITIES AND EQUITY		
Current		
Accounts payable and accrued liabilities (note 21)	170,611	171,112
Unredeemed gift card liability	50,396	50,969
Provisions (note 13)	110	34
Deferred revenue	12,852	13,232
Income taxes payable	360	–
Current portion of long-term debt	–	53
Total current liabilities	234,329	235,400
Long-term accrued liabilities (note 21)	2,378	4,483
Long-term provisions (note 13)	51	109
Total liabilities	236,758	239,992
Equity		
Share capital (note 15)	215,971	209,318
Contributed surplus (note 16)	10,671	10,591
Retained earnings	145,007	124,089
Accumulated other comprehensive income (note 8)	195	–
Total equity	371,844	343,998
Total liabilities and equity	608,602	583,990

See accompanying notes

On behalf of the Board:

Heather Reisman
Director

Michael Kirby
Director

Consolidated Statements of Earnings and Comprehensive Earnings

(thousands of Canadian dollars, except per share data)	52-week period ended April 1, 2017	53-week period ended April 2, 2016
Revenue (note 17)	1,019,845	994,181
Cost of sales	(565,640)	(551,194)
Gross profit	454,205	442,987
Operating, selling, and administrative expenses (notes 9, 10 and 17)	(428,981)	(423,037)
Operating profit	25,224	19,950
Net interest income	2,196	753
Share of earnings from equity investment (note 22)	1,617	1,397
Earnings before income taxes	29,037	22,100
Income tax recovery (expense) (note 12)		
Current	(335)	50
Deferred	(7,784)	6,431
Net earnings	20,918	28,581
Other comprehensive income (note 8)		
Items that are or may be reclassified subsequently to net earnings:		
Net change in fair value of cash flow hedges		
(net of taxes of (496); 2016 – 0)	1,357	–
Reclassification of net realized gain		
(net of taxes of 425; 2016 – 0)	(1,162)	–
Other comprehensive income	195	–
Total comprehensive earnings	21,113	28,581
Net earnings per common share (note 18)		
Basic	$0.79	$1.10
Diluted	$0.78	$1.09

See accompanying notes

Consolidated Statements of Changes in Equity

(thousands of Canadian dollars)	Share Capital	Contributed Surplus	Retained Earnings	Accumulated Other Comprehensive Income	Total Equity
Balance, March 28, 2015	205,871	9,770	95,508	–	311,149
Net earnings	–	–	28,581	–	28,581
Exercise of options (notes 15 and 16)	3,156	(484)	–	–	2,672
Directors' deferred share units converted (note 15)	291	(291)	–	–	–
Share-based compensation (notes 16 and 17)	–	1,212	–	–	1,212
Directors' compensation (note 16)	–	384	–	–	384
Other comprehensive income (note 8)	–	–	–	–	–
Balance, April 2, 2016	209,318	10,591	124,089	–	343,998
Balance, April 2, 2016	209,318	10,591	124,089	–	343,998
Net earnings	–	–	20,918	–	20,918
Exercise of options (notes 15 and 16)	5,983	(1,017)	–	–	4,966
Directors' deferred share units converted (note 15)	670	(670)	–	–	–
Share-based compensation (notes 16 and 17)	–	1,400	–	–	1,400
Directors' compensation (note 16)	–	367	–	–	367
Other comprehensive income (note 8)	–	–	–	195	195
Balance, April 1, 2017	215,971	10,671	145,007	195	371,844

See accompanying notes

Consolidated Statements of Cash Flows

(thousands of Canadian dollars)	52-week period ended April 1, 2017	53-week period ended April 2, 2016
CASH FLOWS FROM OPERATING ACTIVITIES		
Net earnings	20,918	28,581
Add (deduct) items not affecting cash		
Depreciation of property, plant and equipment (note 9)	16,612	14,739
Amortization of intangible assets (note 10)	8,573	9,073
Net reversal of capital asset impairments (notes 9 and 10)	(963)	(1,620)
Loss on disposal of capital assets (notes 9 and 10)	2,770	1,039
Share-based compensation (note 16)	1,400	1,212
Directors' compensation (note 16)	367	384
Deferred tax assets (note 12)	7,784	(7,595)
Assets held for sale (note 11)	(1,037)	–
Other	147	(58)
Net change in non-cash working capital balances (note 19)	(17,196)	(5,102)
Interest expense	36	1,000
Interest income	(2,232)	(1,753)
Income taxes received	51	50
Share of earnings from equity investment (note 22)	(1,617)	(1,397)
Cash flows from operating activities	35,613	38,553
CASH FLOWS FROM INVESTING ACTIVITIES		
Purchase of property, plant, and equipment (note 9)	(19,774)	(20,243)
Addition of intangible assets (note 10)	(10,089)	(9,000)
Short-term investments (note 6)	(100,000)	–
Proceeds from disposal of capital assets	–	6
Distributions from equity investment (note 22)	1,238	702
Interest received	1,190	1,522
Cash flows used for investing activities	(127,435)	(27,013)
CASH FLOWS FROM FINANCING ACTIVITIES		
Repayment of long-term debt	(53)	(175)
Interest paid	(28)	(995)
Proceeds from share issuances (note 15)	4,966	2,672
Cash flows from financing activities	4,885	1,502
Effect of foreign currency exchange rate changes on cash and cash equivalents	887	284
Net increase (decrease) in cash and cash equivalents during the period	(86,050)	13,326
Cash and cash equivalents, beginning of period	216,488	203,162
Cash and cash equivalents, end of period	130,438	216,488

See accompanying notes

Notes to Consolidated Financial Statements

April 1, 2017

1. CORPORATE INFORMATION

Indigo Books & Music Inc. (the "Company" or "Indigo") is a corporation domiciled and incorporated under the laws of the Province of Ontario in Canada. The Company's registered office is located at 468 King Street West, Toronto, Ontario, M5V 1L8, Canada. The consolidated financial statements of the Company comprise the Company, its equity investment in Calendar Club of Canada Limited Partnership ("Calendar Club"), and its wholly-owned subsidiary, Indigo Design Studios Inc. (formerly Soho Studios Inc.) The Company is the ultimate parent of the consolidated organization.

2. NATURE OF OPERATIONS

Indigo is Canada's largest book, gift and specialty toy retailer and was formed as a result of an amalgamation of Chapters Inc. and Indigo Books & Music Inc. under the laws of the Province of Ontario, pursuant to a Certificate of Amalgamation dated August 16, 2001. The Company operates a chain of retail bookstores across all ten provinces and one territory in Canada, including 89 superstores (2016 – 88) under the *Indigo* and *Chapters* names, as well as 123 small format stores (2016 – 123) under the banners *Coles*, *Indigospirit*, *SmithBooks*, and *The Book Company*. In addition, online sales are generated through the *indigo.ca* website and the Company's mobile applications. These digital platforms sell an expanded selection of books, gifts, toys, and paper products. The Company also operates seasonal kiosks and year-round stores in shopping malls across Canada through Calendar Club.

The Company's operations are focused on the merchandising of products and services in Canada. As such, the Company presents one operating segment in its consolidated financial statements.

The Company also has a separate registered charity, the Indigo Love of Reading Foundation (the "Foundation"). The Foundation provides new books and learning material to high-needs elementary schools across the country through donations from Indigo, its customers, its suppliers, and its employees.

3. BASIS OF PREPARATION

Statement of Compliance

These consolidated financial statements have been prepared in accordance with International Financial Reporting Standards ("IFRS") as issued by the International Accounting Standards Board ("IASB") and using the accounting policies described herein.

These consolidated financial statements were approved by the Company's Board of Directors on May 30, 2017.

Fiscal Year

The fiscal year of the Company ends on the Saturday closest to March 31. Under an accounting convention common in the retail industry, the Company follows a 52-week reporting cycle, which periodically necessitates a fiscal year of 53 weeks. The year ended April 1, 2017 contained 52 weeks, while the year ended April 2, 2016 contained 53 weeks. The next 53-week period will be for the fiscal year ending April 3, 2021.

Use of Judgments

The preparation of the consolidated financial statements in conformity with IFRS requires the Company to make judgments, apart from those involving estimation, in applying accounting policies that affect the recognition and measurement of assets, liabilities, revenues, and expenses. Actual results may differ from the judgments made by the Company. Information about judgments that have the most significant effect on recognition and measurement of assets, liabilities, revenues, and expenses is discussed below. Information about significant estimates is discussed in the following section.

Impairment

An impairment loss is recognized for the amount by which the carrying amount of an asset or a cash-generating unit ("CGU") exceeds its recoverable amount. Impairment losses are reversed if the recoverable amount of the capital asset, CGU, or group of CGUs exceeds its carrying amount, but only to the extent that the carrying amount of the asset does not exceed the carrying amount that would have been determined, net of depreciation or amortization, if no impairment loss had been recognized. The Company uses judgment when identifying CGUs and when assessing for indicators of impairment or reversal.

Intangible assets

Initial capitalization of intangible asset costs is based on the Company's judgment that technological and economic feasibility are confirmed and the project will generate future economic benefits by way of estimated future discounted cash flows that are being generated.

Leases

The Company uses judgment in determining whether a lease qualifies as a finance lease arrangement that transfers substantially all the risks and rewards incidental to ownership.

Deferred tax assets

The recognition of deferred tax assets is based on the Company's judgment. The assessment of the probability of future taxable income in which deferred tax assets can be utilized is based on management's best estimate of future taxable income that the Company expects to achieve from reviewing its latest forecast. This estimate is adjusted for significant non-taxable income and expenses and for specific limits to the use of any unused tax loss or credit. Deferred tax assets are recognized to the extent that it is probable that taxable profit will be available against which the deductible temporary differences and the carryforward of unused tax credits and unused tax losses can be utilized. Any difference between the gross deferred tax asset and the amount recognized is recorded on the balance sheet as a valuation allowance. If the valuation allowance decreases as a result of subsequent events, the previously recognized valuation allowance will be reversed. The recognition of deferred tax assets that are subject to certain legal or economic limits or uncertainties are assessed individually by the Company based on the specific facts and circumstances.

Use of Estimates

The preparation of the consolidated financial statements in conformity with IFRS requires the Company to make estimates and assumptions in applying accounting policies that affect the recognition and measurement of assets, liabilities, revenues, and expenses. Actual results may differ from the estimates made by the Company, and actual results will seldom equal estimates. Information about estimates that have the most significant effect on the recognition and measurement of assets, liabilities, revenues, and expenses are discussed below.

Revenue

The Company recognizes revenue from unredeemed gift cards ("gift card breakage") if the likelihood of gift card redemption by the customer is considered to be remote. The Company estimates its average gift card breakage rate based on historical redemption rates. The resulting gift card breakage revenue is recognized over the estimated period of redemption based on historical redemption patterns commencing when the gift cards are sold.

The Indigo plum rewards program ("Plum") allows customers to earn points on their purchases. The fair value of Plum points is calculated by multiplying the number of points issued by the estimated cost per point. The estimated cost per point is based on many factors, including expected future redemption patterns and associated costs. On an ongoing basis, the Company monitors trends in redemption patterns (redemption at each reward level), historical redemption rates (points redeemed as a percentage of points issued) and net cost per point redeemed, adjusting the estimated cost per point based upon expected future activity.

Inventories

The future realization of the carrying amount of inventory is affected by future sales demand, inventory levels, and product quality. At each balance sheet date, the Company reviews its on-hand inventory and uses historical trends and current inventory mix to determine a reserve for the impact of future markdowns that will take the net realizable value of inventory on-hand below cost. Inventory valuation also incorporates a write-down to reflect future losses on the disposition of obsolete merchandise. The Company reduces inventory for estimated shrinkage that has occurred between physical inventory counts and each reporting date based on historical experience as a percentage of sales. In addition, the Company records a vendor settlement accrual to cover any disputes between the Company and its vendors. The Company estimates this reserve based on historical experience of settlements with its vendors.

Share-based payments

The cost of equity-settled transactions with counterparties is based on the Company's estimate of the fair value of share-based instruments and the number of equity instruments that will eventually vest. The Company's estimated fair value of the share-based instruments is calculated using the following variables: risk-free interest rate; expected volatility; expected time until exercise; and expected dividend yield. Risk-free interest rate is based on Government of Canada bond yields, while all other variables are estimated based on the Company's historical experience with its share-based payments.

Impairment

To determine the recoverable amount of an impaired asset, the Company estimates expected future cash flows and determines a suitable discount rate in order to calculate the present value of those cash flows. In the process of measuring expected future cash flows, the Company makes assumptions about certain variables, such as future sales, gross margin rates, expenses, capital expenditures, working capital investments, and lease terms, which are based upon historical experience and expected future performance. Determining the applicable discount rate involves estimating appropriate adjustments to market risk and to Company-specific risk factors.

Property, plant, equipment, and intangible assets (collectively, "capital assets")

Capital assets are depreciated over their useful lives, taking into account residual values where appropriate. Assessments of useful lives and residual values are performed on an ongoing basis and take into consideration factors such as technological innovation, maintenance programs, and relevant market information. In assessing residual values, the Company considers the remaining life of the asset, its projected disposal value, and future market conditions.

4. SIGNIFICANT ACCOUNTING POLICIES

The accounting policies set out below have been applied consistently to all periods presented in these consolidated financial statements.

Basis of Measurement

The Company's consolidated financial statements are prepared on the historical cost basis of accounting, except as disclosed in the accounting policies set out below.

Basis of Consolidation

The consolidated financial statements comprise the financial statements of the Company and entities controlled by the Company. Control exists when the Company is exposed to, or has the right to, variable returns from its involvement with the controlled entity and when the Company has the current ability to affect those returns through its power over the controlled entity. When the Company does not own all of the equity in a subsidiary, the non-controlling interest is disclosed as a separate line item in the consolidated balance sheets and the earnings accruing to non-controlling interest holders are disclosed as a separate line item in the consolidated statements of earnings (loss) and comprehensive earnings (loss).

The financial statements of the subsidiary are prepared for the same reporting period as the parent company, using consistent accounting policies. Subsidiaries are fully consolidated from the date of acquisition, being the date on which the Company obtains control, and continue to be consolidated until the date that such control ceases. Once control ceases, the Company will reassess the relationship with the former subsidiary and revise Indigo's accounting policy based on the Company's remaining percentage of ownership. All intercompany balances and transactions and any unrealized gains and losses arising from intercompany transactions are eliminated in preparing these consolidated financial statements.

Equity Investment

The equity method of accounting is applied to investments in companies where Indigo has the ability to exert significant influence over the financial and operating policy decisions of the company but lacks control or joint control over those policies. Under the equity method, the Company's investment is initially recognized at cost and subsequently increased or decreased to recognize the Company's share of earnings and losses of the investment, and for impairment losses after the initial recognition date. The Company's share of losses that are in excess of its investment is recognized only to the extent that Indigo has incurred legal or constructive obligations or made payments on behalf of the company. The Company's share of earnings and losses of its equity investment are recognized through profit or loss during the period. Cash distributions received from the investment are accounted for as a reduction in the carrying amount of the Company's equity investment.

Cash and Cash Equivalents

Cash and cash equivalents consist of cash on hand, balances with banks, and highly liquid investments that are readily convertible to known amounts of cash with maturities of three months or less at the date of acquisition. Cash equivalents of fixed deposits or similar instruments with an original term of longer than three months are also included in this category if they are readily convertible to a known amount of cash throughout their term and are subject to an insignificant risk of change in value assessed against the amount at inception. Cash is considered to be restricted when it is subject to contingent rights of a third-party customer, vendor, or government agency.

Short-term Investments

Short-term investments consist of guaranteed investment securities with an original maturity date greater than 90 days and remaining term to maturity of less than 365 days from the date of acquisition. These investments are non-redeemable until the maturity date.

Inventories

Inventories are valued at the lower of cost, determined on a moving average cost basis, and market, being net realizable value. Costs include all direct and reasonable expenditures that are incurred in bringing inventories to their present location and condition. Net realizable value is the estimated selling price in the ordinary course of business. When the Company permanently reduces the retail price of an item and the markdown incurred brings the retail price below the cost of the item, there is a corresponding reduction in inventory recognized in the period. Vendor rebates are recorded as a reduction in the price of the products and corresponding inventories are recorded net of vendor rebates.

Prepaid Expenses

Prepaid expenses include store supplies, rent, license fees, maintenance contracts, and insurance. Store supplies are expensed as they are used while other costs are amortized over the term of the contract.

Income Taxes

Current income taxes are the expected taxes payable or receivable on the taxable earnings or loss for the period. Current income taxes are payable on taxable earnings for the period as calculated under Canadian taxation guidelines, which differ from taxable earnings under IFRS. Calculation of current income taxes is based on tax rates and tax laws that have been enacted, or substantively enacted, by the end of the reporting period. Current income taxes relating to items recognized directly in equity are recognized in equity and not in the consolidated statements of earnings (loss) and comprehensive earnings (loss).

Deferred income taxes are calculated at the reporting date using the liability method based on temporary differences between the carrying amounts of assets and liabilities and their tax bases. However, deferred tax assets and liabilities on temporary differences arising from the initial recognition of goodwill, or of an asset or liability in a transaction that is not a business combination, will not be recognized when neither accounting nor taxable profit or loss are affected at the time of the transaction.

Deferred tax assets arising from temporary differences associated with investments in subsidiaries are provided for if it is probable that the differences will reverse in the foreseeable future and taxable profit will be available against which the tax assets may be utilized. Deferred tax assets on temporary differences associated with investments in subsidiaries are not provided for if the timing of the reversal of these temporary differences can be controlled by the Company and it is probable that reversal will not occur in the foreseeable future.

Deferred tax assets and liabilities are calculated, without discounting, at tax rates that are expected to apply to their respective periods of realization, provided they are enacted or substantively enacted by the end of the reporting period. Deferred tax assets and liabilities are offset only when the Company has the right and intention to set off current tax assets and liabilities from the same taxable entity and the same taxation authority.

Deferred tax assets are recognized to the extent that it is probable that taxable profit will be available against which the deductible temporary differences and the carryforward of unused tax credits and unused tax losses can be utilized. Any difference between the gross deferred tax asset and the amount recognized is recorded on the consolidated balance sheets as a valuation allowance. If the valuation allowance decreases as the result of subsequent events, the previously recognized valuation allowance will be reversed.

Property, Plant, and Equipment

All items of property, plant, and equipment are initially recognized at cost, which includes any costs directly attributable to bringing the asset to the location and condition necessary for it to be capable of operating in the manner intended by the Company. Subsequent to initial recognition, property, plant, and equipment assets are shown at cost less accumulated depreciation and any accumulated impairment losses.

Depreciation of an asset begins once it becomes available for use. The depreciable amount of an asset, being the cost of an asset less the residual value, is allocated on a straight-line basis over the estimated useful life of the asset. Residual value is estimated to be nil unless the Company expects to dispose of the asset at a value that exceeds the estimated disposal costs. The residual values, useful lives, and depreciation methods applied to assets are reviewed based on relevant market information and management considerations.

The following useful lives are applied:

Furniture, fixtures, and equipment	5 – 10 years
Computer equipment	3 – 5 years
Equipment under finance leases	3 – 5 years
Leasehold improvements	over the shorter of useful life and lease term plus expected renewals, to a maximum of 10 years

Items of property, plant, and equipment are assessed for impairment as detailed in the accounting policy note on impairment and are derecognized either upon disposal or when no future economic benefits are expected from their use. Any gain or loss arising on derecognition is included in earnings when the asset is derecognized.

Leased assets

Leases are classified as finance leases when the terms of the lease transfer substantially all the risks and rewards related to ownership of the leased asset to the Company. At lease inception, the related asset and corresponding long-term liability are recognized at the lower of the fair value of the leased asset or the present value of the minimum lease payments.

Depreciation methods and useful lives for assets held under finance lease agreements correspond to those applied to comparable assets that are legally owned by the Company. If there is no reasonable certainty that the Company will obtain ownership of the financed asset at the end of the lease term, the asset is depreciated over the shorter of its estimated useful life or the lease term. The corresponding long-term liability is reduced by lease payments less interest paid. Interest payments are expensed as part of net interest on the consolidated statements of earnings (loss) and comprehensive earnings (loss) over the period of the lease.

All other leases are treated as operating leases. Payments on operating lease agreements are recognized as an expense on a straight-line basis over the lease term. Associated costs, such as maintenance and insurance, are expensed as incurred.

The Company performs quarterly assessments of contracts that do not take the legal form of a lease to determine whether they convey the right to use an asset in return for a payment or series of payments and therefore need to be accounted for as leases. As at April 1, 2017, the Company had no such contracts.

Leased premises

The Company conducts all of its business from leased premises. Leasehold improvements are depreciated over the lesser of their economic life or the initial lease term plus renewal periods where renewal has been determined to be reasonably certain ("lease term"). Leasehold improvements are assessed for impairment as detailed in the accounting policy note on impairment. Leasehold improvement allowances are depreciated over the lease term. Other inducements, such as rent-free periods, are amortized into earnings over the lease term, with the unamortized portion recorded in current and long-term accounts payable and accrued liabilities. As at April 1, 2017, all of the Company's leases on premises were accounted for as operating leases. Expenses incurred for leased premises include base rent, taxes, common area maintenance, and contingent rent based upon a percentage of sales.

Intangible Assets

Intangible assets are initially recognized at cost, if acquired separately, or at fair value, if acquired as part of a business combination. After initial recognition, intangible assets are carried at cost less accumulated amortization and any accumulated impairment losses.

Amortization commences when the intangible assets are available for their intended use. The useful lives of intangible assets are assessed as either finite or indefinite. Intangible assets with finite lives are amortized over their useful economic life. Intangible assets with indefinite lives are not amortized but are reviewed at each reporting date to determine whether the indefinite life continues to be supportable. If not, the change in useful life from indefinite to finite is made on a prospective basis. Residual value is estimated to be zero unless the Company expects to dispose of the asset at a value that exceeds the estimated disposal costs. The residual values, useful lives, and amortization methods applied to assets are reviewed annually based on relevant market information and management considerations.

The following useful lives are applied:

Computer application software	3 – 5 years
Internal development costs	3 years
Domain name	Indefinite useful life – not amortized

There are no legal, regulatory, contractual, competitive, economic or other factors that limit the useful life of the domain name to the Company. Therefore, useful life of the domain name is deemed to be indefinite.

Intangible assets are assessed for impairment as detailed in the accounting policy note on impairment. An intangible asset is derecognized either upon disposal or when no future economic benefit is expected from its use. Any gain or loss arising on derecognition is included in earnings when the asset is derecognized.

Computer application software

When computer application software is not an integral part of a related item of computer hardware, the software is treated as an intangible asset. Computer application software that is integral to the use of related computer hardware is recorded as property, plant, and equipment.

Internal development costs

Costs that are directly attributable to internal development are recognized as intangible assets provided they meet the definition of an intangible asset. Development costs not meeting these criteria are expensed as incurred. Capitalized development costs include external direct costs of materials and services and the payroll and payroll-related costs for employees who are directly associated with the projects.

Impairment Testing

Capital assets

For the purposes of assessing impairment, capital assets are grouped at the lowest levels for which there are largely independent cash inflows and for which a reasonable and consistent allocation basis can be identified. For capital assets that can be reasonably and consistently allocated to individual stores, the store level is used as the CGU for impairment testing. For all other capital assets, the corporate level is used as the group of CGUs. Capital assets and related CGUs or groups of CGUs are tested for impairment quarterly and whenever events or changes in circumstances indicate that the carrying amount may not be recoverable. Events or changes in circumstances that may indicate impairment include a significant change to the Company's operations, a significant decline in performance, or a change in market conditions that adversely affects the Company.

An impairment loss is recognized for the amount by which the carrying amount of a CGU or group of CGUs exceeds its recoverable amount. To determine the recoverable amount, management uses a value-in-use calculation to determine the present value of the expected future cash flows from each CGU or group of CGUs based on the CGU's estimated growth rate. The Company's growth rate and future cash flows are based on historical data and management's expectations. Impairment losses are charged pro rata to the capital assets in the CGU or group of CGUs. Capital assets and CGUs or groups of CGUs are subsequently reassessed for indicators that a previously recognized impairment loss may no longer exist. An impairment loss is reversed if the recoverable amount of the capital asset, CGU, or group of CGUs exceeds its carrying amount, but only to the extent that the carrying amount of the asset does not exceed the carrying amount that would have been determined, net of depreciation or amortization, if no impairment loss had been recognized.

Financial assets

Individually significant financial assets are tested for impairment on an individual basis. The remaining financial assets are assessed collectively in groups that share similar credit risk characteristics. Financial assets are tested for impairment whenever events or changes in circumstances indicate that the carrying amount may not be recoverable. Evidence of impairment may include indications that a debtor or a group of debtors are experiencing significant financial difficulty, default, or delinquency in interest or principal payments, and observable data indicating that there is a measurable decrease in the estimated future cash flows.

A financial asset is deemed to be impaired if there is objective evidence that one or more loss events having a negative effect on future cash flows of the financial asset occur after initial recognition and the loss can be reliably measured. The impairment loss is measured as the difference between the carrying amount of the financial asset and the present value of the estimated future cash flows, discounted at the original effective interest rate. The impairment loss is recorded as an allowance and recognized in net earnings. If the impairment loss decreases as a result of subsequent events, the previously recognized impairment loss is reversed.

Assets Held for Sale

Non-current assets are classified as assets held for sale if their carrying amounts will be recovered principally through a sale transaction rather than through continuing use. To qualify as assets held for sale, the sale must be highly probable, assets must be available for immediate sale in their present condition, and management must be committed to a plan to sell assets that should be expected to close within one year from the date of classification. Assets held for sale are recognized at the lower of their carrying amount and fair value less costs to sell and are not depreciated.

Provisions

A provision is a liability of uncertain timing or amount. Provisions are recognized when the Company has a present legal or constructive obligation as a result of past events for which it is probable that the Company will be required to settle the obligation and a reliable estimate of the settlement can be made. The amount recognized as a provision is the best estimate of the consideration required to settle the present obligation at the end of the reporting period, taking into account risks and uncertainties of cash flows. Where the effect of discounting to present value is material, provisions are adjusted to reflect the time value of money. Examples of provisions include decommissioning liabilities, onerous leases, and legal claims.

Borrowing Costs

Borrowing costs are primarily composed of interest on the Company's long-term debt, if any. Borrowing costs are capitalized using the effective interest rate method to the extent that they are directly attributable to the acquisition, production, or construction of qualifying assets that require a substantial period of time to get ready for their intended use or sale. All other borrowing costs are expensed as incurred and reported in the consolidated statements of earnings (loss) and comprehensive earnings (loss) as part of net interest.

Total Equity

Share capital represents the nominal value of shares that have been issued. Retained earnings include all current and prior period retained profits. Dividend distributions payable to equity shareholders are recorded as dividends payable when the dividends have been approved by the Board of Directors prior to the reporting date.

Share-based Awards

The Company has established an employee stock option plan for key employees. The fair value of each tranche of options granted is estimated on the grant date using the Black-Scholes option pricing model. The Black-Scholes option pricing model is based on variables such as: risk-free interest rate; expected volatility; expected time until exercise; and expected dividend yield. Expected stock price volatility is based on the historical volatility of the Company's stock for a period approximating the expected life. The grant date fair value, net of estimated forfeitures, is recognized as an expense with a corresponding increase to contributed surplus over the vesting period. Estimates are subsequently revised if there is an indication that the number of stock options expected to vest differs from previous estimates. Any consideration paid by employees on exercise of stock options is credited to share capital with a corresponding reduction to contributed surplus.

Revenue Recognition

The Company recognizes revenue when the substantial risks and rewards of ownership pass to the customer. Revenue is measured at the fair value of the consideration received or receivable by the Company for goods supplied, inclusive of amounts invoiced for shipping and net of sales discounts, returns, and amounts deferred related to the issuance of Plum points. Return allowances are estimated using historical experience.

Revenue is recognized when the amount can be measured reliably, it is probable that economic benefits associated with the transaction will flow to the Company, the costs incurred or to be incurred can be measured reliably, and the criteria for each of the Company's activities (as described below) have been met.

Retail sales

Revenue for retail customers is recognized at the time of purchase.

Online and kiosk sales

Revenue for online and kiosk customers is recognized when the product is shipped.

Commission revenue

The Company earns commission revenue through partnerships with other companies and recognizes revenue once services have been rendered and the amount of revenue can be measured reliably.

Gift cards

The Company sells gift cards to its customers and recognizes the revenue as gift cards are redeemed. The Company also recognizes gift card breakage if the likelihood of gift card redemption by the customer is considered to be remote. The Company determines its average gift card breakage rate based on historical redemption rates. Once the breakage rate is determined, the resulting revenue is recognized over the estimated period of redemption based on historical redemption patterns, commencing when the gift cards are sold. Gift card breakage is included in revenue in the Company's consolidated statements of earnings (loss) and comprehensive earnings (loss).

Indigo irewards loyalty program

For an annual fee, the Company offers loyalty cards to customers that entitle the cardholder to receive discounts on purchases. Each card is issued with a 12-month expiry period. The fee revenue related to the issuance of a card is deferred and amortized into revenue over the expiry period based upon historical sales volumes.

Indigo plum rewards program

Plum is a free program that allows members to earn points on their purchases in the Company's stores and on *indigo.ca*. Members can then redeem points for discounts on future purchases of merchandise in stores and online.

When a plum member purchases merchandise, the Company allocates the payment received between the merchandise and the points. The payment is allocated based on the residual method, where the amount allocated to the merchandise is the total payment less the fair value of the points. The portion of revenue attributed to the merchandise is recognized at the time of purchase. Revenue attributed to the points is recorded as deferred revenue and recognized when points are redeemed.

The fair value of points is calculated by multiplying the number of points issued by the estimated cost per point. The estimated cost per point is determined based on a number of factors, including the expected future redemption patterns and associated costs. On an ongoing basis, the Company monitors trends in redemption patterns (redemption at each reward level), historical redemption rates (points redeemed as a percentage of points issued) and net cost per point redeemed, adjusting the estimated cost per point based upon expected future activity. Points revenue is included as part of total revenue in the Company's consolidated statements of earnings (loss) and comprehensive earnings (loss).

Interest income

Interest income is reported on an accrual basis using the effective interest method and included as part of net interest in the Company's consolidated statements of earnings (loss) and comprehensive earnings (loss).

Vendor Rebates

The Company records cash consideration received from vendors as a reduction to the price of vendors' products. This is reflected as a reduction in cost of goods sold and related inventories when recognized in the consolidated financial statements. Certain exceptions apply where the cash consideration received is a reimbursement of incremental selling costs incurred by the Company, in which case the cash received is reflected as a reduction in operating, selling, and administrative expenses.

Earnings per Share

Basic earnings per share is determined by dividing the net earnings attributable to common shareholders by the weighted average number of common shares outstanding during the period. Diluted earnings per share is calculated in accordance with the treasury stock method and is based on the weighted average number of common shares and dilutive common share equivalents outstanding during the period. The weighted average number of shares used in the computation of both basic and fully diluted earnings per share may be the same due to the anti-dilutive effect of securities.

Financial Instruments

Financial assets and financial liabilities are recognized when the Company becomes a party to the contractual provisions of the financial instrument. Financial assets are derecognized when the contractual rights to the cash flows from the financial asset expire, or when the financial asset and all substantial risks and rewards are transferred. A financial liability is derecognized when it is extinguished, discharged, cancelled, or expires. Where a legally enforceable right to offset exists for recognized financial assets and financial liabilities and there is an intention to settle the liability and realize the asset simultaneously, or to settle on a net basis, such related financial assets and financial liabilities are offset.

For the purposes of ongoing measurement, financial assets and liabilities are classified according to their characteristics and management's intent. All financial instruments are initially recognized at fair value.

After initial recognition, financial instruments are subsequently measured as follows:

Financial assets

(i)   Loans and receivables — These are non-derivative financial assets with fixed or determinable payments that are not quoted in an active market. These assets are measured at amortized cost, less impairment charges, using the effective interest method. Gains and losses are recognized in earnings through the amortization process or when the assets are derecognized.

(ii) Financial assets at fair value through profit or loss — These assets are held for trading if acquired for the purpose of selling in the near term or are designated to this category upon initial recognition. These assets are measured at fair value, with gains or losses recognized in earnings. Derivatives are classified as fair value through profit or loss unless they are designated as effective hedging instruments.

(iii) Held-to-maturity investments — These are non-derivative financial assets with fixed or determinable payments and fixed maturities that the Company intends, and is able, to hold until maturity. These assets are measured at amortized cost, less impairment charges, using the effective interest method. Gains and losses are recognized in earnings through the amortization process or when the assets are derecognized.

(iv) Available-for-sale financial assets — These are non-derivative financial assets that are either designated to this category upon initial recognition or do not qualify for inclusion in any of the other categories. These assets are measured at fair value, with unrealized gains and losses recognized in other comprehensive income until the asset is derecognized or determined to be impaired. If the asset is derecognized or determined to be impaired, the cumulative gain or loss previously reported in accumulated other comprehensive income is included in earnings.

Financial liabilities

(i) Other liabilities – These liabilities are measured at amortized cost using the effective interest rate method. Gains and losses are recognized in earnings through the amortization process or when the liabilities are derecognized.

(ii) Financial liabilities at fair value through profit or loss – These liabilities are held for trading if acquired for the purpose of selling in the near term or are designated to this category upon initial recognition. These liabilities are measured at fair value, with gains or losses recognized in earnings.

The Company's financial assets and financial liabilities are generally classified and measured as follows:

Financial Asset/Liability	Category	Measurement
Cash and cash equivalents	Loans and receivables	Amortized cost
Short-term investments	Held-to-maturity	Amortized cost
Accounts receivable	Loans and receivables	Amortized cost
Accounts payable and accrued liabilities	Other liabilities	Amortized cost
Derivative instruments	Fair value through profit or loss	Fair value

All other consolidated balance sheet accounts are not considered financial instruments.

All financial instruments measured at fair value after initial recognition are categorized into one of three hierarchy levels for measurement and disclosure purposes. Each level reflects the significance of the inputs used in making the fair value measurements.

Level 1: Fair value is determined by reference to unadjusted quoted prices in active markets.

Level 2: Valuations use inputs based on observable market data, either directly or indirectly, other than the quoted prices.

Level 3: Valuations are based on inputs that are not based on observable market data.

The following methods and assumptions were used to estimate the fair value of each type of financial instrument by reference to market data and other valuation techniques, as appropriate:

(i) The initial fair values of cash and cash equivalents, short-term investments, accounts receivable, and accounts payable and accrued liabilities approximate their carrying values given their short maturities;

(ii) The initial fair value of long-term debt, if any, is estimated based on the discounted cash payments of the debt at the Company's estimated incremental borrowing rates for debt of the same remaining maturities. The fair value of long-term debt approximates its carrying value. These instruments are subsequently measured at amortized cost; and

(iii) The fair value of derivative financial instruments are estimated using quoted market rates at the measurement date adjusted for the maturity term of each instrument. Derivative financial instruments are classified as level 2 in the fair value hierarchy.

Derivative financial instruments and hedge accounting

The Company enters into various derivative financial instruments as part of its strategy to manage foreign currency exposure. All contracts entered into during the year have been designated as cash flow hedges for accounting purposes. The Company does not hold or issue derivative financial instruments for trading purposes. All derivative financial instruments, including derivatives embedded in financial or non-financial contracts not closely related to the host contracts, are measured at fair value. The gain or loss that results from remeasurement at each reporting period is recognized in net income immediately unless the derivative is designated and effective as a hedging instrument, in which case the timing of the recognition in net income depends on the nature of the hedge relationship.

At the inception of a hedge relationship, the Company documents the relationship between the hedging instrument and the hedged item along with the Company's risk management objectives and strategy for undertaking various hedge transactions. Furthermore, at inception and on an ongoing basis, the Company documents whether the hedging instrument is highly effective in offsetting changes in cash flows of the hedged item attributable to the hedged risk. Such hedges are expected to be highly effective in achieving offsetting changes in cash flows and are assessed on an ongoing basis to determine that they actually have been highly effective throughout the financial reporting periods for which they were designated.

Accordingly, the effective portion of the change in the fair value of the foreign exchange forward contracts that are designated and qualify as cash flow hedges is recognized in other comprehensive income (loss) until related payments have been made in future accounting periods. Associated gains and losses recognized in other comprehensive income (loss) are reclassified to earnings in the periods when the hedged item is recognized in earnings. These earnings are included within the same line of the consolidated statement of earnings (loss) as the recognized item. However, when the hedged forecast transaction results in the recognition of a non-financial asset, the gains and losses previously recognized in other comprehensive income (loss) are transferred from equity and included in the initial measurement of the cost of the non-financial asset. The gain or loss relating to the ineffective portion is recognized immediately in the consolidated statements of earnings (loss).

Retirement Benefits

The Company provides retirement benefits through a defined contribution retirement plan. Under the defined contribution retirement plan, the Company pays fixed contributions to an independent entity. The Company has no legal or constructive obligations to pay further contributions after its payment of the fixed contribution. The costs of benefits under the defined contribution retirement plan are expensed as contributions are due and are reversed if employees leave before the vesting period.

Foreign Currency Translation

The consolidated financial statements are presented in Canadian dollars, which is the functional currency of the Company. Sales transacted in foreign currencies are aggregated monthly and translated using the average exchange rate. Transactions in foreign currencies are translated at rates of exchange at the time of the transaction. Monetary assets and liabilities denominated in foreign currencies that are held at the reporting date are translated at the closing consolidated balance sheet rate. Non-monetary items are measured at historical cost and are translated using the exchange rates at the date of the transaction. Non-monetary items measured at fair value are translated using exchange rates at the date when fair value was determined. The resulting exchange gains or losses are included in earnings.

Accounting Standards Implemented in Fiscal 2017

Presentation of Financial Statements ("IAS 1")

In December 2014, the IASB issued amendments to IAS 1 as part of the IASB's Disclosure Initiative. These amendments encourage entities to apply professional judgment regarding disclosure and presentation in their financial statements and are effective for annual periods beginning on or after January 1, 2016. Implementation of these amendments in 2017 did not have a significant impact on the Company's financial statements and annual disclosures.

5. NEW ACCOUNTING PRONOUNCEMENTS

Statement of Cash Flows ("IAS 7")

In January 2016, the IASB issued amendments to IAS 7 as part of the IASB's Disclosure Initiative. These amendments require entities to provide additional disclosures that will enable financial statement users to evaluate changes in liabilities arising from financing activities, including changes arising from cash flows and non-cash changes. These amendments are effective for annual periods beginning on or after January 1, 2017 with early application permitted. Adopting these amendments will not have a significant impact on the Company's results of operations, financial position, or disclosures. The Company applied this standard beginning April 2, 2017.

Revenue from Contracts with Customers ("IFRS 15")

In May 2014, the IASB issued IFRS 15, a new standard that specifies how and when to recognize revenue as well as requiring entities to provide users of financial statements with more informative, relevant disclosures. IFRS 15 supersedes IAS 18, "Revenue," IAS 11, "Construction Contracts," and a number of revenue related interpretations. Application of IFRS 15 is mandatory for all IFRS reporters and it applies to nearly all contracts with customers: the main exceptions are leases, financial instruments, and insurance contracts.

IFRS 15 must be applied retrospectively using either the retrospective or cumulative effect method for annual reporting periods beginning on or after January 1, 2018. The Company plans to apply this standard beginning April 1, 2018 but has not yet determined which transition method it will apply.

Implementation of IFRS 15 is expected to impact the allocation of deferred plum program revenue. Revenue is currently allocated to plum points using the residual fair value method. Under IFRS 15, revenue will be allocated based on relative stand-alone selling prices between plum points and the goods on which points were earned. The Company is currently assessing the impact of this change and other impacts of adopting this standard on its results of operations, financial position, and disclosures.

Financial Instruments ("IFRS 9")

In July 2014, the IASB issued the final version of IFRS 9, which reflects all phases of the financial instruments project and replaces IAS 39, "Financial Instruments: Recognition and Measurement," and all previous versions of IFRS 9. The standard introduces new requirements for classification and measurement, impairment, and hedge accounting. IFRS 9 is effective for annual periods beginning on or after January 1, 2018. The Company plans to apply this standard beginning on April 1, 2018.

IFRS 9 more closely aligns hedge accounting with risk management activities and applies a more qualitative and forward-looking approach to assessing hedge effectiveness. The Company is currently assessing the impact of this change and other impacts of adopting this standard on its results of operations, financial position, and disclosures.

Leases ("IFRS 16")

In January 2016, the IASB issued IFRS 16, which supersedes existing standards and interpretations under IAS 17, "Leases." IFRS 16 introduces a single lessee accounting model, eliminating the distinction between operating and finance leases. The new lessee accounting model requires substantially all leases to be reported on a company's balance sheet and will provide greater transparency on companies' leased assets and liabilities. IFRS 16 substantially carries forward the lessor accounting in IAS 17 with the distinction between operating leases and finance leases being retained. The Company is assessing the impact of adopting this standard on its results of operations, financial position, and disclosures.

The new standard will apply for annual periods beginning on or after January 1, 2019. The Company plans to apply this standard beginning March 31, 2019. For leases where the Company is the lessee, it has the option of adopting a full retrospective approach or a modified retrospective approach on transition to IFRS 16. The Company has not yet determined which transition method it will apply or whether it will use the optional exemptions or practical expedients available under the standard.

6. CASH, CASH EQUIVALENTS, AND SHORT-TERM INVESTMENTS

Cash and cash equivalents consist of the following:

(thousands of Canadian dollars)	April 1, 2017	April 2, 2016
Cash	63,872	102,862
Restricted cash	1,343	3,460
Cash equivalents	65,223	110,166
Cash and cash equivalents	130,438	216,488

Restricted cash represents cash pledged as collateral for letter of credit obligations issued to support the Company's purchases of offshore merchandise.

As at April 1, 2017, the Company held $100.0 million of short-term investments (April 2, 2016 – no such investments). Short-term investments consist of guaranteed investment securities with an original maturity date greater than 90 days and remaining term to maturity of less than 365 days from the date of acquisition. These investments are non-redeemable until the maturity date, and therefore they are classified separately from cash and cash equivalents.

7. INVENTORIES

The cost of inventories recognized as an expense was $571.9 million in fiscal 2017 (2016 – $561.5 million). Inventories consist of the landed cost of goods sold and exclude online shipping costs, inventory shrink and damage reserve, and all vendor support programs. The amount of inventory write-downs as a result of net realizable value lower than cost was $9.0 million in fiscal 2017 (2016 – $10.1 million), and there were no reversals of inventory write-downs that were recognized in fiscal 2017 (2016 – nil). The amount of inventory with net realizable value equal to cost was $2.8 million as at April 1, 2017 (April 2, 2016 – $1.5 million).

8. DERIVATIVE FINANCIAL INSTRUMENTS

The Company's derivative financial instruments consist of foreign exchange forward contracts. These contracts were entered into in order to manage the currency fluctuation risk associated with forecasted U.S. dollar payments, primarily for general merchandise inventory purchases, and have been designated as cash flow hedges for accounting purposes. The fair value of a foreign exchange forward contract is estimated by discounting the difference between the contractual forward price and the current forward price for the residual maturity of the contract using a risk-free interest rate.

During the fiscal year ended April 1, 2017, the Company entered into forward contracts with total notional amounts of C$173.4 million to buy U.S. dollars and sell Canadian dollars. As at April 1, 2017, the Company had remaining forward contracts in place representing a total notional amount of C$70.3 million (April 2, 2016 – no forward contracts). These contracts extend over a period not exceeding 12 months.

The total fair value of the forward contracts as at April 1, 2017 resulted in an unrealized net gain of $0.3 million (April 2, 2016 – no forward contracts) recognized as other comprehensive income. The carrying value of the derivative financial instruments is equivalent to the pre-tax unrealized gain at period end.

During the fiscal year ended April 1, 2017, net gains of $1.2 million from settled contracts (April 2, 2016 – nil) were reclassified from other comprehensive income to inventory and expenses. Reclassified amounts resulting from hedge ineffectiveness were immaterial for the period ended April 1, 2017 (April 2, 2016 – nil).

9. PROPERTY, PLANT, AND EQUIPMENT

(thousands of Canadian dollars)	Furniture, fixtures, and equipment	Computer equipment	Leasehold improvements	Equipment under finance leases	Total
Gross carrying amount					
Balance, March 28, 2015	64,607	11,742	51,270	767	128,386
Additions	8,611	3,207	8,390	–	20,208
Transfers/reclassifications	1	(467)	501	–	35
Disposals	(2,127)	(102)	(372)	(166)	(2,767)
Assets with zero net book value	(2,952)	(2,253)	(5,818)	–	(11,023)
Balance, April 2, 2016	68,140	12,127	53,971	601	134,839
Additions	9,596	3,123	7,859	–	20,578
Transfers/reclassifications	–	(1,032)	997	–	(35)
Disposals	(28)	(17)	(1)	(465)	(511)
Assets with zero net book value	(4,950)	(2,038)	(6,931)	–	(13,919)
Transferred to assets held for sale	(914)	(2)	(501)	–	(1,417)
Balance, April 1, 2017	71,844	12,161	55,394	136	139,535
Accumulated depreciation and impairment					
Balance, March 28, 2015	33,335	5,638	33,990	537	73,500
Depreciation	6,134	2,347	6,092	166	14,739
Transfers/reclassifications	–	(5)	5	–	–
Disposals	(1,265)	(29)	(270)	(166)	(1,730)
Net impairment losses (reversals)	(459)	(5)	(1,156)	–	(1,620)
Assets with zero net book value	(2,952)	(2,253)	(5,818)	–	(11,023)
Balance, April 2, 2016	34,793	5,693	32,843	537	73,866
Depreciation	6,867	2,182	7,502	61	16,612
Transfers/reclassifications	–	–	–	–	–
Disposals	(22)	(3)	(1)	(465)	(491)
Net impairment losses (reversals)	(384)	(4)	(575)	–	(963)
Assets with zero net book value	(4,950)	(2,038)	(6,931)	–	(13,919)
Transferred to assets held for sale	(430)	(1)	(217)	–	(648)
Balance, April 1, 2017	35,874	5,829	32,621	133	74,457
Net carrying amount					
April 2, 2016	33,347	6,434	21,128	64	60,973
April 1, 2017	35,970	6,332	22,773	3	65,078

Property, plant and equipment are assessed for impairment at the CGU level, except for those assets which are considered to be corporate assets. As certain corporate assets cannot be allocated on a reasonable and consistent basis to individual CGUs, they are tested for impairment at the corporate level.

A CGU has been defined as an individual retail store as each store generates cash inflows that are largely independent from the cash inflows of other stores. CGUs and groups of CGUs are tested for impairment if impairment indicators exist at the reporting date. Recoverable amounts for CGUs being tested are based on value in use, which is calculated from discounted cash flow projections. For stores that are at risk of closure, cash flows are projected over the remaining lease terms, including any renewal options if renewal is likely. Cash flows for stores expected to operate beyond the current lease term and renewal options are projected using a terminal value calculation. Corporate asset testing calculates discounted cash flow projections over a five-year period plus a terminal value.

The key assumptions from the value-in-use calculations are those regarding growth rates and discount rates. Cash flow projections for the next three fiscal years are calculated separately for each CGU being tested and are based on management's best estimate of future income. Following these three fiscal years, projections are extrapolated using average long-term growth rates ranging from 0.0% to 3.0% (2016 – 0.0% to 3.0%). Management's estimate of the discount rate reflects the current market assessment of the time value of money and the risks specific to the Company. The pre-tax discount rate used to calculate value in use for store assets was 16.9% (2016 – 19.7%).

Impairment and reversal indicators were identified during fiscal 2017 for certain retail stores. Accordingly, the Company performed testing, which resulted in the reversal of impairment losses for certain Indigo retail stores. There were $1.0 million of property, plant, and equipment impairment reversals recognized in fiscal 2017 (2016 – $2.3 million). The Company did not recognize any impairments in fiscal 2017 (2016 – $0.6 million resulting from a store closure). Impairment reversals in both years arose due to improved store performance and were spread across a number of CGUs. The recoverable amount of the CGUs impacted by impairments or reversals was $7.4 million (2016 – $16.3 million) and was determined using each CGU's value in use. All impairments and reversals are recorded as part of operating, selling, and administrative expenses in the consolidated statements of earnings and comprehensive earnings.

10. INTANGIBLE ASSETS

(thousands of Canadian dollars)	Computer application software	Internal development costs	Domain name	Total
Gross carrying amount				
Balance, March 28, 2015	25,751	14,681	–	40,432
Additions	4,678	4,282	75	9,035
Transfers/reclassifications	(35)	–	–	(35)
Disposals	(16)	–	–	(16)
Assets with zero net book value	(12,561)	(5,543)	–	(18,104)
Balance, April 2, 2016	17,817	13,420	75	31,312
Additions	6,791	3,263	–	10,054
Transfers/reclassifications	35	–	–	35
Disposals	(2,023)	(814)	–	(2,837)
Assets with zero net book value	(5,733)	(4,023)	–	(9,756)
Balance, April 1, 2017	16,887	11,846	75	28,808
Accumulated amortization and impairment				
Balance, March 28, 2015	15,940	7,905	–	23,845
Amortization	5,149	3,924	–	9,073
Disposals	(8)	–	–	(8)
Assets with zero net book value	(12,561)	(5,543)	–	(18,104)
Balance, April 2, 2016	8,520	6,286	–	14,806
Amortization	4,568	4,005	–	8,573
Disposals	(1)	(86)	–	(87)
Assets with zero net book value	(5,733)	(4,023)	–	(9,756)
Balance, April 1, 2017	7,354	6,182	–	13,536
Net carrying amount				
April 2, 2016	9,297	7,134	75	16,506
April 1, 2017	9,533	5,664	75	15,272

The useful life of the domain name has been deemed to be indefinite because there are no legal, regulatory, contractual, competitive, economic, or other factors that limit the useful life of this asset to the Company.

Impairment testing for intangible assets is performed using the same methodology, CGUs, and groups of CGUs as those used for property, plant and equipment. The key assumptions from the value-in-use calculations for intangible asset impairment testing are also identical to the key assumptions used for property, plant and equipment testing. Impairment and reversal indicators were identified during fiscal 2017 for Indigo's retail stores. Accordingly, the Company performed impairment and reversal testing but there were no intangible asset impairment losses or reversals for retail stores in fiscal 2017 (2016 – no impairment losses or reversals). All impairments and reversals are recorded as part of operating, selling, and administrative expenses in the consolidated statements of earnings and comprehensive earnings.

The Company also identified specific projects that did not achieve expected results during the year and reviewed assets capitalized as part of these projects to determine whether they continued to meet the criteria for capitalization. As a result, the Company recorded $2.8 million of intangible asset disposals for derecognized project assets in fiscal 2017.

11. ASSETS HELD FOR SALE

On February 17, 2017, the Company formalized a Letter of Intent with Starbucks Coffee Canada Inc. ("Starbucks") whereby, among other things, the Company and Starbucks mutually agreed to terminate the Company's license to operate Starbucks-branded cafes within 11 retail locations.

Based on the terms of the Letter of Intent, the Company agreed to transfer to Starbucks the café inventories and capital assets from the terminated licensed locations, and the Company classified these inventories and capital assets as assets held for sale. Subsequent to the transfer, the Company will sublease space in each of the previously licensed locations for Starbucks to operate corporate-run cafes, similar to the 72 other Starbucks-branded cafes Starbucks operates in the Company's retail locations. The transfer and subsequent subleasing were completed on May 1, 2017.

12. INCOME TAXES

Deferred tax assets are recognized to the extent that it is probable that taxable profit will be available against which the deductible temporary differences and the carryforward of unused tax credits and unused tax losses can be utilized. As at April 1, 2017, the Company has recorded $44.0 million in gross value of deferred tax assets based on management's best estimate of future taxable income that the Company expected to achieve (April 2, 2016 – $51.8 million gross value of deferred tax assets).

Deferred income taxes reflect the net tax effects of temporary differences between the carrying amounts of assets and liabilities for financial reporting purposes and the amounts used for income tax purposes. Significant components of the Company's deferred tax assets are as follows:

(thousands of Canadian dollars)	April 1, 2017	April 2, 2016
Reserves and allowances	1,300	1,938
Tax loss carryforwards	22,243	23,597
Corporate minimum tax	2,871	2,511
Book amortization in excess of cumulative eligible capital deduction	214	217
Book amortization in excess of capital cost allowance	17,353	23,573
Total deferred tax assets	43,981	51,836

Significant components of income tax expense (recovery) are as follows:

(thousands of Canadian dollars)	52-week period ended April 1, 2017	53-week period ended April 2, 2016
Current income tax expense	360	–
Adjustment for prior periods	(25)	(50)
	335	(50)
Deferred income tax expense (recovery)		
Origination and reversal of temporary differences	6,119	6,586
Change in valuation allowance	–	(12,432)
Deferred income tax expense relating to utilization of loss carryforwards	1,649	–
Adjustment to deferred tax assets resulting from increase in substantively enacted tax rate	–	(451)
Change in tax rates due to change in expected pattern of reversal	38	(134)
Other, net	(22)	–
	7,784	(6,431)
Total income tax expense (recovery)	8,119	(6,481)

The reconciliation of income taxes computed at statutory income tax rates to the effective income tax rates is as follows:

(thousands of Canadian dollars)	52-week period ended April 1, 2017	%	53-week period ended April 2, 2016	%
Earnings before income taxes	29,037		22,100	
Tax at combined federal and provincial tax rates	7,771	26.8%	5,885	26.6%
Tax effect of expenses not deductible for income tax purposes	587	2.0%	793	3.6%
Decrease in valuation allowance	–	0.0%	(12,432)	(56.3%)
Adjustment to deferred tax assets resulting from increase in substantively enacted tax rate	–	0.0%	(451)	(2.0%)
Change in tax rates due to change in expected pattern of reversal	38	0.1%	(134)	(0.6%)
Other, net	(277)	(1.0%)	(142)	(0.6%)
	8,119	27.9%	(6,481)	(29.3%)

As at April 1, 2017, the Company has combined non-capital loss carryforwards of approximately $83.2 million for income tax purposes that expire in 2031 if not utilized.

13. PROVISIONS

Provisions consist primarily of amounts recorded in respect of decommissioning liabilities, onerous lease arrangements, and legal claims. Activity related to the Company's provisions is as follows:

(thousands of Canadian dollars)	52-week period ended April 1, 2017	53-week period ended April 2, 2016
Balance, beginning of period	143	1,023
Charged	85	33
Utilized / released	(67)	(913)
Balance, end of period	161	143

The Company is subject to payment of decommissioning liabilities upon exiting certain leases. The amount of these payments may fluctuate based on negotiations with the landlord. Onerous lease provisions unwind over the term of the related lease and were discounted using a pre-tax discount rate of 19.0%. Legal claim provisions fluctuate depending on the outcomes when claims are settled.

14. COMMITMENTS AND CONTINGENCIES

(a) Commitments

As at April 1, 2017, the Company had operating lease commitments in respect of its stores, support office premises, and certain equipment. The Company also had operating lease commitments related to the future relocation of its corporate home office. The leases expire at various dates between calendar 2017 and 2033, and may be subject to renewal options. Annual store rent consists of a base amount plus, in some cases, additional payments based on store sales. The Company also generates sublease income in respect of some of its premises leases. Over the next five fiscal years and thereafter, the Company expects to generate $5.5 million from these subleases.

The Company's minimum contractual obligations due over the next five fiscal years and thereafter are summarized below. Operating lease expenditures are presented net of their related subleases:

(millions of Canadian dollars)	Total
2018	57.7
2019	45.0
2020	28.8
2021	20.2
2022	14.7
Thereafter	60.2
Total obligations	226.6

(b) Legal Claims

In the normal course of business, the Company becomes involved in various claims and litigation. While the final outcome of such claims and litigation pending as at April 1, 2017 cannot be predicted with certainty, management believes that any such amount would not have a material impact on the Company's financial position or financial performance, except for those amounts that have been recorded as provisions on the Company's consolidated balance sheets.

15. SHARE CAPITAL

Share capital consists of the following:

Authorized

Unlimited Class A preference shares with no par value, voting, convertible into
  common shares on a one-for-one basis at the option of the shareholder

Unlimited common shares, voting

	52-week period ended April 1, 2017		53-week period ended April 2, 2016	
	Number of shares	Amount C$ (thousands)	Number of shares	Amount C$ (thousands)
Balance, beginning of period	25,797,351	209,318	25,495,289	205,871
Issued during the period				
Directors' deferred share units converted	67,108	670	29,142	291
Options exercised	487,025	5,983	272,920	3,156
Balance, end of period	26,351,484	215,971	25,797,351	209,318

16. SHARE-BASED COMPENSATION

The Company has established an employee stock option plan (the "Plan") for key employees. The number of common shares reserved for issuance under the Plan as at April 1, 2017 is 3,452,723. Most options granted between May 21, 2002 and March 31, 2012 have a ten-year term and have one fifth of the options granted exercisable one year after the date of issue with the remainder exercisable in equal instalments on the anniversary date over the next four years. Subsequently, most options granted after April 1, 2012 have a five-year term and have one third of the options granted exercisable one year after the date of issue with the remainder exercisable in equal instalments on the anniversary date over the next two years. A small number of options have special vesting schedules that were approved by the Board. Each option is exercisable into one common share of the Company at the price specified in the terms of the option agreement.

The Company uses the fair value method of accounting for stock options, which estimates the fair value of the stock options granted on the date of grant, net of estimated forfeitures, and expenses this value over the vesting period. During fiscal 2017, the pre-forfeiture fair value of options granted was $2.8 million (2016 – $1.4 million). The weighted average fair value of options issued in fiscal 2017 was $4.19 per option (2016 – $2.35 per option).

The fair value of the employee stock options is estimated at the date of grant using the Black-Scholes option pricing model with the following weighted average assumptions during the periods presented:

	52-week period ended April 1, 2017	53-week period ended April 2, 2016
Black-Scholes option pricing assumptions		
Risk-free interest rate	0.6%	0.5%
Expected volatility	33.8%	32.7%
Expected time until exercise	3.0 years	3.0 years
Expected dividend yield	–	–
Other assumptions		
Forfeiture rate	27.3%	28.4%

A summary of the status of the Plan and changes during both periods is presented below:

	52-week period ended April 1, 2017		53-week period ended April 2, 2016	
	Number #	Weighted average exercise price C$	Number #	Weighted average exercise price C$
Outstanding options, beginning of period	1,751,800	10.07	1,561,150	9.94
Granted	657,000	17.94	597,500	10.34
Forfeited	(257,850)	13.50	(133,930)	10.36
Exercised	(487,025)	10.20	(272,920)	9.79
Outstanding options, end of period	1,663,925	12.60	1,751,800	10.07
Options exercisable, end of period	734,900	9.68	651,550	9.59

A summary of options outstanding and exercisable is presented below:

	April 1, 2017				
	Outstanding			Exercisable	
Range of exercise prices C$	Number #	Weighted average exercise price C$	Weighted average remaining contractual life (in years)	Number #	Weighted average exercise price C$
8.00 – 9.41	322,500	8.30	1.3	322,500	8.30
9.42 – 10.28	306,050	10.09	3.4	75,050	10.09
10.29 – 10.77	343,375	10.56	1.9	258,400	10.59
10.78 – 17.38	172,000	12.92	3.2	78,950	11.91
17.39 – 18.00	520,000	18.00	4.4	–	–
8.00 – 18.00	1,663,925	12.60	3.0	734,900	9.68

Directors' Compensation

The Company has established a Directors' Deferred Share Unit Plan ("DSU Plan"). Under the DSU Plan, Directors annually elect whether to receive their annual retainer fees and other Board-related compensation in the form of deferred share units ("DSUs") or receive up to 50% of this compensation in cash. All fiscal 2017 Directors' compensation was in the form of DSUs (2016 – all DSUs).

The number of shares reserved for issuance under this plan is 500,000. The Company issued 21,788 DSUs with a value of $0.4 million during fiscal 2017 (2016 – 32,175 DSUs with a value of $0.4 million). The number of DSUs to be issued to each Director is based on a set fee schedule. The grant date fair value of the outstanding DSUs as at April 1, 2017 was $3.5 million (April 2, 2016 – $3.8 million) and was recorded in contributed surplus. The fair value of DSUs is equal to the traded price of the Company's common shares on the grant date.

17. SUPPLEMENTARY OPERATING INFORMATION

Supplemental product line revenue information:

(thousands of Canadian dollars)	52-week period ended April 1, 2017	53-week period ended April 2, 2016
Print [1]	598,107	615,410
General merchandise [2]	384,097	343,488
eReading [3]	12,510	14,452
Other [4]	25,131	20,831
Total	1,019,845	994,181

1 Includes books, magazines, newspapers, and shipping revenue.
2 Includes lifestyle, paper, toys, calendars, music, DVDs, electronics, and shipping revenue.
3 Includes eReaders, eReader accessories, Kobo revenue share, and shipping revenue.
4 Includes cafés, irewards, gift card breakage, plum breakage, and corporate sales.

Supplemental operating and administrative expenses information:

(thousands of Canadian dollars)	52-week period ended April 1, 2017	53-week period ended April 2, 2016
Wages, salaries, and bonuses	180,893	178,147
Short-term benefits expense	19,444	19,897
Termination benefits expense	2,922	6,559
Retirement benefits expense	1,575	1,418
Share-based compensation	1,400	1,212
Total employee benefits expense	206,234	207,233

Termination benefits arise when the Company terminates certain employment agreements.

Minimum lease payments recognized as an expense during fiscal 2017 were $60.4 million (2016 – $55.9 million). Contingent rents recognized as an expense during fiscal 2017 were $1.6 million (2016 – $1.6 million).

18. EARNINGS PER SHARE

Earnings per share is calculated based on the weighted average number of common shares outstanding during the period. In calculating diluted earnings per share amounts under the treasury stock method, the numerator remains unchanged from the basic earnings per share calculations as the assumed exercise of the Company's stock options and DSUs do not result in adjustment to net earnings. The reconciliation of the denominator in calculating diluted earnings per share amounts for the periods presented is as follows:

(thousands of shares)	52-week period ended April 1, 2017	53-week period ended April 2, 2016
Weighted average number of common shares outstanding, basic	26,385	25,949
Effect of dilutive securities – stock options	566	212
Weighted average number of common shares outstanding, diluted	26,951	26,161

As at April 1, 2017, 552,000 (April 2, 2016 – 672,500) anti-dilutive stock options were excluded from the computation of diluted net earnings per common share.

19. STATEMENTS OF CASH FLOWS

Supplemental cash flow information:

(thousands of Canadian dollars)	52-week period ended April 1, 2017	53-week period ended April 2, 2016
Accounts receivable	215	(2,767)
Inventories	(13,788)	(9,393)
Income taxes recoverable	(26)	(50)
Prepaid expenses	(416)	(5,813)
Accounts payable and accrued liabilities (current and long-term)	(2,606)	11,109
Unredeemed gift card liability	(573)	2,758
Provisions (current and long-term)	18	(880)
Income taxes payable	360	
Deferred revenue	(380)	(66)
Net change in non-cash working capital balances	(17,196)	(5,102)

20. CAPITAL MANAGEMENT

The Company's main objectives when managing capital are:

• Ensuring sufficient liquidity to support financial obligations and to execute operating and strategic objectives;

• Maintaining financial capacity and flexibility through access to capital to support future development of the business;

• Minimizing the cost of capital while taking into consideration current and future industry, market, and economic risks and conditions.

There were no changes to these objectives during the year. The primary activities engaged by the Company to generate attractive returns for shareholders include transforming physical and digital platforms and driving productivity improvement through investments in information technology and distribution to support the Company's sales networks. The Company's main sources of capital are its current cash position, short-term investments, and cash flows generated from operations. Cash flow is primarily used to fund working capital needs and capital expenditures. The Company manages its capital structure in accordance with changes in economic conditions.

21. FINANCIAL RISK MANAGEMENT

The Company's activities expose it to a variety of financial risks, including risks related to foreign exchange, interest rate, credit, and liquidity.

Foreign Exchange Risk

The Company's foreign exchange risk is largely limited to currency fluctuations between the Canadian and U.S. dollars. Decreases in the value of the Canadian dollar relative to the U.S. dollar could negatively impact net earnings since the purchase price of some of the Company's products are negotiated with vendors in U.S. dollars, while the retail price to customers is set in Canadian dollars. In particular, a significant amount of the Company's general merchandise inventory purchases is denominated in U.S. dollars. The Company also has a New York office that incurs U.S. dollar expenses.

The Company uses derivative instruments in the form of forward contracts to manage its exposure to fluctuations in U.S. dollar exchange rates. As the Company has hedged a significant portion of the cost of its near-term forecasted U.S. dollar purchases, a change in foreign currency rates will not impact that portion of the cost of those purchases.

In fiscal 2017, the effect of foreign currency translation on net earnings was a gain of $0.2 million (2016 – gain of $0.6 million).

Interest Rate Risk

The Company's interest income is sensitive to fluctuations in Canadian interest rates, which affect the interest earned on the Company's cash, cash equivalents, and short-term investments. The Company has minimal interest rate risk and does not use any interest rate swaps to manage its risk. The Company does not currently have any debt.

Credit Risk

The Company is exposed to credit risk resulting from the possibility that counterparties may default on their financial obligations to the Company. Credit risk primarily arises from accounts receivable, cash and cash equivalents, short-term investments, and derivative financial instruments. Fair values of financial instruments reflect the credit risk of the Company and counterparties when appropriate.

Accounts receivable primarily consist of receivables from retail customers who pay by credit card, recoveries of credits from suppliers for returned or damaged products, and receivables from other companies for sales of products, gift cards, and other services. Credit card payments have minimal credit risk and the limited number of corporate receivables are closely monitored.

The Company limits its exposure to counterparty credit risk related to cash and cash equivalents, short-term investments, and derivative financial instruments by transacting only with highly-rated financial institutions and other counterparties, and by managing within specific limits for credit exposure and term to maturity. The Company's maximum credit risk exposure if all counterparties default concurrently is equivalent to the carrying amounts of accounts receivable, cash and cash equivalents, short-term investments, and derivative financial instruments.

Liquidity Risk

Liquidity risk is the risk that the Company will be unable to meet its obligations relating to its financial liabilities. The Company manages liquidity risk by preparing and monitoring cash flow budgets and forecasts to ensure that the Company has sufficient funds to meet its financial obligations and fund new business opportunities or other unanticipated requirements as they arise.

The contractual maturities of the Company's current and long-term liabilities as at April 1, 2017 are as follows:

(thousands of Canadian dollars)	Payments due in the next 90 days	Payments due between 90 days and less than a year	Payments due after 1 year	Total
Accounts payable and accrued liabilities	141,622	28,989	–	170,611
Unredeemed gift card liability	50,396	–	–	50,396
Provisions	7	103	–	110
Long-term accrued liabilities	–	–	2,378	2,378
Long-term provisions	–	–	51	51
Total	192,025	29,092	2,429	223,546

22. EQUITY INVESTMENT

The Company holds a 50% equity ownership in its associate, Calendar Club, to sell calendars, games, and gifts through seasonal kiosks and year-round stores in Canada. The Company uses the equity method of accounting to record Calendar Club results. In fiscal 2017, the Company received $1.2 million (2016 – $0.7 million) of distributions from Calendar Club.

The following tables represent financial information for Calendar Club along with the Company's share therein:

	Total		Company's share	
(thousands of Canadian dollars)	April 1, 2017	April 2, 2016	April 1, 2017	April 2, 2016
Cash and cash equivalents	2,576	3,969	1,288	1,985
Total current assets	5,833	9,713	2,917	4,857
Total long-term assets	363	483	181	242
Total current liabilities	2,596	7,353	1,298	3,677

	Total		Company's share	
(thousands of Canadian dollars)	52-week period ended April 1, 2017	53-week period ended April 2, 2016	52-week period ended April 1, 2017	53-week period ended April 2, 2016
Revenue	38,858	36,200	19,429	18,100
Expenses	(35,438)	(33,166)	(17,719)	(16,583)
Depreciation	(187)	(239)	(93)	(120)
Net earnings	3,233	2,795	1,617	1,397

Changes in the carrying amount of the investment were as follows:

(thousands of Canadian dollars)	Carrying value
Balance, March 28, 2015	726
Equity income from Calendar Club	1,397
Distributions from Calendar Club	(702)
Balance, April 2, 2016	1,421
Equity income from Calendar Club	1,617
Distributions from Calendar Club	(1,238)
Balance, April 1, 2017	1,800

23. RELATED PARTY TRANSACTIONS

The Company's related parties include its key management personnel, shareholders, defined contribution retirement plan, equity investment in Calendar Club, and subsidiary. Unless otherwise stated, none of the transactions incorporate special terms and conditions and no guarantees were given or received. Outstanding balances are usually settled in cash.

Transactions with Key Management Personnel

Key management of the Company includes members of the Board of Directors as well as members of the Executive Committee. Key management personnel remuneration includes the following expenses:

(thousands of Canadian dollars)	52-week period ended April 1, 2017	53-week period ended April 2, 2016
Wages, salaries, and bonus	7,733	7,529
Short-term benefits expense	233	230
Termination benefits expense	424	454
Retirement benefits expense	61	69
Share-based compensation	833	675
Directors' compensation	367	384
Total remuneration	9,651	9,341

Transactions with Shareholders

During fiscal 2017, the Company purchased goods and services from companies in which Mr. Gerald W. Schwartz, who is the controlling shareholder of Indigo, holds a controlling or significant interest. In fiscal 2017, the Company paid $6.0 million for these transactions (2016 – $4.5 million). As at April 1, 2017, Indigo had less than $0.1 million payable to these companies under standard payment terms and $1.0 million of restricted cash pledged as collateral for letter of credit obligations issued to support the Company's purchases of merchandise from these companies (April 2, 2016 – $0.1 million payable and $2.8 million restricted cash). All transactions were measured at fair market value and were in the normal course of business, under normal commercial terms, for both Indigo and the related companies.

Transactions with Defined Contribution Retirement Plan

The Company's transactions with the defined contribution retirement plan include contributions paid to the retirement plan as disclosed in note 17. The Company has not entered into other transactions with the retirement plan.

Transactions with Associate

The Company's associate, Calendar Club, is a seasonal operation that is dependent on the December holiday sales season to generate revenue. During the year, the Company loans cash to Calendar Club for working capital requirements and Calendar Club repays the loans once profits are generated in the third quarter. In fiscal 2017, Indigo loaned $11.6 million to Calendar Club (2016 – $11.1 million). All loans were repaid in full as at April 1, 2017.

Five-Year Summary of Financial Information

For the years ended (millions of Canadian dollars, except share and per share data)	April 1, 2017	April 2, 2016	March 28, 2015	March 29, 2014	March 30, 2013
SELECTED STATEMENTS OF EARNINGS (LOSS) AND COMPREHENSIVE EARNINGS (LOSS) INFORMATION					
Revenue					
Superstores	702.1	695.3	625.2	607.2	615.2
Small format stores	140.7	140.2	127.8	127.4	137.6
Online	148.2	133.3	114.0	102.0	91.9
Other	28.8	25.4	28.4	31.1	34.1
Total revenue	1,019.8	994.2	895.4	867.7	878.8
Adjusted EBITDA[1,2]	52.2	43.1	20.5	0.1	28.5
Earnings (loss) before income taxes	29.0	22.1	(3.2)	(26.9)	4.2
Net earnings (loss)	20.9	28.6	(3.5)	(31.0)	4.3
Dividends per share	–	–	–	$ 0.33	$ 0.44
Net earnings (loss) per common share	$ 0.79	$ 1.10	$(0.14)	$(1.21)	$ 0.17
SELECTED CONSOLIDATED BALANCE SHEET INFORMATION					
Working capital	248.1	217.9	198.7	189.7	224.3
Total assets	608.6	584.0	538.4	512.6	569.1
Long-term debt (including current portion)	–	0.1	0.2	0.8	1.5
Total equity	371.8	344.0	311.1	311.7	350.3
Weighted average number of shares outstanding	26,384,775	25,949,068	25,722,640	25,601,260	25,529,035
Common shares outstanding at end of period	26,351,484	25,797,351	25,495,289	25,298,239	25,297,389
STORE OPERATING STATISTICS					
Number of stores at end of period					
Superstores	89	88	91	95	97
Small format stores	123	123	127	131	134
Selling square footage at end of period (in thousands)					
Superstores	1,953	1,925	2,019	2,163	2,199
Small format stores	304	305	311	321	329
Comparable sales growth[2]					
Total retail and online	4.1%	12.9%	6.5%	(0.3%)	(3.7%)
Superstores	2.9%	12.8%	6.8%	(0.9%)	(4.6%)
Small format stores	0.9%	10.9%	0.8%	(5.0%)	(2.4%)
Sales per selling square foot					
Superstores	360	361	310	281	280
Small format stores	463	460	411	397	418

1 Earnings before interest, taxes, depreciation, amortization, impairment, asset disposals, and equity investment.
2 See "Non-IFRS Financial Measures" in the Company's Management Discussion and Analysis section of the Annual Report.

Appendix B

TYPICAL CHART OF ACCOUNTS FOR CORPORATIONS
Students: Add to this list as you see more account names so you have a record of what is commonly used.

ASSETS	LIABILITIES	SHAREHOLDERS' EQUITY	
Cash	Accounts Payable	Common Shares	**EXPENSES AND LOSSES**
Petty Cash	Notes Payable, Short-Term	Preferred Shares	Cost of Goods Sold
Short-Term Investments	Current Portion of Bonds	Contributed Surplus	Amortization Expense—
Fair-Value Valuation Allowance	Payable	Accumulated Other	(PPE Asset)
Accounts Receivable	Current Portion of	Comprehensive Loss	Bad Debt Expense
Allowance for Doubtful	Long-Term Debt	Retained Earnings	Bank Charge Expense
Accounts	Interest Payable	Dividends	Brokerage Commissions
Note Receivable, Short-Term	Salaries Payable		Expense
Goods and Services Tax	Wages Payable		Commission Expense
Recoverable	Goods and Services Tax		Delivery Expense
Harmonized Sales Tax	Payable		Employee Benefits
Recoverable	Harmonized Sales Tax		Expense
Interest Receivable	Payable		Income Tax Expense
Inventory	Interest Payable		Insurance Expense
Supplies	Income Tax Payable		Interest Expense
Prepaid Insurance	Other Accrued Liabilities		General Expenses
Prepaid Rent	Provisions		Miscellaneous Expense
Notes Receivable, Long-Term	Unearned Service Revenue		Payroll Benefits Expense
Deferred Tax	Notes Payable, Long-Term		Property Tax Expense
Investment Subject to	Bonds Payable		Rent Expense
Significant Influence	Discount on Bonds Payable	**REVENUES AND GAINS**	Salaries Expense
Long-Term Investments	Premium on Bonds	Sales Revenue	Sales Discounts
Other Receivables, Long-Term	Payable	Service Revenue	Sales Returns
(Various PPE Assets such as	Lease Liability	Dividend Revenue	Selling Expenses
Furniture, Buildings,	Non-controlling Interest	Interest Revenue	Supplies Expense
Equipment, etc.)		Equity-Method	Utilities Expense
Accumulated Amortization—		Investment Revenue	Vacation Pay Expense
(PPE Asset)		Foreign-Currency	Wages Expense
Land		Transaction Gain	Warranty Expense
Organization Cost		Gain on Disposal	Foreign-Currency
Franchises		Gain on Sale of	Transaction Loss
Patents		Investments	Loss on Discontinued
Goodwill		Gain on Sale of (Asset)	Operations
Other Assets		Gain on Sale of Equity	Loss on Disposal
		Investment	Loss on Sale of
		Profit on Discontinued	Investments
		Operations	Loss on Sale (or
		Unrealized Gain on	Exchange) of (Asset)
		Short-Term	Loss on Write-down of
		Investments	Goodwill
			Unrealized Loss on
			Short-Term
			Investments

PARTNERSHIP
Same as Proprietorship or Corporation, except for Owners' Equity:
PARTNERS' EQUITY
Partner 1, Capital
Partner 2, Capital
Partner N, Capital
Partner 1, Withdrawals
Partner 2, Withdrawals
Partner N, Withdrawals

Glossary

Accounts receivable turnover Ratio of net credit sales to average net accounts receivable. Measures ability to collect cash from credit customers (p. 1048).

Acid-test ratio Ratio of the sum of cash plus short-term investments plus net current receivables to current liabilities. Tells whether the entity could pay all its current liabilities if they came due immediately. Also called the *quick ratio* (p. 1046).

Actively traded Financial instruments that are easily bought or sold because there are a lot of them in the market and it is easy to find someone who is willing to engage in a transaction (p. 890).

Affiliated company An investment in a company in which there is significant influence and 20 to 50 percent ownership. These investments are accounted for using the equity method (p. 898).

Amortized cost method To account for long-term bond investments, the discount or premium is amortized to more accurately reflect the interest revenue. These bonds are reported at their amortized cost (p. 906).

Appropriations Restriction of retained earnings that is recorded by a formal journal entry (p. 782).

Arrears To be behind or overdue in a debt payment (p. 728).

Articles of incorporation The document issued by the federal or provincial government giving the incorporators permission to form a corporation (p. 714).

Asset revaluation Adjusting asset values to reflect current market values, usually based on an independent appraisal of the assets (p. 679).

Authorization of shares A provision in a corporation's articles of incorporation that permits a corporation to sell a certain number of shares of stock (p. 716).

Authorized shares The number of shares a corporation is allowed to sell according to the articles of incorporation (p. 720).

Basic EPS Earnings per share calculated using the number of outstanding common shares (p. 779).

Bearer bonds Bonds payable to the person that has possession of them. Also called *unregistered bonds* (p. 822).

Benchmarking Comparison of current performance with some standard. The standard often is the performance level of a leading outside organization or the industry average (p. 1041).

Bid price The highest price that a buyer is willing to pay for a bond (p. 823).

Blended payments Payments that are a constant amount, and the amount of interest and principal that are applied to the loan change with each payment (p. 842).

Board of directors A group elected by the shareholders to set policy for a corporation and to appoint its officers (p. 716).

Bond A formal agreement in which a lender loans money to a borrower who agrees to repay the money loaned at a future date and agrees to pay interest regularly over the life of the bond (p. 820).

Bond indenture The contract that specifies the maturity value of the bonds, the stated (contract) interest rate, and the dates for paying interest and principal (p. 820).

Bonds payable Groups of notes payable (bonds) issued to multiple lenders called *bondholders* (p. 820).

Book value The amount of shareholders' equity on the company's books for each of its shares (p. 730).

Book value per common share Common shareholders' equity divided by the number of common shares outstanding (p. 1054).

Bylaws The constitution for governing a corporation (p. 716).

Callable bonds Bonds that the issuer may call or pay off at a specified price whenever the issuer wants (p. 839).

Capital deficiency A partnership's claim against a Partner occurs when a partner's Capital account has a debit balance (p. 685).

Capitalized retained earnings Retained earnings that are not available for distribution. Stock dividends result in retained earnings being moved to contributed capital (p. 765).

Capital lease A lease agreement that substantially transfers all the benefits and risks of ownership from the lessor to the lessee (p. 845).

Carrying value The amount at which an asset is reported on the balance sheet (p. 892).

Cash equivalents Highly liquid short-term investments that can be converted into cash with little delay (p. 951).

Cash flows Cash receipts and cash payments (disbursements) (p. 949).

Cash flow statement Reports cash receipts and cash payments classified according to the entity's major activities: operating, investing, and financing (p. 949).

Certificate of deposit A secure form of investment with a fixed interest rate and term. Unlike a bank account, they must be held to maturity (p. 889).

Chairperson (of board) An elected person on a corporation's board of directors; usually the most powerful person in the corporation (p. 716).

Closely held Describes a corporation with only a few shareholders (p. 731).

Common shares The most basic form of share capital. In describing a corporation, the common shareholders are the owners of the business (p. 718).

Common-size statement A financial statement that reports only percentages (no dollar amounts); a type of vertical analysis (p. 1040).

Companion account An account that is typically paired up with another account (p. 892).

Consolidated financial statements Financial statements of the parent company plus those of majority-owned subsidiaries as if the combination were a single legal entity (p. 898).

Consolidation A decrease in the number of shares outstanding by a fixed ratio. Also called a *reverse split* (p. 768).

Contract interest rate The interest rate that determines the amount of cash interest the borrower pays and the investor receives each year. Also called the *stated interest rate* (p. 822).

Contributed capital A corporation's capital from investments by the shareholders. Also called *share capital* or *capital stock* (p. 717).

Controlling interest Ownership of more than 50 percent of an investee company's voting shares. Also called *majority interest* (p. 898).

Conversion privileges Shareholders with this right may exchange specified bonds or shares into a stated number of common shares (p. 779).

Convertible bond Bonds that may be converted into the common shares of the issuing company at the option of the investor (p. 840).

Convertible note Notes that may be converted into the common shares of the issuing company at the option of the investor (p. 840).

Convertible preferred shares Preferred shares that may be exchanged by the preferred shareholders, if they choose, for another class of shares in the corporation (p. 724).

Counterbalancing transaction Engaging in a second transaction to offset the risk of the first transaction (p. 914).

Coupon rate The contractual rate of interest that the issuer must pay the bondholders (p. 821).

Cumulative preferred shares Preferred shares whose owners must receive all dividends in arrears before the corporation pays dividends to the common shareholders (p. 728).

Currency options A contract that can be purchased to guarantee the right to a future exchange rate (p. 914).

Current ratio Current assets divided by current liabilities. Measures the ability to pay current liabilities from current assets (p. 1046).

Date of record On this date, which is a few weeks after the declaration of the dividend, the list of shareholders who will receive the dividend is compiled (p. 727).

Days' sales in inventory 365 divided by inventory turnover indicates how many days of sales remain in inventory waiting to be sold (p. 1048).

Days' sales in receivables Ratio of average net accounts receivable to one day's sales. Indicates how many days' sales remain in Accounts Receivable awaiting collection (p. 1049).

Debentures Unsecured bonds, backed only by the good faith of the issuer (p. 522).

Debt/equity ratio Ratio of total liabilities to total equity. Gives the proportion of debt financed by those outside the company (p. 1050).

Debt ratio Ratio of total liabilities to total assets. Gives the proportion of a company's assets that it has financed with debt (p. 1050).

Declaration date The date on which the board of directors announces the dividend. There is a liability created on this date (p. 727).

Deficit A debit balance in the Retained Earnings account (p. 719).

Direct method The format of the operating activities section of the cash flow statement that shows cash receipts from and cash payments for operating activities (p. 952).

Discount The amount of a bond's issue price under its maturity (par) value; also called *bond discount* (p. 823).

Dissolution Ending a partnership (p. 661).

Dividends Distributions of retained earnings by a corporation to its shareholders (p. 719).

Dividend yield Ratio of dividends per share to the share's market price per share. Tells the percentage of a share's market value that the company pays to shareholders as dividends (p. 1054).

Double taxation Corporations pay their own income taxes on corporate income. Then, the shareholders pay personal income tax on the cash dividends that they receive from corporations (p. 715).

Downside risk An estimate of the potential loss from a change in market conditions (p. 1054).

Earnings per share (EPS) The amount of a company's net income per outstanding common share (p. 1053).

Effective-interest amortization An amortization method in which a different amount of bond discount or premium is written off through interest expense each year (or period) of the bond's life. The amount of amortization expense is the same percentage of a bond's carrying value for every period over a bond's life (p. 832).

Effective interest rate The interest rate that investors demand in order to loan their money. Also called the *market interest rate* (p. 822).

Efficient capital market A market in which the market prices fully reflect the impact of all information available to the public (p. 1055).

Equity method for investments The method used to account for investments in which the investor generally has 20 to 50 percent of the investor's voting shares and can significantly influence the decisions of the investee. The investment account is debited for ownership in the investee's net income and credited for ownership in the investee's dividends (p. 896).

Face value Another name for the principal or maturity value of a bond (p. 820).

Factors Companies that purchase other firms' accounts receivable at a discount. Receivables are sold so that the cash can be received more quickly (p. 1049).

Fair value method The method of accounting for shares held as short-term investments that values them at their fair, or market, value on the year-end balance sheet date. Any gain or loss resulting from the change in fair value is recognized in net income for the period in which it arises, and fair value becomes the new carrying value of the shares. Also called the *market value method* (p. 890).

Financial instrument A contract that creates an asset for one party and a liability or equity for another (p. 915).

Financing activities Activities that increase or decrease long-term liabilities and equity; a section of the cash flow statement (p. 953).

Foreign-currency exchange rate The measure of one currency against another currency (p. 910).

Foreign-currency transaction gain The gain that occurs when a cash payment is less than the related account payable or a cash receipt is greater than the related account receivable due to a change in exchange rate between the transaction date and the payment date (p. 912).

Foreign-currency transaction loss The loss that occurs when a cash payment is greater than the related account payable or a cash receipt is less than the related account receivable due to a change in exchange rate between the transaction date and the payment date (p. 912).

Forward contract An agreement to purchase at a specified future date and price (p. 914).

Free cash flow The amount of cash available from operations after paying for investments in plant, equipment, and other long-term assets (p. 955).

Fully diluted EPS Earnings per share calculated using the number of outstanding common shares plus the number of additional common shares that would arise from conversion of convertible bonds and convertible preferred shares into common shares (p. 779).

Futures contract A contract that can be purchased to guarantee the right to a product at a specified price in the future (p. 914).

General partnership A form of partnership in which each partner is an owner of the business, with all the privileges and risks of ownership (p. 664).

Hedging A way to protect oneself from losing money in a foreign-currency transaction by engaging in a counterbalancing foreign-currency transaction (p. 914).

Horizontal analysis The calculation and use of percentage changes in comparative financial statements (p. 1033).

Indirect method The format of the operating activities section of the cash flow statement that starts with net income and shows the reconciliation from net income to operating cash flows. Also called the *reconciliation method* (p. 952).

Initial public offering (IPO) The first time a particular class of a corporation's shares are sold to investors (p. 720).

Insider trading According to the Canada Business Corporations Act, the purchase/sale of a security by someone who knows information not known by the general public that might affect the price of that security (p. 773).

Interest allowance An interest component that rewards a partner with an allocation because of his or her investment in the business. This is not the same as interest expense paid on a loan (p. 671).

Inventory turnover The ratio of cost of goods sold to average inventory. Measures the number of times a company sells its average level of inventory during a year (p. 1048).

Investing activities Activities that increase and decrease the long-term assets available to the business; a section of the cash flow statement (p. 952).

Issued shares Shares that are sold to investors (p. 720).

Issue price The price at which shareholders first purchase shares from the corporation (p. 721).

Lease An agreement in which the tenant (lessee) agrees to make rent payments to the property owner (lessor) in exchange for the exclusive use of the asset (p. 844).

Lessee The tenant, or user of the asset, in a lease agreement (p. 844).

Lessor The property owner in a lease agreement (p. 844).

Leverage The use of financial instruments to increase the potential return on investment by earning more income on borrowed money than the related expense, thereby increasing the earnings for the owners of the business. Another name for trading on the equity (p. 1050).

Limited liability No personal obligation of a shareholder for corporation debts. The most that a shareholder can lose on an investment in a corporation's shares is the cost of the investment (p. 715).

Limited liability partnership (LLP) A partnership in which each partner's personal liability for other partners' negligence is limited to a certain dollar amount, although liability for a partner's own negligence is still unlimited. (p. 664).

Limited partnership A partnership with at least two classes of partners: a general partner and limited partners (p. 664).

Liquid assets Assets that can be converted to cash quickly. Often they are financial instruments that can be sold without a discount (p. 1046).

Liquidation The process of going out of business by selling the entity's assets and paying its liabilities. The final step in liquidation of a business is the distribution of any remaining cash to the partners (p. 682).

Liquidation value (redemption value) The amount of capital that a preferred shareholder would receive per preferred share upon liquidation of the corporation (p. 730).

Liquidity A company's ability to meet current payments as they come due (p. 1044).

Long-term investments Investments that a company intends to hold for more than one year (p. 890).

Long-term liabilities Debts due to be paid in more than a year or more than one of the entity's operating cycles if an operating cycle is greater than one year (p. 820).

Long-term solvency The ability to generate enough cash to pay long-term debts as they mature (p. 1032).

Majority interest Another name for controlling interest (p. 898).

Market interest rate The interest rate that investors demand in order to loan their money. Also called the *effective interest rate* (p. 822).

Market value The price for which a person could buy or sell a share (p. 730).

Market value method Another name for the fair value method of accounting for short-term investments in shares (p. 890).

Maturity date The date on which the borrower must pay the principal amount to the lender (p. 820).

Maturity value The amount a company is required to pay back to the lender at the end of the term of the bond. Also another name for a *bond's principal value* or *face value* (p. 820).

Memorandum entry A journal entry without debits and credits (p. 768).

Minority interest Another name for non-controlling interest (p. 903).

Money market fund An investment product generally considered safe because it invests in short-term debt securities, such as certificates of deposit (p. 889).

Mortgage The borrower's promise to transfer the legal title to certain assets to the lender if the debt is not paid on schedule. A mortgage is a special type of secured bond (p. 842).

Mutual agency Every partner can bind the business to a contract within the scope of the partnership's regular business operations (p. 662).

Non-controlling interest A subsidiary company's equity that is held by shareholders other than the parent company. Also called *minority interest* (p. 903).

No-par-value shares Shares that do not have a value assigned to them by the articles of incorporation (p. 722).

Operating activities Activities that create revenue or expense in the entity's major line of business; a section of the cash flow statement (p. 952).

Operating lease Usually a short-term or cancellable rental agreement (p. 844).

Organization costs The costs of organizing a corporation, including legal fees and charges by promoters for selling the shares. Organization costs are an intangible asset under ASPE but are written off as an expense under IFRS (p. 726).

Other comprehensive income Income that arises from a number of sources, including unrealized gains and losses on certain classes of investment securities due in part to the use of fair value measurement (p. 786).

Outstanding shares Shares in the hands of shareholders (p. 721).

Over-the-counter (OTC) market The decentralized market where bonds are traded between dealers. Unlike the stock market, there isn't a central bond exchange where transaction prices are posted for all to see (p. 823).

Parent company An investor company that generally owns more than 50 percent of the voting shares of a subsidiary company (p. 898).

Partnership An unincorporated business with two or more owners (p. 660).

Partnership agreement An agreement that is the contract between partners specifying such items as the name, location, and nature of the business; the name, capital investment, and duties of each partner; and the method of sharing profits and losses by the partners (p. 661).

Par value An arbitrary value assigned when certain shares are initially offered to the public; these types of shares are not common in Canada (p. 722).

Preemptive right Existing shareholders are given the right to purchase additional shares of the company before the shares are offered to others. This would give existing shareholders the opportunity to maintain the same percentage of ownership as they would have had before the new shares were issued (p. 720).

Preferred shares Shares of stock that give their owners certain advantages over common shareholders, such as the priority to receive dividends before the common shareholders and the priority to receive assets before the common shareholders if the corporation liquidates (p. 723).

Premium The excess of a bond's issue price over its maturity (par) value; also called *bond premium* (p. 823).

Present value The amount a person would invest now to receive a greater amount at a future date (p. 824).

President The person in charge of managing the day-today operations of a corporation (p. 716).

Price–earnings ratio (or price-to-earnings ratio, or P/E) The market price of a common share divided by the company's earnings per share. Measures the value that the stock market places on $1 of a company's earnings (p. 779).

Principal value The amount a company borrows from a bondholder. Also called the bond's *maturity value*, *par value*, or *face value* (p. 820).

Prior-period adjustment A correction to Retained Earnings for an error in an earlier period (p. 783).

Private corporation A corporation whose shares are not traded on a stock exchange. (p. 714).

Proportionate share The same amount of shares in relation to others before and after an event such as a new issue of shares (p. 719).

Prospective In the future. For example, changes in accounting estimates are reflected in future financial statements, not in past financial statements (p. 784).

Prospectus A mandatory legal document that describes an investment to potential purchasers (p. 720).

Provisions Accounts that represent a liability of one entity to another entity (p. 845).

Proxy A formal appointment of one person to cast a vote for another person (p. 717).

Public corporation A corporation that issues shares that are traded on a stock exchange (p. 714).

Quick ratio Another name for the acid-test ratio (p. 1046).

Rate of return on common shareholders' equity Net income minus preferred dividends divided by average common shareholders' equity. A measure of profitability. Also called *return on equity* (ROE) or *return on common shareholders' equity* (p. 733).

Rate of return on total assets The sum of net income plus interest expense divided by average total assets. This ratio measures the success a company has in using its assets to earn income for the people who finance the business. Also called *return on assets* (ROA) (p. 732).

Rebuttable assumption A conclusion that something is true unless proven that it isn't (p. 915).

Redeemable bonds Bonds that give the purchaser the option of retiring them at a stated dollar amount prior to maturity (p. 839).

Repurchase shares When a corporation purchases its own shares that it issued previously (p. 769).

Retained earnings A corporation's capital that is earned through profitable operation of the business and is left in the business (p. 717).

Retrospective In the past. For example, changes in accounting policies are reflected in past financial statement figures as if those policies had always been in place (p. 784).

Return on assets (ROA) The sum of net income plus interest expense divided by average total assets. This ratio measures the success a company has in using its assets to earn income for the people who finance the business. (p. 1052).

Return on common shareholders' equity (ROE) Net income minus preferred dividends divided by average common shareholders' equity. A measure of profitability (p. 1052).

Return on sales (ROS) Ratio of net income to net sales. A measure of profitability. (p. 1051).

Reverse split Another name for a share consolidation (p. 768).

Salary allowance Another term for service (p. 670).

Secured bonds Bonds that give the bondholder the right to take specified assets of the issuer if the issuer fails to pay principal or interest (p. 822).

Segmented information Financial information presented in the notes to the financial statements either by industry or by geography (p. 906).

Segment of the business A significant part of a company (p. 776).

Serial bonds Bonds that mature in instalments over a period of time (p. 822).

Service An allocation to a partner based on his or her service to the partnership. This is not the same as salary expense for an employee (p. 670).

Servicing its debt A phrase that means the repayment of principal and interest on loans or bonds (p. 1051).

Share dividend Another name for a stock dividend (p. 765).

Shareholder A person or a company that owns shares in a corporation (p. 714).

Shareholder loans Loans that are obtained from the owner either in the form of cash or in kind. This amount can be shown as a liability or as a receivable on the balance sheet, depending on whether the balance is a credit or a debit (p. 844).

Shareholders' equity Owners' equity of a corporation (p. 717).

Shares Units into which the owners' equity of a corporation is divided (p. 715).

Short-term investments Investments that management intends to hold for less than one year (p. 889).

Short-term liquidity Ability to meet current payments as they come due (p. 1032).

Significant influence When a company participates in the decision making of another company without having full control over it (p. 889).

Stated interest rate The interest rate that determines the amount of cash interest the borrower pays and the investor receives each year. Also called the *contract interest rate* (p. 822).

Stated value An arbitrary amount assigned to a share of stock when it is issued (p. 722).

Statement of equity Another name for statement of shareholders' equity (p. 780).

Statement of shareholders' equity Presents changes in all components of equity. Also called *statement of equity* (p. 780).

Stock Units of ownership into which the owners' equity of a corporation is divided (p. 715).

Stock dividend A proportional distribution by a corporation of its own shares to its shareholders. Also called a *share dividend* (p. 765).

Stock split An increase in the number of authorized and outstanding shares coupled with a proportionate reduction in the book value of each share (p. 767).

Straight-line amortization Allocating a bond discount or a bond premium to expense by dividing the discount or premium into equal amounts for each interest period (p. 829).

Strong currency A currency that is rising relative to other nations' currencies (p. 911).

Subordinated shares Shares with fewer voting rights than other shares within the same corporation (p. 722).

Subsidiary An investee company in which a parent company owns more than 50 percent of the voting shares (p. 898).

Term bonds Bonds that all mature at the same time for a particular issue (p. 822).

Times-interest-earned ratio Ratio of income from operations to interest expenses. Measures the number of times that operating income can cover interest expense. Also called the *interest coverage ratio* (p. 1051).

Trading on the equity Earning more income on borrowed money than the related expense, thereby increasing the earnings for the owners of the business (p. 841).

Translation Another term for a currency conversion or foreign-currency exchange (p. 911).

Treasury bills A short-term debt obligation issued by a government (p. 889).

Treasury shares When a corporation repurchases its own shares and holds the shares in its treasury for resale (p. 770).

Underwriter An independent firm that is hired to sell shares on a corporation's behalf (p. 720).

Unlimited personal liability When a partnership (or a proprietorship) cannot pay its debts with business assets, the partners (or the proprietor) must use personal assets to meet the debt (p. 662).

Unregistered bonds Another name for bearer bonds (p. 822).

Vertical analysis Analysis of a financial statement that reveals the relationship of each statement item to a total, which is 100 percent (p. 1037).

Weak currency A currency that is falling relative to other nations' currencies (p. 911).

Write-down An accounting entry to recognize the decrease in the value of an asset by debiting an expense account and crediting the asset account (p. 898).

Working capital Current assets minus current liabilities; measures a business's ability to meet its short-term obligations with its current assets (p. 1045).

Yield The interest rate that an investor will receive based on a compounding period of one year (p. 823).

Index

A

accounting firms, largest, 660
accounting framework, 784, 848, 906, 956
accounting policy, change in, 784
accounting standards. *See* Accounting Standards for Private Enterprises (ASPE); International Financial Reporting Standards (IFRS)
Accounting Standards for Private Enterprises (ASPE), 714, 764
  see also ASPE-IFRS comparisons
  amortization methods, 848
  cash flow statement, 952–953, 964
  earnings per share, 776, 1053
  effective-interest amortization, 832
  financial statement analysis, 1058
  income statement, 786
  international transactions, 915
  investments, 915
  long-term liabilities, 848
  primary accounting methods under, 890
  share capital, 734
  statement of shareholders' equity, 780, 786
  subsidiaries, accounting for, 898, 899
  summary of accounting for investments under, 905
  types of investments, 890
accounts receivable turnover, 1048–1049, 1063
accrued interest, 825, 826
ACE Bakery, 898
acid-test ratio, 1046–1047, 1063
actively traded, 890, 919
adjusting entries
  effective-interest method, 837–838
  for interest expense, 836–838
  straight-line method, 836–837
admission, of partner, 674–678
  by investment in partnership, 675–678
    bonus to the new partner, 677–678
    bonus to the old partners, 676–677
    at book value—no bonus, 675–676
  by purchasing a partner's interest, 674–675
affiliated company, 898, 919
agreement, partnership, 661, 689
Allowance for Doubtful Accounts, 892
amortization, of bond discount/bond premium, 829–836, 907–908
  effective-interest method, 831–835, 837–838, 848

mortgage amortization schedule, 843
  partial-period, 839
  straight-line method, 829–831, 836–837, 848
amortization expense, 958–959, 972
amortized cost method, 906, 919
annual reports, 1056
annuity
  future value, 875–876
  present value of, 878–879
appropriations, of retained earnings, 782, 791
arrears, 728, 738, 779
articles of incorporation, 714, 715, 727, 738
ASPE. *See* Accounting Standards for Private Enterprises (ASPE)
ASPE-IFRS comparisons
  amortization methods, 848
  bonds, investments in, 915
  cash flow statement, 964
  equity investments, 915
  financial statement analysis, 1058
  foreign-currency transactions, 915
  hedging, 915
  income statement, 786
  investments in debt instruments, 915
  long-term liabilities, 848
  majority interest, 915
  non-strategic investments, 915
  other comprehensive income, 786
  share capital, 734
  statement of shareholders' equity, 786
  strategic investments, 915
asset revaluation, 679, 689
assets
  current, 959–960, 1041, 1046
  intangible, 726, 961–962, 973–974
  liquid, 1046, 1063
  noncash, 685
  overstating, 726
  rate of return on total assets, 732–733
  return on assets, 732–733, 739
  sale at gain, 683–684
  sale at loss, 684
  tangible, acquisitions and sales of, 961–962
authorization of shares, 716, 720, 738
authorized shares, 720, 729, 738

B

Bain Capital Investors, LLC, 713
balance sheet, 732, 773–774

comparative, 1045
consolidated, 900–901, 903–904
elimination entry, 901
horizontal analysis, 1035
mortgage loans, 843–844
note disclosure of cumulative preferred dividends, 729
partnership, 665, 667
shareholders' equity section of, 725, 774
sole proprietorship, 665
vertical analysis, 1039
basic EPS, 777, 779, 791
BDO Canada LLP, 660
bearer bonds, 822, 852
benchmarking, 1041–1043, 1063
  against another company, 1041–1042
  against industry average, 1042–1043
bid price, 823, 852
Blackberry Inc., 720
blended payments, 842, 852
board of directors, 715, 716, 738
Bombardier Inc., 720, 724
bond, 724, 820–821, 848
  amortized cost method, 906
  bearer, 822
  call, 839
  callable, 839, 852
  carrying amount, 834
  certificate, 821, 822
  conversion privileges, 779
  convertible, 840, 852
  coupon rate, 821
  debentures, 821, 822
  defined, 820, 852
  disclosure, 848
  discount. *See* discount
  face value, 820
  interest rates, 822
  investments in, 906–909, 915
  issuing. *See* bond issuance
  long-term investments, 906–909, 915
  market price, 822
  maturity date, 820
  maturity value, 820
  par value, 820
  premium. *See* premium
  present value. *See* present value
  prices, 823
  principal value, 820

bond (continued)
redeemable, 839
retirement of, 839–840
secured, 822
serial, 822
short-term investments, 906, 915
term, 822
types of, 821–822
unregistered, 822
vs. shares, 841
bond discount. See discount
bondholders, 820
bond indenture, 820, 852
bond issuance, 838
advantages, 841
to borrow money, 824–829
disadvantages, 841
at discount, 826–828
journal entry for, 829
and notes between interest dates, 825–826
at par value, 825
at premium, 828–829
price, 823
bond payable, 820, 852
present value of, 879–880
reporting discount on, 827
reporting premium on, 828
bond premium. See premium
book value, 738
in decision making, 731
investing in partnership at, 675–676
per common share, 730, 1063
per preferred share, 730–731
of share, 730–731
withdrawals of partners at, 679–680
book value per common share, 730, 1054–1055, 1063
book value per preferred share, 730–731
borrowing, 841–842
Boston Pizza Royalties Income Fund, 723
business publications, 1043
bylaws, 716, 738

C
callable bonds, 839, 852
call bonds, 839
call value, 730
Canada
largest accounting firm, 660
stock market performance (TSX Composite), 722
Canada Business Corporations Act (CBCA)
and market value of shares issued, 766

no-par-value shares, 722
repurchase shares, 769
sale of repurchased shares, 772
shareholders' rights, 719–720
stated capital, 717
Canada Coal Inc., 768
Canada Goose Holdings Inc., 713, 714, 715, 720, 721, 722, 723, 730, 732, 1041, 1042
Canada Revenue Agency, 663
Canadian dollars, 911, 914
Canadian National Railway Company (CN), 820
Canadian Securities Administrators, 720
Canadian Tire Corporation, Limited, 714, 781
Canopy Growth Corporation, 783
capital deficiency, 685, 689
capital investments, 667, 668–670
capitalized retained earnings, 765, 791
capital lease, 844, 845–847, 852
carrying value, 892, 919
cash, 727, 764, 951
adequacy, measurement of, 955
collections, 970, 972, 979–980
computation, of investing activities, 961–962
Cash account, transactions affecting, 950
cash dividends, 727–729, 766, 768, 782, 891, 894–895
payment of, 974
cash equivalents, 951–952, 986
cash flows, 949, 986
from financing activities, 974
from investing activities, 972–974
from operating activities, 971–972, 979
cash flow statement, 947, 948, 952, 960, 986
basic concepts, 949–950
Cash account, transactions affecting, 950
cash/cash equivalents, 951–952
computing individual amounts for, 961–964
conversion from accrual basis to cash basis, 969
direct method, 952–953, 969–974
discontinued operations, 954
format of, 952–953
free cash flow, 955
indirect method, 952, 956–960
operating section, calculating amounts for, 975–982
payments on, 978
purpose of, 950–952
cash receipts, 978

cash receipts of interest, 972
CBCA. See Canada Business Corporations Act (CBCA)
certificates of deposit, 889, 919
chairperson, 716, 738
CIBC World Markets Inc., 720, 888
circumstances, changes in, 784
classes, of preferred shares, 723–724
closely held corporations, 731, 738
Collins Barrow, 660
common shareholders' equity, 733
common shares, 718, 722–723, 729, 738, 769, 898
book value per, 730, 1054–1055
investors, 722
issuing at stated value, 723
issuing or assets other than cash, 723
no-par-value shares, 722
par value, 722
preferred shares. See preferred shares
rights attached to, 719–720
stated value of shares, 722–723
weighted average number of common shares outstanding, 777
common-size statements, 1040–1043, 1063
common stock, 715
companion account, 892, 919
comparability, of information, 785
compound interest, 874
consistency principle, 783, 784
consolidated financial statements, 898, 899–905, 919
accounting for goodwill, 901–902
consolidated balance sheet, 900–901, 903–904
income of consolidated entity, 904
parent owns all subsidiary's shares, 901–902
parent owns less than 100 percent of subsidiary's shares, 903–904
consolidated statement of earnings and comprehensive income, 787
consolidation, 768, 791
continuing operations, income statement, 774–775
continuous life, of corporations, 715
contract interest rate, 822, 852
contributed capital, 717, 718, 738
controlling interest, 898, 920
see also majority interest
conversion privileges, 779, 791
convertible bonds, 840, 852
convertible notes, 840, 853
convertible preferred shares, 724–725, 738
co-ownership of property, 663

corporate taxation, 715
corporations, 714, 720
  advantages, 716
  articles of incorporation, 714, 715
  authority structure in, 716, 720
  board of directors, 715, 716
  characteristics, 714–716
  closely held, 731, 738
  continuous life, 715
  corporate taxation, 715
  directors' liability, 715–716
  disadvantages, 716
  dividends, 727–729
  evaluation of operations, 732–733
  government regulation, 715
  income statement, 774–779
  limited liability, 715
  mutual agency, 715
  net income, 774
  organization, 716–717
  organization costs, 726
  owners' equity, 715
  private, 714, 739
  public, 714, 715, 739
  retained earnings, 764–765
  rights, 714–715
  separate legal entity, 714–715
  separation of ownership and
    management, 715
  share capital, 717
  shareholders' equity. See shareholders'
    equity
  share repurchase. See repurchase
    shares
  shares. See share
  statement of income and retained
    earnings, 780
  statement of retained earnings, 780
  statement of shareholders' equity,
    780–781
  transferability of ownership, 715
  unique costs, 715–716
  vs. partnership, 664
Corus Entertainment Inc., 947,
  948–949, 952, 954
counterbalancing transaction, 914, 920
coupon rate, 821, 853
CPA Canada Handbook
  capital lease, 845
  consolidation, 899
  financial instruments, 906n
  financing activities, 954
  organization costs, 726
  retroactive restatement of financial
    information, 786
  share investments, 891
  share repurchase, 771
credit agencies, 1043

creditors, 732, 1032, 1050
cumulative preferred shares, 728–729,
  738
currency options, 914, 920
current assets, 959–960, 1041, 1046
current liabilities, 959–960, 1045–1047,
  1046
current ratio, 1046, 1063

D

date of record, 727, 728, 738, 767
days' sales in inventory, 1048, 1063
days' sales in receivables, 1049–1050,
  1063
debentures, 821, 822, 853
debt
  additional, issuance of, 842
  cash received from, 974
  collection of loans, 973–974
  company's ability to pay, 951
  loans to other companies, 973
  long-term, 963, 1050–1051
  long-term loans, 962
  payment of, 974
  reclassification, 1047
  servicing its debt, 1051
  shareholder loans, 844
  vs. equity, 725
debt/equity ratio, 1050–1051, 1063
debt ratio, 1050, 1063
declaration date, 727, 728, 738,
  766–767
deficit, 718, 719, 738, 764
Deloitte LLP, 660, 662
dilution, earnings per share, 779
direct financing leases, 844
direct method, 952–953, 969–974,
  986
  operating activities, 971
directors' liability, 715–716
disclosure
  bond issue details, 848
  EPS information, 786
  non-cash investing and financing
    activities, 954
discontinued operations, 775–776, 954
discount, 823, 853
  amortization of. See amortization, of
    bond discount/bond premium
  bond issuance at, 826–828
  interest expense on bonds issued at,
    827–828
  reporting on bonds payable, 827
discounting, 877
dissolution, 661, 689
distribution date, 727, 728, 767
dividend announcements/notices, 727
dividends, 719, 727–729, 738
  announcement/notice, 727

arrears, 728, 779
cash, 727–729, 766, 768, 782, 891,
  894–895, 974
cash receipts of, 972
company's ability to pay, 951
on cumulative preferred shares,
  728–729
date of record, 727, 728, 767
declaration date, 727, 728,
  766–767
distribution date, 727, 728, 767
division of, 728
effects of, 769
on noncumulative preferred shares,
  729
note disclosure, 729
as operating activities, 954
payments, 727–728, 963–964
preferred, 778–779
restriction on, 782–783
and retained earnings, 764
share of, 897
stock/share. See stock dividend
dividend yield, 1054, 1058
Dollarama Inc., 763, 769, 774,
  888
double taxation, 715, 738
downside risk, 1054, 1063
drawings, 673–674
Dun & Bradstreet Canada, 1043

E

earnings per share (EPS), 776–779,
  786, 791, 842, 1053, 1063
  advantage of borrowing vs. issuing
    shares, 841–842
  basic, 777, 779, 791
  dilution, 779
  fully diluted, 779, 791
  preferred dividends, 778–779
  price-earnings ratio, 779
  stock dividends, 778
  stock splits, 778
  weighted average number of
    common shares outstanding, 777
economic entity assumption, 906
effective-interest amortization,
  831–835, 848, 853
  adjusting entries using, 837–838
  of bond discount, 832–834
  of bond premium, 834–835
effective interest rate, 822, 853
efficient capital market, 1055, 1063
elimination entry, 901
employees, payments to, 972,
  980–981
EnCana Corporation, 732
EPS. See earnings per share (EPS)

equity
  debt *vs.,* 725
  investments, 891
  return on, 733, 739
  shareholders'. *See* shareholders' equity
  statement of, 780–781
  trading on, 841
equity investments. *See* share
    investments
equity method for investments,
    896–898, 900, 920
Ernst & Young LLP, 660, 674
errors, 783–784
ethical considerations
  additional debt, 842
  debt reclassification, 1047
  issuance of shares, 726
  share repurchase, 773
euros, 911
evaluation of operations, 732–733
Excel, 1033
expected sales price, 720

F

face value, 820, 853
factors, 1049, 1063
fair value method, 890, 894, 920
Fair Value Valuation Allowance, 892
financial analysis. *See* financial
    statement analysis; ratios
financial instruments, 906*n*, 915, 920
Financial Post, 1043
financial statement, 734, 960
  see also specific financial statements
  cash flow statement. *See* cash flow
    statement
  common-size statements,
    1040–1043
  consolidated. *See* consolidated
    financial statements
  partnership, 665
  red flags, 1057
  retrospective/prospective changes, 785
  sole proprietorship, 665
  timing of, 950
financial statement analysis
  annual reports, 1056
  benchmarking, 1041–1043
  common-size statements,
    1040–1043
  horizontal analysis, 1033–1036,
    1037
  information sources, 1043
  investor decisions, 1055–1057
  limitations of, 1055
  methods, 1033
  objectives of, 1032–1033
  ratios. *See* ratios

trend percentages, 1036
  vertical analysis, 1037–1039
financing activities, 953–955, 974, 986
  cash dividends, payment of, 974
  cash flows from, 974
  computing cash amounts of,
    963–964
  debt, cash received from, 974
  debt, payment of, 974
  dividend payments, 963–964
  issuances and repurchases of shares,
    963
  share issuance, 974
foreign-currency conversion. *See*
    translation
foreign-currency exchange rates,
    910–911, 920
foreign-currency transaction gain, 912,
    914, 920
foreign-currency transaction loss, 912,
    914, 920
foreign-currency transactions, 910–914
  ASPE-IFRS comparison, 915
  counterbalancing transaction, 914
  foreign-currency exchange rates,
    910–911
  foreign-currency transaction gain,
    912, 914
  foreign-currency transaction loss,
    912, 914
  hedging, 914
  receivables, 912–913
  risk minimization, 914
  strong currency, 911
  translation, 911
  weak currency, 911
forward contracts, 914, 920
free cash flow, 955, 986
fully diluted EPS, 779, 791
futures contracts, 914, 920
future value, 873–876
  of annuity, 875–876
  formula, 876
  tables, 874–875

G

GAAP. *See* generally accepted
    accounting principles (GAAP)
gain
  foreign-currency transaction, 912,
    914, 920
  realized, 893, 895
  on the sale of an equity method
    investment, 897–898
  sale of assets, 959
  sale of assets at, 683–684
  on sale prior to adjustments to fair
    value, 892
  unrealized, 892, 893

generally accepted accounting
    principles (GAAP), 714, 764, 906
general partners, 664
general partnership, 664, 689
George Weston Limited, 898, 899
Gildan Activewear Inc., 972, 1041, 1042
Globe and Mail Report on Business,
    779
Globe and Mail's Report on Business,
    1043
Globe Investor, 1043
government regulation, 715
Grant Thornton Canada, 660
growth investors, 1055

H

hedging, 914, 915, 920
horizontal analysis, 1033–1036, 1037,
    1063

I

IFRS. *See* International Financial
    Reporting Standards (IFRS)
Imperial Oil Limited, 715
income statement, 779
  ASPE, 786
  comparative, 1044
  continuing operations, 774–775
  corporate, 774–779
  discontinued operations, 775–776
  earnings per share. *See* earnings per
    share (EPS)
  horizontal analysis, 1034
  IFRS, 786
  income taxes, 774–775, 776
  multi-step, 774, 775, 785
  partnership, 665
  single-step, 774
  sole proprietorship, 665
  vertical analysis, 1038
income summary account, 668
Income Tax Act, 673
income taxes, 774–775, 776
  payments of, 982
income tax expense, 775
  cash payments for, 972
income trust, 723
incorporators, 716
Indigo Books & Music Inc., 714, 951
indirect method, 952, 956–960, 986
information sources, 1043
initial public offering (IPO), 713, 720,
    721, 738
insider information, 1056
insiders, 773
insider trading, 773, 791
intangible assets, 726
  acquisitions and sales of, 961–962

cash payments for, 973
sale of, cash received from, 973–974
interest, 678
accrued, 825, 826
compound, 874
majority, 898, 920
as operating activities, 953
payments of, 840, 982
interest allowance, 671, 689
interest coverage ratio, 1051
interest expense
adjusting entries for, 836–838
on bonds issued at a discount, 827–828
on bonds issued at a premium, 827–828
carrying amount, 836
cash payments for, 972
interest rates, bonds
market/effective, 822, 853
stated/contract, 822, 852, 853
international accounting, 910
see also foreign-currency transactions
International Accounting Standard (IAS), 786
International Financial Reporting Standards (IFRS), 714, 764
see also ASPE-IFRS comparisons
amortization methods, 848
cash flow statement, 964
effective-interest amortization, 832
financial statement analysis, 1058
income statement, 786
international transactions, 915
investments, 915
long-term liabilities, 848
share capital, 734
statement of shareholders' equity, 786
inventory
days' sales in, 1048
sale of, 1047–1050
inventory turnover, 1047–1048, 1063
investees, 889
investing activities, 953–955, 964, 974, 986
cash flows from, 972–974
collection of loans, 973–974
computing cash amounts of, 961–962
intangible assets, acquisitions and sales of, 961–962
intangible assets, payments for, 973
intangible assets, sale of, 973–974
investments, payments for, 973–974
investments, sale of, 973–974
loan collections, acquisitions and sales of, 962
loans to other companies, 973

long-term investments, acquisitions and sales of, 962
long-term loans, acquisitions and sales of, 962
property, plant, and equipment, payments for, 973
property, plant, and equipment, sale of, 973–974
tangible assets, acquisitions and sales of, 961–962
investment
analysis of shares as, 1053–1055
in bonds, 906–909
capital, 668–670
cash payments for, 973
cash receipts from sale of, 973–974
classification of, 889–890
equity investments. See share investments
equity method for, 896–898
long-term. See long-term investments
non-strategic, 915
in partnership, 675–678
share (equity), 891. See also share investments
short-term. See short-term investments
strategic, 915
transactions, 894, 896
investment trust, 723
investor decisions, 1055–1057
investors, 722, 724, 889, 1032
growth, 1055
value, 1055
IPO. See initial public offering (IPO)
issued shares, 720, 721, 738
issuing shares. See share issuance
issue price, 721, 738, 823

J
Jim Pattison Group, 714, 775
journal entry, 774, 910
for bond issuance, 829
for share repurchase, 772, 773

K
Kinross Gold Corporation, 889
KPMG LLP, 660

L
lease, 844–847, 853
capital, 844, 845–847, 852
direct financing, 844
operating, 844–845, 846
provisions, 845
sales-type, 844
lessee, 844, 853

lessor, 844, 853
leverage, 733, 738, 1050–1051, 1063
LexisNexis, 1043
liability
current, 959–960, 1045–1047, 1046
directors', 715–716
limited, 715
unlimited, 662, 689
limited liability, 715, 738
limited liability partnership (LLP), 664, 689, 715
limited life, partnership, 661–662
limited partners, 664
limited partnerships, 664, 689
liquid assets, 1046, 1063
liquidation, of partnership, 682–685, 689
capital deficiency, 685
sale of assets at gain, 683–684
sale of assets at loss, 684
liquidation value, 730, 738
liquidity, 1044, 1063
LLP. See limited liability partnership (LLP)
loan collections, 962
Loblaw Companies Limited, 714, 767, 899
long-term debt, 963, 1050–1051
long-term investments, 890, 920
acquisitions and sales of, 962
amortized cost method, 906
in bonds, 906–909
long-term liabilities, 820, 853
balance sheet presentation of, 843–844
bonds. See bonds
IFRS, 848
long-term share investments
accounted by consolidation method, 898–899
dividends, share of, 897
equity method for investments, 896–898
fair value method, 894
gain/loss on the sale of an equity method investment, 897–898
income/loss, share of, 896–897
with significant influence, 896–898
summary of, 905
without significant influence, 894–895
long-term solvency, 1032, 1063
loss, 674
foreign-currency transaction, 912, 914, 920
partnership, sharing, 667–673
realized, 893, 895

loss (*continued*)

on the sale of an equity method investment, 897–898

sale of assets, 959

sale of assets at, 684

on sale prior to adjustments to fair value, 892

unrealized, 893

Lululemon Athletica Inc., 767

M

majority interest, 898, 915, 920

Mallette, 660

marketable securities. *See* short-term investments

Market Data, 1043

market interest rate, 822, 853

market value method, 890, 894, 920

see also fair value method

market value/price, 730, 731, 738, 766, 822

marketable securities. *See* short-term investments

maturity date, 820, 853

maturity value, 820, 853

McDonald's Corporation, 820

measurement criteria, 848

memorandum entry, 768, 791

Metro Sportswear Ltd., 713

minority interest, 915, 920

MNP LLP, 660

money market funds, 889, 920

mortgage amortization schedule, 843

mortgages, 842–844, 853

multi-step income statement, 774, 775, 785

mutual agency, 662, 689, 715, 738

N

National Automobile Dealers Association, 1042

National Post, 1043

negative retained earnings, 719

Neilson Dairy, 898

net income, 663, 674, 733, 774, 779

and cash flow, 951

New York Stock Exchange (NYSE), 713, 714

non-controlling interest, 903, 920

noncumulative preferred shares, 729

non-strategic investments, 915

no-par-value shares, 722, 738

Nygård International, 972

O

offering price, 720

online financial databases, 1043

operating activities, 953–955, 974, 986

amortization expense, 972

cash amounts, computation of, 978–982

cash collections from customers, 972, 979–980

cash flows from, 971–972, 979

direct method, 971

dividends, receipt of, 972

employees, payments to, 972, 980–981

income tax expense, 972

income tax payments, 982

indirect method, 956, 958–960

interest, receipts of, 972

interest expense, 972

interest payments, 982

operating expenses, payments for, 981–982

suppliers, payments to, 972, 980

operating leases, 844–845, 846, 853

operations, 953

organization, of corporation, 716–717

organization costs, 726, 738–739

other comprehensive income, 786, 791

outstanding shares, 721, 730, 739, 771

overstating assets, 726

over-the-counter (OTC) market, 823, 853

ownership, 901

separation of, 715

transferability of, 715

owner's investment, recording of, 717

P

parent company, 898, 900, 920

partial-period amortization, 839

partners

admission of. *See* admission, of partner

death of, 682

general, 664

limited, 664

withdrawals, 673–674

partnership, 678. *See also* partners

advantages of, 663–664

agreement, 661, 666, 674, 689

balance sheet, 665, 667

characteristics of, 661–663

co-ownership of property, 663

defined, 660, 689

disadvantages of, 663–664

dissolution, 661

financial statements, 665

formation of, 666–667

general, 664

income statement, 665

limited, 664

limited liability, 664, 689, 715

limited life, 661–662

liquidation of. *See* liquidation, of partnership

mutual agency, 662

sharing profits and losses. *See* sharing partnership profits and losses

taxation of, 663

types of, 664

unlimited personal liability, 662

vs. corporations, 664

withdrawals (drawings). *See* withdrawals, of partners

P/E ratio. *See* price-earnings (P/E) ratio

par value, 722, 739, 820, 853

issuing bonds at, 825

percentage change, in net revenues, 1033

personal liability. *See* liability (personal)

preemptive right, 720, 739

preferred dividends, 778–779

preferred shares, 723–725

book value per, 730–731

classes, 723–724

conversion privileges, 779

convertible, 724–725, 738

cumulative, 728–729, 738

defined, 723, 739

investors, 724

issuing, 724

noncumulative, 729

premium, 823, 853

amortization of. *See* amortization, of bond discount/bond premium

bond issuance at, 828–829

interest expense on bonds issued at, 828–829

reporting, on bonds payable, 828

present value, 824, 845, 853, 876–880

of annuity, 878–879

of bonds payable, 879–880

discounting, 877

formula, 877

tables, 878

president, 716, 739

price-earnings (P/E) ratios, 779, 792, 1053–1054, 1063

principal value, 820, 853

prior-period adjustment, 783, 792

private corporation, 714, 739

see also Accounting Standards for Private Enterprises (ASPE)

profits

partnership, sharing, 667–673

property, co-ownership of, 663

property, plant, and equipment, 973–974

proportionate share, 719, 739
proprietorship. *See* sole proprietorship
prospective treatment, 783, 784, 792
prospectus, 720, 739
provisions, 845, 853
proxy, 717, 739
public corporation, 714, 715, 739
   see also International Financial
     Reporting Standards (IFRS)
PwC, 660

Q
quick ratio, 1046, 1063

R
rate of return on common
   shareholders' equity, 733, 739
ratios, 1044
   ability to pay current liabilities,
     1045–1047
   accounts receivable turnover,
     1048–1049
   acid-test, 1046–1047, 1063
   analysis of shares as investments,
     1053–1055
   book value per common share,
     1054–1055
   current, 1046, 1063
   current liabilities, ability to pay,
     1045–1047
   days' sales in inventory, 1048
   days' sales in receivables,
     1049–1050
   debt, 1050, 1063
   debt/equity, 1050–1051, 1063
   dividend yield, 1054, 1058
   interest coverage, 1051
   inventory, ability to sell, 1047–1050
   inventory turnover, 1046–1047
   price-earnings (P/E), 779, 792,
     1053–1054, 1063
   profitability, 1051–1053
   quick, 1046, 1063
   receivables, ability to collect,
     1047–1050
   return on assets, 1052
   return on sales, 1051–1052
   solvency, 1050–1051
   times-interest-earned, 1051, 1063
   working capital, 1045–1046
RBC Dominion Securities Inc., 720, 888
rebuttable presumption, 915
receivables
   collection of, 1047–1050
   days' sales in, 1049–1050
recognition, 848
redeemable bonds, 839, 853
redemption value, 730

relevance, of information, 785, 848, 956
reliability, 786, 848, 956
repurchase shares, 769, 792
   see also share repurchase
residual ownership, 723
retained earnings, 717, 718–719, 739,
   764–765
   appropriations of, 782
   capitalized, 765, 791
   dividends, declaration of, 727
   dividends and, 764, 765–766
   negative, 719
   restrictions on, 782–783
   statement of, 780
   statement of income and, 780
retirement of bonds, 839–840
retrospective treatment, 783, 784, 792
return on assets (ROA), 732–733, 734,
   739, 1052, 1063
return on equity (ROE), 733, 734, 739,
   1052–1053, 1063
return on sales (ROS), 1051–1052, 1063
reverse split, 768, 792
Richter, 660
Risk Management Association, 1042
RMA Annual Statement Studies,
   1042–1043
ROA. *See* return on assets (ROA)
ROE. *See* return on equity (ROE)
Rogers Communications Inc., 722
ROS. *See* return on sales (ROS)
Royal Bank of Canada, 767

S
salary allowance, 670, 689
sales-type leases, 844
Saputo Inc., 898
Scotiabank, 767
secured bonds, 822, 853
SEDAR (System for Electronic
   Document Analysis and Retrieval),
   720, 1043
segmented information, 906, 920
segment of the business, 776, 792
separate legal entity, 714–715
serial bonds, 822, 853
service, 670–672, 689
servicing its debt, 1051, 1063
share, 715, 717, 739
   authorization of, 716, 720, 738
   authorized, 720, 729, 738
   bonds *vs.,* 841
   book value, 730–731
   common. *See* common shares
   issued, 720, 721, 738
   issuing. *See* share issuance
   market value, 730, 731

no-par-value, 722, 738
outstanding, 721, 730, 739, 771
par value, 722, 739
preferred. *See* preferred shares
proportionate, 719, 739
repurchase. *See* share repurchase
stated value of, 722–723
subordinated, 722, 739
treasury, 770, 792
underpriced, 731
values, 730–731
share capital, 717, 718, 723, 734
   see also share issuance; share
share certificates, 717
share dividend. *See* stock dividend
shareholder loans, 844, 853
shareholders, 714, 732, 739
shareholders' equity, 717–720, 739,
   764
   common, 733
   contributed capital, 717, 718
   dividends, 719
   earnings per common share, 1053
   rate of return on common, 733, 739
   reporting format, 781
   retained earnings, 717, 718–719
   return on common, 1052–1053
   section of balance sheet, 725
   statement of, 780–781, 783, 786
   variations in reporting, 781
shareholders' rights, 719–720
share investments, 888–890, 891
   carrying value, 892
   cash dividend, 891
   cost per share, 891
   investees, 889
   investors, 889
   sale of, 893
   share prices, 888
   significant influence, 889
   stock dividend, 891
share issuance, 720–725, 963
   advantages, 841
   cash received from, 974
   common shares, 722–723
   debt *vs.* equity, 725
   disadvantages, 841
   ethical considerations, 726
   initial public offering, 720, 721
   number of shares, 720–721
   preferred shares, 723–725
   SEDAR, 720
   shareholders' equity section of a
     balance sheet, 725
   underwriters, 720
share repurchase, 769–773, 963
   at average issue price, 770–771

share repurchase (*continued*)
  balance in Contributed Surplus, 771–772
  below average issue price, 771
  ethical considerations, 773
  journal entries for, 772, 773
  no balance in Contributed Surplus, 772
  payment of, 974
  recording, 770, 772
  restriction on, 782–783
  sale of repurchased shares, 772
  transactions, 773
  treasury shares, 770
sharing partnership profits and losses, 667–673
  based on capital investments, 668–670
  based on interest, 671–672
  based on service, 670–672
  based on stated fraction, 668
  negative remainder, allocation of, 671–672
  net loss, allocation of, 672–673
  profit, allocation of, 671
Shopify Inc., 887–888, 889, 912
short-term investments, 889–890, 894, 920
  accounting for, 890–893
  in bonds, 906
  fair value method, 890
  market value method, 890
  reporting, 892–893
  sale of, 893
  share investments, 891
short-term liquidity, 1032, 1063
significant influence, 889, 896–898, 915, 920
single-step income statement, 774
Sleeman Breweries Ltd., 732
Sleep Country Canada Inc, 715
sole proprietorship, 720
  financial statements, 665
  vs. partnership, 664
Spin Master Corp., 1031, 1032, 1033, 1034, 1036, 1038
spreadsheets, 841, 1034
Stanfield's Ltd., 972
stated capital, 717
  see also share capital
stated interest rate, 822, 853
stated value of shares, 722–723, 739
statement of changes in equity. *See* statement of shareholders' equity
statement of comprehensive income, 787
statement of earnings. *See* income statement

statement of equity, 780–781
statement of owner's equity, 665
statement of partners' equity, 665
statement of shareholders' equity, 780–781, 786
stewardship, 785
stock, 715, 739
  common, 715
stock dividend, 765–767, 792
  amount of retained earnings transferred in, 765–766
  earnings per share, 778
  effects of, 765
  reasons for, 766
  receipt of, 891
  recording, 766–767
  and taxable income, 768
  vs. stock splits, 767, 768
stock splits, 767–769, 792
  consolidation, 768
  earnings per share, 778
  effects of, 769
  memorandum entry, 768
  reverse split, 768
  and taxable income, 768
  2-for-1, 768
  vs. stock dividends, 767, 768
stockholders' equity. *See* shareholders' equity
straight-line amortization, 848, 853
  adjusting entries using, 836–837
  of bond discount, 829–830
  of bond premium, 831
strategic investments, 915
strong currency, 911, 920
subordinated shares, 722, 739
subsidiary, 898, 900–904, 920
  accounting for goodwill, 901–902
  parent owns all subsidiary's shares, 900–901, 901–902
  parent owns less than 100 percent of subsidiary's shares, 903–904
suppliers, payments to, 972, 980

T
T-accounts, 961
tangible assets, acquisitions and sales of, 961–962
taxation
  corporate, 715
  double, 715, 738
  income taxes, 774–775
  of partnership, 663
TELUS Corporation Inc., 714, 732, 733, 823, 888
temporary investments. *See* short-term investments

term bonds, 822, 853
times-interest-earned ratio, 1051, 1063
time value of money, 824, 873–879
  see also future value; present value
Toronto Stock Exchange (TSX), 713, 714, 722, 888, 1031
trading on the equity, 841, 853, 1063
transferability of ownership, 715
translation, 911, 920
treasury bills, 889, 920, 951
treasury shares, 770, 792
trend percentages, 1036
TSX Venture Exchange, 888
2-for-1 stock split, 768

U
underpriced share, 731
understandability, 906
Underworld Resources Inc., 889
underwriters, 720, 739
unlimited personal liability, 662, 689
unregistered bonds, 822, 853
US dollars, 911
useful information, 906, 956

V
value investors, 1055
values, share, 730–731
  market, 730
vertical analysis, 1037–1039, 1040, 1043, 1063
vice-presidents, 716

W
weak currency, 911, 920
weighted average number of common shares outstanding, 777
WestJet Airlines Ltd., 820, 888
"what if" analysis, 841
withdrawals, of partners, 673–674, 678–682
  asset revaluation, 679
  at book value, 679–680
  defined, 679
  at less than book value, 681
  at more than book value, 681
working capital, 1045–1046, 1063
write-downs, 898, 909, 920
written partnership agreement, 661

Y
yield, 823, 853